HANDBOOK OF DEVELOPMENT ECONOMICS
VOLUME IIIA

HANDBOOKS
IN
ECONOMICS

9

Series Editors

KENNETH J. ARROW

MICHAEL D. INTRILIGATOR

ELSEVIER

AMSTERDAM • LAUSANNE • NEW YORK • OXFORD • SHANNON • TOKYO

HANDBOOK OF DEVELOPMENT ECONOMICS

VOLUME IIIA

Edited by

JERE BEHRMAN
University of Pennsylvania

and

T.N. SRINIVASAN
Yale University

1995

ELSEVIER
AMSTERDAM • LAUSANNE • NEW YORK • OXFORD • SHANNON • TOKYO

ELSEVIER SCIENCE B.V.
Sara Burgerhartstraat 25
P.O. Box 211, 1000 AE Amsterdam, The Netherlands

Library of Congress Cataloging-in-Publication Data
(Revised for volume 3)

Handbook of development economics.

(Handbooks in economics; 9)
Vol. 3 edited by Jere Behrman and T.N. Srinivasan.
Includes bibliographical references and index.
1. Economic development—Handbooks, manuals, etc.
2. Development economics. I. Chenery, Hollis Burnley.
II. Srinivasan, T. N., 1933–   . III. Handbooks in
economics; bk. 9.
HD82.H275   1988   338.9   87-34960
ISBN 0-444-70339-X (U.S.: set; jacket)
ISBN 0-444-70337-3 (U.S.: v. 1.: jacket)
ISBN 0-444-70338-1 (U.S.: v. 2)
ISBN 0-444-82301-8 (U.S.: v.3A)
ISBN 0-444-82302-6 (U.S.: v.3B)
ISBN 0-444-88481-5 (U.S.: set)

ISBN volume 3A: 0 444 82301 8
ISBN volume 3B: 0 444 82302 6
ISBN set: 0 444 88481 5

This book is printed on acid-free paper.

PRINTED IN THE NETHERLANDS

INTRODUCTION TO THE SERIES

The aim of the *Handbooks in Economics* series is to produce Handbooks for various branches of economics, each of which is a definitive source, reference, and teaching supplement for use by professional researchers and advanced graduate students. Each Handbook provides self-contained surveys of the current state of a branch of economics in the form of chapters prepared by leading specialists on various aspects of this branch of economics. These surveys summarize not only received results but also newer developments, from recent journal articles and discussion papers. Some original material is also included, but the main goal is to provide comprehensive and accessible surveys. The Handbooks are intended to provide not only useful reference volumes for professional collections but also possible supplementary readings for advanced courses for graduate students in economics.

Dedication to HOLLIS CHENERY

Hollis Chenery was a coeditor of the first two volumes of the Handbook of Development Economics. As the present volume was in press, Professor Chenery passed away after a long illness. He was among the pioneers of development economics whose well-known work on Patterns of Development based on an analysis of time series data on a cross section of developing countries was a landmark in policy relevant, and analytically-coherent, though eclectic, empirical analysis of the development process. Both of us knew him well personally and professionally and will miss his wise counsel. We dedicate this volume to Hollis Chenery's memory.

Jere Behrman
T.N. Srinivasan

CONTENTS OF THE HANDBOOK

PREFACE

The first two volumes of the *Handbook of Development Economics* were published in 1988 and 1989 respectively. However, the analysis in various chapters of the two volumes, particularly those relating to debt, capital flows and the analytics of structural adjustment programs initiated by many developing countries in the early eighties, was completed in effect two years or so before publication. By that time the debt crisis had not been resolved and enough data on the experience with structural adjustment programs had not accumulated to allow a serious evaluation of their impact.

More importantly, the collapse of the centrally planned economies of Eastern Europe was in the future. Although the outstanding success of the Chinese reforms abandoning collectivized agriculture in favour of small peasant agriculture based on the household responsibility system was already evident, the rapid growth of Chinese foreign trade, the huge inflow of external capital into China (particularly in the special coastal economic zones), and the phenomenal growth of GDP at annual rates exceeding 10 percent were in the future. Finally and most importantly, the dismal failure of the dominant paradigm of development focusing on state-directed, inward-oriented, import-substituting industrialization on which the development strategies of most developing countries was based, and equally, the outstanding success of East Asian countries that departed early on from the dominant paradigm by emphasizing outward-orientation, was yet to be clearly perceived by policy makers in many, though not all, developing countries.

In part as a result of the mounting evidence against the dominant paradigm, many countries initiated economic reforms in the eighties by reducing state-involvement in the economy through privatization, opening up the economy to a much greater extent to foreign trade and investment and, above all, allowing market forces and the private sector to guide resource allocation to a much greater extent. Many of the reform efforts were undertaken in the context of a less favorable external environment for commodity exports, diminished capital flows (particularly from commercial banks) and a generally unfavorable macro-economic environment. Issues of credibility, sustainability, pace (gradual versus rapid), sequencing (for example, of the liberalization of external capital and current accounts), the response of individual agents to changes in incentives and political economy of reforms came to the fore. A substantial body of new analytical and empirical work on these issues based on the experience with structural stabilization and economic reforms has since become available. Several chapters of the present volume are devoted to this research.

Some significant developments in theoretical and empirical analyses of growth and development were either covered too briefly in the first two volumes or came after their publication. First, it has become possible to apply some relatively new tools of econometric analysis (e.g. kernel estimation of densities, non-parametric regression, ways of controlling for unobserved heterogeneities, cointegration, to mention just a few) for essentially two reasons: a vast increase in computing capability accompanied by a steep fall in computing costs, and the availability of sizeable data sets, particularly data from household surveys (a few of which surveyed the same set of households over a number of periods), and a new data set on real product for 130 countries over the period 1950–1985, put together by Summers and Heston (1988). Second, the applied general equilibrium models discussed in Chapter 18 of Volume 2 have since been generalized and used widely in development policy analyses. Many of these applications have involved extending the analytical scope of the model not only to cover scale economics and non-competitive and incomplete market structures, but also to incorporate macroeconomic aspects arising from the introduction of nominal assets and expectations. Third, interest in growth theory revived with the publication of the pioneering papers of Lucas (1988) and Romer (1986). Since then, a still growing literature variously described as "endogenous growth theory" or "new growth theory" has emerged, which formalizes the externalities from human capital accumulation and learning by doing, and endogenizes technical progress through the profit-seeking actions of agents operating in an imperfectly competitive market which enables them to appropriate the gains from their innovations, at least temporarily. The revived interest in growth theory has also stimulated empirical research on testing the implications of the theory using the Summers–Heston data set. One chapter has been devoted in the present volume to each of the above areas: data and econometric tools, applied general and equilibrium models, and endogenous growth theory.

Some topics which received only a brief attention or none at all in the first two volumes called for a more extensive treatment. For example, even though poverty has been endemic in many developing countries and, understandably, the eradication of poverty has long been, and continues to be, the overarching objective of most development strategies, the first two volumes discussed poverty only briefly. A chapter was devoted to the closely related, but distinct, concept of inequality and there was an extended discussion in it of the Kuznets hypothesis that income inequality will widen during the initial stages of development. But the analytics of poverty measurement, the determinants, correlates and trends in poverty, or the debates as to whether there was an unavoidable trade-off, at least in the short run, between rapid development and poverty alleviation, or whether rapid growth is the most effective strategy to eliminate poverty, were not covered. A second issue, which has become increasingly a matter of public concern around the world, is the need to prevent environmental degradation and to preserve bio-diversity. This concern has led to the search for a balance between the legitimate needs of poor countries to grow rapidly out of their poverty and the possible draft their rapid growth might make on global environmental endowments.

A third issue, which the difficulties experienced by the successor states of the former Soviet Union and its satellites in transforming themselves into market economies has highlighted, is the importance of the existence and effective functioning of appropriate institutions (social, political, legal, administrative and economic) for successful development as well as transition to a market economy. Although institutional economics is an ancient subdiscipline within economics, a rigorous analytical foundation for it is of recent origin. Institutional features of developing economics such as share-cropping, interlinking of land, labor, credit and product markets, etc., which were once thought to be inefficient semi-feudal relics, are now seen in a different light, as possibly efficient contractual arrangements in the absence of a complete set of contingent markets and in the presence of asymmetric information, moral hazard and adverse selection.

One of the crucial processes in development is the process of technological transformation. Kuznets (1966) viewed the epoch of modern economic growth as distinguished by the systematic application of science and technology to production. However, the process through which a technologically backward economy transforms itself not only by adapting and adopting available knowledge from elsewhere but also by beginning to generate new knowledge, is neither simple nor well understood. The first two volumes did not cover this process. Again, a chapter is devoted in the present volume to each of these four topics: poverty, environment, institutions, and technological transformation. Institutions relating to land use are discussed in a fifth chapter.

From early on development economists recognized that lack of infrastructure (then called social overhead capital) constrained development, and saw an important role for state action in ensuring adequate infrastructural investment because of scale economies due to lumpiness of such investment and externalities it generates. For example, Rosenstein-Rodan (1964) argued

"Because of these indivisibilities and because services of social overhead capital cannot be imported, a high initial investment in social overhead capital must either precede or be known to be certainly available in order to pave the way for additional more quickly yielding directly productive investments. This indivisibility of social overhead capital constitutes one of the main obstacles to development of under-developed countries". (p. 435)

In the earlier volumes there was no extended discussion of the role of the state in the development process and infrastructural activities figured primarily in the chapter on project evaluation, and briefly in that on Primary Exporting Countries. The present volume repairs this omission with a chapter devoted to infrastructure. Also, the role of the state in development process figures prominently in the chapter reviewing development experience.

Finally, the present volume also extends and updates the discussion in the earlier volumes on savings and human resource investments and household behavior. There have been recent theoretical developments on intertemporal allocation of resources and risk sharing and distribution in a context where the structure of financial markets is incomplete, existing markets are segmented and imperfect, and when relevant information is asymmetrically distributed among agents. These have major implications of savings and financial intermediation. Besides developments in institutional economics offer new insights on the role of informal savings and credit institutions that are ubiquitous in developing countries in all parts of the world. Formally, transferring resources over time through savings and investment, as well as borrowing and lending, is analogous to transferring resources across uncertain states of nature. Besides, given that future states of nature are often uncertain, intertemporal transfers simultaneously involve transfers across states of nature as well. Thus access to credit could influence an agent's ability to smooth her consumption against fluctuations in income over time as well as across states of nature. Many of these issues were not fully addressed in the earlier volumes and are covered in the present.

Part 3 of the first volume was devoted to Human Resources and Labor Markets. Again, since its publication there have been significant developments in tools of empirical analysis. Further, with the increased availability of micro data from household surveys, there have been several applications of these tools, which in particular pay careful attention to the implications for econometric estimation of the unobserved heterogeneities among individuals and households. The chapter on Human Resources in the present volume covers these recent developments and updates the discussion in the first volume.

Acknowledgements

We owe a deep debt of gratitude to the authors of this volume for their diligent efforts, for commenting on each others' chapters, and responding in their revision to the comments of their fellow authors and editors. We thank the Asian Development Bank for generous support in inviting the authors to present the first drafts of their chapters at the Bank's first Development Economics Conference during October 12–15, 1992. We are grateful to Dr.

S.C. Jha, Chief Economist, and Dr. M.G. Quibria, Head of the Economics and Development Resource Center of the Asian Development Bank, for their hospitality and unstinting cooperation. It is impossible to thank adequately the assistance of Louise Danishevsky of the Economic Growth Center at Yale University in ensuring that the drafts of each chapter were received on time and preparing them for the publishers.

JERE BEHRMAN
University of Pennsylvania

T.N. SRINIVASAN
Yale University

References

Kuznets, S. (1966) *Modern economic growth: Rate, structure and spread.* New Haven: Yale University Press.

Lucas, R. (1988) 'On the Mechanics of Economic Development', *Journal of Monetary Economics*, 22:3–42.

Romer, P. (1986) 'Increasing returns and long-run growth', *Journal of Political Economy*, 94:1002–1037.

Rosenstein-Rodan, P. (1964) 'The "Big-Push" argument', in: G. Meier, ed., *Leading issues in development economics*, New York: Oxford University Press, 431–440.

Summers, R. and Heston, A. (1988) 'A new set of international comparisons of real product and price levels: Estimates for 130 countries', *Review of Income and Wealth*, 34:1–25.

CONTENTS OF VOLUME IIIA

Chapter 35

Applied General Equilibrium Models for Policy Analysis
JAN WILLEM GUNNING and MICHIEL A. KEYZER   2025

PART 8: RESOURCES, TECHNOLOGY, AND INSTITUTIONS

Introduction
JERE BEHRMAN and T.N. SRINIVASAN

Chapter 36
Savings, Credit and Insurance
TIMOTHY BESLEY

PART 7

ANALYTICAL TOOLS

PART 7: ANALYTICAL TOOLS

Introduction

The Preface to the Handbook (Volumes and 2, p. ix) notes that development economics has been defined as the study of the economic structure and behavior of poor (or less developed) countries [Lewis (1984)], "a definition that leaves the core concerns of development economics clear enough, though its outer boundaries are difficult to establish and essentially arbitrary". To understand the economic structure and the behavior of the less developed countries requires conceptual frameworks the critical features of which can be tested against empirical realities. Historically, as the Preface also notes, development economics has been explicitly characterized by competing paradigms. Part 1 of the Handbook considers alternative concepts and approaches the influence of which have waxed and waned over time – neo-classical, Marxian and structuralists – and observes that the divergence in the explanations of stylized facts as put forth by different schools appears to be narrowing.

One important reason for such a narrowing is rigorous analysis made possible by developments in theory and econometrics, and by the availability of a socio-economic data that span a large number of countries and extending over several periods. While "stylized facts" remain important – perhaps too important – in shaping perceptions of what we know about development economics, there also has been a shift towards econometric estimation and statistical hypothesis testing of various propositions about the process of development. In this arguably more "scientific" methodology, theory is tested against evidence that in principle could lead to refutation in contrast to more speculative theorizing based on few hard facts and largely anecdotal evidence. On the other hand, essential dimensions of the development process are not easily quantifiable, and therefore tend to be ignored or underemphasized in more quantitative approaches. There also is a risk that quantitative approaches focus too much on stability of parameters and relationships, particularly if they are estimated with historical data, while the essence of economics is changes in such parameters and relations. One variant of this concern is the so-called "Lucas critique" that policy changes induce behavioral changes that may be offsetting and that may change estimated behavioral reduced-form demand

Handbook of Development Economics, Volume III, Edited by J. Behrman and T.N. Srinivasan
© *Elsevier Science B.V., 1995*

parameters. While such critiques carry substantial weight, nevertheless, quantification of analysis of development issues has been increasing.

This part of the Handbook contains three chapters that are concerned with quantitative analytical tools that are widely and increasingly used for analysis of development problems:

Chapter 33. Angus Deaton, "Data and Econometric Tools for Development Analysis"

Chapter 34. John Strauss and Duncan Thomas, "Human Resources: Empirical Modeling of Household and Family Decisions"

Chapter 35. Jan Willem Gunning and Michiel Keyzer, "Applied General Equilibrium Models for Policy Analysis"

The first two of these chapters focus on the current state of the art regarding empirical analysis of micro phenomena, though the first also addresses some data and estimation issues related to aggregate analysis. These two chapters emphasize the difficulties of understanding behavior and estimating causal relations given that most of our information is based on *choice-based* (and non-experimental) observations, the choices being in part influenced by unobserved individual, household and community characteristics. The second discusses these issues in detail in the context of human resource investments of households and their effects. The third of these chapters considers economy-wide models based on systematic representations of the underlying micro behavior of households and of production units.

Deaton (Chapter 33) presents "Data and Econometric Tools for Development Analysis". Data characteristics, of course, condition empirical analysis. There has been an explosion of sample surveys in developing countries, many of which are directed towards particular purposes such as to monitor living standards, estimate unemployment rates, measure production, or estimate weights in price indices. The units of observation typically are households or production units (firms/farms). These data have been increasingly available from statistical offices, and economists have had at their disposal increasingly powerful computational capabilities for analyzing such data. These data sets are very valuable resources for evaluating the welfare of individuals and the distribution of indicators of that welfare across members of society and for understating the behavioral responses of different individuals, households and firms to changes in markets and in policies.

Most of these micro data sets are cross-sectional, but some are longitudinal (panel), and in a number of cases time series of cross sections are available. Deaton discusses a number of important issues including the definition of households across societies, the seasonality of data collection, the impact of cluster sample design on the estimated variance of community price and policy

effects, the estimation of means and of regression coefficients given complicated stratified sample designs, the measurement of items produced and
consumed by households, and problems of attrition in panel data collection
efforts. Deaton rightly notes that just because developing countries are poorer
than the developed countries are does not mean that data from developing
countries are inferior. In many cases the micro data from developing countries
are of as high or higher quality than data from developed countries, and permit
examination of some issues of general concern more easily than do data from
developed economies. Examples include the nature of intrahousehold allocations and the impact of exogenous shocks (due to the greater sensitivity of
economies to weather shocks). Deaton emphasizes the potential value of panel
data for investigating changes over fairly long periods of time (e.g. 5–10 years
or longer), and observes that there are substantial problems in maintaining
panels for such durations. Promising alternatives are designing one-time
surveys in ways that keep open the possibility of subsequent resurveys,
exploring more the value of recall data, and utilizing time series of cross
sections. He sees limited potential for the use of panel data for analyzing
dynamic processes.

The availability of aggregate data, including national income accounts and
data on human resources and demographic outcomes, has expanded in recent
years in part due to compilations by international agencies such as the World
Bank and the UNDP and in part to the development of purchasing power
parity-based national accounts in the international comparison project based at
the University of Pennsylvania [e.g. Kravis, Heston and Summers (1982),
Summers and Heston (1991)]. A veritable growth industry has emerged in
recent years that explores dimensions of aggregate growth based on these data
[see the review in Romer (1994)]. But there are major problems with these
data, ranging from the standard index number issues to differing definitions
across countries and over time to much of the aggregate data reported by
international agencies being "made up" by extrapolations or interpolations (see
the special section on aggregate data in the June 1994 issue of the *Journal of
Development Economics*). This means that researchers should be critical of
these data and explore the implications of random and systematic measurement
errors, that international organizations should be clearer about the nature of
the data that they disseminate, and that efforts should be made to improve
aggregate data.

The econometric tools used for analyses of data for developing countries, of
course, are no different than those that are used for analyses of data from
developed countries. An important motivation for the development of these
tools has been to permit valid inferences from the available socioeconomic data
that often reflect behavioural responses that are influenced by the unobserved
(in the data) characteristics of individual units such as households, firms or

farms. In Deaton's words (p. 1815), "much of the econometric literature on simultaneity, heterogeneity, selectivity, omitted variables and measurement error can be thought of as finding procedures that can bring the non-experimental results closer to the experimental ideal". He further notes that many of these procedures rest on strong assumptions, but results would be more credible if they hold even with weaker assumptions and methods and if the estimates and the standard errors are calculated in ways that are robust to the failures of the standard underlying assumptions.[1] Deaton then provides a very useful review of many of the cross-sectional, panel and time series parametric and nonparametric tools that have been applied to a range of development issues in recent years. His chapter reinforces that good empirical research with socioeconomic data is indeed hard to accomplish. Therefore, researchers need to be cautious in interpreting their results and explore the robustness of those results to weakening the underlying assumptions.

Strauss and Thomas (Chapter 34) consider empirical models of household and family decisions regarding investments in human resources, and their effects. These topics are related to those in Chapters 12–15 of volume 1 of the *Handbook* (published in 1988) by Birdsall (on population growth), Schultz (education), Behrman and Deolalikar (health and nutrition) and Rosenzweig (labor markets). But there has since been an explosion of studies and applications of new techniques in this area, in part because of the increasing availability of micro survey and panel data noted above and in part because of increasing attention to the implications of models of behavior for empirical studies and to the robustness of empirical results. Therefore, there is considerable value added in Strauss and Thomas' chapter that advances well beyond the four related chapters in volume 1 of the *Handbook*.

Strauss and Thomas consider six major substantive topic areas related to household behavior and human resources: nutrient demands and productivity effects, determinants of human capital investments, production function estimates of the impact of human resources, wages and labor supply, dynamic issues, and links among individuals, households and families. For each of these topics they indicate what the important issues are, why different studies in the

---

[1] Robustness in this sense refers to weakening the underlying assumptions, not, as is sometimes assumed, to finding similar estimates for different data sets under the same strongly maintained assumptions. For example, some advocates of increasing schooling investments point to the large number of positive associations between schooling and "good" outcomes in many different data sets from many different economies as evidence that the strong effect of schooling is robust. But since such associations can be interpreted as causal only under strong assumptions (e.g. that schooling is independent of family background, motivation, abilities, community characteristics, etc. that a priori also might be expected to have direct effects on the outcomes of interest) that are maintained and untested across most of these studies, the robustness across data sets – while a desirable property – is not the same as the robustness with weaker assumptions that is emphasized in the text.

literature may have suggested different empirical magnitudes for critical parameters, what models of household behavior suggest about empirical approaches, and what the remaining open empirical issues are. In some cases they supplement their survey of the existing literature with original empirical analysis. An interesting example is provided by their discussion of the recent controversy over the empirical magnitude of the income elasticity of demand for energy (measured in kilo calories per day) from food intakes, calorie elasticity for short. Energy protein malnutrition is thought to be very wide-spread in the developing world, affecting hundreds of millions of individuals. There has been considerable controversy about how rapidly malnutrition will lessen with income increases that result from the overall process of develop-ment or from policies directed towards increasing the income of the poor. In the early 1980s the conventional wisdom was that the primary means of alleviating malnutrition is through income increases, and several studies of fairly aggregate food expenditure systems were interpreted to imply calorie elasticities with respect to income in the range of 0.6 to 0.8, or even higher for the very poor. Subsequently several studies suggested that these estimates overstated the "true" values by a factor of at least two and as much as ten due to failure to control for intra-food group compositional (quality) changes associated with income, correlated measurement errors in the calorie data and the income (expenditure) data since both depend importantly on food expendi-ture in many studies, and systematic differences associated with income between food acquired by households (the source of calorie data in most studies) and food consumed by household members due to food provided to guests, workers, animals and waste. Once corrected for their over estimation, such estimates suggest that income increases are much less effective in reducing malnutrition than had been claimed earlier. On the other hand, some recent estimates by Strauss and Thomas and others suggest that the calorie elasticity varies with income, with values of about 0.3 for the very poor but close to zero for those somewhat better off. Strauss and Thomas provide a thoughtful discussion of this debate. It is of interest not only because of the substantive concern about the effectiveness of income in alleviating malnutrition, but because it describes the evolution of understanding given various efforts to weaken the underlying maintained assumptions of the previous literature. It is pertinent to note that this literature continues to evolve and is evolving in ways in which the questions being investigated are placed more concretely in the dynamic context in which households operate with differences across stages of agricultural production. For example, a very recent preliminary study [Behr-man, Foster and Rosenzweig (1994)] explores such issues explicitly within the framework of "lean" and "surplus" seasons with costly transfer of some resources across seasons that are thought to typify many rural areas in developing countries (see Chapters 10 (Volume 1) and 35 (this volume) by

Gersovitz and Besley, respectively) and finds calorie elasticities with respect to income of about 0.4 in the lean season when credit constraints are binding and more productive labor has a high payoff in terms of increasing harvest profits, but not significantly different from zero in the surplus harvest season.

The discussion of the calorie-income elasticities illustrates some of the difficulties of empirical analysis with socioeconomic survey data given problems such as simultaneity, measurement errors, and unobserved heterogeneity. Other examples are provided by the other topics that Strauss and Thomas review. In many respects, the better empirical studies on household and family decisions and human resources, advance our understanding and appeal to higher standards of evidence. Also the institutions of and the data from developing countries have permitted greater progress than developed countries in dealing with important but difficult questions that are of general interest – such as coping with exogenous risk and the implications of asymmetric information, moral hazard, and statistical discrimination in labor markets.

Unfortunately not all available studies are concerned with the robustness of the results to the underlying maintained (i.e. untested) assumptions of the analysis. More often than not they deal with such issues in a way that only superficially deals with them and leaves the question of interpretation murky because links between the estimation and the model of behavior are at best tenuous. For example, to control for possible simultaneity, instruments are used. But often the instruments are inappropriate either not being independent of the disturbance term so their use does not lead to consistent estimates, or the first-stage relations are very weak so that the results are not very robust. Therefore the value of such empirical work in this area (and in other areas) is very limited. The discussion of Strauss and Thomas is very valuable in helping the user of empirical studies to separate the wheat from chaff.

While the Deaton chapter and, even more so, the Strauss and Thomas chapter have a micro and econometric (stochastic) orientation, Gunning and Keyzer in Chapter 35 focus on an economy-wide (and largely non-stochastic) perspective and inter-sectoral interactions in their discussion of applied general equilibrium models for policy analysis. Chapter 18 on "Multisectoral Models" by Robinson in volume 2 of the *Handbook* (published in 1989) is on related material. But, as in the case of household modeling and human resources, there has been so much activity in this area recently that the Gunning and Keyzer chapter has considerable value added. Other chapters in this volume of the *Handbook* also cover recent studies using this methodology. For example, Dasgupta and Maler in Chapter 38 give an illustration of the investigation of intersectoral environmental effects that use this analytic tool.

Applied general equilibrium models have been used to analyze a wide range of development issues. These models, unlike the representative-agent mac-romodels, explicitly consider heterogeneity among producers and consumers and are thus able to evaluate the distributional consequences of changes in policies and exogenous variables. Also, unlike partial equilibrium models of individual sectors, such as for example models of market structure, these models are capable of evaluating the *combined* effects and *simultaneous* changes of policies or exogenous variables which affect several sectors. In these two respects there are no other better analytical tools available.

An early and widespread application was the analysis of trade liberalization. The early models generally were limited in their departures from the static perfectly competitive, general equilibrium models. More recent efforts are characterized both by applications to a wider class of policy problems and by greater departures from static general equilibrium applications. The wider class of policy problems investigated ranges from trade in new commodities such as emission rights to international migration to phasing of policies over time. The recent departures from static perfectly competitive general equilibrium models include increasing returns to scale, some aspects of imperfect competition such as mark-up pricing, and some incorporation of dynamic issues related to financial assets, demographic changes, and forward-looking investment (under perfect foresight) with short-run constraints on adjustment.

Through such developments applied general equilibrium models have become even more useful, as well as more used, tools for investigating a set of phenomena in which the economy-wide repercussions through various markets are critical for understanding. Yet there remain major problems with respect to both the specification of such models and their parameterization. With regard to specification, for example, the equilibrium concept is problematic since it rules out false trading, the representation of imperfect competition to date is fairly limited and the assumption of perfect foresight for dynamic models is very strong. With regard to parameterization, the underlying data bases often are quite weak and the approaches to parameterization often cavalier, with little attention to the estimation issues that are central to the other two chapters in Part 7 of the *Handbook*. But it is not obvious that the specification and parametrization problems are much more serious, and hence the results less robust, in the case applied general equilibrium models in comparison to other widely used empirical models for policy evaluation.

Applied general equilibrium models are similar in some important respects to the household models and econometric tools that are discussed in the previous two chapters. For all of these tools there has been substantial recent progress that has increased the possibility of obtaining better understanding of behaviors and policy impacts related to economic development. But at the same time there continues to be a number of applications in which the limitations of the approach are not adequately recognized and there continues to be substantial scope for important future developments.

JERE BEHRMAN
T.N. SRINIVASAN

References

Behrman, J.R., Foster, A. and Rosenzweig, M.R. (1994) 'Stages of agricultural production and the calorie-income relationship', Philadelphia, PA: University of Pennsylvania, mimeo.

Kravis, I.B., Heston, A. and Summers, R. (1982) *World product and income: International comparison of real gross product*, Baltimore and London: The Johns Hopkins University Press.

Lewis, W.A. (1984) 'The state of development theory', *American Economic Review*, 74:1 (March), 1–10.

Romer, P.M. (1994) 'The origins of endogenous growth', *Journal of Economic Perspectives*, 8:1 (Winter), 3–22.

Summers, R. and Heston, A. (1991) 'The Penn world table (Mark 5): An expanded set of international comparisons, 1950–1988', *Quarterly Journal of Economics*, 106:2 (May), 327–368.

Chapter 33

DATA AND ECONOMETRIC TOOLS FOR DEVELOPMENT ANALYSIS

ANGUS DEATON

Princeton University

Contents

*I am grateful to Tim Besley, Jere Behrman, Anne Case, David Card, Alan Krueger, Ron Miller, Christina Paxson, James Powell and T.N. Srinivasan for help in the preparation of this paper.

Handbook of Development Economics, Volume III, Edited by *J. Behrman and T.N. Srinivasan*
© *Elsevier Science B.V.*, 1995

Introduction

Almost all the tools of econometric analysis that have been used in empirical work in economics in general have also been applied to the specific problems of economic development. My choice of topics in this review is therefore to some extent arbitrary, although I have been guided by three considerations. First, there are a number of methods that are so widely encountered in the development literature that they demand some coverage, even when their use raises no issues beyond those encountered in a good standard text. Second, I have been led by the first section of the chapter, on data questions, since discussion of data frequently leads naturally into econometric technique. Third, I have followed much of the recent general econometric literature in emphasizing robustness of inference and estimation. Much recent theoretical work has been devoted to methods that allow applied workers to dispense with unnecessary supporting assumptions, so that, for example, standard errors can be calculated even when standard textbook assumption fail, simultaneity and selection bias can be allowed for without making arbitrary and often incredible assumptions, and key effects can be measured with minimal assumptions about functional form. In keeping with the balance of the development literature, I have chosen to emphasize microeconomic more than macroeconomic applications, although I have included a section on recent results in time-series analysis and their application to problems of economic development.

The plan of the chapter is as follows. Section 1 is concerned with data, and Section 2 with tools and their application. However, since many of the data issues lead directly into the econometrics, I have sometimes found it convenient not to make the separation, and to include both in Section 1. The first and largest part of Section 1 deals with household survey data, with survey design in developing countries, with data collection, with measurement issues, and with the experience of using such data in econometric analysis. Section 1.2 is concerned with national income accounts, and with the index number and other problems that underlie international comparisons of income levels and growth rates. I also give some attention to the quality of country data, looking beyond national incomes to demographic, trade, and other measures.

Section 2 turns to econometric tools. There are three main sections. Section 2.1 is mainly concerned with tools for microeconomic analysis, emphasizing the use of survey data. I work through a range of more or less familiar econometric topics, illustrating their uses in the development literature, discussing methods for strengthening the robustness of inference, and trying to identify common pitfalls and difficulties. Section 2.2 turns to time-series techniques and their uses in the analysis of development questions. The modern time-series literature is very large and is rapidly growing, and I cover only a small selection of the many possible topics. Section 2.3 provides an introduction to non-parametric techniques for estimating density functions, regression functions, and the derivatives of regression functions. Although non-parametric analysis typically requires a great deal of data, there are a number of questions in development economics that are susceptible to a non-parametric treatment using survey data.

1. Data for development economics

1.1. Household survey data

1.1.1. Content and purpose

There are few Less Developed Countries (LDCs) that have not collected survey data of some sort at some time, and many LDCs have multiple surveys that are run on a regular and continuing basis, many of which meet the highest international standards of data collection, editing, and publication of results. Many (perhaps most) of these surveys have a specific *raison d'etre*; household expenditure surveys are used to monitor living standards or to collect weights for the consumer price index, labor force surveys are used to estimate unemployment rates, and censuses to estimate total population. Other surveys, such as surveys of firms or of farms are used to collect production or output data, and use a unit of observation other than a household. In many countries, the statutory authority establishing each survey is explicit about its purpose, and official statisticians design the surveys with these aims in mind. Of course, once the data are collected they can be used for many other purposes, to which they may be more or less suited, and to which government statistical offices may be more or less sympathetic. In the last ten to fifteen years there has been a great expansion in the use of survey data in development economics – as in other branches of the profession – much of it a consequence of better computing facilities, and much of it attributable to the increased willingness of statistical offices around the world to release their data to researchers. Ministers and civil servants are realizing that they have relatively little to fear from econometric analysis, and perhaps something to learn.

The difference between the original statutory purposes of the surveys and the uses to which the data are put in development economics poses a number of problems. In the short run, there are various statistical issues associated with using data for purposes that are different from the original intent and design, and in the longer run, there is the more fundamental (and much more difficult) question of how surveys ought to be redesigned for the broader policy and analytical purposes for which they are increasingly being used. I shall have something to say on both of these topics.

1.1.2. Survey data in policy and development

Why should development economists be interested in household survey data? If the ultimate aim of economic activity is the welfare of individuals, then the data from household surveys are the measure of its success. Although GDP and GNP per capita are often used as summary measures of welfare, in many countries they are derived with the help of household survey data, and even when this is not the case and consumption is derived as a residual, survey data provide a cross-check, and in many cases will provide higher quality data. But even at their best, national income measures can tell us only a very limited amount about distributional issues, about allocation by region, by ethnic group, by poor versus rich, or by rural versus urban. As economic development expands opportunities, we want to know who is benefiting, and who (if anyone) is losing. Indeed, as Stigler (1954) has documented, the first explorations of household budgets were carried out by social activists in the late eighteenth and early nineteenth centuries, and their object was to inform (and shock) policy makers and to lay the basis for reform. Counting the poor, documenting their living-standards (including nutritional standards), and measuring inequality remain important uses of household survey data by development economists.

Household survey data also yield direct measures of the effects of policy changes, whether these operate through price changes or through changes in the provision of public services. They can therefore provide the background information for informed discussion of possible changes in policy. In particular, quantities produced and consumed provide a local approximation to the derivative of welfare with respect to price. To see this in an example, suppose that a farm (or non-farm) household faces output prices p (labor is an output) and input prices v, and receives off-farm income y, that its technology can be represented by the (restricted) profit function $\pi(p, v; a)$ where a is a vector of fixed factors such as land, and that its preferences can be represented by the expenditure or cost function $c(u, p)$ for utility u, since without loss of generality, all consumption goods can be taken to be outputs. Then, since utility must be financed from farm profits or other income, we have

$$c(u, p) = y + \pi(p, v; z) . \tag{1}$$

Equation (1) immediately tells us by how much income y would have to be increased to compensate the household for a change in a price of one of its inputs or outputs. Since the partial derivatives of the cost function with respect to elements of p are the quantities consumed, q, and since the derivatives of the profit function with respect to output and input prices are quantities of outputs, z, and (minus) inputs r, respectively, total differentiation of (1) gives

$$dy = \sum_i (q_i - z_i)\, dp_i + \sum_i r_i\, dv_i . \qquad (2)$$

This is the familiar result, that those who are net producers benefit from a price change, and that those who are net consumers lose, and that, to a first approximation, the *amount* of the money-equivalent benefit (or loss) is the net amount produced (production less consumption) multiplied by the price change. Hence, the survey data not only identify the gainers and losers of a price change, but also quantify the sizes of their gains and losses. All this is obvious enough, but is nevertheless important. In many LDCs, where tax and welfare instruments are limited in number, there is a wide range of commodity taxes and subsidies. Many of these are justified on distributional grounds; imported consumer goods should be taxed because only the rich use them, or bus services should be subsidized to support the poor. By looking at (2) for different households, survey data can be used to check whether such claims are in fact correct, or whether they are simply a cover for special interests.

Provided that we accept the underlying economic assumptions of atomistic maximizing agents in competitive markets with minimal uncertainty, the evaluation of (2) requires only the raw data; no econometric model is required. Of course, there are different ways of presenting the results, and I shall give examples in Section 2.3 below of how non-parametric techniques can be used to illustrate the distributional issues in an immediately assimilable form. Note too that the basic result can be extended in various directions. In particular, (2) is a local approximation and so cannot safely be used except for small price changes. For large changes, a better approximation can be made by including substitution effects, effects that in some circumstances can also be estimated from the survey data, a topic to which I return in Section 2.1.

Note what happens when the policy involves a quantity change rather than a price change, as when additional health, education, or agricultural extension services are provided. If these publicly provided quantities are incorporated into the cost or profit functions, and a compensation is calculated as in (2), the result involves the shadow prices of the public goods, prices that can often be estimated using appropriate behavioral models, [see for example Gertler and van der Gaag (1990) and the studies reviewed in Jimenez (1987)]. However, even without such calculations, the survey data frequently tell us who uses the public goods, and by how much, something that is frequently of direct concern, even where we do not have estimates of how much the households value the services.

Beyond the direct use of survey data for policy, household surveys provide much of the raw material for modeling and trying to understand household behavior. I shall discuss a number of such studies and their results as I illustrate the various techniques.

1.1.3. Survey design and its implications for analysis

I shall use the "typical" household income and expenditure survey as my example, but many of the arguments can be applied to other types of surveys too. Such surveys typically collect data on a household basis – a household usually being defined as a group of people who share the same "cooking-pot" – and ask how much was spent over some reference period on a lengthy list of consumption items; the reference period can be anything from a day to a year, and sometimes varies by category of expenditure, with shorter recall periods for high frequency items like food, and longer periods for unusual purchases, like clothes or durable goods. In countries with near universal literacy, households can be asked to keep diaries; otherwise enumerators verbally ask respondents to recall individual purchases. Data are also collected on the respondents, at the very least covering the numbers, sexes, and ages, or people in the household. This can be extended to a range of household characteristics, such as education, occupation, and race. Data are frequently also collected on quantities consumed as well as expenditures, at least for readily measurable goods such as food. There will also be data on location, and perhaps more if the enumerators collect and retain data on the environment, for example on the size of the village, whether it has a school, and so on. Such surveys are sometimes carried out on an annual basis [Taiwan, Korea, India until 1973–1974 and since 1991], but more usually are done at intervals, often quinquennially, on the grounds that consumption patterns and levels of living and poverty do not change very quickly. The surveys are typically nationally representative, with each remaining in the field for a year, although there are also many special purpose surveys that are restricted in geographical coverage, and which last for a period shorter than a year.

Households are chosen at random, but there is a wide range of designs. The simplest is where each household in the country has an equal chance of being selected, but such simplicity is uncommon, if only because there are very different costs of obtaining data from different types of households. Rural households are more widely scattered than urban households, and in many LDCs, there are some households that live in inaccessible (sometimes even dangerous) areas. Any sample design that minimizes cost for a given degree of precision (or equivalently maximizes precision at given cost) will therefore lead to oversampling of urban and under sampling of rural households. Beyond this, interview procedures usually require more than one visit to each household. For example if a diary is kept, there will be an initial visit, a second visit to check that it is being kept correctly, and a collection visit after seven or fourteen days. In rural areas, where transport is a major cost of the survey, it therefore makes sense for the survey to group households into survey "clusters", often villages, with typically six to fifteen households in each cluster. The optimal number of households in the cluster involves a trade-off between the low marginal cost of drawing another household in a village that is already being visited, and the relatively low contribution to precision of such a household, given that it is likely to look rather similar to other households in the same village. The survey team remains in the village for a week or two, surveying all households in the cluster, and then moves on to a new cluster. Such surveys frequently attempt to give each household an equal chance of inclusion by using a two stage design, in which clusters are selected first, with a probability of inclusion proportional to size (i.e. the number of households in the cluster), while individual households are randomly selected at the second stage. The random selection of clusters and households is made from a "sampling frame", often a census. However, censuses are often badly out-dated, and in some countries are not reliable, either because of political interference – census returns are typically used to make voter rolls and sometimes to allocate resources – or because of difficulties of collection. Problems with censuses can be avoided as in India, where the National Sample Survey (NSS) selects villages from a village frame, and then lists all households in the village at a preliminary stage. The final drawing selects a stratified random sample from their own list, with stratification based on a few variables collected at the list stage, [see Murthy (1977, Chapter 15)] who also describes many of the other features of the design of the NSS, or (more generally) Casley and Lury (1981) for further description.

The relatively simple – and sensible – designs of the previous paragraphs can be complicated ad infinitum. Adjustments can be made for non-response, and for the consequences of replacing non-responders by "look-alike" households, although it should be noted that, unless households are approached at obviously inappropriate times, like harvests, non-response is typically much less of a problem in LDCs than in the United States (US). Probabilities of selection can also be linked to any ancillary information in the sampling frame or listing, such as occupation, housing status, or landholdings. As a result, survey tapes usually report for each household a sampling probability, or its reciprocal, an "inflation factor", which is the number of households in the country for which the household stands proxy. In complex designs, the inflation factors will be different for every household in the survey. Although designs are often "self-weighting", whereby in spite of the many strata and levels of strata each household has an equal chance of being included, refusals or other practical problems often frustrate the intention, and inflation factors remain relevant.

Many survey statisticians, in the US as well as in LDCs, see their role as producing an optimum design that will estimate the target magnitudes – for example the weights for the price index – in a way that trades off precision against cost. From such a perspective, any variable that is observed prior to the survey and is correlated with the target magnitude is a potential candidate for stratification. However, the more complex the design, the greater are the difficulties of using the data for anything other than the original purpose. Households may be stratified by variables that are endogenous to the processes that economists want to model, and even when this is not the case, the fact that samples are not simple random samples raises questions about the extent to which econometric results can be regarded as nationally representative. If it were to be widely recognized that household surveys have a wide range of important uses, then it would also be recognized that complex designs are dysfunctional, with sometimes quite small gains in precision obtained at the price of large compromises in the usefulness of the surveys. While there exist econometric techniques to correct samples for selectivity, as in Heckman (1976) or Manski and Lerman (1977), it is much better not to have to use them, see also the discussion in Section 2.1 below.

Given that development economists only rarely have control over survey protocols, there are a number of implications of design that should be born in mind when using survey data in econometric applications. I focus on three of the most important: the definition of the household, the measurement of dispersion, and the effects of designs other than simple random surveys.

1.1.4. The definition of the household

In many societies, people do not live in households that resemble the typical nuclear families of the US or Europe. Extended families, or members of a common lineage, may live in close proximity to one another, and only sometimes share the same cooking pot. The closeness of the group may vary with economic circumstances, with subunits becoming independent in good times and reuniting in adversity, see for example Ainsworth (1992) on fostering in West Africa. Even when there are separate households undertaking separate economic activities, assets may be held at an extended family level, as with the *chia* in Taiwan, [see Liu (1982) or Greenhalgh (1982)]. In many surveys, the decision whether to count multiple units as one or many households is essentially arbitrary, and in Thailand, a change from one to the other between the 1975–1976 and 1980–1981 surveys caused average household size to drop by about one person per household, [Government of Thailand (1977, 1983)]. Even for identical populations, the survey that distinguishes more households will show higher inequality and higher poverty, since combining households and assuming that each member has the same income or consumption amounts to a mean-preserving reduction in spread, see Haddad and Kanbur (1990). Since most surveys retain the same practices over time, trends in inequality and poverty are unlikely to be misleading, at least for these reasons, but the absolute levels will be incorrect, and international comparisons will be compromised.

1.1.5. Measuring means versus measuring dispersion

Surveys are usually designed to measure *means*, not dispersion, and there is a wide variety of designs that will measure means accurately, but will give very poor estimates of inequality, of poverty, or of other quantities that depend upon higher moments. Consider the measurement of income in an agricultural society where, to take an extreme case, all agricultural income is received in the month of the harvest. A design in which one twelfth of the sample is interviewed in each month and asked to report the previous month's income will generate an estimate of average income that is unbiased. But even if every household has the same annual income, the survey will appear to show that 100 percent of income is concentrated in the hands of 7.5 percent of households, and that 92.5 percent of households are "absolutely poor". Some surveys avoid these problems, at least in part, by revisiting households on a seasonal basis, but most do not. Once again, international comparisons of inequality and poverty are rendered meaningless, and in predominately agricultural societies with variable and weather-affected harvests, there will even be spurious shifts in apparent dispersion between different surveys in the same country, so that even the time path of inequality can be obscured.

The variability of income is one reason why many analysts prefer to use consumption as a basis for measurement. But consumption is not immune to the problem. Different surveys use different reporting periods, from a day to a year. Some purchases are made infrequently, and households stock up when they shop, so that the shorter the reporting period, the larger will be the apparent dispersion. For example, suppose that everyone has consumption c but that purchases are random, with a fraction p of households buying cp^{-1} during the reporting period, and the rest buying nothing. Simple calculation gives:

$$E(x) = p.cp^{-1} + (1-p).0 = c; \quad V(x) = c^2(1-p)p^{-1} \qquad (3)$$

where x is reported expenditure. As the reporting period becomes shorter, p will get smaller, and although the mean is unaffected, the variance will rise. There is no point in comparing distributions of expenditures from different surveys unless we know that the reporting periods are the same. Exactly the same point arises if we attempt to compare two countries one of which has a perishable staple that is bought frequently, while the other uses a storable staple that is bought rarely. Problems over reporting periods and over the definition of the household are two (of the many) reasons why we know so little about international comparisons of inequality and poverty; for others [see Berry (1985) and Fields (1992)].

1.1.6. Estimation of means in stratified samples

When different households have different probabilities of being included in the survey, unweighted sample means will generally be biased for the population means. Consider the simplest example where there are two sectors, sector 1, "urban" and sector 2, "rural", and where households in each are sampled with probabilities π_1 and π_2. We are interested in the random variable x, which is distributed in the populations of the two sectors with means μ_1 and μ_2. There are n observations in total, n_1 urban households and $n_2 = n - n_1$ rural households; these correspond to population figures of N, N_1 and N_2, so that $\pi_s = n_s N_s^{-1}$, $s = 1, 2$. The sample mean is

$$\bar{x} = (n_1 + n_2)^{-1} \sum_i x_i \tag{4}$$

with expectation

$$E(\bar{x}) = \frac{n_1}{n} \mu_1 + \frac{n_2}{n} \mu_2 . \tag{5}$$

The population mean, by contrast, is given by

$$\mu = \frac{N_1}{N} \mu_1 + \frac{N_2}{N} \mu_2 \tag{6}$$

so that the sample mean is biased unless either $\pi_1 = \pi_2$, in which case the sample is a simple random sample, or $\mu_1 = \mu_2$, so that the population is homogeneous, at least as far as the parameter of interest is concerned.

Neither of these requirements would usually be met in practice; for example, rural households are likely to be both poorer and costlier to sample. To get the right answer, we do the obvious thing, and compute a weighted mean. This can be done by defining "inflation factors" for each observation, equal to the reciprocals of the sampling probabilities, so that here

$$\theta_i = \pi_s^{-1}, \quad i \in s, s = 1, 2 . \tag{7}$$

Note that if we multiply each sample observation by its inflation factor and add, we obtain an unbiased estimate of the population *total*, something that is often of separate interest. However, if the inflation factors are scaled by their total to derive sampling weights $w_i = \theta_i / \Sigma\, \theta_k$, and we calculate a weighted mean, when we take expectations we get

$$
E\left(\sum w_i x_i\right) = \frac{n_1 \pi_1^{-1} \mu_1 + n_2 \pi_2^{-1} \mu_2}{n_1 \pi_1^{-1} + n_2 \pi_2^{-1}} = \frac{N_1 \mu_1 + N_2 \mu_2}{N_1 + N_2} = \mu \; .
\tag{8}
$$

which is the right answer. Similar weighting schemes can be applied to the estimation of any other population statistic that can be written as an average, including variances, quantiles, measures of inequality and of poverty. The simple idea to remember is that each household should be inflated to take account of the households that it represents but were not sampled, so as to make the inflated sample "as like" the population as possible.

While the underlying population in these exercises is finite (it is the population of all households in the country at the time of the survey), and although much of the inference in the sampling literature is conducted explicitly from such a perspective, so that expectations are taken over all the possible samples that can be drawn from the finite population, this is not the *only* framework for inference. In particular, the finite population can be regarded as itself being a "sample" from a "superpopulation" of similar households, households that might have existed or might exist in the future. In this way, the parameter μ (for example) is not the mean characteristic for the current population, but a parameter that characterizes the distributional law by which that population was generated. In this way, the superpopulation approach brings survey-sampling theory much closer to the usual sampling theory in econometric analysis where we are usually making inferences about behavioral parameters, not characteristics of finite populations.

1.1.7. Econometric estimation in stratified samples

All this is so familiar and so natural that it seems hardly worth the exposition. However, the simple weighting of observations is less obviously appropriate once we move from the estimation of means to even the simplest of econometric estimates, including ordinary least squares regression. Again, consider the simplest possible case, where there exists a linear relationship between y and x, but with coefficients β_1 and β_2 that differ by sector. Assuming zero means for both variables, write this

$$
y_i = x_i \beta_s + u_i, \quad s = 1, 2 \; .
\tag{9}
$$

Suppose that the parameter of interest is β, the population-weighted average of β_1 and β_2; given the two coefficients, this could be obtained by weighting each by the inflation factor for its sector. For example, if β_i is the marginal propensity to consume in each sector, the population-weighted average β would be the marginal propensity to consume out of a randomly allocated unit of currency, a quantity that is often of interest in discussions of tax and benefit reform.

As with the case of estimating the population mean, it is immediately clear that the (unweighted) OLS estimator using all of the data is biased and inconsistent. Instead, we might follow the principle of the previous subsection, weighting each household by the number of households that it represents in the survey, and compute the weighted estimator

$$\tilde{\beta} = \left(\sum_i w_i x_i^2 \right)^{-1} \left(\sum_i w_i x_i y_i \right) \tag{10}$$

where w_i is the normalized inflation factor. This estimator converges, not to β, but to

$$\text{plim } \tilde{\beta} = \frac{\beta + N_2 N^{-1} \beta_2 (m_2 - m_1) m_1^{-1}}{1 + N_2 N^{-1} (m_2 - m_1) m_1^{-1}} \tag{11}$$

where m_1 and m_2 are the (population) variances of x in each of the two sectors. Unlike the unweighted estimator, this quantity at least has the (limited) virtue of being independent of sample design; indeed, as is to be expected from the general argument for inflation factors, it is what OLS would give if applied to the data from the whole population [see Dumouchel and Duncan (1983)]. However, it is not equal to the parameter of interest β unless either $\beta_1 = \beta_2$, or $m_1 = m_2$; the former is ruled out by hypothesis, and there is no reason to suppose that the latter will hold in general.

Of course, the fundamental issue here is not the sample design but the fact that the regression is not homogeneous within the population being studied. As such, the problem is not a sampling issue – exactly the same issues arise in regressions using pooled time-series for a cross-section of countries – but a heterogeneity issue, and it comes to the fore in the sampling context because it is heterogeneity that justifies the stratification in the first place. As a result, it is often plausible that behavioral parameters will differ across strata, just as they are likely to vary across countries. When this is not the case, and regression coefficients are identical, then both weighted and unweighted regressions are unbiased and consistent, and the Gauss-Markov theorem tells us that the *unweighted* regression is to be preferred. If instead the regression coefficients differ by strata, that fact has to be explicitly faced and cannot be finessed by running regressions weighted by inflation factors. Such recommendations were once standard in econometric texts – [see for example Cramer (1969, pp. 142–143)] – but even so, many regressions using survey data are run in weighted form.

In cases where heterogeneity is suspected, there are several useful strategies. When there are only a few strata – rural versus urban would be the most frequent – it clearly makes sense to run separate regressions, and to use covariance analysis where the homogeneity hypothesis is of separate interest. When the number of strata is large, with relatively few observations in each, random coefficient specifications would seem more useful, and, as a result, analysts should routinely expect heteroskedasticity in OLS regressions. Standard heteroskedasticity tests can be used, for example that given by Breusch and Pagan (1979), which in this case would involve regressing squared residuals on dummy variables for each stratum and comparing half the resulting explained sum of squares with a χ^2 with degrees of freedom equal to the number of strata. Heteroskedastic consistent variance covariance matrices should also be routinely used, see Section 2.1 below.

I should conclude by noting that there is a school of thought that does not accept the argument against weighted regressions, Kish and Frankel (1974) being perhaps the most eloquent example. They argue that the stratification in many surveys is not of substantive interest in its own right, and that the parameters of a hypothetical census regression are indeed of interest. Others, such as Pfefferman and Smith (1985) take a view similar to that here, arguing (among other things) that a complete population is of no great interest since it is only one of the many possible populations with which we might have been confronted.

1.1.8. Estimation and other design features: clustering

Even if the regression coefficients are homogeneous across strata, standard formulae for standard errors may be incorrect depending on the survey design. Two-stage sampling will induce non-independence between households in the same cluster if households who live in the same village are subject to common unobservables, such as weather, tastes, or prices. Under such circumstances, whether we are estimating means or regressions, standard formulae for variances are incorrect and can be seriously misleading.

Consider first the straightforward use of survey data to estimate a mean. Given a set of n observations x_i, standard procedures call for the estimation of the mean and variance according to

$$\hat{\mu} = n^{-1} \sum_{1}^{n} x_j; \quad \hat{\sigma}^2 = (n-1)^{-1} \sum_{1}^{n} (x_1 - \bar{x})^2 . \tag{12}$$

If the observations are independent and identically distributed, the variance of $\hat{\mu}$ is given by

$$V(\hat{\mu}) = n^{-1}\sigma^2 \tag{13}$$

which can be estimated by replacing σ^2 by its estimate from (12). Consider now what happens when the x's are no longer i.i.d., but belong to clusters, and that within each cluster

$$E(x_i - \mu)(x_j - \mu) = \rho\sigma^2 \tag{14}$$

for some quantity ρ, while for two observations in different clusters, we retain the assumption of independence. Then, as shown by Kish (1965), and as may be readily confirmed, (13) must be replaced by

$$V(\hat{\mu}) = n^{-1}\sigma^2 d \tag{15}$$

where d is the Kish design effect, or "deff", defined by

$$d = 1 + (\tilde{n}_c - 1)\rho . \tag{16}$$

The quantity $\tilde{n}_c$ is the number of households in each cluster when the clusters are all the same size; more generally it is the weighted average of cluster sizes, where the weights are the cluster sizes themselves, i.e. $n^{-1}\Sigma n_c^2$ for individual cluster sizes n_c. An estimate of ρ can be obtained from the "intracluster correlation coefficient"

$$\hat{\rho} = \frac{\Sigma_c \Sigma_i \Sigma_{j \neq i} (x_{ci} - \hat{\mu})(x_{jc} - \hat{\mu})}{\hat{\sigma}^2 \Sigma_c n_c(n_c - 1)} . \tag{17}$$

A number of points should be noted. In the presence of positive intracluster correlations, the number of "effective" observations is smaller than the sample size. In the extreme case, when ρ is unity, d is the cluster size, and the effective sample size is the number of clusters, not the number of observations. Even when ρ is 0.5, a high but not unusual figure, the usual formula for the standard error of a mean is optimistic by a factor of 2.34 (the square root of 5), a correction that could make a substantial difference to the conclusions being drawn. Second, although I have illustrated using clusters, the same analysis might be useful within strata, or regions, or sectors, or any other partition of the sample for which there is reason to believe that the observations within each partition are correlated. When the partition is large, ρ is likely to be small, but the size of "deff" depends on the product, and might still be large.

Third, while a similar analysis applies to the residuals in a linear regression, and while it is still true that standard formulas are likely to underestimate the standard errors, the formulas are not exactly the same, and I postpone discussion of the regression case until Section 2.1 below. This is a major issue that has been much neglected, not only in development economics, but in other applied fields using survey data.

1.1.9. General measurement issues

I do not believe that there is any reason to suppose that survey data are always and automatically of lower quality in LDCs, as if "backwardness" were a condition that applied equally to GDP and its measurement. While statistical services are sometimes poorly funded and staffed, especially in Africa, survey data are often relatively cheap to collect in poor countries, and responses are likely to be accurate where there is a high degree of literacy, and where the respondents have time to talk to the enumerators. There are also some very poor countries (such as India) where survey practice is (or at least was) second to none. Indeed, Indian statisticians have played a leading role in the development of sample surveys and of sampling techniques; the surveys of jute production in Bengal by the Indian Statistical Institute under the direction of Mahalanobis were among the first successful large-scale sample surveys [see Mahalanobis (1944, 1946)]. It is also true that respondents tend to be much more patient in LDCs, that they rarely refuse to participate in the survey, and that they will usually tolerate instruments that take several hours to administer. The differences in quality of survey data between poor and rich countries comes, not from survey administration, but from differences in the structure of income and employment. In particular, difficulties in estimating income arise, not because of respondent unwillingness or because of fear that enumerators will pass information to the fiscal authorities, but because a large fraction of poor people in LDCs are self-employed, mostly in agriculture. Self-employment incomes are notoriously difficult to estimate in developed economies, and if income estimates in general are of lower quality in LDCs, it is because self-employment income is a larger fraction of the total.

The problems are easily seen. Self-employed traders or farmers typically have no need of any concept that corresponds to economists' definitions of income. Direct questions about income or profitability cannot therefore generate useful answers, especially for individuals whose personal and business transactions are not clearly separated. Instead, it is necessary for surveys to ask detailed questions about business or agricultural operations, about sales and purchases, about quantities and prices, about taxes and transfers, about multiple business activities, about transactions in kind, and about assets. From this detailed information, an income measure has to be built up by imposing an accounting framework on each household's activities. This is a very time-consuming and complex operation, and the value so obtained is likely to be an extremely noisy estimate of the underlying theoretical magnitude, even supposing that the theory has any behavioral relevance. For example, an appropriate accounting framework might well include some allowance for depreciation of assets, tools, buildings, trees, and animals. Yet unless farmers actually think in those terms, it is unclear that the measure will be useful in understanding the farmer's behavior, however relevant it may be for measuring welfare.

A further major issue is how to handle *autoconsommation*, that fraction of consumption that is produced (or grown, hunted or bartered) by the household without going through a market. Some societies, for example large fractions of rural West Africa, are not extensively monetized, and in extreme cases, non-monetized transactions may account for nearly a half of GDP, [Heston (1994)], and a good deal more of consumption. The standard survey procedure is for values to be imputed to such consumption, typically by surveying quantities, and then by multiplying by some suitable price. The results are added to consumption purchased in markets, as well as to the value of total income. Some mechanical and apparently sensible imputation algorithms can give absurd results. For example, in one comprehensive African survey, values were imputed for water consumption. Where no price was available for a particular transaction, imputation was done at the average of the prices reported by those households who did make monetary purchases. However, the only observed prices for water were for bottled water in the main city, so that rural households were credited with very high levels of total consumption and income, much of it "Perrier" from the local river. Such extreme cases are rare, but the problems are not.

The choice of prices for imputation is rarely obvious; selling prices differ from buying prices, and there are often quality differences (perhaps better, perhaps worse) between goods sold and those retained for home consumption. In extreme cases, where monetization is the exception rather than the rule, *autoconsommation* is the tail that wags the dog; not only is most of consumption measured by making essentially arbitrary assumptions, but there must be legitimate doubts as to the usefulness of imposing a market-based accounting framework on a household or village economy in which markets play little part. Even if all these problems are solved (or ignored), it should always be borne in mind that any errors of imputation will be common to both consumption and income – and perhaps other variables, such as landholdings, or agricultural output – and the communality must be taken into account when the effects of measurement error are being explored.

Note finally that the decision of what to impute is largely arbitrary. By convention, home produced goods are included, but most home produced services are excluded. Meat and vegetables from the home farm are added to both consumption and income, but no similar allowances are made for the value of work in the home, child-minding, or the preparation of meals. While there is a good deal of agreement on the desirability of including these services, and while it is clear that there are systematic biases from failing to do so – the failure to value leisure understates the relative poverty of single parents who have very little of it – there is little agreement on how to value time. If labor markets are sufficiently well-developed so that everyone can work as many hours as they wish at the market wage, then that wage would be the appropriate price for imputing time. But if people have limited opportunities for work, as is often the case for women in many parts of the world, the appropriate rate would be less, perhaps very much less. The mislabelling of unemployment as leisure is injury enough, without adding the insult of labelling the unemployed as wealthy on the basis of their enforced leisure.

1.2. Panel data

1.2.1. Data collection

Most household surveys, in both developed and developing countries, draw new households for each new survey, so that it is generally impossible to track any given household through successive surveys. In a few cases however, most notably the World Bank's Living Standards Surveys (LSS) in Côte d'Ivoire and Ghana, the ICRISAT data from six villages in southern India, and in data collected in Pakistan and the Philippines under the auspices of the International Food Policy Research Institute, have individual households been revisited on a systematic basis at intervals of a year or more. The Living Standards Surveys have a rotating structure, with half of the households from the previous year retained and half replaced, so that data are obtained from each household on two occasions separated by a year. There have been a few other cases where households from a previous survey have been revisited, even though the original survey was not designed to be a panel. The National Council for Applied Economic Research (NCAER) in Delhi revisited a sample of Indian households after a ten year gap, Bevan, Collier, and Gunning (1989) used follow-up surveys in Kenya and Tanzania, and Smith, Thomas and Karoly (1992) report on a 1990 follow-up survey of the households in the 1978 Malaysian Family Life Survey. In all these cases, a large fraction of households or household members was found, nearly three-quarters of the latter in the Malaysian case, which is presumably a much higher fraction of those who are still alive and still resident in the country. Since the fractions reinterviewed would presumably have been higher had the resurvey been planned from the start, these experiences do not support any general supposition that panel data are more difficult to collect in LDCs, because households are "hard to find" or because of attrition in general.

Unlike cross-sections, panel surveys yield data on *changes* for individuals or individual households. Individual changes are of interest in their own right; we want to know how individual living standards change during the development process, the "who is benefiting from development" question, and we want to know whether poverty and deprivation are transitory or long-lived, the income dynamics question. Even beyond the individual, a panel design will allow more precise measurement of *aggregate* changes if the variable being measured is positively autocorrelated in the individual data, [see for example Hansen, Hurwitz, and Madow (1953, pp. 268–272) and Ashenfelter, Deaton, and Solon (1986, pp. 44–51)] for formulae. These results suggest that, even for general purpose surveys, and even when we are interested in levels as well as changes, it will generally be undesirable to replace *all* households from one survey to the next.

Changes over time in the behavior of individuals can also reveal regularities that may be obscured by individual heterogeneity in the cross-section. For example, the cross-section relationship between age and wages usually has a humped shape, with wages rising early in the life cycle, and falling later. However, older workers may be systematically different from younger workers; they may be less educated or have less experience in working with modern techniques, and their wages may have been lower throughout their lives. If so, the cross-section age-wage profile will be quite different from the profile that would result from following an individual or a cohort of individuals through time, something that is possible with panel data. By making comparisons for individuals with their own earlier behavior, each individual is effectively acting as his or her own control. There exists an extensive econometric literature that exploits this insight using panel data, and the techniques are frequently used in work on economic development. I shall return to the topic in Sections 2.1 and 2.2 below.

1.2.2. The Living Standards Surveys

The general usefulness of panel data in LDCs is an issue that is unlikely to be decided for some time, but our knowledge has recently been much expanded by the experience of the World Bank's Living Standards Surveys. These surveys have sometimes been independent cross-sections, but rotating panel data have been collected in Côte d'Ivoire, from 1985 through 1988, and in Ghana, from 1987 on a continuing basis. The LSS was originally seen as a device for monitoring poverty and inequality, and the project was begun in the Bank in response to the then (as now) extremely unsatisfactory situation in respect of international comparisons of poverty and inequality. In one example that was key at the time, it was essentially impossible in the late 1970s to deduce what had happened to distribution in Brazil during the "economic miracle" of the 1960s, whether the poor had benefitted from the income growth, or whether the benefits had flowed to a narrow wealthy group, see the original analysis by Fields (1977) and the criticism by Ahluwalia et al. (1980). Although a set of international comparisons of inequality had earlier been produced within the World Bank by Jain (1975), these were simply compilations of survey data that happened to be available within the organization at the time, with no attempt to allow for differences in definition, or to correct for non-comparabilities between countries. (Given the difficulties, Jain's figures are not a sound basis on which to make international comparisons, and results that rely on them should be viewed with great skepticism, [see for example Anand and Kanbur's (1993) critique of Ahluwalia (1976)], although the lesson is widely ignored in the recent political economy literature, for example Persson and Tabellini (1990) and Alesina and Perotti, (1992).

However, by the time the first LSS surveys were ready to be implemented, as a cross section in Peru in 1984, and with a rotating panel in Côte d'Ivoire a year later, the emphasis within the World Bank had shifted away from poverty more towards a household modelling approach. Influenced by Beckerian models of household behavior, by their extension to integrated farm-household models as in Singh, Squire, and Strauss (1986), as well as by previous experience with RAND's Malaysian Family Life Survey, the philosophy was to collect data from a relatively small number of households, but to attempt to be comprehensive, covering consumption, all income generating activities, agriculture, labor supply, business activities, gifts and transfers, as well as education (including parents' education), migration, demographics, health, and fertility, as well as some limited measurement of anthropometrics. The Ivorian data, for example, come from 1600 households, selected as a simple random sample, 800 of whom were retained as panel members, with a new 800 added each year. The 50 percent rotation pattern comes from a desire to collect at least some panel data combined with doubts about the feasibility of running a much longer panel in Africa, and from the ever present need to produce results relatively quickly.

One of the most impressive achievements of the LSS is its demonstration that microcomputer technology can be used effectively in collecting data in LDCs. A full description of the methodology is given in Ainsworth and Muñoz (1986). Responses were quickly taken to local headquarters, and entered into PCs, and then immediately run through editing programs, so that cross-checks and corrections could be carried out on subsequent visits. The rapid data entry and editing programs also mean that data are available very quickly at the end of the survey, and the teams produced preliminary survey reports within a few months of leaving the last household. The data are thus immediately available for policy analysis, an enormous improvement over previous practice, where survey results were in most countries available only years – in some cases many years – after the end of the survey.

To the extent that it is possible to tell from internal evidence, the LSS data are typically of good quality, although the breadth of the survey clearly carries some price in terms of depth and in the ability to monitor subpopulations. For example, the agricultural modules typically do not produce the sort of reliable harvest estimates that could be obtained from sample crop-cutting in an agricultural survey. But this was by design, and in many applications is offset by knowing the farmer's other activities, his and his parents' education levels, his migration history, ethnic group, and so on. The retrospective questions appear to have worked well, so that, for example, it is possible to use the fertility questions to construct reasonable estimates of changes in infant mortality over time, [see Benefo and Schultz (1993) for estimates for Ghana and Côte d'Ivoire].

Like most surveys, the LSS surveys are designed to collect data, not to experiment with survey methodology, so that it is difficult to use their results to come to general conclusions. The surveys have certainly been expensive relative to most established surveys in LDCs, with costs per household per year ranging between $100–$200 at 1990 prices, although it could be argued that high costs reflect the set-up costs of a new product.

One lesson from these surveys is that in countries where economic development is slow or non-existent, as in much of Africa, and where survey measures of living standards are error prone, as in Africa and elsewhere, measures of change, at both individual and aggregate levels will be dominated by measurement error. Over short periods, living standards in agriculture are variable in any case, so that short panels of a year or two are unlikely to give useful measures either of income dynamics or of the change in living standards, except possibly in the most rapidly developing countries. This is even true for "straightforward" concepts such as household size; in West Africa there is a great deal of genuine mobility among both adults and children – see particularly Ainsworth (1992) – but even here there appears to be a good deal of measurement error.

A second lesson is that it is very difficult to maintain new surveys in the field for any length of time. In the Ivorian case, personnel changes in the World Bank led to a loss of interest, and the survey ceased after 1988 apparently without leaving any permanent enhancement of Ivorien survey capability. This was particularly unfortunate because, in the face of collapsing world prices, procurement prices of cocoa and coffee – the main cash crops in Côte d'Ivoire – were cut by a half, the first such cut since independence. Had the panel been in place, the survey could have observed the process of adaptation as smallholders reacted to the cuts, but the opportunity was lost.

Third, while the computer technology has been successfully applied to the collection of data, it has been much less used for its rapid analysis, particularly in a policy context within the countries themselves. The data are now widely analyzed in academia and in international organizations, but neither analytical capacity nor software exists to make survey data rapidly available to support domestic policy making. As a result, there is less local interest in continuing surveys than is warranted by their potential utility. There have also been difficulties over setting up proper mechanisms to allow access to scholars and to the policy community. The World Bank is an operational entity, not a research foundation, and there are also legitimate interests of countries that have to be protected. Nevertheless, there would have been great benefits to constructing adequate access agreements before any data were collected, agreements that provided for public-use versions of the data at marginal cost.

Fourth and finally, I suspect that if there is a real payoff to panel data, it is over relatively long time periods, five or ten years, or even longer. Perhaps the most interesting and important work using the PSID has come from looking at income changes over long periods of time, or of comparing incomes and consumption patterns of parents and their children [Behrman and Taubman (1990), Solon (1992), Zimmerman (1992), Altonji, Hayashi and Kotlikoff (1989) and Hayashi, Altonji, and Kotlikoff (1991)]. Even here, some of the results are identical to those obtained earlier using recall data, see Sewell and Hauser (1975), and this much cheaper alternative may not be inferior for many applications. Even at best, economic development is far from instantaneous, so that changes from one year to the next are probably too noisy and too short-term to be really useful. It is hard to imagine nationally representative panels being maintained for ten or twenty years, and international organizations and foundations do not have the attention span nor the ability to commit resources over such periods. Perhaps the most promising line of research is one in which one time surveys are designed with at least the possibility of a revisit at some unspecified future date, so that ad hoc panel data can be collected on an opportunistic basis. We also need more evidence on the reliability of recall data for different kinds of information; [again see Smith, Thomas and Karoly (1992) who compare reports of the same migration events obtained in two surveys twelve years apart]. Alternatively, national survey programs might usefully incorporate some panel element, either by deciding in advance to revisit some subsample of households quinquennially or decennially, or by adding a small component of shorter period rotating panel households to their pre-existing surveys.

While there is likely to be some payoff to further experiments with panel data, it is important not to overstate the potential benefits. The PSID in the United States has generated a great deal of important *methodological* work in econometrics, but it is hard to point to any *substantive* conclusion that depends on the existence of these data. Attrition problems, especially in the early years, and the continuing presence of measurement error have made it difficult even to describe the "facts" of dynamic household behavior. Beyond that, the use of the PSID in the more ambitious research programs on life-cycle labor supply and consumption can only be described as a disaster, [see Card (1991) for a review of the labor supply literature and Deaton (1992a, Chapter 5) for the work on the intertemporal allocation of consumption].

1.2.3. Panels from a series of cross-sections

Many countries carry out their household surveys on a regular basis, often using the same instrument over time, in which case there will exist a time-series of cross-sections. Such data can be used for many of the purposes to which panel data are put, and in some respects provide a superior database.

Consider, for example, the Surveys of Personal Income Distribution that have been carried out in Taiwan every year since 1976. While it is not possible to track individuals or households from 1976–1991, it is perfectly feasible to track *cohorts* of individuals. If for example, we are interested in how individual earnings have changed in any economy experiencing very rapid growth, we can follow the mean earnings of the same group through time by looking at the members of the group who are randomly selected into each survey. If our first cohort is those born in 1951, who were 25 years old in 1976, we use the 1976 survey to calculate average earnings – or average log earnings, if that is the variable of interest – for all 25 year-olds, the 1977 survey for the average earnings of 26 year-olds, and so on, up to the average earnings of 40 year-olds in 1991. Figure 33.1, taken from Deaton and Paxson (1994a), shows the results for every fifth cohort; the connected lines track the behavior of each cohort. The figure shows a life-cycle pattern in earnings, together with strong cohort effects, with the younger cohorts earning more. As a result, it is the youngest groups whose earnings have grown the most rapidly; the average 55 year-old in 1976 had relatively little earnings growth over the subsequent fifteen years.

Such data cannot be used to look at income dynamics; even if the membership of the cohort is constant, we can estimate only the marginal distributions of income in each year, whereas estimation of income dynamics require us to observe the joint distributions, which can only come from panel data. That case apart, time-series of cross-sections can perform many of the other functions of panel data. Linear regressions with individual fixed effects can be averaged to give cohort relationships with cohort fixed effects, and can be consistently estimated by differencing the cohort level data or by using within estimators. Note too that, since we start from the individual data, the aggregation can be done over whatever function of the data is prescribed by the theory; averages of logs or of powers are as easily calculated as averages of levels. Since the cross-sections draw new households in each survey, there is no

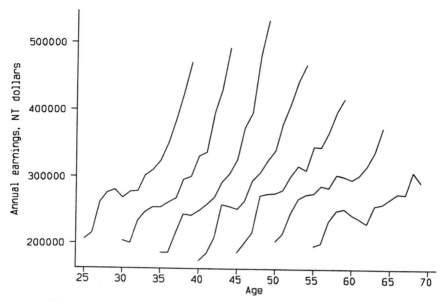

Figure 33.1. Annual earnings of seven age cohorts, Taiwan 1976–1990.

attrition bias as there is in genuine panel data, although with older cohorts, there will be (typically non-random) attrition through death, and immigration and migration will change cohort membership at all ages. The averaging will also yield less measurement error in the cohort than in the micro data provided that, as is plausible, misreporting is sufficiently uncorrelated across members of the cohort. Of course, unless the cohorts are very large, observed cohort means will estimate population cohort means with a sampling error, but the size of the error can be estimated and the appropriate corrections made using what are essentially error-in-variable estimators [see Deaton (1985) and Tan (1991) who applies these methods to life-cycle labor supply in Korea]. I shall return to the theory of these estimators when I come to the econometrics of measurement error in Section 2.1 below.

1.3. National income and other data

I have discussed household survey data at some length because, in that case, it is possible to go beyond ritual complaints about quality and quantity, and to think constructively about the effects on econometric practice of data collection, design, and measurement error. However, a great deal of econometric work in development uses non-survey data. Indeed, there has been a recent explosion of empirical work on economic growth, [see for example, Barro (1991), Barro and Sala-i-Martin (1992), Mankiw, Romer, and Weil (1992), and Levine and Renelt (1992) for four leading examples]. Most of this work is based on (and to some extent inspired by) the internationally comparable national accounts data constructed by the international price comparion project at the University of Pennsylvania, [Kravis, Heston, and Summers (1978)], and whose latest incarnation is the Penn World Table, Mark V, [Summers and Heston (1991)]. Many researchers also use the World Development Indicators, published annually by the World Bank, and which contain, in addition to a large number of social and other indicators, a competing set of national accounts – converted at official exchange rates rather than purchasing power parity exchange rates – and which, like the Summers–Heston data, are conveniently available on diskette. The Bank, the International Monetary Fund, the United Nations, and the International Labor Office all produce a wide range of other data relevant for development work, on trade, on debt, on international finance, on labor, and on social and demographic indicators.

Any sort of evaluation of this multiplicity of sources would quickly fill the whole of this Handbook. I confine myself to (*a*) a discussion of some of the index number problems that underlie international and intertemporal comparisons of income and output, and (*b*) a brief review of quality issues, the latter drawing on a recent set of conference papers on the topic.

1.3.1. Index number problems and international comparisons

Before looking at the *practical* quality issues, it is worth reviewing the *conceptual* index-number problems that underlie international comparisons of income and output. The actual Penn World Tables are a good deal more complex than the examples here, which are chosen to illustrate only the main points. Current price local currency GDP for country *c* at time *t* can be written as the sum of its component goods and services, or

$$y_{ct} = \sum_k p_{ckt} q_{ckt} \, , \tag{18}$$

where *p*'s are prices, *q*'s quantities, and *y* is income or output. Since GDP is an aggregate of value added, not of output, we must assume that there is some quantity or quantity aggregate that represents value added, something that requires suitable separability assumptions on the structure of production [see Sims (1969) and Arrow (1974)]. However, my main concern here is with different index number problems.

Suppose that there is some base country *b*, say, and prices are collected for each good in each country – and this is the main task of an international price comparison project – so that GDP can be repriced, using period *s* prices in country *b* as

$$y_{ct}^{bs} = \sum_k p_{bks} q_{cki} \,.$$

(19)

If country *b* is, for example, the US, and $s = t$, then y_{ct}^{bt} is country *c*'s GDP at US prices, and the ratio of y_{ct} to y_{ct}^{bt} is the purchasing power parity (*PPP*) exchange rate of country *c*'s currency in terms of US dollars. If the *PPP* exchange rate were equal to the official exchange rate – which is not usually the case – GDP at US prices could be obtained without collecting price data simply by conversion, as is done for the data reported in the *WDR*. For measuring real economic growth, we need constant price series, so that, in addition to a base country, we need a base year with a base set of relative prices. Alternatively, as in the recommended and most commonly used series in the Penn World Table, the base can be updated year by year to construct a chain index of GDP.

The problem of choosing base prices and a base country, like all index number "problems", is a conceptual and not a practical one. In principle, there is no reason other than convention to use US prices rather than Korean, Kenyan, or Chilean prices, and since they measure essentially different things, the ratio (for example) of Indian to Chinese GDP will differ depending on the choice. When making comparisons of GDP over time within a single developed country, the same conceptual difficulties arise, but because relative prices change slowly over time, the growth rate of GDP is hardly affected by the choice of base period. For those LDCs where a large share of GDP is concentrated in one or two primary commodities, this is not true, and even comparisons over time become hazardous. These difficulties are perhaps most severe for non-diversified oil exporters, although there are many other commodities (e.g. copper, cocoa, coffee) that have highly variable prices, and that make up a large fraction of GDP for some countries.

Figures 33.2 and 33.3 illustrate the time-series and cross-section implications of the choice of base prices. Figure 33.2 shows real GDP in Nigeria from 1965 to 1985 using two different Summers–Heston measures; according to both sets of estimates, GDP rose until the late 1970s, and has been declining since. The terms-of-trade corrected measure of GDP on the vertical axis allows for the effects on national income of changes in commodity exports and imports, while the chain measure on the horizontal axis does not. Nigeria is a major oil exporter and so has much greater growth using the terms-of-trade corrected measure. Since the Summers–Heston measures are equal by construction in 1985, Nigeria's GDP is very much lower in the earlier years when relative commodity prices are continuously adjusted; in 1965, the adjusted GDP

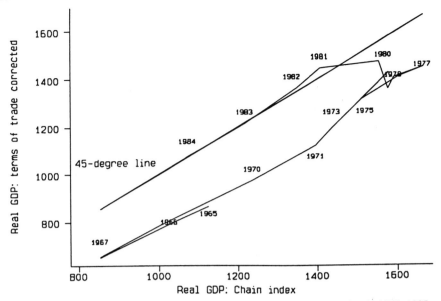

Figure 33.2.   The effects of commodity prices on national income, Nigeria 1965–1985.

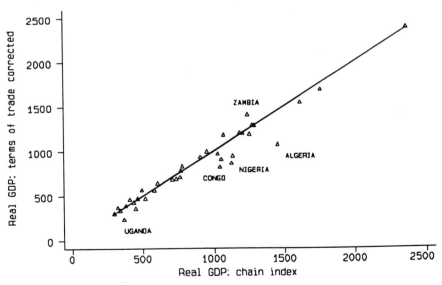

Figure 33.3.   Real GDP in 1970, chain and terms of trade corrected, Africa.

estimate is only 77 percent of the chain estimate. Figure 33.3 shows both estimates for 1970 for all the African economies in the Penn World table. Most countries are close to the 45-degree line, but there are many exceptions: the ratios of adjusted to unadjusted GDP were 69 percent for Algeria, 80 percent for Lesotho, 79 percent for Nigeria, 62 percent for Uganda, and 128 percent for Zambia (the price of copper was *lower* in 1985 than in 1970.) Although some of these differences reflect the difference between output and income measures of GDP–commodity price changes have no (direct) effect on physical output although they make the country richer or poorer – these examples should illustrate the conceptual difficulties of making international comparisons in a many commodity world. (Note that I am not concerned here with measurement error, but with what is essentially an aggregation problem. The Penn World Table take their underlying data from the national accounts of the countries themselves, and these data are repriced, not corrected.)

Although these difficulties are real enough, they are minor compared with those in making comparisons across space. International differences in relative prices are both large and systematic, so that the choice of base country makes a large difference to the estimates. Because labor is relatively cheap in poor countries, the relative price of non-tradeables to tradeables rises with economic development, so that, for example, services and government tend to be relatively cheap, and investment relatively expensive in poorer countries. There are associated substitution patterns in both production and consumption which give rise to the standard biases associated with fixed weight or current weight index numbers. Using American wage rates to revalue Indian labor costs will tend to overstate Indian relative to American GDP, because Indian GDP is (or should be) more specialized in labor-intensive activities, a substitution effect that is turned into apparently high income by applying the prices of a labor-scarce economy. In India, servants – both domestic and civil – are cheap and widely used, so that, at American prices, the real size of the domestic service sector in India is exaggerated. For the same reasons, making comparisons in American prices will bias down the estimated growth rates of the poorer countries, since rising real wages will narrow the relative price differentials, and progressively reduce the exaggeration of GDP in LDCs.

Once we go beyond output measures to interpret GDP as a measure of living standards, then we also have to face the question of whether it makes sense to treat preferences as identical across countries, or at the very least, whether international differences in climate and the conditions of production do not severely compromise international welfare comparisons. The problem of calculating the comparative costs-of-living for an American diplomat in Karachi or Reykjavik is well-defined and calculable to some degree of approximation. It is more of an open question whether it makes sense to compare the living standards of a Nepalese peasant and a Taiwanese fisherman, let alone those of an American lawyer and a Namibian bushman.

1.3.2. Quality issues in development data

This brief review section is based on a set of papers from a conference on databases for development. I have benefitted particularly from the overview paper by Srinivasan (1994), as well as those by Bouis (1994) on nutrition, by Chamie (1994) on demography, by Evenson and Pray (1994) on agriculture, by Rozansky and Yeats (1994) on trade, by Heston (1994) on national income and growth rate comparisons, and by Behrman and Rosenzweig (1994) on labor force and education data. The interested reader should consult these papers; only a few highlights are summarized here.

There are a number of other important *practical* issues in international *national income data*. Heston (1994) points out that the share of non-monetized subsistence in GDP can be greater than 40 percent in the poorest countries, that its measurement is fraught with difficulties, and that the solutions are far from uniform across countries. Many LDCs estimate GDP growth using growth rates of physical indicators, with benchmark weights that are frequently seriously outdated. Given GDP, consumption is obtained as a residual by subtracting net exports from trade flows, government expenditure, and investment in plant and machinery. Over-invoicing of imports and under-invoicing of exports are common methods of transferring funds abroad in countries with exchange controls and overvalued exchange rates, and such practices compromise not only the trade data, but will lead to overstatement of consumption and understatement of saving. In largely agricultural societies, estimation of physical output is difficult, and evidence [in Srinivasan (1994) and Evenson and Pray (1994)] suggests that discrepancies between household survey and national accounts estimates of food consumption and production in India may come more from the national accounts than from the surveys. This is an important lesson with implications beyond India, since national income estimates of income and consumption are nearly always given more weight than survey estimates when there are discrepancies between the two, a practice that has little justification in general.

There have also been suggestions that estimates of GNP are manipulated for political ends. It is certainly true that one of the more widely noted ratios, the relative per capita GDP of India and China is a number about which it is hard to obtain reliable estimates. The Penn World Tables Mark 5 estimate that in 1985 international prices, China's GDP per capita at $1,883 was 2.71 times that of India in 1985. The previous version (Mark 4) of the same tables gives the ratio, again for 1985, at 3.26, now calculated in 1980 prices. Srinivasan (1994) quotes the 1992 WDR figures of $350 for India and $370 for China in 1990, and points out that the respective growth rates over 1965–1990 (in the same publication) are 1.9 percent and 5.5 percent. If these figures are correct, in 1965 GNP per capita in China was only 44 percent of that in India, a statistic that defies belief.

Counting *people, births, and deaths* is also problematic. Chamie (1994) points out that there are a number of LDCs who have yet to carry out their first census, that only a third of LDCs have had a census since 1985, and that 27 percent of countries have a latest census that was conducted prior to 1975. Recent, reliable data on life-expectancy (infant mortality) are available for only a half (a quarter) of LDCs, and two-thirds of African countries have collected no data on life-expectancy since 1970. Many of the figures published in the *World Development Report* and the UN's *Human Development Report* are estimates and projections, not measurements.

There are also puzzles and discrepancies in data on *health, education,* and *nutrition.* Self-reported health data in LDCs typically show a *positive* correlation between living standards and ill-health, something that is usually attributed to better-off people reporting a larger fraction of health problems. Recent work at RAND appears to have made real progress on this issue [see Strauss, Gertler, Rahman, and Fox (1992)]. Questions about ADLs (Activities of Daily Living, such as walking and eating) and IADLs (Instrumental Activities of Daily Living, such as shopping) ask respondents whether, for example, they would find it easy, difficult, or very difficult, to perform a set of specified tasks (climbing stairs, fetching water) that are relevant to everyday life. The results of these questions reveal more sensible, richer, and interesting patterns of health with income and age than do the previous self-reported measures. Education data often exaggerate enrolments, by reporting attendance on the first day of school, or by expressing total enrollments, including those of adult students and grade repeaters as a fraction of the normal age groups for those grades, so that enrolment fractions greater than unity are possible [see Behrman and Rosenzweig (1994)].

Nutritional data are usually obtained from survey data on household purchases of food, and less often from 24-hour food consumption recall data. The latter generate much lower income elasticities of calories and of foods than do the former, Bouis (1994). Bouis argues in favor of the lower figures, on the grounds that traditional food elasticities imply implausible weight patterns. If the food (and calorie) elasticity is 0.4, say, then people in the top decile of the income distribution, who are perhaps six times as well off as people in the bottom decile, consume more than twice as much food and calories as those in the bottom decile, and ought therefore to weigh more than twice as much, something that we do not observe. Not everyone would accept the existence of such a reliable and simple relationship between calories and weight, even in the long-term, nor is it clear that the purchase method of calculating nutrition is necessarily worse than the more invasive and detailed recall surveys. The problem cannot be attributed to imputation biases in the survey data along the lines discussed above [see Bouis and Haddad (1992) and Subramanian and Deaton (1992)]; the latter paper also rules out functional form problems. However, it is possible, as Bouis argues, that there is a very high income elasticity of food wastage and of food gifts to servants, relatives, and even animals, thus reconciling the purchase with the intake data.

Finally, there is an excellent discussion of the quality of international trade data by Rozansky and Yeats (1994) who look for inconsistencies (*a*) across different sources, particularly the U.N., the Fund, and the Bank, (*b*) between trading partners, comparing recorded imports of *A* from *B* with recorded exports from *B* to *A*, (*c*) between trade totals over commodity groups and their component sums, and (*d*) across revisions of SITCs, for those groups not affected by the reclassifications. The results are far from encouraging, and by all criteria, trade data from LDCs show more and greater discrepancies than data for OECD countries, with discrepancies apparently worsening over time. To take just one example, comparisons under (*b*) show that only 2–3 percent of US or French trade gets "lost", compared with more than 50 percent for South Africa (not surprisingly), Venezuela, Seychelles, and Bahrain. The IMF's estimate of Venezuela's 1982 exports is 20 times larger than that compiled by the UN.

1.3.3. Some implications

The news from this section is dismal. National income and growth comparisons across countries are plagued by conceptual index number problems, and by immense practical difficulties. Many frequently used data from LDCs are of poor quality, or only pretend to exist, having their only reality in the mind of bureaucrats in New York or Washington. And while the Penn World Table, which provides probably the best and certainly the most heavily used set of national income data, has provided a great step forward in producing data at a common set of prices, it cannot be better than the raw (and uncorrected) data from the individual countries on which it is based.

What then should be done? Researchers should obviously be encouraged to be critical of the data, and to take every opportunity to explore the consequences of measurement error for their analysis. However, when the data are of such low quality that it is difficult to establish any results – as with much of the official macroeconomic data for Africa – it is difficult to pinpoint specific problems, or to know where to press for improvement. It is also clearly sensible to press for more resources to be devoted to data collection, and it would be a notable improvement if international agencies were to advertise their data more precisely, so that, for example, projections and estimates were clearly separated from genuine measurements. There have been questions as to whether the international organizations have any real interest in improving data collection. Skeptics have argued that the World Bank (or at least its loan staff) is interested in the *quantity* of loans, not ultimately in their *quality*, and that without an interest in the latter, there is little chance that the necessary resources will be committed to the improvement of the data either on its own account, or by helping to improve data collection by its member countries. In defense, it must be remembered that international organizations are responsible to their members, and in many cases are limited in the extent to which they can correct, question, or criticize the data that are provided by the member countries. Unless policy makers can be persuaded that the quality of their decisions are being compromised by poor data, they are unlikely to find the resources to improve matters.

2. Econometric tools for development analysis

2.1. Econometric analysis of survey data

In this second part of the review, I discuss a series of econometric techniques that are particularly appropriate for or are widely used in the analysis of development questions. In this first of three sections, I shall be concerned mostly with techniques used in the analysis of survey data, although a good deal of the material applies more generally. Subsequent sections deal with time-series and non-parametric issues respectively. My focus is on developments in econometric practice over the last ten or fifteen years, and how they relate to practice in published work in economic development. In particular, I attempt to identify a number of topics where best practice is somewhat ahead of what is readily available in the textbooks. One topic that will occur repeatedly is *robustness*. Inferences that rest on arbitrary – sometimes even incredible – assumptions are hard to take seriously, and there has been a major effort in econometrics – as in statistics more generally – to find ways of generating conclusions that are both credible and convincing and that are not the more or less immediate consequence of arbitrary supporting assumptions.

An important role of econometrics is to substitute for experimentation, and much of the econometric literature on simultaneity, heterogeneity, selectivity, omitted variables, and measurement error can be thought of as finding procedures that can bring the non-experimental results closer to the experimental ideal. Many of these procedures rest on strong parametric assumptions, some of them necessarily so, but others do not, and in some cases it is possible to obtain results with quite unobjectionable assumptions. When this is not so, the fact is in itself important, since it implies that robust inferences are not possible, and that the assumptions of the investigator are as necessary as the data for drawing the conclusions.

Even for standard and well-understood techniques, such as linear regression, inferences can be made more robust, either by moving away from OLS to alternatives such as quantile regression, or less radically, by calculating standard errors in ways that are robust against the failures of standard assumptions that are common in survey data. I begin this section with these topics.

2.1.1. Heteroskedasticity and linear regression

As is well-known, the presence of heteroskedasticity in linear regression affects neither the unbiasedness nor the consistency of OLS estimation. However, the assumptions of the Gauss-Markov theorem are violated, so that OLS is no longer efficient, and the usual formula for the variance-covariance matrix of the parameter estimates is no longer valid. In particular, if the regression model is, for $i = 1, \ldots n$,

$$y_i = x_i \beta + u_i; \ E(u_i) = 0; \ E(u_i^2) = d_i > 0, \tag{20}$$

and the OLS estimator is, as usual, $(X'X)^{-1}X'y$, then the variance-covariance matrix is given by

$$V = (X'X)^{-1}X'DX(X'X)^{-1} \tag{21}$$

where D is an $n \times n$ diagonal matrix whose diagonal is the d's from (20). Although V in (21) cannot be evaluated without knowledge of the d's, it has been shown by Eicker (1967), Huber (1967), Fuller (1975) and White (1980), that it can be consistently estimated by replacing D by the diagonal matrix whose elements are the squared OLS residuals. Note that the consistency here is of the matrix V, not of D, the number of elements in which increases with the sample size, and which therefore cannot be consistently estimated. Following White and MacKinnon (1985), this relatively straightforward calculation can be modified and extended in a number of ways, some of which are likely to yield improvements in performance. These methods yield estimates of the variance covariance matrix that are asymptotically valid, and do not require the user to know or to specify the specific form of the heteroskedasticity in (20).

As I argued in Section 1, the stratification of surveys is likely to generate heteroskedasticity, and even without it, experience suggests that residuals are more often heteroskedastic than not. There are a number of tests for heteroskedasticity, of which perhaps the most convenient is that suggested by

Breusch and Pagan (1979), in which the squared OLS residuals are regressed on variables that are thought to be likely candidates for causing the heteroskedasticity, usually including the levels, squares, and interactions of the original explanatory variables. Indeed, as is easily checked, this is the correct specification if β in (20) is taken to be distributed randomly in the population. Under the assumption that the original regression errors are normally distributed, the null of homoskedasticity implies that the explained sum of squares of this supplementary regression will be distributed as χ^2 with degrees of freedom equal to the number of regressors in the supplementary regression. This test is closely related to the information matrix test proposed by White (1980).

It is clearly good practice to calculate and report standard errors and other test statistics that are robust to departures from homoskedasticity. Furthermore, my own experience suggests that it is difficult to pass the Breusch–Pagan test in practical applications, and that heteroskedasticity is usually revealed not just by this test, but by others, such as the quantile regression techniques discussed below. That said, the heteroskedasticity-consistent standard errors and tests are rarely very different from those given by the standard formulas. An upward correction of about 30 percent to standard errors appears to be common, and this correction would not normally lead to startling differences in inference.

2.1.2. Clustering and linear regression

In Section 1 above, I showed that when observations within survey clusters are correlated, survey cluster sampling requires a revision of the formula for the standard error of an estimated mean. In particular, the usual variance, which is the population variance divided by the sample size, has to be multiplied by the Kish design effect (16), which depends on the average number of observations per cluster and the size of the intracluster correlation coefficient. Similar considerations apply to the estimation of linear regressions when there are grounds for believing that the errors are correlated within clusters. The fact that the sample is clustered does not in itself imply that there must be a non-zero intracluster correlation once other explanatory variables have been taken into account. However, survey clusters in rural areas in LDCs are typically geographically dispersed villages, so that there are likely to be unobserved communalities that are shared between households in the same village, and that differentiate them from those in other villages. Note too that there may be intrahousehold correlations between households beyond the cluster levels, for example across provinces or regions, correlations that could come from ethnic factors, from the way in which markets operate, or from the way that the government allocates services across administrative areas.

To illustrate the issues, I shall suppose that the survey is clustered, that there is a regression model such as (20), and that the residuals are positively correlated across observations in the same cluster. As is the case with heteroskedasticity, OLS remains unbiased and consistent, but is inefficient, and as with heteroskedasticity, our main concern is with the invalidity of standard formulas for the variance-covariance matrix of the OLS estimator. A useful result, due to Scott and Holt (1982), is that the Kish design effect is the *maximal* correction that is required, and that, in general, the estimated variances will understate the true variances by a factor that is less than the design effect. However, the maximum is attained when all the right hand side variables in the regression are constant within clusters, as would be the case when the x's are cluster prices, wages, or variables measuring access to schools, health clinics or the like [see also Kloek (1981)]. If some x's vary across members of the cluster, and are correlated between clusters with the other variables, the design effect will overstate the correction.

As with heteroskedasticity, there are parametric and non-parametric methods for correcting the variance-covariance matrix. Among the former would be to specify a variance components model at the cluster level, the estimation of which would allow the calculation of the intracluster correlation coefficient, which can then be used to calculate standard errors. Alternatively, an intracluster correlation coefficient can be calculated from the OLS residuals using (17) and the result used to estimate the correct variance covariance matrix for the OLS estimator. More generally, it is possible to allow for cluster fixed effects, and to work with deviations from village means. This is a useful technique in some contexts, and I shall discuss it below, but note that it does not permit us to estimate coefficients for any regressors that do not vary within the clusters.

A useful procedure is based on the fact that cluster sizes are typically small relative to the total sample size, say 10 or 16 households per cluster, so that it is possible to correct the variance covariance matrix non-parametrically by using the OLS residuals to "estimate" the variance-covariance matrix of the residuals in each cluster, just as the squared OLS residuals are used to "estimate" the variances in the heteroskedasticity-robust calculations. (I use the inverted commas around "estimate" because in neither case are we trying to obtain a consistent estimate of the individual residual variance or individual cluster residual variance covariance matrix.)

Suppose then that we have estimated the regression by OLS, and that for cluster c we have obtained the OLS residuals e_c. We then calculate a robust OLS variance covariance matrix by calculating [see White (1984)],

$$\tilde{V}(\hat{\beta}) = (X'X)^{-1} \sum_{c=1}^{C} X_c' e_c e_c' X_c (X'X)^{-1} \tag{22}$$

where X_c is the submatrix of X corresponding to cluster c, and C is the total number of clusters. Note that in the case where there is only one household per cluster, (22) is the standard formula for the heteroskedasticity-consistent variance covariance matrix. Note too that (22) does not require that there be homoskedasticity, either within clusters or between them, nor that there be a common intracluster correlation coefficient. It is therefore robust against quite general forms of intracluster correlations. The equation is implemented in the software package STATA as part of the huber command, and the corresponding procedure for panel data is described by Arellano (1987).

How much does all this matter? The answer seems to be a great deal, certainly more than is the case for the more familiar heteroskedasticity correction. In many applications, the correction is not much less than the design effect, and in my own work, I have frequently found that the usual formulas give standard errors that are understated by a factor of two to three, a much more serious matter than the 30 percent that seems to be common for the heteroskedasticity correction. The problem is exacerbated by the fact that in so many development applications, the explanatory variables are constant within the clusters, the wage, price, and access variables listed above. It would be invidious to list papers that use clustered data without correction, although [see Deaton (1988, 1990a)] for two selected examples, but there are hundreds of papers in development economics looking at labor market questions, at the demand for commodities and nutrition as a function of prices, and at access to education and health services where the true significance levels for t-values should probably be closer to 6 than to 2. Many of these studies will have to be redone, and I suspect that there will have to be a good deal of revision of conclusions. Of course, these problems are not confined to studies of economic development, and similar considerations apply for example, in labor economics. Indeed, Moulton (1990) has provided a particularly dramatic example using American state level data, where a small intrastate correlation coefficient is combined with large numbers of observations in each state to yield a design effect of nearly 10.

2.1.3. Quantile regressions

The method of quantile regression is not one that has been much used in economics to date, perhaps because of computational considerations. These have now been solved – the qreg command in STATA is an example – so that this extremely useful tool is readily available without the need for special coding. The basic idea was first introduced into economics by Koenker and Bassett (1978) and can be described as follows.

Quantile regression, like linear regression, is concerned with the distribution of a scalar random variable y conditional on a vector of covariates x. In linear regression, it is assumed that one characteristic of this distribution, its mean, is a linear function of x, or at least we attempt to fit a linear function to the conditional expectation, or *regression function*. Instead of the mean, we might choose to work with the median, and to assume that the medians of y conditional on x are linear in x, or at least to fit a linear function to the medians. This would be a median regression, or 0.5 quantile regression. In principle, we can do the same for any other quantile of the distribution, thus constructing the p-quantile regression, where p is any number between 0 and 1.

Given the idea, why should we be interested, and if we are interested, how can such regressions be calculated? Start with the former. First, by looking at a number of different quantile regressions, we can explore different parts of the conditional distribution. For example, consider the relationship between wages and schooling; at any given number of years of schooling, there is a (conditional) distribution of wages, presumably reflecting unobserved abilities and other labor market skills. In general, thereis no reason to require that the rate of return to an additional year's schooling should be the same at all points in the distribution of abilities conditional on schooling, and quantile regression would pick up the differences, see Chamberlain (1991). Used in this way, quantile regression is essentially a non-parametric technique that describes the shape of the empirical distribution without imposing prior restrictions. As such, it can also provide an indication of heteroskedasticity. If the conditional distribution changes shape with one or more of the explanatory variables, quantile regressions at different quantiles will have different slopes, [see Koenker and Bassett (1982)] for a test that uses this property.

Second, just as the median is less sensitive to outliers than is the mean, so are quantile regressions more resistant to outliers than are mean (least-squares) regressions. Median regression is affected by the presence of an outlier, but not by changes in its position, provided of course that it remains above or below the median. As such, quantile regression is one of several regression techniques that have robustness properties superior to OLS [see in particular Huber (1981) and Hampel, Ronchetti, Rousseeuw and Stahel (1986)]. Standard methods of robust regression typically downweight large residuals identified from a previous regression, iterating to convergence. Such procedures require an estimate of the scale of the residuals in order to identify outliers, and thus are sensitive to patterns of heteroskedasticity that are handled naturally by quantile regressions.

Third, quantiles are not affected by monotonic transformations of the data, so that, for example, the median of the logarithm of y conditional on x is the logarithm of the median of y conditional on x. As we shall see in the next subsection, this property has useful consequences.

The estimation of quantile regressions rests on extensions of the well-known result that the median is the point closest to the data in the sense of minimizing the sum of the absolute deviations. Median linear regression parameters are given as the value of the vector β that minimizes

$$\sum_{i=1}^{n} |y_i - x_i'\beta| = \sum_{i=1}^{n} (0.5 - 1(y_i \geq x_i'\beta))(y_i - x_i'\beta) . \tag{23}$$

Koenker and Bassett (1978) show that the p-quantile estimator can be calculated by minimizing a generalization of the second expression in (23),

$$\tilde{\beta} = \text{argmin} \sum_{i=1}^{n} (p - 1(y_i \leq x_i'\beta))(y_i - x_i'\beta) . \tag{24}$$

Although these expressions do not permit explicit solutions, the parameters can be obtained quickly by linear programming methods.

2.1.4. Zeros: probits and Tobits

In development applications, as elsewhere in economics, many variables of interest have limited ranges, either a set of discrete values, or are continuous but limited to some interval. The most frequent example of the latter is when a variable is restricted to positive values; a farmer can produce nothing or something, but cannot grow negative amounts, a consumer may or may not smoke, but cannot sell tobacco, and so on.

Binary discrete choices are typically modelled by using probit or logit models, and often less formally using the linear probability model, in which a dichotomous dependent variable is regressed on the covariates. Provided the standard errors of the linear probability model are corrected for the hetero-skedasticity that is inevitable in such a specification, there is no good reason not to use it, especially when sample sizes are large enough so that computational costs of probit and logit are non-trivial. The fact that linearity is an inappropriate functional form for a probability is unlikely to be problematic provided the bulk of the data are in the range where predicted probabilities are far from either zero or unity.

Cases where the data are a partly discrete and partly continuous are harder to handle. The most common case is where a continuous response is censored at zero, for which the standard model is the Tobit, viz.

$$y_i = \max(0, \beta'x_i + u_i); \quad E(u_i|x_i) = 0; \quad E(u_i^2|x_i) = \sigma^2 . \tag{25}$$

The model is also interpreted as one in which $x_i'\beta + u_i$ is a latent variable, observed when zero or positive, but censored to zero, i.e. replaced by zero, when it would otherwise be negative. A more general version of this model, in which the censoring is controlled by a second latent variable, will be discussed in the subsection on selection below. Estimation is usually done by assuming that the (conditional) distribution of u_i is normal, and following Tobin's (1958) original procedure of estimating the parameters by maximum likelihood. The log likelihood function for this problem is globally concave, so that it is a routine problem in non-linear estimation, typically no more time consuming than the estimation of a probit. Note also that if (25) is correct, OLS will be inconsistent for the parameters β. The regression function is

$$E(y_i|x_i) = (1 - F(-x_i'\beta/\sigma))x_i'\beta + \sigma \int_{-x_i'\beta/\sigma}^{\infty} \tau\, \mathrm{d}F(\tau) \tag{26}$$

where $F(.)$ is the distribution function of $\sigma^{-1}u_i$. (26) will generally not be linear in x_i.

Tobin's maximum likelihood method works well when its assumptions are satisfied. However, the estimates will typically be inconsistent if normality fails, or perhaps more seriously, if there is heteroskedasticity [see Arabmazar and Schmidt (1981, 1982) and Goldberger (1983)]. This is more than a technical problem, and it is straightforward to construct realistic examples with heteroskedasticity where the maximum likelihood estimates are worse than OLS. Particularly in survey data, where heteroskedasticity is endemic, there is no reason to suppose that Tobit will give estimates that are any better than OLS ignoring the censoring. With heteroskedasticity and censoring, neither technique is likely to give satisfactory estimates.

There are two approaches that make sense in practical applications. The first is to abandon this way of thinking about the problem. The standard approach starts from a linear model, and then complicates it to allow for censoring, treating the linearity as a maintained structural hypothesis. In the standard linear regression, this makes sense, because the structural regression coincides with the regression function, and is readily recovered from the data. In many cases, this structural assumption of linearity is merely a convenience, and there is no particular reason to believe that the underlying relationship is genuinely linear. When this is so, the standard procedure for dealing with censoring is not an attractive one, because the original linearity assumption has nothing to support it but convenience, and the convenience is lost with the censoring. The regression function (26) is not a convenient object to handle, and a more suitable alternative would be to start, not from the structure, but from some suitable direct specification for the regression function. Given the presence of the zeros, linearity might not be plausible, but some other flexible functional form might do perfectly well. I shall discuss one particular non-parametric procedure in Section 2.3 below.

The second approach is less radical, and makes sense when there is good reason to retain the linear structure. In this case, it is desirable to use an estimation technique that will deliver consistent estimates in the absence of normality and homoskedasticity. There are a number of these in the literature, all more or less experimental. One that is relatively straightforward to compute is Powell's (1984) censored least absolute deviations estimator, which can be implemented given a program (such as STATA) that allows quantile regression.

Powell's estimator rests on the previously noted fact that medians are preserved by monotone functions. Hence, if $q_{50}(y_i|x_i)$ is the median of the conditional distribution of y_i, then from (25)

$$q_{50}(y_i|x_i) = \max[0, q_{50}(x_i'\beta + u_i)] = \max(0, x_i'\beta) \tag{27}$$

since $\max(0, z)$ is monotone in z, and where the last equality rests on the assumption that the median of u_i is zero. Given (27), consistent estimates of the parameters can be obtained by running a nonlinear median (50th percentile) regression, or equivalently by minimizing

$$\sum_{i=1}^{n} |y_i - \max(0, x_i'\beta)| . \tag{28}$$

Buchinsky (1994) suggests a simple – if not necessarily efficient – computational strategy is to run a median regression of y on x, to calculate predicted values and discard any that are negative before rerunning the regression. Repetition of this procedure, if it converges, will lead to the parameters that minimize (28). In my own – admittedly limited – experience, this works quite satisfactorily even if terminated after five cycles. As is to be expected from a robust procedure, the estimates are a good deal less efficient that Tobit when Tobit's assumptions are correct, and the technique is probably not suitable for a small number of observations. Nevertheless, it is certainly worth trying on survey data, and given large enough samples is likely to be safer than either OLS or Tobit.

2.1.5. Regression bias

Censoring is only one of many cases where the model of interest does not coincide with the regression function, the conditional expectation of y on x. There are a wide range of circumstances where the explanatory variables are correlated with the disturbance, so that least squares regression does not yield consistent estimates of the structural parameters. Omitted variables, simultaneity, heterogeneity, measurement error, and sample selection are all capable of rendering OLS inconsistent, and a great deal of effort in the development literature has gone towards developing techniques that will deliver consistent estimates for a range of specific problems. Some of these techniques draw on panel data when available, and many others rely on one form or another of instrumental variable estimation. In the next few subsections, I review a number of specific topics that illustrate the use of these techniques and some of the issues associated with them.

2.1.6. Agricultural production functions: heterogeneity and panel data

The estimation of farm production functions is a problem that often arises in development applications, whether we are simply attempting to relate physical outputs to physical inputs, or whether we are concerned with more elaborate models of farm-households and the associated integrated models of consumption and production [see for example Singh, Squire, and Strauss (1986)]. Production functions are one of the oldest topics in econometrics; many of the issues reviewed by Marschak and Andrews in 1943 are still relevant, and Mundlak's (1961) paper on agricultural production functions is the first – or at least one of the first – to use fixed effect estimators with panel data as a remedy for unobserved heterogeneity. The simultaneity and omitted heterogeneity problems in this case arise in many other related applications.

A good starting point is the "obvious" procedure, which is to regress outputs on inputs, as for example in

$$\ln(q_i/A_i) = \beta_0 + \beta_1 \ln A_i + \beta_2 \ln h_i + \beta_3 \ln z_i + u_i \tag{29}$$

where A_i is land, so that q_i/A_i is the yield per hectare of farm i, h_i is labor input, and z_i is some other input, such as fertilizer, or perhaps the farmer's education. The sign of β_1 is relevant to the question of whether large or small farms are more "productive", the coefficient β_2 tells us about the marginal productivity of labor on family farms, and the size of β_3 might tell us whether inputs are being efficiently used, since a very large marginal product of fertilizer relative to its costs might be used as an argument for intervention in distribution or extension services.

The problem is that OLS estimation of (29) will tell us none of these things. The finding that $\beta_1 > 0$, that smaller farms have higher yields, is the traditional one since Chayanov's (1925) findings for Russian farmers, and has been widely observed elsewhere [see for example Sen (1962) for India, and Berry and Cline (1979)] for a review of other research. There are many interpretations of the result; that higher output per head is an optimal response to uncertainty by small farmers [Srinivasan (1972)], that there are dualistic labor markets, [Sen (1966, 1975)], or that hired labor requires more monitoring than family labor, [Feder (1985)]. Perhaps the simplest explanation is that (29) omits unobserved heterogeneity, in this case land quality, and that this omitted variable is systematically correlated with the explanatory variables. Farms in low-quality marginal areas (semi-deserts) are typically large, and farms in high-quality land areas are often much smaller. That a garden adds more value-added per hectare than a sheep station does not imply that sheep-stations should be reorganized as gardens. The omitted quality variable is negatively correlated with A_i and so causes the estimated coefficient to be downward biased, from the true value of zero to the observed negative value. Indeed there is some evidence that controlling for quality either reduces or removes the effect [see Bhalla and Roy (1988) and Benjamin (1993)].

Similar arguments apply to the other variables in the production function. For example, it is sometimes found that the returns to fertilizer use, estimated from regression coefficients, are many times larger than would be consistent with productive efficiency [see for example Benjamin and Deaton (1988) for Côte d'Ivoire and Bevan, Collier, and Gunning (1989) for Kenya and Tanzania]. Should fertilizer use be encouraged, and extension services expanded? Not if what we are seeing is that the farms with the higher quality land, or with the most go-ahead farmers, are also those who adopt new technologies. Output is high, not because of the return to inputs, but because of unobservables, land and farmer quality, that are correlated both with inputs and outputs.

Omitted heterogeneity induces correlations between explanatory variables and the error term in a way that has the same consequences as simultaneity bias. Indeed, the production function is likely to suffer from genuine simultaneity bias even in the absence of heterogeneity; inputs, like outputs, are under the control of the farmer, and can have no general claim to exogeneity. The combination of genuine simultaneity and heterogeneity has the further effect of ruling out the use of lags to remove the former; while it is true that seeds have to be planted before the crop is harvested, heterogeneity across farmers will mean that seeds are not exogenous for the harvest, a problem that I shall return to in Section 2.2 in the context of using predetermined variables with panel data. The result of all these considerations is that the regression function of physical output conditional on physical inputs will rarely be informative about the underlying technology.

There are a number of possible econometric solutions to these problems. Note first that, under the standard neoclassical assumptions of the farm-household model, the appropriate exogenous variables for production are not inputs, but the prices of inputs, and the appropriate estimation technique is either instrumental variables applied to the physical production function, or the estimation of a dual specification, in which the technology is specified as a profit function whose derivatives are the demand functions for inputs and the supply functions of outputs, all functions of prices.

There are two problems here, one theoretical and one practical. First, many development economists are comfortable with physical relationships between inputs and outputs, but are unwilling to commit themselves to a neoclassical or "capitalist" view of agriculture in LDCs. Although it is easy to make fun of such "engineering" as opposed to "economic" approaches, there are many cases where misgivings have a real basis. Some markets are not well-developed, and farm inputs are sometimes allocated in ways other than through competitive markets with parametric prices. Second, and consistent with these views, it my impression that it is much more difficult to estimate satisfactory relationships in which inputs and outputs are functions of *prices*, rather than of each other, where the omitted heterogeneity will often guarantee a good if entirely spurious fit. This practical problem will be exacerbated in those cases where there is relatively little price variation across farms. Certainly, it is rare for researchers to report first-stage regressions of inputs on input prices.

When panel data are available, the heterogeneity can be addressed by assuming that it takes the form of additive fixed effects in (29). Consistent estimates of the parameters can then be obtained by OLS applied to differences across periods, or to deviations from individual means. Hence, if (29) is rewritten in standard regression form with i denoting the farm, $i = 1, \ldots, n$, and t the time period, $t = 1, \ldots, T$, we have for the differenced estimator

$$\Delta y_{it} = \beta'.\Delta x_{it} + u_{it} - u_{it-1} \tag{30}$$

for $t = 1, \ldots, T - 1$, while for the within-estimator, we have

$$y_{it} - y_{i.} = \beta'(x_{it} - x_{i.}) + u_{it} - u_{i.} \tag{31}$$

where the suffix $\{i.\}$ indicates the time mean for farm i. Mundlak's (1961) original application of (31) to Israeli farms was designed to remove the effect of "management bias", the heterogeneity that arises from some farmers being better farmers than others.

The ability to deal with heterogeneity does not come without cost, and indeed many of the most important difficulties are recognized in Mundlak's paper. First, the technique depends on the specific functional form for the heterogeneity, that it take the form of an additive fixed effect. There are often good theoretical reasons why this will not be the case, and there is no straightforward way of dealing with fixed effects in nonlinear models. Second, the differencing or demeaning loses n observations, so that if T is small, as is often the case, there will be a substantial loss in precision. Third, when the x's are positively correlated over time, differencing or demeaning reduces variation, so that once again precision is lost. In the extreme case when some of the x's are constant, there is zero precision, and the parameters are not identified. In the agricultural production case, farm size will usually change little or not at all over short periods, which thus precludes any attempt to resolve the "small farms are more productive" question by using fixed effect estimators. Fourth, and perhaps most serious, in the presence of white noise measurement error in the explanatory variables, demeaning or differencing of positively autocorrelated x's will not only reduce the variability of the signal – variability in the true x's – but it will inflate the ratio of noise to signal in the regressors. In the standard case where measurement error induces attenuation bias, the attenuation will be worse using the difference or within estimator. The combination of loss of precision and increased attenuation bias often erases in the difference or within estimates effects that were significant in the cross-section, even when the model is correctly specified and there is no heterogeneity bias. Such results provide no indication that heterogeneity bias is an issue in the cross-section. It clearly makes sense to use Hausman (1978) tests to check whether the estimates from the difference or within estimates are indeed significantly different from the cross-section estimates, although when significant differences are found, further information is needed to discriminate between measurement error or heterogeneity bias as an explanation.

2.1.7. Panel data in practice

Perhaps for the reasons given in the previous paragraph, it is difficult to use panel data – especially short panel data – to generate convincing conclusions and it is particularly difficult to disentangle measurement error from omitted heterogeneity. In particular, it is clear that panel data are no panacea, and that there is no guarantee that difference or within estimates will be preferable to OLS on a cross-section. Even so, panel data have allowed investigators to consider alternatives that could not otherwise have been explored, and to relax previously maintained assumptions.

The techniques that were originally developed for agricultural production functions have been widely applied to other sorts of "production", from the production of health in terms of health inputs – where exactly the same issues of simultaneity and heterogeneity arise – as well as to wage equations, where earnings are a function of schooling and heterogeneity arises because econometricians cannot control for unobserved ability. Such studies are extensively reviewed by Behrman and Deolalikar (1987) and by Strauss and Thomas in this volume. At their best, these studies are sensitive to the difficulties, and much can be done to interpret results by using prior information about the likely size of measurement errors, so that changes between cross-section and within estimates can plausibly be explained. Investigators have also been creative in using the panel data idea, not just for differences over time, but in other applications. A number of studies, for example Behrman and Wolfe (1984, 1989) on education, and Rosenzweig and Wolpin (1988) on child health, use data on siblings to allow for family fixed effects, and to estimate within-family regressions. Fixed effects can also be associated with the villages from which survey clusters are selected, so that village means can be swept out from all the households in each cluster, thus allowing consistent estimation of the effects of quantities that vary within the village in the presence of arbitrary inter-village effects [see for example Deaton (1988) and the further discussion below].

Other studies [Rosenzweig and Wolpin (1986, 1988) and Pitt, Rosenzweig, and Gibbons (1993)] have used panel data to approach the important problem of using regression analysis to aid project evaluation. For example, Pitt et al. look at (among other things) the effects of grade-school proximity on school attendance in Indonesia combining survey with administrative data. One potential problem is that the placement of the schools is unlikely to be random – indeed the whole point of project evaluation would be to avoid random allocation – and that allocation may be influenced by unobservable local factors that themselves have a direct effect on outcomes. The simplest example would be when the government allocates schools to areas with poor attendance, so that an ultimately successful program would be one in which school attendance is the same everywhere, and where a regression analysis would show no effect of school proximity on attendance. (It is also possible that already successful areas are better at getting resources, for example through influential politicians, or by being able to turn money into votes.) Although the Indonesian data are not panels, the same administrative units (*kecamatans*) show up in successive surveys, so that it is possible to compute a difference estimator at *kecamatan* level, a procedure that is closely related to the panel data from cross-sections methodology discussed above. This difference estimator shows much larger effects of school location on school attendance than are visible in the cross-section.

2.1.8. Latent variables and measurement error

Instrumental variables and panel data are only two of the possible ways of dealing with unobserved heterogeneity. In some cases, a more direct approach is available in which the data provide enough information to identify the effects of interest even in the presence of latent variables. These cases fall into the class of multiple indicator and multiple cause, or MIMIC models, which are related both to factor analysis and to models of measurement error [see in particular Goldberger (1974) and Jöreskog (1973)]. Rather than discuss the general case, I look at two particular applications from the development literature.

The first is the model of imperfect fertility control of Rosenzweig and Schultz (1983), used again in Rosenzweig and Schultz (1987) and in Rosenzweig (1990), and in a somewhat different context by Pitt, Rosenzweig, and Hassan

(1990). A skeletal form of the model can be written as

$$y_{1i} = \alpha_1 + \beta y_{2i} + \gamma_1 . z_{1i} + \mu_i + u_{1i}$$
$$y_{3i} = \alpha_2 + \gamma_2 . z_{2i} + \theta \mu_i + u_{2i} \tag{32}$$

where y_1, y_2, and y_3 are endogenous variables, z_1 and z_2 are vectors of exogenous variables, u_{1i} and u_{2i} are error terms, and μ_i is unobserved heterogeneity. In the Rosenzweig and Schultz papers, the first equation explains the number of births in terms of the endogenous contraceptive effort y_2, so that μ_i is couple-specific fecundity. The second equation is used to explain various characteristics of child health which are also influenced by latent fecundity. In the Pitt, Rosenzweig and Hassan paper, which is concerned with nutritional status and consumption, the first equation relates weight for height to calorie consumption (the two endogenous variables) and an individual "endowment" μ_i. In this case, $y_3 = y_2$, which is calorie consumption, and the parameter θ measures the extent to which the household reinforces ($\theta > 0$) or offsets ($\theta < 0$) natural endowments in the intrahousehold allocation of food.

As always with MIMIC models, the major issue is identification, and strong assumptions are required to be able to recover θ. Provided that the β's and γ's are identified – which poses no non-standard issues – θ is identified from the covariance matrix of the residuals provided that u_1 and u_2 are orthogonal – which requires that there be no common omitted variables in the two equations – and provided the instruments are orthogonal to the unobservable μ's, a set of conditions that would seem to be indefensible in any real application. In practice, (32) is usually estimated by applying instrumental variables to the first equation and then using the residuals as a regressor in the second equation, with some allowance for the "measurement error" that comes from the presence of u_1 in the first equation. (Note also that without correction, such a two-step procedure will not generally lead to valid standard errors.) An alternative (and more direct) procedure would be to substitute for μ in the second equation from the first, and to estimate the resulting equation by instrumental variables.

A second example comes from my own work on estimating price elasticities of demand using the spatial price variation that is revealed in cross-sectional household surveys when respondents report, not only how much they have spent, but also the physical quantity bought, so that for each household we can construct a unit value index. This unit value index reflects both local prices and the quality choices of individuals, with unit values usually higher for better-off households who purchase more expensive varieties, even of relatively homogeneous goods. A stripped-down version of the model can be written as follows, see Deaton (1988):

$$
\begin{aligned}
y_{ic} &= \alpha_1 + \beta_1 \ln x_{ic} + \theta \ln p_c + f_c + u_{1ic} \\
\ln v_{ic} &= \alpha_2 + \beta_2 \ln x_{ic} + \psi \ln p_c + u_{2ic}
\end{aligned}
\tag{33}
$$

where i is a household, and c is the cluster or village in which it lives. The first equation explains y_{ic}, the demand for the good – for example the logarithm of quantity or the budget share of the good – in terms of household total expenditure x, the unobservable price p, and village fixed effect f, and a random error term. The price is assumed to be the same for all households in the village and is therefore not indexed on i. The fixed (or random) effect is uncorrelated with the price, but can be correlated with x or with any other included variables that are not constant within the cluster. The unobservable price also manifests itself through the unit value v which is the dependent variable in the second equation. The parameter β_2 is the elasticity of unit value to total expenditure, or quality elasticity – Prais and Houthakker (1955) – while ψ allows for possible quality shading in response to price changes. If price and unit value were identical, ψ would be unity and β_2 would be zero, but quality effects will make $\beta_2 > 0$ and $\psi \leq 1$.

Once again, identification is a problem, and as is intuitively obvious from using the second equation to substitute out for the unobservable log price, only the ratio θ/ψ can be estimated. The β-parameters can be estimated by a within-estimator in which village effects are swept out, a procedure that also provides estimates of the variances and covariances of u_1 and u_2. Given the β's from the within-village estimates, construct the corrected village averages

$$
z_{1c} = y_{.c} - \hat{\beta}_1 \ln x_{.c}, \quad z_{2c} = \ln v_{.c} - \hat{\beta}_2 \ln x_{.c} .
\tag{34}
$$

At the second stage, we calculate the estimate

$$
\hat{\phi} = \frac{cov(z_1 z_2) - n_c^{-1} \hat{\sigma}_{12}}{var(z_2) - n_c^{-1} \hat{\sigma}_{22}}
\tag{35}
$$

where the covariances are taken over villages, where n_c is the number of households per cluster, and the σ's are estimated from the first stage variance covariance matrix of the residuals. Using (33), it is straightforward to show that (35) is a consistent estimate of the ratio θ/ψ.

Note that (35) is a standard errors-in-variables estimator in which the OLS estimator, which is the ratio of the covariance to the variance, is corrected for the component that is attributable to measurement error. The standard error for $\hat{\phi}$ can be obtained from first principles by application of the "delta method", or by adapting the formulas in Fuller (1987) for the effects of the first-stage estimation. The model can also be extended to allow for other covariates both within and between villages, it can be expanded into a system of demand functions with many goods and many prices – [Deaton and Grimard (1992)] – and a simple theory of quality shading can be appended to the model so as to allow θ and ψ to be separately identified, [Deaton (1988)].

2.1.9. Selection models

Selection bias occurs in many different forms; one very general formulation is due to Heckman (1990) and is useful for thinking about a number of issues that arise in development practice. Heckman's formulation has three equations, two regression equations, and a switching equation that governs which of the two determines behavior. The regressions are:

$$y_{0i} = x'_{0i}\beta_0 + u_{0i}, \quad y_{1i} = x'_{1i}\beta_1 + u_{1i} . \tag{36}$$

The dichotomous switch variable d_i takes values 1 or 0 and satisfies

$$d_i = 1(z'_i\gamma + u_{2i} > 0) \tag{37}$$

where the "indicator function" $1(.)$ is defined to take the value 1 when the statement in brackets is true, and 0 otherwise. The dependent variable y_i is thus determined by

$$y_i = d_i y_{0i} + (1 - d_i)y_{1i} . \tag{38}$$

There are several cases in the development literature that use the model in essentially this form. In van der Gaag, Stelcner, and Wijverberg (1989) and Stelcner, van der Gaag and Wijverberg (1989), (36) are wage equations for the formal and informal sectors in Peru, while (37) is the equation determining choice of sector. Pitt and Sumodiningrat (1991) look at the adoption of high yielding versus traditional variety rice in Indonesia, so that the equations (36) are variety specific profit functions, and (37) is the profit maximizing choice between them. Bell, Srinivasan and Udry (1992) model credit markets in the Punjab using a demand equation, a supply equation, and a condition that enforces a ration whenever the supply is less than the demand. In the appropriate notation, all of these fall within the general framework of the previous paragraph. Various special cases of Heckman's model occur even more frequently in development practice.

Consider first setting both β_1 and the variance of u_1 to be zero in the second equation in (36). Given this, we have the Tobit model when the right hand side of the first equation in (36) coincides with the argument of the indicator function in (37). When the two quantities are different, we have the important case generalizing Tobit where the censoring is determined by different factors than determine the magnitude of the dependent variable when it is not censored. This would be the correct model (for example) for the demand for fertilizer if what determines whether a farmer uses fertilizer at all – perhaps the existence of a local extension agent – is different from what determines how much is used conditional on use – perhaps the price of fertilizer, land quality, or the anticipated price of output.

For this generalized Tobit model, (36) and (37) imply that, if we condition on y being positive, the regression function is

$$E(y_i|x_i, z_i, y_i > 0) = x_i'\beta + \lambda(z_i'\gamma) \qquad (39)$$

where I have suppressed the zero suffix and where

$$\lambda(z_i'\gamma) = E(u_{0i}|u_{2i} \geq -z_i'\gamma). \qquad (40)$$

Equation (40) can also be applied to the case of truncation. In contrast to censoring, where we see zeros when the observation is censored, with truncation, the observation does not appear in the sample. In this case, although (40) holds, and although the switching equation (37) still explains the truncation, we cannot use it to estimate the switching parameters in the absence of the information that would have been contained in the truncated observations. We have only (40) to work with, and it is clear from inspection that identification, if it is to be achieved at all, will require strong supplementary assumptions. In cases where truncation cannot be avoided, it will rarely be possible to make a convincing separation between the truncation variables and the variables in the structural equation. With censoring, we have both (37) and (40) and, as we shall see below, identification is easier.

Heckman's general formulation can also be used to analyze the "policy evaluation" or "treatment" case that was discussed in the context of heterogeneity. In (36), set $u_1 = u_2$ and $\beta_0 = \beta_1$ except for the constant term. Equation (38) then becomes

$$y_i = \alpha + \theta\,d_i + x_i'\beta + u_i \qquad (41)$$

where the parameter θ is the difference between the two constant terms and captures the effect of the policy on the outcome. Given the structure of the model, and the determination of d_i by (37), the policy indicator will generally be correlated with the error term in (41) so that the policy effect cannot be consistently estimated by least squares. This is simply another way of looking at the same problem discussed above, that when we want to estimate the effects of a policy or a project, we must take into account what determines it, and having done so, we will usually find that we cannot discover its effects by standard regressions. The basic issue here is the correlation of explanatory variables with the error term, and it matters less whether we think of that correlation as coming from simultaneity, heterogeneity, selection, or omitted variables.

The fully general model (36) through (38) can be estimated as it stands by using maximum likelihood once some joint distribution – typically joint normality – is specified for the three error terms u_0, u_1, and u_3. Given normality, the special case of generalized Tobit can be estimated using a short-cut technique that avoids the need for maximizing a custom built likelihood function. In a famous paper, Heckman (1976) proposed what has come to be known as the "Heckit" or Heckman's probit, by analogy with Tobit or Tobin's probit. At the first stage, the γ-parameters in (37) are estimated up to scale by probit applied to a dichotomous variable that is 0 when y is censored and 1 otherwise. The results are then used to calculate the λ-function in (40), which under normality takes the form of a Mill's ratio, which can then be used on the right hand side of (40) to estimate the β's. This technique is very widely used in the applied development literature, although (notably) not in the study of wage equations among Panamanian males by Heckman and Hotz (1986).

The role of the distributional assumptions in these models has come under increased scrutiny in recent years. As we have already seen, maximum likelihood estimation of the Tobit model is inconsistent when homoskedasticity fails. In the general model, even identification can hinge on the distributional assumptions on the error terms, a situation that is practically little different from lack of identification altogether. The identification of the general model under minimal distributional assumptions has been addressed in papers by Manski (1988), Chamberlain (1986) and Heckman (1990). The identification of the switching equation (38) is straightforward, provided of course that we normalize the variance to unity. The identification of the structural equations in the absence of knowledge of the joint distribution of u_0, u_1, and u_2 requires that there is at least one variable in the switching equation (37) that is absent from the structural equations, although this in itself is not sufficient; for example, at least one of the variables unique to the switching equation must be continuous.

Finding variables that affect switching but are absent from the structure is closely akin to the general problem of finding instruments, and is frequently as difficult. In the paper that introduced selection effects into applied econometrics, Gronau (1973) found that women's wages were systematically higher when they had small children. The implausibility of children directly increasing labor market productivity led to a model in which children acted as selection variables, with higher reservation wages required to bring women with children into the labor force. But this sort of clear separation appears to be rare in practice, and in cases where there are no grounds for excluding the selection variables from the structure, there is little point in pursuing the selectivity through a normality-dependent correction, as opposed to estimating the regression function without any attempt to separate structure from selection.

When the models are identified, it is still desirable to pursue estimation strategies that do not rest on normality. There exist a number of robust techniques for various special cases of the general model. For the "policy evaluation" model given by (37) and (41), the obvious technique is instrumental variables – although see the earlier discussion on heterogeneity – which is dealt with in the next subsection. Robust techniques for dealing with generalized Tobit are still in the experimental stage, and there is little practical experience upon which to draw. However, one straightforward method is given by Newey, Powell, and Walker (1990), who generalize the Heckit to make it robust against departures from normality. At the first stage, they estimate a non-parametric version of probit using the kernel techniques discussed in Section 2.3 below. Alternatively, if we are not too concerned with the role of normality in the probit, the first stage of Heckit can be retained to provide an estimate of the index $z'\gamma$. Indeed, the linear probability model is also a competitive technique for the first stage. At the second stage, Newey, Powell and Walker suggest that the index be entered into the regression, not through the Mill's ratio, but as a polynomial that will mimic the unknown and distribution dependent λ-function in (39). This procedure avoids having to specify a joint distribution for the two error terms, and will force us to confront the lack of identification where it exists. For example, the procedure will break down if the x and z variables are the same.

2.1.10. Instrumental variables and natural experiments

The "policy evaluation" model (37) and (40) is only one of the many regression models where the technique of instrumental variables can be useful. Indeed, whenever there is a correlation between an explanatory variable and the error term, whether induced by heterogeneity, simultaneity, measurement error, omitted variables, or selectivity, instrumentation can be used to generate consistent estimates provided that it is possible to find instruments that are (at least asymptotically) correlated with the explanatory variable and uncorrelated with the error terms. Of course, the variance of IV estimators will be larger than OLS, so that even when the latter is inconsistent, there is no guarantee that the IVE will be closer to the truth; as usual, the price of greater generality is decreased precision, and as usual, it is important not to interpret an insignificant estimate from IVE as evidence that the OLS estimate is spurious.

Once again, the Hausman test is useful for checking whether the IV estimates of the parameters of interest are significantly different from OLS.

In this subsection, I have two points to make in addition to what is contained in any good textbook treatment of instrumental variable estimation. The first concerns the policy evaluation model and the role of "natural" experiments. The second is concerned with some aspects of the finite sample distribution of instrumental variables estimates that are important for the interpretation of results in practice.

Perhaps the best environment for policy evaluation is where the "treatment" is randomly allocated, so that the effects of the policy can be assessed by post-experimental comparison of outcomes for treatment and controls. For obvious reasons, projects and policies in LDCs are typically not allocated randomly, although there is occasional scope for randomization when there are more suitable individuals or localities that would like to be treated than there are funds to support them [see Newman, Gertler, and Rawlings (1993)]. There is also scope for genuine experimentation prior to policy evaluation, something that has been carried furthest in the US [see Grossman (1993) for a review], but is also of increasing interest in LDCs [see again Newman et al.]. When experimentation is not possible, or simply was not done, the question arises as to whether and in what circumstances econometric technique is a substitute.

A good deal of recent attention has been devoted to "natural" experiments, situations where there is no experimental intent, but where the design or implementation of a program has features that allows the construction of good instruments, or of groups of experimentals and controls where it can be convincingly argued that selection into each group is effectively random. Good examples of this technique are provided by papers on veteran status and wages by Angrist (1990) and by Angrist and Krueger (1989). Angrist studies the effects of Vietnam veteran status on wages using the fact that selection for the draft was at least in part random through the allocation of lottery numbers. The comparison of wage rates between those who received high and low lottery numbers reveals the veteran effect without contamination by other omitted variables because the latter cannot be correlated with the selection. Angrist and Krueger note that in the last years of World War II the selection procedures into the military generated a (weak) correlation between the likelihood of induction and the position of an individual's birthday within the year, with those born earlier more likely to be drafted. Using a sample of 300,000 individuals from the 1980 census, Angrist and Krueger show that the positive association between World War II veteran status and wages is reversed when birth dates are used as instruments, and that the subsequent negative wage effect is consistent with the negative effect on wages of having been a veteran of the Vietnam War.

These are impressive studies, and they show how to make good use of natural experiments. However, it is important to note the features of these examples that are responsible for the credibility of the results. In one case, randomization is actually present, so that we are quite close to a genuine experiment. In the other, the birth date effect comes from an accidental feature of the program. In cases where the element of natural experiment comes from deliberate choice by an individual or an institution, the othogonality between the instrument and the error terms can be much harder to defend. In particular, differences in government policy between areas or individuals can rarely be treated as experimental, and indeed one of the achievements of the political economy literature has been to stop economists automatically treating government behavior as an exogenous explanatory variable. Differences in educational policy between two otherwise "similar" countries such as Kenya and Tanzania may provide useful insights on educational outcomes, since at least some hard to observe features are automatically controlled for [see Knight and Sabot (1990)], but the policy differences are neither random nor accidental, and the comparison can hardly be labelled a natural – or any other kind of – experiment. Technological change, such as the green revolution in India – Rosenzweig (1990) – can plausibly be taken as exogenous to Indian farmers, but that is a different matter from the adoption of the technology, which is always likely to be correlated with farm-specific features that make it appear more likely to succeed. Some components of fertility can be thought of as random, such as Rosenzweig and Wolpin's (1980) use of the birth of twins as a natural experiment, but when differences in "the intercouple variation in the biological propensity to conceive" can only be measured as the residuals from a regression, again see Rosenzweig (1990), the validity of the instruments requires that the residuals be uncontaminated by other omitted factors, something that will often not be credible. Even regional price variation, which is routinely treated as exogenous – as in my own work in spatial demand analysis that was discussed above – will not provide valid instruments in the presence of regional taste variation [see Kennan (1989) and Deaton (1994, Chapter 2)].

The natural experiment methodology works best when, as in the Angrist and Krueger examples, it focusses on some detail of the program that is plausibly random. While there is no guarantee that all programs will have this sort of feature, it is possible that a detailed examination of administrative procedures can yield a useful instrument. Although major program outlines are set by politicians or administrators who are well aware of the consequences of their actions, the microstructure of the implementation is often undertaken by bureaucrats who are allowed administrative discretion, whose motivation is no more than completing their task, and whose actions may sometimes be close to random, as when decisions are influenced by birthdates or alphabetical order.

Even in these favorable cases, there are serious econometric problems associated with instrumental variables. Even in the best cases, where samples are large enough to make asymptotic theory useful, the variance covariance matrix of the IV estimator exceeds that of OLS by a positive definite matrix, so the removal of bias – if it is present – comes at the price of precision. But the greatest practical difficulties relate to the finite sample properties of IVEs, and to the fact that practical inference is inevitably based on large-sample distributions that often give very little idea of the true behavior of the estimates. Although general results are available on the finite sample distribution of instrumental variable estimates – see Phillips (1980) – the formulae are not readily calculated and are thus of limited value for applied researchers. Even so, a good deal is known. The finite sample distributions of IVEs can be thick-tailed, so much so that IVEs possess finite sample moments only up to the degree of overidentification [see Davidson and McKinnon (1993, 220–224) for discussion and references]. Thus in the (fairly common) case where there is exact identification, the IVE does not possess a mean. Hypothesis testing in such circumstances is obviously hazardous, especially when asymptotic standard errors are used to compute *t*-values. Even when there is sufficient overidentification to guarantee the exitence of the moments, IVEs are biased towards OLS in finite samples [see Nagar (1959) and Buse (1992)]. In the extreme case, where the first stage regression has no degrees of freedom and fits perfectly, OLS and IVE are mechanically identical. There is therefore a tradeoff between having too many instruments, and risking the close replication of the biased OLS estimates, or of having too few, and risking dispersion and apparently extreme estimates.

Special cases of small sample distributions of IVE have recently been investigated by Nelson and Startz (1990a,b) and by Maddala and Jeong (1992). Nelson and Startz analyze the simplest case of a linear regression with a single right hand side variable and a single instrument. They show that the asymptotic distribution of the IVE will often be a bad approximation to the true distribution when the instrument is a poor one in the sense of being only weakly correlated with the explanatory variable. In particular, there is no guarantee that a "poor" instrument will necessarily result in insignificant estimates when the instrument is used. Indeed, Nelson and Startz produce examples where the opposite occurs, and where apparently significant estimates are generated spuriously by the use of a weak instrument. The moral is that it is important to present the results of the first-stage estimation in two-stage least squares – a practice that is far from routine – and that little credibility should be given to instrumental estimates where the predictive power of the first stage has not been established. Although Nelson and Startz's analysis covers only the univariate case, the natural extension would be to check the joint significance in the first-stage regression of the identifying instruments, for example by calculating an *F*-test for the variables not included in the structural equation.

Buse's results are also concerned with finite sample bias and with the fit of the first-stage regressions. Using Nagar approximations to the moments of the estimator – a technique that will only be valid in those cases where enough moments exist – Buse asks how the finite sample bias changes as the number of instruments is increased. In the case where there is one endogenous right hand side variable, Buse's formula implies that one additional instrument will decrease the approximate bias if

$$R_2^2 - R_1^2 > (L_1 - 2)^{-1}(R_1^2 - R_0^2) \tag{42}$$

where $L_1 > 2$ (the asymptotic approximations are not useful for smaller values) is the number of instruments before the addition, R_0^2 is the fit of the regression of the endogenous right hand side on the exogenous variables included in the structural equation, and R_1^2 and R_2^2 refer to the same regression but with the addition of L_1 and $L_1 + 1$ instruments respectively. Not surprisingly, it is possible for poor instruments to increase the bias, but according to (42) the bias can be exacerbated even by the addition of an instrument that makes a substantial contribution to the fit. These results, like those of Nelson and Startz, underline the importance of examining the first-stage regression in two-stage least squares.

2.1.11. Test statistics

The construction and interpretation of test statistics follows the same general principles in development practice as in the rest of econometrics. The "trinity" of likelihood based tests, Wald, likelihood ratio, and Lagrange Multiplier tests are widely used in the development literature as elsewhere [see Engle (1984) for a review]. Many of these tests are based on the normal distribution, so that in parallel with the increased focus on robust estimation techniques, there has been a move towards robust test statistics. In particular, and as we have already seen, Hausman (1978) tests are frequently useful, since they provide a general framework for comparing efficient estimates obtained under restrictive assumptions with more robust estimators whose consistency is more generally guaranteed but that are less efficient under the conditions that justify the original estimator. The generalized methods of moments (GMM) estimators introduced by Hansen (1982) also provide an integrated framework for estimation and inference. Although GMM estimators are perhaps most frequently used in a time-series context for the estimation of rational expectations models, they also provide a useful way of thinking about many of the techniques discussed above, since it is often the case in development practice that estimation is based on conditional moment restrictions.

For example, suppose that we generalize the instrumental variable models discussed above by writing the structural model in the form

$$f(y_i, x_i, \beta) = u_i \tag{43}$$

and appending the k conditional moment restrictions

$$E(u_i|z_{ij}) = 0, \quad j = 1, \ldots, k. \tag{44}$$

The sample analog of (44) is the condition $n^{-1}Z'u = 0$, and the GMM estimator of β is given by making the quantity as small as possible, or

$$\hat{\beta} = \underset{\beta}{\operatorname{argmin}} \; u'ZW^{-1}Z'u \tag{45}$$

where W is a suitable positive definite weighting matrix. Hansen shows that the optimal choice for W is the variance covariance matrix of the vector $Z'u$, $Z'\Omega Z$ say, in which case the criterion function in (45) is

$$u'Z(Z'\Omega Z)^{-1}Z'u . \tag{46}$$

Under the null that all the instruments are valid, (46) will have an asymptotic χ^2 distribution with degrees of freedom equal to the number of instruments in excess of the number required to identify the parameters. Hence (46) is often referred to as an overidentification test, and it can be used to good purpose in most of the situations described above that involve the use of instrumental variables. In practice, the matrix Ω is not known but is constructed from the residuals analogously with the heteroskedastic and cluster effect models discussed above, see equations (21) and (22) above. Following Newey (1986), we can also estimate the model using a subset of instruments and calculate a Hausman test by comparing the value of the criterion function with that obtained using the full set. As we shall see in the next section, this framework also provides a useful way of addressing a number of important issues in the analysis of macroeconomic and panel data.

When standard test procedures are applied in the context of large scale surveys, the issue often arises as to whether critical values should be adjusted for sample size. In time-series work, including most applied macroeconomics, sample sizes do not vary widely from one application to another, and the issue does not arise. But in survey based econometrics, the number of data points can vary from a few hundred to a few million, and there are arguments that suggest that it is inappropriate to use the same critical values at all sample sizes. In particular, when working with very large sample sizes, investigators often find that standard statistical procedures lead to hypotheses being rejected "too frequently", and that even when the null hypothesis seems like a good approximation, t-tests and F-ratios are large relative to conventional significance levels.

The intuitive argument is that no one believes that hypotheses are literally true, so that when we say $\beta = 0$, we really mean that β is close to zero. With a small sample size, β will not be very precisely estimated, so that an estimate close to zero will not lead to a rejection of the null. However, if β is being consistently estimated, the sampling distribution will tighten as the sample size increases so that even very small values of β can be associated with very large t-statistics when we test the hypothesis that it is zero. Of course, if we literally believe that $\beta = 0$, standard test procedures give the right answer, and the t-test will reject the null 5 percent of the time whatever the sample size.

There are deep issues of statistical philosophy here, which it is not appropriate to rehearse here. Many economists are adherents of classical inference, while others believe that it is inherently nonsensical to test point nulls, and reject testing altogether in favor of estimation. The Bayesian point of view has been eloquently argued by Leamer (1978). He points out that if we hold the probability of Type I error fixed as the sample size increases – which is the classical prescription – all of the increased precision of estimation from the additional observations is being devoted to reducing the Type II error. If β is not zero, the probability of failing to detect the fact may be large with 100 observations, and infinitesimally small with 200,000. The classical procedure, by holding fixed at 5 percent (say) the probability of Type I error, is one that commits us to lexicographic preferences or loss functions over the two types of error; lower Type I error is always preferred, independently of Type II errors. Although classical statisticians emphasize the asymmetry of Type I and Type II errors, as well as the care that should be taken in formulating the null, it is still hard to see why we should subscribe to such preferences, rather than trading-off the two types of error as the sample size increases.

Recognizing the persuasiveness of Leamer's argument is a good deal easier than doing something about it. From the Bayesian perspective argued by Leamer, the solution is to choose models based on posterior probabilities. For example, if we want to test that a parameter or subset of parameters is zero, we compare the posterior probability of the restricted and unrestricted models, and select whichever is the larger. As shown by Schwarz (1978), in sufficiently large samples this rule leads to a simple adjustment to the likelihood ratio test. In particular – see Chow (1983, pp. 300–302) for an exposition – the posterior probability of each of the models is dominated for large enough sample sizes by terms of the form

$$\ln L(\hat{\beta}) - \frac{k}{2} \ln n \qquad (47)$$

where $\hat{\beta}$ is the maximum likelihood estimate, k is the number of parameters, and n the sample size. Hence, standard likelihood ratio tests can be transformed into large sample Bayesian posterior probability tests by comparing twice the log likelihood ratio, not with a χ^2 distribution with q degrees of freedom, where q is the number of restrictions, but with q multiplied by the logarithm of the sample size. For a standard F-test, which in large samples is q times the χ^2, the Schwarz procedure calls for the restrictions to be rejected when the F is larger than the logarithm of the sample size.

While the use of such criteria should ultimately depend on the philosophy of inference, I have frequently found in my own work that the Schwarz criterion gives sensible answers. As far as it is possible to tell on other grounds, it seems to discriminate between what I intuitively think of as "large" and "small" violations of the null; accepting the null according to these sample dependent criteria rarely leads to untoward consequences, while its rejections are ignored at one's peril. However, it should also be emphasized that some of the large test statistics that are frequently encountered using survey data may be attributable to some of the other considerations discussed in this section, such as a failure to treat heteroskedasticity or to allow for cluster effects, and these may provide more mundane explanations for the apparent frequency with which sensible nulls are rejected.

2.2. Econometric issues in time-series

The way that econometricians think about time-series data has undergone major changes in the last ten to fifteen years. Much of the change has come from macroeconomics, and its relevance to development economics lies largely but not exclusively in that area. In this section, I provide a brief introduction to the modern language of time series analysis, and to some of the major issues that have been debated in recent years, particularly those associated with unit roots. I begin with univariate descriptions of time series, and with alternative methods of handling trends. I use illustrations from my own and others' work on modelling commodity prices, one of the leading time-series topics in economic development. Commodity prices are extremely variable, arguably trending, and their behavior generates major problems of macroeconomic stabilization and growth for the large number of LDCs that are dependent on exports of primary commodities. Adequate univariate time-series representations of commodity prices would be a considerable aid to the design of macroeconomic policy in much of the world. The second subsection turns from univariate to multivariate time-series analysis and considers the problems that arise in regression analysis when the variables are trending. These two sections can do no more than scratch the surface of what has become an immense topic. For readers interested in pursuing these questions further, Campbell and

Perron (1991) provide an accessible discussion as well as an excellent synthesis and guide to the literature.

Time-series issues are important not only in statistical description and regression analysis, but also in modelling behavior, particularly when individuals are assumed to behave as dynamic intertemporal optimizers. Such approaches have had a considerable impact on the way we think about saving, and the recent literature on saving and development has begun to make use of the tools of dynamic optimization. I discuss Euler equation approaches to the econometric analysis of these models, as well as the more elaborate structural estimation strategies that have recently made their appearance in development and elsewhere.

The final subsection returns to the topic of panel data, and to the time-series issues involved in its use. Although many of the applications here are again macroeconomic, particularly to the analysis of growth using time-series data from a cross-section of countries, the same issues arise in many microeconomic applications where there are dynamic features, such as lagged dependent or predetermined variables.

2.2.1. Univariate time-series models

For many purposes it is useful to have a simple descriptive model of a time series. Although such models rarely have a direct behavioral content, they can encapsulate the stylized facts about a time-series, whether or not it has a trend, its autocorrelations at different lags, and how long-lived are the effects of unanticipated shocks. In the case of commodity prices, the existence or otherwise of a downward trend in the terms of trade of LDCs has been a topic of debate in economic development since Prebisch and Singer in the 1950s. Similarly, sensible macroeconomic stabilization in the face of shocks to commodity prices is greatly eased if it is possible to come to some sort of understanding of what a given shock means for future prices. In principle, univariate time-series analysis can cast light on these questions.

A useful starting point is the familiar ARIMA formulation of Box and Jenkins (1970). For a univariate time series y_t this can be written

$$A(L)\Delta^d y_t = B(L)\varepsilon_t \qquad\qquad (48)$$

where L is the lag operator, $A(L)$ and $B(L)$ are finite degree polynomials, Δ is the backward difference operator $(1 - L)$ so that Δ^d indicates differencing d times, and ε_t is an independently and identically distributed or "white noise" process. The roots of the polynomials $A(L)$ and $B(L)$ are assumed to lie outside the unit circle, so that the series $\Delta^d y_t$ is stationary. Since the quantity ε_t is white noise, it – or at least the deviation from its mean – is not predictable and is therefore frequently referred to as a shock or innovation. The basic idea of (48) is first to difference the series to induce stationarity, and then to use low order autoregressive and moving average polynomials to capture the autocorrelation structure of the differenced process. If the series is stationary to begin with, d will be zero. However, in many macroeconomic applications, the change or the rate of growth of the series is more naturally thought of as stationary, and there are some cases, such as perhaps the level of prices, where even the rate of growth will be non-stationary, requiring twice-differencing to generate a stationary series. A non-stationary series that has to be differenced d times to induce stationarity is said to be integrated of order d, or $I(d)$, so that a quantity such as GDP would typically be $I(1)$ – or difference stationary – while the price level could be $I(2)$ and unemployment rates or interest rates either $I(0)$ or $I(1)$.

When the parameter d in (48) is greater than 0, then we say that the series y_t has a unit root; the term comes from noting that the left hand side of (48) can be written as $A(L)(1 - L)^d$ which is a polynomial with d unit roots. The simplest case of a unit root model is the random walk with drift, which is written

$$\Delta y_t = \varepsilon_t = \eta + u_t \tag{49}$$

where η is the mean of ε and is the average rate at which y increases in each period. Other more general unit root models come from treating u_t in (49) as a general stationary process, although the restriction in (48) that the roots of $B(L)$ lie outside the unit circle rules out the case where u_t is itself the first difference of a stationary process; otherwise we could write any *stationary* process – including white noise – in the form (49).

Equation (49) is an example of how ARIMA models deal with a trend. With or without additional serial correlation, such models often provide a natural and straightforward method of summarizing the behavior of a series. However, integrated processes are not the only way of modelling trends. The most important competitor is the standard deterministic trend, whereby, instead of differencing the series to induce stationarity, we first remove some deterministic function of time. As we have seen, an $I(1)$ series that is stationary in first-differences is called difference stationary. When $y_t - f(t)$ is stationary for a deterministic function $f(t)$, then we say that y_t is trend stationary. Since 0 is a deterministic function of time, trend-stationary series include stationary series as a special case. For the typical upward trending macroeconomic series, $f(t)$ will usually be linear or exponential, although there is nothing to rule out other possibilities. Note that a series that is stationary about a deterministic linear trend will have a first difference that appears to satisfy (49) (or equivalently (48) with $d = 1$). That it cannot in fact be written in this unit root form follows from the fact that the associated polynomial $B(L)$ would have a unit root, which is ruled out by the definition of (48).

The distinction between trend stationarity and difference stationarity can sometimes be made in terms of econometric convenience, but it is often a good deal more. The long-term behavior of the series and our ability to forecast it depends a good deal on which one is correct. If a series is trend stationary, it is tied to its deterministic trend from which it can never stray too far. However autocorrelated it might be in the short run, and however slowly it comes back to its anchor, come back it must. As a result, once we know the parameters of the process, and once the effects of the original position of the series relative to trend have worn off, our long-term forecasts will be forecasts of the trend. And since the trend is deterministic, there is no more uncertainty about its position in the far distant future than there is in the short or medium term.

For a difference stationary series, the position is quite different. Although the average rate of change per period is fixed, just as it is in the trend stationary case, there is nothing that ties the series to a particular position or particular trend line. For example, the random walk with drift in (49) increases at η per period on average, but in any given period it will increase by more or less depending on the random shock u_t. But once the new position has been attained, the series will increase at an expected rate of η per period from that new position, whatever was the route by which it got there. In particular, there is no non-stochastic trend to which the series is tied, and the series will eventually depart as far as we like from any that we try to delineate. As a result, even when we know the parameters of a difference stationary process, the uncertainty about its future position will grow steadily as we look further into the future. Put another way, because the series is an integrated process, the effects of shocks never wear off; disturbances have permanent effects.

The distinction between trend stationarity and difference stationarity means that in practical work it is necessary not only to estimate the parameters of a given type of model, but it is also necessary to choose a modelling strategy, and to decide which type of model to use. A number of test statistics have been developed to help make the choice. To take the simplest example, suppose that y_t is a trending series and that we consider the model

$$\Delta y_t = a + bt + \pi y_{t-1} + u_t . \tag{50}$$

When $b = \pi = 0$ (50) is a random walk with drift; alternatively, y_t is a stationary AR(1) around the linear trend $(1 - \pi)^{-1}(a + bt)$. The random walk with drift model can therefore be treated as the null hypothesis in (50). However, and although the parameters in (50) are consistently estimated by OLS, conventionally calculated F-tests of the hypothesis that b and π are jointly zero do not have the F-distribution, even asymptotically. Special distributions must therefore be used, and in the case of (50), the appropriate critical values have been calculated and tabulated by Dickey and Fuller (1981).

Although the random walk with drift is a leading special case, we more frequently need to test for a unit root, which requires us to allow for the possibility that y_t is serially correlated even after first-differencing. To do so, (50) is augmented to read

$$\Delta y_t = a + bt + \pi y_{t-1} + \sum_{j=1}^{k} \theta_j \Delta y_{t-j} + u_t \tag{51}$$

where k is selected – typically by some model selection procedure – to be large enough to account for the serial correlation in the differences under the null. Once again, the unit root null can be tested by calculating a standard F-test, and once again the results must be checked against the critical values tabulated by Dickey and Fuller.

The recent literature on unit roots contains a large number of tests that are similar in purpose to those outlined above. There are a variety of different types of trends that can be used, from no trend at all, through polynomials in time, to nonlinear or "breaking" trends. Even in the cases given here, we could consider simply the t-test on π in place of the F-statistic on b and π jointly. These and other possibilities are reviewed by Campbell and Perron (1991) and by Mills (1990). However, the Dickey–Fuller tests shown above illustrate the general principles, and are sufficient background for me to discuss a number of practical implications.

The first point to note is that these tests take the unit root hypothesis as the null, so that if the test results in an acceptance, we have only failed to reject the unit root hypothesis, and we cannot legitimately claim that we have rejected trend stationarity. It is not possible to use these unit root tests to prove that time series have unit roots. The second issue is one of power. In most cases of interest, the data can be equally well represented by both difference stationary and trend stationary formulations. If π in (51) is nonzero but small, which is what the parameter estimates frequently show, it will be difficult to reject the hypothesis that there is a unit root, even though the series is in fact trend stationary. With enough data, it will always be possible to tell difference stationary and trend stationary models apart, but the distinction hinges on the long-run behavior of the series, behavior that can be very difficult to establish in finite samples.

It has become standard practice among some time-series econometricians and macroeconomists to accept the unit root hypothesis when it cannot be rejected, and then to follow the standard Box–Jenkins prescription of estimating a parsimonious (i.e. low-order) ARMA for the differenced series. In many cases, this will be a sensible descriptive strategy, but it is important to recognize it as such, and to note that there are cases where it can be quite misleading. Commodity prices again provide some instructive examples. When deflated by some suitable price index, such as the US consumer price index or an index of imports of manufactures by developing countries, the series are quite volatile but show relatively little trend over long enough periods. (What trends there are are typically negative as suggested by the Prebisch–Singer hypothesis [see for example Grilli and Yang (1988) and Ardeni and Wright (1992)]. The series also display very high first-order autocorrelations, typically 0.9 or higher even in annual data [see for example Deaton and Laroque (1992a) and Cuddington (1992)], and these autocorrelations typically decline only very slowly at higher orders. Such autocorrelation patterns are typically regarded as symptoms of non-stationarity, and indeed it is entirely plausible that commodity prices should be non-stationary over periods long enough to see changes in the technology of material use in production and consumption.

Even so, it comes as somewhat of a surprise to discover to what simple conclusions the unit root methodology leads. Cuddington (1992) looks at 26 commodity prices using long-run annual data, and find that unit roots cannot be rejected for half of them, and that in some cases, such as beef, copper, and rubber, a simple random walk with drift cannot be rejected. Looking at more recent data but at a monthly rather than annual frequency, Deaton (1992b) also finds that low-order unit root models provide an excellent fit to the data for cotton, copper, cocoa, and coffee prices. But these models make neither statistical nor economic sense. The price of annual crops like cotton are influenced by weather shocks that are known to be stationary, so that a model that asserts that all shocks are permanent is essentially absurd. Even with tree crops, where a frost may generate a price increase that can last for several years, the frost is not permanent and the trees will grow again, so that there is no reason to suppose that there will be *any* long term effect on the price. Nor do the data suggest that there are such long term effects, and in spite of the very high levels of volatility, the real prices of many commodities are remarkably close to what they were at the beginning of the century. What seems to be the case is that commodity prices are in fact tied to slowly evolving trends, perhaps deterministic but perhaps also stochastic with low volatility, and that the mechanism that brings them back to their trends operates only very slowly. Because the trend-reversion is small enough in any given month or year, the tests are unable to reject the unit root, and the first-differences of the series are well-approximated by low order autoregressive or moving average processes. But the statistical procedure has effectively discarded all the long-term information in the data, and the fitted process has quite different long-term properties from the data. For policy purposes, such errors can be very serious. If the copper price is a random walk, the income boom that accompanies a price boom can be treated as permanent, and it is appropriate for policy makers to engineer a consumption boom by the full amount of the income boom. But if prices are ultimately trend reverting, the income is ultimately transitory, and can support only a fraction of itself in permanently increased consumption.

A debate along these lines has characterized the estimation of unit roots using American macroeconomic data, where Campbell and Mankiw (1987) found that quarterly data on GDP showed persistence of macroeconomic shocks, while Cochrane (1988) found much less persistence using longer run annual data. Out of these debates came a useful and more direct measure of persistence that can be calculated with minimal parametric assumptions. Suppose that Δy_t is the (demeaned) first difference of the series, and that we write its moving average representation as

$$\Delta y_t = C(L)\varepsilon_t = \varepsilon_t + \sum_{j=1}^{\infty} c_j \varepsilon_{t-j} . \tag{52}$$

Note that (52) does not commit us to either trend or difference stationarity, or indeed to nonstationarity at all; if y_t is white noise, for example, $C(L) = 1 - L$. Campbell and Mankiw (1987) propose that γ defined by

$$\gamma = C(1) = 1 + \sum_{j=1}^{\infty} c_j \tag{53}$$

be used as a measure of persistence. Note that when the series is stationary or trend stationary, the $C(L)$ polynomial will have a unit root and γ will be zero. If the series is a random walk, γ will be unity, if positively correlated in first differences greater than unity, and so on. Note also that if the series is slowly trend reverting, with positive low order autocorrelations that are eventually succeeded by individually small negative ones, the infinite sum $C(1)$ will be much smaller than the sum of its first two terms.

Campbell and Mankiw's persistence measure is closely related to Cochrane's (1988) variance ratio, and both are closely related to the spectral density at frequency zero of the difference Δy_t. This opens the way for the estimation of persistence based on the standard range of non-parametric (window) estimates of the spectral density [see Campbell and Mankiw, Cochrane, and Priestly (1981) for the details]. In the work on quarterly measures of GDP, Campbell and Mankiw's calculations support the persistence measures that are estimated by low-order ARMA processes. However, in the commodity price case, the non-parametric persistence estimates are very much lower than those obtained from the parametric models, and in most cases are not significantly different from zero [see again Deaton and Laroque (1992a)]. Standard unit root modelling of models that are slowly trend reverting will generate a misleading picture of long-run behavior.

2.2.2. Multivariate issues in time-series models

The time-series issues associated with the presence of unit roots arise not only in univariate modelling, but also when we construct models containing several trending regressors. The issue arises most sharply in macroeconomic work, where there is a range of estimation and inference problems associated with the use of regression analysis to estimate relationships between trending variables. In this section, I give only the barest outline of the topic; I am unaware of any issues that are specific to development questions, and fuller treatments are readily available elsewhere [see again Campbell and Perron (1991) and Stock and Watson (1988)].

A useful starting point is a standard linear regression using time-series data,

$$y_t = \beta' x_t + u_t . \tag{54}$$

When all the variables in (54) are stationary, there are no non-standard issues of inference or estimation, so that we suppose some or all of the variables are non-stationary as indeed will be the case in most macroeconomic applications. The knowledge that there can be difficulties with such an apparently innocuous regression goes back to Yule (1926), with later refinements by Granger and Newbold (1974) and Phillips (1986). This is the literature on spurious regression, which is what happens when two essentially unrelated variables are regressed on one another, and appear to be related because, over the period of the sample, they exhibit trend-like behavior. Yule illustrated the point with the correlation at high frequencies of a sine and cosine wave that are orthogonal over frequencies longer than a complete cycle, while Granger and Newbold work with two independent random walks. They show that when two independently generated random walks are regressed on one another, a situation in which the OLS estimate of β converges to zero, there will often be spurious significance with apparently significant values of the t-statistic and of R^2. The very low Durbin–Watson statistics that typically accompany such regressions should indicate that something has gone wrong, although it is not hard to find examples in the literature where it is simply interpreted as evidence of positive autocorrelation, rather than of more fundamental difficulties. Even when investigators are more alive to the dangers, spurious regressions provide a good example of how standard distributional theory can break down in the time-series context.

A central concept in the multivariate analysis of trending variables is *cointegration*, introduced by Engle and Granger (1987). A vector of non-stationary variables z_t is said to be cointegrated when there exists at least one linear combination, $\gamma' z_t$ say, that is stationary. Clearly, if the regression (54) is to make sense, with u_t a zero mean stationary process, the composite vector

$(y_t x_t)$ must be cointegrated with cointegrating vector (1β). By contrast, two independent random walks are clearly not cointegrated, and their failure to be so is part of the problem in spurious regressions. The idea behind cointegration is that two (or more) variables are tied together in the long run, so that while in any given period the cointegrating relationship will never exactly be satisfied, the deviation is always within the bounds defined by a stationary distribution. Indeed, Engle and Granger show that when variables are cointegrated, there exist "error correction" representations of the relationships between them. In the case of two variables, this can be written

$$\Delta y_t = \alpha_0 + \alpha_1 \Delta x_t + \alpha_2(y_{t-1} - \beta x_{t-1}) + u_t \tag{55}$$

where β is the cointegrating parameter, and $y_t - \beta x_t$ is stationary. In many cases, (55) can be interpreted as a causal mechanism running from x to y, whereby y adjusts both to changes in x and to the previous "disequilibrium" in the long-run relationship. However, because (55) is a general consequence of cointegration, there can be many other interpretations.

The error-correction representation is also important because it highlights the consequences of a strategy that used to be recommended by time-series analysts, which is to difference non-stationary variables prior to regression analysis, so that standard inferential procedures can be applied. Equation (55) shows that when variables are cointegrated, a regression in differences ignores the long-run information in the data, and will generate results that do not reflect the long-run behavior of the series. This is analogous to the discussion in the previous section of what happens when a slowly trend-reverting series is modelled by applying a low-order ARMA to its difference. In both cases, the long-run behavior of the series is lost. The same result also applies to the analysis of a set of trending variables among which there may be one or more cointegrating relationships. The dynamics of such systems are often investigated in an atheoretical way by estimating vector autoregressions or VARs, where each variable is regressed on its own lags and those of the other variables. The long-run relationships will be lost if the VAR is estimated using differences.

Given the concept of cointegration, we need procedures for estimation and for inference. Tests for cointegration versus spurious regressions are typically based on the residuals from estimating the cointegrating regression by OLS. In the example of equation (54), we would first estimate by least squares, and then test whether the residuals have a unit root as would be the case if there is no cointegration and the regression is spurious. The recommended way of doing so is to use the augmented Dickey–Fuller test as described above, see equation (51) but without the time trend, and using the Dickey–Fuller tables to test whether the coefficient on the lagged residual is zero. Note once again the structure of the null and alternative hypotheses. Acceptance means that we cannot reject that the residuals have a unit root, which means that we cannot reject the null that there is no cointegration. A significant value of the test leads to the conclusion that the variables are cointegrated. Although the Durbin–Watson statistic may be helpful in indicating the possibility of a spurious regression, it should not be used as a formal test in place of the procedure outlined above.

There remains the question of how inference should be done in relationships like (54) and (55) given cointegration. In general, although OLS will yield consistent estimators, the distributional theory is non-standard, so that it is not possible to rely on the standard normal and χ^2 asymptotic theory. There are a number of alternative approaches. The first was suggested by Engle and Granger and relies on first estimating the cointegrating parameters in a levels regression ignoring any serial correlation in the errors, and then estimating the error-correction equation treating the cointegrating parameters as if they were known. Standard inference applies asymptotically to this second regression in spite of the fact that the cointegrating parameters are estimated not known, a result that hinges on Stock's (1987) proof that the parameters in the first stage regression converge at a rate proportional to $1/T$ rather than the usual $1/\sqrt{T}$. Unfortunately, this procedure does not give a way to make inferences about the cointegrating parameters themselves, nor does it appear to give satisfactory results for the other parameters in the sample sizes usually encountered in macroeconomic applications even in the US, let alone in LDCs, where macro data are often only annual and of relatively short duration.

Several theoretically superior methods are discussed by Campbell and Perron, although it seems that none of these have gone beyond the experimental stage into standard econometric usage. However, it is often possible to avoid the problems altogether. In a number of cases, the cointegrating relationships are "great ratio" relationships, so that a transformation to logarithms gives a cointegrating parameter of unity. If by this or some other argument the cointegrating parameters are known in advance, estimation is straightforward, using for example the error-correction representation. There are other contexts in which non-standard distributions can be avoided, and these have been explored by West (1988) and by Sims, Stock, and Watson (1988). In particular, even in the presence of cointegrating relationships, standard distributional theory applies to OLS estimates of parameters attached to stationary variables, or to parameters that could be attached to stationary variables in an appropriately rewritten regression. This is clearer in an example than it is to state. Consider the regression

$$y_t = \alpha + \beta y_{t-1} + \gamma_0 x_t + \gamma_1 x_{t-1} + u_t \tag{56}$$

which with y as consumption and x as income could be an old-fashioned consumption function as included in innumerable macroeconometric models. This equation can be rewritten in either of the two forms

$$y_t = \alpha + \beta y_{t-1} + \gamma_0 \Delta x_t + (\gamma_0 + \gamma_1) x_{t-1} + u_t \tag{57}$$

or

$$y_t = \alpha + \beta y_{t-1} + (\gamma_0 + \gamma_1) x_t - \gamma_1 \Delta x_t + u_t. \tag{58}$$

If x_t is $I(1)$ so that its first difference is stationary, then (57) and (58) show that both of the γ-parameters can be attached to stationary variables, and that hypotheses concerning either or both can be tested using standard test procedures. Note however that in this example it is not possible to treat β in the same way.

2.2.3. The econometrics of dynamic programs

One of the many recent research programs in macroeconomics has been the use of representative agent dynamic programming models to characterize the economy. Although there is clearly scope for disagreement as to whether it makes sense to model the economy as a fully optimized system – indeed such a program would seem not to leave much scope for traditional development economics – the work has generated a good deal of new econometric tools including techniques for modelling aggregate time-series data. At the same time, there has been an increased interest in using dynamic programming models to help understand microeconomic data. In this section, I briefly review both topics with a focus towards applications in the development literature.

One topic that has been studied at both the macro and micro levels is saving, something that has always been seen as central to the understanding of the development process. Recent papers in development that interpret either micro or macro data using an explicit intertemporal optimization model include Giovannini (1985), Rossi (1988), Corbo and Schmidt-Hebbel (1991), Raut and Virmani (1989), Morduch (1990), and Atkeson and Ogaki (1990). Review papers that cover at least some of this work are Gersovitz (1988) and Deaton (1990b). Deaton (1992a) covers the literature from developed and developing countries, and develops the arguments below at much greater length.

Since the macroeconomic data are often modelled in terms of a single representative agent, we can use the same model to discuss both macro and micro applications. The usual version starts from an intertemporal utility function, whose expected value is the quantity that the agent seeks to maximize. This is typically written as

$$Eu_t = E_t \sum_{k=1}^{\infty} (1 + \delta)^{-k} v(c_{t+k}) \tag{59}$$

where E_t indicates the mathematical expectation conditional on information at time t, δ is the rate of time preference, and the representative agent is assumed to live for ever. Utility is maximized subject to a budget constraint, conveniently written in terms of the evolution of a single asset

$$A_{t+1} = (1 + r_{t+1})(A_t + y_t - c_t) \tag{60}$$

where y_t is labor income – income excluding income from assets – and r_{t+1} is the rate of interest on funds carried from t to $t+1$ and is assumed not to be known in period t. A necessary condition for intertemporal optimality is the Euler equation which for this problem takes the form

$$v'(c_t) = E_t \left[\frac{1 + r_{t+1}}{1 + \delta} v'(c_{t+1}) \right]. \tag{61}$$

A good deal of econometric expertise has been devoted to estimating the parameters of (61) including the parameters of the marginal utility functions, as well as to testing its validity on both aggregate and microeconomic data.

There are several different econometric approaches to the analysis of Euler equations. One of the most straightforward is to select a functional form and to approximate the expectation by taking the first few terms of a Taylor series expansion. The leading example for (61) is to assume isoelastic utility so that the marginal utility is $c_t^{-\rho}$, in which case we can obtain the approximation, see for example Deaton (1992a, p. 64)

$$E_t \Delta \ln c_{t+1} \approx \frac{E_t r_{t+1} - \delta}{\rho} + \frac{\rho \, var_t(\Delta \ln c_{t+1} - \rho^{-1} r_{t+1})}{2} \tag{62}$$

so that, if the last term is small, as is plausibly the case for aggregate (but not micro) data, the Euler equation can be tested by regressing the change in consumption on the real interest rate. The term $E_t r_{t+1}$ can be replaced by r_{t+1} but should then be instrumented using instruments dated period t or earlier, a technique first suggested in the rational expectations literature by McCallum (1976). Variants of (62) are tested on aggregate consumption data for various LDCs by Rossi (1988), Giovannini (1985), and Raut and Virmani (1989).

A more formal estimation and testing technique avoids the approximation by using generalized methds of moments (GMM), an approach pioneered in this context by Hansen and Singleton (1982). Once again, use the isoelastic form for utility and rewrite (61) as

$$\frac{1 + r_{t+1}}{1 + \delta} c_{t+1}^{-\rho} - c_t^{-\rho} = \eta_{t+1} \tag{63}$$

where η_{t+1} is the difference between the outcome and its expectation, or innovation and as such is uncorrelated with any information dated t or earlier. In particular, if we have k such variables z_{it}, we have k conditional moment restrictions $E(\eta_{t+1}|z_{it} = 0)$, whose sample counterparts are the k conditions, $j = 1, \ldots k$,

$$T^{-1} d_j = \frac{1}{T} \sum_{t=1}^{T-1} z_{tj} \left[\frac{1 + r_{t+1}}{1 + \delta} c_{t+1}^{-\rho} - c_t^{-\rho} \right] = 0 . \tag{64}$$

If $k = 2$, so that there are only two instruments, the parameters δ and ρ can be estimated in order to satisfy (64); otherwise, the model is overidentified, and the parameters are estimated by minimizing the quadratic form

$$d'(ZDZ)^{-1}d \tag{65}$$

where D is a diagonal matrix with the estimated η_t^2 on the diagonal, cf. (45) and (46) above.

The theory of GMM estimation requires that both sides of (63) be stationary, something that will typically require some form of detrending prior to estimation. The method also involves nonlinear estimation, which in some cases will make it less attractive than techniques based on the approximations. However, the technique is a clean one that is closely tied to the economics underlying the model, and since the criterion (65) is asymptotically distributed as χ^2 with $k - 2$ degrees of freedom (there are k instruments and two parameters), GMM offers not only estimates, but a natural way of testing the overidentifying restrictions. However, it is not difficult by approximating (64) to show that GMM is closely related to the informal procedure, enforcing very much the same restrictions, and its overidentification test can be regarded as a test of whether the rate of growth of consumption is unpredictable except by variables that predict the real rate of interest.

The final approach to the Euler equation (61) is through a different set of assumptions, that the real rate of interest is constant and equal to the rate of time preference δ, and that preferences are quadratic, so that the marginal utility functions are linear. Together with (61) these assumptions imply that consumption is a martingale, so that the change in consumption is itself an innovation, unpredictable by earlier information

$$\Delta c_{t+1} = \eta_{t+1} . \tag{66}$$

The interest rate question has now been removed from consideration, but (66) can still be tested by finding out whether the change in consumption is in fact predictable by information available in period t, particularly information that is capable of predicting the change in income. This is the approach adopted by many writers in the US, and by Corbo and Schmidt-Hebbel (1991) for a range of Latin American countries together with Ghana, Pakistan, the Philippines, Thailand, and Zimbabwe. However, it is important to note that (66) is not rejected by finding that Δc_{t+1} is correlated with the contemporaneous change in income Δy_{t+1} since the latter will typically contain new information, and thus be correlated with the innovation η_{t+1}. An appropriate procedure, as with the interest rate in (62), is to regress the change in consumption on the contemporaneous change in income by instrumental variables using as instruments any variables dated t or earlier that help predict the next period's income change.

I have discussed these three methods in some detail, partly because the consumption issue is of such great importance, but also because these or similar techniques can be applied to a range of similar problems that generate stochastic intertemporal optimality conditions. Real business cycle models of macroeconomics provide one example; another occurs in finance, where arbitrage conditions are often interpretable as Euler equations, something that will happen quite generally when optimal intertemporal allocations are decentralizable by speculative behavior. For example, Deaton and Laroque (1992a) use GMM to estimate (a subset of) the parameters for the arbitrage conditions for speculative storage of primary commodities.

There are also a number of difficulties with these methods, some of which are general, and some of which are specific to the consumption example. Perhaps most serious is the inherent absurdity of modelling aggregate consumption as the optimal solution to a representative agent problem. Aggregation conditions for these type of models have been discussed (for example) by Grossman and Shiller (1982) and the conditions require (*a*) that people live for ever, (*b*) linearity in functional forms, and (*c*) that information about aggregate macroeconomic variables is known to everyone. In an economy of finitely-lived agents, it is possible for each person's consumption to grow (or to decline) in each year of life, but for aggregate consumption to be constant because the high (low) consumption levels of the old are constantly being replaced by the low (high) consumption levels of the young. The dynamics of individual consumption tells us nothing about the dynamics of aggregate consumption, and vice versa. There is some evidence from developed countries that functional form issues are important in aggregation, Attanasio and Weber (1991), and it is straightforward to use the failure of (*c*) to construct examples where the Euler equation is rejected at the aggregate level even though each agent in the economy is behaving as prescribed, see Pischke (1991) and Deaton (1992a, Chapter 5).

Aggregation problems are avoided by working with individual data, and there is a literature that looks at whether Euler equations like (61) describe the behavior of individual households, or whether there are deviations from (61) in the direction that would be predicted if households were credit constrained. One of the best known (and best) studies for the US is that by Zeldes (1989), and similar work has been undertaken for the South Indian ICRISAT households by Morduch (1990). At least to this writer, these studies make a good deal more sense than do the macroeconomic representative agent models discussed above. However, they are not without technical difficulties. First, these models typically require panel data, and their dynamic structure poses a number of delicate econometric issues that complicate both estimation and inference, see the next subsection. Second, because panel data are typically of short duration, it is impossible to apply the orthogonality conditions that identify these rational expectations models and provide the stuff of hypothesis tests. For example, equation (64) relates to a time average that will not be adequately estimated by two or three observations. In consequence, the panel data studies are forced to replace the time averages in (64) by cross-sectional averages across households or individuals. But the theory has no predictions for the cross-section averages, and in the presence of macroeconomic shocks that are common to many households, the theory can be rejected even when it is correct. Third, it is possible for consumers to be liquidity constrained but for the Euler equation to hold in almost all periods. In Deaton (1990b, 1991) I construct a model of a farmer in an LDC who faces i.i.d. income shocks, and who cannot borrow, but for whom the Euler equation (61) will fail only on the rare equations when it is optimal for him to spend down all his assets. In such circumstances, tests based on the failure of the Euler equation will lack power.

While Euler equations are necessary for optimality, they are not sufficient, so that estimates and tests based on them are less efficient, powerful, or informative than tests based on a complete characterization of behavior. In a few cases, such as the third example above where consumption is a martingale, explicit solutions are available, but this is exceptional and is purchased only at the price of strong assumptions. Recent work in empirical applications of stochastic dynamic programming has taken up this challenge, and attempts to solve for the functions that characterize behavior, not analytically, but numerically. The easiest way to see how this works is to look at an example, and to generalize from it. Since we have the notation at hand, the consumption example is a convenient one.

The basic idea is to have the computer work through the solution to the stochastic dynamic program, mimicking the possibilities that the agent will face. As always with dynamic programming, this is done by starting from the last period and working backwards. Consider then the consumption problem given by (59) and (60), but with a terminal period T. In this final period, since there is no bequest motive, there is an obvious solution to the consumption problem, which is to spend everything. Hence

$$c_T = g_T(A_T + y_T) = A_T + y_T. \tag{67}$$

We can think of this (trivial) solution as period T's decision rule, by which the decision variable c_t is related to the current state variables, here the sum of assets and labor income. This is a clumsy way to describe this obvious result, but the language is useful later.

Given last period behavior, we can begin to work backwards using the Euler equation. In period $T - 1$, (61) implies that

$$v'(c_{T-1}) = E_{T-1}\left[\frac{1 + r_T}{1 + \delta} v'(y_T + (1 + r_T)(A_{T-1} + y_{T-1} - c_{T-1}))\right]. \tag{68}$$

In order to solve (68) for consumption, we need an explicit functional form not only for the marginal utility function but also for the joint distribution of one period ahead interest rates conditional on information at $T - 1$. For example, if this conditional distribution depends only on current values of income and interest rates, the solution to (68) will be of the form

$$c_{T-1} = g_{T-1}(A_{T-1}, y_{T-1}, r_{T-1}; \beta) \tag{69}$$

where β contains parameters of both preferences and the distribution function of interest rates and income. The solution (69) could contain more variables if for example income and interest rates are not first-order Markovian, or if utility depends on variables other than consumption, or less variables, if income and/or interest rates were i.i.d. In any case, there will usually not be an analytical solution for (69), although it will be possible to find it numerically given values of the state variables and of the parameters.

As we pursue the recursion back through time, the equations and the calculations become more complex, but the general principle remains the same. For any period t, there will exist some solution

$$c_t = g_t(s_t; \beta) \tag{70}$$

where s_t is a vector of state variables, for this problem, current and lagged values of income, assets, and interest rates, plus anything else that appears in preferences. There will also be a set of "updating" equations that relate the state variables to their earlier values; the budget constraint (60) is one, and others will represent the dynamic structure of the exogenous or forcing variables, here income and interest rates. Equation (70) is the "policy function" for time t, and is the equation that forms the basis for the econometric analysis of the relationship between consumption and the state variables. In some cases, the functions g_t may converge to a period in-dependent or stationary policy function; this will typically require stationarity of the environment together with restrictions on preferences, conditions that have to be determined on a case by case basis.

This framework, together with a discussion of empirical applications has recently been reviewed by Rust (1992). Most of the empirical work, including Rust's (1987) own path-breaking study of engine replacement at the Madison, Wisconsin bus depot, has been concerned with cases where the choice is over a finite number of alternatives. In such a case, the econometric analysis proceeds as follows. Starting from a parametric form for preferences and for the laws of motion of the exogenous state variables, and a set of trial parameters, the computer first solves the decision problem. In the stationary case, and with discrete state variables, this essentially involves tabulating the function (70) for all possible values of its arguments conditional on the trial parameters. These solutions require iterative methods, and can be (extremely) computationally expensive for large problems with many choices and many state variables. Once the tabulation has been done, the actual values of the state variables can be inserted and the predicted choices compared with actuals. To avoid point predictions, at least one unobservable state variable is introduced, the dis-tribution of which will induce probabilities on each of the outcomes, so that a likelihood function can be constructed in the usual way, the maximization of which is the outer loop of the estimation procedure.

Examples of the use of these techniques in the development literature include Wolpin's (1984) model of fertility using the Malaysian Family Life Survey, and Rosenzweig and Wolpin's (1993) examination of bullocks and pump-sets using the ICRISAT data. The latter study displays both the strengths and weaknesses of the general approach. The strength is the model's close links to the theoretical structure, especially the fact that solutions are genuine solutions of the dynamic problem rather than ad hoc intertemporal allocation rules whose costs and benefits are largely unknown. In principle, functional forms for preferences and distributions can be chosen for their plausibility and suitability to the problem at hand, here the agroclimatic and production conditions in the Indian semi-arid tropics. However, the costs are also high. Even with the use of supercomputers, it is necessary to keep down the number of state variables and to restrict the heterogeneity of individual agents, restrictions that can compromise the realism of the model. For example, Rosenzweig and Wolpin are forced for essentially computational reasons to have only a single asset, bullocks, so that all intertemporal transactions have to pass through the bullock market. There is no money, no jewelry, and no other assets. Note also that these models, by their heavy reliance on parametric functional forms, are extreme examples of the detailed structural specifications that are being increasingly discarded in other applications.

At least in simple cases, it is possible to implement dynamic stochastic programming models where the choice and state variables are continuous. An example is provided by Deaton and Laroque (1992b), who formulate and estimate a model of speculatively determined commodity prices. Under the assumptions that the commodity is an agricultural one whose harvests are i.i.d. from year to year, that demand is a linear function of price, that speculators will store the commodity whenever its one-period ahead expected price exceeds the current price by the costs of storage, and that storage cannot be negative, it is possible to write price as a function of the amount on hand, defined as this year's harvest plus any storage from the previous year. The observed price is thus a function of the unobserved state variable, the amount on hand, which is itself updated by the amount of the new harvest less consumption and the amount taken into storage by the speculators. In consequence, price follows a stationary but nonlinear first-order Markov process. As in the discrete case, estimation is done by nesting two sets of calculations, one to calculate the functions, and one to do the estimation. The function relating prices to the amount on hand can be characterized by a functional equation, the solution of which can be obtained by contraction mapping techniques for any given set of parameter values. The practical difficulty here is that instead of filling in a table, as in the discrete case, we have to solve for a continuous function, and much of the work is concerned with finding suitable discrete approximations that allow us to tabulate the function with interpolation methods (cubic splines) used to fill in the other values. Once the function has been obtained, the Markov process for prices is determined, and likelihood techniques are used to match outcomes to the data, with the results used to modify the parameters.

While these techniques are currently at the frontiers of computational complexity, they are no more difficult than were the now standard nonlinear estimation calculations when they were first explored twenty years ago. Calculations that require supercomputers now will be undertaken on notebook computers in only a few years. I suspect that the limitations to these methods lie not in the computation, but in their reliance on strong parametric assumptions. Robustness issues for both identification and estimation remain to be explored.

2.2.4. Time-series issues in panel data

In this final subsection, I return to the topic of panel data, and to the special problems that arise in using them to examine dynamic issues. I have two sets of applications in mind. The first is those studies that pool time-series from a cross-section of countries to explore the political and economic determinants of economic growth, see for example the references at the beginning of section 1.2. The second is provided by microeconomic studies of household or farm behavior, such as those using the ICRISAT panel data. The difference between the two lies less in methodology than in sample sizes. The country data usually have 20 to 30 years of observations, combined with a cross-section size of between 20 and 120, depending on how many countries are selected into the study. However, many authors work with five or ten year averages of growth rates, so that the time dimension is often reduced to three or four observations. The micro panel studies usually have many more observations in the cross-section but with a smaller number of years. The ICRISAT data, which covered 240 households in six villages for 10 years, have fewer observations and more time periods than is typically the case.

When panel data are used to confront dynamic issues, such as whether countries with low initial levels of GDP will subsequently grow faster, whether political changes cause economic changes or vice versa, or how assets affect current consumption, the regression equations will contain lagged dependent and predetermined variables. A useful model is the following:

$$y_{it} = \alpha + \beta y_{it-1} + \gamma' x_{it} + \eta_i + \varepsilon_{it} \tag{71}$$

where the x's are covariates whose degree of exogeneity and predeterminateness will be discussed, η_i is an individual (or country) specific effect that might or might not be correlated with the x's, and ε_{it} is an error term that will be treated as uncorrelated both across individuals and over time, assumptions than can be relaxed in special cases.

There is a substantial econometric literature on the estimation of (71) [see in particular Chamberlain (1984), Holtz-Eakin, Newey and Rosen (1988), Arellano and Bond (1991), and Schmidt, Ahn, and Wyhowski (1992)], the last three offering particularly clear and accessible treatments that are useful for practical work. As usual, the basic issue is correlation between right-hand side variables and error-terms, with the additional complications involved in dealing with fixed effects by differencing or using within estimators.

Consider first the case where there are no η's. There is no special problem with estimating (71) by OLS, and the model can be estimated using all the data without differencing or sweeping out means. Now suppose that there is individual heterogeneity, that we treat η_i as random, and that there is no lagged dependent variable. Provided the x's are uncorrelated with the random effects, this is a standard random-effects model of the Balestra and Nerlove (1966) variety, and estimation should be by (feasible) GLS. The problem here is that it is often quite implausible that the x's and the η's should be uncorrelated. In particular, if the x's are endogenous but predetermined, the random effects estimator will be inconsistent. For example, if the dependent variable is almost any aspect of household behavior and one of the x's is a measure of assets in any previous period, see for example Rosenzweig and Binswanger (1993), households with high η's will have high y's, and thus high or low x's. Because the η's are present in every period, they determine not only the current value of the dependent variable, but also all previous values, so that any feedback between dependent and independent variables will generate inconsistency, no matter how far lagged are the independent variables. Consistency of OLS (IVE) – or of the random effects estimator – requires that the x's (instruments) be strictly (strongly) exogenous, that they be uncorrelated with the compound error at all leads and lags. For the lagged dependent variable, strict exogeneity is logically impossible, so that OLS or GLS are automatically inconsistent in this case.

If the individual heterogeneity parameters are treated as fixed effects with no further structure, they must either be estimated – which is equivalent to sweeping out the individual means – or the data must be differenced to remove them. The former, whether implemented by estimating individual specific constants or by sweeping out means, is also inconsistent unless the explanatory variables are strictly exogenous. To see why, suppose that there is no lagged dependent variable, and that we sweep out the means from (71):

$$y_{it} - y_{i.} = \gamma'(x_{it} - x_{it-1}) + (\varepsilon_{it} - \varepsilon_{i.}) . \tag{72}$$

The fixed effects have been removed, but only at the price of introducing the average of the ε's. Hence, if there is any feedback from y's to x's the x's will be correlated with the new compound error term. This is a problem of small numbers of time periods, since as T becomes large the time-average of the ε's will converge to its limit of zero. However, in many panel applications, the time dimension is small relative to the cross-section, and large n will not provide consistent estimates. It certainly makes more sense to use the within-estimators on cross-country data with 25 observations per country than it does to use them on a three period cross-sectional panel or on country data that has been averaged by decade.

How then should (71) be estimated? Holtz-Eakin, Newey and Rosen suggest that the equation be differenced to give

$$y_{it} - y_{it-1} = \beta(y_{it-1} - y_{it-2}) + \gamma'\Delta x_{it} + (\varepsilon_{it} - \varepsilon_{it-1}) \tag{73}$$

and that the parameters be estimated by instrumental variables using the fact that x's and y's lagged at least two periods are orthogonal to the differenced error terms. GMM approaches can also be used and will generate efficient estimates, see the elegant treatments in Arellano and Bond and in Schmidt et al. In practice, it may well be difficult to find instruments that are well-correlated with the right hand side variables in (73); especially in micro data, changes are often much harder to predict than are levels. In consequence, the within estimator may be worth considering in spite of its inconsistency, especially if there are more than a few time-periods.

2.3. Introduction to non-parametric methods

Many policy questions can be illuminated from survey data using only very straightforward concepts and techniques. In countries where there is little statistical information, the characterization of univariate and bivariate distributions from survey data is often extremely useful, in much the same way that simple unconditional forecasts are useful for time-series. Poverty measurement typically relies on univariate distributions of income and consumption, while questions of the distributional incidence of price changes depend on the joint distribution of living standards and net purchases. Simple multivariate relationships are often also useful, as when we disaggregate Engel curves by region or by family type. Basic "facts" such as these are routinely obtained from survey data using histograms, cross-tabulations, scatter diagrams, and linear regressions. While there is nothing wrong with any of these techniques, they are frequently not the best that can be done, particularly given the richness of survey data, and the typically large sample sizes. The numerical outputs of cross-tabulations and regressions are harder to communicate to policy makers or non-specialists than is graphical evidence, yet graphs of scatter diagrams are not very informative with very large samples, and plots of linear regressions have the opposite problem of compressing too much information into one graphic. Non-parametric estimation of densities and regressions is often useful in these situations, and allows the analyst to extract and display many more features of the data in a way that is sensitive to sample size. These techniques come in many varieties and flavors, from those that are obvious cousins of cross-tabulations and scatters, through non-parametric regression, to semi-parametric estimation, where a balance is struck between sample and prior information. There is a large and rapidly growing literature on these topics, and I only pick out a few development related applications. Readers interested in following these issues further should begin with the splendid book by Silverman (1986), and then draw from Bierens (1987), Härdle (1991), Stoker (1991), Powell (1992) and Härdle and Linton (1993).

2.3.1. *Estimating densities*

A histogram is the standard and most familiar non-parametric method for representing a univariate density, for example that of incomes in a household survey. For continuous data, however, the discrete steps in histograms usually do not have any counterpart in the underlying population, but are arbitrary artifacts of the selection of the discrete bins into which the observations are separated.

Instead of using a fixed bin, we might use a "sliding" bin or band, so that at each point x, say, we count the number of observations that fall in a symmetric band around x. If the sample points are $x_1, x_2, \ldots, x_N$, the estimated density, $\hat{f}_r(x)$ is given by

$$\hat{f}_r(x) = (2hN)^{-1} \sum_1^N I(x - h \le x_i \le x + h) \tag{74}$$

where $I(e)$ is the indicator function, which is unity if the statement e is true, and zero otherwise, and where the positive number h controls the width of the band. According to (74), the density at x is estimated by the fraction of the sample per unit length (the band is $2h$ long) that is close to (i.e. within h of) x. The procedure here is akin to taking a moving average in time series; rather than take the fraction of the sample *at* x, which can only be zero or j/N for positive integer j and so is very variable from point to point, we average over a nearby interval.

Like the time-series moving average, (74) has the disadvantage of being discontinuous at every point where an observation comes into or falls out of the band. As a result, if (74) is applied to a finite amount of data, the resulting estimator will have a "step" for every data point. This roughness can be removed by calculating a weighted average of the number of points near x, with maximum weight when points are at x, and with the weight steadily declining for points that are further away, and becoming zero for points that are just about to drop out of the band. We write this in the form:

$$\hat{f}_h(x) = \frac{1}{hN} \sum_1^N K\left(\frac{x - x_i}{h}\right) \tag{75}$$

where $K(z)$ is a positive symmetric function, so that $K(z) = K(-z)$, which is declining in the absolute value of its single argument, and which integrates to unity. The function $K(z)$ is a *kernel*, and (75) is a kernel estimator of the density. Note that the naive estimator (74) is a special case of (75) with $K(z) = 0.5I(|z| \le = 1)$; for obvious reasons it is known as the rectangular kernel estimator. The intuition of (75) is exactly the same as that of (74); we are adding up the number of points per unit of line in an interval around x, but we use weights, that sum to unity but that weight more heavily the points near x.

There are several kernels that give good results in practice; three of the most commonly used are the Epanechnikov

$$K_e(z) = 0.75(1 - z^2)I(|z| \le 1) .\tag{76}$$

the Gaussian

$$K_n(z) = (2\pi)^{-0.5} \exp(-0.5z^2)\tag{77}$$

and the quartic

$$K_q(z) = \tfrac{15}{16}(1 - z^2)^2 I(|z| \le 1) .\tag{78}$$

For estimating densities (and regression functions) the choice between these (and other) kernels appears not to be of great importance, see Silverman (1986, p. 43). The Gaussian kernel does not require a separate line of code to detect whether the observation is or is not in the kernel, but many computers are unhappy exponentiating large negative numbers. The Epanechnikov and quartic kernels do not have this problem; the latter has the advantage of being everywhere differentiable, a property that is necessary if we want the estimated density – and later regression function – also to be differentiable, as will be the case in several of the applications discussed below.

More important than the choice of the kernel is the choice of the bandwidth. When the bandwidth is large, the estimator averages over a wide interval around each point, the estimated density will be relatively smooth, but we risk bias by missing genuine features of the underlying density. When the bandwidth is small, sample irregularities will be transmitted to the estimate, and while we will not miss real irregularities, and so will be protected against bias, we risk having too much variability. In any case, as the sample size increases, the bandwidth should shrink, so that with infinite amounts of data, the bandwidth will be zero, and we measure the fraction of the sample – and the population – at each data point. But the bandwidth must decrease more slowly than the sample size expands, so that the number of points in each band increases fast enough to ensure that consistent estimates are obtained at each point. If the bandwidth decreased in proportion to N^{-1}, there would be the same number of points in each band no matter what the sample size, and the variance of the estimate would never decrease. It turns out that it is optimal for the bandwidth to decrease in proportion to the fifth root of the sample size. Beyond that, there are a large number of methods of determining the constant of proportionality, each with its own adherents. Silverman (1986, pp. 45–46) suggests the following as a useful bandwidth when using a Gaussian kernel

$$h = 1.06 \min(\sigma, \chi/1.34)N^{-0.2},$$ (79)

where σ is the standard deviation of the sample, and χ is its interquartile range, i.e. the difference between the 75th and 25th percentiles. The same formula can be used with the Epanechnikov and quartic kernels if the 1.06 is modified to 2.34 and 2.42 respectively.

Figure 33.4 shows densities for the logarithm of household income (deflated by a single price index in each year) in Taiwan for the years 1976 through 1990 inclusive. The underlying data come from the fifteen household surveys discussed in Section 1; there are 9,000–10,000 households in 1976 and 1977, and thereafter between 14,000 and 16,000. Each graph is calculated using (75) and a Gaussian kernel with bandwidth given by (79), and so varying from survey to survey. The densities are estimated at each point on a grid of 100 evenly spaced points for each survey; in order to draw graphs, it is unnecessary (and expensive) to estimate the density for each individual sample point. Note that the underlying distribution of incomes in levels is positively skewed, with observations much more densely distributed at low values than at high values. In such circumstances, it would be better to use smaller bandwidths at low incomes than at high. The logarithmic transformation is a simple way of avoiding having to do so, and the plots of the roughly symmetric densities are easier to see. The graphs show clearly the pattern of real income growth in

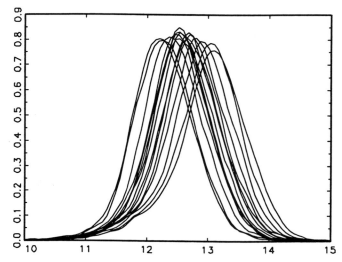

Figure 33.4.   Non-parametric estimates of densities of log real income, Taiwan 1976–1990.

Taiwan, and modal real household income approximately doubles from 1976 to 1990. The graphs also show that the *shape* of the income distribution has been changing over time, with the lower tail stretching out as some households are left behind, and the density at the mode falling. Taiwan has had, and continues to have one of the world's most equal distributions of income, but inequality has been widening over the last decade [see also Government of Taiwan, (1989) and Deaton and Paxson (1994b)].

It is also possible to look at income distribution non-parametrically by plotting cumulative distribution functions or Lorenz curves. I have focussed here on density estimation, not because it is necessarily superior, but because the estimation of distribution functions or Lorenz curves using the individual data is straightforward because it is not usually necessary to smooth the estimates. The empirical estimator of the distribution function

$$\hat{F}(x) = N^{-1} \sum_{1}^{N} I(x_i \leq x) \tag{80}$$

is discontinuous for the same reasons as is the naive estimator, but for reasonable sample sizes, the discontinuities will not usually be apparent to the naked eye, and will not usually generate difficulties for the calculation of poverty or other measures. The same is true for Lorenz curves.

Non-parametric methods can also be used to estimate multivariate densities, although the "curse of dimensionality" means that very large numbers of observations are required when the dimensionality is high, see Silverman (1986, pp. 93–94). In practice, it is frequently useful to disaggregate by discrete variables, and to estimate densities by region, or by ethnic group, and these estimates present no new issues of principle. Estimates of the joint density of two continuous variables are practical and often informative, and can be constructed using the bivariate extensions of the methods given above. The standard procedure is to transform the data using its variance covariance matrix so as to make the scatter spherical, and then to make a weighted count of the number of observations in a circle around each point (x, y). The details are again in Silverman, pp. 65–80. To illustrate using the quartic kernel, the joint density estimator is

$$\hat{f}(z) = \hat{f}(x, y) = 3(\pi \sqrt{|S|} Nh^2)^{-1} \sum_{1}^{N} (1 - h^{-2}t_i^2)^2 I(|t_i| \leq h) \tag{81}$$

where S is the sample variance-covariance matrix, $|S|$ is its determinant, and t^2 is the quadratic form $(z - z_i)'S^{-1}(z - z_i)$, the squared distance of $z_i = (x_i, y_i)$ from z.

Figure 33.5 shows a contour map of the joint density of log consumption and log income using the Taiwanese data for 1979. This was calculated from 16,424

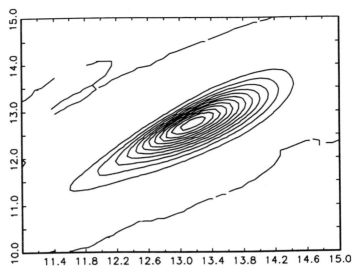

Figure 33.5.   Non-parametric estimate of joint density of log income and log consumption, Taiwan 1990.

observations using (81), a 99 by 99 point grid, and a bandwidth of 1. (The calculations took a little less than an hour using GAUSS on a 66-Mhz PC.) Once again, the fact that the contours are not far from elliptical shows that the transformation to logs has induced something close to normality, not only for the marginals but also in the joint distribution of log income and log consumption. Even so, the contours are more egg-shaped than elliptical, so that although the regression function of log consumption on log income will be approximately linear, it will not be homoskedastic. The contour map is the preferred way of showing detail in the joint distribution, although for some purposes, a rapid appreciation of its general shape can be better seen from "net-maps", which provide a projection of the three dimensional object, see Deaton (1989) for net-maps of the joint distributions of living standards and net rice consumption across different regions of Thailand.

2.3.2. *Non-parametric regression*

Joint densities, such as that illustrated in Figure 33.5, contain the information that goes into regression functions, whether the conditional density of x on y, or the conditional density of y on x. More generally, the regression (function) of y on a vector $(x_1, x_2, \ldots, x_k)$ is defined as the expectation of y conditional on the x's, or

$$m(x_1, x_2, \ldots, x_k) = E(y/x_1, x_2, \ldots, x_k).$$

If two variables x and y are jointly normally distributed, then both regression functions (of x on y and of y on x) will be linear and homoskedastic, but in general we cannot expect this to be the case. Indeed, there are a number of examples in development econometrics where nonlinearity has been an important issue, and perhaps the leading example is the relationship between nutrition and income. As emphasized by Ravallion (1990), it is likely that very poor people, who are close to subsistence, will spend a large fraction of any additional available resources on calories, but that this fraction will become much less as basic needs are met. As a result, the regression function of calories on income (or total expenditure) may be steeply sloped at low income levels, and flatten out as income increases. A transformation to logs may help, but there is no reason to suppose that the relationship is exactly of the form that would thereby become linear. The obvious procedure, especially when data are plentiful, is to estimate a non-parametric regression.

The procedures are closely analogous to those for density estimation, and the basic ideas are, if anything, even more transparent. With an infinite amount of data, the regression function of y on x could be calculated by averaging all the observations on y at each point x. With finite data, such a procedure is impractical, but we can use the same idea as in density estimation, and take an average over some interval around x. An early form of such non-parametric regression is Mahalanobis' (1960) fractile graphical analysis by which the x's are first sorted and then partitioned into fractile groups, such as deciles, so that averages of y can be calculated and plotted for each fractile. This method is analogous to the construction of histograms to represent densities, and like the latter can be improved by calculating averages for each x, and by weighting within the averages.

Alternatively, and more formally, we can write the regression function of y on x, $m(x)$ as

$$m(x) = \int yf(y|x)\, dy = f(x)^{-1} \int yf(x, y)\, dy \tag{83}$$

for which we can construct an estimate

$$\hat{m}(x) = \left[\frac{1}{Nh} \sum y_i K\left(\frac{x - x_i}{h}\right) \right] \div \left[\frac{1}{Nh} \sum K\left(\frac{x - x_i}{h}\right) \right] \tag{84}$$

which is known as the Nadaraya–Watson kernel regression estimator. Procedures for choosing the kernel and the bandwidth are similar to those in density estimation, though the kernel and bandwidth that optimally trade-off bias and variance for the density will generally not do so for the regression function. However, if the main object of the exercise is graphical representation of the regression function, a bandwidth can be selected by trial and error, with some preference for erring on the side of too small a bandwidth, since it is easier for the eye to smooth over irregularities than to uncover invisible features from an over-smoothed curve.

One useful feature of (84) is that since these methods estimate regression functions, and not the underlying structure, they require no modification for dichotomous or limited dependent variables. If the y's are 1 or 0, the regression function will be a conditional probability, and that is what the nonparametric regression will estimate. If the true model is Tobit, a linear model with censoring at zero, the nonparametric regression will deliver the Tobit regression function, equation (26).

One useful feature of (84) is that it allows straightforward estimation, not only of the regression function at each point, but of its derivatives, which are often of as much or more interest. Direct calculation gives:

$$\hat{m}'(x) = \left(h \sum K(t_i) \right)^{-1} \left(\sum K'(t_i)(y_i - \hat{m}(x)) \right) \qquad (85)$$

where $t_i = (x - x_i)/h$. These derivatives are readily calculated at the same time as the estimates of the regression function. Note however that, at the same bandwidth, the derivatives will be much less smooth than the regression as a function of x, so that higher bandwidths are typically desirable, see also Härdle (1991).

Figure 33.6, reproduced from Subramanian and Deaton (1992), shows the derivatives of the regression of the logarithm of calories on the logarithm of per capita household total expenditure for a sample of 5,600 households in rural Maharashtra in India. Since the regression function is in logs, the figure shows the elasticity of calories with respect to per capita total expenditure at each level of the latter. The results for two different bandwidths are shown; the smaller value is clearly too small and introduces what is almost certainly spurious fluctuations as total expenditure changes. Using the larger of the two bandwidths, there is some evidence of a slow decline as per capita expenditure rises, but not of any critical (or subsistence) point where the elasticity falls sharply. This is in contrast to Strauss and Thomas' (1990) results for Brazil, obtained using Cleveland's (1979) LOWESS estimator – an alternative nonparametric regression method – where elasticities are found to be much higher for poor than for rich households. The fact that the Indian households are much poorer may be relevant; perhaps they are all poorer than the cut-off

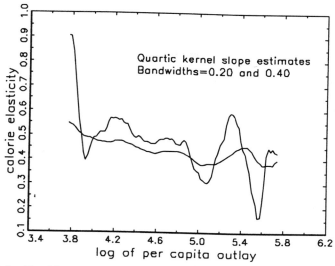

Figure 33.6. Elasticity of the calorie-expediture relationship with different bandwidths, Maharashtra, India 1983.

point in the Brazilian data. Note too that the elasticities in the figure are all a great deal higher than the figures that Bouis (1992) and Bouis and Haddad (1992) regard as sensible, perhaps because of the fact that nothing has been done to eliminate plate wastage, or food passed on to other people. These varying estimates are also fully consistent with that obtained by Behrman and Deolalikar (1987) using panel data from the ICRISAT data, from a nearby part of India. However, Behrman and Deolalikar's estimate of 0.37, based on a much smaller sample, and obtained from the first-differences of panel data, is not significantly different from zero, and the authors choose to interpret their result as showing that there is no relationship between calories and income.

2.3.3. Other non-parametric estimation methods

I have emphasized kernel regression methods in this presentation, but there are many other possibilities. I have already referred to Cleveland's (1979) LOWESS procedure, whereby the regression function is estimated by a series of local OLS regressions, appropriately weighted. Non-parametric regressions can also be estimated using splines, see Engle et al. (1986) and Härdle (1991), or by nearest-neighbor methods, which are similar to kernel methods, but the averaging is done, not over a fixed bandwidth centered on the point, but over the k nearest neighbors of the point, with k playing the role of the bandwidth. Such estimators are very similar to variable kernel estimators, with the bandwidth small in regions of high density, and large in regions of low. It is also possible to approximate regression functions using series expansions, with polynomial and Fourier series the obvious choices; for the latter see Gallant (1981), El-Badawi, Gallant, and Souza (1983), and Gallant and Souza (1991). Such estimators are convenient because they can be estimated by OLS, but can be dangerous with "dirty" survey data. A few outliers can have a major effect on fitted polynomials, while, with Fourier series, the regression function tends to "send out" tailored sine waves to pick up individual outliers. Kernel estimators have the advantage that observations beyond the bandwidth do not have any effect on the regression line at a point, so that the effect of outliers is limited. Kernel estimators of densities and of regression functions are also readily generalizable from the univariate and bivariate cases to multivariate analysis.

All of these nonparametric estimation techniques are most valuable in low dimensional situations, for one or two dimensional densities, or for regressions with at most two or three right hand side variables. In higher dimensions, data requirements are usually prohibitive, even by the standards of household survey data, and even armed with several million observations, it is unclear how one would display the results of a high dimensional density or regression. (Although programs such as *Mathematica* will draw three-dimensional netmaps with color variation representing the fourth dimension.) While there are many problems in development economics where the problems are low dimensional – calorie expenditure curves, Engel curves, and income distributions, for example – there are many other problems that require a different approach.

There has been a good deal of recent work on *semi-parametric* estimation techniques, where the idea is to mix parametric and non-parametric approaches, using prior structure where data are weak or scarce, and letting the data speak for themselves through non-parametric specifications where they are capable of doing so. One possibility is to write a regression function that is a mixture of linear and unspecified parts

$$E(y|x, z) = m(x, z) = \beta'x + f(z) \tag{86}$$

where z is a variable about which the data are likely to be quite informative, and x is a vector of variables where prior structure is required. For example, z might be income in an Engel curve, and x a set of sociodemographic variables whose effects are likely to be less well-defined in even a very large data set. Techniques for estimating (86) have been investigated by Robinson (1988).

2.3.4. Average derivatives and index models

Perhaps even more useful for many problems in empirical development is the *index* model, in which the regression function is written in the form

$$E(y|x) = m(x) = \theta(\beta'x) \tag{87}$$

so that while the standard linear structure is retained in the index $\beta'x$, the function $\theta(.)$ is left unspecified. This index model has the obvious attractions of mixing parametric and non-parametric specifications, something that is necessary if we are to bring some element of non-parametric methodology to higher dimensional problems. It also arises naturally in limited dependent variable models; for example, the regression function of Tobit – equation (26) – is of this form. Stoker (1991) shows that a range of other models – logit and probit models, truncation models, Box – Cox and Generalized Linear Models, and duration models – can all be written in the index form (87). While estimation of the parameters of (87), which are clearly identified only up to scale, will typically not provide estimates of all the parameters of these models, it can provide some information, and can do so without the distribution assumptions that are required for traditional maximum likelihood procedures.

Estimation of index models has been studied by Powell, Stock, and Stoker (1989), who show that it is possible to estimate the β's consistently and with convergence to the true values at the usual rate of root-N not at the much slower rates, typically the fifth root of N, that characterize non-parametric regressions. The basic idea comes from Stoker (1986). Write $f(x)$ for the marginal density of the x's, the conditioning variables in the regression, and define the vector of "scores" $z(x)$, by, $j = 1, \ldots, K$,

$$z_j = -\partial \ln f(x)/\partial x_j \tag{88}$$

so that, for each of the K x-variables, we have a value of its score for each observation. Consider then the population expectation of $z_j(x)y$, where the expectation is taken over both y and x. Note first that, from (88),

$$E(z_j y) = \int \int z_j(x)yf(y, x)\, dy\, dx = -\int \int f_j(x)yf(y|x)\, dy\, dx \tag{89}$$

where $f_j(x)$ is the jth partial derivative of the joint density. If the right hand side of (89) is integrated by parts, and if $f(x)$ is zero on the boundary of x, then

$$E(z_j y) = \int \int f(x)yf_j(y|x)\, dy\, dx = E_x\left(\frac{\partial E_y(y|x)}{\partial x_j}\right). \tag{90}$$

The last term on the right hand side of (90) is the vector of population average derivatives of the regression function, while the left hand side involves the scores z_j which can be estimated by the kernel methods discussed above; note that estimates of the derivatives of the joint densities can be obtained by differentiating (75) or its multivariate extension. Replacing population quantities by their estimates in (90) yields the *average derivative estimator*

$$\hat{\delta}_j = N^{-1} \sum_{i=1}^{N} \hat{z}_j(x_i) y_i \tag{91}$$

$\hat{\delta}_j$ will converge to the average over the population of the jth partial derivative of the regression function.

There are a number of complications and improvements to this basic idea that make it work better in practice. First, note that the scores are *logarithmic* derivatives of the joint density, and so will be very badly estimated where the joint density is small. This problem is dealt with by "trimming", which means dropping such observations from the sum in (91). Second, note from (90) that the $E(z_j x_k)$ is the derivative with respect to x_j of the expectation of x_j conditional on x, which is 1 if $j = k$, and is otherwise zero. As a result, if the scores are placed in an N by K matrix Z, the "instrumental variable estimator" $(Z'X)^{-1}(Z'y)$ also converges to the vector of average derivatives. To trim this, define the diagonal N by N matrix W by its typical element

$$w_{ii'} = \delta_{ii'} I(\hat{f}(x_i) > \alpha) \tag{92}$$

for some small positive number α. We then construct the "practical" estimator

$$\hat{\delta} = (\hat{Z}'WX)^{-1}(\hat{Z}'Wy) \tag{93}$$

where $\hat{Z}$ is the matrix of estimated scores.

Härdle and Stoker (1989) and Stoker (1991) discuss a number of other possible variants of this average derivative estimator. The remarkable thing about these estimators is not that they consistently estimate the average partial derivatives of the regression, but that they converge at the standard rate of $1/\sqrt{N}$. Although the kernel estimates may give very imprecise and slowly converging estimates of the scores, the averaging over the sample cancels out the variability in the components of the estimator, and allows the δ's to converge at the standard rate.

Consider first the application of average derivative estimators to the index models discussed above. If the expectation is given by (87), the average derivative estimator $\hat{\delta}_j$ will converge to β_j multiplied by the average derivative of θ, a quantity that is independent of j. For such index models, Powell, Stock,

and Stoker (1989) actually recommend a "density-weighted" average derivative estimator which differs from (93) in replacing the matrix W by one with
the estimated densities on its diagonal.

Perhaps the most enticing potential application of average derivative estimators is to the case where the regression function is unspecified, in which
case it offers a non-parametric estimate of the derivatives. A good example
comes from the theory of tax reform, and its application to problems of pricing
in LDCs. The basic material is discussed at length in Newbery and Stern
(1987), Deaton (1987), and for India and Pakistan in Ahmad and Stern (1991).

A policy reform of increasing the price of good i is under consideration. The
welfare cost of an infinitesimal price change Δp_i is the sum over each agent h of
$\xi^h q_i^h \Delta p_i$, where q_i^h is net consumption of good i by h, and the weight ξ^h is the
marginal social utility of money to individual h, independent of h for
unrepentant Harbergians, see Harberger (1978, 1984), or varying with income
(or ethnicity or region) if we want to apply distributional or other weights. The
benefit of the price change is the value of additional revenue that it generates,
so that the cost to benefit ratio of increasing the price can be written

$$\lambda_i = \frac{H^{-1} \Sigma_h \, \xi^h q_i^h}{H^{-1} \Sigma_h \, q_i^h + \Sigma_k \, t_k (H^{-1} \Sigma_h \, \partial q_k^h / \partial p_i)} \tag{94}$$

where t_k is the tax rate (or shadow tax rate, see Stern, 1987) on good k, and H
is the population size. Commodities that have large λ-ratios are those through
which it is (socially) harmful to raise government revenue, and whose prices
should ideally be reduced, and vice versa for commodities with low λ-ratios.

The standard practice for evaluating tax reform proposals is to use household
survey data to evaluate the equity effects in the numerator, weighting the
consumption patterns of different groups by whatever importance policy-
makers attach to their consumption at the margin. In practice this is usually
done by using an Atkinson (1970) social welfare function, in which ξ^h is taken
to be proportional to income (or per capita expenditure) to the power of $-\varepsilon$.
Calculations are then done for a range of values of ε, with zero representing
indifference to distribution, and larger values representing greater concern for
the poor. Survey (or administrative) data can also be used to estimate mean
consumption, the first term on the denominator, so that all but the second term
in the denominator can be calculated without need of a parametric model. This
last term is usually obtained by using time-series data or spatial variation in
prices to estimate a demand system in which quantities are a function of prices,
incomes, and household characteristics, and to calculate the responses using
the estimated parameters, see for example Ahmad and Stern (1991) or Deaton
and Grimard (1992) for alternative specifications applied to Pakistan. However, the term can be estimated without a parametric demand system using

average derivative estimators. Not only can we avoid distributional assumptions about unobservables, but we do not even require a functional form for demand. In cases like this, and the general point applies to any average or weighted average of behavioral responses, the use of a functional form is essentially a detour, and an unnecessary one at that. Note too that in these sort of cases, there is no loss in precision from the non-parametric treatment, at least asymptotically.

The point made, a number of caveats ought to be entered. Practical experience with average derivative estimators in real situations is essentially nil, although see the experimental calculations in Deaton and Ng (1993). Although the asymptotic theory has been fully worked out, we do not know how difficult are the computational problems with data sets of several thousand observations, nor what is the best way to select the bandwidth for the estimation of the scores. Nor does the fact that these estimators are root-N consistent in itself guarantee that they will perform well in small samples. Indeed, the literature provides no guidance on what sample sizes are required to make the methods work. Nevertheless, these techniques are exceptionally promising, and provide a potential antidote to that body of empirical work that derives its results using restrictive functional forms and arbitrary distributional assumptions.

References

Ahluwalia, M.S. (1976) 'Inequality, poverty, and development', *Journal of Development Economics*, 3:307–342.

Ahluwalia, M.S., Duloy, J.H., Pyatt, G. and Srinivasan, T.N. (1980) 'Who benefits from economic development? Comment', *American Economic Review*, 70:242–245.

Ahmad, E. and Stern, N. (1991) *The theory and practice of tax reform in developing countries*, Cambridge. Cambridge University Press.

Ainsworth, M. (1992) 'Economic aspects of child fostering in Côte d'Ivoire', The World Bank, processed.

Ainsworth, M. and Muñoz, J. (1986) 'The Côte d'Ivoire living standards study', LSMS Working Paper 26, The World Bank, Washington, D.C.

Alesina, A. and Perotti, P. (1992) 'Income distribution, political instability, and investment', Washington, D.C. Institute for Policy Reform Working Paper No. 53, (September.)

Altonji, J., Hayashi, F. and Kotlikoff, L.J. (1992) 'Is the extended family altruistically linked? Direct tests using micro data', *American Economic Review*, 82:1177–1198.

Anand, S. and Ravi Kanbur, S.M. (1993) 'Inequality and development: a critique', *Journal of Development Economics*, 41:19–44.

Angrist, J.D. (1990) 'Lifetime earnings and the Vietnam era draft lottery: evidence from social security administrative records', *American Economic Review*, 80:313–336.

Angrist, J.D. and Krueger, A.B. (1994) 'Why do World War II veterans earn more?' *Journal of Labor Economics*, 12:74–97.

Arabmazar, A. and Schmidt, P. (1981) 'Further evidence on the robustness of the Tobit estimator to heteroscedasticity', *Journal of Econometrics*, 17:253–258.

Arabmazar, A. and Schmidt, P. (1982) 'An investigation of the robustness of the Tobit estimator to non-normality', *Econometrica*, 50:1055–1063.

Ardeni, P.G. and Wright, B. (1992) 'The Prebisch – Singer hypothesis: a reappraisal independent of stationarity hypotheses', *Economic Journal*, 102:803–812.

Arellano, M. (1987) 'Computing robust standard errors for within-groups estimators', *Oxford Bulletin of Economics and Statistics*, 49:431–434.

Arellano, M. and Bond, S. (1991) 'Some tests of specification for panel data: Monte Carlo evidence and an application to employment equations', *Review of Economic Studies*, 58:277–297.

Arrow, K.J., 1974, 'The measurement of real value added', in P. David, and M. Reder, eds., *Nations and households in economic growth: essays in honor of Moses Abramovitz*, New York. Academic Press, 3–19.

Ashenfelter, O., Deaton, A. and Solon, G. (1986) 'Collecting panel data in developing countries: does it make sense?' LSMS Working Paper 23, The World Bank, Washington, D.C.

Atkeson, A. and Ogaki, M. (1990) 'Engel's law and saving', University of Chicago and University of Rochester (July), mimeo.

Atkinson, A.B. (1970) 'On the measurement of inequality', *Journal of Economic Theory*, 2:244–263.

Attanasio, O. and Weber, G. (1991) 'Consumption growth, the interest rate and aggregation', Stanford University and University College, London (June), mimeo. (*Review of Economic Studies*, forthcoming).

Balestra, P. and Nerlove, M. (1966) 'Pooling cross-section and time-series data in the estimation of a dynamic model: the demand for natural gas', *Econometrica*, 34:585–612.

Barro, R.J. (1991) 'Economic growth in a cross-section of countries', *Quarterly Journal of Economics*, 106:407–444.

Barro, R.J. and Sala-i-Martin, X. (1992) 'Convergence', *Journal of Political Economy*, 100:223–251.

Behrman, J.R. and Deolalikar, A.B. (1987) 'Will developing country nutrition improve with income? A case study for rural south India', *Journal of Political Economy*, 95:108–138.

Behrman, J.R. and Deolalikar, A.B. (1988) 'Health and nutrition', Chapter 14 in H. Chenery, and T.N. Srinivasan, eds., *Handbook of Development Economics*, 1:631–711.

Behrman, J.R. and Rosenzweig, M.R. (1994) 'The quality of aggregate inter-country, time-series data on educational investments and stocks, economically active populations, and employment', *Journal of Development Economics*, forthcoming.

Behrman, J.R. and Taubman, P. (1990) 'The intergenerational correlation between children's adult earnings and their parents' income: results from the Michigan panel survey of income dynamics', *The Review of Income and Wealth*, 36:115–127.

Behrman, J.R. and Wolfe, B.L. (1984) 'The socioeconomic impact of schooling in a developing country', *Review of Economics and Statistics*, 66:296–303.

Behrman, J.R. and Wolfe, B.L. (1989) 'Does more schooling make women better nourished and healthier?' *Journal of Human Resources*, 24:644–663.

Bell, C., Srinivasan, T.N. and Udry, C. (1992) 'Segmentation, rationing and spillover in credit markets: the case of rural Punjab', New Haven. Yale University, processed (February)

Benefo, K. and Schultz, T.P. (1993) 'Determinants of fertility and child mortality in Côte d'Ivoire and Ghana', New Haven. Yale University, processed (March)

Benjamin, D. (1993) 'Can unobserved land quality explain the inverse productivity relationship?' University of Toronto, processed. (February)

Benjamin, D. and Deaton, A. (1988) 'The Living Standards Survey and price policy reform: a study of cocoa and coffee production in Côte d'Ivoire', Living Standards Measurement Working Paper No. 44, Washington, D.C., The World Bank.

Berry, A.R. (1985) 'On trends in the gap between rich and poor in less developed countries: why we know so little', *Review of Income and Wealth*, 31:337–354.

Berry, A.R. and William R. Cline, 1979, *Agrarian structure and productivity in developing countries*, Baltimore. Johns Hopkins University Press.

Bevan, D., Collier, P. and Gunning, J.W. (1989) *Peasants and government: An economic analysis*, Oxford. Clarendon.

Bhalla, S.S. and Roy, P. (1988) 'Mis-specification in farm productivity analysis: the role of land quality', *Oxford Economic Papers*, 40:55–73.

Bhalla, S.S. and Roy, P. (1988) 'Mis-specification in farm productivity analysis: the role of land quality', *Oxford Economic Papers*, 40:55–73.

Bierens, H.J. (1987) 'Kernel estimators of regression functions', in: T.F. Bewley, ed., *Advances in Econometrics: Fifth World Congress*, 1:99–144.

Bouis, H.E. (1994) 'The effect of income on demand for food in poor countries: are our databases giving us reliable estimates?' *Journal of Development Economics*, forthcoming.

Bouis, H.E. and Haddad, L.J. (1992) 'Are estimates of calorie-income elasticities too high? A recalibration of the plausible range', *Journal of Development Economics*, 39:333–364.

Box, G.E.P. and Jenkins, G.M. (1970) *Time-series analysis: forecasting and control*, San Francisco: Holden–Day.

Breusch, T.S., and Pagan, A.R. (1979) 'A simple test for heteroskedasticity and random coefficient variation', *Review of Economic Studies*, 47:1287–1294.

Buchinsky, M. (1994), 'Changes in the U.S. wage structure 1963–1987: application of quantile regression; *Econometrica*, 62:405–465.

Buse, A. (1992) '*The bias of instrumental variables estimators*', *Econometrica*, 60:173–179.

Campbell, J.Y. and Mankiw, N.G. (1987) 'Are output fluctuations transitory?' *Quarterly Journal of Economics*, 102:857–880.

Campbell, J.Y. and Perron, P. (1991) 'Pitfalls and opportunities: What macroeconomists should know about unit roots', in: O.J. Blanchard and S. Fischer, eds., *Macroeconomics Annual 1991*, Cambridge, MA: MIT Press for NBER, 141–201.

Card, D.E. (1991) 'Intertemporal labor supply: an assessment', Cambridge, MA: NBER Working Paper No. 3602, processed. (January)

Casley, D.J. and Lury, D.A. (1981) *Data collection in developing countries*, Oxford: Clarendon.

Chamberlain, G. (1984) 'Panel data', in: Z. Griliches and M.D. Intriligator, eds., *Handbook of Econometrics, Volume 2*, Amsterdam: North-Holland. 1247–1322.

Chamberlain, G. (1986) 'Asymptotic efficiency in semiparametric models with censoring', *Journal of Econometrics*, 32:189–192.

Chamberlain, G. (1991) 'Quantile regression, censoring, and the structure of wages', Cambridge, MA: Harvard University, processed, (June.)

Chamie, J. (1994) 'Population databases in development analysis', *Journal of Development Economics*, forthcoming.

Chayanov, A.V. (1966) *The theory of peasant economy*, Homewood, IL: Irwin. (Originally published in Russian, 1925.)

Chow, G.C. (1983) *Econometrics*, New York: McGraw-Hill.

Cleveland, W.S. (1979) 'Robust locally weighted regression and smoothing scatter plots', *Journal of the American Statistical Association*, 74:829–836.

Cochrane, J.H. (1988) 'How big is the random walk in GNP?' *Journal of Political Economy*, 96:893–920.

Corbo, V. and Schmidt-Hebbel, K. (1991) 'Public policy and saving in developing countries', *Journal of Development Economics*, 36:89–115.

Cramer, J.S., 1969, *Empirical econometrics*, Amsterdam: North-Holland.

Cuddington, J.T. (1992) 'Long-run trends in 26 primary commodity prices: a disaggregated look at the Prebisch–Singer hypothesis', *Journal of Development Economics*, 39:207–227.

Davidson, R. and MacKinnon, J.G. (1993) *Estimation and inference in econometrics*, Oxford: Oxford University Press.

Deaton, A.S. (1985) 'Panel data from time series of cross-sections', *Journal of Econometrics*, 30:109–126.

Deaton, A.S. (1987) 'Econometric issues for tax design in developing countries', in: D. Newbery and N. Stern, eds., *The theory of taxation for developing countries*, Oxford: Oxford University Press for The World Bank, 92–113.

Deaton, A.S. (1988) 'Quality, quantity and spatial variation in price', *American Economic Review*, 78:418–430.

Deaton, A.S. (1989) 'Rice prices and income distribution in Thailand: a non-parametric analysis', *Economic Journal*, 99:(Supplement) 1–37.

Deaton, A.S. (1990a) 'Price elasticities from survey data: extensions and Indonesian results', *Journal of Econometrics*, 44:281-309.

Deaton, A.S. (1990b) 'Saving in developing countries: theory and review', *World Bank Economic Review*, Special Issue, Proceedings of the First Annual World Bank Conference on Development Economics, 61–96.

Deaton, A.S. (1991) 'Saving and liquidity constraints', *Econometrica*, 59:1221–1248.

Deaton, A.S. (1992a) *Understanding consumption*, Oxford: Oxford University Press.

Deaton, A.S. (1992b) 'Commodity prices, stabilization and growth in Africa', Washington, D.C. Institute for Policy Reform Working Paper No. 40, processed. (September)

Deaton, A.S. (1994) *The analysis of household surveys: microeconomic analysis for development policy*, Research Program in Development Studies, Princeton University, processed. (423 pp.) (Apr.)

Deaton, A.S. and Grimard, F. (1992) 'Demand analysis for tax reform in Pakistan', Princeton, N.J. Princeton University, Research Program in Development Studies, processed. (January)

Deaton, A.S. and Laroque, G. (1992a) 'On the behavior of commodity prices', *Review of Economic Studies*, 59:1–23.

Deaton, A.S. and Laroque, G. (1992b) 'Estimating the commodity price model', Research Program in Development Studies, Princeton University, processed.

Deaton, A.S. and Ng, S. (1993) 'Parametric and non-parametric approaches to price and tax reform', Princeton, N.J. Princeton University, Research Program in Development Studies, processed. (March)

Deaton, A.S. and Paxson, C.H. (1994a) 'Saving, growth, and aging in Taiwan', in: D. Wise, ed., *Studies in the economics of aging*, Chicago: Chicago U. Press for National Bureau of Economic Research.

Deaton, A.S. and Paxson, C.H. (1994b) 'Intertemporal choice and inequality', *Journal of Political Economy*, 102:437–468.

Dickey, D.A. and Fuller, W.A. (1981) 'Likelihood ratio statistics for autoregressive time series with a unit root', *Econometrica*, 49:1057–1072.

Dumouchel, W.H. and Duncan, G.J. (1983) 'Using sample survey weights in multiple regression analysis of stratified samples', *Journal of the American Statistical Association*, 78:535–543.

Eicker, F. (1967) 'Limit theorems for regressions with unequal and dependent errors', in: *Proceedings of the Fifth Berkeley Symposium on Mathematical Statistics and Probability*, 1, Berkeley, CA: University of California Press, 59–82.

El-Badawi, I., Gallant, A.R. and Souza, G. (1983) 'An elasticity can be estimated consistently without knowledge of functional form', *Econometrica*, 51:1731–1751.

Engle, R.F. (1984) 'Wald, likelihood ratio, and Lagrange multiplier tests in econometrics', in: Z. Griliches and M.D. Intriligator, eds., *Handbook of Econometrics, Volume 2*, Amsterdam: North-Holland, 775–826.

Engle, R.F. and Granger, C.W.J. (1987) 'Co-integration and error correction: representation, estimation, and testing', *Econometrica*, 55:251–276.

Engle, R.F., Rice, J. and Weiss, A. (1986) 'Semiparametric estimates of the relation between weather and electricity sales', *Journal of the American Statistical Association*, 81:310–320.

Evenson, R.E. and Pray, C.E. (1994) 'Measurement of food production and consumption', *Journal of Development Economics*, forthcoming.

Feder, G. (1985) 'The relation between farm size and farm productivity', *Journal of Development Economics*, 18:297–313.

Fields, G.S. (1977) 'Who benefits from economic development? A re-examination of Brazilian growth in the 60's', *American Economic Review*, 67:570–582.

Fields, G.S. (1992) 'Data for measuring poverty and inequality changes in the developing countries', Ithaca, N.Y.: Cornell University, processed. (June)

Fuller, W.A., 1975, 'Regression analysis for sample survey, *Sankhya*, Series C, 37:117–132.

Fuller, W.A. (1987) *Measurement error models*, New York: John Wiley.

Gallant, A.R. (1981) 'On the bias in flexible functional forms and an essentially unbiased form: the Fourier flexible form', *Journal of Econometrics*, 15:211–245.

Gallant, A.R. and Souza, G. (1991) 'On the asymptotic normality of Fourier flexible form estimation', *Journal of Econometrics*, 50:329–353.

Gersovitz, M. (1988) 'Saving and development', in: H. Chenery and T.N. Srinivasan, eds., *Handbook of Development Economics, Volume 1*, Amsterdam: North-Holland, 381–424.

Gertler, P. and van der Gaag, J. (1990) *The willingness to pay for medical care: evidence from two developing countries*, Baltimore, MD: Johns Hopkins University Press for The World Bank.

Giovannini, A. (1985) 'Saving and the real interest rate in LDCs', *Journal of Development Economics*, 18:197–217.

Goldberger, A.S. (1974) 'Unobservable variables in econometrics', in: P. Zarembka, ed., *Frontiers of Econometrics*, New York: Academic Press, 193–213.

Goldberger, A.S. 1983, 'Abnormal selection bias', in S. Karlin et al., eds., *Studies in econometrics, time series, and multivariate statistics*, New York: Academic Press.

Government of Thailand (1977) *Report of the 1975/6 Socio-Economic Survey: Whole Kingdom*, Bangkok: National Statistical Office.

Government of Thailand (1983) *Report of the 1981 Socio-Economic Survey: Whole Kingdom*, Bangkok: National Statistical Office.

Government of Taiwan (1989) *Report on the survey of personal income distribution in Taiwan area of the Republic of China*, Taipei: Directorate General of Budget, Accounting and Statistics Executive Yuan.

Granger, C.W.J. and Newbold, P. (1974) 'Spurious regressions in econometrics', *Journal of Econometrics*, 2:111–120.

Greenhalgh, S. (1982) 'Income units: the ethnographic alternative to standardization', *Population and Development Review*, 8:(Supplement), 70–91.

Grilli, E. and Yang, M.C. (1988) 'Primary commodity prices, manufactured goods prices, and the terms of trade in developing countries', *World Bank Economic Review*, 2:1–47.

Gronau, R. (1973) 'The effects of children on the housewife's value of time', *Journal of Political Economy*, 81:S168–99.

Grossman, S.J. and Shiller, R.J. (1982) 'Consumption correlatedness and risk measurement in economies with nontraded assets and heterogeneous information', *Journal of Financial Economics*, 10:195–210.

Grossman, J.B. (1994) 'Evaluating social policies: principles and U.S. experience', *World Bank Research Observer*, 9:159–180.

Haddad, L.J. and Ravi Kanbur, S.M. (1990) 'How serious is the neglect of intra-household inequality', *Economic Journal*, 100:866–881.

Hampel, F.R., Ronchetti, E.M., Rousseeuw, P.J. and Stahel, W.A. (1986) *Robust statistics: the approach based on influence functions*, New York: Wiley.

Hansen, L.P. (1982) 'Large sample properties of generalized method of moments estimators', *Econometrica*, 50:1029–54.

Hansen, L.P. and Singleton, K.J. (1982) 'Generalized instrumental variables estimation of nonlinear rational expectations models', *Econometrica*, 50:1269–1286.

Hansen, M.H., Hurwitz, W.N. and Madow, W.G. (1953) *Sample survey methods and theory*, 2, New York: Wiley.

Harberger, A.C. (1978) 'On the use of distributional weights in social cost benefit analysis', *Journal of Political Economy*, 86:S87–120.

Harberger, A.C. (1984) 'Basic needs versus distributional weights in social cost benefit analysis', *Economic Development and Cultural Change*, 32:455–474.

Härdle, W. (1991) *Applied nonparametric regression*, Cambridge: Cambridge University Press.

Härdle, W. and Stoker, T.M. (1989) 'Investigating smooth multiple regression by the method of average derivatives', *Journal of the American Statistical Association*, 84:986–995.

Härdle, W. and Linton, O. (1993) 'Applied nonparametric methods', Humbolt-Universität zu Berlin and Nuffield College Oxford, processed. (June), in: R.F. Engle and D. McFadden, eds., *Handbook of Econometrics, Volume 3* (1994), Amsterdam: North-Holland.

Hausman, J. A. (1978) 'Specification tests in econometrics', *Econometrica*, 46:1251–72.

Hayashi, F., Altonji, J. and Kotlikoff, L.J. (1991) 'Risk-sharing, altruism, and the factor structure of consumption', NBER working paper no. 3834 (September), processed.

Heckman, J.J. (1974) 'Shadow prices, market wages, and labor supply', *Econometrica*, 42:679–693.

Heckman, J.J. (1976) 'The common structure of statistical models of truncation, sample selection and limited dependent variables and a simple estimator for such models', *Annals of Economic and Social Measurement*, 5:475–492.

Heckman, J.J. (1990) 'Varieties of selection bias', *American Economic Review* (paps. and procs.), 80:313–318.

Heckman, J.J. and Hotz, V.J. (1986) 'An investigation of the labor market earnings of Panamanian males: evaluating the sources of inequality', *Journal of Human Resources*, 21:507–542.

Heston, A.C. (1994) 'A brief review of some problems of using national accounts data in level comparisons and growth studies', *Journal of Development Economics*, forthcoming.

Holtz-Eakin, D., Newey, W. and Rosen, H. (1988) 'Estimating vector autoregressions with panel data', *Econometrica*, 56:1371–1395.

Huber, P.J. (1967) 'The behavior of maximum likelihood estimates under non-standard conditions', *Proceedings of the Fifth Berkeley Symposium on Mathematical Statistics and Probability*, 1:221–233.

Huber, P.J. (1981) *Robust statistics*, New York: John Wiley.

Jain, S. (1975) *Size distribution of income: a compilation of data*, Washington, D.C.: The World Bank.

Jimenez, E. (1987) *Pricing policy in the social sectors: cost recovery for education and health in developing countries*, Baltimore: Johns Hopkins University Press for The World Bank.

Jöreskog, K.G. (1973) 'A general method of estimating a linear structure equation system', in: A.S. Goldberger and O.D. Duncan, eds., *Structural equation models in the social sciences*, New York: Seminar Press, 85–112.

Kennan, J. (1989) 'Simultaneous equations bias in disaggregated econometric models', *Review of Economic Studies*, 56:151–156.

Kish, L. (1965) *Survey sampling*, New York: John Wiley.

Kish, L. and Frankel, M.R. (1974) 'Inference from complex samples' (with discussion), *Journal of the Royal Statistical Society*, Series B, 36:1–37.

Kloek, T. (1981) 'OLS estimation in a model where a microvariable is explained by aggregates and contemporaneous disturbances are equicorrelated', *Econometrica*, 49:205–207.

Knight, J.B. and Sabot, R.H. (1990) *Education, productivity, and inequality: the East African natural experiment*, Oxford: Oxford University Press for The World Bank.

Koenker, R. and Bassett, G. (1978) 'Regression quantiles', *Econometrica*, 46:33–50.

Koenker, R. and Bassett, G. (1982) 'Robust tests for heteroscedasticity based on regression quantiles', *Econometrica*, 50:43–61.

Kravis, I.B., Heston, A. and Summers R. (1978) *International comparisons of real product and purchasing power*, Baltimore: Johns Hopkins University Press.

Leamer, E.E. (1978) *Specification searches: ad hoc inference from non-experimental data*, New York: Wiley.

Levine, R. and Renelt, D. (1992) 'A sensitivity analysis of cross-country growth regressions', *American Economic Review*, 82:942–963.

Liu, P. (1982) 'Determinants of income inequality over the family development cycle: the case of Taiwan', *Population and Development Review*, 8 (Supplement), 53–69.

Maddala, G.S. and Jeong, J. (1992) 'On the exact small sample distribution of the instrumental variable estimator', *Econometrica*, 60:181–183.

Mahalanobis, P.C. (1944) 'On large scale sample surveys', *Philosophical Transactions of the Royal Society*, Series B, 231:329–451.

Mahalanobis, P.C. (1946) 'Recent experiments in statistical sampling in the Indian Statistical Institute', *Journal of the Royal Statistical Society*, 109:325–370.

Mahalanobis, P.C. (1960) 'The method of fractile graphical analysis', *Econometrica*, 28:325–351.

Manski, C.F. (1988) 'Identification of binary response models', *Journal of the American Statistical Association*, 83:729–738.

Manski, C.F. and Lerman, S. (1977) 'The estimation of choice probabilities from choice-based samples', *Econometrica*, 45:1977–1988.

Mankiw, N.G., Romer, D. and Weil, D. (1992) 'A contribution to the empirics of economic growth', *Quarterly Journal of Economics*, 107:407–437.

Marschak, J. and Andrews, W.H. (1944) 'Random simultaneous equations and the theory of production', *Econometrica*, 12:143–205.

McCallum, B.T. (1976) 'Rational expectations and the natural rate hypothesis: some consistent estimates', *Econometrica*, 44:43–52.

Mills, T. (1990) *Time series techniques for economists,* Cambridge: Cambridge University Press.

Morduch, J. (1990) 'Risk, production, and saving: theory and evidence from Indian households', Harvard University, processed.

Moulton, B.R. (1990) 'An illustration of a pitfall in estimating the effects of aggregate variables on micro units', *Review of Economics and Statistics,* 72:334–338.

Mundlak, Y. (1961) 'Empirical production function free of management bias', *Journal of Farm Economics,* 43:44–56.

Murthy, M.N. (1977) *Sampling theory and methods,* Calcutta. Statistical Publishing Society. (2nd ed.)

Nadaraya, E.A. (1964) 'On estimating regression', *Theory of Probability and Applications,* 10:186–190.

Nagar, A.L. (1959) 'The bias and moment matrix of the general k-class estimators of the parameters in simultaneous equations', *Econometrica,* 27:575–595.

Nelson, C. and Startz, R. (1990a) 'The distribution of the instrumental variable estimator and its t-ratio when the instrument is a poor one', *Journal of Business,* S125–140.

Nelson, C. and Startz, R. (1990b) 'Some further results on the exact small sample properties of the instrumental variable estimator', *Econometrica,* 58:967–976.

Newbery, D., and Stern, N. eds. (1987) *The theory of taxation for developing countries,* Oxford: Oxford University Press for The World Bank.

Newey, W.K. (1986) 'Maximum likelihood specification testing and conditional moment tests', *Econometrica,* 53:1047–1070.

Newey, W.K., Powell, J.L. and Walker, J.R. (1990) 'Semiparametric estimation of selection models: some empirical results', *American Economic Review,* 80:324–328.

Newman, J., Gertler, P. and Rawlings, L. (1994) 'Using randomized central designs in evaluating social sector programs in developing countries', *World Bank Research Observer,* 9:181–201.

Persson, T. and Tabellini, G. (1991) 'Is inequality harmful for growth?' Cambridge, MA: NBER Working Paper No. 3599, processed. (January)

Pfefferman, D. and Smith, T.M.F. (1985) 'Regression models for grouped populations in cross-section surveys', *International Statistical Review,* 53:37–59.

Phillips, P.C.B. (1980) 'The exact distribution of instrumental variables estimators in an equation containing $n + 1$ endogenous variables', *Econometrica,* 48:861–878.

Phillips, P.C.B. (1986) 'Understanding spurious regression', *Journal of Econometrics,* 33:311–340.

Pischke, J.-S. (1991) 'Individual income, incomplete information, and aggregate consumption', Industrial Relations Section Working Paper no. 289, Princeton University, mimeo.

Pitt, M.M., Rosenzweig, M.R. and Gibbons, D.M. (1993) 'The determinants and consequences of the placement of government programs in Indonesia', *World Bank Economic Review,* 7:319–348.

Pitt, M.M., Rosenzweig, M.R. and Hassan, M.N. (1990) 'Productivity, health and inequality in the intrahousehold distribution of food in low-income countries', *American Economic Review,* 80:1139–1156.

Pitt, M.M. and Sumodiningrat, G. (1991) 'Risk, schooling and the choice of seed technology in developing countries: a meta-profit function approach', *International Economic Review,* 32:457–473.

Powell, J.L. (1984) 'Least absolute deviations estimation for the censored regression model', *Journal of Econometrics,* 25:303–325.

Powell, J.L. (1992) 'Estimation of semiparametric models', Princeton, N.J.: Princeton University, processed. (September)

Powell, J.L., Stock, J.H. and Stoker, T.M. (1989) 'Semiparametric estimation of index co-efficients', *Econometrica,* 57:1403–1430.

Prais S. and Houthakker, H.S. (1955) *The analysis of family budgets,* Cambridge: Cambridge University Press.

Priestly, M.B. (1981) *The spectral analysis of time-series,* London: Academic Press.

Raut, L. and Virmani, A. (1989) 'Determinants of consumption and savings behavior in developing countries', *World Bank Economic Review,* 3:379–393.

Ravallion, M. (1990) 'Income effects on undernutrition', *Economic Development and Cultural Change,* 38:489–515.

Robinson, P.M. (1988) 'Root-N-consistent semiparametric regression', *Econometrica,* 56:931–954.

Rosenzweig, M.R. (1990) 'Population growth and human capital investments: theory and evidence', *Journal of Political Economy*, 98:S38–70.

Rosenzweig, M.R. and Binswanger, H. (1993) 'Wealth, weather risk and the composition and profitability of agricultural investments', *Economic Journal*, 103:56–78.

Rosenzweig, M.R. and Schultz, T.P. (1983) 'Estimating a household production function: heterogeneity, the demand for health inputs, and their effects on birth weight', *Journal of Political Economy*, 91:723–46.

Rosenzweig, M.R. and Schultz, T.P. (1987) 'Fertility and investments in human capital: estimates of the consequences of imperfect fertility control', *Journal of Econometrics*, 36:163–184.

Rosenzweig, M.R. and Wolpin, K.J. (1980) 'Testing the quantity-quality model of fertility: results of a natural experiment – twins', *Econometrica*, 48:227–240.

Rosenzweig, M.R. and Wolpin, K.J. (1986) 'Evaluating the effects of optimally distributed public programs', *American Economic Review*, 76:470–487.

Rosenzweig, M.R. and Wolpin, K.J. (1988) 'Migration selectivity and the effects of public programs', *Journal of Public Economics*, 37:265–289.

Rosenzweig, M.R. and Wolpin, K.J. (1993) 'Credit market constraints, consumption smoothing, and the accumulation of durable production assets in low-income countries: investments in bullocks in India', *Journal of Political Economy*, 101:223–244.

Rossi, N. (1988) 'Government spending, the real interest rate, and the behavior of liquidity-constrained consumers in developing countries', *IMF Staff Papers*, 35:104–140.

Rozansky, J. and Yeats, A. (1994) 'On the (in)accuracy of economic observations: an assessment of trends in the reliability of international trade statistics', *Journal of Development Economics*, forthcoming.

Rust, J. (1987) 'Optimal replacement of GMC bus engines: an empirical model of Harold Zurcher', *Econometrica*, 55:999–1033.

Rust, J. (1992) 'Do people behave according to Bellman's principle of optimality?' Stanford, CA: Hoover Institution, processed. (May)

Schmidt, P., Ahn, S.C. and Wyhowski, D. (1992) 'Comment', *Journal of Business and Economic Statistics*, 10:10–14.

Schwarz, G. (1978) 'Estimating the dimensions of a model', *Annals of Statistics*, 30:461–464.

Scott, A.J. and Holt, D. (1982) 'The effect of two-stage sampling on ordinary least squares methods', *Journal of the American Statistical Association*, 77:848–854.

Sen, A.K. (1962) 'An aspect of Indian agriculture', *Economic Weekly*, 14, Annual Number.

Sen, A.K. (1966) 'Peasants and dualism with and without surplus labor', *Journal of Political Economy*, 74:425–450.

Sen, A.K. (1975) *Employment, technology, and development*, Oxford: Clarendon Press.

Sewell, W.H. and Hauser, R.M. (1975) *Education, occupation and earnings: Achievement in the early career*, New York: Academic Press.

Silverman, B.W. (1986) *Density estimation for statistics and data analysis*, London: Chapman and Hall.

Sims, C.A. (1969) 'Theoretical basis for a double deflated index of real value added', *Review of Economics and Statistics*, 51:470–471.

Sims, C.A., Stock, J.H. and Watson, M.W. (1988) 'Inference in linear time-series models with some unit roots', *Econometrica*, 58:113–144.

Singh, I., Squire, L. and Strauss, J. eds. (1986) *Agricultural households models: extensions, applications, and policy*, Baltimore, MD: Johns Hopkins University Press for The World Bank.

Smith, J.P., Thomas, D. and Karoly, L.A. (1992) 'Migration in retrospect: differences between men and women', Santa Monica, CA: Rand Corporation, processed. (April)

Solon, G.R. (1992) 'Intergenerational income mobility in the United States', *American Economic Review*, 82:393–408.

Srinivasan, T.N. (1972) 'Farm size and productivity – implications of choice under uncertainty', *Sankhya*, Series B, 34:409–420.

Srinivasan, T.N. (1994) 'Data base for development analysis: an overview', *Journal of Development Economics*, forthcoming.

Stelcner, M., van der Gaag, J. and Wijverberg, W. (1989) 'A switching regression model of public – private sector wage effects in Peru, 1985-6', *Journal of Human Resources*, 24:545–559.

Stern, N. (1987) 'Aspects of the general theory of tax reform', Chapter 3 in: D. Newbery and N. Stern, eds., *The theory of taxation for developing countries*, Oxford: Oxford University Press for the World Bank.

Stigler, G.J. (1954) 'The early history of empirical studies of consumer behavior', *Journal of Political Economy*, 42:95–113.

Stock, J.H. (1987) 'Asymptotic properties of least-squares estimators of cointegrating vectors', *Econometrica*, 55:1035–1056.

Stock, J.H. and Watson, M.W. (1988) 'Variable trends in economic time-series', *Journal of Economic Perspectives*, 2:147–174.

Stoker, T.M. (1986) 'Consistent estimation of scaled coefficients', *Econometrica*, 54:1461–1481

Stoker, T.M. (1991) *Lectures on semi-parametric econometrics*, Louvain-la-Neuve, Core Foundation.

Strauss, J. and Thomas, D. (1990) 'The shape of the calorie expenditure curve', New Haven: Yale University, processed.

Strauss, J., Gertler, P., Rahman, O. and Fox, K. (1992) 'Gender and life-cycle differentials in the patterns and determinants of adult health', RAND Corporation and Ministry of Health, Government of Jamaica, processed. (June)

Strauss, J. and Gertler, P. (1993) 'Human resources: household decisions and markets', *this volume*.

Subramanian, S. and Deaton, A. (1992) 'The demand for food and calories: further evidence from India', Princeton, N.J.: Princeton University, Research Program in Development Studies, processed. (February)

Summers, R. and Heston, A.C. (1991) 'The Penn World Table (Mark 5): an expanded set of international comparisons, 1950–1988', *Quarterly Journal of Economics*, 106:327–368.

Tan, C.C.H. (1991) 'Drawing out the life cycle of Korean households with synthetic panels of rational consumers', Yale University and University of Hong Kong, processed. (November)

Tobin, J. (1958) 'Estimation of relationships for limited dependent variables', *Econometrica*, 26:24–36.

van der Gaag, J., Stelcner, M. and Wijverberg, W. (1989) 'Wage differentials and moonlighting by civil servants: evidence from Côte d'Ivoire and Peru', *World Bank Economic Review*, 3:67–95.

Watson, G.S. (1964) 'Smooth regression analysis', *Sankhyā*, Series A, 26:359–372.

West, K.D. (1988) 'Asymptotic normality when regressors have a unit root', *Econometrica*, 56:1397–1418.

White, H., and MacKinnon, J.G. (1985) 'Some heteroskedasticity-consistent covariance matrix estimates with improved finite sample properties', *Journal of Econometrics*, 29:305–325.

White, H. (1980) 'A heteroskedasticity consistent covariance matrix estimatorand a direct test for heteroskedasticity', *Econometrica*, 48:817–838.

White, H. (1984) *Asymptotic theory for econometricians*, New York: Academic Press.

Wolpin, K.J. (1984) 'An estimable dynamic stochastic model of fertility and child mortality', *Journal of Political Economy*, 92:852–874.

Yule, G.U. (1926) 'Why do we sometimes get nonsense correlations between time-series?' *Journal of the Royal Statistical Society*, 89:1–64.

Zeldes, S.P. (1989) 'Consumption and liquidity constraints: an empirical investigation', *Journal of Political Economy*, 97:305–346.

Zimmerman, D.J. (1992) 'Regression toward mediocrity in economic stature', *American Economic Review*, 82:409–429.

Chapter 34

HUMAN RESOURCES:
EMPIRICAL MODELING OF HOUSEHOLD AND FAMILY DECISIONS

JOHN STRAUSS[†]

Michigan State University

DUNCAN THOMAS[†]

RAND and UCLA

Contents

[†] Financial support from NICHD Grants P01-HD28372 and 5R01-HD27650 is gratefully acknowledged; Strauss was also supported by the Human Capital Department, RAND. We have benefitted enormously from the comments of the editors, Harold Alderman, Will Dow, John Maluccio, Anne Pebley, Jim Smith and Chris Udry and from the editorial advice of Gary Bjork.

Handbook of Development Economics, Volume III, Edited by J. Behrman and T.N. Srinivasan
© *Elsevier Science B.V., 1995*

1. Introduction and overview

There has been nothing short of an explosion in both the quantity and quality of household and individual level data that have become available for research purposes from poor countries in recent years. Paralleling this, there have been important advances in both economic models and econometric methods to handle difficulties inherent in the analysis of micro-level data. As a result, understanding household behavior and how it relates to economic growth and development has been substantially enriched.

It is well recognized that in many developing economies, the household and family[1] are key economic decision-makers and intermediaries, whereas, as development progresses, some of these roles are taken over either by the market or the state. Some of the most important choices households make revolve around the human capital of children and adults. The fact that human capital investments are associated with higher standards of living and welfare has been repeatedly demonstrated both in aggregate data and in studies that have used individual or household level micro data. This chapter reviews recent advances in the empirical literature on the role that households and families play in investing in human resources, focusing on education and health.

In the rest of this introductory section, we place the literature in historical context. The work of Gary Becker, the 1992 Nobel laureat, and others on the economic model of the household has been critical in bringing a series of fundamental issues into the domain of economic research. Insights from these models are described very briefly.[2] Along with these theoretical developments, the nature of data collection has changed and we review how the two have become intimately linked.

Armed with both a modeling framework and an abundance of data from developing countries, economists have set about attempting to estimate relationships between welfare and human resources. Many of the studies have followed in the footsteps of the empirical labor and consumer demand literature which underwent a similar progression of integrating economic and microeconometric theory with empirical evidence. Indeed, today all of these literatures have much in common, especially in terms of their empirical and theoretical methodologies. We follow this trend and discuss the body of evidence that has accumulated on a number of human capital issues but pay

---

[1] For the purposes of this survey, we will define households as comprised of people living together. By families, we mean related kin who may or may not be living together.

[2] For a more extensive discussion, see the chapter in the first volume of this Handbook by Behrman and Deolalikar (1988).

special attention to identifying results that seem to be more robust, problems that seem to be more serious and approaches that seem to work better.

The next section addresses a pair of issues that have been central in development economics: the effects of income on nutritional status and the reverse influence of nutrition (and more broadly, health) on labor productivity and thus income. We use these examples to not only highlight some of the controversies in the literature but also to illustrate, in some depth, many of the difficulties that arise in empirical research on human capital. Identifying problems is easy; choosing among the array of solutions is harder and requires a good dose of judgement. See Deaton (this volume) for a discussion.

It is certainly true that many empirical results have ambiguous interpretations and unobserved heterogeneity of various forms is ubiquitous in this literature. Yet, the reader should not despair and lose sight of the fact that a good number of critical empirical regularities have been established. There can be little dispute, for example, that both market and non-market productivity is enhanced by the accumulation of human capital, particularly education and health. These investments have been shown to affect labor market outcomes, fertility, child health and child educational attainment.[3] While the magnitudes of the effects may be disputed, it seems most unlikely that sensible attempts to rid the estimates of potential biases due to omitted variables or unobserved heterogeneity will overturn this general conclusion.

Considerably less is known, however, about the mechanisms that underlie these relationships. The next two sections focus on this issue. Section 3 is concerned with the estimation of reduced form demands for human capital, particularly education and health. Special attention is paid to the measurement and interpretation of the impact of household resources, particularly parental education and income, as well as the impact of community resources, namely prices and infrastructure. The process underlying the production of human capital is discussed in Section 4. We pay particular attention to the difficulties in measuring inputs and input quality and the associated issues of estimation and interpretation.

In Section 5, we return to labor productivity and relate it to education. Placing the spotlight on recent studies that have attempted to understand why the estimated returns to schooling in developing countries have consistently been very high, we focus on evidence regarding the influence of family background, school quality, ability and self-selection.

The final two sections of the chapter discuss recent developments in the empirical literature and identify some of the most active areas in current

---

[3] See the reviews in the first volume of this Handbook by Rosenzweig (1988c), Birdsall (1988) and Behrman and Deolalikar (1988), respectively. See also the review of education by Schultz (1988a).

research. Models of household behavior in a dynamic setting are reviewed in Section 6. Section 7 discusses extensions to the model that are concerned with the flow and allocation of resources both across and within households as well as to extensions that treat household boundaries as fluid. Before launching into a discussion of some of the economic issues that are of most current concern, we take a step back and place this literature in some historical perspective.

1.1. Historical developments: modeling

Economic models of household behavior have their roots in both Becker's (1965) model of household production and in the farm household model [Tanaka (1951), Nakajima (1957, 1969, 1986), Sen (1966)].[4] The idea in both sets of models is much the same: the household allocates time and goods to produce commodities, some of which are sold on the market, some of which are consumed at home and for some, no market exists at all.

We begin with a very simple model due to Gronau (1977) and Jorgenson and Lau (1969). Assume the household has preferences that can be characterized by the utility function, U, which depends on consumption of a vector of commodities, X, and leisure, L, which is also vector-valued with one element per household member:

$$U = U(X, L) \tag{1}$$

Consumption may be either purchased in the market, X_M, or produced at home, X_H, and these are assumed to be perfect substitutes (an important assumption that will be relaxed below)

$$X = X_M + X_H \tag{2}$$

Although it is straightforward to allow market-purchased inputs and exogenous household characteristics to affect the production of home produced goods, X_H, without loss of generality, we treat it as depending on only the vector of household labor supplies, H:

$$X_H = f(H) \tag{3}$$

The household picks the optimal consumption bundle, given the production function (3) and a budget constraint:

$$pX_M = wN + V \tag{4}$$

---

[4] Gronau (1973, 1977) and Pollak and Wachter (1975) have also made important contributions to the household production model, as have Krishna (1964), Jorgenson and Lau (1969) and Hymer and Resnick (1969) to the farm household model. Singh, Squire and Strauss (1986) synthesize the literature.

That is, given prices, p, total market consumption, pX_M, cannot exceed total income, the sum of non-labor income, V, and labor earnings which depend on a vector of exogenous wages, w, and household market labor supply, N. For each household member, total time, T, cannot exceed the sum of leisure, time in home production and time working in the market, $L + H + N$. Incorporating this identity and [2] into the budget constraint, then total consumption, including the value of time spent in leisure activities, cannot exceed "full income"

$$pX + wL = wT + (pX_H - wH) + V \tag{5}$$

full income is the sum of the value of time available to all household members, wT, "profits" from home production, $pX_H - wH$, and nonlabor income, V.

In this simple model, it is optimal to maximize "profits" from home production and thus allocate labor so that the value of the marginal product in home production is equal to its opportunity cost, which is the market wage. Given those profits, the household can then choose its consumption and leisure bundle. The model is, therefore, recursive in the sense that production decisions can be solved independently of preferences. The reverse is not true: commodity and leisure choices are affected by home production decisions, through full income. The key for our purposes is that the reduced form demands for commodities and leisure (and thus total labor supply) depend on commodity prices, wages and full income, all of which are exogenous in this one-period model.

While the model embodies many assumptions, it has been shown to be a useful representation of behavior in many circumstances. For example, the framework has been very powerful in explaining decisions of farm households.[5] However, to explain household decisions regarding human capital, the model requires modification.

Home produced and market goods have been assumed to be perfectly substitutable. Yet, in reality, most human capital outcomes, such as health and education, cannot even be purchased in the market. Incorporating this fact, and relaxing the assumption of perfect substitutability, changes the nature of the household equilibrium [Gronau (1973)]. Now households will choose to allocate labor to home production so that the marginal product in that activity is equal to the marginal rate of substitution between leisure and the home produced good. If the household participates in some market labor, then this condition can be reformulated so that the marginal product of labor is equated

---

[5] For a more complete discussion and consideration of circumstances in which recursion fails (and associated empirical evidence), see Singh, Squire and Strauss (1986), the studies therein, and Benjamin (1992).

to the market wage divided by the shadow price of the home produced commodity, p^*. This shadow price is simply the marginal utility of the home produced commodity divided by the marginal utility of income, λ. Thus, in equilibrium:

$$\partial X_H/\partial H = w/p^* = w/[(\partial U/\partial X_H)/\lambda] \tag{6}$$

The model is no longer recursive as now home production decisions do depend on preferences as well as the technology of home production. Reduced forms for home production outputs and inputs will depend not only on exogenous variables, such as input prices, from the home production side, but also factors from the consumption side, such as prices of market purchased commodities or education of household members.

In the reduced form demands for X_H, there are substitution and income effects, both with respect to market prices and shadow prices of home output (Strauss, 1986b). Thus, it is not, in general, possible to sign comparative statics and so data need to be brought to bear on these models in order to learn about *both* the magnitude *and* direction of key variables such as prices.

Household production models have been extremely influential in modeling many non-marketed investments, including human capital outcomes. Indeed the origins of interest among economists in topics such as fertility and child and adult health can be traced to the household production model.

It is natural to model human capital outcomes in this framework as it lends itself to the integration of biological, demographic and economic considerations, all of which are almost certainly at work. Taking child growth as an example, it is sensible to think of weight or height as being generated by a biological production function (see the detailed discussion in Section 4) in which a number of the input allocations, such as type of infant feeding or nutrient intakes, result from household decisions. The production technology corresponds closely to the demographer's notion of proximate determinants. Where the household production approach differs from other frameworks in the social and certainly the biological sciences is the explicit modeling of behavior in which households choose allocations to maximize their welfare given the resource and information constraints they face.[6] It is the combination of ideas from a range of different disciplines, which is inherent in the household production approach, that has fostered a richer set of analyses of human capital outcomes than is likely to be achieved through the lens of any one perspective in isolation.

The household production model has also proved to be a useful tool in empirical research. It provides guidance (and discipline) on what should be

[6] See Mosley and Chen's (1984) discussion of child mortality for a similar perspective.

estimated and how to interpret those estimates. For example, estimating the production technology, often together with input demands, can be useful when one wishes to examine the pathways through which underlying exogenous factors affect the outcomes of interest. On the other hand, reduced forms provide information about the ultimate (or "total") impact of exogenous factors, net of the effects that work through all endogenous inputs. Third, in some instances interest focuses on outcomes (such as child health) that are conditional on one or more choices (such as the number of children).[7]

Critical insights into what types of factors should be treated as exogenous, as opposed to endogenous, can be gleaned from the household production approach. For example, production function inputs, over which the household has control, ought to be treated as endogenous. For child growth, these might include duration of breastfeeding, when supplementation begins and what types of supplementation are given. In thinking about what variables may be plausible instruments for endogenous inputs, the household approach is, once again, informative. In the case of child growth, prices of inputs such as milk, or the availability and quality of child health services are a potential source of identifying information.

However, as is true with most economic models, guidance in this dimension is seldom unambiguous; changes in the model assumptions often change what one would consider to be endogenous. If, for instance, a household chooses its location based on services available in a community, then any variables related to those characteristics (such as the quality of child health services) should be treated as endogenous [Rosenzweig and Wolpin (1988b)]. Furthermore, endogeneity can, and often does, arise from considerations apart from true simultaneity. Blind reliance on theory (or dogma) is unlikely to be a good strategy: solid empirical work requires judiciousness in the choice of issues that are deemed the most critical in a particular application.

Having argued that household production models are well-suited to the analysis of human capital decisions, it is but a short step to use this framework to design data collection efforts. In this domain, too, the household production approach has had a major impact in development economics.

1.2. Historical developments: data collection

Many of the early empirical applications of the household production approach, such as modeling the demand for children, used aggregate data

---

[7] These are not production functions since estimates are conditional on only a subset of choice variables. This class of models includes conditional demand functions [Pollak (1969)] and first order conditions such as Euler equations.

because adequate micro-level data were not available, [e.g. T.P. Schultz (1973)]. At that time, most micro-level data sets did not have the requisite breadth of information necessary to estimate the kinds of models suggested by the home production framework.

Farm management surveys had information on farm outputs and inputs; demographic surveys typically did not contain information on economic variables and were often narrowly designed even within demographic interests; household budget surveys and labor market surveys were typically narrowly focused.

Yet, even simple, static models that seek to explain human capital outcomes such as fertility [e.g. Willis (1974)] suggest that a wide variety of information is needed. They call for information on female and male market wages and their underlying determinants (including education, age and family background characteristics), nonlabor income or household assets, and local community characteristics such as prices and the availability and quality of any family planning or health centers. To examine the impact of child mortality on births, information on all children, including those who have died, would be necessary. To estimate production functions, the analyst would need detailed information on inputs into home production including contraceptive usage. The data requirements quickly become overwhelming.

Thus, beginning in the late 1960s and early 1970s, several attempts were made to collect data that provided the breadth of information needed to apply the household production approach to answer specific sets of questions. Very early examples include the Additional Rural Incomes Survey (ARIS), fielded by the National Council of Applied Economic Research (NCAER) in India; the Malaysian Family Life Survey, fielded by RAND [Butz and DaVanzo (1978)]; the RAND-Institute for Nutrition in Central America and Panama (INCAP) surveys in Guatemala and a series of linked household cross-sectional surveys fielded by a team of economists and nutritionists in Laguna Province, Philippines [Evenson (1978)]. In all cases, the surveys were informed by the household economics approach (indeed former students of Becker and T.W. Schultz helped design the latter three) and have had a direct and substantial influence on subsequent socio-economic surveys.

To illustrate, with one example, the first Malaysian Family Life Survey (MFLS-1) was explicitly designed as an implementation of the household production approach in economic and demographic analysis [Butz and DaVanzo (1975)]. With a sample of about 1,200 households, a conscious choice was made to forgo a larger sample in return for a more comprehensive interview that collected far more information and with greater quality control than was possible in a census or large scale demographic survey. Many innovations were incorporated in collecting detailed retrospective data on such topics as work, migration marital and pregnancy histories, along with information on the local community, including health, schooling and family planning infrastructure. Extremely detailed information was collected on incomes as well. The richness and breadth of the MFLS-1 has been widely exploited in analyses of the interrelationships between economic and demographic decisions; one important reason for its extensive use is the fact that the data were placed in the public domain.[8]

These early surveys have had a substantial influence on many of the vast number of household surveys that have been fielded since the mid-1970s. Among these surveys, two merit explicit mention because they have been so extensively used in the empirical household production literature: the south India village level surveys of the International Crops Research Institute for the Semi-Arid Tropics (ICRISAT) and the World Bank's Living Standards Surveys (LSS).[9]

The ICRISAT village-level studies (VLS) along with the NCAER's ARIS survey represent the first major panel survey using a household framework in a developing country. The ICRISAT VLS were collected from 1975 to 1985 in six villages in three regions in semi-arid India [Walker and Ryan (1990)]. Guided, in part, by the experiences of the Guatemala, Malaysia and Laguna surveys, the ICRISAT VLS covered a broad array of topics but these studies were also extremely intensive. Enumerators lived in the sample villages and visited the households very frequently which enabled them to accurately measure flows, such as time allocation, that often varies significantly across time (seasons). The familiarity built up between the enumerator and sample household may also have resulted in the collection of good data on such sensitive topics as credit and assets. The price of the intensity comes in sample size: only 240 households are included in the ICRISAT VLS. The unique feature of these data is its longitudinal nature which has enabled researchers to pose a wide array of questions related to risk, consumption smoothing and its impact on farm household decisions and household welfare. The intensiveness of the surveys has also been profitably used in the analysis of a variety of other issues.

The Living Standard Surveys have a different scope. The first two surveys

---

[8] Unfortunately, many data collection groups still restrict use of their data to an intimate group of researchers even though, in many cases, public funds have been used to support the data collection effort. This is one critical dimension in which development economists have lagged behind those working in labor economics.

[9] Numerous other very good surveys have been fielded, including the Bicol Multipurpose [Surveys (1978, 1980)], the Cebu Longitudinal Health and Nutrition Survey (1983–1986), the second Malaysian Family Life Survey (1988) and surveys fielded by the International Food Policy Research Institute. Some have special features motivated by either the household production approach or by empirical difficulties commonly encountered in empirical analyses. An example of the latter is the survey fielded by Behrman, Belli and Wolfe in Nicaragua, which collected data on matched sisters, enabling the inclusion of sister fixed effects in studies [see, for example, Behrman and Wolfe (1984)].

were conducted in 1985–1986 in the Côte d'Ivoire and Peru.[10] The LSSs were intended to measure multiple dimensions of economic welfare and simultaneously support analysis of human capital (and other) choices from a household perspective [Ainsworth and Munoz (1986)]. These national samples contain a range of information on household socio-demographic characteristics including income, health, education and fertility. A key innovation in the LSSs is the integration of household budget data in a broad purpose socio-demographic survey. This has proved to be a useful addition, both to analyze consumption and savings decisions as well as an indicator of longer-run income (see the discussion in Sections 3 and 6).

In these and other data collection efforts, attempts have been made to broaden the scope of the survey instruments and gather even more information on household choices, options and constraints. As researchers become more involved in the design of socio-economic surveys, data from developing countries are likely to provide analysts with opportunities to pose increasingly subtle and potentially more useful questions regarding the complexities underlying household decisions. Empirical research on household behavior in developing countries will surely continue to increase rapidly both in terms of its quality and quantity.

2. Nutrient demands, income and productivity: Evidence on their interrelationships

Two related issues that have been widely debated in the literature are examined in this section: the impact of income on the demand for nutrients and the reverse effects of nutrient intake (and more generally health) on wages, labor supply and thus income. These questions are not only of substantial interest, in and of themselves, but this discussion will serve as a good vehicle to review some of the generic difficulties, and potential solutions, that are frequently encountered in empirical work on human resources.

2.1. Nutrient intakes and income

Low nutrient intakes of the poor has occupied a central place in the study of poverty, both in developing and industrial countries. Substantial resources have been allocated to alleviate this problem, particularly through income related programs or subsidies which have been justified on the basis of the

---

[10] Subsequent LSSs have been fielded in several other countries, including Bolivia, Ghana, Jamaica, Mauritania, Morocco and Pakistan.

Table 34.1
Income and expenditure elasticities of calorie demand

Author(s)	Year	HH resources	Measure of Calories	Country studied	Estimation Method	Elasticity (at Mean)
A. INDIRECT ESTIMATES (Calculated from food demand equations):						
Behrman & Deolalikar	1987	X	Availability	India	2SLS	0.77
Behrman & Deolalikar	1987	X	Availability	India	FE	1.18
Pinstrup-Andersen & Caicedo	1978	Y	Availability	Colombia	System	0.51
Pitt	1983	X[a]	Availability	Bangladesh	Tobit	0.78–0.82
Sahn	1988	X	Availability	Sri Lanka	Heckit	0.62
Strauss	1984	X	Availability	Sierra Leone	System	0.82
B. DIRECT ESTIMATES (Calculated from calorie demand equations):						
Alderman	1987	X	Availability	India	2SLS	0.41–0.44
Bouis & Haddad	1992	X	Availability[b]	Philippines	OLS	0.43
Bouis & Haddad	1992	X	Availability[b]	Philippines	2SLS	0.32
Bouis & Haddad	1992	X	Availability[b]	Philippines	FE	0.59
Deaton & Subramanian	1992	X	Availability	India	Nonparam	0.45
Edirisinghe	1987	X	Availability	Sri Lanka	OLS	0.56
Garcia & Pinstrup-Anderson	1987	X	Availability	Philippines	OLS	0.12–0.34
Timmer & Alderman	1979	X	Availability	Indonesia-rural	OLS	0.51
Timmer & Alderman	1979	X	Availability	Indonesia-urban	OLS	0.26
Chernichovsky & Meesook	1984	X	Intake-7 day recall	Indonesia	OLS	0.54
Ravallion	1990	X	Intake-7 day recall	Indonesia	OLS	0.15
Strauss & Thomas	1990	X	Intake-7 day weighed	Brazil	OLS	0.20

Author	Year	X/Y	Measure	Country	Value
Strauss & Thomas	1990	X	Intake-7 day weighed	Brazil	0.11
Behrman & Deolalikar	1987	X	Intake-24 hr recall	India	0.17[c]
Behrman & Deolalikar	1987	X	Intake-24 hr recall	India	0.37[c]
Bouis & Haddad	1992	X	Intake-24 hr recall	Philippines	0.12
Bouis & Haddad	1992	X	Intake-24 hr recall	Philippines	0.08
Bouis & Haddad	1992	Y	Intake-24 hr recall	Philippines	0.14
Bouis & Haddad	1992	Y	Availability[b]	Philippines	0.11
Bouis & Haddad	1992	Y	Availability[b]	Philippines	0.28
Trairatvorakul	1984	Y	Availability	Thailand	0.27–0.33
Ward & Sanders	1980	Y	Availability	Brazil	0.24
Ward & Sanders	1980	Y	Availability	Brazil	0.53
von Braun, Puetz & Webb	1989	Y	Intake-7 day recall[d]	Gambia	0.37–0.48
Behrman & Wolfe	1984	Y	Intake-24 hr recall	Nicaragua	0.05
Bouis & Haddad	1992	Y	Intake-24 hr recall	Philippines	0.03
Bouis & Haddad	1992	Y	Intake-24 hr recall	Philippines	0.09
Wolfe & Behrman	1983	Y	Intake-24 hr recall	Nicaragua	0.01

Measures of household resources are expenditure (X) or income (Y). Calorie measures are household availability based on food purchases and changes in stocks of own production (Availability), intake based on food consumption recall for last 7 days (Intake-7 day recall), recall for last 24 hours (Intake-24 hr recall) or intake weighed prospectively (Intake-weighed). Estimation methods are demand system (System), two stage least squares (2SLS), fixed effects (FE), Heckman selection (Heckit), OLS (ordinary least squares) or nonparametric (Nonparam).

[a] Food, not total, expenditure is used.
[b] Meals to guests & workers removed from availability.
[c] Not significant at 5 per cent significance level.
[d] Based on meal-specific recall for every meal over last 7 days.

conventional wisdom that low nutrient intakes are largely a consequence of low incomes. Yet despite numerous studies, there appears to be little agreement in the literature about the responsiveness of household nutrient intake (or availability) to income [see the surveys by Alderman (1986, 1993), Behrman (1990) and Behrman and Deolalikar (1988)].

To begin, we focus on the relationship between one nutrient, calories, and income. Several recent influential studies have questioned the conventional wisdom, suggesting that, even among the *very poor*, as income rises households purchase *only* additional taste and non-calorie nutrients: the calorie-income curve, it is argued, is essentially flat [Wolfe and Behrman (1983), Behrman and Deolalikar (1987), Behrman, Deolalikar and Wolfe (1988), Bouis and Haddad (1992)].[11] At the other extreme, some studies have estimated the elasticity of demand for calories to be close to one [Pitt (1983), Strauss 1984)]. Table 34.1 contains estimates from a score of recent studies.

Some of the range in estimated calorie-income elasticities can be explained by methodological differences [see Bouis and Haddad (1992) for a discussion]. Estimates in the first panel, which tend to be high, are calculated *indirectly*. That is, elasticities of demand for a series of food groups are computed first and then those are converted to calorie elasticities using standard food composition tables. This is a convenient empirical strategy since it may be applied to *any* expenditure survey. Implicitly, it is assumed that within each food group, there is no substitution from, say, lower-priced calories to higher-priced calories [Behrman and Deolalikar (1987)]. Clearly the extent of substitution will depend both on the level of aggregation in the definition of food sub-groups and on the scope for substitution within these groups. Bias due to this aggregation may explain the very high elasticities for India estimated by Behrman and Deolalikar (1987). However, it has very little impact on the high elasticity found in Sierra Leone [Strauss and Thomas (1990)] and only a moderate impact in some other data sets, such as the Indian National Sample Survey [Subramanian and Deaton (1992)].

Potential bias due to aggregation can be avoided by *direct* estimation of the calorie-income relation. This requires information on quantities of each food consumed to calculate nutrient intakes, which are then used to estimate the relationship with income. While direct estimates, presented in the second panel of Table 34.1, are generally lower, there is still considerable heterogeneity, even within these estimates. Part of this variation may also be ascribed to methodological differences.

---

[11] This is consistent with the controversial hypothesis that it is rare for individuals to be truly malnourished because of short- and long-run body adaption to food shortages. Sukhatme (1988), Beaton (1983) and Payne (1989) discuss the issue of body adaption to deprivation, which is unresolved both as to its magnitude and the extent to which it prevents functional disabilities.

Elasticities based on current income tend to be lower than those based on expenditure. In the absence of complete smoothing, expenditures tend to be lumpy and so current expenditure is a noisy measure of long-run resources. It may, however, be a better indicator than income, which is even more difficult to smooth in the short run. Invoking a standard errors-in-variables argument, the income elasticity will be less than that based on expenditure, as long as measurement error is random. This ranking turns out to be true in ENDEF (*Estudo Nacional da Despesa Familiar*), a Brazilian household survey: the expenditure elasticity is 0.21, but the income elasticity is only 0.11 [standard errors are less than 0.01 in both cases, Strauss and Thomas (1990)]. Alternatively, instrumenting income with factors associated with permanent income, such as land owned, may raise the income coefficient, as it does in the Ward and Sanders (1980) and Bouis and Haddad studies.[12]

However, it is reasonable to suppose that income is properly treated as endogenous. For example, it may be that increased nutrient intake raises productivity and/or labor supply, particularly among low income households. In this case, the estimated elasticity will be biased upward and the bias is probably greater for lower income households. It is also plausible that unobserved taste for work may be correlated with taste for nutrients, although the sign of the correlation, and thus bias, is not obvious. Of course, expenditure, which is a function of income, might also be considered as jointly determined.

There may also be systematic biases arising from measurement errors in nutrient consumption that are correlated with expenditure or income (see Bouis and Haddad for a detailed discussion). In this case there is an important distinction between errors that are common between nutrient consumption and expenditure, but uncorrelated with income or other resource measures, and errors in nutrient consumption that are systematically related to income.

Part of these common measurement errors are probably due to wastage and leakages that are difficult to capture and so not taken into account. For example, nutrient intake will be overstated for households that give away or waste relatively more food or have relatively more visitors at meals (typically higher income households) and understated for households that receive food or

---

[12] Using the ICRISAT south India village-level survey, [Behrman and Deolalikar (1990)] create a measure of permanent income (namely mean income over 9 years) and include it, along with current income, in nutrient demand equations. The coefficient on current income thus captures the effect of transitory flows. Neither income measure is significant, in line with their earlier results. Since only one year of income is measured prior to the two years in which nutrient intake data were collected, Behrman and Deolalikar make strong assumptions about stationarity of the income process and also about the impact of nutrient intakes now on future income. In addition, a substantial part of current income, which is measured on an annual basis, is obtained in months after nutrient intakes are taken. If households do not have perfect foresight, this measure of current income will be a noisy proxy for transitory income, biasing the coefficient towards zero.

are absent from many meals (typically lower income households).[13] This will tend to bias upwards the elasticity. As another example, it is usually assumed that meals away from home have the same calorie content as meals taken at home; if poor workers eat better on the job (where most of their meals out are taken) than they eat at home, then measurement errors will be correlated with income.

The nature and importance of these sources of bias is likely to be related to the way nutrient consumption data are collected. One method is to infer household nutrient *availability* from food purchases and imputed values based on the part of own production or in-kind wages that is consumed. This is a cost-effective strategy in budget surveys which collect detailed food expenditures as a matter of course since the only additional information needed is quantities (or prices) of each food. It has, therefore, been carried out in many countries (including, for example, India and Sri Lanka). However, since nutrient consumption and total expenditure are derived from the same source, there are likely to be common random measurement errors which will result in estimates of nutrient-expenditure elasticities that are biased (although the sign is a priori ambiguous).

A second method of collecting nutrient consumption is to obtain information on *intakes* rather than *availability*. In the Brazilian ENDEF survey, for example, nutrient data were collected in seven daily visits to the household at which the enumerator measured the quantity of food to be consumed that day and also wastage from the previous 24 hours. In addition, the enumerator listed all household members and guests present at every meal during the 7 day period. This is a very intensive and expensive way to collect these data and consequently seldom used. Some budget surveys (in Indonesia, for example) have asked respondents about food consumed during the reference period (usually a week).

It has been argued that it may be better to collect nutrient intakes based on *actual meals consumed* and the ingredients that went into those meals, rather than making the respondent add them over the reference period herself; these recalls are usually based on the last 24 hours and have also been used to assign intakes to individuals within the household (as in the ICRISAT and Bukidnon surveys).

It is not obvious which of these three methods for collecting intakes is the most cost-effective. The intensive ENDEF method is expensive to field. It is, however, quite accurate although it does not collect information on food eaten out of the home. That information is, in principle, collected in intake recalls, but little is known about their accuracy. Furthermore, those based on only the

[13] Leakages due to guests present and members absent from meals can be taken into account if a roster of all people present at every meal during the survey period is reported.

last 24 hours are probably very noisy (especially when one respondent provides information for all household members) as there is much daily variation in eating habits. With longer recalls (such as seven days) it may be difficult to capture leakage due to guests eating meals in the home.

Looking at Table 34.1, there is some evidence that elasticities based on *availability* tend to be higher than those based on *intakes* suggesting that accounting for leakages may be important. It is difficult to see a general pattern when comparing estimates based on the different methods for calculating calorie intakes although, perhaps, those based on seven day recalls are larger. This may also be due to leakages.

Two classes of estimators have been used to address the general set of concerns discussed above: instrumental variables and analysis of covariance (fixed effects). Both estimators have been widely adopted in the empirical human resource literature, and we will discuss general problems that arise when applying these estimators in the context of the nutrient-income example.

We begin with instrumental variables. Identification of valid instruments is seldom easy and assumptions need to be made about the reasons for the correlations between observables and unobservables. In practice, instruments need to not only be uncorrelated with the error term but also be informative in the sense they are sufficiently highly correlated with the covariate of interest. In the human resource literature, identifying good instruments is no mean feat.

For the example of common measurement error in nutrient intake and total expenditure, asset or wealth measures and, possibly, income are potential instruments, provided that reporting error and purchase frequency is not systematically related to wealth or income and that measurement errors in income are uncorrelated with errors in consumption. For household surveys that measure leakages well, such as ENDEF, this seems at least possible. In the example above, when per capita expenditure is instrumented with house-hold income, the calorie elasticity falls from 0.21 to 0.12 (standard error 0.01).

A different approach might be to argue that since imputing the value of own production is inherently difficult, all correlated measurement error is contained in these values. In this case, the value of purchased commodities is a valid instrument for total consumption. More generally, Subramanian and Deaton (1992) show that if the measurement error in food consumption and non-food consumption are uncorrelated, then an IV estimator with non-food consumption as the instrument provides a lower bound of the true elasticity.

It was argued above that income may be endogenous, in which case neither it nor non-food expenditures (which are a function of income) are appropriate instruments. In a static model, current productivity should be unaffected by nonlabor income, a measure of wealth, and so it may be a valid instrument. Under this assumption, the estimated elasticity in the ENDEF data drops further, to 0.05 (standard error 0.02), a level which is among the lowest estimates in Table 34.1. However, since nonlabor income is the return to assets built up with previous labor earnings, it may be argued that in a dynamic model (and possibly even in a static framework), nonlabor income is not an appropriate instrument.

Ignoring endogenous labor earnings, components of measurement error in nutrient intakes may still be systematically correlated with income, wealth or purchased consumption in which case none of the instruments proposed above is valid and 2SLS using them will be biased. These circumstances could arise, as argued by Bouis and Haddad, if the nutrient measure fails to take account of income-related leakages such as the amount of food that is wasted; gifts of food made into or out of the household; food eaten in the household by visitors or servants; or the quantity and quality of food eaten away from home.

A fixed effects estimator, provided panel data are available, will remove the time-persistent part of this bias. Apart from requiring data with repeated observations, fixed effects estimates have two disadvantages. First, all time invariant characteristics are swept out of the model: in many instances, those effects are of greatest interest. Second, random measurement error in covariates will bias estimated coefficients downwards. In our example, this may well be a serious problem for income for the reasons discussed above.

Bouis and Haddad (1992) use four rounds of household data collected in Bukidnon Province in Mindanao, Philippines, to examine the robustness of elasticities to variation in the measurement of calories and income. Results are reported for a series of estimators: OLS, instrumental variables using land operated and characteristics of the house as instruments, fixed effects and Hausman–Taylor random effects.[14] Estimated elasticities based on 24-hour food intake recalls using instrumental variables or fixed effects range between 0.08 and 0.14. These, they argue, are their best estimates.

In general, Bouis and Haddad report that elasticities based on 24 hour food recalls tend to be considerably lower than those using calories calculated by availability. They argue this is because disappearance methods fail to account for transfers of food into and out of the household. Yet, according to their own data, only a small percentage of food is consumed by guests and workers, even for higher income households (just 8 percent) and, in fact, they take account of this consumption in their calculation of net calorie availability. The IV and FE estimates for net calorie availability should, therefore, be unbiased, barring other leakages. These estimates range from 0.28 to 0.59. The authors discard these estimates because, they argue, other leakages are important, invalidating the instruments (cultivated land area and characteristics of the house). While

---

[14] Per capita expenditure and household size are allowed to be correlated with the time-persistent error, while other household composition variables and food prices are maintained as uncorrelated. This treatment of demographics is somewhat inconsistent.

given the evidence presented by the authors, there is no statistical basis for the claim, it may well be true; this is taken up again below.

As corroborating evidence to support their conclusions regarding the choice of best estimates, [Bouis and Haddad (1992) and Bouis (1993)] argue that differences in weight across income groups ought to be equi-proportional to differences in calorie intakes. In their Bukidnon data, however, they find more spread in measured calorie intakes than in weights. Further, they note that a calorie-income elasticity of even 0.2 would imply much greater dispersion of weights than exists. However, their assumption that weights and calorie intakes move equi-proportionately is based on very strong assumptions, which are, in turn, based on a slim scientific knowledge base. In particular, in addition to the very strong functional form assumption between changes in weight and energy intake, it is assumed that no inter-individual differences exist in energy requirements to maintain weight given gender, age, weight and energy expenditure. But there is evidence suggesting that rather large differences in energy intakes can be required by persons of similar weights in order to maintain body weight, given roughly equal energy expenditure [Pacey and Payne (1985) Edmundson and Sukhatme (1990)].[15] In view of the uncertainty surrounding these issues, it is not obvious the choice of "best" estimates should rely on the argument that weight and calories are very highly correlated.

How calories are calculated, how income is defined, the role of measurement error, as well as endogeneity of income or expenditure, and the validity of instruments are all very important concerns. But other specification issues warrant attention. It is generally agreed that as income (or expenditure) rises, households switch to higher valued foods, not necessarily with higher nutrient content [Poleman (1981), Alderman (1986), Behrman and Deolalikar (1987) Strauss and Thomas (1990), Subramanian and Deaton (1992)]. Intuitively, among the poor, calorie intakes are likely to respond positively to income, but as income rises the elasticity will decline, possibly to zero, or even become negative at high enough income levels. This suggests that nonlinearities may be key. Several studies that have included quadratic terms in expenditure or

---

[15] This could well result in greater proportionate variation in intakes relative to weights by income-level. If body adaptation exists such that persons with lower weight or ingesting lower energy intakes process with greater efficiency [e.g. Sukhatme and Margen (1982)], this will further raise the energy requirements as a function of weight. Reports by committees convened by the Food and Agricultural Organization and the World Health Organization [FAO/WHO (1973, 1985)] do suggest that calorie requirements move equi-proportionately, or less, with weight. However, these reports do not carefully investigate potential nonlinearities and make the same assumptions regarding no inter-individual variation in efficiency of intake conversion into energy, and the 1985 report notes this at the end, calling for more research. For example, the regressions on which the 1985 report bases its predictions of basal metabolic rate (as a function of weight, height, gender and age, for prime-aged adults) have R^2s of only 0.36 or less suggesting there is, in fact, considerable (unexplained) individual variation.

income find a concave relationship.[16] However, quadratic forms may not always be sufficient to adequately capture the shape of the calorie-expenditure relationship. For instance, in descriptive studies, Poleman (1981) and Lipton (1983) argue that the calorie-income curve may be elbow-shaped. A related, but stronger hypothesis, also postulated by them, is that the budget share of foods may actually increase with income for very poor households. There is some evidence to support this view [Thomas (1986)] and it is hard to imagine the budget *share* allocated to food rising without a concomitant increase in calorie intake.[17]

Nonparametric regression provides a powerful set of tools that can be extremely useful for data analysis when there is little a priori knowledge of the shape of the function to be estimated and, especially, when that shape may vary over the distribution of the covariate. Strauss and Thomas (1990) and Subramanian and Deaton (1992) use these methods to investigate the relationships between nutrient intakes, the price of calories and per capita expenditure (treated as exogenous).[18] Essentially, nonparametric regression seeks to estimate the regression function, $\mu(y) = E(y|x)$ by computing an estimate of location of y within a specific band of x. If that band is constant in width across the distribution of x, then these are called kernel estimators and if the bands maintain a constant share of the sample, then they are nearest neighbor estimators.

Figure 34.1 presents nearest neighbor type nonparametric estimates of the bivariate relationship between household per capita calorie consumption and per capita expenditure for three different measures of calorie consumption. All figures are drawn to a log scale and so the slopes can be interpreted as elasticities.[19]

Estimates based on the Brazilian ENDEF survey, in panel (a), use calorie intakes weighed on a daily basis for a week. Wastage is explicitly subtracted and adjustments made to account for guests at each meal; meals away from home are assumed to have the same nutrient content as meals at home. This measurement approach addresses part of the concerns raised by Bouis and

---

[16] For example, Timmer and Alderman (1979), Pitt (1983), Behrman and Wolfe (1984c), Chernichovsky and Meesook (1984), Garcia and Pinstrup-Andersen (1987), Sahn (1988) and Ravallion (1990).

[17] Part of this may be attributed to the fact that household budget surveys are based on samples of households who must thus spend some minimum amount on housing. Very poor households are more likely to be included in a survey if they spend less of their budget on food and this will result in upward biased estimates of income-nutrient elasticities. Empirically, the magnitude of this effect is quite small in Sri Lanka [Thomas (1986)].

[18] See also Anand, Harris and Linton (1993).

[19] The estimates are locally weighted smoothed scatterplots (LOWESS) which are nearest neighborhood type estimators. The tails of the distribution of PCE are trimmed so that attention is focussed on the remaining 90–95 percent of households.

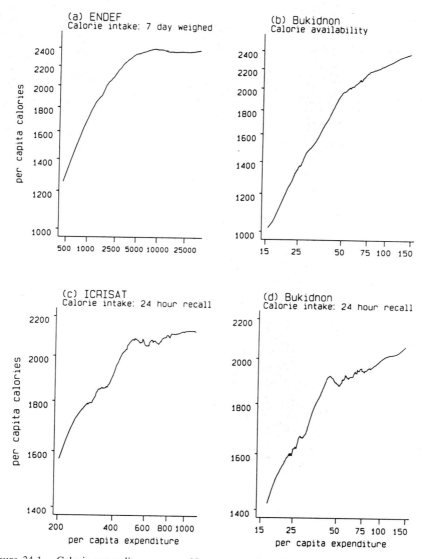

Figure 34.1.   Calorie-expenditure curves; Non parametric estimates; (Logarithmic scales).

Haddad. The shape of the calorie-expenditure relation is very clear: it is positive to about 2,400 calories per capita per day and then, somewhere around the sixth decile of PCE, it completely flattens out. For households below median PCE, the slope is 0.29 (with a standard error of 0.004). See Strauss and Thomas (1990) for more details.[20]

The lower half of Figure 34.1 presents non-parametric estimates of the relationship between calorie intakes, based on 24-hour intake recalls, and per capita expenditure. The ICRISAT data, used by Behrman and Deolalikar are presented in panel (c) and the first round of the Bukidnon data, used by Bouis and Haddad, in panel (d). The shapes of these functions are strikingly similar to the Brazilian case in panel (a): at low levels of expenditure, the calorie intakes and expenditure are positively correlated but when per capita calories reach about 2,000 per day, the curves flatten out. The functions are not very smooth reflecting the small sample sizes and, the fact that there is a good deal of noise in 24 hour recall data. For households with per capita expenditure below the median, the elasticity is 0.30 (with a standard error of 0.04) in the ICRISAT data and 0.33 (0.10) in Bukidnon.[21]

Panel (b) of Figure 34.1 presents the relationship between calorie *availability* and per capita expenditure, again using the first round of the Bukidnon data. The shape is rather different. There is less curvature and the estimated elasticity remains high for all households; for those below the median it is 0.67 (with a standard error of 0.03). Although the calorie availability measure used in this picture excludes leakages associated with meals given to workers and guests (as described in Bouis and Haddad), comparing panel (b) with (d) we see that among low expenditure households availability is substantially less than intake whereas the reverse is true among households at the top of the expenditure distribution. (Note that the scales of the two panels are different). For example, households in the bottom decile of PCE report intakes that are about 40 percent above availability; according to the latter, per capita consumption is only about 1,100 calories per day which seems very low. On the other hand, households in the top decile report availability that is about 20 percent above intakes, and per capita availability is a more reasonable 2,400. This asymmetry probably reflects the way in which leakages were measured. Any transfers of food *into* low income households were not measured, while foods provided to workers or guests were and this occurs largely in higher income households. Other leakages are left unaccounted.

Subramanian and Deaton (1992) estimate the elasticities non-parametrically using data on calorie availability from Maharashtra state, India, in the 1983

[20] A similar shape is reported for Sri Lanka in Anand, Harris and Linton (1993) although in their case the elasticity is zero somewhere between the first and sixth decile of expenditure (depending on window width).

[21] This is nearly three times the OLS estimate from Bouis and Haddad's linear model using data from all four rounds. The elbow shape is less apparent when the four rounds are aggregated together although within rounds (apart from 2), the shapes are similar to that in Figure 34.1(c). We are grateful to Mark Rosenzweig for providing the ICRISAT data and Howdy Bouis and Lawrence Haddad for the Bukidnon data.

round of the National Sample Survey (NSS). They report a shape very similar to the one for availability in the Bukidnon data in panel (b), with elasticities which range from 0.55 at the bottom of the PCE distribution to 0.40 at the top.[22] Since meals given to workers and guests are recorded in the NSS, but waste is not, some of the concerns regarding availability measures raised by Bouis and Haddad may be at issue. Subramanian and Deaton argue that the waste-income elasticity would have to be very large to account for the size of the estimated calorie-income elasticity. This presumes that other leakages have been fully taken into account and, as suggested by comparing panels (b) and (d), that may be quite difficult in household survey data.

One important determinant of household per capita calorie consumption is household composition: adults tend to consume more calories than children and men more than women.[23] Controlling for demographics in the ICRISAT data turns out to be key. The sample size is too small to estimate the calorie-expenditure function separately for different household types but when demographics are included in a parametric specification, the estimated elasticity for households below median PCE falls to 0.12 and it is no longer significant (consistent with the results reported in Behrman and Deolalikar (1987). This is not the case in Brazil. Exploiting the large sample size, panel (a) of Figure 34.2 presents the calorie-expenditure curve for households with only two adults and two children under 15. The shape is essentially identical to Figure 34.1(a) and the elasticity remains large and significant among poorer households. The Bukidnon data report intakes at the individual level: panel (b) of Figure 34.2 presents the relationship between calorie intake of male heads of households and PCE (again using the first round of the survey). Although the curve is quite noisy, it displays the same general shape as the household function except that it is shifted upwards (with intakes stabilizing around 3,000 calories).

These simple non-parametric estimates seem to indicate that among poor households there is a positive correlation between expenditure and calorie intakes but when some threshold level of intake has been attained the correlation is close to zero. The nonlinearities appear to be clearer when using data on intakes then when availability measures are used.

While nonparametric methods will surely yield substantial pay-offs in a broad range of applications in the empirical human resource literature, we are often interested in more than bivariate relationships and would like to

---

[22] Pitt (1990) uses spline functions to estimate the calorie-expenditure relationship using the 1980 SUSENAS from Indonesia. He reports a similar shape.

[23] Controlling for demographics is not straightforward. On the one hand, household age and gender composition may be properly treated as endogenous. On the other hand, nutrient requirements and intakes vary systematically with age and gender and failure to take this into account could impart bias due to omitted variables. For example, households with higher PCE tend to have fewer children and so per capita calorie consumption will appear to be higher than it would when conditioning on household composition: expenditure elasticities will be upward biased.

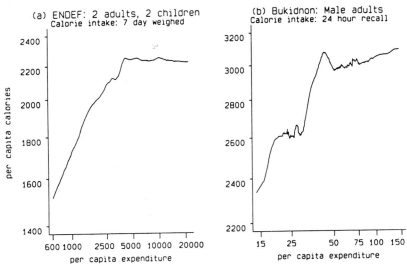

Figure 34.2.   Calorie-expenditure curves; Controlling for demographics; Non parametric estimates; (Logarithmic scales).

simultaneously control for a range other factors including family size and composition, seasons and market prices. Implementation of nonparametric methods with a small number of discrete covariates is straightforward. In the case of multiple covariates, they are very demanding of data, not to mention technology. Furthermore, very little is known about these estimators when covariates are endogenous. We might resort to parametric techniques but draw on the nonparametric results as a guide to suggest appropriate functional forms.

It turns out that in the Brazilian ENDEF data, the inverse of lnPCE and its square capture the shape in Figure 34.1 rather well. The elasticity at the bottom semi-decile of PCE is 0.45, dropping to 0.38 at the bottom decile, 0.21 at the median and 0.10 at the top decile.[24] To investigate some of the issues discussed above, Strauss and Thomas also experiment with instrumental variable estimators. When total income is used as the identifying variable, OLS estimates are clearly rejected in Wu-Hausman specification tests and the elasticity estimates fall to 0.32 at the bottom semi-decile, 0.26 at the bottom decile, 0.11 at the median (notice this is close to the IV and fixed effects estimates Bouis and Haddad obtain using intake data) and 0.03 at the top

---

[24] The standard errors in each case are around 0.01. Other covariates included in the regression include local price indices for 12 foods, education of the head and spouse, age and gender of the head, existence of the spouse, seven region dummies and dummies for month of interview.

decile of PCE. Thus the nonlinearities remain and the calorie response of low income households is substantially above those with middle or high incomes.

Subramanian and Deaton likewise use parametric analysis and examine potential biases from common measurement errors, using nonfood expenditures to instrument for total expenditures. Their lower bound estimate is 0.28, compared to their estimate of 0.40 when common measurement error is ignored. This is actually close to the 0.37 estimate of Behrman and Deolalikar based on the small ICRISAT sample (100 households), but one which is estimated with greater precision.

As discussed above, if labor supply is endogenous, or there are nutrition-wage feedbacks, then total income is not a valid instrument. Strauss and Thomas attempt to address this issue using nonlabor income to explore the robustness of the IV estimates to changes in the instrument set and find that the elasticities are somewhat (but not significantly) smaller at the bottom of the PCE distribution. If, however, a third term expenditure term is added to the regression (lnlnPCE) then the elasticities increase by a factor of 10 (and the standard errors explode). In contrast, when the instrument is total income, the elasticity at the bottom decile in this more flexible specification is only slightly larger than its estimate in the quadratic inverse-log expenditure model.

Apparently there is an interaction between the power of the instruments and the flexibility of the functional form. Even though there are 13,000 observations in the dataset and the F-statistic for nonlabor income in the first stage is 398,[25] there is just not sufficient information to support a third order polynomial. Fortunately, the standard errors are also large and so there are good reasons to be suspicious of these estimates.[26] This is similar to the results in [Bound, Jaeger and Baker (1993)], who demonstrate that even with the very large samples used by [Angrist and Krueger (1991)], the IV estimates break down when enough interactions are included in the model. At the very least, running two stage least squares when there is little or no explanatory power in the first stage is unlikely to be a good empirical strategy. These results, however, suggest that even if good first stage predictions are obtained, interactions with functional form may wreak havoc with IV estimators.

Strauss and Thomas and Subramanian and Deaton examine other dimensions of nutrient intakes. The implicit price of calories (total expenditure divided by total calories) is an indicator of the quality of calories and it tends to increase with PCE in both India and Brazil. Subramanian and Deaton estimate the elasticity to be about 0.30, which is close to the estimates reported by

---

[25] Although half the sample reports no nonlabor income.

[26] Not all problems with instruments are readily detected; see, for example, [Nelson and Startz (1990) and Staiger and Stock (1993)] who present theoretical results demonstrating that the bias in IV estimates can be greater than OLS and that precision of the IV estimates can be misleading (since the "t" statistics are not distributed as ts).

Strauss and Thomas as well as to earlier estimates (from several countries) in Alderman (1986). Strauss and Thomas also estimate the relationship between protein and expenditure, finding the elasticity is positive and higher than the calorie elasticity (0.4 at the bottom decile of PCE and 0.1 at the top). These studies confirm the argument of Behrman and Deolalikar, that as expenditure increases, even the poorest households switch into higher-valued foods and foods that are more intensive in proteins. But they are also consuming more calories.

The elasticities for low income households reported by Strauss and Thomas, Subramanian and Deaton and others are not the large elasticities found by Pitt, Strauss and argued to exist by Lipton. Nor are they zero, or even close to zero, as claimed by Behrman, Bouis, Deolalikar, Haddad and Wolfe. On balance, the evidence suggests there is at least some scope for income-based policies to alleviate low nutrient intakes. At the same time, income is by no means a panacea: households do care about dimensions of welfare other than calorie consumption.

2.2. Health, productivity and labor supply

The previous section focused on the effect of poverty and income on nutrient intakes. In this section, we look at its inverse: the impact of nutrients and, more generally health, on incomes. These relationships have historically played a prominent role in the economic development literature and their behavioral consequences are the intellectual genesis of several forms of the efficiency wage theory.[27] A number of recent papers have explored the empirical basis for the health and nutrition variants of these models,[28] concentrating on the estimation of the effects of different dimensions of better health on wages, labor productivity and labor supply.

Health status is multi-dimensional (see the discussion in Section 3) and different dimensions of health are likely to have different effects on labor market outcomes. Thus, a range of health indicators have been adopted in empirical analyses including morbidities, anthropometrics and nutrient intakes.

Morbidity data are usually based on self-reports which are, therefore, subjective and prone to reporting errors. As argued below, these errors may be

---

[27] Early papers were largely theoretical and include [Leibenstein (1957), Mazumdar (1959), Stiglitz (1976), Mirrlees (1975), Bliss and Stern (1978a) and more recently Dasgupta and Ray (1986, 1987)]. For a recent review see Rosenzweig (1988c).

[28] Surveys of the empirical literature from an economics perspective can be found in [Bliss and Stern (1978b), Binswanger and Rosenzweig (1984), Strauss (1986a), Behrman and Deolalikar (1988), Rosenzweig (1988c), Behrman (1993a) and Strauss (1993)]. [Spurr (1983), Martorell and Arroyave (1988) and Latham (1993)] provide perspectives from nutritionists.

related to information, education and thus to income. If higher income individuals are more likely to report themselves ill, ceteris paribus, then it will be very hard to separate the effect on wages of the incidence of illness from reporting error.

Anthropometric measurements – in particular height and weight – have been suggested as more objective indicators of health status, although clearly they measure different dimensions of health. Height may be directly related to productivity and is fixed by adulthood. The ratio of weight to height or the related measure of body mass index (BMI)[29] does vary in the short run, and BMI has been shown to be related to maximum physical capacity independent of energy intake. Furthermore, energy can be stored in the body and some jobs may require extreme strenuous activity, in which case employers could screen on the basis of body size.

Current nutrient intakes may be useful in enhancing productivity for some jobs; for instance calorie intake increases maximum oxygen uptake (which is related to maximum work capacity; Spurr, 1983). On the other hand many jobs do not require maximum physical effort, so it is not obvious that energy or other nutrient intakes should be correlated with either productivity or labor supply. Furthermore, there is some evidence that the body adapts to changes over some range in energy intakes in such a way as to keep functioning intact (see footnote 11). If this hypothesis is true then it is only at extremely low levels of calorie intakes that productivity or labor supply should suffer; these relationships should exhibit very nonlinear shapes. Other nutrient intakes, such as of proteins or iron, may also affect labor productivity [e.g. Basta, et al. (1979)].

Over and above concern with measurement of different dimensions of health, it seems likely that the impact of health on income will depend on the nature of work. A laborer, for example, may suffer a larger decline in income because of physical injury than would a more sedentary worker. This also raises the issue of the joint determination of occupation and health status.

To empirically describe the relationships between different dimensions of health and income, Thomas and Strauss (1992b) use nonparametric methods to relate hourly market wages to height, BMI, and household-level per capita calorie and per capita protein intakes. Bivariate regressions are presented in Figure 34.3 (in log scales) for men in urban Brazil, using the ENDEF data. The relationship between height and wages is essentially log-linear (and this is true for women as well). The BMI curve is sigmoidal, suggesting some kind of threshold effects. Wages and per capita calories are positively correlated until 2,400 calories per day, at which point the correlation is essentially zero.

---

[29] This is defined as weight (in kilograms) divided by height (in meters) squared.

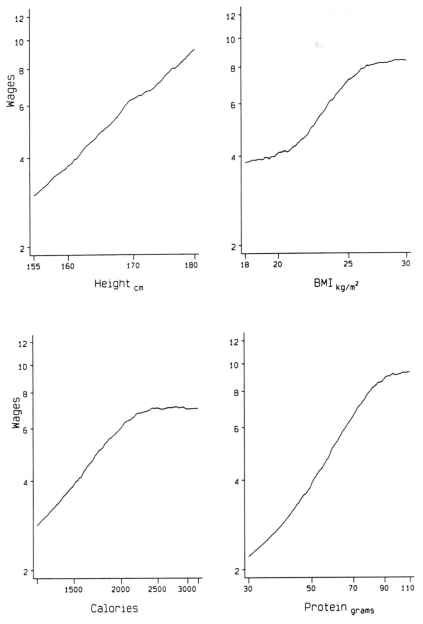

Figure 34.3.   Relationship between wages and health; Males in urban Brazil; Non parametric estimates; (Logarithmic scales); Data source: ENDEF.

Flattening out is less apparent in the protein curve. These wage-nutrient shapes are consistent with the nutrient-expenditure curves presented in Section 2.1.

While the shapes in Figure 34.3 are suggestive, their interpretation is complicated since correlations between any component of income (such as wages or labor supply) and measures of health that depend on current behavior could reflect causality in either direction. While better health may result in a worker being more productive, higher income may be spent on improving one's health. Furthermore, correlations with past behavior could reflect unobserved, time-persistent heterogeneity. For example height is certainly predetermined for adults but it may reflect, in part, previous health investments made primarily early in life. These investments may be correlated with other unobserved dimensions of human capital and, thus, with the disturbance term in a wage function. BMI will reflect both current and previous health investments and thus may suffer from both true simultaneity as well as unobserved heterogeneity. As discussed in the last section, nutrient intakes and income are likely to be jointly determined. Indeed, the issue of endogeneity of health status has been one of the dominant themes in the current literature on this topic.

As in the nutrient-income literature discussed in the previous section, both instrumental variables and fixed effects estimators have been used to address these concerns. Strauss (1986a) estimates a farm production function, using food prices and number of adults in the household to instrument for per capita household calorie availability and for family and hired labor input use. Similar approaches, using measures of assets, food prices and local infrastructure as instruments in wage functions are followed by Sahn and Alderman (1988), Foster and Rosenzweig (1992), Schultz and Tansel (1992) and Thomas and Strauss (1992b)]. Deolalikar (1988), Behrman and Deolalikar (1989) and Haddad and Bouis (1991) use individual-level fixed effects techniques, taking advantage of longitudinal data. Although the fixed effects estimators sweep out time-invariant heterogeneity, they will not correct for bias induced by simultaneity between time-varying heterogeneity and the health variables, which, as discussed, there is reason to believe exists in this case.[30]

Following the pioneering work of Heckman (1979), most studies attempt to take account of the fact that people select into the labor force or into a particular sector, albeit with varying success. Household assets, nonlabor income or household composition are typically used to identify these choices, although good arguments may be made for treating these "instruments" as

---

[30] Instrumental variables will correct for both simultaneity and unobserved heterogeneity provided the instruments are valid; however, as noted, their validity cannot be taken for granted. Haddad and Bouis attempt to use instrumental variables techniques, in addition to fixed effects, to estimate their wage functions; their predictions of calorie intake and BMI are so collinear that they are unable to obtain robust coefficient estimates.

outcomes of decisions made over the life cycle (see the more general discussion in Section V).

Those studies that have considered the relationship between incidence of illness and income have typically found no, or fairly small, effects [Pitt and Rosenzweig (1986) Schultz and Tansel (1992)]. As argued by Pitt and Rosenzweig for rural Indonesia, this could indicate that it is possible to hire in healthy labor to replace sick family labor and that the two types of labor are homogeneous. Incidence of ill health is likely to be a short term measure (unless the illness is chronic) and for many bouts of illness, incomes are likely to be little affected, at least among workers in the market sector.

Many of the recent economic studies of the relation between health and productivity have included measures of calories consumed (either at the individual or household level). Strauss (1986a) and Sahn and Alderman (1988) use per capita household calorie availability measures. Strauss estimates a farm production function for households in Sierra Leone and finds a significant calorie effect, while Sahn and Alderman estimate market wage equations for men and women in rural Sri Lanka, finding a significant effect for men, but not for women. According to the body adaptation view it should only be at very low levels of calorie intakes that productivity should suffer. This type of nonlinearity between calorie intake and productivity has not been closely examined. Strauss allows for a simple quadratic and reports a concave relationship; the adaptation point of view, however, hypothesizes a much more nonlinear structure.

Calories alone may well be proxying for other health characteristics, with which they are correlated, such as body size. Deolalikar (1988) and Behrman and Deolalikar (1989) include calorie intake data at the individual level and also control for the ratio of weight to height in market wage and farm production functions using the ICRISAT Indian data. Deolalikar finds that it is weight-for-height and not calories that matters for both farm self-employment and market labor productivity. In an extension, Behrman and Deolalikar find that during the season of peak labor demand, it is calorie intake that has a significant effect, but that during the off-peak season it is weight-for-height. Upon disaggregating by gender they find that this is true only for men. These results are consistent with BMI increasing labor productivity through enhanced strength, maximum work capacity, or as a store of calories which are drawn upon during work.

Haddad and Bouis (1991) estimate market wage functions for adults (pooling men and women) in which they control for three health variables: individual-level calorie intake, BMI and height. They find a strong effect of height on market wages in Bukidnon, Philippines, but not of BMI nor of current calorie intake. This association could represent the direct influence of height on wages,[31] but it could also result from unobserved factors related both to an individual's human capital and to his or her height.[32] This finding raises the question of whether earlier results reflect anything other than the impact of prior human capital investments which are correlated with current health status.

Thomas and Strauss (1992b) use the ENDEF data to investigate the impact on wages of urban workers of four indicators of health: height, body mass index, and per capita calorie and protein intakes. The latter three measures are treated as endogenous, with relative food prices serving to identify them.[33] Their effects are examined individually as well as all together. Wage functions are estimated for both men and women. The choice to work is taken into account and wages are also disaggregated into those earned in the market and self-employment sectors, allowing for endogenous selection into each sector, with nonlabor earnings as the identifying instrument.

All four measures of health are found to significantly affect wages even after accounting for endogeneity. Height has a particularly large impact: taller men and women earn more even after controlling for education and other dimensions of health. Body mass index has a positive effect on the wages of men, but not those of women. Disaggregated by level of education, body mass is associated with higher log wages for poorly educated men in all sectors and for women in the market sector, suggesting, perhaps, a return to strength. Nutrient intakes are also important in the market wage sector for men and women. More calories are associated with higher wages, but only at very low intake levels. Conditional on calorie intake, mass and height, additional protein has the greatest return at high levels of intakes. Since additional protein, conditional on calorie intake, is indicative of a higher quality diet, this suggests there is a significant return to raising diet quality.

Foster and Rosenzweig (1992, 1994) use the same data as Haddad and Bouis to examine the effects of calorie intake, body mass index and height on market wages for farm work. They advance the literature by examining the impact of health on piecework and time wages separately. Some dimensions of health, such as body mass index, may be more easily observable, relative to, say, calorie intakes. While food can be given on the job, there is no guarantee that intrafamily substitution will not occur at home, with other persons being fed more than otherwise. Furthermore, there may be worker incentive problems

---

[31] Many of the workers in the survey are sugarcane cutters, for whom height may well enhance productivity.

[32] Such as might result from prior health and human capital investments when the respondent was a child.

[33] A region-specific, overall price index is included as a covariate in the (nominal) wage functions.

on daily-wage contracts; workers have an incentive to shirk unless monitoring can prevent this or contracts can be structured to provide proper incentives. Piece-rate contracts are much less likely to suffer from incentive problems. Thus, Foster and Rosenzweig argue, only observable health measures should be rewarded in time wages, while among piece-rate workers, observability of health should play no part in the reward structure. This argument is dependent, however, on imperfect monitoring of worker effort by employers, a point not acknowledged by Foster and Rosenzweig. If employers can observe and reward worker effort and if effort is positively related to health, then a positive correlation between health and wages will exist in the data even though employers cannot directly observe health.

Foster and Rosenzweig estimate piece-rate and time-rate wage functions for harvest activities. Keeping the activities identical for the two types of contracts is useful because then any differences in productivity effects are less likely to result from different contract types being used for different activities. Foster and Rosenzweig (1992) first pool all wage payments and then disaggregate by payment scheme. They find significant effects of calorie intake on piece-rates but not on time rates.[34] Many workers report both piece-rate and time-rate wages, which enables Foster and Rosenzweig to include individual fixed effects in their model and test for different effects across the two contract types. Consistent with their hypothesis, they report that calories (which are difficult to observe) have a significantly larger effect on piece-rate wages.

In Foster and Rosenzweig (1994) body mass index is added to the fixed effects specification. Conditional on calories and height, BMI is found to differentially raise time-rate wages. This is consistent with body mass being used as a signal for caloric intake by employers. Height is found to have a significantly larger effect on piece-rate wages. Why *both* calories and height should have a larger effect on piece-rate wages is not clear since height is certainly easy to observe. While shirking on daily-wage jobs is a possibility, the greater effect of BMI on time-rate jobs is inconsistent with this hypothesis.

More direct evidence on the possibility of moral hazard by workers in daily-wage contracts is provided in Foster and Rosenzweig (1994). They estimate a dynamic health production function for body mass and an Euler equation for changes in individual-level calorie consumption to assess how these vary with days working on different types of contracts. They distinguish working in self-employment on owned land, on sharecropped land, and working for others by the piece or by daily wage. If worker effort is provided differentially across contract types, then this should be reflected in energy expenditures. Energy expenditure may come from drawing down body mass or

---

[34] In Foster and Rosenzweig (1994) account is taken of selectivity into the type of contract. This turns out to make very little difference to the results.

current calorie intake. By estimating a production function for body mass, holding constant for energy intake, lagged body mass and other inputs, it is, in principle, possible to infer how much energy is expended on different contract types if it is known how many days are worked on each. Foster and Rosenzweig disaggregate days worked by contract type as separate inputs into the body mass production function. They find that working on one's own land or for piece-rate wages reduces body mass significantly more than does working for daily wages.[35] They also find no significant differential effect of working on sharecropped land, consistent with perfect monitoring of effort by landlords. To explore whether calorie intake varies directly with work expenditure, Foster and Rosenzweig derive a dynamic model and solve a linear approximation to the Euler conditions to express changes in individual energy intake as a function of changes in food prices, wages, illness and in days worked on different contract types.[36] They find results that are consistent with the BMI production function estimates; that working more days for piece rates or on one's own farm is associated with greater calorie intake than daily-wage work.

Taken together, this evidence may be viewed as supporting the notion that worker effort and the effects of hard to observe dimensions of health on productivity are greater on forms of contracts that have the most incentive effects. Consistent with this, Foster and Rosenzweig (1992) also find that more productive workers tend to self-select into piece-rate jobs. Their results are, however, highly dependent on both the costliness of monitoring worker effort and on the form of contract.[37] Furthermore, it is not clear why, if information and moral hazard are problems, there are not more long-run contracts such as sharecropping or permanent worker contracts. Instead, there may be something common in piece-rate work that is different from time wage work in their sample.[38]

---

[35] These inputs are treated as endogenous. Instruments include education, height, household land owned and demographic composition, survey round and community dummy variables. It is arguable that community influences would affect body mass directly, such as water and sanitation quality or the disease environment.

[36] The Euler equation that is estimated amounts to an individual fixed effects specification. Since there are potentially endogenous variables on the right hand side, differencing may not purge all correlations with the unobserved error. However, Foster and Rosenzweig report that according to a Wu-Hausman test there is no evidence for endogeneity after controlling for individual fixed effects.

[37] Thomas and Strauss (1992b) report that in urban Brazil the impact of nutrient intakes is actually stronger in the market wage sector relative to self-employment, suggesting that observability of health is not a key issue. Both the observability of worker effort and the nature of the labor contracts may differ from rural Bukidnon, Philippines, however.

[38] One possibility is that piece-rate harvesting is done largely on sugarcane farms, while time-wages are typically paid for harvesting on maize farms. Attributes, such as height, have been shown to be related to sugarcane harvest productivity [Immink and Viteri (1981)]. In their analysis, Foster and Rosenzweig do control for the crop being harvested, although interactions with worker attributes are not included.

Pitt, Rosenzweig and Hassan (1990) adopt an entirely different approach to examine the impact of weight for height on occupational choice, income and calorie consumption of men and women in Bangladesh. Beginning with a weight for height production function, they treat estimated residuals as indicative of health endowments, a methodology suggested by Rosenzweig and Schultz (1983).

For men, one's own health "endowment" is positively associated with the probability of working in exceptionally active occupations, conditional on average household endowments. The average endowment for males over 12 years of age is positively related to household income, net of landholding, schooling of the head and some household composition covariates. Male adults who have better endowments also consume more calories. Thus, adult men who are better endowed (by this measure) are fed more, work in more strenuous occupations and contribute more to household income. For women, weight for height endowments have no impact on any of the outcomes.

Treating estimated residuals from production function as endowments is not without its problems. The most worrisome in this case relates to omitted inputs (see Section 4). Due to data constraints, Pitt, Rosenzweig and Hassan make a number of simplifying assumptions, including pooling men and women in one production function, and they only have measures of contemporaneous inputs. These include individual calorie consumption, indicators for working in a strenuous occupation, for being pregnant or lactating and for source of water. Although weight-for-height can vary in the short run, it still has a long-run component, making the problem of omitted inputs potentially important. To the extent that the residuals incorporate the role of these omitted factors or specification error, then they may be correlated with a propensity to work in higher return, more strenuous occupations.

Since they have repeated observations on the same individual, Pitt, Rosenzweig and Hassan account for random measurement error in the endowment residuals by using endowment estimates from other periods as instruments. This assumes the errors are not systematic across periods. If, however, unobserved inputs are correlated over time, the resulting estimates would still be biased because they would be correlated with the lagged endowment measures used as instruments. Autocorrelation in unobserved inputs is quite likely since they are influenced by common time-invariant factors such as long-run household resources, education, water quality and sanitation.

In this case, the fact that endowments are calculated at both the household (for men and women separately) and individual-levels is potentially helpful. If omitted inputs vary across households, but not across individuals within households, they would be subsumed in a household fixed effects specification. Since fixed effects estimates in small samples with qualitative variables are in general inconsistent, Pitt, Rosenzweig and Hassan include the estimated gender-specific mean household endowment as a covariate, along with the estimated individual endowment. While the purpose of this specification is to measure the effect of an individual's endowment relative to the household endowment, the latter should subsume any effects of omitted family-level inputs. Of course, omitted individual-specific inputs remain problematic. This discussion illustrates some of the difficulties in identifying nutrition-labor supply effects as well as using estimated production function residuals to represent endowments. Yet it is still the case that Rosenzweig, Pitt and Hassan's paper is the only serious attempt to date, that models the impact of nutrient intake on the likelihood of being able to work in strenuous but high paying jobs.

In summary, since the skeptical reviews of Bliss and Stern (1978a,b) and Binswanger and Rosenzweig (1984), evidence has been accumulating that better health, specifically nutrition-related dimensions of health, are associated with higher labor productivity. Confirming the causal nature in these relationships is difficult and each study has weaknesses. Taken together, however, it seems that there does appear to be an effect of health on productivity. Exactly which dimensions of health matter remains at issue, as does the importance of threshold effects. Research on precisely what labor market consequences derive from these health-productivity relationships is still in its early stages.

3. Human capital investments: Reduced form and conditional function estimates

3.1. Introduction

As discussed in Section 1, models of human capital investments fall into three broad groups. Production functions seek to understand the underlying production process; reduced form models integrate this process with a model of household choices; and conditional functions are a hybrid of the two which focus attention on how human capital investments are affected by (typically) a small number of endogenous characteristics such as the relationship between quantity and quality of children within a family. What can be learned from these different models varies, and thus the choice of tool in any case will depend on the nature of the question posed. Reduced forms and conditional functions are discussed in this section; production functions are deferred to Section 4.

Human capital is multi-dimensional, spanning a wide array of investments; we focus on education and health, both broadly defined. We begin with a discussion of measurement of these investments and then turn to their determinants. Time and time again, it has been shown that parental education has a powerful influence on all indicators of human capital. We pay careful attention to interpretation of this result, taking into account an issue that has plagued this literature, namely the role of unobservables (omitted variables and measurement error). For example, we ask whether parental education reflects anything other than the effect of unobserved background on child investments. We go on to discuss household resource availability and then turn to the role of public policy as it influences the environment in the community. There are good reasons to expect interactions among these groups of characteristics and we draw out some of the evidence on these relationships. The next sub-section is devoted to the concern that community characteristics should not be treated as exogenous. It is followed by a discussion of the importance of potential biases from selecting samples of people who are currently alive (or included in the survey).

3.2. Measurement of human capital

In many studies, human capital is measured by completed years of schooling or the highest grade achieved. In virtually every case, the two measures are treated as interchangeable although, in the presence of grade repetition, they will diverge. Perhaps more importantly, they represent but one dimension of a very complex set of investments which are unlikely to be captured by a single indicator. Both measures ignore questions of the quality of schooling, the time spent at school in any day and time spent during the year, all of which are likely to be intimately related to educational attainment. Furthermore, for many purposes, we are interested in the value added associated with schooling, in which case it becomes important to control for innate ability. These concerns affect both the measurement of outcomes (such as child schooling) and the measurement of determinants (such as parental education).   Human capital is much broader than just schooling and includes health, which is, itself, multidimensional. One health indicator, child mortality, has been frequently analyzed, primarily because it is relatively easy to measure.[39] It is, however, a somewhat gross indicator of health, providing little, if any, information about the incidence or acuteness of specific diseases. Furthermore, it is information on health of the living that may be key in an assessment of the impact of ill-health as well as for policy evaluation. For example, among children, measures of incidence of acute illness, such as diarrhea, may reflect rather

---

[39] In retrospective data, deaths tend to be under-reported and the extent of under-reporting tends to be greater by mothers of lower socio-economic status. Thus, estimated mortality rates, the ratio of deaths to the number ever born, tend to be under-estimated more for this group than those with higher socio-economic status. Furthermore, vital statistics data are also weak in many countries.

different factors and have different consequences from, say, chronic respiratory problems. Certain diseases, such as cholera, may have acute, short-run consequences, but matter little for survivors in the long-run. Researchers and policy-makers have more recently turned, therefore, to indicators of morbidity.

The measurement of morbidity is, however, beset by notoriously difficult problems. This is especially true in the case of self-evaluations or proxy reports.[40] For example, in Peru, the correlation between maternal education and child mortality is overwhelmingly negative, but the relationship between education and the reported incidence of child illness follows an inverted-U shape [Sindelar and Thomas (1991)]. In the Ghana and Côte d'Ivoire Living Standards Surveys, the propensity for adults to report being ill is a positive function of own education [Schultz and Tansel (1992)]. It has been argued that more specific indicators of symptoms or indicators of severe illness may be less subject to these biases [e.g. Hill and Mamdani (1989)]. But even this turns out to not always be the case.[41] Various reasons have been proposed why higher socio-economic status may be positively associated with the probability of reporting an illness: these include better information and greater awareness, stemming perhaps from more experience with health care providers.

Indicators that are likely to be related to the economic consequences of ill-health, such as the number of days of restricted activity, have also been suggested. While these are negatively correlated with socio-economic status in some datasets [Hill and Mamdani (1989)], in others the correlation is positive [see, for example, the evidence in Schultz and Tansel (1992)]. A negative correlation between ill-health and education is not, by itself, evidence that this is a good indicator. The true relation may be even more negative. And it may reflect people with a high opportunity cost of time being less likely to let a given illness interfere with their normal activities. All of this suggests that measurement of physical health with morbidity data is hard.

A promising set of self-reported measures have to do with an individual's ability to function at particular tasks, such as performing certain vigorous activities, walking uphill, bending, eating or bathing. Such self-reported measures of physical functioning have been used in analyses of health of the elderly in the United States[42] but have only recently been used in developing countries. Thus far, the evidence in poorer countries suggests that these

---

[40] See Kroeger (1985), Hill and Mamdani (1989) for discussion.

[41] Sindelar and Thomas (1991) show that there is a negative relationship between reporting a child's diarrhea and mother's education but that better educated mothers are *more* likely to report a respiratory infection in her child. They suggest that since respiratory infections are less easily diagnosed than digestive problems, measurement error is likely to be greater among those diseases that are more difficult to detect (especially among mothers with little education). Clearly these kinds of problems may be ameliorated by careful data collection; see, for example, evidence in the Cebu Child Nutrition and Health Survey.

[42] For example, Manning, Newhouse and Ware (1982).

measures may be useful not just for the elderly but for adults over the entire life-cycle.[43]

As alternatives to self-reported measures, researchers have attempted to find more "objective" indicators of health. One set includes direct observation by survey enumerators of difficulties with activities of daily living (such as climbing stairs or carrying a heavy load). Secondly, there is a long tradition of using anthropometric measurements as indicators of nutritional status; some have argued they may also be indicative of health. Child height for age is thought to be an indicator of longer-run health (and nutrition), whereas weight conditional on height (or body mass index) as a shorter-run measure.[44] A key advantage of anthropometrics lies in the fact that individuals can be measured in the field inexpensively and that errors are likely to be random rather than systematic.[45]

Anthropometrics are not very specific indicators of health status and it may be argued that behavioral decisions are made on the basis of health perceptions. In this case self-reported health (including morbidity and activity) measures may be appropriate for analyzing such decisions as curative health care demand [see Ware, et al. (1980)] and even labor effort. As new data are collected that attempt to address these concerns, much will probably be learned about the meaning and interpretation of a range of indicators of health status.

3.3. Determinants: Effects of education

Our discussion of the determinants of human capital investments is divided into three sub-sections. We begin with the role of education, followed by household resources more generally and then resources in the community.

3.3.1. Measuring the effect of education

The positive association between education and labor market outcomes is well-documented (and discussed below in Section 5). Similarly, education plays an important role in affecting nonmarket outcomes and input allocations. Here

---

[43] See Strauss, Gertler, Rahman and Fox (1993) for a discussion.

[44] See Waterlow, et al. (1977) or Falkner and Tanner (1986) for a discussion. Fogel (1986) and his many collaborators use height to measure the long-run economic well-being of a population; Fogel, Costa and Kim (1992) describe the relationship between BMI and survival. See also Waaler (1984).

[45] Although even this advantage is lost in the United States where anthropometrics are often collected by self-reports as in the Health Interview Surveys.

we concentrate on the impacts of parental or own education on child or adult health and on child schooling. Most studies report very strong associations between parental education and infant or child mortality as well as child schooling attainment.[46] Parental education has also been shown to be positively associated with child anthropometrics, particularly when true reduced forms have been estimated.[47]

As is the case with the labor earnings literature, the interpretation of the impact of education is debated; in particular, there is disagreement about how much of it represents the effect of human capital accumulation in school and how much the effects of correlated, but unobserved, family background factors.

Two broad approaches have been adopted to address these issues: attempts to measure various omitted variables (or a subset of them) and attempts to use control groups and fixed effects procedures.[48] A handful of studies have explicitly included measures of school quality (such as average teacher education in the school area); others have attempted to proxy "ability" with scores on so-called ability tests (such as Raven's test). Several studies have incorporated indicators of human capital accumulated during childhood; these have included height (which is determined early in a child's life) or information on family background (such as parents' education and height). Indeed, it has been argued that it is not even clear parents' education should be treated as exogenous in a model that seeks to explain child human capital investments. All of these issues are quite general and will be raised again in the discussion of the relationship between education and labor market outcomes in Section 5.

We argue that on balance the evidence indicates family background is important but that estimated education effects do represent, at least in part, real effects of schooling per se. Given that, identifying the pathways of influence remains an important and largely unresolved issue.

An empirical regularity about which there is little debate is the powerful negative association between maternal education and infant or child mortality. Since Caldwell's (1979) pioneering work on maternal education differentials in

---

[46] See Cochrane, O'Hara and Leslie (1982), Behrman and Deolalikar (1988), Cleland and van Ginneken (1988), Schultz (1988a, 1990), Behrman (1990) and Alderman (1990) for reviews of the development literature.

[47] Much of the early anthropometric literature was plagued by studies mixing the concepts of reduced forms and production functions and not dealing with the endogeneity of many of the covariates. See Behrman and Deolalikar (1988) and Strauss (1990, 1993). Some of the data sets have small samples, which may be partly responsible for estimated parental education effects not being significant.

[48] This follows a very long tradition in the human capital literature in industrial countries. See, for example, Altonji (1991), Behrman, Hrubec, Taubman and Wales (1980), Card and Krueger (1992a,b), Featherman and Hauser (1978), Griliches (1977, 1979), Hauser and Sewell (1986), Leibowitz (1974), Willis (1986) and Willis and Rosen (1979).

infant mortality in Nigeria, this pattern has been confirmed in many studies[49] and has been interpreted as evidence for the importance of education in non-market, home production activities as well as of the critical role women play in these activities.

Education reflects, in part, household resources and so it is important to also control for income, assets, location and environmental conditions such as water and sanitation quality. After including these controls, the impact of maternal education persists and it is often significantly larger than that of paternal education. Controls for family background characteristics, which may pick up some unobserved dimensions of human capital such as school quality or health of the mother are typically not available in data sets that are used to analyze child mortality.[50]

Parental education also has a significant positive effect on child anthropometric outcomes, especially height for age, the longer-run indicator. For example, in the urban Northeast of Brazil, children of mothers who have completed primary school are 2.5 percent taller than those of illiterate mothers (who account for 30 percent of the sample; [Thomas, Strauss and Henriques, (1990)]).[51] Like the results for child mortality, these effects persist after controlling for household and community resources such as income, assets and health infrastructure. Several analyses have attempted to include additional controls related to family background, including parental height [Barrera (1990a), Horton (1986, 1988), Strauss (1990), Thomas, Strauss and Henriques (1990)] and the characteristics of grandparents, including their education, occupation and presence [Wolfe and Behrman (1987)]. While parents' height has a strong genetic effect on child height, and so is a good predictor of child height, it also represents the investments made by the grandparents when the parents were still young. To that extent, it may be interpreted as another control for human capital of the parents.

The estimated magnitudes of parental education have been found to be somewhat sensitive to the inclusion of family background controls.[52] But, even after including these controls, parental education remains an important determinant of child height.

---

[49] See, for example, Rosenzweig and Schultz (1982b), Farah and Preston (1982), Habicht, DaVanzo and Butz (1986) and Mensch, Lentzner and Preston (1985) and the references in footnote 46.

[50] This is the case for the World Fertility Surveys or national censuses. Thomas, Strauss and Henriques (1990) provide an exception, see below.

[51] Weight given height seems to be a far more noisy measure of health and results for that measure are usually much more imprecise although Strauss (1990) finds it is significant affected by mother's and father's education (jointly) in rural Côte d'Ivoire.

[52] For example, Barrera reports that in the Philippines, estimates for mother's education fall by between 20 to 50 percent, depending on the child's age group, when mother's height is controlled. Thomas, Strauss and Henriques report similar rates in Brazil when both parents' height are included.

Significant positive effects of maternal schooling have been reported for a series of inputs into child health and, once again, this is true after controlling for household resources (income and assets) as well as background. These inputs into the health production function have included the number of prenatal visits, the likelihood of obtaining well-baby care and immunizations for women [Akin, Griffin, Guilkey and Popkin (1986), using data from Bicol province in the Philippines] as well as the timeliness in seeking pre-natal care and obtaining it from modern (rather than traditional) sources [Wong, Popkin, Akin and Guilkey (1987), Guilkey, Popkin, Akin and Wong (1989), using data from Cebu, in the Philippines]. Other studies, such as the Cebu Study Team (1991), Guilkey and Stewart (1994), or Wolfe and Behrman (1987) find strong negative impacts of maternal education on breastfeeding, especially exclusive breastfeeding; formula feeding by better educated women may reflect their higher value of time[53].

A small number of studies have examined the correlates of adult health which is found, in many, but not all cases, to be positively associated with own education. Strauss, Gertler, Rahman and Fox (1993) report this to be the case using self-reported general health status as well as measures of physical functioning for adult men and women in Jamaica, while controlling for age and location. Behrman and Wolfe (1989) find negative own education effects among adult women in Nicaragua on whether certain diseases had ever been contracted, after controlling for variables related to the woman's background (such as parental education) and for some community-level covariates.[54] The evidence on anthropometrics is more ambiguous; in the Côte d'Ivoire, education is positively associated with body mass index but this effect largely disappears after controlling for household resources (except for urban women).[55]

Finally, there is abundant evidence that child schooling outcomes, in particular years of schooling attainment and current school enrollment are positively correlated with the education of the parents.[56] Again, this result is robust to the inclusion of household and community resources.

Despite the use in many of these studies of numerous controls for family

[53] Earlier studies of infant feeding, like earlier studies of health outcomes, suffer from many endogenous variables being used without instrumentation. For instance, in their multinomial logit analysis of infant feeding practices, Akin, Griffin, Guilkey and Popkin (1986) include labor force participation, use of child care, knowledge of health practices (which is likely to be related to use of health facilities) and several fertility related covariates such as contraceptive use.

[54] See also Wolfe and Behrman, (1984) and Pitt and Rosenzweig (1985).

[55] Thomas, Lavy and Strauss (1992); see Alderman (1990b) for evidence on women in Ghana.

[56] See, for example, DeTray (1988), King and Lillard (1987), Lillard and Willis (1993) and Pong (1992) for Malaysia, Deolalikar (1992) for Indonesia, Birdsall (1985), Harbison and Hanushek (1992), Barros and Lam (1994) for Brazil, King and Bellew (1991) for Peru, Rosenzweig and Wolpin (1982) for India, Hossain (1989) for Bangladesh, Parish and Willis (1993) for Taiwan, Behrman and Sussangkarn (1990) for Thailand.

background, resource availability and community infrastructure, there may still be important unobservables which confound a true education effect. This has been explored with both fixed effects and explicit modeling of the heterogeneity. Wolfe and Behrman (1987), Horton (1988), Behrman and Wolfe (1989) and Strauss (1990) use family or household fixed effects estimators of child or adult health, while Lillard and Willis (1993) model the unobserved components of the correlations between parents' and children's education in a child schooling equation.

Wolfe and Behrman and Behrman and Wolfe, using data from Nicaragua, exploit the fact that they have data on outcomes of sisters and their children so that they are able to remove a sister (or family) fixed effect for both child (Wolfe and Behrman) and adult (Behrman and Wolfe) health. The survey includes half-sisters as well as biological sisters, allowing the effects of parental characteristics to be explored, even using fixed effects. The authors find that controlling for these sister effects, the significant influence of parental education disappears on child health outcomes.[57] However, fixed effects removes much of the variation in the data and indeed very few variables come close to significance; for the case of child height none is significant.[58] Of the few coefficients that are significant, several measure characteristics of the sister's background. This raises a question because only 1/6 of the adult sisters are half-siblings, who may have different background characteristics – a relatively small group on which to estimate these effects. The same potential problems affect the adult health "fixed effects" estimates of Behrman and Wolfe.

Horton and Strauss use household-level fixed effects estimators of child height and weight given height for children in Bicol, the Philippines, and rural Côte d'Ivoire respectively. Strauss tests explicitly for correlation between unobserved household fixed effects and observed covariates, using a Wu-Hausman test of a random effects against a fixed effects specification. He does not find evidence for correlation of parental education with unobservables, but does for household composition variables.[59] In Côte d'Ivoire, extended family members living together allows one to estimate effects of parental education while using household-level fixed effects. Although variation is lost, Strauss still finds positive parental education effects on weight given height.

The potential difficulties of fixed effects estimators can be overcome at the cost of modeling how observables and unobservables are related. This is the approach taken by Lillard and Willis (1993) in their paper on child schooling attainment in Malaysia. Lillard and Willis use a sequential probit model to

---

[57] But not for two inputs, intakes of nutrients or whether children are being breastfed.

[58] In their Table 1, Wolfe and Behrman show that not all variation is removed, but that it is reduced by roughly 40 percent for child height.

[59] These include whether extended family members are living in the same household or whether the head has multiple wives.

analyze the progression of schooling enrollment for an individual. They define levels of schooling and model the probability of achieving the first level of schooling, followed by conditional probabilities of continuing to the next level. By using an open interval for children still enrolled, they allow for incomplete schooling.[60] They allow each child to have a time-invariant heterogeneity component, which allows for correlation of unobservables across equations for the different levels of educational attainment. Time-dated information on covariates allows them to identify and estimate the sequence of schooling decisions.[61] In some of their models they also allow for errors on the years of mother's and father's education, decomposing them into time-invariant and time-varying components. They then allow the time-invariant components to be correlated across parents and between parents and children, which explicitly allows for unobserved family heterogeneity. Joint normality is assumed and the errors are integrated out of the likelihood function. In addition to parents' schooling, these specifications allow for a variety of observed family background characteristics including father's occupation and characteristics of the house during the relevant schooling period (from retrospective data). Lillard and Willis find that the parental education coefficients fall by roughly 30 percent, but remain significantly positive, when unobserved family-level heterogeneity is added to the model. A correlation of between 0.2 and 0.3 is found between the parents' and children's random effects.

3.3.2. Pathways of influence

Taking all the results together, we interpret the evidence on child health and schooling outcomes as indicating that while part of the measured education effect can be attributed to family background, community and other confounding factors, an important positive effect remains after these are taken into account to the extent possible with available data. This raises the question of how education affects these outcomes and this is the issue to which we now turn.

Following T.W. Schultz (1964) and Welch (1970) economists have usually posited that education affects human capital outcomes by raising the technical efficiency with which inputs are used or by increasing the allocative efficiency of input use. The latter effect is usually hypothesized to be paramount, particularly during periods of rapid technological change, when past routine experience may no longer be a good guide [T.W. Schultz (1964, 1975)].

---

[60] King and Lillard (1987) use an ordered probit specification to model completed education of Malaysian children. They therefore assume that the coefficients of covariates are identical for each stage of education, an assumption which is also implicit in the more typical OLS formulation, which ignores the incompleteness of schooling.

[61] This approach is essentially a discrete-time hazard model.

Reduced form (and conditional) estimates typically reflect the influence of both allocative and technical efficiency. Nevertheless, it is possible to learn something about the role of allocative efficiency from examining the determinants of input demands which are discussed in more detail in Section 4, below.

Taking an example from the child health literature, the Cebu Study Team (1991) traces through the effect of maternal education on the incidence of diarrhea among children from birth to 1 year. Their specification of the production function treats feeding practices, health service use and certain health practices such as use of soap and poor excreta disposal as endogenous and allows the technology to differ by age of the infant. They report that maternal education has a positive effect on levels of excreta disposal and on the amount of non-breastmilk calories given to the child which are, in turn, negatively associated with the incidence of diarrhea. Offsetting these effects, education has a negative effect on breastfeeding, especially exclusive breastfeeding which has a strong negative impact on diarrheal incidence.[62] On balance, the net effect of maternal education is to lower diarrheal incidence as indicated by reduced form estimates which show that a one-year increase in maternal education lowers diarrheal incidence by 5 percent.

Estimates of human capital production and input demand functions can provide insights into understanding the pathways of influence as mediated by endogenous covariates such as input choices. They do not, however, fully address the deeper questions of *how* education affects these investments. We cannot assess, for example, how much of the effect is working through increased income, how much through better processing of information and how much through changing preferences. Some useful hints regarding these sorts of pathways can be gleaned from reduced form and conditional function results.

In a reduced form model with no measures of household resources, part of the effect of education will surely reflect the role of income. But, as discussed above, the weight of the evidence in the child health and schooling literature indicates that parental, and especially maternal, education effects persist even after controlling for resources. This is true not only when resources are measured by current income (in which case education may reflect the role of permanent or long-run income) but also with a series of measures of correlates of permanent income.[63]

Thomas, Strauss and Henriques (1990) explicitly examine the extent to

---

[62] Guilkey and Stewart (1994) provide a more detailed analysis of infant feeding determinants using the Cebu data.

[63] Studies have conditioned on predicted household expenditure, predicted total household income, income excluding the mother's contribution (non-mother income), or assets and still tend to find that the effect of mother's education remains. Other studies have controlled for father's or husband's education (which may have more than income effects) and find the same.

which the effect of parental education on child height and survival is picking up the impact of household resources. Using data from Brazil, they begin with a baseline specification that excludes all household resources, first add household non-labor income and then add instrumented per capita household expenditure. The magnitudes of the maternal education effects on child height do not decline as nonlabor income is added and in general decline only slightly when the expenditure variable is used instead.[64] In their child survival regressions more of the maternal education effect comes through income, as evidenced by declines of between 1/4 and 1/3 in the maternal education coefficients, yet mother's education remains highly significant, positively affecting child survival. While part of the effect of father's education does operate through income, with up to declines of 30 percent when instrumented household expenditure is added, its effect remains on both child height and on child survival. Similar results are reported using a different dataset from the Brazilian Northeast in Thomas, Strauss and Henriques (1991). This strongly suggests that, in Brazil at least, the effect of both parents' education operates over and above an income effect. This is consistent with both parents playing an active role in the production of child health.

More education may also be related to the quantity and quality of public services available to the household. Thomas, Strauss and Henriques (1991) and Behrman, Ii and Murillo (1993) find the impact of parental education on child height and child schooling outcomes, respectively,[65] to fall once community infrastructure or community dummy variables are controlled. Yet significant parental education effects remain in both studies.

If education enables people to process information better and if this leads to improvements in both technical and allocative efficiency, then education should condition the effect of community infrastructure on child investments. The impact of community resources on these outcomes is discussed more fully below; for now, additional insights into the role of parental education may be revealed by examining the interaction between education and constraints at the community level in reduced form output or input demand models. Since reduced forms subsume both preferences and technology, care is needed in interpreting the evidence.

Caldwell (1979) hypothesizes and offers some evidence that more educated women are better able to understand information in the media as well as from medical and public health personnel. Thus, he argues, these women benefit more than uneducated women from better infrastructure. Caldwell provides limited evidence that medical personnel spend more time with better educated

---

[64] There is some variation in this result across regions and urban and rural areas, but even the largest decline is only 18 percent.

[65] Behrman, Ii and Murillo examine a variety of schooling outcomes in Bolivia.

patients. In contrast, Rosenzweig and Schultz (1982b) and Schultz (1984) argue that the benefits of health infrastructure and the information provided will be greater for the least educated, which seems plausible if the underlying health messages are easily understood and targeted towards the poorest.

In addition to this "information processing" effect, education-infrastructure interactions may pick up the role of income. A positive interaction may arise, for example, if higher income (or better educated) households are the only ones that actually use local services. Also, if quality of infrastructure or services is not observed (or heterogeneous) and the better educated enjoy better quality services then, once again, we would expect a positive education interaction. Clearly, the magnitude and sign of these interactions is an empirical issue; it is also one on which there is no clear consensus.

Several studies indicate that, in terms of child mortality and anthropometry, the least educated benefit most from the availability of community health infrastructure such as doctors, clinics and hospitals,[66] although this is by no means a universal finding.[67] While the evidence may suggest that infrastructure is a "substitute" for maternal education, the interpretation is not straight-forward. Availability is frequently interpreted as indicative of price [Acton (1975)], in which case the evidence is consistent with the finding that lower income households are more price responsive [Gertler, Locay and Sanderson (1987), Gertler and van der Gaag (1990)]. That is, if the effective price of health care is lowered (by increasing availability), then the probability that the poor use these services will be increased.

The evidence on interactions between education and community sanitation is similarly ambiguous. There is no clear pattern in the relationship between child health and modern water sources as we move along the education distribution.[68] But having modern toilets in the community tends to have a greater impact on child health if the mother is better educated.[69] It seems likely that this reflects an income-quality effect rather than the role of information processing.

---

[66] Rosenzweig and Schultz (1982b) use census data on mortality in Colombia. Rosenzweig and Wolpin (1988b) examine child weight for height in Colombia. Thomas, Strauss and Henriques (1991) and Thomas, Lavy and Strauss (1992) look at child height in Brazil and Côte d'Ivoire, respectively.

[67] Pitt, Rosenzweig and Gibbons (1993) and Frankenberg (1994) find no significant interactions between female education and measures of the availability of health, schooling or family planning programs on child mortality in Indonesia. In Bicol, Philippines, Barrera (1990a) reports a positive interaction. Similarly ambiguous results are reported in the education literature.

[68] In terms of child height, children of mothers with little education benefit most from piped water in Bicol, Philippines [Barrera, (1990a)]. In Malaysia, the reverse is true for child mortality [Esrey and Habicht (1988)]. But in Brazil, there are no interactive effects between maternal education and water supply on child height [Thomas, Strauss and Henriques (1991), Thomas and Strauss (1992a)].

[69] Barrera (1990a), Thomas, Strauss and Henriques (1991) and Thomas and Strauss (1992a).

Food intake is an important component of child nutrition and there is some evidence that maternal education helps to mitigate the deleterious effects of higher food price variation on child health. Thomas and Strauss (1992a) find that while higher prices of both dairy products and sugar negatively affect child height in Brazil, the impact is smallest for children whose mothers have some education. Since the authors also find that higher income households are *more* responsive to variation in (most) prices (including sugar), this suggests that the price-education interaction does not reflect the role of income. Similar, if weaker, results are reported for weight for height in Côte d'Ivoire [Thomas, Lavy, Strauss (1992)].

Another way to examine the impact of parental education on child health is to stratify the sample on child age. It is argued in Section 4 that child health production functions differ by age, in which case the reduced form parameters should also vary by age. It is usually argued that the period from 6 to 24 months is especially critical because of weaning and the introduction of non-breastmilk liquid and solid nutrients. Barrera hypothesizes that the impact of maternal education on child height or weight should be enhanced during this critical child age if education is playing an information processing role. When he stratifies his sample by child age, he finds evidence consistent with the conjecture: mother's education coefficient is almost 2.5 times greater for 0 to 24 month olds than for 11 to 15 year olds. Thomas, Strauss and Henriques (1990) find the same pattern: maternal education has a larger positive impact on heights of children age 6 to 23 months than on children age 5 to 9 years.

A different cut at the information role of maternal education is taken by Preston and Haines (1991), who compare determinants of child mortality at the turn of the 19th century in the United States with developing countries today. Using data from the 1890 U.S. census, as well as selected other data, Preston and Haines estimate a fairly small female education differential in child mortality in the United States at the turn of the 19th century. They also report only a small advantage for children whose fathers worked in professional classes relative to other occupations, which is in sharp contrast to the situation in developing countries today. They argue that given the rudimentary state of medical knowledge at the turn of the century, there was little opportunity for education to play an informational role; this is much like T.W. Schultz's argument regarding low returns to education in areas having traditional agriculture.[70]

Thomas, Strauss and Henriques (1991) attempt to provide additional direct evidence concerning the informational role of education. The Demographic and Health Survey in Brazil (and other countries) contains information on whether an individual regularly listens to the radio, watches television or reads

---

[70] Low quality of schooling is an alternative, though not mutually exclusive, explanation.

a newspaper. By engaging in these activities, a mother may gather useful health-related information. Since these activities also reflect (observed and unobserved) underlying individual and household heterogeneity, it is inappropriate to treat them as exogenous. The authors adopt an instrumental variables estimator, using as instruments independently collected community data on such factors as whether local communities had access to television, radio or newspapers. Whereas mother's education does affect child height (after controlling for household income and partner education), the impact becomes insignificant when controls for information gathering are also included. But the information variables are jointly significant and positively related to child height in both urban and rural areas. Furthermore, when the information variables are added to a specification with interactions between mother's education and community infrastructure variables, the education interactions are no longer jointly significant but the information, literacy and years of education variables are jointly significant. Reading newspapers appears to have a positive, significant effect on child height in rural areas. This suggests that part of the way in which education modifies community health infrastructure and service availability may be through information acquisition and processing.

3.4. Determinants: *Effects of household resources*

Depending on the data available, different covariates have been used to measure the effect of resources on human capital outcomes. In a static household production model, nonlabor income or assets may be treated as exogenous. But they are endogenous in a dynamic model or when tastes for work are taken into account, are difficult to measure accurately and many households report having none. In the case of child outcomes, household income has been proxied by the earnings of the husband (or father) and treated as exogenous under the assumption that the man's time allocation is not endogenous in human capital investment decisions [Willis (1974)]. This is a convenient but strong assumption and implies both that the father does not participate in the production of child human capital and that household preferences are separable in father and mother leisure. In a reduced form model of child human capital outcomes, total household income is inappropriate if female time allocation is likely to be endogenous; it may, however, be used in a conditional function framework (and treated as endogenous). Since current income is a mixture of long-run and short-run resources, several studies have used household (per capita) expenditure as a proxy for permanent income.

Assumptions about what resources, or resource components, are exogenous are important but seldom tested. An exception is provided by Thomas, Strauss and Henriques (1990) who analyze the impact of per capita expenditure on child height and child survival using the Brazilian ENDEF data. Maintaining that non-labor income is exogenous, they test for the exogeneity of income of all household members other than the mother. Wu-Hausman tests are unable to statistically discriminate between the two sets of instruments when differences in all coefficients are considered but exogeneity of non-mother income is rejected when differences in only the expenditure coefficients are tested. This is important since estimated expenditure effects are quite sensitive to the choice of instruments in both child height and survival regressions: they are zero when only nonlabor income is used, but positive and significant with non-mother income. In contrast, using a different data set, the Brazilian Demographic and Health Survey, Thomas, Strauss and Henriques (1991) maintain land owned is exogenous for instrumenting total household income and are unable to reject exogeneity of nonlabor income. Then, maintaining nonlabor income as exogenous, they are unable to reject exogeneity of non-mother income.

There is some evidence that stock measures of child health (e.g. height) are positively affected by measures of long-run resources.[71] While these effects are significant, their magnitudes are typically fairly small. Shorter run measures of income typically have an even weaker impact on stocks of child health. In contrast, shorter-run measures of health (e.g. weight given height) are more responsive to current income but not to permanent income.[72] However, these results are far from universal[73] and the fact that there are mixed empirical results regarding the effects on human capital outcomes of resources should not be a surprise given the difficulties in their measurement.

Part of the effect of income may reflect the fact that households with higher income tend to live in less crowded areas with better hygiene, cleaner water, and better health care services. It is of interest, therefore, to see how the effect of income varies as one adds controls for these community covariates. Thomas, Strauss and Henriques (1991) find that doing so reduces the effect on child height of per capita household income by over half and it becomes insignificant. Behrman, Ii and Murillo, (1990) however, do not find household

---

[71] For instance, Horton (1986) reports a positive influence of land owned on child height in Bicol Province, Philippines and per capita household expenditure is found to be positively related to height by Thomas, Strauss and Henriques (1990) for Brazil, Sahn (1990) and Thomas, Lavy and Strauss (1992) for urban Côte d'Ivoire. Thomas, Strauss and Henriques (1991) find that predicted per capita household income positively influences child height in northeast Brazil.

[72] As examples, Wolfe and Behrman (1987) report a positive effect of current income on weight, but not height, of children in Nicaragua. Thomas, Strauss and Henriques (1989) find that current non-mother's earned income has a larger effect on weight for height than on height. Barrera finds that current non-mother income has no effect on child height.

[73] Strauss (1990) finds that measures of longer run household assets, such as land, has a significant impact on weight for height, but not on height, in rural Côte d'Ivoire.

income coefficients change when community fixed effects are added to their schooling demand equations for Bolivia.

Furthermore, other human capital outcomes show different levels of responsiveness to different definitions of income. Infant and child mortality has been found to respond to current household income (uninstrumented) in Nigeria, Sri Lanka and Thailand by Mensch, Lentzner and Preston (1985), while for other countries they find that father's occupation has an independent, measurable impact. Likewise, Casterline, Cooksey and Ismail (1989) find that household income, treated as exogenous, helps to predict child (though not infant) mortality even when controls include a number of community sanitation and water quality covariates. Thomas, Strauss and Henriques (1990) find a strong, positive impact of predicted household expenditure on child mortality, a much stronger effect than they find on child height.

In an analysis of adult health, Strauss, Gertler, Rahman and Fox (1993) find that measures of general health and physical functioning (which are stock measures) do not respond to per capita household expenditure provided expenditure is treated as endogenous to adult health.[74] Since measures of physical functioning reflect health inputs over a long period, it is certainly possible that current household expenditure (even predicted from long-run covariates) may not reflect well initial period wealth or discounted life-cycle income. An adult health measure which is more susceptible to short-run fluctuations is body mass index. Thomas, Lavy and Strauss (1992) find a nonlinear, positive relationship between predicted household expenditure and BMI of men and women in Côte d'Ivoire.

In a pure investment model of schooling, income should have no effect on schooling if the interest rate faced by the household is independent of income, [Becker and Tomes (1979)].[75] But measures of current income are often found to have positive effects on educational outcomes including current enrollments and years of completed schooling. This suggests that either household income affects access to credit access (or interest rates) or that schooling has consumption returns. For example, DeTray (1988) and King and Lillard (1987) find higher current (unpredicted) total household income raises enrollment rates and years of completed schooling in Malaysia. Levison (1991) finds the same for enrollments in Brazil as does Deolalikar (1993), using current nonlabor income, in Indonesia. Asset measures also have positive effects on schooling decisions as shown by King and Lillard (using the value of land owned) in Bicol Province, Philippines and King and Bellew (1991) (using

---

[74] Instruments include characteristics of the senior male and senior female in the household.

[75] In the strong version of Becker and Tomes's (1979) efficient schooling model parents invest in their children's schooling by equating expected marginal value products of schooling with resource costs.

housing characteristics) in Peru. Gertler and Glewwe (1990) report that income affects the choice of public or private school in Peru.

3.5. Determinants: Effects of community resources

In addition to education and resources, considerable attention has been paid to the effects of community-level influences. These include infrastructure, such as water and sanitation quality; measures related to price and quality of health, education and family planning facilities; and prices of other health or education inputs such as foods (also see Jimenez, this volume, and the discussion above).

Often interest is focussed on a particular policy or set of policies, such as a specific health intervention or a structural adjustment program; frequently these policies can only be time-dated, rather than quantified, and so inference is based on changes that occur simultaneously. These sorts of before-and-after comparisons have been a source of many so-called "natural experiments" in the U.S. health, education and labor literatures and they have been widely used by epidemiologists studying health interventions in developing countries.

3.5.1. Measurement issues

An issue that warrants careful thought is the level at which infrastructure or prices are measured. For infrastructure, there may be a relevant distinction between household use and community availability. Use of different infrastructure, such as good quality water, sanitation or the local health facility, is likely to depend on household resources (including education) and will often be related to unobserved characteristics (such as tastes); their use may, therefore, be endogenous in human capital investment decisions. Likewise, prices measured as unit costs from household expenditure data may be endogenous if prices reflect quality variation, which responds to factors such as income [Deaton (1988)]. However, availability or prices, measured at the community level, may be thought of as a constraint, in which case they could be treated as exogenous and may be preferred.[76]

The definition of "community" is seldom clear and is often driven by data. Many studies attempt to measure variables at the local community level, often using data collected independently from the household. At other times household data are aggregated to the community-level. How problematic this is will depend on local community sample sizes. Sample sizes of ten or fifteen

---

[76] If programs are placed purposively, or if there is migration to a location because of its amenities and infrastructure, then community characteristics will be endogenous. This caveat is potentially important and will be taken up below.

households within a sampling unit, which is not unusual, are worrisome as a basis for aggregation.

As an example, Thomas, Lavy and Strauss (1992) use independently collected community data at the village level for rural areas in Côte d'Ivoire, while for urban areas they aggregate local areas within a city on the assumption that travel opportunities within cities are much better than between rural villages. Thomas and Strauss (1992a) form regional food price indices at a more aggregate level (urban and rural areas within a Brazilian state). While this may be a larger than optimal geographic distinction, prices are based on household unit cost data and although there are some 55,000 households in the survey, smaller geographical units would result in small cell sizes in the calculation of commodity-specific prices for infrequently purchased goods.

Health prices provide a different example. Since user fees for medical facilities, schools, or family planning clinics often either do not exist or are very small, the opportunity cost of time may be a large fraction of the full price. Measures of service availability have therefore been used as covariates. These include distance or travel time to the nearest facility of a particular type, or the number of facilities or staff (e.g. doctors). If people travel beyond the nearest facility because there are important quality differences, then local measures of availability are not appropriate and the notion of "community" will have been defined too narrowly.

Estimated impacts of service availability or prices can be biased if service quality is not also measured. For instance, if a higher price is associated with better quality, then it is likely that estimated price responses will be understated. Few surveys measure aspects of infrastructure quality, though that is beginning to change. Sometimes density measures, such as number of local doctors per capita in the community, will pick up very crude dimensions of quality.

However, quality or even availability measures may be quite inaccurate depending on the source. Thomas, Lavy and Strauss (1992) use a special health facility survey conducted as part of the LSS in Côte d'Ivoire. Two measures of staffing are available: the numbers that are listed in official records and the number who had been present in the 24 hours preceding the interview.[77] The authors show that using the actual number of doctors present in a reduced form equation for child height results in a positive, significant effect on child height, whereas using the number on the books indicates no impact. They argue that it is likely the difference stems from measurement error, and failure to take this into account may lead to incorrect inferences about the efficacy of public policies.

---

[77] In some countries the number of staff present on the interview date would be misleading because some staff are on outreach missions.

A somewhat different problem involves the timing of measurement. Most commonly, measures of service availability or quality are recorded as of the survey date and matched to past events. Sometimes the events are recent, such as analyzing anthropometrics for pre-school aged children [e.g. Thomas and Strauss (1992a)] but in many cases the outcomes reflect investments over many years prior to the survey, as in the case of adult health. In a few instances data on past availability or quality can be matched to the relevant time for the event. Examples are provided by DaVanzo and Habicht (1986) and DaVanzo (1988), who use the Malaysian Family Life Survey, which enables matching of retrospective data on water and sanitation quality to past mortality events. But, even in this case there may be lagged effects, so that matching past infrastructure with concurrent outcomes could still miss part of the impact.

A difficult modeling issue stems from the existence of many potential community influences, ranging from prices to the underlying disease environment, to water and sanitation quality, to the availability and quality of health, education and family planning facilities. This may present both an omitted variables and a degrees of freedom problem. It is hard to account for all the potential influences: even those that are probably important often constitute a long list. Moreover, many of these influences may move together over time and be highly spatially correlated as well. Disentangling their effects is not easy. If there are only a few local areas represented in the data, fewer community variables can be controlled. In addition, many community characteristics may be correlated with income; if income is not properly controlled, some income effects may be incorrectly attributed to community factors. All of these issues associated with measurement, along with potential problems involving systematic program placement and selective household migration (both of which are discussed below), call for caution in the interpretation of reduced form estimates of program effects. Next, we review some of the empirical evidence.

3.5.2. Selected results

Schultz (1973), Rosenzweig and Evenson (1977), Rosenzweig (1982), Rosenzweig and Schultz (1982b) and Rosenzweig and Wolpin (1982) provide early attempts to measure the reduced form impacts of community factors on human capital outcomes. The Schultz study focuses on the impact of family planning programs on fertility outcomes, the Rosenzweig and Schultz, and Rosenzweig and Wolpin studies try to quantify effects of one type of program, such as family planning, on other outcomes, such as child mortality, while the Rosenzweig and Evenson and Rosenzweig studies examine the impact of community level child and adult wages on fertility and child schooling. Measuring cross-price and program effects is potentially important; subsequent studies have focused on the effects of wages, food prices and three types of programs: health, schooling and family planning, on child health, schooling and fertility outcomes.

Rosenzweig (1982, 1990) considers a rather different kind of program, namely one designed to raise agricultural productivity. He investigates, for India, the hypothesis of T.W. Schultz (1975) that technological progress should raise the return to schooling, resulting in more human capital investment and concomitant declines in the numbers of children. Market returns to primary schooling are indeed found to be higher in areas in which the government carried out agricultural intensification activities, and school enrollments are found to be higher and fertility lower for farm households in those areas. As Rosenzweig notes, however, these agricultural programs were placed in better agro-climatically endowed areas, thus confounding interpretation of results. This issue, which affects the entire program evaluation literature, is dealt with more fully in Section 3.6.

It is difficult to draw general conclusions about the impact of health infrastructure on health outcomes. On one hand, several studies indicate that child health and infrastructure are positively correlated. For example, Rosenzweig and Schultz (1982b) show that more health clinics per population are associated with lowered child mortality and fertility in rural Colombia, but not in urban areas. Rosenzweig and Wolpin (1982) and Hossain (1989) show a negative relationship between clinics per capita and child mortality in India and Bangladesh respectively, also using density measures. Thomas, Strauss and Henriques (1991) find that health facilities with specialists are associated with taller children in the urban northeast of Brazil, but not in rural areas. Thomas, Lavy and Strauss (1992) show a positive relationship between doctors and child height in urban Côte d'Ivoire, and Deolalikar (1992) finds a positive relation between health expenditures per capita and child weight among low income households in Indonesia.[78] But there are also some studies that suggest more health infrastructure is associated with worse health outcomes. For example, Rosenzweig and Wolpin find that health facilities other than hospitals and clinics are associated with higher child mortality, and both Thomas and Strauss and Thomas, Lavy and Strauss show similar relationships between nurses per capita and child height in Brazil and Côte d'Ivoire respectively.

Distance measures of health service availability show less of a pattern with health outcomes; for instance Strauss (1990) shows that distance to facilities are orthogonal to child height or weight for height in rural Côte d'Ivoire, while Barrera (1990a) shows the expected inverse relationship in Bicol Province,

---

[78] Children of middle and high income households exhibit no such relationship.

Philippines. Distances are particularly difficult for respondents to measure accurately, and thus may suffer from random measurement error.

A growing literature relates distance or time traveled to health facilities to utilization of curative care and choice of type of provider.[79] Because of multiple potential providers, multinomial logit or conditional logit analysis has been used. Consistent with results in industrial economies [Manning et al. (1987)], the evidence indicates that price of care does affect demand, but, in developing countries, lower income households tend to be more price responsive [e.g. Gertler, Locay and Sanderson (1987), Alderman and Gertler (1989), Mwabu (1989), Gertler and van der Gaag (1990)]. Akin, Griffin, Guilkey and Popkin (1986), however, find no impact of price on demand but they do not consider interactions between prices and household resources.[80]

Having a price-expenditure interaction ensures that when differences are constructed in the utilities, conditional on choice of each potential provider (to examine under which provider, utility will be highest), expenditure will not be differenced out.[81] This allows estimation of an income effect. If this effect is linear, however, then it will be differenced out except in the case that income effects vary by the choice of provider. Gertler et al. [also see Gertler and van der Gaag (1990)] argue that this implies two alternatives which provide the same health improvement and the same nonhealth consumption will provide, in general, different levels of utility and, thus, may give rise to inconsistent

---

[79] Choice of schools has also been considered, e.g. Gertler and Glewwe (1990).

[80] A weakness in models of curative health care demand has to do with the treatment of illness. These models restrict their samples to persons reporting an illness; thus, at best, the estimated responses of income, prices or education are conditional on being ill. In some ways, this makes good sense. One might expect, for example, that education or income would be associated with a lower probability of being ill (ignoring reporting bias), but, conditional on being ill, the better educated may be more likely to seek care from private physicians. This may occur because of shorter waiting times at private physicians' offices and the better educated have a higher value of time; or, it may be that private care is of higher quality and demand for quality is responsive to income. In addition to these conditional models, estimates from unconditional demand functions would also be of interest since education, income and prices are likely to be associated with the conditioning variables, health outcomes. However, inferring unconditional demands from conditional demands is not straightforward as there exist good reasons to believe illness is endogenous in this process.

[81] Gertler, Locay and Sanderson define non-health consumption to be household expenditures net of the cost of obtaining care, where cost is defined as the per visit full price (including the value of travel and waiting time). In this way, non-health expenditure is made to differ by provider. The conditional utility is then allowed to have a quadratic term in non-health consumption, which creates an interaction between household expenditure and visit price. Comparisons are made across the conditional utilities, including the utility from not seeking care, and the outcome with the greatest value is chosen. There exist other ways to include nonlinearities in non-health expenditures, for instance by allowing for nonadditivity between health and non-health consumption in the conditional utility functions.

orderings. Testing whether income effects do differ by choice of provider is, thus, one way of testing the adequacy of the underlying specification.[82]

Availability of schooling infrastructure has been shown to have positive impacts on schooling completed or enrollments by Birdsall (1985) in urban Brazil, DeTray (1988) and Lillard and Willis (1994) in Malaysia, Alderman et al. (1993) in Pakistan and Hossain (1989) in Bangladesh.[83] For instance, Alderman, et al. show a large effect of availability of local schools for girls on female educational attainment in rural Pakistan (where schools are segregated by gender). Likewise, Lillard and Willis show that the presence of Chinese language schools has a large impact on schooling completion of Chinese in Malaysia. It may be, however, that schools for girls or local language schools for Chinese are located in areas where there is demand for these services. This would confound interpretation of the results (see below).[84]

Family planning programs have also been found to be correlated with lower fertility in some cases [Schultz (1973, 1992), Rosenzweig and Schultz (1982b), Rosenzweig and Wolpin (1982), Hossain (1989)]. In addition, cross-program effects have been found of family planning on child mortality [Rosenzweig and Wolpin, Hossain].

As noted above, estimates of service availability are likely to be biased if quality dimensions are not also taken into account. It is only recently that data on quality of health facilities or schools have begun to be collected and analyzed. Data on water and sanitation quality have been more frequently analyzed and are discussed below. Birdsall (1985) uses census data to compute mean education of teachers within local areas in Brazil. She uses this, plus the income of local teachers per school-aged population (as a measure of expenditure per child), in reduced form equations for years of schooling completed for children aged 8–15 and finds significant, positive teacher education effects in rural areas. Since the data on completed years of schooling are drawn from the same census, one has to the assume that the distribution of quality has not

---

[82] One major advantage of estimating the utility functions underlying provider choice is that it is possible, then, to calculate welfare gains and losses from changes in exogenous variables. Much of the focus has been on health care prices [see Jimenez, this volume, for a detailed discussion of social sector pricing policies]. For instance, it is possible to calculate the willingness to pay for having better access to facilities, in the sense of reduced travel time [e.g. Gertler and van der Gaag]. This can be helpful in setting user fees as well as in deciding where to place more facilities. Gertler and van der Gaag find, in rural Côte d'Ivoire and Peru, that setting user fees equal to a level that would recover half of the expected facility costs would likely price households out of the health care market in poor villages, but not in wealthy ones.

[83] Gertler and Glewwe (1990, 1992) show significant effects of availability on the type of secondary school chosen in Peru. However, Rosenzweig and Wolpin fail to find any effect on enrollments in India.

[84] Alderman et al. show that within regions, no correlations exist between school availability and village characteristics, suggesting that, in Pakistan, demand-side influences may be unimportant.

changed over the relevant period. For the younger age-group, 8 to 11 year olds, this is probably a reasonable assumption. As another example, Harbison and Hanushek (1992) find that measures such as having books and writing implements is associated with higher probabilities of grade promotion in the rural northeast of Brazil.

In a health application, Strauss (1990) uses information on the quality of local health infrastructure, as reported in focus group interviews, in his regressions for child height and weight for height in rural Côte d'Ivoire. He finds strong, positive quality effects, particularly of health facilities which have drugs available and are not congested. Using a later round of the LSS in Côte d'Ivoire, plus a special survey of health facilities, Thomas, Lavy and Strauss (1992) find that having antibiotics in stock and providing birth services is associated with higher child heights in urban areas, while availability of quinine-based drugs and of immunization services leads to positive effects in rural areas. The magnitude of the drug availability effect is large; providing drugs where none is available would reduce the height deficit of an Ivorian child relative to a U.S. child by one-third. Similarly, Mwabu, Ainsworth and Nyamete (1993) find significant, positive effects of drug availability on utilization of health care facilities in Kenya.

Estimates of impacts of water and sanitation infrastructure have been more plentiful. Negative, significant effects on child mortality have been found by, among others, Mensch, Lentzner and Preston (1985) using several data sets, by Merrick (1985) in urban Brazil, by Habicht and DaVanzo (1986) and DaVanzo (1988) in Malaysia and by Rosenzweig and Wolpin (1982) in India. Moreover, this evidence is consistent with epidemiological evidence suggesting the importance of clean water and good sanitation on such outcomes as child diarrhea [Esrey, Feachem and Hughes (1985)]. In related evidence, Barrera (1990a) has shown the importance of absence of excreta on child heights (although he does not obtain significant results for water and type of toilet); Strauss (1990) shows that having piped water in rural Côte d'Ivoire is associated with greater height and Thomas and Strauss show that children are taller in urban Brazil in areas that have more buildings with sewerage hookups and electricity. The evidence is not uniform, however, particularly with respect to measures of water [see, for instance, Thomas, Strauss and Henriques, Barrera, Hossain]. In part this may reflect the difficulty in measuring water quality.

A rather different set of community influences are prices. The time-prices of health care facilities have been discussed above. In addition it is of substantial interest to examine the influence of adult and child wages and food prices, since adult and child time and food intake are major human capital inputs. As is the case for income, measuring price effects using a cross-section is tricky because it is difficult to disentangle permanent from transitory movements and because some of the outcomes of interest are flows (which are likely to respond to price fluctuations) but others are stocks (which reflect longer run influences).

Rosenzweig and Evenson (1977) and Rosenzweig (1982, 1990) examine the effects of child, female and male wages on child schooling and fertility in India.[85] These studies find that higher child wages are associated with lower enrollment rates and higher levels of childbearing. Higher female wage rates seem to lower fertility, though this effect is not robust across different samples. Higher male wages have a positive income effect on schooling and thus raise enrollments.

Pitt and Rosenzweig (1986) provide an early study which measures food price impacts on the probability of Indonesian adults reporting an illness. They find few statistically significant results, which, given that the outcome is reported illness of adults, is perhaps not surprising. Behrman and Deolalikar (1989) find positive effects during the lean season of staple prices on child weight for height in the ICRISAT villages,[86] although the impact on nutrient intake is estimated to be negative, which presents a puzzle. Higher sugar and dairy prices are associated with lower child heights in Brazil [Thomas and Strauss (1992a)], whereas in rural Côte d'Ivoire [Thomas, Lavy and Strauss (1993)] and Bicol Province, Philippines [Barrera (1990a)] food prices do not have significant effects on child heights. However, Thomas, Lavy and Strauss (1993) do find significant, negative effects of a broad range of food prices on child weight given height and on adult body mass index in Côte d'Ivoire.

Sometimes it is possible to evaluate a broad policy using time-varying data. Evaluations of Malaysia's New Economic Policy (NEP) are examples [Govindasamy and DaVanzo (1992), Pong (1992), Lillard and Willis, (1994)]. Begun in 1971, the objective of the NEP was to provide economic opportunities for ethnic Malays, albeit at the expense of Chinese and Indian Malays. Laws were passed mandating minimum levels of Malay ownership in businesses; banning instruction in Chinese, English or Tamil; requiring Malay language certification for government employment; and reserving strict quotas at the university level for ethnic Malays. These policies should have had the effect of reducing incentives for Chinese and Indian families to invest in their children's education and perhaps reducing the incentives to have children at all.

Using both waves of the Malaysia Family Life Surveys, Govindasamy and DaVanzo (1992) examine the impact of the NEP on fertility, by ethnic group. They estimate reduced form equations for desired completed fertility capturing the impact of the NEP with a dummy variable equal to one for younger women, who would have potentially been affected by the NEP. They find that,

---

[85] Also see Skoufias (1993b, 1994).
[86] Most of the households are net sellers of the staple, so the net income effect of a price rise is positive.

among Malay women, the NEP is associated with an increase in the desired number of children, net of socio-economic influences; but it is associated with lower numbers of desired children among Chinese and Indians. While the NEP variable is really a measure of cohort-time effects and may therefore reflect other influences, it is reasonable to suppose that it is measuring effects inclusive of the NEP. Consistent with this view are the results of Lillard and Willis (1994) and Pong (1992), who measure effects of the NEP on schooling continuation and attainment of children. Lillard and Willis find, as noted above, a strong effect of the local presence of Chinese language schools on schooling continuation of Chinese. They also find for older cohorts, not exposed to the NEP when their schooling decisions were made, that Malay children are at a disadvantage compared to Chinese and Indian children, while for younger cohorts, this is reversed, especially for transition into secondary and post-secondary schools. The relative advantage of Malays increases as socio-economic variables are added to the model, the opposite pattern from what would be expected if socio-economic differentials were responsible for the ethnic differences.

3.6. Endogenous program placement and selective migration

The estimates of program and pricing impacts just discussed assume that no correlations exist between program variables and unobserved components in the outcome being analyzed. Two sources of such bias have been discussed in the literature: purposive program placement and selective migration.

Some programs may be placed using criteria that are related to the outcomes being studied [Rosenzweig and Wolpin (1986)]. For instance, health clinics may be placed first in less healthy areas. In the absence of perfect measurement of the health environment, clinics will appear to be less effective than they are in reality. Indeed, observing a negative correlation between public health investments (numbers of nurses, say) and health outcomes might be construed as indicating that nurses make people less healthy; but the correlation may, in fact, reflect effective targeting of public investments. The implications of these two interpretations for public health policy are completely different and so it becomes important to understand the mechanisms underlying program placement. This is an area that has been under-explored in the socio-economic literature. Along the same lines, secondary schools may be located in areas with high demand for schooling; without taking account of the reasons for the location of those schools, evaluations will overstate the impact of secondary schools on school enrollments or completion.

Selective migration will also contaminate estimates of program effectiveness if different levels of infrastructure or subsidies across regions attract people with selectively different tastes for the particular service or endowment level [Rosenzweig and Wolpin (1988b), Schultz (1988b)]. For instance, if residential location is related to quality of local schools for families with unobserved higher tastes for education, or an ability to better complement learning in schools, then school effectiveness will be over-rated.

This class of problems has been faced in much of the program evaluation literature (including training, welfare reform, technological innovation and health interventions). The standard solution is to use statistical procedures that mimic the quasi-experimental design of pre- and post-program comparisons for experimental and control groups. That is, one compares *changes* in outcomes across areas with and without a program (policy). This may be accomplished by using individual-level longitudinal data with individual fixed effects [Rosenzweig and Wolpin (1986)], or by aggregating individual-level observations into time series-cross section data and using regional fixed effects [Schultz (1973), Montgomery and Casterline (1993), Pitt, Rosenzweig and Gibbons (1993), Gertler and Molyneaux (1994) and Frankenberg (1995)].[87]

These estimates will be unbiased if the source of individual-level heterogeneity is fixed and so it is swept out by the fixed effect and if other regional characteristics, which may be correlated with the program changes, are not also changing. However, the assumption that all unobserved heterogeneity is swept out by these methods may not be innocuous. There may be interactions between program effectiveness and unobserved community characteristics, such as between a health program and the underlying healthiness of an area. Alternatively, if new programs are located in areas where there is an increase in demand for the service (that is if the source of unobserved heterogeneity is not fixed), then fixed effects estimates will obviously be biased. Similarly, they will be biased if there are changes in other community-level factors that are, in turn, correlated with program changes.[88] Intuitively, examining the impact of changes in programs on outcomes naturally raises questions about what

---

[87] Frankenberg uses a difference-in-difference type estimator as she randomly pairs two children per local area, born in different periods and thus with different program exposure, and examines subsequent survival.

[88] Pitt, Rosenzweig and Gibbons allow for a constant term in their fixed effects estimates, which implies a time trend in the level estimates. They find that inclusion of the constant reduces the significance of program variables. Similarly, Montgomery and Casterline allow for time effects. Clearly, if there is a strong trend component to the program, controlling for time will result in an underestimate of program effectiveness, just as omitting a time variable will result in an overestimate if other factors are trending together. A somewhat different approach would be to examine whether two or more series of program changes are cointegrated and with how many underlying factors. However, this would require a longer time series than is typically available in survey data.

determines those changes and one may suppose that they are even *more* endogenous than levels of services.

In general, survey data do not follow a strict control-experimental group pattern. Instead, spatial variation in the intensity of a program [Schultz; Pitt, Rosenzweig and Gibbons; Frankenberg, Gertler and Molyneaux] or the length of exposure to it [Rosenzweig and Wolpin] is used to identify the program effect. An exception is provided by Foster and Roy (1993), who analyze data from the quasi-experimental family planning program run by the International Center for Diarrheal Disease Research-Bangladesh (ICDDR,B) in the Matlab region. ICDDR,B began a family planning program in 1978 in one part of Matlab, whereas in a contiguous area no such program was initiated.[89] While one might expect program leakages due to diffusion of information, apparently this did not occur on a large-scale. As documented by Foster and Roy and Phillips, et al. (1988), contraceptive rates rose and age-specific fertility rates fell in the experimental area as compared to the control area with both starting from similar levels. What Foster and Roy show is that the family planning program had a major impact on child schooling as well.[90] In the year prior to the program's initiation, schooling completion rates were similar for both areas, whereas twelve years after program initiation, schooling levels for both boys and girls were significantly higher in the treatment area. Moreover, the gender differential in schooling attainment had narrowed considerably in the treatment area, but not in the control area. This estimated program effect survives controls for parental education, owned land, and distance to local schools. It is possible that unmeasured factors differ between the two areas and may contribute to increasing differences in fertility and schooling levels. To check this possibility, Foster and Roy also use mother-level fixed effects and, if anything, find the results to be strengthened.

In most of the studies to date, estimates of program impacts are quite different when individual-level fixed effects are used. However, the pattern is not uniform, which is to be expected since any bias should depend on how programs are distributed, and this is apt to differ across programs and between countries. For instance, Rosenzweig and Wolpin examine changes in standardized child heights and weights over a four year period using data from Laguna Province in the Philippines. They calculate measures of the time

---

[89] A maternal and child health program, including oral rehydration therapy and vaccinations, was later gradually initiated in the experimental area.

[90] Infant mortality rates were not much affected, although child mortality rates were lowered; [see Koenig, Fauveau and Wojtyniak (1991)]. The lowered child mortality rates may have affected both fertility and schooling.

children were exposed to health and family planning programs, using changes in the fraction of life children were exposed as regressors along with child-level fixed effects.[91] The fixed effects results show that exposure to family planning increases growth in both standardized height and weight, in contrast to results based on cross-sectional data, which show insignificant effects.[92] Evidently health programs were placed in areas with less healthy children.[93] Similarly, Montgomery and Casterline find the estimated impact of family planning on fertility in Taiwan to increase three-fold when fixed effects are used; Schultz, using a different and shorter time series, also finds the effectiveness of family planning programs on birth outcomes in Taiwan increases with fixed effects, as do Duraisamy and Malathy (1991) for fertility in India.

On the other hand, Pitt, Rosenzweig and Gibbons demonstrate that negative and significant impacts of family planning clinics on school attendance by young children in Indonesia disappear when a fixed effects procedure is used.[94] However, the impact of availability of local schools remains significantly, positively related to schooling. In child fertility equations, the impacts of schools and family planning clinics also disappear with fixed effects. Gertler and Molyneaux, using somewhat different Indonesian data, also find that school and health clinic availability become insignificant in birth probability models once community-level fixed effects are controlled. They find that measures of family planning intensity do not affect birth probabilities on balance, but do increase the odds of using contraceptives and also lower the age at which women marry; these two effects cancel each other. Frankenberg examines child mortality in Indonesia. She finds that a large effect of having a private toilet, estimated with cross-sectional data, turns insignificant when fixed effects are used but the availability of maternity clinics and doctors become significantly and negatively correlated with child mortality.

As noted by Foster and Roy, the fixed effects estimates may suffer from

---

[91] Rosenzweig and Wolpin aggregate all ages under 18. This combines adolescents with infants, who have distinct growth trajectories. Standardizing on levels, rather than growth rates, is unlikely to correct for this adequately. Indeed, there exist distinct age-profiles in standardized heights and weights [see Martorell and Habicht (1986) or Thomas, Strauss and Henriques (1990)]. Thus, the estimated program exposure effects are also likely to be picking up age effects. Moreover, it is also likely that it matters *when* during childhood the program is experienced, just as the effect of maternal education differs by age of the child [Barrera (1990a), Thomas, Strauss and Henriques (1990)]. Most of the children who have differences in program exposure between the two time periods, measured as a fraction of lifetime, are likely to be older, with a spell of non-exposure early in life.

[92] It is arguable that even fixed effects estimates are inappropriate in this case because of the stock nature of height and weight. A dynamic production function might relate growth (or changes) to levels of current and past inputs and to a child-level unobservable [see Section 4]. In that case, a reduced form in differences will not sweep out child heterogeneity.

[93] This is corroborated by a regression of local health facilities on locally averaged predicted child heights.

[94] The data they use are aggregated to a regional level.

inattention to lag structure, a problem driven by data availability. For instance, Pitt, Rosenzweig and Gibbons relate changes in schooling, fertility and mortality from 1980 to 1985 to program changes from 1980 to 1986. Yet if family planning programs provide information, not just subsidies, and this information diffuses gradually by area, longer lags might be expected. The estimates of Frankenberg and Gertler and Molyneaux may be similarly affected. Schultz accounts for this by cumulating man-months of program exposure over a period of time and relating changes in these stock measures of family planning inputs to changes in children born over a five-year period. This amounts to relating the fertility changes to a cumulative measure of inputs over the same five-year period. Montgomery and Casterline use a dynamic model with lagged fertility levels in the same and nearby districts to examine the possibility of diffusion.[95] Rosenzweig and Wolpin's (1986) results are less susceptible to this difficulty because they are using data on length of exposure, although they do not allow effects to differ depending on when the program was experienced. Foster and Roy, however, are able to allow the impact of the family planning program to differ for different dates of exposure.

Less work has focused on biases from selective migration. Schultz (1988b) shows that urban female migrants in Colombia have fewer children than women of equivalent age and education levels in origin areas, but have more children than like women in the urban destination area. If this behavior is related to possible underlying heterogeneity of the women and not to program effects, then migration selection will bias estimates of program effects. One way to circumvent this problem is to compare program effectiveness among those who are not migrants. Rosenzweig and Wolpin (1988b) pursue this line of reasoning in analyzing weight gains of children in a city in Colombia who were exposed to a program of nurse volunteers. Rosenzweig and Wolpin use child-level fixed effects to purge unobserved heterogeneity which might cause bias in such a comparison.[96] They compare their estimates from the sample of non-migrants to estimates from an inclusive sample and find that program impacts are overestimated for children in high income households, but underestimated for children of low income households.[97]

The general problem in all these models may be cast as one of omitted variables: some studies have shown that the inclusion of additional characteristics can mitigate apparent selectivity bias. For example, Behrman and Birdsall (1983) find the effect of schooling on wages in Brazil is different for migrants relative to non-migrants, indicating there may be migration selection. How-

---

[95] This requires good data on other time- and district-varying covariates. Montgomery and Casterline use information on child mortality rates, local population density, percent of population employed in agriculture and a schooling variable.

[96] The issues of dynamics and age standardization raised above also apply in this case.

[97] Interactions are included between income and program exposure.

ever, when the authors take school quality into account, this difference disappears. Few studies have attempted to include controls for the process underlying program placement although this seems like a natural next step.

On balance it appears that evidence is emerging that systematic program placement can severely bias program evaluations. The evidence on selective migration is more limited. It may be a less severe source of bias than purposive program placement to the extent that the prime motivating forces behind migration are relative wages, spreading income risk or marriage and not programs [see, for instance, Stark (1991)] and to the extent that sources of underlying individual heterogeneity can be measured.

3.7. Sample selectivity: Fertility and mortality selection

Reduced form human capital models are by necessity estimated on samples of the living. It is possible that a woman whose children have very poor health status (possibly having died) may stop having more. If so, those children who were born would be healthier and possibly have more schooling than the set of all children who could have potentially been born. In addition, it is possible that a disproportionately high number of the most frail children will have died prior to the survey. These twin potential problems of fertility and mortality selection may bias estimates from both reduced forms and production functions. For instance, Pitt and Rosenzweig (1989) demonstrate that if the costs of children increase, then if fertility responds positively to the expected human capital endowment of the child, the average endowment of children born in a population should rise. How large a potential problem these selection issues represent has only begun to be investigated. Two major reasons for this are the very strong data requirements[98] and the difficulties in obtaining data on plausible identifying variables for the selection terms.

In their paper, Pitt and Rosenzweig estimate reduced forms for birthweight and for schooling attainment using the Malaysian Family Life Survey and attempt to correct for both fertility and mortality selection. In their birthweight equation they do not have identifying variables and use nonlinearities of the selection functions (which they estimate nonparametrically) for identification. They obtain strong, but not particularly sensible, results. In particular they estimate a *negative* correlation between the probability of having birth and birthweight. This result completely changes the estimated relation between mother's age at birth (from age 20 to 35) and child birthweight, from an upward sloping, concave shape to a U-pattern. It is hard to imagine a plausible

---

[98] Data are needed, for instance, on all potential mothers and their households and on children who died.

explanation for such a pattern, although there are good reasons why an upwards, concave shape might emerge.[99] Pitt and Rosenzweig also estimate schooling demand models. While in one set of models they do have identifying restrictions,[100] they still estimate a negative correlation between the probability of having children and years of schooling attained or expected. Further, their estimate of the correlation coefficient is over 0.99 (in absolute value) with extremely high t-statistics (over 180), which is a good indication that regularity conditions are being violated.[101] Again, the evidence should be treated with caution.

Mortality selection has been investigated by Pitt and Rosenzweig, the Cebu Study Team (1992) and Lee and Rosenzweig (1992). Pitt and Rosenzweig do not find mortality selection to be important in their birthweight equations. The Cebu Study Team uses the prospective data on infant mortality available in the Cebu Longitudinal Health and Nutrition Survey. Given that they are correcting for selectivity in production functions, identifying instruments such as prices are available; however, the sample size (and the corresponding number of infant deaths) is too small to enable meaningful estimates to be obtained. Lee and Rosenzweig correct for mortality selection in the estimation of weight production functions using data from Bangladesh and Bukidnon Province, Philippines. The part of Bangladesh that their data come from is a high mortality environment, while the Philippine data come from a lower mortality area. The authors use semiparametric methods to correct for mortality selection which is identified with prices, household assets and head's characteristics. The production function specifications are very simple, with only current calorie intake, water source and sanitation variables as inputs, stratified for children aged 1 to 6 years and 7 to 14.[102] Even so, they are unable to find significant mortality selection effects.

Based on these attempts it may be that mortality selection is not very important, especially when compared with the many other problems discussed in this chapter. While mortality levels in the Philippine and Malaysian samples are low (under 40 per 1,000 live births) compared to high mortality countries,

---

[99] Younger mothers are more likely to be having their firstborn, whose birthweights tend to be lower.

[100] The authors impose the assumption of efficient income maximization on the part of parents [see Becker and Tomes (1979)], which has the implication that efficient schooling decisions are made based only on relative income payoffs and are independent of parental preferences and resources. Thus, parental income or measures of costs of children should not influence schooling decisions under this model and can serve as instruments.

[101] The correlation should be between 0 and 1; the fact that it is so close to -1 indicates that true convergence of the likelihood may not have been achieved. If that point is indeed the maximum, then there is a different problem: maximum likelihood estimates do not in general retain their well-behaved statistical properties at a boundary.

[102] For children age 1 to 2 years, the form of feeding will still matter, as will disease patterns and many of the other factors discussed in Section 4.

such as in south Asia or sub-Saharan Africa, even analysis using the sample from Bangladesh fails to show an important effect. Likewise, while fertility selection could be troublesome in some cases, based on the evidence to date, it would be imprudent to conclude that it is.

4. Production functions

4.1. Empirical issues in estimation of static production functions

Researchers have been concerned with estimating production functions for a variety of human capital outcomes, including inter alia: child health, education achievement and fertility outcomes. Since Rosenzweig and Schultz (1983), the overriding concern has been with potential biases that arise when there are correlations between input usage and error terms in the production function.[103] As in the reduced form and conditional function literature, the major sources of bias that have been discussed stem from unobserved heterogeneity in the outcomes. Under general conditions, input use will vary with factors known to the household but not to the analyst. For instance, in a production function framework, birthweight is a function of factors such as gestational age; the timing, quantity and quality of prenatal health care; and health-related behaviors of the mother during pregnancy (such as smoking, alcohol consumption, *etc.*). It may be that less healthy mothers are more likely, *conditional on observables such as education*, to seek prenatal care early in pregnancy. If so, any positive effect of early prenatal care will be understated. The sign of the bias will, in general, be indeterminate without knowledge of how input allocations respond to these unobservables.

Paralleling the reduced form literature, instrumental variables and fixed effects estimators have been employed to address this concern. It is, in principle, straightforward to enumerate plausible instruments for production functions. Input and output prices and measures of exogenous resource availability are candidates. In practice, money prices are not observed (or do not exist) for many inputs into health, education or fertility production functions, such as water quality or use of prenatal care. If the time cost of using these inputs is large, then measures of distance (or time) to a health facility are part of the full price of service and may serve to identify the input.[104] Guilkey, Popkin, Akin and Wong (1989) and the Cebu Study Team (1992) provide examples of this approach for estimating birthweight and child weight pro-

---

[103] Also see Schultz (1984), Rosenzweig and Wolpin (1988a), Briscoe, Akin and Guilkey (1990), and the surveys by Behrman and Deolalikar (1988) and Behrman (1990).

[104] This approach assumes, however, that non-random program placement and selective migration are not important.

duction functions. Other service availability measures used include the number of facilities or professional service personnel in an area. For example, Rosenzweig and Schultz analyze birthweight production functions using data on doctors and OB/GYNs per capita and public health expenditures to predict inputs such as timing of prenatal care. Measures of resource availability used as identifying instruments have included education of family members (which imposes the strong assumption that technical efficiency is unrelated to education), assets, non-labor or husband's income.

It is one matter to worry about a potential problem. It is another to show that it matters. In their study of diarrheal incidence in children aged 0 to 2 years in Cebu Province, Philippines, the Cebu Study Team (1991) found the effect of poor excreta disposal to be insignificant when input endogeneity was ignored, but that it was a significant, positive cause of higher diarrheal incidence when endogeneity was controlled using instrumental variables. Similarly, the estimated negative impact of exclusive breastfeeding (as opposed to breastfeeding supplemented with liquid or solid nutrients) increased almost tenfold and became highly significant when endogeneity of inputs was controlled. This evidence, which is not unique, indicates that instrumental variables methods can make a substantial difference in these models.

We have noted several times, however, that, in practice, instrumental variables estimators can be quite fragile, and the production function literature provides many examples of how these methods may perform poorly. It is difficult to measure all the inputs that enter human capital production functions, let alone the quality of these inputs. If omitted inputs, or input quality, are correlated with inputs that are included, or with instruments, then estimates will be biased. For example, better quality inputs may be correlated with household resources. If quality is either not measured or imperfectly captured, then measures of resources are not valid instruments. Similarly, if inputs that cost more are of higher quality, then prices may be correlated with omitted quality, in which case they are also not valid instruments.

A related problem, which has not been given the attention it deserves, is the question of functional form. If the marginal productivity of inputs is not constant, or if there are interactions among inputs, then these omitted higher order moments will be correlated with both endogenous inputs and exogenous constraints. Once again, instruments will not be valid.

For example, the effects on child growth of (supplemented and unsupplemented) breastfeeding are likely to vary with the age of the child. For very small children, unsupplemented breastfeeding will provide strong immunity effects, which wear off as the child ages, particularly past 6 months. On the other hand, a 9 month old who is still being breastfed with no supplementation is likely to not be getting sufficient nutrients for proper growth. Continuing unsupplemented breastfeeding well into infancy may be correlated (negatively) with the mother's education, household resources, or the quality of household water supplies. These characteristics will not be valid instruments if data are pooled across ages. Studies by Barrera (1990b) and the Cebu Study Team (1992) allow for interactions between child age and health inputs in their analyses of child height, weight and diarrheal incidence. Such attention to the underlying biology is, however, unusual in the economics literature.

When instrumental variables fail, many turn to fixed effects. But fixed effects will also be biased if non-linearities are omitted from the model. Indeed, fixed effects are only appropriate when the unobservables are, in fact, fixed. Yet, it seems plausible that the effect of a time-invariant child unobservable on child growth may change as the child ages, as might the effect of observed inputs. This is essentially identical to turning a time-invariant unobservable into a time-varying effect. There are many similar examples of unobservables affecting the production of human capital which are unlikely to be swept out by fixed effects procedures.

Fixed effects approaches may have additional difficulties. To begin with, it is key to difference out at the appropriate level(s) of the underlying heterogeneity. For instance, a mother-level fixed effects will not sweep out errors that vary over time and thus children. These will include all child-specific effects. Rosenzweig and Wolpin (1988a) argue that one might expect child effects to be important and that parents may use information learned about prior-born children in their input allocations for the later-born. They assume there is a time-persistent, child-specific unobservable (such as an innate child health component), known to the household after the child is born, but not before. If so, the household's health decisions concerning a child should also incorporate information learned about the healthiness of prior-born children. Since the error term of an equaton which is differenced across children will contain unobservables from prior-born children, this should be correlated with input decisions for the later-born. Thus, even though the family or mother-specific error components have been swept out, child-specific components can cause a family or mother fixed effects procedure to be inconsistent.

There is a special case in which it is possible to use inputs for the prior-born children as instruments for the difference in inputs between the later- and prior-born. In the case of birthweight, the unobserved characteristics of the later-born are unknown at the time prenatal input decisions are made for the prior-born. Thus the prior-born's prenatal inputs should be uncorrelated with the later-born's *child-specific* errors. However, prenatal inputs used for the prior-born should be correlated with later-born child inputs because many common factors (including mother or household-specific unobservables) affect both.[105] Thus, it is argued by Rosenzweig and Wolpin, inputs for the prior-born

---

[105] In any case inputs of the prior-born will be correlated by construction with the difference in inputs between children.

are appropriate instruments for differences in inputs in a household or mother-level fixed effects procedure. Note, however, that if there are time-varying mother or household effects, then prior-born input allocations will be correlated with the underlying error term. A time-varying error might result from measurement errors in time-varying inputs, such as the quality of prenatal care across different children.

4.2. Empirical issues in estimation of dynamic production functions

Thus far we have been assuming that the production function is static so that current output is a function of only current inputs. However, many human capital variables we are concerned about are stocks, not flows. For instance, many health variables, such as child height or weight or measures of adult physical functioning, are cumulative measures that depend on inputs in past periods and possibly on past health outcomes as well.[106] Indeed, Grossman's (1972) seminal paper on the demand for health treats health as a capital stock, which depends on past values as well as current inputs. Likewise, educational achievement is a cumulative process, depending on prior schooling and prior home inputs [Hanushek (1986)].

Taking child growth in height (or weight) as an example, write a general production function as:

$$H_t = f(H_{t-1}, X_i, X_h, X_c, \mu) \tag{7}$$

where subscript i denotes a child-level, h a household-level and c a community-level covariate and μ represents unobserved heterogeneity. The input vector may include inputs of past periods as well as health, lagged several periods. Substituting out lagged health, then current health is a function of only lagged inputs. Alternatively, one may estimate a growth function like (7) directly. In the special case that lagged health, in this case height, is a sufficient statistic for past inputs, then *current* height would be a function of *lagged* height and *current* period inputs. The data needed to estimate this model are dramatically reduced to only current output and inputs along with output lagged one period. This is the approach used in the Cebu child growth studies [Cebu Study Team (1991, 1992)] and in some of the education production function literature [Harbison and Hanushek (1992), Jimenez, Lockheed and Wattanawaha (1988)].

Introducing dynamics by having the current period outcome depend on past

---

[106] Some outcomes, such as incidence of nonchronic diseases, may be more reasonably treated as flows, although they too might be a function of lagged stocks of other health dimensions. For instance, resistance to particular infectious diseases is often a function of the cumulative exposure to the particular pathogen.

outcomes complicates estimation. If the error in the production function has a time-persistent component then it will be correlated with lagged output even though output is predetermined. Simple fixed effects estimation does not solve the problem because these estimators are inconsistent in the presence of lagged endogenous variables unless the number of time periods is quite large [Nerlove (1971), Nickell (1981)].[107] In principle, lagged exogenous variables are valid instruments for lagged endogenous variables. In the child growth case this might include lagged information on local infrastructure and the economic environment, which is the strategy followed by the Cebu Study Team (1991, 1992) in their estimation of child growth functions.

4.3. Applications to child health

Children's health has been a major focus of the human capital production function literature in development economics. Production functions have been estimated for child height, weight, weight given height, birthweight, gestational age and diarrheal incidence. Special emphasis has been given to the role of food in promoting child health, especially methods of infant and child feeding. The roles of household sanitation and quality of water supply have also been highlighted, as have the roles of timely prenatal care, birth spacing and birth order on birthweight.

4.3.1. Birthweight

Guilkey, Popkin, Akin and Wong (1989) provide an example of a detailed specification of a birthweight production function in a developing country using the Cebu Longitudinal Health and Nutrition Survey. Taking advantage of its extraordinary richness in data on child health, they include a wide range of inputs in their model and treat all those related to maternal health as endogenous.[108] In urban Cebu, they find a positive effect on birthweight of mother's height, gestational age and fat area during pregnancy and a negative

---

[107] Substituting lagged inputs for the lagged outputs will result in the addition of time-invariant heterogeneity terms. Differencing the dynamic production functions written in terms of only lagged inputs does not sweep out these heterogeneity terms, and so fixed effects estimators will be biased.

[108] The inputs include, inter alia, the number of prenatal care visits to private, public and traditional practitioners before 30 weeks of pregnancy, gestational age, time from the end of the prior pregnancy to conception, mother's fat area during the pregnancy, whether the mother smoked, drank alcohol or took vitamins during pregnancy, time engaged in "stressful" activity, age at birth (all of which are endogenous) and maternal height. Arguing that there are quality differences in infrastructure in the rural and urban sector, they stratify the sample. In the rural sample, mother's height is the only significant determinant of birthweight. This may be a reflection of the difficulty in obtaining precise estimates when using instrumental variables with so many endogenous inputs.

impact of the mother being ill just prior to birth. Except for mother's height, these covariates are treated as endogenous, with identifying information coming from household assets, non-mother household income, household size and age composition, education of the mother, prices of basic staples and prices (including cash and the value of travel and waiting times) of prenatal care facilities.

However, Guilkey et al. do not treat birth history variables in a symmetrical way, despite the strong argument that they, too, are outcomes of optimizing behavior. For example, having had a previous child is found to have a strong positive effect on birthweight, but it is treated as exogenous. Likewise, previous conception interval, parity and household composition are treated as exogenous. Incorrectly treating fertility related covariates as exogenous will, in general, contaminate the coefficients of all covariates, including the health variables.

Rosenzweig and Schultz (1987), following their pioneering estimates of birthweight production function for children in the United States [Rosenzweig and Schultz (1983)], estimate birthweight production functions for Malaysian children. They use a family fixed effects procedure with parent's education, husband's income and local community program variables as instruments for the differenced inputs to purge them of correlation with any child-specific heterogeneity. Rosenzweig and Schultz use children of order two or three, and thus restrict their sample to families with at least three children. Rosenzweig and Wolpin (1988a) follow a similar strategy but use families with at least two children. In contrast to the more complete set of inputs used by Guilkey et al., both studies focus on birthspacing and birth order.[109] They use a simple linear specification and do not test for interactive effects, although the biological evidence suggests there is at least one interaction that may be especially important: the birth interval contains two elements, conception interval and gestation length, and their impacts are likely to be very different.[110] [See Guilkey et al. (1989), Miller (1989) and Miller, Trussell, Pebley and Vaughan (1992)].

A disadvantage of the estimation procedure used by Rosenzweig and Schultz and Rosenzweig and Wolpin is that much of the variance is removed from the data, making it harder to detect statistical relationships. It is the *differences* between child birthweight outcomes that is being explained by differences in input allocations. Moreover, by requiring their sample households to have at least two young children, the Rosenzweig and Wolpin sample contains only 238 births; the Rosenzweig and Schultz sample is even smaller. Not surprisingly,

---

[109] Although some of the inputs are differenced away by the fixed effects procedure.
[100] While the Malaysian Family Life Survey does contain retrospective information regarding length of pregnancy, it is not clear how reliable these data are.

the Rosenzweig and Schultz estimates are very noisy, although they do suggest that longer prior birth intervals are associated with greater birthweight. Rosenzweig and Wolpin's estimates are a little more precise and they also find a positive effect of prior birth interval. In addition, they find that children of higher birth order have lower birthweights. This is somewhat surprising since in the medical and epidemiological literature, there is evidence that first borns tend to have lower birthweight than subsequent births. It is possible that birth order is picking up a nonlinearity in mother's age at birth, which is entered linearly in this specification. For instance, if the impact of mother's age is first increasing and then decreasing, birth order may well pick up the decreasing portion. However, with a small sample and much of the variation differenced away, these subtleties are hard to capture.

4.3.2. Child anthropometrics and morbidity

There have been many attempts to model the biology underlying child health measured in terms of both anthropometrics and morbidity. We will focus here on recent work; see Behrman and Deolalikar (1988) for a review of earlier studies.

Using data from Bicol Province, Philippines, Barrera (1990b) examines the effects of breastfeeding on the height of children aged 0 to 2 years. He allows the effect to vary over the child's life and distinguishes supplemented from unsupplemented feeding, both of which are treated as endogenous.[111] This distinction is important since unsupplemented breastfeeding is likely to have a strong beneficial impact when the child is young, especially during the first six months of life when the immunological advantages of breast milk are greatest. However, as the child ages, unsupplemented breastfeeding is unlikely to supply sufficient nutrients. Consistent with this hypothesis, Barrera finds that between four and six months, the effects of unsupplemented feeding are positive and significant but then turn negative. The positive effects persist for a longer period among children of less educated mothers, which may reflect better educated women being more able to offset the potentially deleterious effects of supplementation, for instance by supplying clean water and providing more nutritious supplements.

The Cebu Study Team (1991, 1992) estimate production functions for three different dimensions of child health: weight,[112] diarrheal incidence and respira-

---

[111] The model also includes maternal age, height and schooling, along with household-level food supplies and use of sanitary toilet facilities. The latter two are treated as endogenous with identifying instruments including household income, prices of major foods, local female wages, and local community characteristics having to do with water quality and sanitation.

[112] Rosenzweig and Wolpin (1988a) also estimate child weight production functions, but their data are not nearly as rich as those used by Barrera and the Cebu Study Team.

tory infection. They use the first year of the Cebu Longitudinal Health and Nutrition Survey, which follows infants bimonthly from birth to twelve months. The longitudinal dimension of the data are exploited to estimate dynamic relationships in which lagged health outcomes appear in the production functions. For example, the child weight production function includes lagged child weight, recent (previous week) and lagged incidence of diarrhea and respiratory infection. Likewise, diarrhea incidence is posited to depend on lagged weight. All lags of the health variables, including the initial condition and birthweight, are treated as endogenous to account for the possibility of unobserved heterogeneity. Individual random effects are also incorporated into the estimation, further taking advantage of the longitudinal nature of the data. In these papers, the potentially endogenous fertility-related variables are not included as instruments, making the results more compelling than the birth-weight results discussed above.[113]

As in the birthweight analysis, the input specification is extensive. It includes whether the infant was breastfed during the week prior to the survey and, if so, whether it was exclusive, with non-nutritive nutrients added, or with a nutritive supplement. Calories fed from supplemental foods are included as a separate input. The study finds that, conditional on lagged weight, breastfed children under one year grow faster than non-breastfed children, but that those receiving nutritive supplements grow fastest. Consistent with this is a positive effect on growth of calories fed, although this effect is significant only in urban areas. On the other hand, exclusive breastfeeding is found to significantly lower the probability of having diarrhea in urban, but not rural, areas. One reason for this difference may be that the quality of water is lower in urban areas. For instance, the study finds that water contamination raises the chances of a child contracting diarrhea in urban, but not rural, areas. The negative impacts of water quality and sanitation on diarrhea are also consistent with Barrera's finding from Bicol Province, Philippines, and both are consistent with a large epidemiological literature [e.g. Esrey, Feachem and Hughes (1985)].

In this paper, the production function dynamics indicate that lagged standardized weight is unrelated to the incidence of both diarrheal and respiratory disease. Yet, in the Cebu Study Team's 1991 paper, lagged weight velocity is negatively and significantly related to diarrheal incidence (in urban areas) and this effect dissipates with higher levels of lagged weight. The reason for this contradiction across the two papers is unclear and not addressed by the authors. It seems unlikely that it can be explained by differences in the input

---

[113] Otherwise, the instrument set is similar to that used for the birthweight study. It includes maternal and paternal education levels, non-mother income, household assets, prices of various foods and infant foods, local wages, recent local rainfall, travel times to local health facilities and average prices for prenatal care.

specification (which are very similar) although differences in the instruments (which are not presented) may be the key.

The Cebu Study Team (1991) also traces through the impact of increasing maternal education on the probability of diarrheal incidence which is, on net, negative. Most of the benefits of education operate through better sanitation and increased non-breastfed calories, although there is an important counter-vailing effect because education is associated with a decline in the probability of exclusive breastfeeding. This simulation helps illustrate the usefulness of simultaneously estimating the production functions and input demands.

4.4. Applications to educational achievement

Relative to health, there is less research on estimation of education production functions, and many of the studies that do exist have ignored problems associated with unobserved heterogeneity. There are, in addition, specification issues such as endogeneity of the level of school attainment, whether school choice (if available) is treated as subject to choice and how dynamics are introduced.

4.4.1. School attainment, school choice and sample selection

Being in a particular level or grade of school is surely endogenous and is likely to depend in part on past schooling outcomes (achievement). The type of school chosen, such as private or public, may also reflect past achievement or household resources.[114] Using school-based samples rather than population-based samples runs the risk of introducing significant selection bias. The problem is likely to be more pronounced the more select the sample. For instance, Cox and Jimenez (1990a) analyze reading and math scores for secondary school students in academic tracks in Tanzania. However, only 4 percent of children of secondary school age are enrolled and only one-quarter of those are in the academic track.

Correcting for selection in completed schooling is difficult with most data sets, partly because identifying variables are not usually available. For instance, Harbison and Hanushek (1992) estimate educational production functions for changes in achievement in math and Portuguese for children in the poor Northeast region of Brazil. The longitudinal survey is based on a sample of schools and covers children who were in the second grade at the beginning of the survey and who, two years later, had progressed to the fourth

---

[114] See Cox and Jimenez (1990a) and Jimenez, Lockheed and Wattanawaha (1988) who attempt to control for choice of school type.

grade. In addition to possible selection because not all children in the Northeast are educated through second grade, selection into fourth grade (that is, on-time promotion from second grade conditional on having been in that grade) is unlikely to be random. Harbison and Hanushek recognize the potential for promotion selection and model repetition, using those estimates to correct their achievement score equations. However, they have no information that can identify repetition selection in the achievement equations and so end up using functional form for identification. They find that promotion selection is not significantly related to achievement test scores, but given no identifying instruments, caution may be called for in interpreting this evidence.

A somewhat different example is given by Glewwe and Jacoby (1994), who use the Living Standards Survey from Ghana to estimate production functions for math and reading achievement scores of children enrolled in middle school. Although this survey is household based, selection may be a problem since tests were only given to children who were currently enrolled in school. In Ghana education levels are very low: most children never make it to middle school. For instance, of 1,395 children aged 11 to 20 in the sample, almost 300 never attended any school and only 324 are currently enrolled in middle school. Glewwe and Jacoby attempt to correct for two sources of sample selection: beginning school at a later than normal age and dropping out of school prior to the survey. They use local community average characteristics of primary and middle schools to identify these effects. Since characteristics of the middle school actually attended are used in the test score equations, Glewwe and Jacoby are assuming that primary school characteristics help to determine grade achieved, but not achievement in middle school conditional on middle school characteristics.[115] Test score data from past years are unavailable, although an imputed ability score is used as a proxy. If ability is not a sufficient statistic for past schooling inputs (as it would not be if it measures an attribute unchanged by schooling) then this is a poor assumption. In this case, current scores should be a function of all past inputs, including primary school characteristics. The authors report that selection is not empirically important, although this is surely partly explained by the fact that the primary school variables do a very poor job of explaining years of school attainment: only one of seven primary school variables is significant in the grade attainment equation.

As one more, still different, example, Alderman, Behrman, Khan, Ross and Sabot (1993) use a population-based sample in rural Pakistan to estimate production functions for reading and math scores for a sample of adults aged

---

[115] If there exists variation in school characteristics within communities, use of community averages will also serve to identify the selection terms.

20 to 44. In this survey, tests were administered to all individuals regardless of current schooling status. Yet selection is still an issue because Alderman et al. specify their measures of achievement to be a function of the level of schooling attained, in addition to other inputs. They use distance to local primary and middle schools and the cost of books for identification. These restrictions seem plausible and are significant predictors of school enrollment. Indeed, predicted years of schooling has a powerful influence on test scores, although even in this case, the selection coefficients are not significant.

These examples raise the issue foursquare about whether one should worry about the different types of selection. The answer must depend on whether plausible identifying variables, such as ones measuring availability or prices, are available in the data. However, simply because the data may not support an adequate accounting of selection does not mean that it is not a problem.

4.4.2. Dynamic issues

Two methods have been adopted to account for the fact that schooling test scores represent a stock of knowledge. One approach focuses on the flow by including lagged test scores as covariates and has been adopted by Harbison and Hanushek (1992) and Jimenez, Lockheed and Wattanawaha (1988). In both cases, lagged scores are treated as exogenous (as are all inputs), which seems inappropriate.

A second method includes a measure of aptitude, or innate ability, in the production function. In principle, if this is truly a measure of ability and it does not vary with a child's education, then past as well as current school inputs should be included in the achievement equation. This is a very demanding data requirement, especially in the case of adult achievement [Alderman et al. (1993)]. Glewwe and Jacoby and Alderman et al. have information only on schools *currently* serving the local area and, in the case of Alderman et al., on when schools were introduced into the area. Both studies assume that school characteristics (such as prices or dimensions of quality) have not changed and that there has been no migration. This seems unlikely in view of the growth in school availability and investment in school quality in both countries.

4.4.3. What affects learning in low income countries?

All these studies attempt to assess the impact on education of a wide variety of inputs, particularly on the school side. In their study of fourth grade children in Northeast Brazil, Harbison and Hanushek report rather strong results regarding certain school-related inputs. Indices of a school having writing materials and electricity are associated with higher Portuguese performance (conditional on past achievement) whereas writing materials and an index of school hardware are positively related to math achievement. The authors also find that teacher quality matters; specifically, teachers who are stronger in math have students with higher rates of increase in achievement in both Portuguese and math, while teachers who score better in Portuguese tests have students who show greater improvement in Portuguese.[116] Alderman et al. and Glewwe and Jacoby show that children with more schooling perform better at both math and reading, after accounting for selectivity to the extent possible. Glewwe and Jacoby also find that schools with blackboards and fewer leaking classrooms have children with higher math test scores, while students in schools with more books, fewer leaking classrooms and more usable classrooms achieve higher reading scores. Alderman et al., like Harbison and Hanushek, find teacher quality to be important. Teachers with higher scores on reading and math tests are associated with higher student scores for both reading and math, although this effect disappears when region dummies are added to the specification. They also find that high student-teacher ratios are associated with lower math scores (though not reading), an unusual finding in the test score production function literature [see Hanushek (1986)].[117] These results jointly suggest that improvements in dimensions of school quality that are relatively simple and are taken for granted in high income countries may have a substantial payoff in at least some low income settings.

5. Wages and labor supply

5.1. Introduction

There have been an enormous number of studies that estimate Mincer-type earnings or wage functions with data from developing countries. These studies have almost universally demonstrated that (private) returns to education tend to be high [Psacharopoulos (1973, 1981, 1985, 1989), Colclough (1982)]. A good deal of effort has been put into assessing the extent to which these estimated returns are affected by omitted measures of ability, family background and schooling quality [see the reviews in Schultz (1988a) and Behrman (1990)]. In the industrial country literature the problem of selection into the labor force has been widely discussed for women and there are, at least conceptually, standard methods available to address the concern [Smith (1980), Killingsworth (1983), Killingsworth and Heckman (1986)]. In view of the

[116] One does need to guard against the possibility that students are grouped into classrooms by ability, with high ability students being matched with high ability teachers.
[117] Glewwe and Jacoby control for several household background characteristics, such as education of the parents, their constructed measure of individual ability and predicted household per capita expenditure. Alderman, et al. find family background variables to be insignificant.

prevalence of self-employment in developing countries, self-selection is also potentially important for men. When data from only the wage sector (or formal sector) are used, sectoral choice becomes a serious issue for both men and women [Sumner (1981), Anderson (1982)]. Yet while these factors do affect the magnitudes of estimated returns, even after accounting for them (to the extent possible), it is the case that the estimated returns to education remain high in a preponderant number of studies.

5.2. Data issues: Measurement and sample selection

Since earnings incorporate labor supply decisions, wages are a better measure of labor productivity. Whereas wages in the market sector may also embody elements of signalling, this may be a less serious concern among the self-employed. But self-employment income is very difficult to measure. First, the so-called wage from self-employment includes a return to entrepreneurship, to risk taking and, depending on how self-employment income is measured, to physical capital. Second, many of the self-employed are operating family enterprises, such as family farms, which employs unpaid family labor. Not only is it difficult to value this family labor but it is also not clear how net income should be allocated among family workers. Since self-employment does account for a large fraction of the labor force in many parts of the developing world, this is not just a minor detail.

From a theoretical point of view, it is inappropriate to estimate wage functions without either imputing a shadow wage for those who are not working in the market sector or, alternatively, accounting for the fact that the decision to work for a wage is a choice. The analyst thus needs data not only on those who work (or work in that sector) but also those who do not. This puts a premium on data from household-based surveys. Just as is the case for school-based surveys or clinic-based surveys (see Section 4), establishment survey data (which cannot be linked to household data) are difficult to use reliably in labor market analyses.

The most commonly used method to control for participation or sectoral choice relies on now standard procedures introduced by Heckman (1979). In principle, this involves joint estimation of reduced forms for participation and wages. The sectoral choice/participation decision will depend not only on factors that influence actual wages but also shadow wages.

For the market (or labor force) participation decisions, these factors might include owned assets, such as land, or the income from them (nonlabor income). Since assets will typically depend on previous labor supply, in a dynamic model, they are properly treated as endogenous [Smith (1977)]. Inherited assets, which in some countries would include land owned, remain possible instruments although even they may be correlated with unobserved heterogeneity (such as investments in the individual during childhood).[118] In some regions very few people inherit assets, so that relying on only that information to identify the choice to work is unlikely to be a good empirical strategy; see the discussion in Section 2.

Parental occupation and the occupation of siblings may also be instruments under the assumption that these measures of background have no direct effect on productivity. If one were willing to treat marital status as exogenous, then characteristics of one's spouse or partner (and that person's parents) are potential instruments, as is household composition if fertility were assumed to be exogenous. Exogenous fertility is counter to the spirit of the household model in which it is natural to assume that female labor supply and fertility decisions are jointly determined. One could argue that marital status, too, should be considered as endogenous, or at least correlated with unobserved heterogeneity [Korenman and Neumark (1991, 1992)].

In practice, identifying good instruments is not easy [see Griffin (1987) for a useful discussion]. Problems of identification are compounded when studying income or earnings, rather than wages. Since income incorporates labor supply, all factors that affect labor supply (such as assets and household composition) belong in the income function and so cannot be used as instruments.

If identification of labor force or market work participation is empirically difficult, it is even harder to account for sectoral choice within the market. Within the market work sector, employment in the public sector is sometimes distinguished from private sector employment [Van der Gaag and Vijverberg (1988), Glewwe (1991)]. These distinctions have also been used to "test" hypotheses regarding market segmentation [e.g. Mazumdar (1983)]. However, as Heckman and Hotz (1986) point out in their study of labor markets in Panama, in order to properly test for market segmentation it is key to control for potential selectivity in labor sector allocations. The problem is that the types of exclusion restrictions for identification discussed above are unlikely to be powerful in explaining choices within the market sector, conditional on working there. Thus, many studies have relied on functional form to identify selection.[119]

Comparisons of self-employment and market wage functions have been used

---

[118] For instance, Quisumbing (1991) provides evidence that parents in the Philippines use investments in education for girls to compensate for land inheritances going largely to boys.

[119] Even if sectoral selection were satisfactorily accounted for, finding different coefficients in a wage function is, by itself, not conclusive evidence in favor of segmentation or signalling. The reason is that elements of human capital may have different productivities in alternative uses [Heckman and Sedlacek (1985)]. For instance, education may not be rewarded heavily in simple repetitive tasks such as harvesting sugarcane, whereas strength may be; the opposite may well apply to certain clerical jobs.

to provide insights into the role of signalling in wage determination [Wolpin (1977), Riley (1979)]. Identification in self-employment wage functions, however, is also hard.[120] Self-employment wages depend in general on both preferences and production technology, including prices of outputs and variable inputs as well as quasi-fixed inputs. To be valid instruments, assets need to be measured exclusive of those associated with the business enterprise. More problematic, perhaps, is that household assets must also be uncorrelated with time-invariant individual characteristics, such as entrepreneurship; this seems most unlikely. Furthermore, if the business is a family enterprise, then household composition will not serve as valid instruments.

Self-employment net income is arguably better analyzed in terms of production, cost or profit functions [see, for instance Jamison and Lau (1982), Blau (1985b), Singh, Squire and Strauss (1986), Lopez (1986), Jacoby (1993), Lambert and Magnac (1991), Vijverberg (1991) and Newman and Gertler (1993)]. Indeed if self-employment production and household consumption decisions are not recursive, so that there are possible feedbacks between production and consumption decisions, then net income must be analyzed within a firm-household framework [e.g. Gronau (1973, 1977), Singh, Squire and Strauss (1986), Benjamin (1992)], in which case preferences as well as technology affect input choices and thus net income.

Newman and Gertler (1994) provide an example that simultaneously takes account of sectoral selection while treating self-employment in a restricted (i.e. conditional) profit function framework. Using the Peruvian Living Standards Survey, they extend Lopez (1986), deriving the first order conditions from a farm household model which does not impose recursiveness. Three types of equations are modeled: the marginal rate of substitution between leisure and household consumption, a market wage function and a marginal return to farm work function. The latter is derived from a restricted (conditional on family labor use) farm profit function and is the partial derivative with respect to farm labor of an individual family member. Newman and Gertler model the marginal return to work function holding constant family farm labor, output price, quasi-fixed inputs and human capital-related factors. This marginal return provides an estimate of the shadow wage of an individual's farm labor. If the individual also works off-farm then the shadow wage equals the market wage offer, which is estimated by a standard Mincer-type wage function. The fact that some individuals work off-farm allows Newman and Gertler to estimate the marginal farm returns functions without using farm income

---

[120] For recent examples, see Strauss and Thomas (1994) or Vijverberg (1993).

data.[121] Likewise, the equation of the market wage and the marginal rate of substitution of leisure for income allows estimation of parameters of the marginal rate of substitution function. Allowing for corner solutions, however, greatly raises the econometric complexity.[122]

The family farm labor variables in the farm shadow wage functions are endogenous. They are identified by using demand shifters in the market wage functions, as well as by exogenous taste shifters that belong in the marginal rate of substitution between individual leisure and household consumption. Of course identification is also conditional on strong functional form assumptions for both the restricted farm profit function and the utility function. While in principle, it is plausible to use taste shifter and market wage demand factors as identifying variables for family on-farm labor in the farm shadow wage functions, in practice it is not easy to find such variables. For example, Newman and Gertler use distance to a permanent market in the market wage function, but not in the farm shadow wage equation. However, a number of studies have found such factors to be important in determining farm output and input use [Antle (1984), Binswanger, Khandker and Rosenzweig (1993)]. A more serious difficulty is the use of market wage experience as an exogenous variable, serving to identify hours of an individual's own farm labor. Likewise, experience of other family members in farm work is used to identify their hours of farm labor. If years of specific job experience reflects underlying abilities as well as job match, both of which would affect productivity and thus shadow wages, experience will be correlated with unobserved heterogeneity [Mroz (1987), Topel (1991)].

An alternative to selectivity-based approaches using market wage data to derive shadow wages is to use self-employment output, input and/or net income data to estimate production functions [Blau (1985b), Jacoby (1993), Lambert and Magnac (1991)], restricted cost or profit functions, or restricted input functions [Lopez (1986), Lambert and Magnac (1991)].[123] Once marginal products are estimated, they can be used as proxies for shadow wages. For instance, Jacoby uses constructed shadow wages for men and women to estimate labor supply functions. The shadow wages are the estimated marginal

[121] Only data on market wages, for workers, are needed, along with household consumption, individual family member labor hours on the farm, quasi-fixed assets and prices. While information on family labor allocations are typically expensive to collect and error-ridden, it is not obvious that income data are any worse or more difficult to collect. Use of income information can aid in estimating shadow wages as we discuss below.

[122] Newman and Gertler report that a single run of this model takes all night on a 25 megahertz 486 PC.

[123] Restricted in the sense that they are conditional on the quantities of family labor used.

products of a farm production function, which Jacoby estimates while treating variable inputs, such as labor, as endogenous, using community-level prices, household composition and characteristics of the house as instruments.

Of course estimating self-employment marginal products directly raises the data requirements considerably, because now information is needed on outputs and inputs of the self-employment enterprise. Given the difficulty in measuring inputs and input quality accurately one might well be suspicious of resulting estimates of marginal productivity;[124] indeed this is one reason why this approach has not been more widely used.[125]

The production or cost function approaches used by Jacoby and Lambert and Magnac do not attempt to model sectoral labor allocations.[126] For instance, Jacoby restricts his sample to households in which there is both an adult and female who work on-farm. One-third of his potential households are thereby discarded.

In spite of the fact that so much emphasis has been placed on sectoral selection in the literature, there may actually be much more severe problems associated with understanding wage determination in poor countries. These include the omission from wage functions of such factors as ability, family background or school quality; the use of plausibly endogenous variables such as job-specific experience (either directly or as instruments) and the adoption of restrictive functional forms.

5.3. Functional form: Certification and self-selection

A large fraction of wage function studies have restricted the impact of education to be linear and this often turns out to be a poor assumption. In many studies that have used more flexible formulations, returns to schooling often rise with education, potential certification may become apparent, as may self-selection into different levels of schooling. Restricting the function to be

---

[124] See Vijverberg (1992) for a good discussion of the problems in measuring even revenues and net income from nonfarm enterprises.

[125] Jacoby's production function estimates imply a large number of violations of regularity conditions, such as having negative estimated marginal products of female labor. Lambert and Magnac find only weak correlations between estimated marginal productivity for females and local female wage rates. Both these studies use data from Living Standards Surveys, Jacoby from Peru and Lambert and Magnac from Côte d'Ivoire. The LSSs are not specialized farm management surveys and lack detail on many basic aspects of input use as well as on outputs produced. This limits their usefulness in estimating production functions.

[126] The Newman and Gertler and Blau (1985b) papers are exceptions. Blau includes selection corrections in his farm and non-farm production functions, but uses education, age and ethnicity to identify sectoral choice; a very strong assumption.

linear can also lead to an overstatement of the importance of unobserved heterogeneity, such as from school quality.

A number of studies have shown that there are positive returns to completing particular levels of schooling.[127] These effects have been interpreted as representing the use of certification as a market signal in the face of imperfect information on an individual's productivity. Sometimes market segmentation is inferred. However, these inferences may be incorrect for at least two reasons. First, it may be that certification is associated with greater human capital accumulation at school; those who pass examinations may have achieved more. Second, those who complete a particular level of schooling may be a select group in ability and their higher productivity may reflect this selection. Of course, if this is known by firms, they may use this information to screen able workers; however, this need not imply market segmentation or imperfection within skill (or ability) classes.

Evidence that selection may be important is provided by Strauss and Thomas (1994) who use labor force data from urban Brazil to estimate semi-parametric wage functions which use dummy variables for each year of schooling and therefore place no restrictions on the effect of any year of completed education. Illustrative estimates for men from the South and Northeast are displayed in Figure 34.4 with vertical bars identifying the ends of the first and second halves of primary school, and the end of secondary school.[128] On average, for men (and women), returns to education are large, positive and tend to increase with education (after controlling for age, race, family background and state of residence). Furthermore, the estimated wage functions are not smooth but characterized by steps which could not possibly be picked up by polynomials; even spline functions would have difficulty tracing all the flats and jumps.[129]

While there is a tendency for the return to be higher at the completion of primary school (eight years), there are also jumps in the return function at other grades, not associated with completion of particular levels. In addition, the jumps do not occur at the same levels across all regions (in spite of a common education system); they also differ between men and women. There

---

[127] See Boissiere, Knight and Sabot (1985), Van der Gaag and Vijverberg (1989), King (1990), Glewwe (1991), Stelcner, Arriagada and Moock (1987), Dougherty and Jimenez (1991), Khandker (1991). These studies use both years completed (sometimes splined) and dummy variables for completion of particular levels.

[128] Hungerford and Solon (1987) and Lam and Schoeni (1993) use a similar specification for the United States and Brazil, respectively.

[129] The samples are large with 24,000 men in the market sector and 9,000 self-employed. The differences in the by year education coefficients are often significant, suggesting that the steps are not due just to sampling variation, but represent something real.

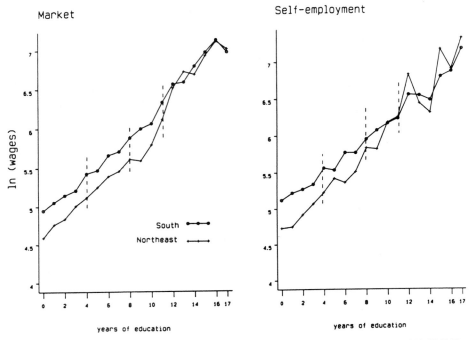

Figure 34.4.   Wages and years of education; Males in urban Brazil; Data source: 1982 PNAD.

are jumps in the returns to self-employment, and this is hard to reconcile with a credentialism explanation, given the nature of self-employment in Brazil. Finally, in several cases, predicted wages are actually lower for people who dropped out of school soon after starting a new level, relative to those who moved into the labor force upon completion of that level; this is particularly clear for men in the Northeast who dropped out after completing only one year of secondary school.

The upward slope in both the market and self-employment sectors is consistent with a human capital explanation. However, given the nature of the steps, credentialism seems not to be key. Rather, the evidence is consistent with there being selection of higher ability individuals into certain grades and into higher levels of education. This would suggest that taking account of the endogeneity of schooling may be productive in a developing country context.[130]

[130] Recent evidence in the United States suggests that endogeneity of schooling may not be key but, instead, measurement error is a more serious problem [Ashenfelter and Krueger (1992), Ashenfelter and Zimmerman (1993)]. See Lam and Schoeni (1993) for related evidence from Brazil.

Many studies have found that market returns to schooling are convex.[131] There are several plausible explanations for this fact and each explanation probably plays some role. Credit market constraints may restrict higher education to the more affluent, who may also be more productive.[132] Children who stay at school longer may have parents who invest not only in formal education but also in their home environment; the convexity may be reflecting the role of background. Students who go on to higher education may have had better quality primary level education, or schools of higher education may be of better quality on average than primary schools. If continuation at school is a function of past performance, then those with higher levels of education will be a self-selected group of the more able.[133] The extent to which these factors matter is clearly an empirical issue: we discuss some of the evidence in the next sections.

5.4. Ability

Measuring "ability" is not easy and few socio-economic surveys in developing countries contain measures of achievement over and above crude indicators of school completion, let alone ability. A small number of studies have used data on market workers to estimate wage functions that include, in addition to years of schooling, scores from numeracy and literacy tests along with Raven's tests, which involve recognition of changes in patterns across a series of four pictures. [Boissiere, Knight and Sabot (1985), Glewwe (1991), Psacharopoulos and Velez (1992), Alderman, Behrman, Khan, Ross and Sabot (1993)]. All the authors (except Glewwe) assert that the Raven's test is a measure of innate ability and is therefore maintained as exogenous. Literacy and numeracy test scores are modeled to be a function of years of schooling, which is modeled as a function of the Raven's test and parental characteristics.[134]

---

[131] In addition to Strauss and Thomas, see Blau (1985a) on Malaysia, Dougherty and Jimenez (1991), Lam and Schoeni (1993) and Barros and Ramos (1991) for Brazil, Behrman and Deolalikar (1993) for Indonesia, van der Gaag and Vijverberg (1989) for Côte d'Ivoire, Moll (1992b) for South Africa and Khandker (1991) for Peru.

[132] Although as discussed in Jimenez (this volume), fees for university education are often highly subsidized.

[133] There is evidence that in many developing countries, grade repetition is important and it is a function, in part, of past performance [see Jamison (1978) and Harbison and Hanushek (1992)]. The impact of repetition on labor market outcomes has received very little attention in the literature (largely because of lack of data), although Behrman and Deolalikar (1991a) provide illustrative calculations from Indonesia that indicate estimated schooling returns can be overstated by as much as 100 percent if repetition is not taken into account.

[134] In the Alderman, et al. study, for example, family income and parental education along with school quality and village dummies are instruments. However, unless the achievement scores are perfect measures of human capital accumulation, background and school quality may have a direct impact on wages. Village dummies, of course, should also enter the wage functions to control for differences in prices, infrastructure and labor demand.

In all four studies, the samples are very small and the results are rather mixed. Typically, the Raven's test scores tend to have little direct impact on wages, but affect achievement scores which, in turn, significantly affect wages. The addition of these test scores substantially reduces the estimated effect of schooling. Since the achievement test scores are not observed by employers, significant effects of these scores are interpreted to mean that education is productive. As many have noted, however, interpreting the impact of years of schooling and in this case test scores, is ambiguous since they may also embody signalling effects. Key to the productivity interpretation is the assumption that the Raven's test perfectly measures underlying ability.

However, the arguments about the appropriate meaning of the two sets of tests are not entirely persuasive. In two of the four studies, the Raven's test scores are significantly higher for men relative to women; this is especially so in the Pakistan data used by Alderman et al.[135] It is hard to imagine that girls are less able than boys, and so the evidence certainly raises doubts about the interpretation of the Raven's test as a measure of "ability" rather than achievement in abstract reasoning. It seems likely that the difference in test scores in Pakistan is related to the fact that boys spend much more time in school than girls, and so one would imagine that whatever does underlie the gender difference in tests is, in fact, related to schooling and school achievement.

While it is true that employers do not see the results of the survey tests, employers may see the results of school examinations and can administer their own tests. Furthermore, it is quite possible that the skills underlying good test performance can be signalled to employers. It is thus not obvious that better performance on the tests conducted in the surveys (which may have very little to do with productivity on a particular job) implies that education, or more precisely test-taking, is in and of itself productive. Test scores could be used for screening purposes by some employers.[136]

5.5. Family background

Since measuring ability is fraught with problems, many studies have resorted to examining the impact of family background on wages. These measures are

---

[135] The mean score is 17 (out of a maximum of 35) but, on average, men score 6 points higher than women.

[136] Boissiere, Knight and Sabot argue that the effects of screening should dissipate with worker job experience (and thus better information by the firm), which they do not find. It is not at all clear, however, that this should be the case. If the screen does capture underlying job-related ability, on-the-job human capital accumulation and wage growth may be correlated with the screen as well.

intended to proxy not only for ability but also for human capital investments made by parents during one's childhood which are not captured by completed years of schooling.

Education and/or occupation of the parents has been one of the more common family background controls. In an early study in this genre, Carnoy (1967) found that father's occupation had a powerful effect on wages of males in Mexico, but that the effect of own education was little affected by the addition of this background variable. Although many studies since then have found that the effect of years of schooling is sensitive to the addition of indicators of parental background, in general, schooling remains an important determinant of earnings or wages even when using these controls.

Many of the studies that have used parental education or occupation covariates focus on Latin or Central American economies, where intergenerational economic mobility has often been alleged to be low (e.g. Medeiros, 1982). In one of the most careful studies in this genre, Heckman and Hotz (1986) examine the robustness of own education coefficients in earnings functions for Panamanian men, to the inclusion of mother's and father's education. They find that both have positive effects on earnings, with the mother's education having a larger effect. The addition of family background in these data results in the own education effects falling by 25 percent. Stelcner, Arriagada and Moock (1987) and Behrman and Wolfe (1984) report similar results for men and women respectively in Peru and Nicaragua.

Outside of Latin American, returns to own schooling tend to remain high even after controlling for family background. Sahn and Alderman (1988) find that among market wage workers in Sri Lanka, (predicted) father's wage has a positive effect on the son's wage, but that the marginal returns to the son's schooling are unaffected. Smith (1991) reports that even after controlling for parents' education, father's occupation and number of siblings, education continues to be a powerful predictor of wages in Malaysia. Armitage and Sabot (1987) interact schooling with parental education using data from Kenya and Tanzania and find that the marginal returns to own education rise sharply with parents' schooling, especially in Kenya. This may reflect better quality of schooling for those who achieve higher levels, or it may result from non-linearities in the returns to schooling, which are not being captured.

Lam and Schoeni (1993), in a twist on this literature, show that not only does parent's education affect earnings, controlling for years of schooling, but that education of the spouse's parents does as well! Using labor force data from Brazil, they show that the effect of the spouse's father is even greater than the effect of one's own father. They also find that marginal returns increase somewhat with higher levels of parental schooling. In this paper, total earnings is the subject of interest, so some of the effect of spouse's parents could operate through increased resource availability for self-employment activities, some could reflect better connections and some could reflect positive assortive mating in marriage and thus represent unobserved individual human capital.

Behrman, Birdsall and Deolalikar (1991) exploit the idea that with assortive mating in the marriage market, characteristics of one's spouse contains information about unobserved human capital. Instead of using spouse characteristics directly, as Lam and Schoeni do, they use residuals from predictions of the wife's schooling, net dowry and age at marriage, as covariates in wage functions for males, using the ICRISAT data. This, they argue, captures the unobserved human capital of the man.

Partner characteristics are predicted using the man's own schooling, plus characteristics of his family. While own schooling has no measurable impact on rural farm wage rates for men, those whose wives are more educated than predicted enjoy higher wage levels and higher average growth in wages.

Of course, the residuals also capture unobserved heterogeneity of the spouse. To the extent that spouse characteristics *directly* influence wage rates (they might, for example, be correlated with better nutritional status of the man through higher efficiency in farm or home production) and assortive mating is imperfect, then the residuals will also capture this effect. Further, for these residuals to be unbiased estimates of unobserved human capital, it must be the case that coefficients in the marital sorting equations are unbiased. This is difficult to achieve for exactly the same reasons as in the case of the wage regressions.

Behrman and Wolfe (1984b) use unusual data from Nicaragua on sisters and their parents which enable them to control for family background using both parental covariates and fixed effects procedures.[137] They estimate household income functions, which means they are incorporating labor supply effects of both the woman and her husband. In addition they are capturing a return in the marriage market to female education, through assortive mating. They find a return to female education of just over 11 percent when parental education and certain other childhood background variables are controlled. This drops to 8.5 percent when a sister's fixed effects specification is maintained. The decline in the estimated return may indicate that parental education, number of siblings and urban upbringing do not capture all unobserved family-level heterogeneity. In this sample, however, controlling for own education, only the education of the woman's father has a significant impact on household income, and its effect is quite weak. This contrasts with the results discussed above which indicate that parental education does affect wages or earnings of men.

---

[137] Behrman, Sussankarn, Hutaserani and Wattanalee (1993) also incorporate sibling fixed effects using Thai labor force data. Other recent studies have used marriage partner fixed effects to control for family background [e.g. Khandker (1991), Behrman and Deolalikar (1993)]. However, this requires the very strong assumption that perfect marital sorting exists. Given imperfect marital sorting, not all person-specific heterogeneity will be swept out by the fixed effect procedure.

5.6. School quality

Part of the impact of family background on wages is likely to reflect choices by parents such as type and quality of school their children attend. The fact that achievement test scores affect wages, over and above years of education, indicates that years, alone, are a crude measure of the benefits of schooling. The test scores are likely to be proxying for quality of education, as it seems most implausible that the effectiveness of schooling would be unrelated to its quality.

It is, however, not obvious how school quality should be measured, and few labor force surveys have even attempted to collect this information. In addition, there is a potential behavioral complication since people with more education may have attended better quality schools, and so it may be especially important to treat school choice as endogenous in this context.

A key difficulty in examining the impact of school quality on wages is lack of (historical) data on the schools that were attended by adults in a typical labor force survey or census. In the face of this difficulty, data on school quality at the survey date have been used. An exception, and probably the most convincing work on school quality effects to date, has been done for the U.S., comparing the effectiveness of segregated black and white schools in the south on subsequent black and white earnings [Card and Krueger (1992a,b), also see Margo (1990), and Orazem (1987)]. The Card and Krueger studies allow the return to years of schooling to depend on the cohort, state of birth and current region of residence. Current location is intended to pick up interactions between demand and education, while interactions with location at birth will pick up effects of school quality. The estimated cohort-state coefficients are assumed to depend on a variety of school quality indicators, average state income and a series of family background measures. The key to their work is their ability to find state-level public school quality indicators that match the same years that those in the sample were in school. Both studies find that higher school quality, particularly pupil-teacher ratios, are associated with significantly higher returns to education.

In the only such studies conducted to date in a developing country, Behrman and Birdsall (1983) and Behrman, Birdsall and Kaplan (1994) interact a regional-level indicator of school quality with individual years of schooling. The original study estimates earnings functions for men in Brazil using 1970 census data, while the latter estimates both wage and earnings functions using the 1980 census.

As measures of school quality, Behrman and Birdsall (1983) construct averages of the years of education of all teachers within each state. Since these data are drawn from the current year, and not the years during which the respondents were at school, the sample is restricted to men aged 15 to 35 years.

Aside from the obvious problem of mismatching the time periods for the school quality variable, the only regional characteristic used in the specification is teacher years of schooling. Any demand-side factors that vary with region and influence earnings or returns to education will thus be forced to operate through this school quality measure.

Without any controls for school quality, the return to schooling is estimated to be 20 percent (in a linear model). When quality is added, the return falls to only 11 percent (at the mean level of quality) and so Behrman and Birdsall conclude that failure to include school quality results in upward biased estimates of the return to schooling. In addition, they report the return rises with school quality and there is a positive interaction between the constructed measure of school quality and years of schooling.

One interesting finding, not highlighted by Behrman and Birdsall, is that when they enter a quadratic in schooling, and allow for a full set of interactions with teacher schooling, they find that the rate of return is an increasing function of years of schooling. The gradient with respect to school quality is now much reduced, although it is still rising. In the paper Behrman and Birdsall discount this result because it indicates convexity in the returns, although as discussed, other studies have found similar patterns in developing countries. Thus, part of the quality effect may result from nonlinearities in the returns to schooling due to schooling selection or imperfect credit markets. Further, Behrman and Birdsall are unable with the census data they use, to include any family background characteristics such as parental education. To the extent that this is correlated with the human capital of teachers, then the impact of background on wages may also be captured in the school quality measures. Finally, if households choose location based in part on school quality or if investments in schools responds to local characteristics, then estimates of school quality effects will be biased.

In sum, selection and unobserved heterogeneity are no doubt important factors in studies of labor market outcomes in developing countries. But, the overwhelming body of evidence indicates that returns to schooling are high and that education is a good investment for any household.

The next two sections discuss a series of issues over which there is considerably less agreement. We begin with a discussion of the role of dynamics in household behavior and then turn to studies that have questioned the meaning of the household (or family) itself. Both are active areas of ongoing research and these literatures are bound to develop rapidly in the near future.

6. Dynamic issues

Most of the empirical models discussed thus far have been static in nature. One class of models takes the perspective of a lifetime, treating it as a single period.

These models are usually concerned with an outcome that may be treated as a stock, such as children ever born, completed schooling or child height. An alternative strategy focuses on a single-period outcome, such as labor supply. Typically, it is assumed that life cycle choices are made in a two-stage budgeting framework, with the first-stage allocation of resources across time periods relegated to the background.

For some cases, however, researchers and policy makers are interested in the dynamics, themselves. For example, one issue that has attracted attention is the impact of unexpected events (shocks) on human capital outcomes, an interest spawned by factors such as warnings of deleterious impacts of structural adjustment programs on children and other vulnerable groups [Cornia, Jolly and Stewart (1987)].

Analyses of the effects of economy-wide shocks on human capital outcomes suggest a mixed picture. It is to be expected that the effects of aggregate shocks will vary by country. This may result from differences in levels of socio-economic development, market structure and sectoral mixes and also levels of publicly and privately provided safety nets. The impacts are also likely to vary depending on the particular outcomes. Some studies suggest a Malthusian response of age at marriage or marital fertility to changes in aggregate income,[138] while others suggest that the child mortality response may be limited.[139] It has even been the case, albeit rarely, that economic retrenchment has coincided with a reduction in poverty, as in Indonesia during the 1980s [Ravallion and Huppi (1991)].

These studies of economy-wide shocks have not examined specific differences in country characteristics that may explain differential responses. Nor can they differentiate between aggregate-level shocks and more local shocks, let alone the possibility that households' ability to adjust to shocks may be associated with their characteristics. For example, are the poor more vulnerable to the impact of adverse economic shocks? It is necessary to turn to micro-level evidence to answer these questions.

Some research has emerged that focuses on both household responses ex-post to adverse shocks and ex-ante to perceived risks. Much of this recent literature has addressed the question of whether households are able (both by themselves and using community-level mechanisms) to perfectly smooth their consumption against all risks; a subset of these studies have been interested in

---

[138] See, for instance, Hill and Palloni (1992), Palloni, Hill and Aguirre (1993), the National Research Council (1993), and Rutenberg and Diamond (1993). Much of this literature follows the work of Lee (1980) and Galloway (1988), who use long time-series data to explore effects of short-run swings in food staple prices on demographic outcomes in pre-industrial Europe.

[139] Palloni, Hill and Aguirre (1992), National Research Council (1993), and Behrman and Deolalikar (1991b). Palloni and Hill (1992), however, find in Latin America that macro shocks do affect infant and child mortality from respiratory tuberculosis and diarrhea.

modeling effects on human capital-related outcomes. In doing so, a set of common modeling problems have arisen, which we now discuss.

Static models of flow outcomes, such as current labor supply, generally assume that preferences are separable over time and that perfect capital markets exist. In this case one can invoke a two-stage budgeting framework and model current supply as a function of current prices and current full income [e.g. Deaton and Muellbauer (1980)]. Alternatively, the first order conditions from this intertemporal optimization problem imply that households adjust their consumption and labor supplies so that the discounted marginal expected value of wealth is the same in every period [Heckman (1976)]. This generates price of utility constant, or Frisch, demand functions, which are a function of current prices and the expected value of the discounted marginal utility of current period wealth.[140] By imposing further restrictions on preferences, tractable estimating equations can be derived with a linear term in the marginal utility of wealth or its inverse, the price of utility [Browning, Deaton and Irish (1985)]. Given panel data, it is possible to estimate the Frisch demand functions by differencing out the unobserved price of utility [MaCurdy (1981)].

Very few studies, such as Blau (1985a) and Skoufias (1993a), have used the Frisch framework in a developing country.[141] The Frisch demand approach allows one to measure responses along the anticipated time trajectories of prices, but fails to allow measurement of the effects of shocks, which operate through the marginal utility of wealth. In addition the approach breaks down in a number of instances that are likely to exist in many developing countries. These include, for example, the presence of credit constraints, due, perhaps, to imperfect information and uncertainty. As discussed by many authors [e.g. Besley, this volume or Hoff and Stiglitz (1990)], such assumptions as perfectly competitive credit markets fly in the face of recent theorizing and evidence regarding the nature of credit markets.

An issue in using the two-stage budgeting or Frisch approaches to model human capital investment is that many outcomes are stocks rather than flows. Examples include child height, measures of adult physical functioning, completed fertility, achievement test scores or years of completed schooling. In this case, as discussed in Section 4, current outcomes depend on past as well as current inputs. This has the same effect on two-stage budgeting as assuming that preferences are not intertemporally separable. In general, therefore, reduced form solutions will include the entire history (including expected

---

[140] Past and expected future prices enter the functions only through the marginal utility of wealth.

[141] Blau (1985a) estimates Frisch supplies for total (market and self-employment) labor of men and women using longitudinal data from the Malaysian Family Life Survey. Skoufias (1993a) uses the ICRISAT data to estimate Frisch demands for total and market labor supply.

future values) of exogenous influences. It is rare that data sets have available such historical data on individual, household and community-level characteristics, let alone information on the future. An important subset of covariates, such as parental education, are time-invariant; provided they are uncorrelated with the omitted time-varying variables, their effects in child health or education reduced forms will be estimated without bias. Estimates of measures that vary over time, such as income, prices or possibly community infrastructure will, however, be biased. Because data are typically unavailable, this is ignored in most of the reduced form literature.

When the empirical literature has addressed the stock nature of many human capital outcomes the method has varied depending on data availability. With only cross-section data, attempts have been made to relate covariates that measure time-invariant or long-run factors. As discussed earlier, the existence of total household expenditure data has been exploited in a number of papers to represent the effect of long-run resources.

Strictly speaking, use of expenditure is theoretically justified only if it is possible to derive a reduced form or conditional demand function for human capital outcomes which is a function of permanent income. Central to permanent income models, as for Frisch demands, is the assumption that capital markets exist and function perfectly. Typically, it is also assumed that there are no motives for precautionary saving so that marginal utility of consumption is linear.[142] Either credit constraints or precautionary saving may result in expenditure tracking income, invalidating a permanent income model [Zeldes (1989), Deaton (1992c), Besley, this volume].

Recent studies, such as Deaton (1992a,b) and Paxson (1992), attempt to test the permanent income hypothesis.[143] They find little support for the strong form although Paxson finds a weaker version does rather well for Thai farm households. Using estimated impacts of regional time-series shocks in rainfall on current household income to identify transitory income,[144] she finds that large fractions of transitory income are saved and so household expenditures are little affected. Nevertheless, a strict form of the hypothesis, that all transitory income is saved, can be rejected.

A different set of evidence has been provided in the studies prompted by Townsend's (1994) work on testing for complete risk pooling.[145] The intuition

---

[142] There are exceptions. For example, if utility displays constant absolute risk aversion and income is independently, identically distributed as a normal variate, then the variance of income as well as expected (or permanent) income will matter [Paxson (1992)].

[143] See also surveys in Gersovitz (1988), Deaton (1989a) and Besley (this volume).

[144] Current income is regressed on exogenous household-level characteristics, long-run measures of rainfall and short-run deviations. Transitory income is then defined as that part of predicted income due to the rainfall shocks.

[145] See Townsend (1994), Rosenzweig and Stark (1989), Morduch (1990, 1991) and Deaton (1992b). Alderman and Paxson (1992) and Besley (this volume) provide more detailed summaries.

for Townsend's tests is that if households are able to perfectly smooth their consumption (or at least smooth against idiosyncratic risk), then conditional on a household fixed effect and aggregate village consumption (or alternatively a village-specific time effect),[146] consumption should be unrelated to household income. With panel data, household fixed effects can be used, so that consumption growth is regressed on a village-specific time effect and the lagged level or changes in household income. Many of the empirical tests to date, most using ICRISAT's India data, are consistent with Paxson's tests of the permanent income hypothesis; full pooling is rejected (as is the strong form of permanent income), as household income is found to affect changes in consumption over and above village-time specific fixed effects. However the estimated income effects on consumption are small. These studies suggest that using household expenditure (per capita) as a measure of long-run income in human capital studies may be reasonable.

    In addition to strong assumptions regarding credit markets, permanent income models treat both permanent and transitory income as exogenous. This is very restrictive when there exist many potential income sources and more so in dynamic models. As an alternative, dynamic models have been used that allow for endogenous income or credit market imperfections. These range from highly structural to reduced form models. Rosenzweig and Wolpin (1993a) and Fafchamps (1993) specify dynamic programming models of farmer behavior in response to shocks. Rosenzweig and Wolpin model bullock investment and disinvestment decisions, incorporating the tradeoff in livestock sales between the potential need for current cash and foregoing future output due to the loss of livestock for traction. Fafchamps is concerned with the degree of flexibility farmers have in changing their labor input decisions. He estimates the intertemporal substitution of labor demand across stages of the cropping cycle and the technical rate of substitution between labor and cumulative crop growth for a given stage. Each of these approaches relies on strong assumptions, including functional form assumptions on preferences and production functions.[147]

    In contrast, other papers have eschewed such a structural approach, preferring to directly measure the impacts of expected values and surprises of the shock variables in a more reduced form setting, rather than forcing them to

---

[146] Deaton (1992b) provides this formulation.

[147] For instance, Rosenzweig and Wolpin assume that there exists a minimum consumption level that households cannot fall below and that households cannot use other smoothing mechanisms. These assumptions are made to ensure that households will have to sell assets if income becomes low enough. Clearly, however, many other avenues are open to households to use to respond to negative shocks (some being the focus of other papers by the same authors).

work through income.[148] In this case, the shocks are allowed to have direct effects, and underlying measures of exogenous assets (e.g. beginning-period assets, such as inherited land) are used to replace estimates of permanent income. For example, Razzaque, et al. use information on whether a birth occurred during a famine period to examine subsequent mortality of Bangladeshi children. Udry uses measures of plot-level crop damage to investigate its impacts on household credit transactions and savings.

For those studies that model the effects of shocks through income, a key issue is how income is measured. The concept of permanent income assumes that all income is exogenous. Including endogenous components in the income measure will result in the volatility of transitory income being systematically understated. Rejecting risk pooling in tests such as the Townsend-type test [Townsend (1994)] may then be more difficult (see the discussion below).

If one wants to measure a pure income shock, it is desirable that this measure be purged of all ex-ante and ex-post actions to smooth income. This is especially important if the object is to explain partial income smoothing mechanisms such as the amount of transfer or extra labor income. Measuring only exogenous swings in income is extremely difficult to achieve in practice. For studies of risk-pooling, not only is labor income likely to be endogenous, but so, too, are asset sales, transfers and remittances from temporary migration and even farm profits net of the value of family labor.[149]

In view of the difficulty associated with measuring purely exogenous swings in income, instrumental variables and household fixed effects techniques have been used to purge models of unobserved error. Wolpin (1982) uses regional, time-series data on rainfall to construct long-run moments to instrument current income (which measures permanent income with error) in a savings equation. Paxson extends Wolpin's study by using deviations of rainfall from its long-run mean (and functions thereof) to construct a measure of the transitory component of income for use in her savings equation. Measures of permanent income and the (expected) variance of income are likewise constructed. Rosenzweig and Stark also use rainfall, plus interactions with a household's dry and irrigated landownings, to instrument for the household-level mean and variance of farm profits in explaining the variance of food consumption.

Rosenzweig (1988a) uses household fixed effects to model the impacts of

---

[148] See for example, Rosenzweig (1988a), Razzaque, Alam, Wai and Foster (1990), Rose (1992); or Udry (1990, 1993, 1994).

[149] Morduch (1990) and Rosenzweig and Binswanger (1993) find that poor Indian farmers are likely to adjust their farm investments in ways that lower expected profits, but decrease profit variation. Fafchamps finds that weeding labor is adjusted to rainfall received earlier, at planting time.

household *full* income surprises on net transfers into the household and on household net indebtedness. Likewise, many of the full income pooling tests implicitly use household fixed effects by transforming the estimating equation so that consumption growth is the dependent variable [e.g. Townsend, Morduch (1991), Deaton (1992b)].[150]

Given a measure of transitory shock, ex-ante and ex-post strategies used to smooth consumption can be modeled. To the extent that households are successful in smoothing consumption, it is less likely that shocks will affect human capital investment decisions. A set of studies have tried to estimate the impacts of unanticipated income changes on various dimensions of ex-post (mostly household and family level) methods of consumption smoothing, including transfers, credit transactions, asset sales and labor force participation.[151]

The empirical risk pooling literature has been quite concerned with the differential ability of households to pool risks. A central hypothesis has been that wealthier households are better able to pool their risk. This may arise because wealthier households have more access to credit markets, because they have more assets to sell in case of need, because they may have more diversified income sources (such as nonfarm self-employment),[152] or because relatives living apart may be better able to afford help during times of distress. For instance, Townsend (1994) and Morduch (1990) stratify their analyses on land owned and find that perfect risk pooling is more likely to be rejected among the landless or small farmers.[153] Rosenzweig and Stark find that inherited assets help mitigate the impact of farm profit variability on the variability of food consumption.

Studies of responses of human capital investments to shocks have examined expenditures on human capital inputs, such as food [Rosenzweig and Stark, Morduch (1990, 1991), Rosenzweig and Binswanger (1993)], individual nutrient intakes [Behrman and Deolalikar (1990)], child growth [Foster (1995)]; schooling attendance [Jacoby and Skoufias (1992)] and infant and child mortality [Ravallion (1987), Razzaque, Alam, Wai and Foster (1990)]. A

---

[150] A number of these studies [Morduch (1990), Jacoby and Skoufias (1992), Deaton (1992a)] worry about potential measurement error in income, random and possibly systematically related to errors in consumption. Lagged rainfall is used, for example, as an instrument for income deviations.

[151] For example, Rosenzweig (1988a, 1988b), Rosenzweig and Stark, Rosenzweig and Binswanger (1993), Rosenzweig and Wolpin (1993), Udry (1990, 1993, 1994) and Rose (1992).

[152] Liedholm and Kilby (1991) report that nonfarm self-employment earnings are especially important both for extremely poor and relatively better off rural households, in a number of different countries. Von Braun and Pandya-Lorch (1991) report the importance of nonfarm self-employment income among better off rural households in numerous Latin American, African and Asian surveys.

[153] Townsend also estimates separate risk pooling equations for each household, finding that poorer households are less likely to be fully insured.

different set of studies have decomposed effects of child mortality on fertility into expected (hoarding) and shock (replacement) effects [Olsen and Wolpin (1983), Olsen (1988)].

Ravallion and Razzaque et al. estimate the impact of the 1974 Bangladesh famine on subsequent child mortality. Ravallion shows that in the Matlab area, time-series mortality rates closely track rice prices. Rice prices rose by 50 percent over a very short (3 month) period at a time when Bangladesh did not have any public safety net programs, such as the food-for-work program adopted in later years. Household, family and village mechanisms were, in many cases, overwhelmed. Using vital event data linked to census records from the Matlab area, Razzaque et al. demonstrate that higher mortality was not uniformly distributed: smaller increases were registered among wealthier households. These vital records, collected by the International Center for Diarrheal Disease Research, Bangladesh (ICDDR,B), are considered to be of very high quality, in contrast with most vital statistics. Information is used on whether a child was born or conceived during the famine period (July 1974 to June 1975) to predict subsequent mortality. The authors control, albeit crudely, for the household's asset holdings using a measure of the number of owned articles. This measure is used both directly and interacted with whether the birth occurred during the famine period. Being conceived during the famine raises the risk of neonatal, but not post-neonatal mortality. On the other hand, being born during the famine significantly raises the risk of mortality between 1 and 23 months, with a larger effect during the first year of life. However, in both cases, these added risks were either nonexistent (for neonatal mortality) or were much lower for children in households with more assets.

Foster (1995) examines the impact of a major flood in rural Bangladesh on growth in child weight during the subsequent three months. He derives an Euler equation that represents changes in household utility associated with changes in a child's weight. Changes in child weight are expressed as a function of changes in rice prices, changes in the rate of change of rice prices, changes in the incidence of illness (instrumented by lagged illness incidence), child age and gender and the elapsed time between the initial weighing and the follow-up. Interest rates are captured by the amount of borrowing by the household and in aggregate by the village.

To explore differential ability to smooth child growth outcomes by wealth, Foster splits the sample by whether the household owns more than a very modest amount of land. He finds that a higher price of rice is associated with significantly lower growth for children in landless households, but the effect is not significant for children of better off households; this is consistent with the hypothesis of differential ability to smooth. The duration of time between weighings is significant and positively related to growth, but again only for children in landless households. This is consistent with children of landless households at least partially catching up in growth rates to children from landed households.

A principal question in Foster's results is robustness to specification. For instance, borrowing is treated as exogenous, which is a very strong assumption.[154] Illness by contrast is treated as endogenous, lagged illness being used as the identifying instrument. However, lagged illness will be endogenous if the production function is dynamic, which Foster assumes it is. Then, in general, looking at changes in weight without conditioning on lagged weight will not eliminate unobserved health heterogeneity terms, either in the production function, reduced form or Euler equations. Also, as is usual in estimating Euler equations, numerous strong assumptions need to be made for data reasons. In this case Foster has no data on consumption or leisure and so must assume additive separability in utility between each of these and child health. Likewise, a sparse specification of inputs into the weight production function is necessary (these, or at least the time varying ones, belong in the Euler equation), unlike some of the studies discussed in Section 4.

Jacoby and Skoufias (1992) use four years of the ICRISAT data, divided into two cropping seasons, in each year, to examine whether changes in the time allocated to school attendance responds to changes in measured full income,[155] controlling for changes in the local child wage and for village-season effects. Changes in income do have a significant impact on school attendance, net of the opportunity cost of children's time, which the authors interpret as indicating a lack of perfect consumption smoothing. They also find that changes in child wages negatively affect school attendance, similar to Rosenzweig and Evenson's (1977) and Rosenzweig's (1982, 1990) evidence. In a second step, Jacoby and Skoufias replace the village-season by village-season-year dummies. Adding the year dimension to the village-time dummies is important because it isolates the idiosyncratic household risk, as in Townsend's specification. Significant effects of changes in income in this regression are interpreted as indicating a lack of perfect intra-village consumption smoothing. That is, idiosyncratic risk is not fully insured within the village. Again, changes in income are found to significantly affect school attendance.

Jacoby and Skoufias explore the robustness of their results to a number of changes in specification. In particular, the income term becomes insignificant in a specification with both village-season-year dummies and full income in-

---

[154] In general, it is not possible to sign the effect of the flood on borrowing. Greater damage implies a larger demand, holding interest rates constant; but interest rates may rise because there is less standing crop in the field to use as collateral. Further, since Foster is unable to control for flooding damage, the borrowing variables should pick up those effects as well.

[155] The value of potential time of family members is included, plus the value of nonlabor farm income. Transfers are considered to be ex-post income and are excluded.

strumented with village rainfall measured on a quarterly basis. However, when the sample is then stratified by owned land, instrumented full income becomes significant for landless households. Jacoby and Skoufias then use Paxson's method to decompose full income into permanent and transitory components, conditional on village-season-year effects. They find that transitory income is only significant for landless households, while anticipated effects are not significant for either type. This evidence is consistent with landless households using their children as assets to borrow against during bad times.

A rather different, yet related, set of evidence comes from the attempt to separate the impacts of mortality on fertility into anticipated and unanticipated effects. This is usually done in the context of conditional demands, in which measures of child mortality are added to otherwise reduced form equations for child demand. Interest in estimating the impacts of child mortality on subsequent fertility is long-standing [see Schultz (1976), Preston (1978), Lee (1980), and reviews in Behrman and Deolalikar (1988), and Schultz (1992)].

One might think of observing how long it takes after a child death for a woman to have another conception. This would help measure what is called the "direct replacement" effect, which corresponds in part to a behavioral response resulting from a mortality surprise. One might also be interested in a "precautionary savings" effect: households that have greater expected mortality may hoard children. This is analogous to allowing the expected variance of income to affect savings decisions, as in Paxson (1992) and would require a measure of expected family mortality. There are some potential complications in trying to estimate and disentangle these dynamic effects; such as endogeneity of mortality because of both unobserved heterogeneity and potential simultaneity (high fertility usually leads to shorter birth intervals, which may raise child mortality) and the fact that a child death will lead to an earlier stopping of breastfeeding, which has a strong contraceptive effect.[156]

Olsen (1988), building on earlier work by Olsen and Wolpin (1983) and Olsen (1980), uses the Malaysian Family Life Survey to derive a waiting time regression approach to account for some dynamics as well as for censoring of birth intervals. He defines the unit of observation to be the fraction of a potential conception interval until a conception occurs. Time-dated covariates, such as the date of a mortality event or length of breastfeeding, can then be used as regressors. Clearly the prior mortality and breastfeeding variables are endogenous. This is treated using a couple-specific fixed effect, which requires that the sample be restricted to couples with at least two births. Using this method has the disadvantage that a hoarding effect cannot be estimated.[157] In

---

[156] Williams (1977) has an early statement on some of these issues.

[157] Olsen and Wolpin use the waiting time regression approach for time to conception, but without family fixed effects, to estimate the impact of the mortality fixed effect, the hoarding effect, on time to conception. However, they do not attempt to estimate a replacement effect.

addition, it requires data on pregnancy intervals, not just birth intervals. This is a significantly stronger data requirement, since it presumes accurate memory of events such as miscarriages.

In a separate analysis to estimate the hoarding effect, Olsen (1988) follows Olsen and Wolpin and models expected family mortality by using the same waiting time regression approach, with family fixed effects, to estimate a child "mortality" production function.[158] The estimate of the family fixed effect is the estimate of expected mortality, which is then used together with the methods developed in Olsen (1980) to estimate a hoarding effect. Olsen finds a total replacement effect of 0.35 in Malaysia, with direct replacement, hoarding and early stopping of breastfeeding each accounting for one third of the effect. The use of fixed effects in both the mortality and conception waiting time regressions is supported against the alternative of ignoring family hetero-geneity.

In sum, there are rather few studies that have attempted to measure effects of resource shocks on human capital outcomes and how existing assets may condition those effects. This is certainly a question which is raised directly by the issue of whether economic adjustment hurts the poor disproportionately as claimed by Cornia, Jolly and Stewart (1987). The few studies reviewed here suggest that there are some impacts, certainly in the case of a major event such as a flood or famine, and the effects seem to hit the poor hardest, consistent with intuition. Whether smaller changes have negative impacts, though, or whether households are able to adjust in ways not detrimental to human capital investment is still unclear. Furthermore, the aggregate time-series evidence indicates differences among countries, which may be partly a function of the existence and quality of social safety nets as well as of the level of market and human capital development and thus households' ability to adjust.

7. Links among individuals, households and families

There is much discussion in the social science literature regarding differential investments in household members – especially between males and females, between the first and later born, and between older and younger household members. We begin this section with a review of the evidence regarding differences in human capital outcomes, focusing on gender and birth order. This discussion is brief as much of the literature has recently been reviewed [Behrman (1992, 1993b)]. We next turn to studies that have sought to explain

---

[158] Use of family or couple-fixed effects to purge health production functions of heterogeneity bias depends on there existing no systematic intrafamily allocations in response to differing endowments. See the discussion of the birthweight and child weight production function estimates of Rosenzweig and Wolpin (1988a) in Section 4.

these differences and, in particular, consider whether there is evidence that household investment patterns are efficient and/or equitable. All this is considered in the context of the economic model of the household outlined in Section 1 above; the final section considers alternative models of household and family decision-making and we discuss the meaning of the household as a decision-making unit.

7.1. Gender differences in human capital investments and outcomes

Sen (1990) argues that "over 100 million women are missing" in Asia and North Africa, where female mortality rates are substantially higher than those for men.[159] Data on completed family size or parental intentions have been used to argue there is evidence for gender preference in fertility outcomes.[160] Other studies have looked at gender differences in a series of health inputs and outputs. Broadly speaking, in south Asia, and possibly southeast Asia, females tend to fare worse than males,[161] but the evidence elsewhere seems weaker.[162] In terms of schooling, however, there is evidence in a variety of countries all over the world that women are significantly less well educated than men, although this difference seems to dissipate with GDP [Schultz (1993a)].

Why might households appear to discriminate against daughters? First, the (expected) returns to investing in sons might be higher. If households seek to maximize total family income, then in the absence of credit constraints, they should invest differentially in each child's human capital to fulfill this goal. The household may then use financial transfers to re-distribute incomes among the children [Becker and Tomes (1979)]. Although it is far from clear why a household would seek to maximize income rather than utility, the assumption of no credit constraints is strong (particularly for low income households) and

---

[159] See, also, evidence regarding infant and child mortality in Bangladesh [D'Souza and Chen (1980)] and in India [Rosenzweig and Schultz (1982a)].

[160] See van de Walle (1992) for a review and Rosenzweig and Wolpin (1993b) for a good discussion of some of the problems in interpretation of attitudinal and intention questions.

[161] Sen (1984), Sen and Sengupta (1983) and Behrman (1988a) argue, on the basis of anthropometric indicators, that boys receive preferential treatment in India. Several studies indicate that boys tend to be favored in the intrahousehold distribution of nutrients [Behrman and Deolalikar (1989), for India, Evenson, et al., 1980, and Senauer, et al. (1988), for the Philippines, Chen, Huq and D'Souza (1981), for Bangladesh, Chernikovsky and Meesook (1984), for Indonesia]. Strauss, Gertler, Rahman and Fox (1993) present evidence that women are more likely to have functional disabilities than men; this is true for older people in Malaysia and Bangladesh and at all ages in Jamaican families.

[162] For reviews of the anthropometrics literature see Behrman (1990), Svedberg, (1990), on Africa and Schofield, (1979), on Latin America. In the equivalence scale literature, there is little evidence for gender bias in the allocation of expenditures in the Côte d'Ivoire and Thailand, [Deaton (1990b)], or in the United States, [Gronau (1988)].

so greater market returns to investments in sons is a potentially powerful reason for discrimination.

In many traditional societies, parents rely on their sons to look after them in old age, while daughters contribute resources to their husband's families [Caldwell (1977), see also Tang (1981), Greenhalgh (1985) and Das Gupta (1987)]. In such cases it would be efficient (for the parent) to invest more in a son, rather than a daughter. If parents care solely about themselves, then it is only expected net returns to the parent that matter in their investment calculation; both benefits and costs need to be included. Notice also that returns need not be measured only in terms of income (or remittances) but might also take account of time spent caring for parents. Indeed, with the development of pension and social security programs, these aspects are likely to take on increasing importance.

Higher expected lifetime earnings of men is not sufficient to explain greater investments in sons relative to daughters, since parents must also be able to extract more resources from sons than daughters. Furthermore, if investing in a daughter leads to a better marriage and that married daughter provides resources to her parents, then discrimination may not be explained by (market) returns alone.

Using district-level data on mortality outcomes in rural India, Rosenzweig and Schultz (1982a) argue that male and female mortality rates respond to expected relative market wages and find evidence to support this view. However, since expected wage differentials are measured by current labor force participation rates rather than an explicit model of expectation formation, the interpretation of these results is not entirely unambiguous.

Direct evidence on gender wage differentials is abundant in both developed and developing economies and the vast majority of the literature indicates that women earn lower wages.[163] But, since similar gaps are not typically observed

---

[163] Foster and Rosenzweig (1991, 1992) argue there is no evidence for taste discrimination in rural labor markets (in India and the Philippines). Using a difference-type estimator, they compare piece-rate wages with time-rates for the same individuals (and thus include fixed effects to control for unobservables). Making the argument that piece rates reflect productivity, then differences between time- and piece-rates for the same individual provide a measure of discrimination, both statistical and taste, that might arise, for example, through information asymmetries. They find men are paid more on a time-rate basis than women and that differences in piece rates account for much of the difference. They decompose the remainder into statistical and taste discrimination and find essentially no taste discrimination. These results are among the most compelling evidence on the issue. They are, however, based on rather small samples and it is not clear that men and women who work in both the piece- and time-rate sectors are a random draw from the working population. If men and women are allocated to different piece rate tasks or if the factors that affect productivity in piece-rate work have a different effect on productivity in time-rate activities, the piece rate may not be a good measure of productivity in the time-rate sector.

in terms of male and female child mortality, it seems likely that other explanations for gender discrimination play important roles.

Differences in the costs of boys and girls may be a second source of apparent discrimination within the household. For example, in a dowry system girls incur an extra cost compared to boys. In some societies with dowries, the women's origin household is even responsible for making contributions to the husband's family after marriage [Das Gupta]. Bardhan (1988) has noted the overlap between areas in India which have dowries and areas with higher girl mortality.

Investment costs may also differ. Young girls may provide child care or household services if they do not go to school, in which case the cost of schooling a daughter, inclusive of costs of time, maybe higher than the price of schooling a son. However, the argument can easily be reversed if sons provide help on the farm, which raises the question of why these costs might be different, an issue about which there has been little scientific research. Notice that all these motivations for differential investments in sons and daughters can arise even with equal concern of parents towards each of their children.[164]

There might, however, be differences in resource allocations simply because of tastes, which may reflect social and cultural norms. Parents might just derive more pleasure (utility) from investing in sons, rather than daughters. Differential human capital investments might also reflect attempts by parents to compensate for other investments (or endowment differences) in their children so that all their offspring are equally well-off. Quisumbing (1994), for instance, finds that Filippino households give more land inheritances to sons, but more education to daughters. While no conclusions can be drawn regarding the extent of equalization, the direction seems clear.

Behrman, Pollak and Taubman (1982) construct a structural model of family utility maximization which Behrman (1988a) adopts to examine intra household resource allocations. He examines the relationship among a series of health outcomes (weight, weight for height, and arm circumference) and five nutrient inputs. The model posits specific functional forms for the production of health and parental preferences, with a simple parameterization of both gender preference and aversion to inequality among children. Using the Indian ICRISAT data, Behrman reports there is very little difference in the mean outputs or inputs (relative to norms) of boys and girls. However, after imposing the model structure on the data, he finds that there is, in fact, significant pro-male bias during the lean season which evaporates during the

---

[164] If it is only net returns that parents care about, then why not invest in only one son? Parents may be risk averse and that son could turn out to be a lemon, or die.

surplus season.[165] The bias is only apparent among the bottom castes, with the top caste indicating some pro-female bias. There is also evidence for inequality aversion among parents, but only during the surplus season. Behrman interprets the results as indicating that parents follow a pure investment strategy during the lean season but when they can afford to (in the surplus season) they display considerable inequality aversion.

However, not all results in the paper are consistent with this interpretation. For example, Behrman finds that more β-Carotene has a *negative* effect on anthropometrics (are parents dis-investing in their children?) and the gender preference parameters in the lean and surplus season are not significantly different from each other. One prediction, consistent with Behrman's interpretation, would be that longer- run measures of nutritional status (height for age) would diverge substantially and this gap would widen with age as the lean season pro-male bias cumulates over time. Unfortunately, although the data include height, results for this indicator are not included in the study.

There is a more general concern with this genre of studies. While evidence of substantial mortality and education differentials between boys and girls is unequivocal, other (more subtle) evidence regarding gender differences in health inputs and outputs is less readily interpreted. For example, simple comparisons of nutrient intakes of men and women tell us nothing about differences in resource allocations unless we also know the *needs* of these men and women. Needs, however, are very difficult to measure and are related to many factors, including activity levels, body size and previous nutrient intakes, all of which are endogenous. As an alternative, many studies use standards derived from healthy populations. This too raises a degree of arbitrariness and will give little insight regarding the reasons for the allocations.

Using food recall data, Haddad and Kanbur (1990) demonstrate that there is in fact considerable intra-household heterogeneity in the proportion of calories consumed relative to "requirements" (as set by international standards). They show, for example, that ignoring intra-household variation (that is using household averages) results in a 20 to 40 percent underestimate of the poverty rate that would be estimated with individual data. However in light of the concerns about "needs" just raised, it is not entirely obvious how to interpret these results.

Indeed, there is evidence that taking account of (typically unobserved)

---

[165] Unfortunately, the implications of the model leads to a regression of ratios of outputs (child weight) of separate individuals to ratios of inputs (nutrient intakes) used. As discussed in Section 4, estimation of such an equation using OLS in general results in biases due to unobserved heterogeneity and simultaneity; Behrman argues the bias is likely to be upwards for the inequality aversion parameter. Furthermore, it is difficult to find plausible instruments within the model, because any instruments should differ in value by individuals if they are to have any predictive power and many potential instruments such as food prices are identical across household members.

heterogeneity in energy output and body size can completely change inferences regarding evidence of gender differences in nutrient intakes. Using a very rich survey from Bangladesh, Pitt, Rosenzweig and Hassan (1990) report that men tend to consume more calories than women. At first blush, this might be interpreted as pro-male bias. However, men tend to be engaged in more active occupations than women: clearly, to assess whether men (or boys) are treated preferentially in the allocation of energy intakes, it is necessary to at least take account of energy output. Pitt, Rosenzweig and Hassan examine the impact of health endowments on calorie consumption where endowments are measured by the "residual method" in a series of anthropometric production functions. While the results rely on a series of strong assumptions (see Section 4), they are certainly provocative. Higher own endowments increase nutrient intakes only for men and not women. That is, households seem to allocate more resources to members with better health endowments, who are more likely to work at energy-intensive activities which pay relatively high wages. When the data are stratified by age, the authors find that endowments affect intakes for men older than 12 and for both boys and girls aged 6 to 12 which, they argue, are the individuals in the household with the greatest scope for varying energy intensity. Of course, this sidesteps the question of whether there is gender discrimination in the allocation of tasks, but at least the study directs us towards the questions that do need to be addressed.

We can avoid the types of problems raised by norms by asking whether additional resources available to a household are allocated differently to boys and girls. For example, if the household were to be given more income, who would benefit most?

Drawing on the equivalence scale literature, Deaton examines the impact of additional resources on *household* expenditure patterns, distinguishing not only adult from child goods but also female from male goods. As children join a household, expenditures on adult goods are likely to fall; if this decline is smaller when additional boys join the household, relative to girls, then this may be evidence for discrimination in favor of boys.[166] Using data from the Côte d'Ivoire [Deaton (1989b)], India [Subramanian and Deaton (1990)] and Bangladesh [Ahmad and Morduch (1993)] there seems to be little evidence for gender differences in household allocations [see Gronau (1988) for related evidence for the United States]. The results from south Asia are a bit surprising in view of the perceived wisdom that boys are favored over girls and so raises questions about the power of these tests.

Thomas (1994) takes a different approach and examines the effects of

---

[166] These tests are indirect in contrast to examining gender-specific mortality rates. Problems arise as comparisons are drawn between households with different numbers and composition of children, implicitly treating child quantity as exogenous. See Browning (1992) for a discussion.

household resources on a child specific outcome, height for age. He finds that maternal education and non-labor income have a bigger impact on the height of a daughter, relative to a son and that paternal education has a bigger impact on a son, relative to a daughter. These results are robust to the inclusion of household fixed effects and suggest that mechanisms underlying intra-household allocations among boys and girls may be quite complex. See, also, Thomas (1990).

Several studies have compared the impact of community resources on individual welfare indicators of boys and girls such as education, health inputs and outputs. There is some evidence that price and income elasticities of human capital investments are higher for girls, relative to boys. That is, according to several studies, if prices are raised, then girls are more likely to drop out of school (or not receive medical attention) than boys. See, for example, De Tray (1988) and Gertler and Glewwe (1992) who examine the demand for schooling in Malaysia and Peru respectively and Schultz (1984) using cross-national data on schooling. Behrman and Deolalikar (1988) also find a greater price responsiveness of girls' anthropometric outcomes in India and Alderman and Gertler (1989) find the same for the demand for health care in Pakistan. Using data on individual nutrient intakes from the ICRISAT survey in India, Behrman and Deolalikar (1990) report that estimated price and wage elasticities of intakes are in many cases substantially and significantly lower (algebraically) for females relative to males. Thus, for nutrients with negative elasticities (which is not all of them), women and girls share a disproportionate burden of rising food prices.

7.2. Differences between siblings

Not only might there be differential investments in sons and daughters, but investments might differ by birth order, either because of biological factors (working through birthweight, for example) or through behavioral influences. These may complement or counteract each other and are likely to operate differently at different ages of the child (and parent). For instance, first borns tend to have lower birthweights for biological reasons, yet if parents favor them in resource allocations, they may grow faster than later- born children.

For social scientists, behavioral influences are of most interest. For example, it may be that parents prefer their first born or, perhaps, the youngest child more than the others. Part of this may reflect tastes but part may also reflect expected future returns, particularly if traditionally one of the children (the oldest or youngest) tends to maintain closer links with the parents later in life.

A hypothesis with a more economic foundation is that there is resource crowding within the household so that as more children are born, household resources are stretched and there is less available *per* child. If the household is able to perfectly smooth inter-temporal consumption (or investment) then resource crowding should have no impact on child well-being. In a world of credit constraints, this is an unlikely scenario. Whether the first born or last born is the best off is not unambiguous and clearly depends on the life cycle pattern of household income.

Wages tend to rise over the life cycle, thus mitigating resource crowding, though they may not rise sufficiently fast to fund new investments as additional children join the household. Older children, however, may enter the labor market and thus free up resources for their siblings or augment household resources which could be spent on their younger siblings. Younger siblings might also benefit from asset accumulation by parents who are later in their own life cycle and so have had time to accumulate resources; these assets might be spent down to finance the schooling of their children or used as collateral for borrowing.

Higher birth order children may also learn from the experience of their older siblings. Along the same lines, parents are likely to learn through experience and may be more efficient at raising later children. Thus, it may be useful to distinguish older from younger siblings and perhaps boys from girls (as they may have different roles in the household).

Studies of the effects of birth order on child schooling and health differ in whether the composition of siblings is considered and by whether interactions are allowed between number of children and birth order. Also, most studies of birth order or household composition ignore possible heterogeneity bias resulting from the correlation of higher birth order or number of siblings with children ever born, although a few studies have attempted to struggle with this issue.[167]

Birdsall (1979, 1991) examines the impact of birth order on the schooling attainment of urban Colombian children, distinguishing between different sized households, whether the mother is working for a market wage and household income. These stratifications allow a number of subtle questions to be examined, at the cost, however, of using arguably endogenous variables for the stratifications, with the number of children and whether the mother is working being particularly worrisome. She finds that being both first- and last-born in a family of three children with a non-working mother is associated with higher

---

[167] Behrman and Deolalikar (1988) review the child quantity-quality literature. The essence of the problem is that prices of having or avoiding children are typically unobserved. Use of twins has been proposed as one way of avoiding heterogeneity (Rosenzweig and Wolpin, 1980), another is to estimate biological fecundity as a residual from a fertility production function and use the residuals in reduced form equations for health or other quality outcomes [Rosenzweig and Schultz (1985, 1987)]. These studies do not examine the influence of birth order or other potential sibling influences.

schooling attainment relative to age-specific norms. This effect is not found among children with working mothers and yet it persists among high income families. The latter result suggests that credit constraints are not the entire story; Birdsall hypothesizes that time constraints may be partly responsible for the pattern among high income families.

Several other studies have examined the effect of birth order on child schooling outcomes, controlling for a fuller range of parental, household and community characteristics, although they also ignore potential heterogeneity bias associated with the number of siblings or birth order. Exploiting an unusual dataset from Taiwan, Parish and Willis (1993) include a richer set of household and sibling composition variables to examine completed education, along with timing of marriage and work among both adults and children.[168] Controlling for birth order, they find that additional siblings are associated with less education among both men and women and this effect is largest among the most recent cohorts. Since higher birth order children (who are in more recent cohorts) tend to be better educated, it is the middle children who pay the largest penalty for having many siblings. The gender of the sibling turns out to be key. For both men and women, more younger siblings of the same sex are a threat to educational attainment. The effect of older siblings is quite different: whereas older brothers reduce the educational attainment only of men, additional older sisters are associated with more education for *both* men and women. Parish and Willis argue this is because older sisters reduce the resource constraint on the family, either by marrying early (and reducing demands on the family as well as providing a brideprice) or, to a lesser extent, by working (and possibly sending money home). All this suggests that households are not discriminating against all women, but rather that resource constraints are binding and older daughters bear a good part of that burden.

To test this view, the authors stratify their sample on a measure of socio-economic security and find that the deleterious impact of larger sibsize is concentrated among those with low economic security and, furthermore, that additional older sisters are the least damaging to one's educational prospects. Since family size has declined dramatically over time in Taiwan, one might expect resource constraints to be less binding among the more recent cohorts. Apparently, however, the negative effect of sibsize on education is highest among the most recent cohorts. Parish and Willis speculate that this reflects increasing opportunity costs of education (in terms of lost labor income) for recent cohorts and so this trade-off is most apparent for younger women, who are increasingly entering the labor market.

The story, as told by Parish and Willis, suggests that this has less to do with preferences and more to do with resource constraints, which contrasts with

---

[168] See, also, King and Lillard (1987) and Lillard and Willis (1993).

Birdsall's results for Colombia. What is clear, however, is that it seems sibsize affects investments in children and that the gender and relative age composition of one's family are critically important.

These studies are potentially affected by heterogeneity bias although exactly how much is not clear. In a study that does attempt to control for heterogeneity, Horton (1988) uses household fixed effects to model the impact of birth order in reduced form equations for height for age and weight for height of Philippine children. Using the Bicol sample, she finds a negative effect of birth order on height, with a weak degree of concavity although, unlike Parish and Willis, this effect is not offset by better educated mothers or greater household assets. She does find a significant positive, although very small, interactive effect of birth order and number of children in the household, but since these effects are not interacted with gender or composition of siblings, they cannot be directly compared with those of Parish and Willis. In contrast, however, she finds essentially no effects of birth order on the shorter-run measure of nutritional status, weight for height, except for a small negative effect in households with more than two children. She interprets the differences between the impact on height for age and weight for height as reflecting the impact of household resources although since assets are included in the model and have little impact on either outcome, it is not clear that the interpretation is correct. It is striking that the magnitude of the negative birth order variable increases six-fold when household fixed effects are incorporated, compared with OLS, indicating that either heterogeneity or measurement error may be very important. At the very least, these results suggest that it is prudent to be cautious when interpreting birth order effects.

7.3. Interactions among household members

Implicit in many of these studies is the notion that there might be trade-offs among household members either in long-run investment strategies or in responses to short-run opportunities or shocks. While a good deal can be surmised from this research, rather few studies have explicitly examined these sorts of interactions. One reason is that it is hard.

In their study of the relationship between productivity and health, Pitt, Rosenzweig and Hassan (1990) also ask whether there are interactions among household members by looking for cross-effects in the impacts of endowments on calorie intakes. If the household behaves as a pure income-maximizing unit, then there will be no cross-effects of the endowments of others in the household on any given member's calorie allocation. To test this, they examine the impact on individual calorie consumption of not only one's own endowment, but also those of other household members. Capturing the latter with the estimated mean endowment of all household members, they find no evidence of cross-effects; but when the average endowments of males and females are distinguished, then there is some evidence of a negative effect of the endowments of other males on any particular man's consumption.[169] However, since significance is marginal, the authors' interpretation that men are bearing the brunt of the household compensation mechanism seems somewhat strong.

Pitt and Rosenzweig (1990) examine the impact of morbidity among infants on time allocation of other household members. They point out that time allocations within the household are likely to be interdependent and also that infant morbidity is not only affected by time allocation but may also affect these allocations. Focusing on mothers, sons and daughters, they distinguish three activities (at school, home work and leisure), each of which is measured as an indicator variable. Allocations across pairs of activities are compared using a Chamberlain fixed effects conditional logit model to sweep out all household invariant effects. The difference in the latent variables for activities across types of people (e.g. mothers, daughters, sons) is then related to exogenous factors, plus the latent health variable for the infant. Infant's health is treated as endogenous and identification is achieved by assuming that community infrastructure and prices affect activity levels of different people in the same way, conditional on infant health. This implies that the impact of infrastructure on time allocation is identical for wives, sons and daughters; thus infrastructure is swept out in the fixed effects specification and so may be used as instruments for infant health in the conditional logit equation.[170] Treating infant morbidity as endogenous, they find that, as it increases, the time allocation of sons is little affected but the time of mothers and daughters is significantly re-arranged. Mothers tend to shift out of the labor force into home care whereas daughters move out of school into the home although the differences between mothers and daughters are not significant.

The dichotomous nature of the outcomes, ill in the previous year and the crude measures used for time allocation (over the previous week), is troubling – especially in a fixed effects framework. Essentially, the estimates rely exclusively on those pairs in which time allocations differ – that is comparisons, for example, of sons who do no home work with their sisters who

---

[169] Rosenzweig and Wolpin (1988a) look at a similar question, examining the impacts of family and individual child health endowments, measured as residuals from a weight production function, on the probability of having a subsequent short birth interval, breastfeeding and being innoculated. Controlling for the family health endowment, they find that children with healthier endowments tend to be followed by shorter birth intervals.

[170] The effects of other characteristics are allowed to vary across the demographic groups. This assumption is, perhaps, weaker than an ad hoc exclusion restriction, but it is nonetheless strong. It implies, for instance, that food prices only act as prices of health in their effects on time allocation.

do no school work. This both limits the observations which are effectively used and creates a potentially very selected sample if the error term is not additive.

Newman and Gertler (1994) explicitly model time allocation in a multi-person, farm-household model and estimate three functions for each demographic group – a market wage function, marginal return to on-farm work and a marginal rate of substitution between leisure and household consumption. As discussed in Section 5, the model is complex and computationally burdensome even after making several very strong but simplifying assumptions. Generally, they find that the hours of work of other family members affects the marginal return to farm work of every individual – especially in the case of men. They also find that increases in the leisure of other members has an impact on one's own evaluation of the marginal rate of substitution between leisure and consumption. The study is clearly another step towards understanding the interactions among household members and how their choices are all interrelated.

7.4. Concept of the household

The research reviewed above suggests that delving inside the household is likely to have a substantial pay-off in understanding household behavior. In much of the literature, furthermore, precisely what is meant by "the household" is seldom clearly articulated and in empirical work the definition is often dictated by survey data practice. In most cases, the household is defined as a group of people who share a common cooking pot (or kitchen): in complex societies, it is far from clear that this is always an appropriate definition, at least from the point of view of understanding behavior of families and their members.

In this section, we discuss two related issues. First, we consider some recent models of the household that treat it as a collection of individuals who may have different preferences. It is a natural step from permitting preference heterogeneity within the household to consider a broader conception of the household. In the second section, we focus on linkages across (data-based definitions of) households.

7.4.1. Intra-household allocations: Collective models of the household

The vast majority of the literature on household decisions has been predicated (explicitly or implicitly) on the assumption that the household maximizes a unique utility function given a set of constraints dictated by the household budget and available technology; see Section 1 above. Although treating the household as a "black box" (or more precisely as a single homogeneous unit) has the virtue of simplicity and convenience, the micro-economic theory of demand is predicated on the behavior of individuals. Aggregating individuals into households involves invoking assumptions that may not be innocuous. In essence, it amounts to assuming either that all household members have identical (or *common*) preferences or that there is one household member (a *dictator*) who determines all allocations (from the point of view of pure self-interest or behaving as an altruist). Under these assumptions, the household is, to all intents and purposes, the elementary decision unit. In consequence, it may be treated as if all resources are pooled and then allocated according to some (common) rule. The model thus imposes restrictions that are not entirely consistent with the notion in micro-economic theory of a decision-maker being a single individual, characterized by his (or her) own preferences.

The extent to which these simplifying assumptions are inappropriate is clearly an empirical issue and will certainly depend on the research or policy issue at hand. Indeed, it is hard to overstate the contribution of this simple model to our understanding of many behavioral choices in the context of a developing economy. There are, nevertheless, some decisions that are difficult to examine in the framework of the traditional model including, for example, the formation, dissolution and partition of households. Furthermore, for some purposes, it is key that we have a good understanding of the mechanisms underlying individual choices.

For example, public policy may change the structure of decision-making within the household and the implications of these changes need to be taken into account. As an example, investments in irrigation to raise the productivity of rice in the Gambia, which has been traditionally grown by women, resulted in changes in the allocation of labor. With the advent of higher yielding, irrigated rice, men took primary control over the crop [see, for example, von Braun and Webb (1989), Dey (1982)]. Whether women (and other household members) were better or worse off as a result of these innovations is not at all clear. However, in order to evaluate the impact of these kinds of programs on the welfare of all households members, we need to consider the potential behavioral responses of individuals within the household: it is sometimes the case that these issues can be adequately addressed only in the context of an individualistic model of the household.

Recently, there has been a resurgence of interest in developing theoretically more appealing models of households that explicitly take account of the fact that individuals within a household may have different preferences. Realism, however, does not come for free: it carries along with it complexity and thus the need for additional assumptions.

One class of models in this literature suggests that household allocation decisions are the outcome of a bargaining process in which household members seek to allocate resources over which they have control to goods they especially care about. While the exact nature of this bargaining process may take a number of forms, the intuition underlying all these models is quite simple.

Each household member has some fall-back position (level of utility) and non-cooperative behavior will occur if his (her) welfare falls below this "threat point" level. This will occur if the sum of utilities associated with these fall-back positions is greater than total household welfare. Any utility gain from household activities over and above the sum of the individuals' threat points is shared in a cooperative solution among household members, presumably in accordance with their bargaining strength. We clearly need to assume some kind of structure for this process and thus place additional restrictions on the model such as to what state of the world the threat points correspond as well as to the equilibrium concept.[171] Failure to reject the traditional *common preference* model of the household in favor of one of these models does not necessarily mean that treating the household as a single unit is appropriate; it may simply mean that these additional restrictions are false [Chiappori (1988)].

Chiappori (1988, 1992) has proposed a more general, *collective* model of the household in which members allocate resources in such a way that no allocation could result in one member being better off without some other member being worse off: that is resource allocations are *Pareto efficient*. It turns out that even under fairly general conditions, this imposes testable restrictions on data.

Assume, for simplicity, that there are two people in a household and each has altruistic preferences in the sense that each cares about the other's consumption of a private good; they may also consume public goods. Browning and Chiappori (1993) show that for all Pareto-efficient allocations, there exists a set of individual welfare weights such that the household welfare function may be written as the weighted sum of two utility functions, one for each individual, which is then optimized subject to expenditures equaling total household income. The demand for any private good, x_i, will depend on all prices, p, total household income, y, and these welfare weights, μ:

$$x_i = x_i(p, y; \mu) \tag{8}$$

The weights, themselves, are a function of prices, *individual* incomes and

---

[171] Many studies have drawn on the seminal work of Manser and Brown (1980) and McElroy and Horney (1981) who consider the threat point to correspond to being divorced. Ulph (1988) and Lundberg and Pollak (1993) examine threat points based on noncooperative solutions *within* the household. In Lundberg and Pollak, the threat points correspond to gender roles which arise from tradition. In a game-theoretic framework, it is also necessary to define the appropriate concept of equilibrium. McElroy and Horney focus on a cooperative Nash equilibrium; see also refinements in McElroy (1990a,b). Manser and Brown, Ulph and Bjorn and Vuong (1984) consider alternative equilibria. Related class-based models of conflict are discussed in Folbre (1986) and Hartmann (1981).

possibly other factors. Thus conditional on total income, individual income affects demands only through the welfare weights. Conditional on these weights, the demand functions satisfy all the usual properties such as homogeneity and symmetry. Treating them as endogenous leads to a further series of Slutsky-like conditions and a potentially rich set of testable restrictions on the data.

If there are three sources of income, $y = y^1 + y^2 + y^0$, say, then it is easy to see from differentiating the demand function, [8], that the ratio of any two income effects, $(\partial x_i/\partial y^1)/(\partial x_i/\partial y^2)$ is independent of i – since differential effects of y^1 and y^2 can appear only through the implicit welfare weight. This is a very powerful result as it suggests a simple test for Pareto efficient allocations with few additional restrictions on the model; in particular, it says nothing about a specific bargaining structure, or even whether a bargaining structure underlies the equilibrium. Rather, the restrictions say, for example, that the ratio of male income effects to female income effects will be constant across all pairs of goods. In contrast, the "traditional" model of the household implies that it matters not a wit who controls income and so male and female income effects should be equal and their ratio should be unity (Chiappori, 1992).

Chiappori shows that the collective model can also be given an interpretation in the context of income pooling. Assume public good allocations are given, X^*. Further, let preferences be "caring" (in the sense of Becker) so that one person cares about the other's allocation only to the extent it gives that person individualistic welfare. This imposes weak separability in each individual's utility function, $U^i(x^i, X^*, \omega[x^j, X^*])$, where x^i is individual i's consumption of private goods. Under these assumptions, the household optimization problem may be rewritten as a two stage process. We can treat the household as if all members pool their income and then allocate it according to some sharing rule. Thereupon, in the second stage, each household member maximizes his (her) own utility given their income share (conditional on making choices about public goods within the household). The income-sharing rule is clearly related to the weights, μ, and so is a function of, inter alia, prices, wages and incomes. The rule also has a very nice intuitive interpretation as an indicator of relative bargaining power of household members: the more powerful the individual, the bigger that person's share of the pie. In fact, since co-operative bargaining outcomes are Pareto efficient, those models are a special case of this more general framework.

7.4.2. Empirical evidence

There is a substantial literature that argues men and women have different preferences: it is often asserted that, relative to fathers, mothers care more about the health, education and well-being of their children. If true, then this would suggest that women will seek to allocate more resources towards improving child health than would men.

Some of the evidence for this view seems to be based on the observation that those children whose mothers work are also healthier (although this is not a universal finding).[172] Even if the empirical facts were clear, their interpretation is not straightforward. The observation may simply reflect a positive correlation between child health and household income, if households with working women have higher total income. Another confounding factor is that family members choose time allocation along with commodity consumption. Even if incomes are pooled, child health outcomes and income earned by the mother may be positively related, after controlling for total household income. For example, sicker children may divert time of the mother away from market work [consistent with Pitt and Rosenzweig's (1990) evidence], while the father may work longer to compensate for any loss in income.

Nor is there a simple interpretation of this observation in the collective model of the household allocation, without explicating the income sharing rule. A woman working outside of the home may bring in income but that does not *necessarily* mean she gets a bigger share of the pie to allocate. It may be, for example, that a woman's share depends on the assets she owns (or controls), what she will take away with her if she leaves the household, her options in the re-marriage market or even the (expected) wealth of her (future?) extended family.

A theoretically more compelling test of the hypothesis of different preferences of household members might examine the impact on intrahousehold allocations of exogenous individual level characteristics which are plausibly related to any income sharing rule. Measurement of such characteristics is not straightforward, however, and this raises another set of thorny problems. Most studies that have attempted this strategy, using data from developing countries, have used non-labor income (or the value of assets) as indicators of control over resources (although some studies have also tried to take account of marriage market opportunities).[173]

Schultz (1990) finds that in Thailand resources in the hands of women tends to reduce fertility more than non-labor income held by men and, furthermore, that the impact of non-labor income has different effects on labor supply outcomes depending on who controls that income. Thomas (1990) reports that

---

[172] For a review of the sociological literature, see Blumberg (1988), Behrman (1992) provides an excellent summary of the evidence in economics. More recent evidence includes von Braun, de Haen and Blanken (1991), Kennedy and Peters (1992) and Engle (1993).

[173] See Carlin (1991) who exploits the fact that in the United States divorce laws generosity varies across states. Schultz (1991) demonstrates that marital choice is affected by an individual's non-labor income in the United States and these effects differ substantially for whites and blacks. See also Rao and Greene (1991) who examine marriage markets in Brazil.

child health (survival probabilities, height for age and weight for height) along with household nutrient intakes tend to rise more if additional (non-labor) income is in the hands of women rather than men. Using the same data, Thomas (1993) reports that income in the hands of women is associated with increases in the share of the household budget spent on health, education and housing as well as improvements in child health.[174] Evidence in India indicates that children are more likely to attend school and receive medical attention if the mother has more assets, mostly jewelry [Duraisamy (1992), Duraisamy and Malathy (1991)]. Quisumbing (1994) finds that among Philippine households, bequests to children are a function of resource control, with sons tending to get more land inheritances relative to daughters when fathers have more education or the household has more land.

While this literature is small, the results are suggestive that resources in the hands of different individuals within a household do not have the same impact on the welfare of all members. In particular, there is some evidence that a reallocation of resources among men and women may affect household commodity patterns along with the health and welfare of children. The results, however, are certainly not universal [see, for example, McElroy and Horney (1981)].

In sum, there appears to be evidence that, in specific cases, the restriction of equality of income effects in the "traditional" model of the household is rejected by the data. Contrary to the interpretation of some authors, this obviously does not imply that bargaining models are appropriate. Unfortunately, to date, there have been few tests of the implications of Pareto efficiency. Using data from France and Canada, Bourguignon, Browning, Chiappori and Lechene (1993, 1995) find that the ratio of income effects is not unity (and thus they reject income pooling), but the ratios are constant across a range of commodities and so the data are consistent with the collective model; see Thomas and Chen (1994) for similar evidence from Taiwan.

Many of these studies are, however, subject to at least one common caveat. They ignore the fact that income is neither exogenous nor likely to be measured without error. Labor income (and time allocation) is a choice and so should be modelled as part of the household allocation. Several of the studies use non-labor, either directly or, in the case of Thomas, 1993, as an instrument for total income. Since non-labor income is, in large part, the accumulation of previous savings and thus a function of prior labor supply, it too is endogenous in a dynamic model of choices [Smith (1977)]. This concern may be less critical

---

[174] It turns out that this result holds for total (non-labor and labor) income (measured at the individual level) where labor income is treated as endogenous (and instrumented with non-labor income). See also the work on commodity demand in France and Canada in Bourguignon, Browning, Chiappori and Lechene (1993, 1995).

in those studies that focus on children (and thus households early in the life cycle) and in those that rely on measures of wealth that are typically inherited or given at the time of marriage (such as jewelry in India).

Thomas (1990) does attempt to address the measurement error issue. Using data on multiple outcomes, he assumes that measurement error in income is additive (and uncorrelated with any observables). The equality of true income effects for male and female non-labor income on any one outcome translates into the equality of the ratios of (observed) male and female income effects across any pair of outcomes (a result that is similar to the Chiappori observation regarding Pareto efficiency). This equality cannot be rejected by the data and so the joint hypothesis of measurement error in income and income pooling cannot be rejected.

Taking a different strategy, Thomas (1994) has shown that (non-labor) income in the hands of women has a bigger impact on the anthropometric outcomes of her daughters relative to her sons. But this is not true for fathers. This result is robust to the inclusion of household fixed effects which amounts to a comparison of the impact of parental income on brothers and sisters. It is also consistent with patterns observed in the impact of parental education on the height of their sons and daughters. It is very hard to explain this rejection of income pooling by appealing to either measurement error, endogeneity or other sources of unobserved heterogeneity.

It seems clear that at this point, we need to know a lot more about the practical importance of modeling the household in this more general framework. A better understanding of how household allocations differ depending on who controls resources is a critical first step. We cannot, however, stop there: from the point of view of policy, we also need to know whether there are feasible and cost-effective mechanisms for affecting the intra-household balance of power. It does seem, at least, that this may be a useful direction for further empirical research, especially in the context of complex household formation such as exists in many societies. It is to these issues we now turn.

7.4.3. Household formation and partition

Discussion of relationships within households, families or larger kin-groups focuses the analytical spotlight on the meaning of the "household" or "family" as a unit of decision-making. It is not clear that the usual definition of the household in survey data (the common cooking pot) is appropriate in all contexts. Given the prevalence of extended family members living in the same household, or multiple households living within a compound, these concerns may be especially important in the context of developing countries.

As Guyer (1986) points out, households within a kin-group (in west Africa) may farm separately but consume some goods jointly. Grain storage may be centralized at a compound level, perhaps to gain some economies of scale or save on transactions costs, even though field production is at the household-level. Clearly, the appropriate definition of the "household" or "family" will depend critically on the nature of the research or policy question at hand. Given a definition, implementation in the field is not likely to be easy – especially when there is no clear concept of a "household" in the community. As an example, ICRISAT household data from Burkina Faso contain multiple household lists taken at roughly the same time, but by different investigators. Large discrepancies exist between these different rosters. In part this results from different sub-households, which may or may not be farming or consuming separately, being included in different lists.

In addition to identifying the proper level(s) of analysis and interactions among them, analyses need to take account of the possibility that these boundaries change and may be responsive to economic forces. This raises a number of complex issues that have been little explored. There are many dimensions in which household composition may change, ranging from marriage and divorce, to childbearing and fosterage, to migration, partition and extended living arrangements. As yet, there are few precise descriptions of links between households, let alone appropriate models for analyzing them, although the theoretical and empirical analyses discussed in the previous sub-section may be usefully applied to address these questions. For example, tests of the nature of resource pooling across different household or sub-household groupings within a family- or kin-network may provide useful information.

Drawing on unusual longitudinal data from Bangladesh (the Demographic Surveillance System in Matlab), Foster (1993) matches household rosters from two surveys so that he can link households that were partitioned in 1982 but that reside in the same *bari* as the origin household in 1974.[175] He uses data on child education outcomes to test for income pooling within the extended households in order to determine whether partitioned households are different from those that remain intact.

If partitioned households have no ties with their origin (or linked) household, then characteristics of the latter households should have no impact on resource allocations. This hypothesis is unambiguously rejected: in particular, land ownership and education of the head in the origin household are positively associated with educational attainment of children in the partitioned household. He finds, furthermore, that income pooling is not perfect since own land ownership has a significantly different effect from that of the origin

---

[175] A *bari* is a collection of usually related households that live in a larger compound and typically remain economically connected.

household. A stronger form of the test controls for (extended) household fixed effects and still finds a significant effect of land ownership in the partitioned household. This implies that the *bari* (or extended household) is not the exclusive decision-making unit, at least with respect to child education.

There are a host of reasons why there may be economic links across households, and these linkages manifest themselves in a variety of ways, including transfers of money, goods and time. First, households may be altruistic, in which case the income pooling model of Chiappori (1992) can be extended to the multiple household case. Second, transfers may be motivated by exchange through an implicit contract or strategic behavior [Bernheim, Schleifer and Summers (1985), Cox (1987)]. A particular form of exchange, insurance against income shocks, may be a key motive for inter-household links in a developing country context [Rosenzweig (1988a), Rosenzweig and Stark (1989)]. If so, then this suggests the pool of potential donors and recipients may be very large (see Section 6 and the discussion of risk-pooling in a village context).

Several studies have attempted to disentangle altruism from exchange motives for transfers.[176] For concreteness, we focus on links between parents and children. If parents are altruistic, then those children whose consumption is lower than its long-run level should receive transfers.[177] Exchange, on the other hand, need not be negatively related to the child's resources [Lucas and Stark (1985), Cox].

The timing of transfers is also key. If old age support is the primary motivation for transfers, then transfers will be made from parents to children when the children are young, but from children to parents when the parents are old. Further, there may be inheritances by children to help ensure their good behavior during the parents' lives [Bernheim, Schleifer and Summers, Lucas and Stark]. Using cross-section data from Peru, Cox and Jimenez (1992) find that net transfers are greatest among households with the youngest and oldest aged heads, which is consistent with the exchange interpretation.

Risk sharing has quite different implications for the timing of transfers [Rosenzweig (1988a, 1988c)]. The direction of net transfers should depend on which party has faced positive or negative shocks and is unrelated to the life-cycle. This hypothesis is very hard to test without a (long) time series of

---

[176] Altonji, Hayashi and Kotlikoff (1992a), for example, use evidence on expenditures of adult children and their non-coresident parents in the United States.

[177] This statement is true for an individual's lifetime consumption path. It is *not* the case that in a cross-section, altruism implies a negative relationship between transfers and income as argued by several authors [see, for example, Cox and Jimenez [1990b]]. In fact, if higher income households are more altruistic, then in a cross-section, there would be a positive association between income and transfers. Studies based on cross-section data are, therefore, very difficult to interpret.

data on both sides of the contract (and possibly on all households in the pool): few, if any, datasets of this nature exist.[178]

Using the Bangladeshi data described above, Foster (1993) finds, not surprisingly, that larger households are more likely to partition. He notes that even in rural Bangladesh, the vast majority of any individual's life is spent as a head, spouse or child of the head although not necessarily in a simple nuclear family. He points out that households often include siblings of the head or are vertically extended.

While the nature and timing of household partitioning is likely to be importantly influenced by social considerations, there may also be economic reasons for household partitioning. Presumably, when the (present discounted value of the expected) benefits associated with the public goods (or externalities) provided within the household are outweighed by the perceived costs, household members will split off and set up their own households.

Rosenzweig and Wolpin (1985) argue that in an agricultural setting with heterogeneity in land quality and weather, there is a return to investing in land-specific human capital, especially in an environment with little technological innovation. This suggests that adult children will seek to benefit from the experience of their elders by tilling the family farm with them. The model also predicts that there will be few land sales, that land-owners will tend not to migrate and that there will be a tendency for families facing greater income risks to be vertically extended since the advantage of farm-specific experience will be more valuable in that environment. Using NCAER data from India, the authors present evidence that is consistent with this view of the world. Using the Indian ICRISAT data, Rosenzweig (1988b) shows that specific farm experience contributes significantly to agricultural profits and also mitigates the influence of rainfall (although not significantly).

Households may choose to mitigate risk through spatial diversification in living arrangements [see Rosenzweig (1988a), for an excellent discussion]. Rosenzweig and Stark (1987) argue that in south India where women, rather than men, tend to move to new households, families will seek to locate daughters in different places if risk is a concern. The authors find almost complete diversification, and that the extent of diversification is greatest for the least wealthy, who are, presumably, those at greatest risk in the face of a weather shock. Furthermore, daughters tend to marry kin, who, it is argued, are more likely to be concerned about the origin family after marriage. Rosenzweig (1988b) reports that, conditional on wealth, variability of agricul-

[178] See Lucas and Stark (1985), Kaufman and Lindauer (1986), Ravallion and Deardon (1988), Cox and Jimenez (1990b, 1992) and Hoddinott (1992) who all use cross-section data. Apart from Ravallion and Deardon (who use predicted household expenditure as a measure of long-run income), these studies also suffer from problems associated with measuring income; see Section 6.

tural profits positively affects the number of co-resident daughters-in-law, which he interprets as a measure of intergenerational and spatial extension. The effect is not, however, precisely estimated.

In sum, exactly what is meant by the "family" or "household" is likely to depend on the nature of any particular study of the behavior of individuals. To the extent that household composition and boundaries are endogenous, analysis of household behavior becomes far more complicated. And even if these boundaries are treated as exogenous, endogenous intrahousehold allocations are difficult to study. Until more work has been done on models of the household that take account of these concerns – both from a theoretical and empirical point of view – we cannot judge how important these considerations are from a practical point of view. Tests of income pooling are suggestive that research along these lines may be fruitful but much remains to be learned.

8. Conclusions

The fact that there is a very large literature on investments in human capital is hardly surprising in view of its importance as a factor underlying economic growth and development. Some of the recent empirical research has been reviewed in this chapter with a particular focus on the role of the household, in and of itself, and as an intermediary between the individual and community.

A good deal of the work has used the household production model as an organizing principle which we view as testimony to the power of that approach. But theory alone is not sufficient; we also need to test our models and assess the magnitude as well as significance of effects predicted by theory. In fact, the integration of survey data collection with a theoretical framework has proved itself to be a key factor in the development of this area of intellectual inquiry. Continued close collaboration in this vein is bound to yield a substantial pay-off.

Whereas much of the early work in this literature was rather cavalier in its approach towards estimation and interpretation, over the last decade or so, the pendulum has swung in the opposite direction. A good deal of the literature is now preoccupied with concerns that revolve around unobserved heterogeneity and measurement error of one sort or another. There is no doubt in our minds that many of these are legitimate concerns and we have tried in this chapter to discuss their importance in the context of particular models. We have also sought to demonstrate that recipe-book approaches to resolving these problems are, in some cases, counter-productive. At times, the subset of problems addressed is less important than others that are ignored. It is indisputable that problems in estimation warrant the thoughtful attention of empirical researchers in the field.

In spite of all the difficulties empirical researchers have faced (or ignored), our understanding of individual and household behavior has been significantly enhanced in a number of critical dimensions. Much has been learned about the production of human capital, especially health, and knowledge about this process has been substantially enriched by the integration of biomedical and social science approaches. Production function estimation is also an area in which the collection of data with a conceptual model in mind has proved to be extremely fruitful: the Cebu Longitudinal Health and Nutritional Survey provides an excellent example.

Taking the household production model seriously has led to the estimation of reduced form models that examine the ultimate determinants of human capital accumulation. There is little disagreement that human capital investments in children are critically influenced by the human capital of their parents. The role that household resources play has been harder to pin down although, on balance, longer-run measures of human capital investments do seem to respond to increases in permanent income. The evidence is rather less clear with respect to shorter-run measures, including inputs into the production function such as nutrients (calories and protein). The extent to which community resources matter is far from resolved. On the one hand, there are substantial problems in definition and measurement. On the other hand, it seems that evaluations need to take seriously the possibility that programs are not randomly located.

Considerable progress has been made in understanding the nature of returns in the labor market to human capital accumulation, broadly defined. Several recent studies have examined the impact of not only schooling, but health, in addition to interactions among them. Some useful insights have been generated by studies that focus on allocations to individuals within a household in response to market returns to these investments. More generally, research on interactions among individuals within households and across households (such as extended families) has generated some provocative results. Recent work on a series of related questions regarding how individuals and families respond to risk, imperfect information and surprises such as price shocks or fluctuations in transitory income suggests this will be a very productive area for research.

The spectacular growth in the availability and quality of data has played a key role in the maturation of research on families and households in developing countries. As this research has evolved, the questions posed have become more subtle and complex. In turn, new data collection enterprises have attempted to incorporate additional information that will enable researchers to address these issues along with a new set of questions. Social science research in this field is bound to be even more exciting.

References

Acton, J. (1975) 'Nonmonetary factors in the demand for medical service: Some empirical evidence', *Journal of Political Economy*, 83.3:595–614.

Ahmad, A. and Morduch, J. (1993) 'Identifying sex bias in the allocation of household resources: Evidence from linked household surveys from Bangladesh', Harvard Institute of Economic Research Discussion Paper No. 1636, Harvard University.

Ainsworth, M. (1992) 'Economic aspects of child fostering in Côte d'Ivoire', Living Standards Measurement Study No. 92, World Bank.

Ainsworth, M. and Munoz, J. (1986) 'The Côte d'Ivoire Living Standards Survey: Design and implementation', Living Standards Measurement Study No. 26, World Bank.

Akin, J., Griffin, C., Guilkey, D. and Popkin, B. (1986) 'The demand for primary health care services in the Bicol region of the Philippines', *Economic Development and Cultural Change*, 34.4:755–782.

Alderman, H. (1986) 'Effects of price and income increases on food consumption of low income consumers', mimeo, International Food Policy Research Institute, Washington D.C.

Alderman, H. (1990) 'Nutrition status in Ghana and its determinants', Social Dimensions of Adjustment Working Paper No. 3, World Bank.

Alderman, H. (1993) 'New research on poverty and malnutrition: What are the implications for research and policy?', in: M. Lipton and J. van der Gaag, eds., *Including the Poor*, Washington D.C.: World Bank.

Alderman, H. and Gertler, P. (1989) 'The substitutability of public and private health care for the treatment of children in Pakistan', Living Standards Measurement Study No. 57, World Bank.

Alderman, H. and Paxson, C. (1992) 'Do the poor insure?: A synthesis of the literature on risk sharing institutions in developing countries', Research Program in Development Studies Discussion Paper No. 164, Woodrow Wilson School, Princeton University.

Alderman, H., Behrman, J.R., Khan, S., Ross, D.R. and Sabot, R. (1993) 'Public schooling expenditure in rural Pakistan: Efficiently targeting girls and a lagging region', mimeo, World Bank.

Altonji, J. (1991) 'Relationships among the family incomes and labor market outcomes of relatives', mimeo, Department of Economics, Northwestern University.

Altonji, J., Hayashi, F. and Kotlikoff, L. (1992a) 'Is the extended family altruistically linked? Direct tests using micro data', *American Economic Review*, 82.5:1177–1198.

Altonji, J., Hayashi, F. and Kotlikoff, L. (1992b) The effects of income and wealth on time and money transfers between parents and children, mimeo, Department of Economics, Northwestern University.

Anderson, K.H. (1982) 'The sensitivity of wage elasticities to selectivity bias and the assumption of normality: An example of fertility demand estimation', *Journal of Human Resources*, 17.4:594–605.

Anand, S., Harris, C. and Linton, O. (1993) 'On the concept of ultrapoverty', Harvard Center for Population and Development Studies Working Paper No. 93.02, Cambridge, Massachusetts.

Angrist, J. and Krueger, A.B. (1991) 'Does compulsory school attendance affect schooling and earnings?', *Quarterly Journal of Economics*, 106.4:979–1014.

Antle, J. (1984) 'Human capital, infrastructure and the productivity of Indian rice farmers', *Journal of Development Economics*, 14:163–182.

Armitage, J. and Sabot, R. (1987) 'Socioeconomic background and the returns to schooling in two low-income countries', *Economica*, 54:103–108.

Ashenfelter, O. and Krueger, A.B. (1992) 'Estimates of the economic returns to schooling from a new sample of twins', mimeo, Department of Economics, Princeton University.

Ashenfelter, O. and Zimmerman, D. (1993) 'Estimates of the returns to schooling from sibling data: Fathers, sons and brothers', National Bureau of Economic Research Working Paper No. 4491, Cambridge, Massachusetts.

Bardhan, P.K. (1988) 'Sex disparity in child survival in rural India', in: T.N. Srinivasan and P. K. Bardhan, eds., *Rural Poverty in South Asia*, New York: Columbia University Press.

Barrera, A. (1990a) 'The role of maternal schooling and its interaction with public health programs in child health production', *Journal of Development Economics*, 32.1:69–92.

Barrera, A. (1990b) 'The interactive effects of mother's schooling and unsupplemented breastfeeding on child health', *Journal of Development Economics*, 34:81–98.

Barros, R. and Lam, D. (1994) 'Income inequality, inequality in education and the demand for schooling in Brazil', in: N. Birdsall, B. Bruns and R. Sabot, eds., *Opportunity foregone: Education, growth and inequality in Brazil*, World Bank, forthcoming.

Basta, S., Soekirman, Karyadi, K. and Scrimshaw, N. (1979) 'Iron deficiency anemia and productivity of adult males in Indonesia', *American Journal of Clinical Nutrition*, 32:916–925.

Beaton, G. (1983) 'Energy in human nutrition: Perspectives and problems', *Nutrition Reviews*, 41.11:325–340.

Becker, G. (1960) 'An economic analysis of fertility', in: *Demographic and Economic Change in Developed Countries*, Princeton: Princeton University Press for the National Bureau of Economic Research.

Becker, G. (1965) 'A theory of the allocation of time', *Economic Journal*, 75:493–517.

Becker, G. and Lewis, H.G. (1973) 'On the interaction between the quantity and quality of children', *Journal of Political Economy*, 81.2:S279–S288.

Becker, G. and Tomes, N. (1979) 'An equilibrium theory of the distribution of income and intergenerational mobility', *Journal of Political Economy*, 87.6:1153–1189.

Behrman, J.R. (1988a) 'Intrahousehold allocation of nutrients in rural India: Are boys favored? do parents exhibit inequality aversion?', *Oxford Economic Papers*, 40.1:32–54.

Behrman, J.R. (1988b) 'Nutrition, health, birth order and seasonality: Intrahousehold allocation in rural India', *Journal of Development Economics*, 28.1:43–63.

Behrman, J.R. (1990) 'The action of human resources and poverty on one another: What we have yet to learn', Living Standards Measurement Study Working Paper No. 74, World Bank.

Behrman, J.R. (1992) 'Intrahousehold allocation of nutrients and gender effects: A survey of structural and reduced-form estimates', in: S.R. Osmani, ed., *Nutrition and Poverty*, Oxford: Oxford University Press.

Behrman, J.R. (1993a) 'The economic rationale for investing in nutrition in developing countries', *World Development*, 21.11:1749–1772.

Behrman, J.R. (1993b) 'Intrahousehold distribution and the family', in: M.R. Rosenzweig and O. Stark, eds., *Handbook of Population and Family Economics*, Amsterdam: North-Holland, forthcoming.

Behrman, J.R. and Birdsall, N. (1983) 'The quality of schooling: Quantity alone is misleading', *American Economic Review*, 73.5:928–946.

Behrman, J.R. and Deolalikar, A.B. (1987) 'Will developing country nutrition improve with income? A case study for rural South India', *Journal of Political Economy*, 95.3:492–507.

Behrman, J.R. and Deolalikar, A.B. (1988) 'Health and Nutrition', in: H. Chenery and T.N. Srinivasan, eds., *Handbook of Development Economics, Volume 1*, Amsterdam: North-Holland.

Behrman, J.R. and Deolalikar, A.B. (1989) 'Agricultural wages in India: The role of health, nutrition and seasonality', in: D. Sahn, ed., *Seasonal variability in third world agriculture*, Baltimore: Johns Hopkins University Press, 107–117.

Behrman, J.R. and Deolalikar, A.B. (1990) 'The intrahousehold demand for nutrients in rural south India: Individual estimates, fixed effects and permanent income', *Journal of Human Resources*, 25.4:665–696.

Behrman, J.R. and Deolalikar, A.B. (1991a) 'School repetition, dropouts, and the rates of return to schooling: The case of Indonesia', *Oxford Bulletin of Economics and Statistics*, 53.4:467–480.

Behrman, J.R. and Deolalikar, A.B. (1991b) 'The poor and the social sectors during a period of macroeconomic adjustment: Empirical evidence for Jamaica', *World Bank Economic Review*, 5.2:291–314.

Behrman, J.R. and Deolalikar, A.B. (1993) 'Unobserved household and community heterogeneity and the labor market impact of schooling: A case study for Indonesia', *Economic Development and Cultural Change*, 41.3:461–488.

Behrman, J.R. and Sussangkarn, C. (1990) 'Parental schooling and child outcomes: Mother versus father, schooling quality and interactions', mimeo, Department of Economics, University of Pennsylvania.

Behrman, J.R. and Wolfe, B.L. (1984a) 'Labor force participation and earnings determinants for women in the special conditions of developing countries', *Journal of Development Economics*, 15:259–288.

Behrman, J.R. and Wolfe, B.L. (1984b) 'The socioeconomic impact of schooling in a developing country', *Review of Economics and Statistics*, 66.2:296–303.

Behrman, J.R. and Wolfe, B.L. (1984c) 'More evidence on nutrition demand: Income seems overrated and women's schooling underemphasized', *Journal of Development Economics*, 14:105–128.

Behrman, J.R. and Wolfe, B.L. (1987) 'How does mother's schooling affect family health, nutrition, medical care usage and household sanitation?', *Journal of Econometrics*, 36:185–204.

Behrman, J.R. and Wolfe, B.L. (1989) 'Does more schooling make women better nourished and healthier?', *Journal of Human Resources*, 24.4:644–663.

Behrman, J.R., Birdsall, N. and Deolalikar, A.B. (1991) 'Marriage markets, labor markets and unobserved human capital: An empirical exploration for south-central India', mimeo, Department of Economics, University of Pennsylvania.

Behrman, J.R., Birdsall, N. and Kaplan, R. (1994) 'The quality of schooling in Brazil and labor market outcomes: Some further explorations', in: N. Birdsall, B. Bruns and R. Sabot, eds., *Opportunity foregone: Education, growth and inequality in Brazil*, World Bank, forthcoming.

Behrman, J.R., Deolalikar, A.B. and Wolfe, B.L. (1988) 'Nutrients: Impacts and determinants,' *World Bank Economic Review*, 2.3:299–320.

Behrman, J.R., Ii, M. and Murillo, D. (1993) 'Household schooling demands in urban Bolivia', mimeo, Department of Economics, University of Pennsylvania.

Behrman, J.R., Pollak, R. and Taubman, P. (1982) 'Parental preferences and provision for progeny', *Journal of Political Economy*, 90.1:52–73.

Behrman, J.R., Hrubec, H., Taubman, P. and Wales, T.J. (1980) *Socioeconomic success: A study of the effects of genetic endowments, family environment, and schooling*, Amsterdam: North-Holland.

Behrman, J.R., Sussangkarn, C., Hutaserani, S. and Wattanalee, S. (1993) 'Private versus public schooling impact on wage rates', mimeo, Department of Economics, University of Pennsylvania.

Benjamin, D. (1992) 'Household composition, labor markets, and labor demand: Testing for separation in agricultural household models', *Econometrica*, 60.2:287–322.

Ben-Porath, Y. (1980) 'The f-connection: Families, friends and firms and the organization of exchange', *Population and Development Review*, 6.1:1–30.

Bernheim, D., Shleifer, A. and Summers, L. (1985) 'The strategic bequest motive', *Journal of Political Economy*, 93.6:1045–1076.

Besley, T. (1995) 'Savings, credit and insurance', chapter 36 in: J. Behrman and T.N. Srinivasan, eds., *Handbook of Development Economics, Volume 3*, Amsterdam: North-Holland.

Bhalla, S. (1980) 'The measurement of permanent income and its application to savings behavior', *Journal of Political Economy*, 88.4:722–744.

Binswanger, H. and Rosenzweig, M.R. (1984) 'Contractual arrangements, employment and wages in rural labor markets: A critical review', in: H. Binswanger and M. Rosenzweig, eds., *Contractual arrangements, employment and wages in rural labor markets in Asia*, New Haven: Yale University Press, 1984.

Binswanger, H., Khandker, S. and Rosenzweig, M.R. (1993) 'How infrastructure and financial institutions affect agricultural output and investment in India', *Journal of Development Economics*, 41.2:337–366.

Binswanger, H., Evenson, R.E., Florencio, C.E. and White, B., eds. (1980) *Rural household studies in Asia*, Singapore: Singapore University Press.

Birdsall, N. (1979) 'An economic approach to birth order effects', Economic Growth Center Discussion Paper No. 313, Yale University.

Birdsall, N. (1985) 'Public inputs and child schooling in Brazil', *Journal of Development Economics*, 18.1:67–86.

Birdsall, N. (1988) 'Economic approaches to population growth', in: H. Chenery and T.N. Srinivasan, eds., *Handbook of Development Economics, Volume 1*, Amsterdam: North-Holland.

Birdsall, N. (1991) 'Birth order effects and time allocation', in: T.P. Schultz, ed., *Research in Population Economics, Volume 7*, Greenwich, CT: JAI Press, 191–213.

Bjorn, P. and Vuong, Q. (1984) 'Simultaneous equations models for dummy endogenous variables:

A game theoretic formulation with an application to labor force participation', Working paper, California Institute of Technology.

Blau, D. (1985a) 'The effects of economic development on life-cycle wage rates and labor supply behavior in Malaysia', *Journal of Development Economics*, 19:163–185.

Blau, D. (1985b) 'Self-employment and self-selection in developing country labor markets', *Southern Economic Journal*, 52.2:351–363.

Bliss, C. and Stern, N. (1978a) 'Productivity, wages and nutrition: part I: The theory', *Journal of Development Economics*, 5.4:331–362.

Bliss, C. and Stern, N. (1978b) 'Productivity, wages and nutrition: part II: Some observations', *Journal of Development Economics*, 5.4:363–398.

Blumberg, R. (1988) Income under female versus male control: Hypotheses from a theory of gender stratification and data from the third world, *Journal of Family Issues*, 9.1:51–84.

Boissiere, M., Knight, J.B. and Sabot, R. (1985) 'Earnings, schooling, ability and cognitive skills', *American Economic Review*, 75.5:1016–1030.

Bouis, H.E. (1994) 'The effect of income on demand for food in poor countries: Are our databases giving us reliable estimates?', *Journal of Development Economics*, 44.1:199–226.

Bouis, H.E. and Haddad, L.J. (1992) 'Are estimates of calorie-income elasticities too high? a recalibration of the plausible range', *Journal of Development Economics*, 39.2:333–364.

Bound, J. and Johnson, G. (1992) 'Changes in the structure of wages in the 1980's: And evaluation of alternative explanations', *American Economic Review*, 82.3:371–392.

Bound, J., Jaeger, D. and Baker, R. (1993) 'The cure can be worse than the disease: A cautionary tale regarding instrumental variables', Technical Working Paper No. 137, National Bureau of Economic Research, Cambridge, Massachussetts.

Bourguignon, F., Browning, M., Chiappori, P.-A. and Lechene, L. (1993) 'Intrahousehold allocation of consumption: Some evidence on French data', *Annales d'Economie et de Statistique*, 29:137–156.

Bourguignon, F., Browning, M., Chiappori, P.-A. and Lechene, L. (1995) 'Incomes and outcomes: A structural model of intra-household allocation', *Journal of Political Economy*, forthcoming.

Briscoe, J., Akin, J. and Guilkey, D. (1990) 'People are not passive acceptors of threats to health: Endogeneity and its consequences', *International Journal of Epidemiology*, 19:147–153.

Browning, M. (1992) 'Children and household behavior', *Journal of Economic Literature*, 30.3:1434–1475.

Browning, M. and Chiappori, P.-A. (1993) 'Efficient intra-household allocations: A general characterization', mimeo, McMaster University.

Browning, M., Deaton, A. and Irish, M. (1985) 'A profitable approach to labor supply and commodity demands over the life cycle', *Econometrica*, 53.3:503–544.

Butz, W. and DaVanzo, J. (1975) 'Economic and demographic family behavior in Malaysia: A conceptual framework for analysis', R-1834-AID, RAND, Santa Monica, California.

Butz, W. and DaVanzo, J. (1978) 'The Malaysian Family Life Survey: Summary report', R-2351-AID, RAND, Santa Monica, California.

Buzina, R. et al. (1989) 'Workshop on functional significance of mild-to-moderate malnutrition', *American Journal of Clinical Nutrition*, 50:172–176.

Caldwell, J.C. (1977) 'The economic rationality of high fertility: An investigation illustrated with Nigerian survey data', *Population Studies*, 31.1:5–27.

Caldwell, J.C. (1979) 'Education as a factor in mortality decline: An examination of Nigerian data', *Population Studies*, 33.3:395–413.

Card, D. and Krueger, A.B. (1992a) 'Does school quality matter? returns to education and the characteristics of public schools in the United States', *Journal of Political Economy*, 100.1:1–40.

Card, D. and Krueger, A.B. (1992b) 'School quality and black-white relative earnings: A direct assessment', *Quarterly Journal of Economics*, 107.1:151–200.

Carlin, P. (1991) 'Intra-family bargaining and time allocation', in: T.P. Schultz, ed., *Research in Population Economics, Volume 7*, Greenwich, CT: JAI Press, 215–243.

Carnoy, M. (1967) 'Earnings and schooling in Mexico', *Economic Development and Cultural Change*, 15:408–419.

Casterline, J., Cooksey, E. and Ismail, A.F. (1989) 'Household income and child survival in Egypt', *Demography*, 26.1:15–36.
Cebu Study Team. (1991) 'Underlying and proximate determinants of child health: The CEBU longitudinal health and nutrition study', *American Journal of Epidemiology*, 133.2:185–201.
Cebu Study Team. (1992) 'A child health production function estimated from longitudinal data', *Journal of Development Economics*, 38.2:323–351.
Chen, L.C., Huq, E. and D'Souza, S. (1981) 'Sex bias in the family allocation of food and health care in rural Bangladesh', *Population and Development Review*, 7.1:55–70.
Chernichovsky, D. and Meesook, O. (1984) 'Urban-rural food and nutrition consumption patterns in Indonesia', World Bank Staff Working Paper no. 670, Washington D.C.
Chiappori, P.-A. (1988) 'Rational household labor supply', *Econometrica*, 56.1:63–89.
Chiappori, P.-A. (1992) 'Collective labor supply and welfare', *Journal of Political Economy*, 100.3:437–467.
Clark, C. (1981) 'Children's economic activities and primary school attendance in rural Guatemala', RAND Paper Series P-6603.
Cleland, J. and van Ginneken, J. (1988) 'Maternal education and child survival in developing countries: The search for pathways of influence', *Social Science and Medicine*, 27.12:1357–1368.
Cochrane, S., O'Hara, D. and Leslie, J. (1982) 'Parental education and child health: intracountry evidence', *Health Policy and Education*, 2:213–250.
Colclough C. (1982) 'The impact of primary schooling on economic development: A review of the evidence', *World Development*, 10.3:167–185.
Cornia, G.A., Jolly, R. and Stewart, F., eds. (1987) *Adjustment with a human face, volume 1*, Oxford: Clarendon Press.
Cox, D. (1987) 'Motives for private income transfers', *Journal of Political Economy*, 95.3:508–546.
Cox, D. and Jimenez, E. (1990a) 'The relative effectiveness of private and public schools: Evidence from two developing countries', *Journal of Development Economics*, 34:99–121.
Cox, D. and Jimenez, E. (1990b) 'Achieving social objectives through private transfers', *World Bank Research Observer*, 5.2:205–218.
Cox, D. and Jimenez, E. (1992) 'Social security and private transfers in developing countries: The case of Peru', *World Bank Economic Review*, 6.1:155–169.
D'Souza, S. and Chen, L. (1980) 'Sex differentials in mortality in rural Bangladesh', *Population and Development Review*, 6.2:257–270.
Das Gupta, M. (1987) 'Selective discrimination against female children in rural Punjab, India', *Population and Development Review*, 13.1:77–100.
Dasgupta, P. and Ray, D. (1986) 'Inequality as a determinant of malnutrition and unemployment: Theory', *Economic Journal*, 96:1011–1034.
Dasgupta, P. and Ray, D. (1987) 'Inequality as a determinant of malnutrition and unemployment: Policy', *Economic Journal*, 97:177–188.
DaVanzo, J. (1988) 'Infant mortality and socioeconomic development: Evidence from Malaysian household data', *Demography*, 25.4:581–595.
DaVanzo, J. and Habicht, J.-P. (1986) 'Infant mortality decline in Malaysia, 1946-1975: The roles of changes in variables and changes in the structure of relationships', *Demography*, 23.2:143–160.
Deaton, A. (1988) 'Quality, quantity and spatial variation in price', *American Economic Review*, 78.3:418–430.
Deaton, A. (1989a) 'Saving in developing countries: Theory and review', *Proceedings of the World Bank Annual Conference on Development Economics*, 61–96.
Deaton, A. (1989b) 'Looking for boy-girl discrimination in household expenditure data', *World Bank Economic Review*, 3.1:1–15.
Deaton, A. (1990) 'Price elasticities from survey data: Extensions and Indonesian results', *Journal of Econometrics*, 44.3:281–309.
Deaton, A. (1992a) 'Saving and income smoothing in Côte d'Ivoire', *Journal of African Economies*, 1:1–24.
Deaton, A. (1992b) 'Household saving in LDCs: Credit markets, insurance and welfare', *Scandinavian Journal of Economics*, 94.2:253–273.
Deaton, A. (1992c) *Understanding Consumption*, Oxford: Oxford University Press.

Deaton, A. (1995) 'Data and econometric tools for development economics', chapter 35 in: J. Behrman and T.N. Srinivasan, eds., *Handbook of development economics, Volume 3*, Amsterdam: North-Holland.

Deaton, A. and Muellbauer, J. (1980) *Economics and consumer behavior*, Cambridge: Cambridge University Press.

Deolalikar, A.B. (1988) 'Nutrition and labor productivity in agriculture: Estimates for rural South India', *The Review of Economics and Statistics*, 70.3:406–413.

Deolalikar, A.B. (1992) 'Does the impact of government health expenditure on the utilization of health services by children and on child health outcomes differ across expenditure classes?', mimeo, Department of Economics, University of Washington.

Deolalikar, A.B. (1993) 'Gender differences in the returns to schooling and in schooling enrollment rates in Indonesia', *Journal of Human Resources*, 28.4:899–932.

de Tray, D. (1988) 'Government policy, household behavior, and the distribution of schooling: A case study of Malaysia', in: T.P. Schultz, ed., *Research in Population Economics, Volume 6*, Greenwich, CT: JAI Press.

Dey, J. (1981) 'Gambian women: Unequal partners in rice development projects?', *Journal of Development Studies*, 17.3:110–122.

Dos Reis, J.G.A. and de Barros, R.P. (1991) 'Wage inequality and the distribution of education: A study of the evolution of regional differences in inequality in metropolitan Brazil', *Journal of Development Economics*, 36.1:117–143.

Dougherty, C. and Jimenez, E. (1991) 'The specification of earnings functions: Tests and implications', *Economics of Education Review*, 10.2:85–98.

Duraisamy, P. (1992) 'Gender, intrafamily allocations of resources and child schooling in south India', Economic Growth Center Discussion Paper No. 667, Yale University.

Duraisamy, P. and Malathy, R. (1991) 'Impact of public programs on fertility and gender specific investment in human capital of children in rural India: Cross sectional and time series analyses', in: T.P Schultz, ed., *Research in Population Economics, Volume 7*, Greenwich, CT: JAI Press, 157–187.

Edmundson, W. and Sukhatme, P.V. (1990) 'Food and work: Poverty and hunger?', *Economic Development and Cultural Change*, 38.2:263–280.

Ellis, R. and Mwabu, G. (1988) 'The demand for outpatient medical care in rural Kenya', mimeo, Department of Economics, Boston University.

Engle, P. (1993) 'Influences of mothers' and fathers' income on children's nutritional status in Guatemala', *Social Science and Medicine*, 37:1303–1312.

Esrey, S. and Habicht, J-P. (1988) 'Maternal literacy modifies the effect of toilets and piped water in infant survival in Malaysia', *American Journal of Epidemiology*. 127.5:1079–1087.

Esrey, S., Feachem, R. and Hughes, J. (1985) 'Interventions for the control of diarrhoeal diseases among young children: Improving water supplies and excreta disposal facilities', *Bulletin of the World Health Organization*, 63:757–772.

Evenson, R.E. (1978) 'Symposium of household economics: Introduction', *The Philippine Economic Journal*, 36:1–31.

Evenson, R.E., Popkin, B. and King-Quizon, E. (1980) 'Nutrition, work and demographic behavior in rural Philippine households: A synopsis of several Laguna household studies', in: H. Binswanger, R. Evenson, C. Florencio and B. White, eds., *Rural Household Studies in Asia*, Singapore: Singapore University Press.

Fafchamps, M. (1993) 'Sequential labor decisions under uncertainty: An estimable household model of West African farmers', *Econometrica*, 61.5:1173–1198.

Falkner, F. and Tanner, J.M. (1986) *Human growth: A comprehensive treatise, Volume 3*, New York: Plenum Press.

Farah, A-A. and Preston, S. (1982) 'Child mortality differentials in the Sudan', *Population and Development Review*, 8.2:365–384.

Featherman, D. and Hauser, R. (1978) *Opportunity and Change*, New York: Academic Press.

Fogel, R. (1986) 'Physical growth as a measure of the economic well-being of populations: The eighteenth and nineteenth centuries', in: F. Falkner and J.M. Tanner, eds., *Human growth: A comprehensive treatise, Volume 3*, 2nd edition, New York: Plenum Press.

Fogel, R., Costa, D. and Kim, J. (1992) 'Secular trends in the distribution of chronic conditions at young adult and late ages, 1860–1888: Some preliminary findings'. mimeo, University of Chicago.

Folbre, N. (1986) 'Cleaning house: New perspectives on households and economic development', *Journal of Development Economics*, 22.1:5–40.

Food and Agricultural Organization/World Health Organization. (1973) *Energy and Protein Requirements*, Report of the Joint Consultative Meeting of Experts From FAO/WHO/UNU. Geneva: World Health Organization Technical Report Series No. 522.

Food and Agricultural Organization/World Health Organization. (1985) *Energy and Protein Requirements*, Report of the Joint Consultative Meeting of Experts From FAO/WHO/UNU. Geneva: World Health Organization.

Foster, A. (1993) 'Household partition in rural Bangladesh', *Population Studies*, 47.1:97–114.

Foster, A. (1995) 'Rice prices, credit markets and child growth in rural Bangladesh', *Economic Journal*, forthcoming.

Foster, A. and Rosenzweig, M.R. (1991) 'Unequal pay for unequal work: Asymmetric information, sex discrimination and the efficiency of casual labor markets', mimeo, Department of Economics, University of Pennsylvania.

Foster, A. and Rosenzweig, M.R. (1992) 'Information flows and discrimination in labor markets in rural areas in developing countries', *Proceedings of the World Bank Annual Conference on Development Economics*, 173–204.

Foster, A. and Rosenzweig, M.R. (1993) 'Information, learning and wage rates in low-income rural areas', *Journal of Human Resources*, 28.4:759–790.

Foster, A. and Rosenzweig, M.R. (1994) 'A test for moral hazard in the labor market: Effort, health and calorie consumption', *Review of Economics and Statistics*, 76.2:213–227.

Foster, A. and Roy, N. (1993) 'The dynamics of education and fertility: Evidence from a family planning experiment', mimeo, Department of Economics, University of Pennsylvania.

Frankenberg, E. (1995) 'The effects of access to health care on infant mortality in Indonesia', *Health Transitions Review*, forthcoming.

Friedman, G. (1982) 'The heights of slaves in Trinidad', *Social Science History*, 6:482–515.

Galloway, P. (1988) 'Basic patterns in annual variations in fertility, nuptuality, mortality and prices in pre-industrial Europe', *Population Studies*, 42.2:275–302.

Garcia, M. and Pinstrup-Andersen, P. (1987) 'The pilot food price subsidy scheme in the Philippines: Its impact on income, food consumption and nutritional status', International Food Policy Research Institute Research Report no. 61. Washington D.C.

Gersovitz, M. (1988) 'Savings and development', in: H. Chenery and T.N. Srinivasan, eds., *Handbook of development economics, Volume 1*, Amsterdam: North-Holland.

Gertler, P. and Alderman, H. (1989) 'Family resources and gender differences in human capital investments: The demand for children's medical care in Pakistan', mimeo, RAND, Santa Monica, CA.

Gertler, P. and Glewwe, P. (1990) 'The willingness to pay for education in developing countries: Evidence from rural Peru', *Journal of Public Economics*, 42.3:251–275.

Gertler, P. and Glewwe, P. (1992) 'The willingness to pay for education for daughters in contrast to sons: Evidence from rural Peru', *The World Bank Economic Review*, 6.1:171–188.

Gertler, P. and Molyneaux, J. (1994) 'How economic development and family planning combined to reduce Indonesian fertility', *Demography*, 31.1:33–64.

Gertler, P. and van der Gaag, J. (1990) *The willingness to pay for medical care: Evidence from two developing countries*, Baltimore: Johns Hopkins University Press.

Gertler, P., Locay, L. and Sanderson, W. (1987) 'Are user fees regressive? The welfare implications of health care financing proposals in Peru', *Journal of Econometrics*, 36 (supp.):67–88.

Glewwe, P. (1991) 'Schooling, skills, and the returns to government investment in education: An exploration using data from Ghana', World Bank LSMS Working Paper No. 76.

Glewwe, P. and Jacoby, H. (1994) 'Student achievement and schooling choice in low-income countries: Evidence from Ghana', *Journal of Human Resources*, 29.3:843–864.

Goldin, C. and Margo, R. (1992) 'The great compression: The wage structure in the United States at mid-century', *Quarterly Journal of Economics*, 107.1:1–34.

Govindasamy, P. and DaVanzo, J. (1992) 'Ethnicity and fertility differentials in peninsular Malaysia: Do policies matter?', *Population and Development Review*, 18.2:243–267.

Greenhalgh, S. (1985) 'Sexual stratification in East Asia: The other side of "growth with equity" in East Asia', *Population and Development Review*, 11.2:265–314.

Griffin, C. (1987) 'Methods for estimating value of time with an application to the Philippines', Economic Growth Center Discussion Paper No. 549, Yale University.

Griliches, Z. (1957) 'Specification bias in estimates of production functions', *Journal of Farm Economics*, 39:8–20.

Griliches, Z. (1977) 'Estimating the returns to schooling: Some econometric problems', *Econometrica*, 45.1:1–22.

Griliches, Z. (1979) 'Sibling models and data in economics: Beginnings of a survey', *Journal of Political Economy*, 87.5:S37–S64.

Gronau, R. (1973) 'The intrafamily allocation of time: The value of housewive's time', *American Economic Review*, 63.4:634–651.

Gronau, R. (1977) 'Leisure, home production and work: The theory of the allocation of time revisited', *Journal of Political Economy*, 85.6:1099–1123.

Gronau, R. (1988) 'Consumption technology and the intrafamily distribution of resources: Adult equivalence scales reexamined', *Journal of Political Economy*, 96.6:1183–1205.

Grossman, M. (1972) 'On the concept of health capital and the demand for health', *Journal of Political Economy*, 80.2:223–255.

Guilkey, D., Popkin, B., Akin, J. and Wong, E. (1989) 'Prenatal care and pregnancy outcome in Cebu, Philippines', *Journal of Development Economics*, 30.2:241–272.

Guilkey, D. and Stewart, J. (1994) 'Infant feeding patterns and the marketing of infant foods in the Philippines', *Economic Development and Cultural Change*, forthcoming.

Guyer, J. (1986) 'Intra-household processes and farming systems research: Perspectives from anthropology', in: J. Moock, ed., *Understanding Africa's Rural Households and Farming Systems*, Boulder: Westview Press.

Habicht, J.-P., DaVanzo, J. and Butz, W.P. (1986) 'Does breastfeeding really save lives or are the apparent benefits due to biases?', *American Journal of Epidemiology*, 123.2:279–290.

Haddad, L.J. and Bouis, H.E. (1991) 'The impact of nutritional status on agricultural productivity: Wage evidence from the Philippines', *Oxford Bulletin of Economics and Statistics*, 53.1:45–68.

Haddad, L.J. and Kanbur, R. (1990) 'How serious is the neglect of intra-household inequality?', *Economic Journal*, 100:866–881.

Hanushek, E. (1986) 'The economics of schooling: Production and efficiency in public schools', *Journal of Economic Literature*, 24.3:1141–1177.

Harbison, R. and Hanushek, E. (1992) *Educational performance of the poor: Lessons from rural northeast Brazil*, Oxford: Oxford University Press.

Hartmann, H. (1981) 'The family as the locus of gender, class and political struggle: The example of housework', *Signs*, 6:366–394.

Hauser, R.M. and Sewell, W. (1986) 'Family effects in simple models of education, occupational status and earnings: Findings from the Wisconsin and Kalamazoo samples', *Journal of Labor Economics*, 4.3:S83–S115.

Hausman, J. and Taylor, W.E. (1981) 'Panel data and unobservable individual effects', *Econometrica*, 49.6:1377–1398.

Heckman, J.J. (1976) 'A life-cycle model of earnings, learning and consumption', *Journal of Political Economy*, 84.4: S11–S44.

Heckman, J.J. (1979) 'Sample selection bias as specification error', *Econometrica*, 47.1:153–161.

Heckman, J.J. and Hotz, V.J. (1986) 'An investigation of the labor market earnings of Panamanian males: Evaluating the sources of inequality', *Journal of Human Resources*, 21.4:507–542.

Heckman J.J. and Sedlacek, G. (1985) 'Heterogeneity, aggregation and market wages functions: An empirical model of self-selection in the labor market', *Journal of Political Economy*, 93.6:1077–1125.

Hill, A. and Mamdani, M. (1989) 'Operational guidelines for measuring health through household surveys', mimeo, Centre for Population Studies, School of Hygiene and Tropical Medicine, University of London.

Hill, K. and Palloni, A. (1992) 'Demographic responses to economic shocks: The case of Latin

America', mimeo, Department of Population Dynamics, School of Public Health, Johns Hopkins University.

Hoddinott, J. (1992) 'Rotten kids or manipulative parents: Are children old age security in western Kenya?', *Economic Development and Cultural Change*, 40.3:545–565.

Hoff, C. and Stiglitz, J. (1990) 'Imperfect information and rural credit markets-puzzles and policy perspectives', *World Bank Economic Review*, 4.3:235–250.

Horton, S. (1986) 'Child nutrition and family size in the Philippines', *Journal of Development Economics*, 23.1:161–176.

Horton, S. (1988) 'Birth order, and child nutritional status: Evidence from the Philippines', *Economic Development and Cultural Change*, 36.2:341–354.

Hossain, S. (1989) 'Effect of public programs on family size, child education and health', *Journal of Development Economics*, 30.1:145–158.

Hymer, S. and Resnick, S. (1969) 'A model of an agrarian economy with nonagricultural activities', *American Economic Review*, 59.4:493–506.

Hungerford, T. and Solon, G. (1987) 'Sheepskin effects in the returns to education', *Review of Economics and Statistics*, 69.1:175–177.

Immink, M. and Viteri, F. (1981) 'Energy intake and productivity of Guatemalan sugarcane cutters: An empirical test of the efficiency wage hypothesis', parts 1 and 2, *Journal of Development Economics*, 9.2:251–287.

Jacoby, H. (1993) 'Shadow wages and peasant family labor supply: An econometric application to the Peruvian Sierra', *Review of Economic Studies*, 60.4:903–921.

Jacoby, H. and Skoufias, E. (1992) 'Risk, seasonality and school attendance: Evidence from rural India', Rochester Center for Economic Research working paper no. 328, Department of Economics, University of Rochester.

Jamison, D. (1978) 'Radio education and student repetition in Nicaragua', in P. Suppes, B. Searle and J. Friend (eds.), *The Radio Mathematics Project: Nicaragua, 1976–1977*, Institute for Mathematical Studies in the Social Sciences, Stanford University.

Jamison, D. and Lau, L. (1982) *Farmer education and farm efficiency*, Baltimore: Johns Hopkins University Press.

Jimenez, E. (1995) 'Human and physical infrastructure: Public investment and pricing policies in developing countries', chapter 43 in: J. Behrman and T.N. Srinivasan, eds., *Handbook of Development Economics, Volume 3*, Amsterdam: North-Holland.

Jimenez, E., Lockheed, M. and Wattanawaha, N. (1988) 'The relative efficiency of private and public schools: The case of Thailand', *World Bank Economic Review*, 2.2:139–164.

John, M. (1988) 'Plantation slave mortality in Trinidad', *Population Studies*, 42.2:161–182.

Jorgenson, D. and Lau, L. (1969) 'An economic theory of agricultural household behavior', paper read at the 4th meeting of the Far Eastern meeting of the Econometric Society.

Kaufman, D. and Lindauer, D. (1986) 'A model of income transfers for the urban poor', *Journal of Development Economics*, 22.2:337–350.

Kennedy, E. and Peters, P. (1992) 'Household food security and child nutrition: The interaction and income and gender of household head', *World Development*, 20.8:1077–1085.

Khandker, S.R. (1991) 'Labor market participation, returns to education, and male-female wage differences in Peru', in: B.K. Herz and S.R. Khandker, eds., *Women's work, education and family welfare in Peru*, World Bank Discussion Paper No. 116, World Bank.

Killingsworth, M. (1983) *Labor Supply*, Cambridge: Cambridge University Press.

Killingsworth, M. and Heckman, J.J. (1986) 'Female labor supply: A survey', in: O. Ashenfelter and R. Layard, eds., *Handbook of Labor Economics, Volume 1*, Amsterdam: North-Holland.

King, E.M. (1990) 'Does education pay in the labor market? The labor force participation, occupation and earnings of Peruvian women', Living Standards Measurement Study Working Paper No. 67, World Bank.

King, E.M. and Bellew, R. (1991) 'Gains in the education of Peruvian women, 1940 to 1980', in: B.K. Herz and S.R. Khandker, eds., *Women's Work, Education and Family Welfare in Peru*, World Bank Discussion Paper No. 116, World Bank.

King, E.M. and Lillard, L. (1987) 'Education policy and schooling attainment in Malaysia and the Philippines', *Economics of Education Review*, 6.2:167–181.

Knight, J.B. and Sabot, R. (1983) 'Educational expansion and the Kuznets effect', *American Economic Review*, 73.5:1132–1136.

Knight, J.B. and Sabot, R. (1987) 'Educational expansion, government policy and wage compression', *Journal of Development Economics*, 26.2:201–221.

Knight, J.B. and Sabot, R. (1990) *Education, Productivity and Inequality: The East African Natural Experiment*, Oxford: Oxford University Press.

Kochar, A. (1992) 'Credit constraints and land tenancy markets in rural India', mimeo, Department of Economics, Stanford University.

Koenig, M., Fauveau, V. and Wojtyniak, B. (1991) 'Mortality reductions from health interventions: The case of immunization in Bangladesh', *Population and Development Review*, 17.1:87–104.

Korenman, S. and Neumark, D. (1991) 'Does marriage really make men more productive?', *Journal of Human Resources*, 26.2:282–307.

Korenman, S. and Neumark, D. (1992) 'Marriage, motherhood and wages', *Journal of Human Resources*, 27.2:233–255.

Krishna, R. (1964) 'Theory of the firm: Rapporteur's report', *Indian Economic Journal*, 11:514–525.

Kroeger, A. (1985) 'Response errors and other problems of health interview surveys in developing countries'. *World Health Statistics Quarterly*, 38.1:15–37.

Lam, D. and Levison, D. (1991) 'Declining inequality in schooling in Brazil and its effects on inequality in earnings', *Journal of Development Economics*, 37.1/2:199–225.

Lam, D. and Schoeni, R. (1993) 'Effects of family background on earnings and returns to schooling: Evidence from Brazil', *Journal of Political Economy*, 101.4:710–740.

Lam, D., Sedlacek, G. and Duryea, S. (1992) 'Increases in women's education and fertility decline in Brazil', Population Studies Center Research Report No. 92-255, University of Michigan.

Lambert, S. and Magnac, T. (1991) 'Measurement of implicit prices of family labour in agriculture: An application to Côte d'Ivoire', mimeo, INRA, Paris.

Langoni, C.G. (1973) *Distribuicao de renda e desenvolvimento economico do Brasil*, Rio de Janeiro: Editora Expressao e Cultura.

Latham, M. (1993) 'The relationship of nutrition to productivity and well-being of workers', in: P. Pinstrup-Andersen, ed., *The Political Economy of Food and Nutrition Policies*, Baltimore: Johns Hopkins Press.

Lavy, V. and Quigley, J. (1993) 'Willingness to pay for the quality and intensity of medical care: Evidence from low income households in Ghana', Living Standards Measurement Study No. 94, World Bank.

Lee, L.-F. and Rosenzweig, M.R. (1992) 'The effects of improved nutrition, sanitation and water purity on child health in high-mortality populations', mimeo, Department of Economics, University of Michigan.

Lee, R. (1980) 'Short term variation: Vital rates, prices and weather', in: E.A. Wrigley and R.S. Schofield, eds., *The population history of England 1541–1871: A reconstruction*, Cambridge: Cambridge University Press.

Leibenstein, H. (1957) *Economic backwardness and economic growth; studies in the theory of economic development*, New York: Wiley & Sons.

Leibowitz, A. (1974) 'Home investments in children', *Journal of Political Economy*, 82.2:S111–S131.

Levison, D. (1991) 'Are work and school incompatible? The labor market activity of Brazilian children, mimeo, Economic Growth Center, Yale University.

Levison, D. and Lam, D. (1991) 'Declining inequality in schooling in Brazil and its effects on inequality in earnings', *Journal of Development Economics*, 37:199–225.

Liedholm, C. and Kilby, P. (1991) 'The role of nonfarm activities in the rural economy', in: J. Williamson and V. Panchamukhi, eds., *The balance between industry and agriculture in economic development*, New York: Macmillan Press.

Lillard, L. and Willis, R. (1994) 'Intergenerational educational mobility: Effects of family and state in Malaysia', *Journal of Human Resources*, 29.4:1126–1166.

Lipton, M. (1983) 'Poverty, undernutrition and hunger', World Bank Staff Working Paper no. 597, Washington D.C.

Lipton, M. and Ravallion, M. (1995) 'Poverty and policy', chapter 41 in: J. Behrman and T.N. Srinivasan, eds., *Handbook of Development Economics, Volume 3*, Amsterdam: North-Holland.

Lopez, R. (1986) 'Structural models of the farm household that allow for interdependent utility and profit-maximization decisions', in: I. Singh, L. Squire and J. Strauss, eds., *Agricultural Household Models: Extensions, Applications and Policy*, Baltimore: Johns Hopkins Press.

Lucas, R.E.B. and Stark, O. (1985) 'Motivations to remit: Evidence from Botswana', *Journal of Political Economy*, 93.5:901–918.

Lundberg, S. and Pollak, R. (1993) 'Separate spheres bargaining and the marriage market', *Journal of Political Economy*, 101.6:988–1010.

MaCurdy, T. (1981) 'An empirical model of labor supply in a life-cycle setting', *Journal of Political Economy*, 89.6:1059–1085.

Magnac, T. (1991) 'Segmented or competitive labor markets?', *Econometrica*, 59.1:165–187.

Manning, W., Newhouse, J.P. and Ware, J. (1982) 'The status of health in demand estimation; or, beyond excellent, good fair, poor', in: V. Fuchs, ed., *Economic aspects of health*, Chicago: University of Chicago Press.

Manning, W., Newhouse, J.P., Duan, N., Keeler, E., Leibowitz, A. and Marquis, S. (1987) 'Health insurance and the demand for medical care: Evidence from a randomized experiment', *American Economic Review*, 77.3:251–277.

Manser, M. and Brown, M. (1980) 'Marriage and household decision-making: A bargaining analysis', *International Economic Review*, 21.1:31–44.

Margo, R. (1990) *Race and schooling in the south, 1880–1950: An economic history*, Chicago: University of Chicago Press.

Margo, R. and Steckel, R. (1982) 'The heights of American slaves: New evidence on slave nutrition and health', *Social Science History*, 6:516–538.

Martorell, R. and Arroyave, G. (1988) 'Malnutrition, work output and energy needs', in: K. Collins and F. Roberts, eds., *Capacity for Work in the Tropics*, Cambridge: Cambridge University Press.

Martorell, R. and Habicht, J.-P. (1986) 'Growth in early childhood in developing countries', in: F. Falkner and J.M. Tanner, eds., *Human Growth: A Comprehensive Treatise, Volume 3*, New York: Plenum Press.

Mazumdar, D. (1959) 'The marginal productivity theory of wages and disguised unemployment', *Review of Economic Studies*, 26:190–197.

Mazumdar, D. (1983) 'Segmented labor markets in LDCs', *American Economic Review*, 73.2:254–259.

McElroy, M. (1990a) 'The empirical content of Nash-bargained household behavior', *Journal of Human Resources*, 25.4:559–583.

McElroy, M. (1990b) 'Nash-bargained household decisions: Reply', *International Economic Review*, 31.1:237–242.

McElroy, M. and Horney, M.J. (1981) 'Nash-bargained household decisions: Toward a generalization of the theory of demand', *International Economic Review*, 22.2:333–349.

Medeiros, J. (1982) 'Alcance e limitacoes de teoria do capital humana: Diferencas de ganhos no Brasil em 1973', Serie Ensaios Economicos, Volume 17, Instituto de Pesquisas Economcos, Sao Paulo.

Mensch, B., Lentzner, H. and Preston, S. (1985) *Socio-economic differentials in child mortality in developing countries*, ST/ESA/SER.A/97, Department of International Economic and Social Affairs, United Nations, New York.

Merrick, T. (1985) 'The effect of piped water on early childhood mortality in urban Brazil 1970 to 1976', *Demography*, 22.1:1–24.

Miller, J.E. (1989) 'Is the relationship between birth intervals and perinatal mortality spurious? Evidence from Hungary and Sweden', *Population Studies*, 43.3:479–495.

Miller, J.E., Trussell, J., Pebley, A.R. and Vaughan, B. (1992) 'Birth spacing and child mortality in Bangladesh and the Philippines', *Demography*, 29.2:305–318.

Mirrlees, J. (1975) 'A pure theory of underdeveloped economies', in: L. Reynolds, ed., *Agriculture in Development Theory*, New Haven: Yale University Press.

Moll, P. (1992a) 'Quality of education and the rise in returns to schooling in South Africa, 1975–1985', *Economics of Education Review*, 11.1:1–10.

Moll, P. (1992b) 'Primary and secondary schooling returns in South Africa', mimeo.

Montgomery, M.R. and Casterline, J.B. (1993) 'The diffusion of fertility control in Taiwan: Evidence from pooled cross-section, time-series models', *Population Studies*, 47.3:457–479.

Moock, P., Musgrove, P. and Stelcner, M. (1990) 'Education and earnings in Peru's informal nonfarm family enterprises', Living Standards Measurement Study Working Paper No. 64, World Bank.

Morduch, J. (1990) 'Risk, production and saving: Theory and evidence from Indian households', mimeo, Department of Economics, Harvard University.

Morduch, J. (1991) 'Consumption smoothing across space: Tests for village-level responses to risk', mimeo, Department of Economics, Harvard University.

Mosley, H. and Chen, L. (1984) 'An analytical framework for the study of child survival in developing countries', in: H. Mosley and L. Chen, eds., *Child Survival: Strategies for Research, Supplement to Population and Development Review*, 10, 25–45.

Mroz, T. (1987) 'The sensitivity of an empirical model of married women's hours of work to economic and statistical assumptions', *Econometrica*, 55.4:765–799.

Mwabu, G. (1989) 'Nonmonetary factors in the household choice of medical facilities', *Economic Development and Cultural Change*, 37.2:383–392.

Mwabu, G., Ainsworth, M. and Nyamete, A. (1993) 'Quality of medical care and choice of medical treatment in Kenya: An empirical analysis', *Journal of Human Resources*, 28.4:838–862.

Nakajima, C. (1957) 'Equilibrium theory of the farm household', (in Japanese) *The Economic Review of Osaka University*, 7:2.

Nakajima, C. (1969) 'Subsistence and commercial family farms: Some theoretical models of subjective equilibrium', in: C. Wharton, ed., *Subsistence Agriculture and Economic Development*, Chicago: Aldine.

Nakajima, C. (1986) *Subjective equilibrium theory of the farm household*, Amsterdam: Elsevier Press.

National Research Council. (1993) *Population dynamics of sub-Saharan Africa, volume 5, Demographic effects of economic reversals in sub-Saharan Africa*, National Academy of Sciences, Washington D.C.

Nelson, C.R. and Startz, R. (1990) 'The distribution of the instrumental variables estimator and its t-ratio when the instrument is a poor one', *Journal of Business*, 63.1: S125–S140.

Newman, J., and Gertler, P. (1994) 'Family productivity, labor supply and welfare in a low income country', *Journal of Human Resources*, 29.4:989–1026.

Newman, J., Jorgensen, S. and Pradhan, M. (1991) 'How did workers' benefits from Bolivia's Emergency Social Fund', *World Bank Economic Review*, 5.2:367–393.

Nerlove, M. (1971) 'Further evidence on the estimation of dynamic economic relationships from a time series of cross sections', *Econometrica*, 39.2:359–382.

Nickell, S. (1981) 'Biases in dynamic models with fixed effects', *Econometrica*, 49.6:1417–1426.

Olsen, R. (1980) 'Estimating the effect of child mortality on the number of births', *Demography*, 17.4:429–443.

Olsen, R. (1988) 'Cross-sectional methods for estimating the replacement of infant deaths', in: T.P. Schultz, ed., *Research in Population Economics, Volume 6*, Greenwich, CT: JAI Press.

Olsen, R. and Wolpin, K. (1983) 'The impact of exogenous mortality on fertility: A waiting time regression with dynamic regressors', *Econometrica*, 51.3:731–749.

Orazem, P. (1987) 'Black-white differences in schooling investment and human capital production in segregated schools', *American Economic Review*, 77.4:714–723.

Over, M., Ellis, R., Huber, J. and Solon, O. (1992) 'The consequences of adult ill-health', in: R. Feachem, T. Kjellstrom, C. Murray, M. Over and M. Phillips, eds., *The Health of Adults in the Developing World*, Oxford: Oxford University Press.

Pacey, A. and Payne, P. (1985) *Agricultural development and nutrition*, Boulder: Westview Press.

Palloni, A. and Hill, K. (1992) 'The effects of structural adjustment on mortality by age and cause in Latin America', mimeo, Center for Demography and Ecology, University of Wisconsin.

Palloni, A., Hill, K. and Pinto Aguirre, G. (1993) 'Economic swings and demographic changes in the history of Latin America', mimeo, Center for Demography and Ecology, University of Wisconsin.

Parish, W.L. and Willis, R.J. (1993) 'Daughters, education and family budgets: Taiwan experiences', *Journal of Human Resources*, 28.4:863–898.

Paxson, C. (1992) 'Using weather variability to estimate the response of savings to transitory income in Thailand', *American Economic Review*, 82.1:15–33.

Payne, P. (1989) 'Public health and functional consequences of seasonal hunger and malnutrition', in: D. Sahn, ed., *Seasonal variability in third world agriculture*, Baltimore: Johns Hopkins University Press.

Pencavel, J. (1986) 'Labor supply of men: A survey', in: O. Ashenfelter and R. Layard, eds., *Handbook of Labor Economics, Volume 1*, Amsterdam: North-Holland.

Phillips, J., Simmons, R., Koenig, M. and Chakrobarty, J. (1988) 'Determinants of reproductive change in a traditional society: Evidence from Matlab Bangladesh', *Studies in Family Planning*, 19:313–334.

Pinstrup-Andersen, P. and Caicedo, E. (1978) 'The potential impact of changes in income distribution on food demand and human nutrition', *American Journal of Agricultural Economics*, 60:402–415.

Pitt, M. (1983) 'Food preferences and nutrition in rural Bangladesh', *Review of Economics and Statistics*, 65.1:105–114.

Pitt, M. (1990) 'An analysis of the nutritional levels of Indonesian households based upon household expenditure surveys', mimeo, Department of Economics, Brown University.

Pitt, M. and Rosenzweig, M.R. (1986) 'Agricultural prices, food consumption and the health and productivity of Indonesian farmers', in: I. Singh, L. Squire and J. Strauss, eds., *Agricultural household models: Extensions, applications and policy*, Baltimore: Johns Hopkins University Press.

Pitt, M. and Rosenzweig, M.R. (1989) 'The selectivity of fertility and the determinants of human capital investments: Parametric and semi-parametric estimates', Bulletin Number 89-9, Economic Development Center, Department of Economics, University of Minnesota.

Pitt, M. and Rosenzweig, M.R. (1990) 'Estimating the intrahousehold incidence of illness: Child health and gender-inequality in the allocation of time', *International Economic Review*, 31.4:969–980.

Pitt, M., Rosenzweig, M.R. and Hassan, Md.N. (1990) 'Productivity, health and inequality in the intrahousehold distribution of food in low-income countries', *American Economic Review*, 80.5:1139–1156.

Pitt, M., Rosenzweig, M.R. and Gibbons, D. (1993) 'The determinants and consequences of the placement of government programs in Indonesia', *World Bank Economic Review*, 7:319–348.

Poleman, T. (1981) 'Quantifying the nutrition situation in developing countries', *Food Research Institute Studies*, 18.1:1–58.

Pollak, R. (1969) 'Conditional demand functions and consumption theory', *Quarterly Journal of Economics*, 83:60–78.

Pollak, R. (1985) 'A transaction cost approach to families and households', *Journal of Economic Literature*, 23.2:581–608.

Pollak, R. and Wachter, M. (1975) 'The relevance of the household production function and its implications for the allocation of time', *Journal of Political Economy*, 83.2:255–277.

Pong, S.-L. (1992) 'Preferential policies and secondary school attainment in peninsular Malaysia', *Sociology of Education*, 66.4:245–261.

Popkin, B., Adair, L., Akin, J., Black, R., Briscoe, J. and Flieger, W. (1990) 'Breast-feeding and diarrheal morbidity', *Pediatrics*, 86.6:874–882.

Preston, S. (1978) *The effects of infant and child mortality on fertility*, New York: Academic Press.

Preston, S. and Haines, M. (1991) *Fatal years: Child mortality in late nineteenth century America*, Princeton: Princeton University Press.

Psacharopoulos, G. (1973) *Returns to education; an international comparison*, San Francisco: Jossy Bass-Elsevier.

Psacharopoulos, G. (1981) 'Returns to education: An updated international comparison', *Comparative Education*, 17:321–341.

Psacharopoulos, G. (1985) 'Returns to education: A further international update and implications', *Journal of Human Resources*, 20.4:583–604.

Psacharopoulos, G. (1989) 'Time trends of the returns to education: Cross-national evidence', *Economics of Education Review*, 8.3:225–231.

Psacharoloulos, G. and Velez, E. (1992) 'Schooling, ability and earnings in Colombia, 1988', *Economic Development and Cultural Change*, 40.3:629–643.

Quisumbing, A. (1994) 'Intergenerational transfers in Philippine rice villages: Gender differences in traditional inheritance customs', *Journal of Development Economics*, 43.2:167–196.

Rahman, O., Foster, A. and Menken, J. (1992) 'Older widow mortality in rural Bangladesh', *Social Science and Medicine*, 34.1:89–96.

Rao, V. (1993) 'The price of a spouse: A hedonic analysis of dowry and brideprice in rural India', *Journal of Political Economy*, 101:666–677.

Rao, V. and Greene, M. (1991) 'Marital instability, inter-spouse bargaining and their implications for fertility in Brazil: A multi-disciplinary analysis', Population Research Center Discussion Paper No. OSC-PRC 91-3, NORC/University of Chicago.

Ravallion, M. (1987) *Markets and famines*, Oxford: Clarendon Press.

Ravallion, M. (1990) 'Income effects on undernutrition', *Economic Development and Cultural Change*, 38.3:489–515.

Ravallion, M. and Dearden, L. (1988) 'Social security in a "Moral Economy": An empirical analysis for Java', *The Review of Economics and Statistics*, 70.1:36–44.

Ravallion, M. and Huppi, M. (1991) 'Measuring changes in poverty: A methodological case study of Indonesia during an adjustment period', *World Bank Economic Review*, 5.1:57–82.

Razzaque, A., Alam, N., Wai, L. and Foster, A. (1990) 'Sustained effects of the 1974–5 famine on infant and child mortality in a rural area of Bangladesh', *Population Studies*, 44.1:145–154.

Riley, J. (1979) 'Testing the educational screening hypothesis', *Journal of Political Economy*, 87.5:S227–S252.

Rose, E. (1992) 'Ex-ante and ex-post labor supply response to risk in a low income area', mimeo, Department of Economics, University of Pennsylvania.

Rosenzweig, M.R. (1980) 'Neoclassical theory and the optimizing peasant: An econometric analysis of market family labor supply in a developing country', *Quarterly Journal of Economics*, 94.1:31–55.

Rosenzweig, M.R. (1982) 'Educational subsidy, agricultural development and fertility change', *Quarterly Journal of Economics*, 97.1:67–88.

Rosenzweig, M.R. (1988a) 'Risk, implicit contracts and the family in rural areas of low-income countries', *Economic Journal*, 98:1148–1170.

Rosenzweig, M.R. (1988b) 'Risk, private information, and the family', *American Economic Review*, 78.2:245–250.

Rosenzweig, M.R. (1988c) 'Labor markets in low-income countries', in: H. Chenery and T.N. Srinivasan, eds., *Handbook of development economics, Volume 1*, Amsterdam: North-Holland.

Rosenzweig, M.R. (1990) 'Population growth and human capital investments: Theory and evidence', *Journal of Political Economy*, 98.5:S38–S70.

Rosenzweig, M.R. (1993) 'Women, insurance capital and economic development in rural India', *Journal of Human Resources*, 28.4:735–758.

Rosenzweig, M.R. and Binswanger, H. (1993) 'Wealth, weather risk and the composition and profitability of agricultural investments', *Economic Journal*, 103:56–78.

Rosenzweig, M.R. and Evenson, R.E. (1977) 'Fertility, schooling and the economic contribution of children in rural India: An econometric analysis', *Econometrica*, 45.5:1065–1079.

Rosenzweig, M.R. and Schultz, T.P. (1982a) 'Market opportunities, genetic endowments and intrafamily resource distribution: Child survival in rural India', *American Economic Review*, 72.4:803–815.

Rosenzweig, M.R. and Schultz, T.P. (1982b) 'Child mortality and fertility in Colombia: Individual and community effects', *Health Policy and Education*, 2:305–348.

Rosenzweig, M.R. and Schultz, T.P. (1983) 'Estimating a household production function: Heterogeneity, the demand for health inputs and their effects on birth weight', *Journal of Political Economy*, 91.5:723–746.

Rosenzweig, M.R. and Schultz, T.P. (1985) 'The demand for and supply of births: Fertility and its life-cycle consequences', *American Economic Review*, 75.5:992–1015.

Rosenzweig, M.R. and Schultz, T.P. (1987) 'Fertility and investments in human capital: Estimates of the consequences of imperfect fertility control in Malaysia', *Journal of Econometrics*, 36:163–184.

Rosenzweig, M.R. and Stark, O. (1989) 'Consumption smoothing, migration and marriage: Evidence from rural India', *Journal of Political Economy*, 97.4:905–926.

Rosenzweig, M.R. and Wolpin, K.I. (1980) 'Testing the quantity-quality fertility model: The use of twins as a natural experiment', *Econometrica*, 48.1:227–240.

Rosenzweig, M.R. and Wolpin, K.I. (1982) 'Government interventions and household behavior in a developing country: Anticipating the unanticipated consequences of social programs', *Journal of Development Economics*, 10:209–225.

Rosenzweig, M.R. and Wolpin, K.I. (1985) 'Specific experience, household structure and intergenerational transfers', *Quarterly Journal of Economics*, 100(5), Supplement: 961–987.

Rosenzweig, M.R. and Wolpin, K.I. (1986) 'Evaluating the effects of optimally distributed public programs: Child health and family planning interventions', *American Economic Review*, 76.3:470–482.

Rosenzweig, M.R. and Wolpin, K.I. (1988a) 'Heterogeneity, intrafamily distribution and child health', *Journal of Human Resources*, 23.4:437–461.

Rosenzweig, M.R. and Wolpin, K.I. (1988b) 'Migration selectivity and the effects of public programs', *Journal of Public Economics*, 37.2:265–289.

Rosenzweig, M.R. and Wolpin, K.I. (1993a) 'Credit market constraints, consumption smoothing and the accumulation of durable production assets in low-income countries: Investments in bullocks in India', *Journal of Political Economy*, 101.2:223–244.

Rosenzweig, M.R. and Wolpin, K.I. (1993b) 'Maternal expectations and ex post rationalizations: The usefulness of survey information on the wantedness of children', *Journal of Human Resources*, 28.2:205–258.

Rutenberg, N. and Diamond, I. (1993) 'Fertility in Botswana: The recent decline and future prospects', *Demography*, 30.2:143–157.

Sahn, D. (1988) 'The effect of price and income changes in food-energy intake in Sri Lanka', *Economic Development and Cultural Change*, 36.2:315–340.

Sahn, D. (1990) 'Malnutrition in Côte d'Ivoire: Prevalence and determinants', Social Dimensions of Adjustment Working Paper No. 4, World Bank.

Sahn, D. and Alderman, H. (1988) 'The effects of human capital on wages, and the determinants of labor supply in a developing country', *Journal of Development Economics*, 29.2:157–183.

Schofield, S. (1979) *Development and the Problems of Village Nutrition*, London: Croom Helm.

Schultz, T.P. (1973) 'Birth rate changes over space and time: A study of Taiwan', *Journal of Political Economy*, 31.supplement: 238–274.

Schultz, T.P. (1976) 'Interrelationships between mortality and fertility', in: R. Ridker, ed., *Population and Development: The Search for Selective Interventions*, Baltimore: Johns Hopkins Press.

Schultz, T.P. (1984) 'Studying the impact of household economic and community variables on child mortality', in: H. Mosley and L. Chen, eds., *Child survival: Strategies for research, Supplement to Population and Development Review*, 10:215–235.

Schultz, T.P. (1988a) 'Education investments and returns', in: H. Chenery and T.N. Srinivasan, eds., *Handbook of development economics, Volume 1*, Amsterdam: North-Holland.

Schultz, T.P. (1988b) 'Heterogeneous preferences and migration: Self-selection, regional prices and programs and the behavior of migrants in Colombia', in: T.P. Schultz, ed., *Research in Population Economics, Volume 6*, Greenwich, CT: JAI Press.

Schultz, T.P. (1988c) 'Population programs: Measuring their impact on fertility and the personal distribution of their effects', *Journal of Policy Modeling*, 10.1:113–139.

Schultz, T.P. (1990) 'Testing the neoclassical model of family labor supply and fertility', *Journal of Human Resources*, 25.4:599–634.

Schultz, T.P. (1991) 'Marriage, own and spouse's characteristics', mimeo, Department of Economics, Yale University.

Schultz, T.P. (1992) 'The relationship between local family planning expenditures and fertility in Thailand, 1976–1981', Economic Growth Center Discussion Paper No. 662, Yale University.

Schultz, T.P. (1993a) 'Returns to women's education', in: E.M. King and M. Hill, eds., *Women's education in developing countries: Barriers, benefits, and policies*, Baltimore: Johns Hopkins University Press.

Schultz, T.P. (1993b) 'The demand for children in low income countries', in: M.R. Rosenzweig and O. Stark, eds., *Handbook of Population and Family Economics*, Amsterdam: North-Holland, forthcoming.

Schultz, T.P. and Tansel, A. (1992) 'Measurement of returns to adult health: Morbidity effects on wage rates in Côte d'Ivoire and Ghana', Economic Growth Center Discussion Paper No. 663, Yale University.

Schultz, T.W. (1963) *The economic value of education*, New York: Columbia University Press.

Schultz, T.W. (1964) *Transforming traditional agriculture*, Chicago: University of Chicago Press.

Schultz, T.W. (1975) 'The value of the ability to deal with disequilibria', *Journal of Economic Literature*, 13.3:827–846.

Sen, A. (1966) 'Peasants and dualism with and without surplus labor', *Journal of Political Economy*, 74:425–450.

Sen, A. (1984) 'Family and food: Sex bias in poverty', in: A. Sen, ed., *Resources, Value and Development*, London: Blackwell.

Sen, A. (1990) 'More than 100 million women are missing', *New York Review of Books*, 37:20 (December 20, 1990):61–66.

Sen, A. and Sengupta, S. (1983) 'Malnutrition of rural children and sex bias', *Economic and Political Weekly*, 18:855–864.

Senauer, B., Garcia, M. and Jacinto, E. (1988) 'Determinants of the intrahousehold allocation of food in the rural Philippines', *American Journal of Agricultural Economics*, 70.1:170–180.

Sindelar, J. and Thomas, D. (1991) 'Measurement of child health: Maternal response bias', Economic Growth Center Discussion Paper No. 633, Yale University.

Singh, I., Squire, L. and Strauss, J., eds., (1986) *Agricultural household models: Extensions, applications and policy*, Baltimore: Johns Hopkins University Press.

Skoufias, E. (1993a) 'Seasonal labor utilization in agriculture: Theory and evidence from agrarian households in India', *American Journal of Agricultural Economics*, 75.1:20–32.

Skoufias, E. (1993b) 'Labor market opportunities and intrafamily time allocation in rural households in South Asia', *Journal of Development Economics*, 40.2:277–310.

Skoufias, E. (1994) 'Market wages, family composition and the time allocation of children in agricultural households', *Journal of Development Studies*, 30.2:335–360.

Smith, J.P. (1977) 'Assets, savings and labor supply', *Economic Inquiry*, 15.4:551–573.

Smith, J.P. (1980) *Female labor supply: Theory and estimation*, Princeton: Princeton University Press.

Smith, J.P. (1991) 'Labor markets and economic development in Malaysia', in: T.P. Schultz, ed., *Research in Population Economics*, 7:131–156.

Smith, J.P. and Thomas, D. (1993) 'On the road: Marriage and mobility in Malaysia', Labor and Population Program Working Paper No. 93-11, RAND.

Spurr, G.B. (1983) 'Nutritional status and physical work capacity', *Yearbook of Physical Anthropology*, 26:1–35.

Staiger, D. and Stock, J. (1993) 'Asymptotics for instrumental variables regressions with weakly correlated instruments', mimeo, Kennedy School, Harvard University.

Stark, O. (1991) *The Migration of Labor*, Cambridge: Basil Blackwell.

Stark, O. (1992) 'Nonmarket transfers and altruism', *European Economic Review*, 37.7:1413–1424.

Stelcner, M., Arriagada, A.-M. and Moock, P. (1987) 'Wage determinants and school attainment among men in Peru', Living Studies Measurement Study Working Paper No. 38, World Bank.

Stewart, A., Ware, J., Brook, R. and Davies-Avery, A. (1978) *Conceptualization and measurement of health status for adults in the Health Insurance Study: Volume II, physical health in terms of functioning*, R-1987/2-HEW, RAND, Santa Monica, California.

Stewart, J., Popkin, B., Guilkey, D., Akin, J., Adair, L. and Flieger, W. (1991) 'Influences on the extent of breast-feeding: A prospective study in the Philippines', *Demography*, 28:181–200.

Stiglitz, J. (1976) 'The efficiency wage hypothesis, surplus labor and the distribution of income in LDCs', *Oxford Economic Papers*, 28.2:185–207.

Strauss, J. (1984) 'Joint determination of food consumption and production in rural Sierra Leone: Estimates of a household-firm model', *Journal of Development Economics*, 14:77–103.

Strauss, J. (1986a) 'Does better nutrition raise farm productivity?', *Journal of Political Economy*, 94.2:297–320.

Strauss, J. (1986b) 'The theory and comparative statics of agricultural household models: A general approach', in: I. Singh, L. Squire and J. Strauss, eds., *Agricultural Household Models: Extensions, Applications and Policy*, Baltimore: Johns Hopkins University Press.

Strauss, J. (1990) 'Households, communities and preschool child nutrition outcomes: Evidence from rural Côte d'Ivoire', *Economic Development and Cultural Change*, 38.2:231–261.

Strauss, J. (1993) 'The impact of improved nutrition on labor productivity and human resource development', in: P. Pinstrup-Andersen, ed., *The Political Economy of Food and Nutrition Policies*, Baltimore: Johns Hopkins Press.

Strauss, J. and Thomas, D. (1990) 'The shape of the calorie expenditure curve', Economic Growth Center Discussion Paper No. 595, Yale University.

Strauss, J. and Thomas, D. (1994) 'Wages, schooling and background: Investments in men and women in urban Brazil', in: N. Birdsall, B. Bruns and R. Sabot, eds., *Opportunity foregone: Education, growth and inequality in Brazil*, World Bank, forthcoming.

Strauss, J., Gertler, P., Rahman, O. and Fox, K. (1993) 'Gender and life-cycle differentials in the patterns and determinants of adult health', *Journal of Human Resources*, 28.4:791–837.

Subramanian, S. and Deaton, A. (1990) 'Gender effects in Indian consumption patterns', Research Program in Development Studies Discussion Paper No. 147, Woodrow Wilson School, Princeton University.

Subramanian, S. and Deaton, A. (1992) 'The demand for food and calories: Further evidence from India', mimeo, Woodrow Wilson School, Princeton University.

Sukhatme, P.V. (1988) 'Energy intake and nutrition: On the autoregulatory homeostatic nature of the energy requirement', in: T.N. Srinivasan and P.K. Bardhan, eds., *Rural Poverty in South Asia*, New York: Columbia University Press.

Sukhatme, P.V. and Margen, S. (1982) 'Autoregulatory homeostatic nature of energy balance', *American Journal of Clinical Nutrition*, 35:355–365.

Sumner, D. (1981) 'Wage functions and occupational selection in a rural less developed country setting', *Review of Economics and Statistics*, 63.4:513–519.

Svedberg, P. (1990) 'Undernutrition in sub-Saharan Africa: Is there a gender bias?', *Journal of Development Studies*, 26.3:469–486.

Tanaka, O. (1951) 'An analysis of economic behavior of the farm household', (in Japanese) *Journal of Rural Economics*, 22.

Tang, S.L.W. (1981) 'The differential educational attainment of children: An empirical study of Hong Kong', Ph.D. dissertation, University of Chicago.

Thomas, D. (1986) 'Can the food share be used as a welfare measure?', Ph.D. dissertation, Department of Economics, Princeton University.

Thomas, D. (1990) 'Intra-household resource allocation: An inferential approach', *Journal of Human Resources*, 25.4:635–664.

Thomas, D. (1991) 'Gender differences in household resource allocations', Living Standards Measurement Studies Working Paper No. 79, World Bank.

Thomas, D. (1993) 'The distribution of income and expenditure within the household', *Annales de Economie et de Statistique*, 29:109–136.

Thomas, D. (1994) 'Like father like son, or, like mother, like daughter: Parental education and child health', *Journal of Human Resources*, 29.4:950–988.

Thomas, D. and Chen, C.-L. (1994), 'Income shares and shares of income: Empirical tests of models of household resource allocations', RAND Labor and Population Program Working Paper 94-08, Santa Monica, California.

Thomas, D. and Strauss, J. (1992a) 'Prices, infrastructure, household characteristics and child height', *Journal of Development Economics*, 39.2:301–331.

Thomas, D. and Strauss, J. (1992b) 'Health, wealth and wages of men and women in urban Brazil', mimeo, Department of Economics, Yale University.

Thomas, D., Lavy, V. and Strauss, J. (1992) 'Public policy and anthropometric outcomes in the

Côte d'Ivoire', Living Standards Measurement Study Working Paper no. 89, World Bank, Washington D.C.

Thomas, D., Strauss, J. and Henriques, M-H. (1989) 'Child survival, nutritional status and household characteristics: Evidence from Brazil', *Pesquisa e Planejamento Economico*, 19:427–482, Instituto de Planejamento Economico e Social, Rio de Janeiro, Brazil.

Thomas, D., Strauss, J. and Henriques, M-H. (1990) 'Child survival, height for age and household characteristics in Brazil', *Journal of Development Economics*, 33.2:197–234.

Thomas, D., Strauss, J. and Henriques, M-H. (1991) 'How does mother's education affect child height?', *Journal of Human Resources*, 26.2:183–211.

Timmer, C.P. and Alderman, H. (1979) 'Estimating consumption parameters for food policy analysis', *American Journal of Agricultural Economics*, 61.5:982–994.

Topel, R. (1991) 'Specific capital, mobility and wages: Wages rise with job seniority', *Journal of Political Economy*, 99.1:145–176.

Townsend, R. (1994) 'Risk and insurance in village India', *Econometrica*, 62.3:539–592.

Trairatvorakul, P. (1984) 'The effects on income distribution and nutrition of alternative rice price policies in Thailand', Research Report 46, International Food Policy Research Institute, Washington D.C.

Udry, C. (1990) 'Credit markets in northern Nigeria: Credit as insurance in a rural economy', *World Bank Economic Review*, 4.3:251–269.

Udry, C. (1993) 'Risk and saving in northern Nigeria', mimeo, Department of Economics, Northwestern University.

Udry, C. (1994) 'Risk and insurance in a rural credit market: An empirical investigation in northern Nigeria', *Review of Economic Studies*, 61.3:495–526.

Ulph, D. (1988) 'A general non-cooperative Nash model of household consumption behavior', mimeo, Department of Economics, Bristol University.

van der Gaag, J. and Vijverberg, W. (1988) 'A switching regression model of wage determinants in the public and private sectors of a developing country', *Review of Economics and Statistics*, 70.2:244–252.

van der Gaag, J. and Vijverberg, W. (1989) 'Wage determinants in Côte d'Ivoire: Experience, credentials and human capital', *Economic Development and Cultural Change*, 37.2:371–381.

van de Walle, E. (1992) 'Fertility transition, conscious choice and numeracy', *Demography*, 29.4:487–502.

Vijverberg, W. (1991) 'Profits from self-employment: The case of Côte d'Ivoire', *World Development*, 19.6:683–696.

Vijverberg, W. (1992) 'Measuring income from family enterprises with household surveys', *Small Business Economics*, 4.4:287–305.

Vijverberg, W. (1993) 'Educational investments and returns for women and men in Côte d'Ivoire', *Journal of Human Resources*, 28.4:933–974.

von Braun, J. and Pandya-Lorch, R., eds. (1991) *Income sources of malnourished people in rural areas: Microlevel information and policy implications*, Working Papers on Commercialization of Agriculture and Nutrition no. 5, International Food Policy Research Institute.

von Braun, J. and Webb, P. (1989) 'The impact of new crop technology on the agricultural division of labor in a West African setting', *Economic Development and Cultural Change*, 37.3:513–534.

von Braun, J., Puetz, D. and Webb, P. (1989) *Irrigation technology and commercialization of rice in the Gambia: Effects on income and nutrition*, International Food Policy Research Institute Research Report No. 75, Washington D.C.

von Braun, J., de Haen, H. and Blanken, J. (1991) *Commercialization of agriculture under population pressure: Effects on production, consumption and nutrition in Rwanda*, International Food Policy Research Institute Research Report No. 85, Washington D.C.

Walker, T. and Ryan, J. (1990) *Village and household economies in India's semi-arid tropics*, Baltimore: Johns Hopkins University Press.

Waaler, H. (1984) 'Height, weight and mortality: The Norwegian experience', *Acta Medica Scandinavia*, supplement no. 679., Stockholm.

Ward, J. and Sanders, J. (1980) 'Nutritional determinants and migration in the Brazilian northeast: A case study of rural and urban Ceara', *Economic Development and Cultural Change*, 29.1:141–163.

Ware, J., Davies-Avery, A. and Brook, R. (1980) *Conceptualization and measurement of health status for adults in the Health Insurance Study: Volume VI, analysis of relationships among health status measures*, R-1987/6-HEW, RAND, Santa Monica, California.

Waterlow, J.C., Buzina, R., Keller, W., Lane, J., Nichaman, M. and Tanner, J.M. (1977) 'The presentation and use of height and weight data for comparing the nutritional status of groups of children under the age of 10 years', *Bulletin of the World Health Organization*, 55:489–498.

Welch, F. (1970) 'Education in production', *Journal of Political Economy*, 78.1:35–59.

Welch, F. (1979) 'Effects of cohort size on earnings: The baby boom babies' financial bust', *Journal of Political Economy*, 87.5:S65–S97.

Williams, A.D. (1977). 'Measuring the impact of child mortality on fertility: A methodological note', *Demography*, 14:581–590.

Willis, R.J. (1974) 'Economic theory of fertility behavior', in: T.W. Schultz, ed., *The Economics of the Family: Marriage, Children, and Human Capital*, Chicago: University of Chicago Press.

Willis, R.J. (1986) 'Wage determinants: A survey and reinterpretation of human capital earnings functions', in: O. Ashenfelter and R. Layard, eds., *Handbook of Labor Economics, Volume 1*, Amsterdam: North-Holland.

Willis, R.J. and Rosen, S. (1979) 'Education and self-selection', *Journal of Political Economy*, 87.5:S7–S36.

Wolfe, B.L. and Behrman, J.R. (1983) 'Is income overrated in determining adequate nutrition?', *Economic Development and Cultural Change*, 31.3:525–549.

Wolfe, B.L. and Behrman, J.R. (1984) 'Determinants of women's health status and health care utilization in a developing country: A latent variable approach', *Review of Economics and Statistics*, 66.4:696–703.

Wolfe, B.L. and Behrman, J.R. (1987) 'Women's schooling and children's health: Are the effects robust with adult sibling control for the women's childhood background', *Journal of Health Economics*, 6.3:239–254.

Wolpin, K.I. (1977) 'Education and screening', *American Economic Review*, 67.5:949–958.

Wolpin, K.I. (1982) 'A new test of the permanent income hypothesis: The impact of weather on the income and consumption of farm households in India', *International Economic Review*, 23.3:583–594.

Wong, E., Popkin, B., Akin, J. and Guilkey, D. (1987) 'Accessibility, quality of care, and prenatal care use in the Philippines', *Social Science and Medicine*, 24.11:927–944.

Zeldes, S. (1989) 'Optimal consumption with stochastic income: Deviations from certainty equivalence', *Quarterly Journal of Economics*, 104.2:275–298.

Chapter 35

APPLIED GENERAL EQUILIBRIUM MODELS FOR POLICY ANALYSIS[1]

JAN WILLEM GUNNING* and MICHIEL A. KEYZER**

Free University, Amsterdam

Contents

[1] We gratefully acknowledge valuable comments on an earlier version by Jere Behrman, Stanley Fischer, Celito Habito, Larry Lau, T.N. Srinivasan and other participants at the First ADB Conference on Development Economics and of Victor Ginsburgh, Geert Overbosch and Claus Weddepohl. A very large number of researchers active in this field have responded to our request for information on ongoing and recently completed research and their cooperation was very valuable.
   * Department of Agriculture and Development Economics, Faculty of Economic and Econometric Sciences.
   ** Centre for World Food Studies.

Handbook of Development Economics, Volume III, Edited by J. Behrman and T.N. Srinivasan
© *Elsevier Science B.V., 1995*

1. Introduction

Policy makers are commonly interested in the effects of particular policy measures, like a change in income tax, on the wellbeing of various socio-economic groups and on the government budget. Often these effects can be studied in a partial setting. Similarly, when there is a change in the rate of subsidy on a particular commodity the effect on other markets may be limited, so that again partial analysis will do. It is only when there are substantial indirect effects on other groups or on other markets that an economywide analysis is needed.

This calls for multi-agent, multi-commodity models. General equilibrium models can fulfil this purpose and bring the additional advantage that the response of the model to imposed shocks satisfies the conditions of optimality of agents' behaviour, technological feasibility and resource constraints. This point is particularly relevant when the shocks are large, as is typically the case under trade liberalization or financial deregulation.

General equilibrium analysis used to be confined to pure theory but it has increasingly become a tool of applied policy work. This involves two crucial steps. First, in theory equilibrium is only a possible, though often desirable state, but in applied models it is treated as a representation of reality. It implies optimizing behaviour, budget balance (all expenses have to be covered) and clearing of markets. It also involves an assumption which is more controversial: all trading is assumed to take place in equilibrium (no false trading) so that agents receive no signals corresponding to non-equilibrium allocations. Secondly, one has to specify the set of commodities for which (spot and future) markets exist.

While general equilibrium theory remains a very active field of research, since the mid-seventies policy analysts have come to see the theory as descriptively useful. This is partly due to its improved capability to move beyond the assumptions of the Arrow–Debreu competitive equilibrium. Initially this was largely limited to taxes and tariffs but recent general equilibrium models also include imperfect competition, increasing returns, price rigidities and many other extensions.

Whatever the descriptive value of the general equilibrium concept, it has an important normative value. This is because of the relation, known from the welfare theorems between, a general equilibrium and a welfare optimum. This relation makes it possible to use general equilibrium models to design welfare improving reforms. For this reason this survey will often use a form of presentation which makes welfare analysis easier than with the form commonly used in applied general equilibrium work.

Moreover, the approach facilitates data collection and organization because it provides, like input-output analysis, a coherent framework, namely a social accounting matrix in which accounts are disaggregated by agent (households, firms and government).

The Korea model of Adelman and Robinson (1978) marked the beginning of applied general equilibrium models for developing countries.[2] In fact for a great many countries one or more models now exist. At the same time international general equilibrium models were developed, usually by linking country and regional models.

The field has become much more accessible in recent years. Principles of construction of general equilibrium models are discussed in Dixon et al. (1992) and Shoven and Whalley (1992). Kehoe (1991) gives an excellent treatment of many theoretical and computational aspects. Brooke, Kendrick and Meeraus (1988) and Codsi et al. (1992) document two useful software packages [Gams and Gempack].

There have been several surveys including Shoven and Whalley (1984), Manne (1985), Devarajan et al. (1986), de Melo (1988), Decaluwé and Martens (1989) and Robinson (1989) in Chapter 18 of this Handbook. Since several recent surveys exist, this chapter will not attempt to be exhaustive. It will focus on areas which have received relatively little attention in these surveys such as welfare analysis of reforms, money, dynamic aspects, external effects and imperfect competition. The survey will cover some promising examples in these fields for developed countries and even some theoretical models which have not yet been applied. The aim of this chapter is to provide a classification of existing and potential applications which is explicitly related to the theoretical literature.

The structure of the chapter is as follows. In the next Section we introduce the simplest applied general equilibrium model, which we will refer to as the basic Computable General Equilibrium (CGE) model and we describe some of its extensions. Section 3 is devoted to the use of the CGE-model in policy analysis. While the CGE-model accounts for the bulk of the applications, it imposes a number of restrictions: it does not allow bounds on endogenous variables (e.g. quantitative constraints on imports), government interventions are necessarily distortionary and financial markets are not modelled explicitly. These limitations are addressed in the subsequent sections where we consider models that do not belong to the CGE-class as we define it. In Section 4 we allow for inequality constraints and for non-distortionary government interventions justified by external effects or non-convexities. In Section 5 we discuss intertemporal aspects, both under finite and infinite horizons, and we pay

---

[2] Also "archetype" models have been developed which do not describe a specific economy but are designed to explore numerically particular policy issues.

particular attention to the modelling of money and financial assets. Section 6 concludes.

2. The CGE-model

In this section we first present the basic CGE-model. We briefly discuss some important aspects of implementation (social accounting, parameter estimation, dynamics and welfare measures). We also present and compare alternative formats for representing a model which will facilitate later exposition. The section concludes with the specification of extensions of the basic CGE-model which define the CGE-models that are commonly used in applications.

2.1. Specification

2.1.1. The basic CGE-model

The basic CGE-model is specified as follows. There are r commodities, m consumers and n firms. Some commodities (factors) are not produced: $n < r$. Those which are produced are called goods.[3]
Consumer i, $i = 1, \ldots, m$ has preferences given by a utility function u_i: $R_+^r \to R$ which is strictly concave, nonsatiated and increasing for at least one consumer (say consumer 1). Each consumer owns nonzero endowments of factors but there are no endowments of goods. Factor endowments of consumer 1 are strictly positive.[4]
Firm j, $j = 1, \ldots, n$ produces a single commodity and there is at most one firm producing each commodity.[5] Its production function f_j: $R_+^r \to R_+$ requires positive inputs of at least one factor (like labour). It is monotonic, has constant returns to scale, strictly convex isoquants and inaction is allowed ($f_j(0) = 0$).
We denote consumption by x_i, input demand by v_j, gross production by q_j and prices by p.
A competitive equilibrium of the basic CGE-model[6] is an allocation x_i^*, q_j^*, v_j^* supported by a price vector p^*, such that:

---

[3] The index set $\{1, \ldots, r\}$ for commodities is partitioned into $G = \{1, \ldots, n\}$ for goods and $F = \{n + 1, \ldots, r\}$ for factors; $J = \{1, \ldots, n\}$ is the set of firms.
[4] The assumptions on consumer 1 ensure that prices are positive in equilibrium.
[5] This assumption is restrictive and will be relaxed. It ensures that no commodity is produced by firms with different constant returns to scale technologies. This avoids discontinuities in response which can arise when two constant returns to scale firms compete.
[6] The basic CGE-model differs from the standard Arrow–Debreu specification in three respects: (a) constant returns to scale are imposed, (b) there is at most one firm for each commodity, (c) there is at least one consumer whose utility function is increasing and whose endowment is positive.

(1) Consumer i maximizes his utility subject to a budget constraint:[7]

$$\max_{x_i \geq 0} u_i(x_i)$$

subject to

$$p^* x_i \leq h_i^*$$

for given prices p^* and income from endowments $h_i^* = p^* \omega_i$, where ω_i is the vector of endowments.

(2) Firm j maximizes its profits:

$$\pi_j(p^*) = \max_{y_j \in Y_j} p^* y_j$$

where the production set Y_j is defined as:

$$Y_j = \{y_j | y_j \leq q_j b_j - v_j, \ q_j \leq f_j(v_j), \ q_j \geq 0, \ v_j \geq 0\}$$

and b_j is a vector of constants and f_j denotes the production function; for ease of notation we assume that the first n commodities are produced, so that $b_{jj} = 1$ for $j = 1, \ldots, n$ and 0 otherwise. Let y_j^* be optimal in this program.[8]

(3) Markets clear with free disposal:

$$\sum_i x_i^* - \sum_j y_j^* - \sum_i \omega_i \leq 0 \perp p^* \geq 0 \,^9$$

Utility maximization (1) and profit maximization (2) imply that consumption and input-output coefficients are homogeneous of degree zero in prices. Therefore, the model (1)–(3) determines only relative prices, as usual. It has a solution with (as yet unnormalized) positive prices, so that the commodity balance in (3) will hold with equality.

---

[7] We write ab for the inner product $a \cdot b$. The variables under the maximand are the arguments of the optimization (in this case x_i).

[8] Since the production function has constant returns to scale, y_j^* is not unique. Profits are zero in equilibrium and scale independent so that the producer is indifferent as to the scale of production. Since there is a single firm for each produced commodity, the level of output will be determined from the demand side. Because profits are zero the consumer's income consists only of the value of endowment.

[9] We use the notation $a \leq 0 \perp b \geq 0$ to represent $a \leq 0$, $b \geq 0$ and $ab = 0$. The left-hand inequality indicates that there cannot be positive excess demand, the right-hand inequality that prices cannot be negative and complementarity implies that if a commodity is in excess supply in equilibrium its price is zero. In this case the inequalities themselves are already sufficient, $ab = 0$ is implied by Walras' Law.

2.1.2. The CGE-format

We have written the model in the Arrow–Debreu format, using the optimization problems of consumers and firms. However, the CGE-model is usually represented in a format which contains explicit consumer and input demand functions. One therefore specifies analytical forms of the (Marshallian) demand functions $x_i(p, h_i)$ for the consumer implied by the utility maximization problem (1). For the producer profit maximization problem (2) implies cost minimization:

$$C_j(p, q_j) = \min_{v_j \geq 0} pv_j$$

subject to

$$f_j(v_j) \geq q_j$$

for given gross output q_j, where $C_j(p, q_j) = c_j(p) q_j$ because of constant returns to scale. Demand by firm j for commodity k can be obtained by applying Shephard's lemma:

$$v_{jk}(p, q_j) = a_{kj}(p)q_j$$

where $a_{kj}(p) = \partial c_j(p)/\partial p_k$ is the input-output coefficient.[10]

Denoting goods and factors by superscripts g and f respectively, one obtains consumer demand functions $x_i^g(p^g, p^f, h_i)$ and $x_i^f(p^g, p^f, h_i)$ and input coefficient functions $A^g(p^g, p^f)$ and $A^f(p^g, p^f)$ for goods and factors. This leads to the following representation:

$$\sum_i x_i^g(p^g, p^f, h_i) + A^g(p^g, p^f) q^g = q^g \tag{4}$$

$$\sum_i x_i^f(p^g, p^f, h_i) + A^f(p^g, p^f) q^g = \sum_i \omega_i^f \tag{5}$$

$$p^g = p^g A^g(p^g, p^f) + p^f A^f(p^g, p^f) \tag{6}$$

$$h_i = p^f \omega_i^f \tag{7}$$

Here, (4) and (5) are the commodity balances for goods and factors. The matrices A^g and A^f contain the input-output coefficients for goods and factors respectively. Since under constant returns to scale profits are zero, the goods

---

[10] Thus, the resulting matrix of input output coefficients $A(p) = [a_{kj}(p)]$ has r rows and n columns.

price in (6) is set equal to unit cost, that is, the value of goods and factors used as inputs.[11]

Note that part of the model is recursive. For given input-output coefficients and given p^f, one can solve for p^g from the linear equation (6); income h_i follows from (7), so that consumption $x_i^g(p^g, p^f, h_i)$ is determined. Hence equation (4) can be solved for q^g. Factor input demand $A^f(p^g, p^f) q^g$ in (5) can then be computed. Since demand for factors $x_i^f(p^g, p^f, h_i)$ can also be calculated, one can determine whether (5) is satisfied.[12] In equilibrium the input coefficients will be equal to their function value.

We will say that a model is written in CGE-format when it is specified as a system of simultaneous equations consisting of commodity balances [like (4) and (5)] for goods and factors, price equations for goods [like (6)] and budget equations (7).[13] This is a wide class which contains all the models of Section 2 and 3. The class excludes models with inequality constraints,[14] with an infinite number of commodities or agents or periods, or with multiple firms under constant or increasing returns to scale.

2.1.3. Trade in the CGE-model

The model (4)–(7) is closed in the sense that there is no external trade.[15] We can introduce external trade by relaxing some of the factor balances. We distinguish tradeable and nontradeable factors with index sets T and N and partition the index set F accordingly. Trade may be physically impossible but nontradeability may also be the result of trade policy. For example, labour may be non-tradeable because migration is not allowed.

The factor balance (5) can now be rewritten as:

$$\sum_i x_{ik}(p^g, p^f, h_i) + A_k(p^g, p^f)q^g = \sum_i \omega_{ik}, \quad k \in N \tag{5a}$$

---

[11] To ensure that prices of goods are positive at all nonzero values of p^f (rather than at equilibrium only) it is commonly assumed that the economy is productive, i.e. for all (p^g, p^f) there exists some positive q^g such that $q^g \geq A^g(p^g, p^f) q^g$, with at least one strict inequality. This guarantees that $(I - A^g(p^g, p^f))$ has a non-negative inverse.

[12] A fixed point algorithm may be used to adjust factor prices until this condition is satisfied.

[13] The system may also include other equality constraints with associated to them additional endogenous variables, called closure variables. We will discuss this and other extensions in section 2.4.

[14] Introducing inequality constraints transforms the problem from a nonlinear system of equalities $F(x) = 0$ into the nonlinear complementarity problem $F(x) \geq 0 \perp x \geq 0$ which requires more sophisticated computational methods. For a discussion of solution algorithms see Kehoe (1991).

[15] International trade can be represented in the closed model by treating consumers as members of different nations and by assigning firms to nations. The model then describes trade between and within the nations covered but, of course, not trade with external agents. Hence, such a model necessarily describes either an autarkic region or the whole world.

$$\sum_i x_{ik}(p^g, p^f, h_i) + A_k(p^g, p^f)q^g = \sum_i \omega_{ik} + z_k, \quad k \in T \qquad (5b)$$

where z_k is net imports demand of commodity k.

For tradeable factors, prices are given exogenously[16], endowments may be zero (the factor will then be imported) and net imports z^f_k adjusts. The budget equations and commodity balances imply that $\Sigma_{k \in T} p_k \ z^f_k = 0$, so that the external deficit is zero. These prices can be normalized arbitrarily and determine the normalization of the domestic prices.

This treatment of trade can be extended to goods. However, this may introduce practical problems. First, at a given world price for a particular good profits may become negative, so that the good is not produced domestically. Secondly, if profits are zero then output is indeterminate since the producer is indifferent and supply cannot be determined from the demand side as it was in (4) since foreign demand is completely price elastic.[17]

In practice modellers avoid this difficulty in two ways. One is to specify demand for exports as demand of foreign consumers. These consumers face prices p^g (possibly corrected for tariffs). The specification serves a dual purpose. One thereby drops the small-country assumption, since external prices are no longer all treated as given. It also avoids the difficulty of the trader being indifferent between internal and external destinations for supply. In these models there are imports, but not of commodities produced domestically under constant returns to scale.

Another way to avoid the difficulty is to define a firm-specific factor. This will avoid indifference of the producer, provided the production function is increasing in this factor.

2.2. Implementation

2.2.1. Choice of classifications

In applied models one has to choose a classification of consumers, firms and commodities, whereas in theoretical analysis one only has to specify index sets. Choosing this classification is one of the most decisive steps in applied work. To keep the costs involved in checking of data, parameter estimation and

---

[16] In practice this poses a problem: the external price used for commodity k will be either an import or an export price. This imposes a sign restriction on z_k, which is, however, not included in the model. For example, if an import price has been used while in a policy experiment the solution for z_k is negative, there is an inconsistency.

[17] The case of positive profits cannot arise as it would lead to infinite demand for nontradeable factors.

monitoring of simulation results manageable the extent of disaggregation will have to be limited.

For consumers for example two criteria should be taken into account. One important consideration is whether groups are expected to be differentially affected by policy changes. On this ground one may want to distinguish groups such as landless labourers or rural households with access to remittances. One may also want to distinguish vulnerable groups like orphans, but this is difficult to implement empirically. A second criterion is that, within each group, heterogeneity should be as limited as possible. Income distribution within classes can be represented by imposing fixed (discrete or continuous) income distribution. At this point it must be recognized that all applied general equilibrium models suffer from problems involved in the representative agent construction: aggregation of individual net trades does not preserve microeconomic properties other than continuity, homogeneity and adding up. This is a fundamental problem from which any level of disaggregation suffers. For a further discussion see Kirman (1992).

For commodities it is inevitable that some of the commodity aggregates, particularly in the manufacturing and in the service sector, are heterogeneous. One implication is that domestic and foreign production of the "same" commodity are imperfect substitutes. This has led to the "Armington-specification", discussed in Section 2.4.3.

2.2.2. The social accounting matrix (SAM)

A solution to the model (4)–(7) makes it possible to write balances for all commodities (in volume and value terms) and budget constraints for all agents which constitute the basic elements of a Social Accounting Matrix (SAM). Often a SAM is written only in value terms and is (like an input-output table) organized to highlight the flow of payments by commodity between agents. A simple SAM is shown in Table 35.1.[18]

In terms of equations (4)–(7) the SAM can be interpreted as follows. Let k denote a good. Its commodity balance can be written in value terms by premultiplying the kth row by the associated price. The left-hand side of the balance equation (4) represents demand and appears in this table as one of the goods rows. The two expenditure components appear in the columns for firms and consumers. The demand of firms $(p_k A_k(p^g, p^f) q^g)$ is booked as "input"; similarly, the demand of consumers $(p_k x_{ik}(p^g, p^f, h_i))$ is booked as "consumption". The right hand side of equation (4) represents supply

---

[18] The term "SAM-based model" is sometimes used but is misleading since a SAM does not define a model. Rather, any model which satisfies commodity balances and budget constraints defines a SAM.

Table 35.1
Structure of a SAM

	Goods	Factors	Firms	Consumers	External
Goods			Input	Consumption	
Factors			Input	Consumption	Export
Firms	Production				
Consumers		Endowments	Profits		
Externals		Import			

from production and appears in the kth goods column. Obviously, since the entries are derived from a balance equation, the row and column totals are equal.

For factors, the same applies with two qualifications. First, in model (4)–(7) factors are not produced. Secondly, the basic CGE-model allows for international trade in factors but not in goods.

For generality there is an entry for profits in the SAM of Table 35.1, although profits are zero due to constant-returns.

Once a SAM (in values) has been obtained, estimates of prices are derived.[19] This yields estimates of h_i, p^f, p^g, q^g in (4)–(7). It also gives estimates for consumption x_i^f, x_i^g and input coefficients A^f and A^g. If the functions which determine these variables are also "calibrated" in order to ensure that they generate the observed values, then, by construction, the model will fully replicate the SAM. Hence such a base year solution does not provide any new information for the period covered by the SAM.[20]

2.2.3. Parameter estimation

To implement the CGE-model, one needs to provide analytical specifications for the demand functions $x_i(\cdot)$ (possibly including the export demand functions) and the input-output matrix $A(\cdot)$. Usually the input-output coefficients are obtained as derivatives of some postulated unit-cost function e.g. a Cobb–

[19] In many applications prices are set equal to one through an appropriate choice of units. The disadvantage of this procedure is that price and volume results cannot be compared directly with published data. A more serious drawback is that the information contained in price differences e.g. on transport costs is likely to be lost. For example, if rice is produced in different locations then interregional price differences will be attributed to product heterogeneity rather than to transportation costs, even if the products are in fact physically identical. We shall return to this point in Sections 2.4.3 and 4.1.2.

[20] It does provide consistency checks and this is an important advantage of using a SAM. When the outcomes of the model do not coincide with those of the SAM, one may be able to identify the error by comparing all row and columns totals. There are two possible sources of differences: either the SAM violates model restrictions (like non-negativity of income) or the model does not follow the SAM structure (due to a programming error or a difference in design).

Douglas or a CES function but more flexible forms have also been used. For consumer demand one may also apply Cobb–Douglas or CES-forms for indirect utility functions as well as more elaborate forms like translog.[21,22]

Full system econometric estimation of parameters in equations (4)–(7) is usually impossible. There are two reasons for this. First, there are identification problems since the number of endogenous variables is very large. One could, of course, attempt to instrumentalize at least some of these endogenous variables, but this is rarely done.

Secondly, full system estimation is also hampered by lack of data. For consumption, household budget surveys may be available for a few years, possibly supplemented by aggregate time series data. For inputs one rarely has access to more than one or two input-output tables, supplemented with time series of a more specialized nature (e.g. agricultural production series). This severely limits the scope for a more than rudimentary treatment of the intertemporal correlation of disturbances.

Modellers often react to these econometric problems by resorting to simple benchmarking methods. This typically involves borrowing elasticities from the literature and adjusting some coefficients to force the model to reproduce a selected set of base year data. This is clearly unsatisfactory. Although full system estimation is rarely feasible, it is, of course, possible to estimate components of the model, e.g. consumer demand and input demand, separately but such a modular approach has its econometric limitations.

2.2.4. Static versus dynamic simulation

The CGE-model as we have formulated it so far is basically static (atemporal). In many applications the model indeed applies to a single period which may range from a year to a lifetime. Obviously, in the latter case substantial time aggregation is involved. This has the attraction that short run effects can be disregarded but it introduces two problems. First, very few observations will remain if available time series have to be aggregated over long periods. Secondly, time aggregation obscures uncertainty and the process of accumulation. Hence the approach seriously limits the scope for empirical implementation: a lifetime-SAM is required and very few degrees are left to validate the model for years other than the base period validation. Therefore, it seems

---

[21] While forms like the CES are restrictive the standard flexible forms fail to satisfy globally concavity and monotonicity requirements imposed by the underlying theory [see Diewert and Wales (1987)]. Although functional forms have been developed which do meet these requirements without losing flexibility [see Barnett (1991)], it remains difficult to obtain the parameters of such forms.

[22] In these specifications the utility function is often strictly quasi-concave rather than strictly concave.

advisable to choose as short a time period as the data allow and to reserve the use of static models to single, short period applications.

We will discuss several representations where time enters explicitly: recursive dynamics (discussed in Section 2.4.8) and models with intertemporal optimization (Section 5).[23] For these models there is more scope for validation since time series observations can be used. The differences between simulation results and observed values are then used to adjust the values of parameters for which only a base-year observation is available. This procedure is necessarily informal but has the advantage that the performance of the model over time can be reported. This appears to be a reasonable minimum requirement but unfortunately in current modelling practice it is not customary to publish such tests.

The CGE-model derives its usefulness from the possibility of simulation experiments (scenarios) whereby some exogenous variables (typically policy variables) are changed with respect to a reference run,[24] which is the final outcome of the validation process: for the past it reproduces observed values as closely as possible and for the future it incorporates baseline assumptions, for example unchanged government policies.

2.2.5. Welfare measures

In order to be able to assess the outcomes of simulation experiments the modeller needs performance criteria. These may be indicators such as GDP or calorie consumption or utility based measures such as compensated or equivalent variations,[25] which are relatively straightforward to compute and are often reported in applied work.

The consumer surplus, which is popular in partial analysis, is not so readily obtained; obviously in general equilibrium welfare triangles cannot be used, as

---

[23] Such dynamics models may have static solutions, e.g. those corresponding to a steady state. A specification of a steady state must be derived from the dynamic model. Since it is unlikely that any observed year corresponds to a steady state, equilibrium values for the steady state have to be computed as a model solution rather than being equated to observed values. It should be noted that the steady state may not be a state to which dynamic paths converge, so that it may be of limited practical interest (see Section 5.2).

[24] Strictly speaking such an exercise is meaningful only if the equilibrium solution is unique. Unfortunately, uniqueness cannot be guaranteed. All that can be said is that, generically, when the demand functions are continuously differentiable at positive prices, the equilibrium will be locally unique. We then say that it is regular in the sense of Dierker (1972). Methods are now available to compute all equilibria using polynomial approximation [cf. Garcia and Zangwill (1981)]. In applied models the determinant of the Jacobian is often found to be rather insensitive under a gradual shift from the base run to the policy alternative, so that it may be acceptable to neglect other equilibria, as (only) the new equilibrium can be seen as a continuous deformation of the original one.

[25] Equivalent variation is the change in expenditure at old prices needed to achieve the change in utility. Compensating variation uses new prices.

these are only defined for partial demand curves. In general equilibrium consumer surplus for consumer i is $u_i(x_i) - \partial u_i(x_i)/\partial x_i x_i$ [26] when measured in terms of utility. Alternatively, it can be measured in money terms as $u_i(x_i)/\lambda_i - px_i$, after dividing both terms by marginal utility of income λ_i and substituting the first-order conditions $\partial u_i(x_i)/\partial x_i\, x_i = \lambda_i px_i$. The two measures can easily be computed from the solution of the model. The value u_i/λ_i can be decomposed into income $h_i(=px_i)$ and consumer surplus. Therefore, it is sometimes called "full income" or "full expenditure".

Producer surplus is in partial equilibrium analysis defined as maximal profits $\pi_j(p)$ for producer j and $\Sigma_j\, \pi_j(p)$ in the aggregate. In general equilibrium one must also account for the value of endowments $\Sigma_i\, p\omega_i$ as part of supply and hence of producer surplus. Aggregate welfare can then be measured in money terms as the sum of aggregate consumer surplus and aggregate producer surplus, including the value of endowments. Since the budget constraints imply that total expenditures equal total profits (if any) plus the value of endowments, aggregate welfare is equal to the sum of full incomes $\Sigma_i^r\, u_i(x_i)/\lambda_i$. Hence it can be called "full social income". It can be written as the linear social welfare function:

$$W = \sum_i \alpha_i u_i \tag{8}$$

with given positive welfare weights $\alpha_i = (1/\lambda_i)$.

2.3. Alternative formats

Any general equilibrium model can be represented in alternative formats. One of these is called for in welfare analysis but usually the model specification determines which format is most suitable. In this section we will consider some of these formats for the basic CGE-model and discuss their relative merits. We will stress that without the appropriate representation, some forms of analysis can become extremely cumbersome. In the Sections 2.1 and 2.2 we have already encountered two representations: the Debreu-format of Section 2.1.1 and the CGE-format (4)–(7). We now present three other formats.

2.3.1. Negishi-format

The linear welfare function (8) provides a link with welfare economics. To

---

[26] Recall that $\partial u_i(x_i)/\partial x_i\, x_i$ denotes the inner product.

show this we consider the following welfare program[27]:

$$W = \max \sum_i \alpha_i u_i(x_i)$$

$$x_i \geq 0, \, y_j, \, i = 1, \ldots, m, \, j = 1, \ldots, n$$

subject to

$$\sum_i x_i \leq \sum_j y_j + \sum_i \omega_i \qquad (p)$$

$$y_j \in Y_j$$

for given positive welfare weights α_i, restricted to add up to one[28]; the notation (p) indicates that p is the vector of Lagrange multipliers associated with the constraint.

The solution to this program is a Pareto-efficient allocation.[29] If it were not, then one could find an alternative allocation which gives higher utility for at least one consumer while no consumer's utility is reduced. Since all welfare weights are positive this new allocation must yield a higher value for W which contradicts optimality.

Conversely, any Pareto-efficient allocation is a welfare optimum. This can be seen as follows. Consider the program:

$$\max \tilde{\alpha}_1 u_1(x_1)$$

$$x_1, x_i \geq 0, \, y_j, \, i = 2, \ldots, m, \, j = 1, \ldots, n$$

subject to

$$\sum_i x_i \leq \sum_j y_j + \sum_i \omega_i \qquad (p)$$

$$y_j \in Y_j$$

$$u_i(x_i) \geq u_i^0 \qquad (\tilde{\alpha}_i)$$

where u_i^0 denotes a feasible level of utility and $\tilde{\alpha}_1$ is a given positive welfare weight. The associated welfare program can be obtained by using the values $\tilde{\alpha}_1, \tilde{\alpha}_2, \ldots, \tilde{\alpha}_m$ as weights (after normalizing their sum to unity). The two programs will have the same Lagrangean.

The Pareto efficient allocation (and hence the welfare program) can be

---

[27] This is a convex program. The constraint set is nonempty since a zero value for all x_i, y_j is feasible. It is bounded since production functions are increasing in a nonproduced input. Moreover since aggregate endowments are positive, there exist positive x_i's such that all commodity balances hold with strict inequality. Therefore Slater's constraint qualification [see Avriel (1976)] is satisfied, so that nonzero, non-negative Lagrange multipliers p exist.

[28] This normalization of welfare weights determines the normalization of Lagrange multipliers p.

[29] The relation between welfare optimality and Pareto efficiency is discussed in many textbooks, e.g. Varian (1984, pp. 207–209).

decentralized, in accordance with the Second Welfare Theorem, as a competitive equilibrium with transfers T_i. Using p from the set of Lagrange multipliers, the transfers, which sum to zero (because commodity balances are satisfied), can be calculated from the budget constraint as:

$$T_i = px_i - p\omega_i$$

Negishi (1972) has shown that welfare weights α_i^* exist such that $T_i = 0$ for all consumers, so that a competitive equilibrium (1)–(3) is obtained.[30] This gives the program which we will refer to as the Negishi-format:

$$\max \sum_i \alpha_i^* u_i(x_i)$$

$$x_i \geq 0, y_j, i = 1, \ldots, m, j = 1, \ldots, n$$

subject to

$$\sum_i x_i \leq \sum_j y_j + \sum_i \omega_i \qquad\qquad (p) \qquad\qquad (9)$$

$$y_j \in Y_j$$

where the weights α_i^* are nonnegative, add up to one and are such that:

$$p^* x_i^* = p^* \omega_i$$

The main attraction of the Negishi-format is that the competitive equilibrium is described in a format in which the welfare implications are immediately apparent. For the applied modeller, Negishi's format is important because it enables him quickly to see the implications both for decentralization and for welfare of a change in the model structure. We will see this when the model is extended. In addition, production sets much less restrictive than those of the CGE-model can be accommodated, for example linear production sets.

For the small open economy the CGE-model (4), (5a), (5b), (6), (7) can be represented in the Negishi-format as:

$$\max \sum_i \alpha_i^* u_i(x_i)$$

$$e_k, m_k, q_j, v_{jk}, x_{ik} \geq 0, i = 1, \ldots, m, j = 1, \ldots, n$$

subject to

$$\sum_i x_{ik} + \sum_j v_{jk} \leq q_k, \quad k \in G \qquad\qquad (p_k)$$

---

[30] The weight α_1 will be positive since ω_1 is positive and since at least one Lagrange multiplier must be positive.

$$\sum_i x_{ik} + \sum_j v_{jk} \leq \sum_i \omega_{ik}, \quad k \in N \qquad\qquad (p_k) \qquad\qquad (10)$$

$$\sum_i x_{ik} + \sum_j v_{jk} + e_k \leq \sum_i \omega_{ik} + m_k, \quad k \in T \qquad\qquad (p_k)$$

$$\sum_{k \in T} (p_k^m m_k - p_k^e e_k) \leq 0 \qquad\qquad (\rho)$$

$$q_j \leq f_j(v_j)$$

with given import and export prices p_k^m and p_k^e, such that $p_k^m \geq p_k^e \geq 0$, $p_k^m > 0$. The Negishi welfare weights α_i^* should be such that $p^* x_i^* = p^* \omega_i$ for all i.

In the program, rather than writing net imports z_k, a distinction is made between exports and imports.[31] Since import and export prices are given this balance of payments condition is like a technological constraint which defines how imports can be produced from exports. In this format this constraint is necessary to constrain demand (in the CGE-format of Section 2.1.3 balance of payments equilibrium is implied by budget constraints and balance equations).

Writing the first-order conditions for exports and imports of tradeables one obtains:

$$p_k \leq \rho p_k^m \perp m_k \geq 0, \quad k \in T \qquad\qquad (11a)$$

$$p_k \geq \rho p_k^e \perp e_k \geq 0, \quad k \in T \qquad\qquad (11b)$$

$$\sum_{k \in T} (p_k^m m_k - p_k^e e_k) \leq 0 \perp \rho \geq 0 \qquad\qquad (11c)$$

At equilibrium ρ must be positive (otherwise p_k would be zero) so that the balance of payments constraint will be binding.

Note that the model now has two normalizations: one for welfare weights and one for world prices. As before the normalization of welfare weights determines the normalization of p. If we renormalize prices p by dividing them by ρ then all prices are expressed in the same unit. Conditions (11a) and (11b) then imply that price p_k equals the import price when the commodity is imported, the export price when it is exported and that it lies in between the two for autarky.

2.3.2. Full format

Ginsburgh and Waelbroeck (1981) work with a generalization of the Negishi-format which they call the Full format. Ginsburgh and Keyzer (forthcoming) show that this format is particularly useful in general equilibrium models with

---

[31] However, when $p_k^m = p_k^e$ the program can only determine the difference between m_k and e_k.

financial constraints. In our present setting budget constraints are the only financial constraints. Adding these constraints to the Negishi program (9) leads to:

$$\max \sum_i \bar{\alpha}_i u_i(x_i)$$

$$x_i \geq 0, \; y_j, \; i = 1, \ldots, m, \; j = 1, \ldots, n$$

subject to

$$\sum_i x_i \leq \sum_j y_j + \sum_i \omega_i \qquad\qquad (p)$$

$$\bar{p} x_i \leq \bar{p} \omega_i \qquad\qquad (\rho_i)$$

$$y_j \in Y_j$$

for given prices $\bar{p}$ and welfare weights $\bar{\alpha}_i$. Prices $\bar{p}$ are to be set in such a way that in equilibrium they belong to the set of shadow prices of the program (possibly up to a normalization) and weights $\bar{\alpha}_i$ are such that in equilibrium the values ρ_i are equal among consumers (possibly zero).

Obviously, for $\bar{\alpha}_i = \alpha_i^*$ and $\bar{p} = p^*$, a solution to this problem can be obtained from the Negishi program (9) since adding the budget constraint to that program maintains feasibility and therefore optimality of the old allocation. One can also obtain such an equilibrium directly from the Full format by mapping p to $\bar{p}$ and adjusting $\bar{\alpha}_i$ on the basis of ρ_i to satisfy the two requirements (proportionality of $\bar{p}$ *and* p and equality of ρ_i among consumers).

The Full format has a number of theoretical advantages which will become apparent in models with overlapping generation (Section 5.2.2) and in models with money and financial assets (Section 5.3).[32]

2.3.3. *Mathematical program with feedback*

The Negishi-format has two drawbacks. First, it cannot accommodate strictly quasi-concave utility functions, that is the wider class of functions used in theoretical work.[33] Secondly, when the Negishi-format is used in applications one is forced to specify an analytical form for the (primal) utility and

---

[32] In that case some of the shadow prices ρ_i may differ among consumers. As a result there may exist an other price vector which corresponds to an equilibrium that is Pareto-superior. However, at the prevailing price there is no scope for Pareto-improvement. Such an equilibrium can therefore be said to be locally Pareto-efficient.

[33] The assumption of strict concavity is not restrictive in applied work since Varian (1982) has shown that the assumption of strictly concave utility cannot be rejected by a finite set of data that satisfy the weak axiom of revealed preference. However, some of the demand systems used in applied work (e.g. some of the flexible forms) can only be related to strictly quasi-concave utility functions.

production functions and as we noted above a primal representation in general is not suited for econometric estimation.[34]

The format of Mathematical program with feedback overcomes these limitations. The formulation starts with a trade surplus maximization for an open economy model, subject to the same constraints as in the Negishi program (9) but with given consumer demand:

$$\max p^e e - p^m m$$

$$e, m \geq 0, \ y_j, \ j = 1, \ldots, n$$

subject to

$$\sum_i \hat{x}_i + e \leq \sum_j y_j + \sum_i \omega_i + m \qquad\qquad (p) \qquad\qquad (12)$$

$$y_j \in Y_j$$

for given $0 < p^e \leq p^m$ defined for all commodities and given $\hat{x}_i$. For some p belonging to the set of shadow prices of the program, consumption satisfies the feedback[35] condition[36]:

$$\hat{x}_i = \mathrm{argmax}\{u_i(x_i) \mid px_i \leq p\omega_i\} \qquad\qquad (13)$$

In this setup there is a circularity: the program (12) generates a set of shadow prices from which a price vector is taken and used in the consumer problem (13). Program (12) in turn takes the resulting consumption values as given. Note that all commodities can be traded. Fischer et al. (1988) have shown that the mapping thus defined has a fixed point which is an open economy competitive equilibrium. Since export prices are strictly positive domestic prices p must also be positive. They have also shown that by setting all export prices sufficiently close to zero a closed economy equilibrium is obtained. In addition, when only some export prices are reduced toward zero one obtains an equilibrium with tradeables and nontradeables, where goods have $e_k = m_k = 0$; this yields the basic CGE-model.

As in the Negishi-format we now introduce the distinction between goods and factors. Recall that goods were defined as commodities produced under constant returns to scale with one firm for each product and no joint production. Like in the CGE-equations (4)–(5) we use the matrix of input

---

[34] For example, for many widely used demand systems like the translog form, there is no primal representation.

[35] We will use the term feedback for a function of optimal primal or dual variables from a mathematical program which generates parameters for the same program.

[36] Here the utility function may be strictly quasi-concave rather than strictly concave.

output coefficients and formulate the following linear program with feedback:

$$\max p^e e - p^m m$$
$$e, m, q \geq 0$$

subject to

$$\sum_i \hat{x}_i + \hat{A}q + e \leq q + \sum_i \omega_i + m \qquad (p) \qquad (14)$$

where (for some p belonging to the set of shadow prices of the program) the parameters $\hat{x}$ and $\hat{A}$ satisfy the feedback conditions:

$$\hat{x}_i = x_i(p, h_i), \; h_i = p\omega_i \qquad (15)$$

and

$$\hat{A} = A(p) . \qquad (16)$$

Here consumer demand and input-output coefficients are determined as in the CGE-model. Many general equilibrium models have been constructed which are not (fully) based on optimizing behaviour [see Taylor (1990)]. Therefore, it is important to note that the program with feedback will also have a solution when (15) and (16) are not derived from optimization (provided both are continuous at all $p^e \leq p \leq p^m$), but then the connection to welfare analysis is lost.[37] Hence the format covers a wide class of specifications and tools such as existence proofs can be used outside the class of general equilibrium models with optimizing agents. However, to maintain the link with micro-economic principles we will restrict ourselves to this narrower class.

In practice it is useful to impose one further restriction that brings the model closer to the CGE-formulation. We can ensure that only factors are traded by appropriate choice of import and export prices. This ensures continuity in response to parameter changes.

The CGE-model (4)–(7) can be seen as a special case of the linear program with feedback. Any given basic solution of the linear program (14) determines which of the non-negativity constraints on q^g, e, m are binding and therefore whether a commodity is produced, exported or imported. This removes all inequality constraints and thereby transforms the model into a CGE. In fact, the CGE-model appears in the present format as an input-output model with feedbacks (15) and (16), so that both final demand and input coefficients are endogenous.

Hence the present model is more flexible than the CGE-model in two

---

[37] Also (15) can represent demand aggregated over heterogeneous utility maximizing consumers in group i. Income in the group is distributed according to some density function [see Deaton (1989)].

respects. First, it does not need the highly restrictive assumption on viability[38], which in the CGE-model ensures that all goods will be produced at positive levels. A parameter change can in program (14) result in some q_j becoming zero. Secondly, one need not impose in advance whether z_k is positive, zero or negative: the trade regime can change endogenously. This avoids the possible inconsistency between assumed external prices and the resulting trade regime.

2.3.4. Relative merits of the formats

So far, we have presented five alternative formats for a general equilibrium model: the formats of Debreu, the CGE, Negishi, the Full format and the Mathematical program with feedback.

Under the assumptions made for the CGE-model, the CGE-format is the easiest to work with in applied modelling. Its equivalence to the Debreu-format makes clear that it generates a competitive equilibrium and further properties are then known from theory. However, when the model is extended, the choice of the most suitable format will depend on the nature of the extension.

The Debreu-format is the natural point of reference whenever micro-foundations are considered desirable. Therefore, under any extension of the CGE-model it is natural to investigate the implications for the Debreu-format. In particular one may wish to identify the signals to the individual agents which are needed for decentralization of a particular welfare optimum.

The CGE-format is convenient for performing simulation experiments involving changes in taxes and tariffs and for the representation of markup pricing and marginal pricing under increasing returns to scale. Also, the format has been used to represent variable entry and exit of firms when there are no indivisibilities. These possibilities will be illustrated later on.

We have already indicated that the Negishi-format provides a direct link to welfare analysis and that it makes it possible to use weaker assumptions on the production technology. Sometimes (for example with externalities or noncon-vexities) it is easier to use the Negishi-format, that is to formulate a centralized welfare program, than to specify its decentralized counterpart (in Debreu or CGE-format). The Full format is an extension of the Negishi-format and hence has the same advantages. It is particularly useful to represent financial constraints. We will see that it is helpful to view financial constraints as defining the opportunities for transactions i.e. the transaction technology. Treating the financial and the physical constraints in the same program makes it possible to

---

[38] The non-negativity of the inverse of $(I - A^g(p))$.

clarify the links between real and financial sphere and to use weaker assumptions than are common in the monetary literature.

Some advantages of the Mathematical program with feedback have been mentioned already: by exploiting duality, one can make use of forms that are well suited for econometric estimation; one can incorporate non-optimizing behaviour; and, more importantly, one can handle inequality constraints (this is also possible in the Negishi and in the Full format). The incorporation of inequality constraints makes it possible to represent buffer stocks, trade regimes, transport and rationing.

2.4. Extending the specification

The basic CGE-model contains all the essential characteristics of applied general equilibrium models but it obviously is highly restrictive. Many applications of the CGE-model incorporate decreasing returns, government consumption, external trade, taxes, savings and investment and capital accumulation. We now consider these extensions in turn. In practice a single model will contain several of these extensions.

2.4.1. Decreasing returns; entry and exit

In the basic CGE-model we have assumed a constant-returns-to-scale technology, so that in equilibrium profit maximization leaves the scale of production indeterminate. Obviously, when one or more factors are firm specific (like land or a capital good once installed), the indeterminacy disappears, provided the production function is increasing in such a factor. Since the firm specific inputs will be utilized fully, they can be treated as a vector of fixed stocks k_j and the production function exhibits decreasing returns to scale in the remaining inputs. The fixed stocks can be left out of the commodity list but intersectorally mobile capital goods should be represented explicitly as commodities leased by "capital rental" firms.

Profit maximizing formulation (2) will now yield positive profits which are redistributed to consumers according to fixed ownership shares θ_{ij}. Income is then defined as:

$$h_i = p\omega_i + \sum_j \theta_{ij}\pi_j(p)$$

Hotelling's lemma can be used (since isoquants have been assumed to be strictly concave) giving net supply as the derivative of the (restricted) profit function:[39]

$$y_j(p, k_j) = \partial \pi_j(p, k_j)/\partial p \quad \text{for } j \in J^f \tag{17}$$

In practice it is not always possible to observe all elements of the vector k_j. In that case the production function exhibits decreasing returns in the observed factors.

Equation (17) is a substantial extension of the basic CGE-model since it allows factors to be produced, possibly by more than one firm. In virtually all applied CGE-models this formulation is used.

Under decreasing returns it is possible to specify an extended production function that has constant returns to scale: $\tilde{f}_j(v_j, n_j) = n_j f(v_j/n_j)$ with $n_j = 1$. Equation (17) then applies, with the vector k_j replaced by the scalar n_j (when no confusion arises the variable n_j can be dropped). Note that n_j stands for the number of firms of type j. This number need not be kept equal to one and can be determined endogenously by treating it as a commodity used as an input. However, the number of firms is then treated as a real rather than an integer number and under imperfect competition this may introduce a serious error. If there is no upper bound imposed on the number of firms and no cost involved in creation or closing of firms, profits will be zero and the sector will have constant returns. We will encounter applications with a variable number of firms in Section 3.2.

2.4.2. Government consumption

A government can be introduced as a new consumer, to be denoted by the subscript g.[40] This implies that the government has endowments, owns shares in firms and maximizes utility subject to a budget constraint.[41] This specification is quite common but it has the serious drawback in welfare analysis that government consumption is modelled as waste: in the model it does not add to (private) consumers' utility, since no preference for public goods has been introduced. Hence abolishing government would increase the welfare of private consumers.

In the simplest version (without taxes) for the government to have any income, some endowments and/or profit shares must be transferred from consumers to the government. Clearly this will reduce consumer welfare. On

---

[39] J^f is the set of firms producing with a fixed factor or under decreasing returns and J^g the set of firms producing goods (under constant returns).

[40] There may be more than one government e.g. to represent local and central government levels.

[41] Very often the utility function will be very simple, e.g. Leontief.

the other hand consumers may benefit to the extent public consumption enters their utility function. However, Pareto-efficient decentralization requires additional signals to determine the level of public consumption. We will return to this in our discussion of non-rivalness (Section 4.2.1).

2.4.3. External trade

In many applications, imported and domestically produced commodities are treated as imperfect substitutes. The justification for this is that the model cannot be disaggregated so far that only homogeneous commodities are represented. Imports then appear as z_k in (5b) and there is no domestic supply, either from production or from endowments.[42] This is often referred to as the Armington-specification. In implementation a CES-cost function is often used to determine the demand for imported and domestically produced inputs. Similarly, a CES-utility function determines consumer demand for imported and domestic commodities, which has the disadvantage that any commodity which is imported in the base year will continue to be imported.

As noted before, demand for exports is often specified as a demand of goods by a consumer who represents the rest of the world. This agent demands domestic goods and tradeable factors and supplies tradeable factors. Since he is subject to a budget constraint, trade will balance. To do this properly one has to construct a complete two-country world model. This is clearly very demanding. It is customary therefore to introduce a small-country assumption and keep the factor prices exogenously fixed (Keller (1980)), with foreign net demand import of tradeable factors adjusting to the net export of the home country.

In this setup trade in goods and trade in factors are treated asymmetrically: the country is only facing exogenous prices in its trade of factors. By contrast in Heckscher-Ohlin models all external prices are exogenous but this has the consequence that, in the presence of constant returns to scale, net imports will no longer be a continuous function of prices.

A further possibility is that demand for goods by the rest of the world is treated exogenously or as some function of prices [see Robinson (1989)] without any budget constraint imposed. This is problematic since Walras' Law is not satisfied out of equilibrium, so that equilibrium cannot be achieved in general without additional mechanisms such as rationing.

Consumers may receive exogenously given income F_i from abroad. These income components sum to F and appear in the balance of payments:

---

[42] Then the commodity will always be imported and use of the import price is appropriate.

$$\sum_{k \in T} (p_k^m m_k - p_k^e e_k) = F$$

where F is expressed in the same unit as p^e and p^m.

2.4.4. Quantitative restrictions

Nontradeability of factors, like labour, may be the result of a policy decision. This gives rise to a rent (positive or negative) because the domestic price will differ from the external price. In fact it may be seen as an extreme case of a constraint on trade and clearly when the constraint is binding, relaxing it will improve welfare. Between the extremes of tradeability and non-tradeability there exist non-zero quotas that limit trade to some interval. These have to be modelled through inequality constraints. This cannot be handled in the CGE-format and will be discussed in Section 4.1.

2.4.5. Taxes and tariffs

Once a government has been identified as an agent, taxes and tariffs can readily be introduced. We first distinguish indirect and direct taxes. Indirect taxes create wedges between prices paid and received by firms and consumers. Direct taxes (which may be positive or negative) operate like transfers (T_i).

Wedges make it necessary to distinguish various prices. From now on we will reserve the term "price" for the variable p_k dual to the commodity balance in (3). With a consumer tax rate τ_k^c, this gives the consumer price as:

$$p_k^c = (1 + \tau_k^c)p_k \tag{18}$$

In the case of subsidies τ_k^c is negative. The budget constraint of consumer i is now written as:

$$p^c x_i \leq h_i \tag{19}$$

The rate τ_k^c need not be fixed; if it is determined by a function, the function should be continuous. The tax is ad valorem if τ_k^c is fixed. It is in nominal terms if $\pi_k^c p_k$ is fixed and it is a variable levy if p_k^c is fixed and τ_k^c adjusts accordingly. In all three cases τ_k^c is a continuous function of prices and quantities consumed. However, only in the first case is the homogeneity (of degree zero) of demand in terms of prices maintained.[43] We will restrict ourselves to τ_k^c-functions which are homogeneous.

---

[43] In this way one can model tariffs and levies on imports, taxes or refunds on exports, excise taxes on production, input taxes and subsidies. Value added tax can be represented as indirect taxes levied on domestic final demand. Tax rates may differ between agents. This makes it possible to model consumer or producer specific taxes or subsidies.

The revenue generated by the indirect tax (or the expenditure in the case of a subsidy) can in principle accrue to any agent in the model. However, taxes accruing to private agents are usually neglected. In the case of consumer tax, the proceeds will be:[44]

$$T = \sum_i \sum_k \tau_k^c p_k x_{ik} \tag{20}$$

These proceeds accrue to the government which then either uses them for its own consumption or redistributes them to consumers as transfers.

In CGE-models direct taxes are often levied on total income, measured as the value of endowments plus profits.[45] In practice governments are unable to implement such a tax. For example, it is difficult to tax leisure, only net labour supply can be taxed. This makes taxes commodity specific and therefore indirect. Let h_i^0 denote pre-tax income and τ_i the direct tax rate, so that:

$$h_i = (1 - \tau_i)h_i^0, \quad \text{for all } i \neq g \tag{21}$$

Government income is then given by:

$$h_g = h_g^0 + \sum_{i \neq g} \tau_i h_i^0 + T \tag{22}$$

As long as all tax rates τ_i, τ_k^c are non-negative, with τ_i less than unity, taxes will leave all agents' income positive. Such requirements are rarely satisfied because of subsidies. As a result, there is no guarantee that the government's income is positive (obviously, if income becomes negative the model is infeasible). This problem can be avoided by setting tax rates τ_i through a continuous function which ensures that the incomes of all agents are positive and that the right hand side of (22) is non-negative in equilibrium. More formally, (21) and (22) can be written as:

$$h_i = h_i^0 + T_i(p, T, h_1^0, \ldots, h_m^0), \quad \text{for all } i .^{46} \tag{23}$$

Indirect taxes on production, input demand and external trade can be treated in a similar way.

---

[44] The summation over i includes the government, so that the government may pay indirect tax to itself.

[45] This is not standard practice: many modellers include in income the value of sales (or lease) of endowments rather than the value owned. For example, actual employment is exogenous to the consumer's decision subject to labour availability (although this constraint is not always imposed explicitly). This can be interpreted as the outcome of a rationing process, as we shall see in Section 4.1.

[46] Here $T_i(\cdot)$ is continuous, homogeneous of degree one, yields positive income and satisfies $\sum_i T_i \geq T$ with equality whenever $T + \sum_i h_i^0 > 0$ [see Ginsburgh and Keyzer (forthcoming)].

2.4.6. Savings and investment

So far capital stocks have only appeared [in equation (17)] as exogenous variables and neither savings nor investment have as yet been introduced. We begin by keeping capital stocks exogenous. Savings and investment can then be specified by assuming that each consumer makes a separate investment decision. Savings is then modelled like a direct tax, with the "revenue" accruing to these consumers. Therefore, at all prices, savings will add up to investment. Investors buy capital goods which they allocate to firms according to their "preferences", which are represented through the utility function $\tilde{u}_i(I_i)$. The capital goods are modelled as composite goods of fixed composition at given prices. The problem for an investor i can be written:

$$\max \tilde{u}_i(I_i)$$
$$I_i \geq 0$$

subject to   (24)

$$p(KI_i) \leq H_i$$

where I_i is the vector of investments by destination j, K is the so-called capital matrix with element K_{kj} representing the requirement of capital good k per unit of investment in firm j and H_i are the savings available to the investor. The capital matrix describes the technology of capital goods and its coefficients are determined through cost minimization.

This makes it possible to define a single-period equilibrium as a competitive equilibrium with saving and investment, where investment does not affect capital stocks within the period. This has been criticized on two grounds. First, in this formulation investment is explicitly constrained by savings only. The allocation of investment is not affected by rates of return differentials or by financial variables such as interest rates. Such issues have received attention in the macroeconomic literature. In development economics this has led to the formulation of closure rules which we consider below. Secondly, because this treatment of saving and investment is not based on intertemporal optimization, the resulting allocations will not possess any property of intertemporal efficiency. This makes welfare analysis problematic since the Negishi weights have no direct interpretation in terms of consumer welfare: for consumption zero savings and investment would be preferable. We will return to this in Section 5.

2.4.7. Closure rules

In the above formulation I_{ij} is determined endogenously by investor i. However, in many models it is set exogenously as part of a public investment program. In this case the savings generated by the "tax"-functions will not be equal to investment unless an additional adjustment mechanism is specified. The association of a particular endogenous variable to an exogenous demand component is commonly referred to as a closure rule [Sen (1963), Taylor and Lysy (1979)]. Closure rules have been defined not only for investment but also for exports and government expenditures.

To balance savings and investment there is a choice between several mechanisms. First, all exogenous investments may be scaled. Secondly, components F_i of foreign savings may adjust. Thirdly, (part of) public consumption may adjust or tax rates may be adjusted.

Such mechanisms have been explained in terms of rationing schemes. A natural next step was to introduce an interest rate as an equilibrating variable $[S(p, r) = I(p, r)$, Adelman and Robinson (1978)]. This has been extended to segmented credit "markets" where one sector refers to formal, rationed credit and the other to credit in the curb market [van Wijnbergen (1982), Nsengiyumva and Decaluwé (1992)]. The closure rule has served as a tool to incorporate macroeconomic mechanisms into general equilibrium models. Macroeconomic equations were grafted onto these models, by introducing for each new macroeconomic variable a new equilibrating constraint. These did not necessarily relate to markets. The flexibility is operationally attractive since it makes it possible to introduce many variables which are central to policy discussions but this is obtained at the expense of theoretical rigour.

First, savings and investment are not derived from optimizing behaviour. As a consequence there is no possibility to perform meaningful welfare analysis. Secondly, the interest rate when used as equilibrating variable is not part of the return on an explicitly represented financial asset and this is misleading. Finally, one would like consumer savings to be decided upon in relation to consumer wealth. After all, savings in any period are merely a change in wealth (a stock) but typically in these models the accounting applies only to flows.[47]

2.4.8. Recursive dynamics

In static applications a model solution is only obtained for a single-period and in other applications a time sequence of single-period equilibria is computed for periods $t = 1, 2, \ldots$ (recursive dynamic simulation). Periods are related through updating of some exogenous variables like the capital stock or demography.

The simplest rule for updating capital stock k_{jt}, treating it as a scalar, is to

---

[47] The wealth constraint typically appears in a life cycle model of an individual or in the intergenerational model of a dynasty (see Section 5.2).

use fixed rates of depreciation and to ignore gestation lags:

$$k_{j,t+1} = (1 - \delta_j)k_{jt} + \sum_i I_{ijt}, \quad t = 1, 2, \ldots \tag{25}$$

Equation (25) is linear so that capacity can be increased under constant returns to scale. This assumption is sometimes dropped to represent adjustment (or installation) costs ($\sum_i I_{ijt}$ is then replaced in (25) by a decreasing returns function of k_{jt} and $\sum_i I_{ijt}$, which is typically quadratic in total investments). The effect of this is to smooth adjustments under a reform, since instantaneous adjustment now is more costly. The theoretical justification for such a specification is unclear. A more explicit representation would specify installation or construction sectors with gestation lags and possibly decreasing returns. Installation cost specifications are more commonly found in the intertemporal models to be discussed in Section 5 than in recursively dynamic models.

Recursive dynamics is a mode of operating a CGE-model that is widely used in the context of development. It has the capability to address some of the concerns which have characterized development planning in the 1960s and 1970s. Traditionally, development planning focused on the design and assessment of public investment programs, taking into account private consumer demand and balance of payments constraints. The recursive dynamic use of a CGE is particularly suitable for assessing given investment plans,[48] especially for checking their feasibility. However, it does not satisfy any intertemporal optimality criterion. To this we return in Section 5. Compared to statics, recursive dynamics has the important advantage that simulation results can be compared with time-series evidence. This contrasts with the static use where all available data have been used to construct the SAM. Typically, one will adjust some parameters so as to improve the fit. Adjustment is commonly restricted to parameters which have not been estimated econometrically over a time series but it has to be recognized that this is not a formal process.[49]

3. Policy analysis with the CGE-model

We will first discuss the use of CGE-models to evaluate policy packages and then focus on tax and tariff reform, the area where they have been used most frequently (Section 3.1). Then, we turn to two fields of more recent research: models with markup pricing and imperfect competition (Section 3.2) and finally models in which monetary neutrality is dropped (Section 3.3).

---

[48] Since this investment is then exogenous it requires a closure rule.
[49] The reasons for this have already been given in our discussion of the estimation of the SAM.

3.1. Policy packages

CGE-models have been used to evaluate a wide range of policy issues, including changes in indirect taxes, trade policy, income redistribution and public investments. Well-known examples include Adelman and Robinson (1978), Dervis et al. (1982), Dixon et al. (1987), Whalley (1985, 1986). Usually the changes modelled are based on existing reform proposals. The evaluation is commonly in terms of GDP, incomes of various socioeconomic groups or formal welfare criteria as well as nutrition, market shares, production in various sectors etc.

Applied general equilibrium models can be particularly useful in such applications since the welfare effects of the policy proposals cannot be predicted only on theoretical grounds. This is so because the reforms typically do not involve full compensation of the losers and because they do not remove all distortions.

Several studies use models which do not belong to the class of CGE-models. For example, they often contain inequality constraints to represent downward real wage rigidity or import quota. However, in this section we focus on a simulation model which, while possibly more complex, can be understood in terms of the more restrictive CGE-model.

Policy packages typically involve simultaneous changes in variables under the control of the government such as taxes and public investments. The CGE-models have the advantage that specific policy measures as proposed can be accommodated without excessive simplification and aggregation.[50] The classification can correspond closely to the one the policy maker is used to.

Using CGE-models not only has the advantage that general equilibrium effects are taken into account but also that the interaction of different policy measures can be studied. For example, Narayana et al. (1991) show that the combination of infrastructural investment with food-for-work programs is a more effective way of reducing poverty than food subsidies. Clarete and Roumasset (1990) analyze trade liberalization for agricultural commodities and factors for the Philippines. They find that the results are to an important extent determined by the remaining quantitative restrictions in industry. Bevan et al. (1990) analyze the effect of world coffee price increases combined with partial trade liberalization in Kenya. They conclude that a large part of the benefit to smallholder producers accrues as rents to owners of trade quota.

Perhaps most importantly, when used in the recursive dynamic mode, the CGE-models make it possible to evaluate lagged effects of policies, in particular of public investment. This can be done by distinguishing investment

---

[50] However, as discussed in Section 2.2.4 there is excessive time aggregation when the model is static and refers to a "lifetime".

projects of various degrees of completion [for example in irrigation see Salauddin Ahmad et al. (1986)]. The policy packages can also refer to the past: the model is then used for counterfactual simulation. For example, Maasland (1990) uses a model for Sri Lanka to explore whether policies other than those actually adopted would have been more successful in alleviating poverty.

The results from simulation runs with alternative policy packages can be compared in terms of various welfare measures. Typically, some groups will gain and others will lose and although an aggregate welfare measure can be computed it will not satisfy the Pareto-criterion. We will now discuss the design of reform packages that do satisfy this criterion.

3.1.1. Welfare analysis of tax and tariff reform

To specify reform packages in which no agent loses, it is helpful to use the Negishi-format. We illustrate this, first for a consumer subsidy and then for a tariff.

Tax reform. We represent consumer taxes as discussed in Section 2.4.5 within the Negishi-format. For this, we amend the formulation (9) by introducing a pseudo consumer with a "utility" function that is linear in total consumption x and who has a unit welfare weight. This does not change the constraint set but the pseudo consumer's utility competes with the utility of all other consumers, since he has a nonzero welfare weight. Hence the welfare $\Sigma_i \, \alpha_i^* u_i(x_i)$ of the other consumers will be reduced (or at best unchanged) through this construction. The program may now be written as:

$$\max \sum_i \alpha_i^* u_i(x_i) - \xi^{c*} x$$

$$x, x_i \geq 0, \, y_j, \, i = 1, \ldots, m, \, j = 1, \ldots, n$$

subject to

$$x \leq \sum_j y_j + \sum_i \omega_i \qquad\qquad\qquad (p)$$

$$\sum_i x_i \leq x \qquad\qquad\qquad (p^c) \qquad (26)$$

$$y_j \in Y_j$$

for given nonnegative welfare weights α_i^*, which again sum to one, and given tax rates ξ^{c*}. In equilibrium the nominal tax ξ^{c*} is set for fixed rates τ^c as:

$$\xi_k^{c*} = \tau_k^c p_k^* \qquad\qquad\qquad (27)$$

and welfare weights are set in such a way that the consumers and the government are on their budget constraints:

$$p^c * x_i = h_i^*$$ (28)

for h_i defined for equilibrium prices as in (23) and T given by (20).

In the objective function the value of taxes is subtracted from social welfare ($\Sigma_i \, \alpha_i u_i$) which is also measured in value terms like in equation (8). Since taxes are subtracted, the program (26) can be seen to maximize full social expenditure (evaluated at prices p instead of consumer prices p^c i.e. full income minus tax).[51]

Of course this model does not maximize social welfare but it can be shown that the solution to (26)–(28) is a competitive equilibrium with consumer taxes [cf. Fischer et al. (1988)]. To see the relation between the Negishi-format and the CGE with consumer taxes, note that since $x*$ will be positive the first-order conditions of (26) imply that:

$$p_k^c * = \xi_k^c * + p_k^*$$

Hence in equilibrium:

$$p_k^c * = (1 + \tau_k^c) p_k^*$$

Many Pareto-improving reforms can be designed by reducing the weight of this pseudo consumer below unity (obviously Pareto-improvement refers to the "real" consumers and excludes the pseudo consumer). We consider three types of such reforms: a proportional reduction in nominal taxes with compensation, a non-proportional reduction with compensation and a transition to a uniform (possibly zero) tax rate without compensation.

A proportional reduction of nominal taxes $\xi^c *$ can be interpreted as a lowering of the welfare weight of the pseudo consumer and cannot be Pareto-inferior.[52] This result makes it possible to specify a reform in which welfare changes monotonically with the weight of the pseudo consumer. Such a formulation may be useful if reforms have to be designed in sequence where each step of the reform is Pareto-improving, provided no future step is anticipated by consumers or producers.

Under the second type of reform, an arbitrary reduction of taxes with

---

[51] Recall that expenditure is full in the sense that it includes consumer surplus.

[52] Formally one should add constraints $u_i(x_i) \geq u_i^0$, for all consumers except consumer 1 (whose utility function is increasing), where the superscript 0 denotes the pre-reform value. One keeps the welfare weight α_1 for consumer 1 and one sets welfare weights to zero for the other consumers. One then tests for Pareto-superiority by checking whether this agent gains. Alternatively, one can check whether $\Sigma_i \, \alpha_i \, u_i$ increases, keeping weights constant. Then, one is only interested in testing whether at old weights, collectively consumers gain. Obviously these two tests may give different results but in the theoretical experiments which we discuss they point in the same direction. We will use the second test.

compensation, the welfare gains (if any) may not be sufficient to compensate losers, that is, the reform is not weakly Pareto-superior. Only if the initial distortion is sufficiently small will there be a gain.

Now consider the third type, where all consumer tax rates are made equal, possibly set to zero, but no compensation is given. This is the standard case in the public finance literature. One immediately sees in the consumer's problem that this is equivalent to a proportional tax on total income and therefore to a direct (non-distortionary) tax.[53] The new solution will be Pareto-efficient, although generally it is not Pareto superior to the original solution. Without compensation, theory currently has no more to say on the impact of tax reform, which is unfortunate, not only because compensation is hard to achieve, since policy changes all the time, but also because even if feasible, it is not self-evident that one would always want to compensate losers. This is an ethical issue which is beyond our scope.

In program (26) we have analyzed consumer taxes by adding a term $(-\xi^c *x)$ to the objective function. This is a powerful tool for analyzing distortions and also applies to indirect taxes other than consumer taxes. We will use this approach repeatedly.

Tariff reform. In a world model, tariffs and subsidies on trade can be treated like commodity taxes on net demand, so that the earlier discussion applies. However, in a model for a small open economy, which takes external prices as given, taxes on trade require separate treatment. This is because it is natural to attribute value only to increases in utility of internal agents. For example, in the analysis of national policies it would be unusual to compensate external agents but it must be recognized that external agents impose a balance of payments constraint.

First, we discuss tariffs on factors and then tariffs on goods.

In the Negishi-program (10) the balance of payments (for trade in factors) was incorporated directly, while in the objective function only the utility of "internal" agents was represented. Trade taxes appear in the objective function in the same way as commodity taxes in program (26) as a deduction from full income. As before, the distortion appears as the linear "utility"-function of a pseudo consumer with unit welfare weight. We now write the program as:

$$\max \sum_i \alpha_i^* u_i(x_i) - \xi^e e - \xi^m m$$

$$e_k, m_k, q_j, v_{jk}, x_{ik} \geq 0, \ i = 1, \ldots, m, \ j = 1, \ldots, n$$

subject to

[53] As before this amounts to taxing leisure.

$$\sum_i x_{ik} + \sum_j v_{jk} \le q_k, \quad k \in G \qquad (p_k)$$

$$\sum_i x_{ik} + \sum_j v_{jk} \le \sum_i \omega_{ik}, \quad k \in N \qquad (p_k) \qquad (29)$$

$$\sum_{k \in T} (p_k^m m_k - p_k^e e_k) \le 0 \qquad (\rho)$$

$$q_j \le f_j(v_j)$$

$$e_k = m_k = 0 \text{ for } k \notin T$$

for given import and export prices p^m and p^e, nominal tariffs ξ_k^m and ξ_k^e. For fixed rates τ_k^m, τ_k^e the nominal tariffs ξ_k^m and ξ_k^e for imports and exports are given by:

$$\xi_k^m = \tau_k^m p_k^m$$

$$\xi_k^e = \tau_k^e p_k^e \qquad (30)$$

where tariff rates are such that domestic prices of exports do not exceed domestic prices of imports. The welfare weights α_i^*, which again sum to one, are set in such a way that the consumers and the government are on their budget constraints:

$$p^* x_i^* = h_i^* \qquad (31)$$

for h_i^* defined as in (23) and T is given by:

$$T = \sum_{k \in T} (\xi_k^m m_k^* + \xi_k^e e_k^*) \qquad (32)$$

The relation between the Negishi-format and the CGE with tariffs may be verified from the first-order conditions of (29) evaluated in equilibrium.

$$p_k \le \rho p_k^m + \xi_k^m \perp m_k \ge 0, \quad k \in T \qquad (33)$$

$$p_k \ge \rho p_k^e - \xi_k^e \perp e_k \ge 0, \quad k \in T \qquad (34)$$

$$\sum_{k \in T} (p_k^m m_k - p_k^e e_k) \le 0 \perp \rho \ge 0 \qquad (35)$$

As before ρ will be positive and welfare weights and nominal tariffs (ξ^m, ξ^e) can be renormalized so that prior to any reform, in equilibrium $\rho = 1$. Conditions (33) and (34) then reduce to the standard conditions. It is again clear from the objective function of the program (29) that tariffs reduce welfare. Moreover, any proportional reduction of ξ cannot be welfare decreasing. This again illustrates how the Negishi-format can be used to design reforms under which no consumer's utility is reduced. Along the path of this reform, the nominal tariff will (in general) not move in proportion with pre-reform rates. Since for example for imports the nominal tariff will become equal to the new value of ξ^m plus $(\rho - 1) \; p^m$. Hence while ξ changes proportionately tariff rates do not.[54]

This approach to tariff reduction is of relevance for the discussion on sequencing of reforms only in a recursively dynamic context where agents have naive expectations. Conversely if they plan with foresight they must be given a time-path of future prices such that ξ^m and ξ^e are reduced proportionally. In this sense sequencing is not necessarily Pareto-improving: all instruments have to be adjusted simultaneously.

We now consider tariffs on goods. This is similar to the analysis of trade reform in a multi-country model of the world economy. Recall that in the CGE-model exports of goods are determined through an external consumer. This consumer will face external rather than tariff ridden prices.[55] One then has to compensate the external consumer, so that he can be dealt with like any other consumer and the above treatment applies where the tariff is a tax on the net demand by the external consumer.

The above discussion follows a first-best approach, hence disregarding problems of mobilizing lump-sum transfers. Mitra (1992) performs a second-best analysis to design tariff structure for India which avoids lump-sum transfers.

Environmental taxes and property rights. In applications environmental problems are typically dealt with through taxes. The tax rate is chosen such that emissions do not exceed some chosen level. The tax is then used as a substitute for the market price.[56] In general this will not yield an efficient solution since the tax applies only to the using up of clean air (the Polluter Pays Principle) rather than to total use, that is including rental by those who do not pollute but derive utility from the resource (possibly indirectly). Therefore, rather than considering emissions (a flow) one should focus on the use of (a renewable stock of) resources like clean air. For such resources competitive markets should be organized, where obviously the user will have to pay the owner. For this, endowments must be defined and property rights must be distributed. This is an issue of distributive justice about which general equilibrium theory has nothing to say. However, current proposals and regulations for environmental

---

[54] In the standard CGE-formulation it would seem natural to change all tariff rates in the same proportion but this is not Pareto-efficient.

[55] In several CGE-models the budget is expressed in domestic prices, so that in general balance of payments will not be in equilibrium at world prices [for example, see Keller (1980)].

[56] Clearly, one then has to drop the assumption of free disposal. This may lead to negative prices and may require the introduction of commodities in which utility is decreasing (like unclean air). This undermines basic assumptions of the two welfare theorems.

taxes clearly imply extreme distributions since they amount to assigning all property rights to the government[57] which levies the tax, or to the polluter if there is a tax rebate.

If markets for environmental resources were to be established they would restore Pareto-efficiency but this may not be possible because of the excludability problem or because of nonrivalness or nonconvexity. To overcome such problems, government intervention is required and a welfare model may be helpful. One then introduces a market in the model which does not yet exist in the real world. The model can be used to compute prices and quantities which can serve as a basis for taxation. We return to these issues in Sections 4.2 and 4.3.

3.1.2. Applications of tax and tariff reform

Taxes and tariff reforms at national level. It was recognized early in the public finance literature that the study of tax reform calls for numerical simulation because tax changes typically involve opposing effects. For example, a reduction of a consumer subsidy directly affects consumer prices. But in addition market prices may change and this leads to changes both on the expenditure and on the revenue side of the consumer's budget. It may also affect production. The consumer may gain more from these indirect effects than he loses from the direct effect of the removal of the subsidy. This can happen because the consumer shifts his demand towards other goods, the price of which falls. It is possible that the resulting income gain for suppliers of those goods raises the utility of the consumers who were the main beneficiaries of the subsidy and could therefore have been expected to be the principal losers. This possibility was of course implied in the theoretical literature. It was elaborated later in the trade theoretical literature [Bhagwati et al. (1983)] on transfer "paradoxes".[58] There it is recognized that "paradoxical" outcomes are crucially dependent on functional specifications and numerical values of parameters. This dependence makes it important to develop models with a sound empirical basis.

It is impossible to review the use of CGE-models for analysis of unilateral tax and tariff reforms since virtually every national CGE-model has at least once been used for this purpose. De Melo (1988) gives a survey of trade policy applications. Chenery et al. (1986) use a model for Korea to assess to what

---

[57] This is often based on the mistaken belief that the government must be given the resources to pay for cleaning activities. In fact when the market for clean air is organized firms will perform these activities profitably (provided their technology set is convex).

[58] The possibility that a donor is enriched by a gift and/or a recipient is immiserized by it. This is an expression of the lack of generic properties of excess demand functions as established by Debreu, Mantel and Sonnenschein [see Kirman (1992)].

extent past growth can be attributed to price reform including trade liberalization. They conclude that liberalization has only a limited explanatory power. This point is more general. Many authors find only modest welfare gains from trade liberalization, using standard CGE-models. One response to this finding has been to argue that the important channels through which liberalization leads to growth are absent from the standard model. First, trade liberalization improves access to technology, either because it is incorporated in imported goods or because it is tied to foreign investment. Secondly, trade liberalization improves competition but this effect is not well captured in the standard model which assumes perfect competition, ignores rent-seeking and keeps trade margins fixed. Hence in such models the initial situation may be insufficiently distorted so that the potential gains are underestimated.

Later applications have been able to show larger effects in various ways: by introducing rent-seeking [for example Grais et al. (1986)] or imperfect competition (see Section 3.2) or by considering capitalization effects through an intertemporal model (see Section 5).

International trade reform. CGE-models have also been used to study multilateral trade reform by linking national CGE-models. International prices are taken as given in each country model and adjusted so that total net imports balances with total net export for each commodity.

Whalley (1985) has used various multiregional models to assess Tokyo Round Proposals. One of his results is that regions often gain less from their own proposal than from the proposals of other negotiating partners. The reason for this is that their own proposal usually maintains more internal protection. He also shows that a single developing country is likely to gain from unilateral trade liberalization (partly because consumers will gain from lower domestic prices of imports). The country will also gain when trade liberalization is global (so that developing countries have better access to markets in developed countries). However, when a group of developing countries liberalizes (without reciprocation by developed countries), they may lose because of an induced terms of trade loss. Similar results are obtained by Deardorff and Stern (1986).

The emphasis placed in the Uruguay Round on reform of agricultural policies has led to the use of models tailored to this issue. Examples are the Basic Linked System models described in Parikh et al. (1987) and Fischer et al. (1988) and the RUNS model used by the OECD [Gunning et al. (1982), Burniaux and van der Mensbrugghe (1990)]. A comparison of results of agricultural trade liberalization scenarios in various (general equilibrium and other) models is given in Goldin and Knudsen (1990). One of the results of many of these models is that poor groups in developing countries may lose from trade liberalization because they are net buyers of food and world food prices rise as a result of reform [see also Srinivasan (1989)]. Welfare gains are usually limited because factor mobility is restricted in the short run. Experiments for multilateral liberalization show much larger gains than for unilateral liberalization and losers can easily be compensated.

In Hamilton and Whalley (1984) and Fischer et al. (1991) it is emphasized that barriers which are usually ignored in trade negotiations, namely constraints on international migration are very important: the welfare gains which can be obtained by allowing migration are significantly larger than those obtained through trade liberalization.

Other models show gains from trade liberalization which are attributable to increasing returns to scale and improved competition. To this we return in Section 3.2.

Environmental taxes and property rights. Recently general equilibrium models have been used to evaluate environmental policies in particular taxes on carbon dioxide emissions. Usually pollution is represented as a byproduct that cannot be disposed of freely. Emission constraints are imposed to limit it and the impact on allocations is studied under various timings and rules for distributing and trading emission rights. Tax rates are adjusted until constraints defined by emission permits are satisfied and welfare comparisons are made between various timings and rules. In fact these uses of CGE-models must be seen as tax reform scenarios. The recognition of emission rights introduces a new commodity used by firms and owned by the government. The tax revenues are therefore effectively proceeds from endowments and therefore non-distortionary (given the chosen emission level) and the scenarios effectively compare alternative regimes of taxation.

Whalley and Wigle (1991) formulate a static model, Burniaux et al. (1991) a recursively dynamic one. Intertemporal models with perfect foresight are used by Manne and Richels (1990), Jorgenson and Wilcoxen (1993), Goulder (1991). These models were originally developed to obtain efficient investment decisions in the energy sector. This made them well-suited to analyze carbon dioxide emissions. All these models were for developed countries or for the international economy. Blitzer et al. (1986, 1994) have developed intertemporal models for Mexico and Egypt.

As stressed by Goulder (1991) one of the problems with these formulations is that pollution does not enter utility, production functions or welfare criteria. As a result environmental degradation has no effect and leaving emission rights unused cannot bring a welfare gain. Welfare comparisons between scenarios with different emission rates are impossible.

The intertemporal perfect foresight formulation is particularly relevant to assess the long run profitability of existing and alternative technologies under different scenarios. It will be discussed further in Section 5.2.

3.2. Markup pricing and imperfect competition

Specification. When the income from price wedges accrues to private agents rather than to government, we call the wedges markups. In CGE-models they can be treated like indirect taxes. Markups may be seen as attempts to represent various deviations from pure competitive conditions. This may be because (a) a commodity has been left out of the model, (b) a commodity is represented in the model but there is no market for it, (c) firms supply quantities such that their marginal cost is equal to the price of the output, (d) there is imperfect competition. We consider these four possibilities in turn.

First, the case of a missing commodity arises because it is impossible to account completely for value added in terms of returns to inputs. Some inputs are not measured. If they are in fixed supply then this leads to a decreasing returns specification. However, if constant returns to scale is maintained (in terms of the measured inputs) then revenue accruing to the unmeasured input would be zero. In such cases a markup is introduced [for example in Dervis et al. (1982) as a wedge between price and average cost to cover the value of these inputs]. This is commonly implemented by making the markup a function of other prices. Often the markup is made proportional to variable cost. It thus operates like an indirect tax and is distortionary. Hence in models with markups first-best welfare analysis does not apply.

Secondly, when there is no market for a commodity its price cannot be obtained from market clearing conditions. To account for the transaction value of such a commodity prices must be determined in some way. This is commonly done by treating this price as a markup cost for activities which use the commodity.

Thirdly, under increasing returns to scale Pareto-efficient pricing requires the price to be set equal to marginal cost.[59] Since in this case average exceeds marginal costs this gives rise to a negative markup. Dixon (1990) applies this for the pricing of public utilities.

Finally, the markup is often used to represent imperfect competition. Although constant returns to scale is compatible with imperfect competition, for example when there is licensing, in applied models it is commonly used in conjunction with increasing returns or setup costs. The markup is intended to avoid losses for the firm. However, there is no guarantee that an arbitrary markup function will lead to nonnegative profits, since as we shall see it depends on demand and not on costs. Under increasing returns the specification has the additional advantage that it may help to make the constraint set of

---

[59] This is necessary but not sufficient for Pareto-efficiency. Also such pricing gives rise to losses which the owners may not be able to cover. We return to this when we discuss nonconvexities (Section 4.3).

the firm convex, so that the producer problem can be formulated as profit maximization.[60]

In this problem profits are maximized subject to a possibly non-convex technology set and a perceived demand schedule as in partial equilibrium analysis. The resulting markup rate is then calculated from this demand schedule. The number of firms is fixed, at one (monopoly) or higher (cartel). The demand schedule should be homogeneous of degree zero in prices. This requirement is satisfied if the demand function is expressed in relative prices. In early applications the price elasticities of the demand schedule were taken as given [see Harris (1984)]. More recent specifications follow the conjectural variations approach. Perceived reactions of the other agents are then taken into account by making these reactions explicit functions of the own actions.[61]

However, such a borrowing of partial equilibrium concepts for general equilibrium models is problematic. Conjectural variations are supposed to reflect the workings of the model. In applications a convenient functional form is chosen, such that the demand function is continuous, single valued and sufficiently convex to ensure that the producers optimization problem has a unique solution. However, there is no theoretical justification for such a specification, it excludes for example the case with multiple equilibria and therefore with multiple demands. Even if the demand schedule happens to be single valued it is doubtful that it will generate continuous supply functions in the producer's problem.

An even more fundamental problem is that profit maximization is assumed. As pointed out by Gabzewicz and Michel (1992) profit maximization is in principle not rational when firms are not competitive. When all prices are taken as given by the household which maximizes utility subject to a production set and a budget constraint, the problem can be decomposed so that household utility maximization implies profit maximization subject to the technology set. This is no longer true when agents set prices. In that case the fundamental

---

[60] This is because in the single output case with (inverse) perceived demand curve $p(q)$ profit can be written as $p(q)q - c(q)$ and convexity of the first term with respect to q can make up for non-concavity of the second term. Profit maximization yields the well-known Amoroso–Robinson formula: $p(1 + \eta) = \partial c(q)/\partial q$, where $\eta = q/p \partial p/\partial q$ is the flexibility of the demand curve. The value $(p/c(q) - 1)$ is the resulting markup rate.

[61] Coefficients of these functions are usually obtained numerically from sensitivity analysis with the model as the algorithm proceeds in its search for equilibrium prices. This may create convergence problems, path dependence of the solution and even nonhomogeneity. Conjectural variations may be seen as midway house between the extremes of given reaction functions and strategic games with "true" reactions [for a comparison of approaches see Norman (1990)]. Published descriptions are often insufficiently detailed to allow the reader to judge whether these problems occur. While for simple demand schedules the equilibrium solution found can be expected to be independent of the choice of algorithm, this may not be true for the more sophisticated conjectural variations used in recent models. Mercenier and Schmitt (1992) confirm this.

rationale for imposing profit maximization as an objective disappears so that there is no alternative to utility maximization. In this spirit Berthélémy and Bourguignon (1994) study imperfect competition between trading blocks where each block maximizes its utility rather than profits.

Finally, it is important to keep in mind that since a markup is like an indirect tax it is Pareto-efficient to abolish a markup that is due to imperfect competition. This indicates that imperfect competition may be vulnerable to buyout as those who abolish or reduce markups can be compensated.[62] No imperfect competition can do better than a competitive solution. However, limitations on entry, information and possibility of side payments may prevent buyouts.

Applications. In applications, models which combine imperfect competition and increasing returns have been used to analyze tariff reductions and market integration.

In such models experiments with tariff reductions tend to find very much higher welfare gains than under constant or decreasing returns to scale [Harris (1984), de Melo and Roland-Holst (1994), Delorme and van der Mensbrugghe (1990)]. Since a tariff reduction lowers the input cost of a sector with increasing returns, it allows the sector to reduce its markup and therefore its price, which leads to an increase in demand. The efficiency gain then comes from the resulting exploitation of scale economies.

The main effect of market integration is to increase the number of competing producers on a single market. Each producer will then perceive a higher price elasticity and will react by lowering his markup [see Burniaux and Waelbroeck (1992) and Mercenier (1992) on European integration and de Melo and Tarr (1991) on voluntary export restraints in the automobile industry].

So far we have considered specifications in which the number of firms is fixed. Some models allow for free entry [Harris (1984) and Devarajan and Rodrik (1991)]. The number of firms is then endogenously determined at a level where profits are zero. For this the markup is set so that price equals average unit cost, including setup costs per unit. This leads us back to the case with variable entry discussed in 2.4.1 above. Each firm will produce at minimum average cost (provided this minimum exists, which will be the case if increasing returns are limited to a closed interval) and the scale of production will be fully determined by the number of firms. The disadvantage of this procedure is that the number of firms is treated as a real variable, which amounts to assuming perfect divisibility, in which case neither setup costs nor

---

[62] This applies to imperfect competition where firms maximize profits. Obviously under other behavioral assumptions, say those which value independence of the firm, the vulnerability is not evident.

increasing returns are relevant. Under imperfect competition the number of firms is likely to be small, so that ignoring the integer nature of the number of firms may introduce a serious error.

3.3. Dropping monetary neutrality

3.3.1. Determination of the absolute price level

The basic CGE-model of the closed economy only determines relative prices. In the small open economy that faces at least one given factor price, the absolute price level is determined through this given factor price in terms of international prices. Alternatively, a (single) domestic price may be kept fixed. In both cases the fixed price acts as a scaling factor which does not affect equilibrium allocations. Typically values are measured in terms of domestic (or foreign) currency but money then serves only as a unit of account. There is neither transaction nor asset demand for money.

In some CGE-models the homogeneity requirement on the specification of the tax, tariff and markup functions is abandoned but one maintains a homogeneous specification for the consumer and producer problems (no money illusion). Existence of equilibrium will obviously depend on the properties of these functions.[63] In such models all prices are determined in absolute terms so that there is no scope for any scaling factor.

Nonhomogeneities may arise in various ways. First, it may be an empirical fact that contracts cannot be adjusted instantaneously, so that for example some wages may be nominally rigid in the short-run.

Secondly, the income of the consumer may contain nominally fixed components, positive or negative,[64] for example as a result of debt servicing but this is more adequately represented in a model with financial assets. Thirdly, sometimes the government intervenes in a market by setting a fixed price through a variable indirect tax; more generally, prices may be set within some nominally fixed band. Fourthly, direct tax schedules are rarely fully indexed to prices and therefore contain nonhomogeneities. Many of these specifications are not unrealistic but they are only reduced forms. Much current research aims at a more explicit representation of the process which generates them. Nonhomogeneities obviously destroy the classical dichotomy between the real

---

[63] The mathematical program with feedback (14)–(16) still applies, with some modifications: the indirect taxes and markups must be entered in the objective function like in the Negishi-program (24). Hence a solution still exists but it is possible that, for p^e approaching zero, export remains positive, so that the economy exports a commodity that should be nontradeable in equilibrium.
[64] Negative claims will have to balance with positive claims. Of course, claims should be such that all incomes remain positive.

and financial spheres. This makes it difficult to pursue an analysis of the consequences of nonhomogeneities without an explicit representation of financial assets and transaction demand for money.

3.3.2. Exchange rates

Before discussing such representations, we now consider models where the exchange rate is the only monetary variable [like in some of the models in Dervis et al. (1982)]. We will discuss two cases, one of pure renormalization and one where the exchange rate is an adjustment mechanism.

In the simplest case the exchange rate is simply a conversion factor which allows one to express foreign and domestic values in their respective currencies. All the exchange rate does is to scale prices. Alternatively one can choose some basket of domestic goods as numéraire and express the exchange rate as the value of the basket measured in international currency. The exchange rate is then only an indicator, that is a variable which changes endogenously without affecting other endogenous variables. This amounts to no more than a renormalization. Obviously, in the absence of a money market one should not equate this indicator with the market exchange rate and no policy implications can be derived from changes in the value of the indicator.

Sometimes adjustment of the exchange rate is part of a closure rule to satisfy, say a balance of payments constraint [see Condon et al. (1990) and Dewatripont and Michel (1987)]. At the same time a normalization is imposed by setting the price of some commodity basket equal to unity. Hence there are two numéraires, the foreign prices and this basket. The domestic prices of tradeables are assumed to be affected directly by changes in the exchange rate while nontradeables are included in the basket. Therefore, under a devaluation of the exchange rate, the price of the basket will remain unaffected, so that the domestic price of tradeables will tend to rise relative to that of nontradeables.

This approach has two serious shortcomings. First, the general criticism of the use of closure rules applies: the exchange rate is not the equilibrating variable on the money market, indeed these models often do not specify the demand for money. Secondly, if the choice of numéraire is only meant as a normalization then changes in the exchange rate should have no real effects. If it is more than a normalization, it must represent a nominal price rigidity, possibly due to a lag in adjustment. In this case it is better to model the mechanism (like the taxation discussed above or rationing or stockholding) which supports the price rigidity explicitly.

3.3.3. Money and financial assets

In models with money and financial assets the exchange rate will appear as the relative price of currencies, or for example in Bourguignon et al. (1992) and

Feltenstein et al. (1988), of foreign bonds. This obviously is the natural way to obtain such rates.

If money serves no asset function there only is transactions demand. This is sometimes represented by appending a Cambridge equation with money demand proportional to expenditure [Lewis (1994)]. For given money supply and in the absence of nonhomogeneities in any other equations in the model, this determines the price level, without affecting the real sphere. In Section 5.3.1 we shall discuss the limitations of this approach and introduce a (cash-in-advance) model where the price level affects the real sphere.

Usually more general money demand functions are introduced, to arrive at a specification inspired by macro-economics. This leads to demand functions, not derived from any utility maximization, that depend on interest rates and are not homogeneous in prices. Hence money is non-neutral even if there are no other nonhomogeneities in the model. To go beyond this one must change the problems of the consumer and the firm to incorporate money demand.

Sometimes initial transactions holdings and demand appear in the budget constraint, so that money serves as a store of value. Rosensweig and Taylor (1990) and Bourguignon et al. (1992) have developed this further. They specify a function which distributes wealth over four different assets: money, domestic bonds, foreign bonds and real capital. This makes it possible significantly to increase the number of policy variables which the model can accommodate. For example in the context of structural adjustment it permits to distinguish fiscal policies, exchange rate adjustment and external borrowing. Wealth is measured as the discounted value of bonds at an expected interest rate which differs between assets. The expectation is purely static over an infinite horizon, which is, of course, in contradiction with the simulation path generated (time-inconsistency).

The allocation depends on relative prices, income and wealth levels according to behavioral equations not derived from utility maximization let alone intertemporal optimization. An intertemporal treatment of asset holdings will be considered in Section 5.3.2 (incomplete asset markets).

The introduction of financial assets makes it possible to derive financing costs of firms related to their debt, working capital requirements, dividend and tax obligations etc. Similar models have been implemented by de Janvry et al. (1991), Morrisson (1991), Thorbecke (1992).[65] The work by Easterly (1990) is closely related.

Financial assets may introduce nonhomogeneities e.g. when debt is fixed in

---

[65] Keyzer et al. (1992) perform counterfactual simulations for structural adjustment policies in Indonesia using a model without a financial sector or nonhomogeneities. Their findings do not differ very much from the ones in Thorbecke (1992).

nominal terms. Obviously in such cases a change in the price level, for example as a result of an adjustment in the money supply, or when there is a change in the exchange rate will necessarily have real effects. However, these effects are due to the nonhomogeneity of initial stocks of money [see Collier and Gunning (1992)], or other unindexed claims e.g. bonds, rather than to the introduction of financial portfolio decisions. For example when working capital require-ments enter the markup equation, then, if the model is homogeneous, a change in the money supply will lead to a proportional increase in the nominal cost of capital and of all prices. The real interest rate remains unaffected. Similarly when initial money holdings are given an increase in the price level will have a real balance effect. McMahon (1990) has reviewed the results of models with money and financial assets and reports that such effects dominate.

Bourguignon and Morrisson (1992) see it as the main advantage of the portfolio approach that it allows to represent constraints on transactions explicitly. This improves the model's capacity to address issues of phasing of reform [see also Goldin and Winters (1992)]. They generally find that gradual reforms are superior to shock therapy.

4. Regime switches, externalities and nonconvexity

In the previous section we have covered what so far have been the major fields of application: taxes and tariffs, imperfect competition (markup pricing), financial assets including money (portfolios). All these applications could be understood in terms of the CGE-model. The treatment of regime switches, externalities and nonconvexity which are so important in the theoretical literature forces us to leave the relatively simple CGE-format. However, the other formats introduced in Section 2.3 are well suited to incorporate these departures from the standard assumptions.

Regime switches arise when the pattern of flows changes, for example when a country switches from importing to exporting a particular commodity or when a government operates a buffer stock or when alternative transport routes exist. Regime switches can also be used to represent price rigidities within a general equilibrium model. We use the Mathematical program with feedback introduced in Section 2.3.3 to represent them.

It also is difficult to handle externalities in the CGE-format. We apply the Negishi-format (see Section 2.3.1) to represent a number of important externalities in consumption: non-rivalry, empathy and efficiency-wage effects. Finally, we discuss how nonconvexities in production affect the possibilities of decentralization.

4.1. Regime switches

As discussed in Section 2.3.3 the CGE-format can be seen as a basic solution of a linear program. Since the basis does not change in the CGE-format regime, switches as discussed above cannot be represented.

4.1.1. Price rigidities

There are two interpretations of price rigidities. The first regards rigidities as the norm in the short run. This is a compromise between the extreme positions of Walrasian tâtonnement and the non-tâtonnement approach [see Arrow and Hahn (1971)]. The compromise consists of maintaining price equalization (buying and selling prices are the same for all agents), while restricting trading opportunities in order to model non-instantaneous achievement of Walrasian equilibrium. The second possibility is to consider only explicit cases of government or private intervention as causes of price rigidities. Here we choose to follow the second interpretation because it is particularly relevant for developing countries, where many interventions exist which can result in price rigidities.

Buffer stocks. We have already encountered the simplest case of price rigidity,[66] namely the small country model where prices of tradeable factors were fixed exogenously. Alternatively, fixed prices (p^l and p^u) may apply to sales to and purchases from a buffer stock (s^l and s^u respectively).

The buffer stock formulation can be used for various purposes. First, it can represent publicly operated schemes for price stabilization [see for example Narayana et al. (1991)], particularly in a recursively dynamic, possibly stochastic simulation. Secondly, it may describe stocks held by private traders, where the p^l and the p^u are determined by (common) future expectations, which here are taken as given, but this will be relaxed in Section 5. Thirdly, price rigidities may be used to represent price fixing by a cartel where the chosen fixed price is supported by stock changes rather than by adjustment in production. Here one may think of a cartel of oil producers (when we treat the oil in the ground as a stock) or of an unemployment scheme (which buys labour at p^l, the unemployment benefit level and sells at p^u, the wage rate).[67] Finally, the scheme may be seen as a way of representing sluggish adjustment where p^l and p^u are the bounds on price adjustment relative to an initial solution.

---

[66] The term rigidity should not be interpreted in a temporal sense (e.g. sluggish adjustment). It is commonly used to indicate that prices are constrained.

[67] Here it is assumed that since the scheme buys the labour of the unemployed, these are not allowed to enjoy leisure during "labour" hours. Such a model has been applied by Ginsburgh and van der Heyden (1985).

One difference from external trade is that costs of the buffer stock are not borne by a foreign agent: domestic consumers are charged for it through a tax function (or receive the revenue). Another difference is that it is natural to impose bounds $\bar{s}^l$, $\bar{s}^u$ on trade with the buffer stock since stocks cannot become negative and the capacity of warehouses is limited. We ignore physical storage costs. Using the Mathematical programming format (12)–(13) this can be written[68] as:

$$\max p^e e - p^m m + p^l s^l - p^u s^u$$

$$e, m, s^l, s^u \geq 0, \ y_j, \ j = 1, \ldots, n$$

subject to

$$\sum_i \hat{x}_i + e + s^l \leq \sum_j y_j + \sum_i \omega_i + m + s^u \qquad (p)$$

$$y_j \in Y_j \qquad\qquad\qquad\qquad\qquad\qquad\qquad\qquad (36)$$

$$s^l \leq \bar{s}^l$$

$$s^u \leq \bar{s}^u$$

for given $0 < p^e < p^l \leq p^u < p^m$ defined for all commodities[69] and given $\hat{x}_i$. For some p belonging to the set of shadow prices of the program, consumption is calculated in the feedback such that:

$$\hat{x}_i = \operatorname{argmax}\{u_i(x_i) \mid p x_i \leq h_i\} \qquad (37)$$

with income h_i determined as in (23) and "tax" revenue given by:

$$T = p(s^u - s^l) \qquad (38)$$

Analogously to the complementarity conditions for external trade in (11a) and (11b), optimality of (36) implies that p_k will equal p_k^l whenever the buffer stock buys and its purchase remains below bound. Conversely $p_k = p_k^u$ whenever the buffer stock sells and sales are below bound.

When p^e approaches zero, (36)–(38) describe a closed economy: exports go to zero due to nonsatiation and this also makes imports go to zero because

---

[68] Here we allow some firms to produce under decreasing returns to scale but, as before, whenever a particular commodity is produced under constant returns to scale it is produced by only one firm.

[69] Previously we have assumed that $p^e \leq p^m$, while here the inequality is strict. If in fact $p_k^e = p_k^m$ for some k the model cannot determine whether trade is external or with the buffer stock. To resolve this some additional restriction has to be imposed (like $\bar{s}_k^l = \bar{s}_k^u = 0$) and then one can accept $p_k^e = p_k^m$. Hence at given prices there is no ambiguity as to whether trade is with the buffer stock, with the rest of the world or with domestic agents only. Buffer stocks can only be held in positive amounts for factors. For goods we will assume, that p_k^l is sufficiently close to zero and p_k^u is sufficiently large, so that at equilibrium $e_k = m_k = s_k^l = s_k^u = 0$.

trade balance has to be maintained. Then, buffer stocks can be made self-financing. This may be verified as follows: when the consumer is not taxed ($T = 0$), the complementarity conditions, the budget equations and commodity balances imply self-financing of all buffer stock schemes combined: $ps^u = ps^l$. However, this only holds in the aggregate, not for an individual commodity and not for individual agents: for example private stock holders may gain at the expense of a public buffer stock. Although buffer stocks may be self-financing, price rigidities do generate distortions. This may be seen with the aid of the Negishi program (26). For this we simply need to make consumption endogenous, by adding the term $\Sigma_i \, \alpha_i^* \, u_i(x_i)$ to the objective of (36) and by replacing $\hat{x}_i$ by x_i, and by introducing a balance of payments constraint. The term $p^e e - p^m m$ can then be dropped from the objective. The resulting objective function is $\Sigma_i \, \alpha_i^* u_i(x_i) + p^l s^l - p^u s^u$. The discussion of Section 3.1.2 now applies, which establishes that price rigidities supported by buffer stocks reduce welfare. Moreover, any proportional reduction of both p^l and p^u cannot be welfare decreasing. This is not immediately obvious. One might have thought that by reducing the purchase price and raising the selling price the buffer stock would become inactive so that the distortion would disappear. However, since the stock is then not released for domestic use, this is wasteful.

There are several ways of financing a buffer stock. The first is the central income transfer scheme of equation (23) with total transfers set according to (38). Alternatively, the scheme can be made commodity specific; (38) is then modified so that it applies separately for (subsets of) commodities and the cost is distributed over subsets of consumers.

Rationing in support of price rigidities. Buffer stocks can be supported by rationing instead of by taxation. Agents then face quantity constraints in their trades. Obviously there are many ways in which this can be done. Rationing schemes studied in the literature have a number of characteristics in common: (i) rationing occurs only when a price is at bound p^l or p^u, (ii) exchange is voluntary (no forced trade), (iii) only one side of the market is rationed (net buyers and net sellers do not face binding constraints at the same time for the same commodity), (iv) there is one commodity which is not rationed.

Rations are generated as part of adjustment mechanisms: like for the buffer stock there is either quantity adjustment (when prices are at bound) or price adjustment. Unlike for buffer stocks this rule is not implied by the mathematical program. It therefore has to be specified as part of the feedback.[70]

Different views on the functioning of the market in the short-run have led to

---

[70] This rule (e.g. the Drèze mapping) may become rather complicated (particularly since we have a model with production) and we will not give it here. In addition the mathematical program has to be adjusted to account for the implicit tax on the consumer.

the formulation of various rationing schemes. We briefly mention some of these.

First, there is the so-called uniform rationing [Drèze (1975)] whereby all consumers face the same bounds on net trade. Here rationing is only applied to non-produced commodities and rationing of net sellers is associated with $p_k = p_k^l < p_k^u$, while net buyers are rationed when $p_k^l < p_k^u = p_k$. Obviously, since consumers differ, under this scheme shadow prices will differ between consumers. Secondly, there is virtual tax rationing [Cornielje and van der Laan (1986)] where the rations are distributed so as to equalize the shadow price across rationed consumers. This shadow price (rather than the ration) can then be seen as the adjustment mechanism [Neary and Roberts (1980)]. Thirdly, there is Benassy rationing [Benassy (1982)] which differs from Drèze rationing in two respects: rationing is not necessarily uniform and $p^l = p^u$. Because of this equality it is no longer obvious which side of the market has to be rationed. This is resolved by letting agents indicate whether they feel rationed and if so on which side.[71] The Benassy-concept has been very influential in neo-Keynesian macroeconomics particularly by popularizing the concepts of classical and Keynesian unemployment and of repressed inflation.[72] In addition there is a substantial econometric literature on this model, possibly because it is more easily formally estimated due to the exogeneity of prices which simplifies the identification problem [Kooiman (1984)].

Fixed rations, black markets. In all the above approaches rations have to adjust freely. This may be unrealistic. Also the adjustment may reach its bound. Program (36) with buffer stocks has price bands and aggregate quantity restrictions on stock changes ($\bar{s}^l$, $\bar{s}^u$). When these restrictions become effective, the price cannot be kept within the band [p^l, p^u] and must adjust. Consider a non-produced commodity and assume that the buffer stock sells. Consumers who buy will pay the price p_k^u unless the buffer stock is exhausted, in which case the price will rise until p_k^m is reached. Hence as a group consumers can only buy a limited quantity at the price p_k^u. Thus, they are facing rations (not necessarily effective).

Such rations can also be specified for individual consumers: they receive nontradeable rights to buy a given quantity r_i^u at price p_k^u. If they wish to buy more they have to pay the going market price p. We call this soft rationing.

---

[71] For this, Benassy defines effective demand as: $d_{is} = x_{is}^s - \omega_{is}$ where x_{is}^s is element s of the vector x_i^s defined by $x_i^s = \text{argmax } \{u_i(x_i)|px_i \leq h_i, r_{ik}^l \leq x_{ik} - \omega_{ik} \leq r_{ik}^u, k \neq s\}$. Hence effective demand for commodity s is calculated by taking all constraints on trade r_{ik}^l, r_{ik}^u into account except the constraints for commodity s. The consumer will feel rationed on market s when his effective demand exceeds the ration.

[72] This was done for the three-commodity case with one consumer, in which case the rationing rule becomes very simple.

This is equivalent to the case of a consumer subsidy with the important difference that the price wedge applies only for the ration. The consumer problem can be written as:

$$\max u_i(x_i)$$

$$x, x_i^u, x_i^f \geq 0$$

subject to

$$p^u x_i^u + p x_i^f \leq h_i$$

$$x_i^u \leq r_i^u$$

$$x_i = x_i^u + x_i^f$$

In the Negishi-format this can be represented by adding the last three constraints to program (26) and replacing the last term in the objective term by $-\xi^u \Sigma_i x_i^u$, with $\xi_k^u = \min (p_k^u - p_k, 0)$. This yields $T = \Sigma_i \Sigma_k \xi_k^u x_{i\,k}^u$ to be shared among consumers. There now are two distortions: the excise tax in the objective and the rationing constraints.

When fixed rations are tradeable they are equivalent to income transfers.[73] In the consumer problem the rationing constraints disappear and the rations appear only as an additional term $\xi_i^u r_i^u$ in the income equation (23), funded out of taxes. There will be no distortion.

Fixed rations can also be imposed on net trades by agents rather than on consumption only. In this way uniform rationing (with fixed rations) can be represented. The difference with Drèze rationing will be that agents may exceed their rationing by trading at prices outside bounds.[74] An example of fixed rations on net trade is subsidized procurement whereby limited amounts can be sold at an above market price.

Models with fixed rations have been applied to India by Narayana et al. (1991) and to Bangladesh by Salauddin Ahmad et al. (1986). They find these rations to be an effective tool for income redistribution to the poor (particularly as part of food for work programs).

Nguyen and Whalley (1985) and Devarajan et al. (1989) have developed a variant in which a market with price controls coexists with a black market. The actual clearing takes place on the black market but there are fines and other risks which introduce special transaction costs on this market. They find, not unexpectedly, that higher fines reduce welfare.

[73] The right to buy at a subsidized price may be seen as a form of commodity (as opposed to fiat) money (see Section 5.3.1).
[74] One can view Drèze rationing as a scheme for adjusting the rations and the excise until no one wishes to trade at prices outside bounds p', p''.

4.1.2. Transport

Investment in transportation has figured prominently in many development plans. There have been two types of concerns: the need for publicly provided transport infrastructure and, more recently, the impact of the transport cost e.g. through higher oil prices. The first concern requires the representation of indivisibility features of networks and hence involves nonconvexity. This we do not pursue here. The second concern has led to applications which focus on the impact of transport policy on regional development e.g. through induced income effects and changes in specialization.

In the model with buffer stocks, commodities are exchanged between consumers, firms, the buffer stock and the rest of the world. When this is given a spatial interpretation, there are physical distances between agents and the flow of commodities requires routing, possibly involving transport costs. In the case of transport costs, the commodity the consumer buys is different from the one supplied to the transport firms. Under the assumption that there is at most one constant-returns-to-scale firm for each commodity, it is immediately clear which constant returns firm will supply but this assumption can be relaxed.[75] Allowing for this in the model means relaxing our assumption that there is at most constant returns to scale firm supplying one commodity. Clearly, the model can easily accommodate this generalization, since it brings us back to the standard assumptions in Debreu (1959) (the restriction was made mainly to introduce the CGE-model). However, in applications the discontinuity in response which may result from this relaxation may be considered undesirable, particularly because it makes it hard to estimate the parameters of the model.

Elbers (1992) formulated a model where regions import from each other. When prices change switches may occur, so that one exporter is replaced by another one.[76] Although the approach was applied for a national model, it is more general and can be used to model international trade with transport costs. This has the advantage of attributing price differences to transport costs rather than explaining them artificially as product heterogeneity as is done in the Armington approach (see Section 2.4.3).

---

[75] Transport usually involves several transport firms which supply the same commodity at one location, procured from different sources. Routing is unambiguous if these firms produce under decreasing returns to scale because then the scale of production is set by prices. If they produce under constant returns, routing can be ambiguous as the commodity may be supplied at the same price via two channels.

[76] There are different routes between any two regions, so that there will be ambiguity when two routes are equally costly but under the conditions of the model the ambiguity only affects transport activities.

4.2. External effects

External effects occur when prices and incomes are not the only variables consumers are faced with. Whenever such effects occur, the welfare theorems no longer apply: a decentralized solution is not necessarily Pareto-efficient and it may not be possible to decentralize a welfare optimum. If in policy analysis Pareto-efficiency and the possibility of decentralization are considered desirable, it is convenient to start with a welfare program. Optimality conditions are then used to derive signals which induce agents to behave in such a way that a welfare optimum is achieved.

While desirable in principle, this approach has as yet hardly found empirical applications for developing countries. We will concentrate on external effects in consumption. We distinguish three types of externalities: non-rival consumption, empathy and productivity effects of consumption.

4.2.1. Non-rival consumption

To represent non-rivalness we write the utility function as $u_i(x_i, x_g)$, where consumption x_g is non-rival, say government consumption, so that it benefits all consumers simultaneously. For notational convenience the set of consumers is taken to exclude g. The welfare program may be written as:

$$\max \sum_i \alpha_i u_i(x_i, x_g)$$

$$x_i, x_g \geq 0, \; y_j, \; i = 1, \ldots, m, \; j = 1, \ldots, n$$

subject to

$$\sum_i x_i + x_g \leq \sum_j y_j + \sum_i \omega_i + \omega_g \qquad\qquad (p)$$

$$y_j \in Y_j$$

for given welfare weights α_i. In this form this program does not lend itself to decentralization because it does not indicate that consumers may wish to consume different quantities x_g^i of the non-rival commodity. Obviously, the quantity consumed must be the same for all agents, so that $x_g^i = x_g$ for all i. The equilibrium model can now be written in Negishi-format as:

$$\max \sum_i \alpha_i^* u_i(x_i, x_g^i)$$

$$x_i, x_g^i, x_g \geq 0, \; y_j, \; i = 1, \ldots, m, \; j = 1, \ldots, n$$

subject to

$$\sum_i x_i + x_g \leq \sum_j y_j + \sum_i \omega_i + \omega_g \qquad\qquad (p) \qquad\qquad (39)$$

$$x_g^i = x_g \tag{ϕ_i}$$

$$y_j \in Y_j$$

with α_i^*, which are nonnegative and add up to unity, are such that (for p^* and ϕ_i^* in the set of Lagrange multipliers and x_i^*, $x_g^i{}^*$ optimal in the welfare program) for all consumers budget constraints are satisfied:

$$p^* x_i^* + \phi_i^* x_g^i{}^* = h_i^0{}^* \tag{40}$$

where $h_i^0{}^*$ is pretax income.

The consumption x_g^i in program (39) denotes what consumer i would like to consume of the non-rival commodity. Agreement[77] among consumers is imposed through the constraint $x_g^i = x_g$. Since utilities are nondecreasing in x_g^i, the dual variable ϕ_i will be nonnegative. By the optimality conditions clearly $p = \Sigma_i \phi_i$. Consumers only pay for commodities from which they derive (positive marginal) utility. In fact when there are consumers groups who have no non-rival goods in common, one can partially decentralize the program (39) into separate problems for consumer groups who face given prices, satisfy a group budget constraint and demand x_i and x_g (based on agreement within the group). Signals ϕ_i are relevant only within the group. This is known as the principle of subsidiarity: only those who benefit have to agree on, and pay for, the provision of the non-rival good.

Decentralization proceeds as follows. Producers maximize profits as in the competitive model. Consumers solve:

$$\max u_i(x_i, x_g^i)$$

$$x_i, x_g^i \geq 0$$

subject to

$$p^* x_i + \phi_i^* x_g^i \leq h_i^0{}^* \tag{41}$$

for given p^*, ϕ_i^*. Prices ϕ_i^* are called Lindahl prices. Hence consumers decide independently on x_g^i[78] and at equilibrium p^* and ϕ_i^* are such that the commodity balance is satisfied and that consumers agree on x_g.

By contrast, in applied modelling government consumption is usually modelled as having no effect on the utility of (private) consumers, like in Section 2.4.2, and this is hard to justify. Also, the level of provision is not determined through agreement among consumers. This may be realistic but it is not Pareto-efficient.

---

[77] Since preferences and welfare weights differ, agreement only means that the same quantity is consumed.

[78] There exists an extensive public economics literature on the incentives to reveal x_g^i.

The distinguishing characteristic of Lindahl-pricing is that consumers agree. The process of reaching agreement and clearing prices is left unspecified, just like the market clearing process is not specified in the standard competitive equilibrium. The finding of Lindahl prices may be viewed as a hypothetical political process in which consumers are allowed to choose any vector x_g^i they like, rather than restricting them to select one of the vectors offered by some finite set of political parties.[79]

One can use alternative equilibrium concepts. For example, rather than basing his decision on ϕ_i, the consumer may conjecture that his share of the cost is fixed. When this leads to a solution where his share in the cost is less than proportional, one can say that he is free-riding, while if he pays more he is facing a so-called assurance problem. Obviously, it will be difficult to realize a Lindahl equilibrium since consumers have an incentive not to reveal their preferences. Non-rival consumption is of particular relevance for environmental issues since the benefits which the consumer derives from the biosphere are largely non-rival.

Non-rivalness can also occur for inputs into production but in that case joint profit maximization at given prices will ensure efficiency. Alternatively, when all the production sets Y_j are known to all producers, every one can pay according to the marginal value productivity of the non-rival input which is then known to all.

4.2.2. Empathy

We have just seen how non-rivalness can be used to obtain Pareto-efficient government consumption. We now discuss a way to obtain Pareto-efficient income transfers (including development aid). Non-rival consumption can be interpreted as the demand of a consumer whose consumption raises utility of other consumers. A special case is empathy where utility (rather than consumption) of consumer g affects utility of consumer i: $u_i(x_i, u_g(x_g))$. As long as consumer g does not care about any other consumer the earlier model applies.

Based on his empathy consumer i will be willing to pay transfers to consumer g who will receive income px_g, to which consumer i contributes $\phi_i x_g$. Consumers need not have the same perception of the utility curve of consumer g. All that is required for efficient decentralization is that they agree on x_g. Again, in the absence of Lindahl pricing there will be an assurance or a free-rider problem. Of course this representation is simplified. In fact when there is empathy consumer i's utility will not only depend on the utility of consumer g but also on the utility of all other consumers. In this case the

---

[79] This is formally equivalent to the completeness of financial markets (see Section 5.3.2).

model with non-rival consumption no longer applies since it is no longer possible to distinguish between donors and recipients. The utility function is now written as $w_i(x_i, u^i)^{80}$ where u^i is the vector of all consumers' utilities, with elements u_h^i, as "demanded" by consumer i. The Negishi problem is then:

$$\max \sum_i \alpha_i^* w_i(x_i, u^i)$$

$$x_i \geq 0, u^i, u, y_j, i = 1, \ldots, m, j = 1, \ldots, n$$

subject to

$$\sum_i x_i \leq \sum_j y_j + \sum_i \omega_i \qquad\qquad (p)$$

$$u^i = u \qquad\qquad (\psi^i) \qquad (42)$$

$$w_i(x_i, u^i) = u_i^i$$

$$y_j \in Y_j$$

with α_i^* on the unit simplex such that for all consumers budget constraints are satisfied:

$$p^* x_i^* + \sum_h \psi_h^{i*} u_h^{i*} = h_i^{0*} + \sum_h \psi_i^{h*} u_i^{h*}$$

for p^*, ψ^{i*} in the set of Lagrange multipliers and x_i^*, u^{i*} optimal in the welfare program, where h_i^{0*} is pretax income.

This problem can again be decentralized. Each consumer i maximizes his utility, takes transfers received $(\sum_h \psi_i^{h*} u_i^{h*})$ as given and decides on the transfers to give $(\sum_h \psi_h^{i*} u_h^{i*})$. In equilibrium consumers agree on the utilities. Arrow (1981) has studied the efficiency properties of equilibria with empathy.

Hence it is conceptually straightforward to incorporate empathy. However, program (42) assumes that each consumer is able to measure the utility of other consumers (although it does not require interpersonal comparability). If this is not the case, it is still possible to proceed along the line of (42) but agreement will have to apply to, for example, consumption. Then the utility function may be written as $w_i(x_i, x^i)$ and agreement is required on x^i, which has the advantage of being observable. Now the transfer will not be lump-sum: only consumption of specific commodities will be subsidized. This tied form of aid is referred to as paternalism.[81] This makes it possible to model transfers

---

[80] The function $w_i(x_i, u^i)$ is strictly concave and monotonic. It must also satisfy an additional "selfishness" assumption which ensures that the welfare program (42) will be bounded: consumers should not be happy only because the other consumers are happy, even if they consume little.

[81] In a different interpretation of this specification, consumers do not care about the other agent but benefit directly from his consumption: it may be nice to see the neighbour's garden in good order. The transfers and subsidies then pay for joint consumption and the consumers who are interrelated in this way can be thought of as forming a club. While this interpretation has nothing to do with empathy, the model is identical.

such as bequests and development aid in a theoretically satisfactory way. However, it is obviously very difficult to estimate models with empathy because, while transfers can be observed, the signals ψ (and the utilities) cannot.

4.2.3. Efficiency wage

External effects may also arise when endowments are treated as endogenous. This is studied in efficiency wage theory where the basic assumption is that endowments, in particular labour, are dependent on (rival as well as non-rival) consumption: $\omega_i(x_i)$.[82] Such a dependence is called an efficiency wage relation. In poor countries food, shelter, health care are likely to be important determinants of productivity and there exists an extensive econometric literature which documents this [Behrman and Deolalikar (1989) and Strauss and Thomas in the present volume]. More generally, education and consumer durables can raise productivity.

In this empirical literature[83] it is often suggested that such relations call for interventions. For example if health care[84] appears as a significant variable in a regression explaining some proxy of ω, then one usually concludes that government should promote health care. This may be misleading. Indeed no conclusions can be drawn without a comprehensive welfare analysis. The central question introduced by the efficiency wage relation is whether it calls for intervention.[85]

In welfare analysis it is necessary to extend the efficiency wage relation by including labour hours worked (n_i) as an argument. For the time being we assume that $\omega_i(x_i, n_i)$ is concave and nondecreasing in x_i, and increasing in n_i. There is an upper bound $\bar{n}_i$ on labour hours so that the consumer's problem remains a convex program which will set n_i at its upper bound. The resulting aggregate excess demand function possesses the continuity properties that are necessary for existence of equilibrium. We distinguish five cases.

First, with zero transfers (hence no taxes) the equilibrium is Pareto-efficient, so that in this case there is no need for intervention.

Secondly, when there are income taxes then Pareto efficiency may be lost.

---

[82] Here labour power is the commodity. It is either employed or consumed as leisure. Note that this covers the standard case with ω_i constant.

[83] Unfortunately there still appears to exist a gap between this econometric literature and the micro-economic models with contain $\omega(x)$-relations. This is mainly due to the fact that in the econometric formulation many properties of the micro-model such as concavity or adding-up are neglected.

[84] Often health care is considered endogenous in the household model and therefore replaced in the regression by some instrumentalization.

[85] This implies general equilibrium analysis, whereas most of the theoretical efficiency wage literature [e.g. Stiglitz (1976)] uses partial equilibrium methods, with Dasgupta and Ray (1986) as an important exception.

This is because the tax may reduce consumer's income below a well defined critical level so that $\omega_i(x_i, n_i)$ becomes too low.[86] To restore efficiency incomes must be raised by lowering the tax rate or instituting transfers.

Thirdly, since measuring of labour supply is difficult a market for labour hours is more easily organized than a market for labour power. Then, incentives are distorted. An equilibrium will exist (possibly involving rationing) but it will not be Pareto efficient unless corrective action is taken. This can take the form of consumer subsidies and income transfers paid by the government but this requires accurate measurement of labour power by the government. Alternatively, the producer who may be in a better position to grade labour, can pay worker specific wage supplements (in Stiglitz' terminology: efficiency wage premia). Obviously, there is a free rider problem: there is an external effect for employers who prefer to see the government pay.

Fourthly, when employers have monopsony power and workers are satiated in leisure, the efficiency wage relation will make the employer offer a positive wage. This is an important difference from the standard model (with constant ω_i) in which under monopsony a zero wage will arise and lead to a Pareto efficient equilibrium, since labour supply is fixed and hence independent of income.

Finally, when we drop the assumption on concavity of $\omega_i(x_i, n_i)$, possibly to account for setup costs, it may be efficient to provide income supplements and consumer subsidies to some workers while leaving others unemployed. Here efficiency has the unusual effect of social stratification: identical consumers will be treated differently. This is a form of efficient rationing, a topic considered in the Section 4.3.[87]

Issues which arise in these five cases have received considerable attention in the development literature but surprisingly little welfare analysis and general equilibrium modelling has been conducted.

4.2.4. Scope for applications

All three examples of external effects (non-rivalness, empathy and efficiency wage) are of special relevance in the context of development. In none of the applied models reviewed does non-rival consumption enter private consumers utility. This severely limits the possibilities for welfare analysis of changes in public policies since these often involve non-rival goods. In developing countries transfers often form a substantial part of household income. In most

---

[86] Income taxes must here be interpreted broadly, for example they would include rent payment to a landowner under a sharecropping agreement.

[87] Dropping the concavity assumption tends to create possibility of non-existence of an equilibrium with zero transfers. Dasgupta and Ray (1986) prove existence for a continuum of "sufficiently different" consumers.

applied models they are treated like income taxes, through functions and not derived from maximizing behaviour. Finally, the relevance of the efficiency wage theory for developing countries has been indicated earlier. Here empirical work has been going on for a long time but the results have not been incorporated in applied general equilibrium models. Hence there is substantial scope for expansion in this direction.

4.3. Nonconvexity in production

Nonconvexities (setup costs and increasing returns to scale) were already discussed in relation to markup pricing and imperfect competition in Section 3.2. Here we consider welfare aspects and decentralisation.

Nonconvexity in production can arise at different levels, of which four are particularly relevant. First, they can arise within the firm. To the extent the production process is divisible the nonconvexity is not problematic, as for variable entry models with a real-valued number of firms (Section 2.4.1) above. For example, in agriculture a nonconvex relation may exist for an individual plant and the area of the plot can be treated as the real-valued number of firms. Secondly, nonconvexity can apply at firm level due to setup cost, or, thirdly, due to increasing returns to scale. Finally, there may be a similar nonconvexity with respect to a non-rival input (for example accumulated knowledge); this may be seen as nonconvexity at the level of the economy.

The first case need not be discussed since it can be dealt with in a competitive equilibrium. The other three cases present two sorts of problems: the welfare program is nonconvex and the decentralization may not be possible without transfers.

The second case (setup costs) can be modelled by redefining the production set as:

$$Y_j(\delta_j) = \{y_j | y_j \le q_j b_j - v_j - v_j^0, \; q_j \le \delta_j f_j(v_j), \; \delta_j \le \delta_j f_j^0(v_j^0), \; q_j \ge 0,$$
$$v_j^0, v_j \ge 0\} \tag{43}$$

where δ_j is the (integer) number of active firms (zero or one but possibly larger); firm activity is "produced" through the setup inputs v_j^0 incurred by each firm.

This transforms the welfare program (9) into a mixed integer program which endogenously determines the number of active firms. There are several problems in decentralizing the optimum, all related to the integer nature of δ_j.

First, it is not clear what decentralisation means in this context. Unlike in the case of convex technologies, optimal decisions for a group of firms need not coincide with decisions which are optimal for its members individually. This is because a change in the δ_j affects prices. A conglomerate will take this into account while an individual firm does not. Secondly, in the welfare optimum some producing (group of) firms may make a loss. This calls for intervention in the form of subsidies or for mergers of firms. Conversely, firms which should not produce (in the sense that $\delta_j = 0$ in the welfare optimum) may, taking prices as given, want to produce but should be prevented from doing so. Thirdly, a competitive equilibrium (without transfers) need not exist. If it does it is not necessarily Pareto-efficient since the set of active firms may not be Pareto-efficient.

Since all these problems are related to the integer nature of δ_j, once the δ_j has been obtained in the welfare program, the optimum can be achieved as a competitive equilibrium with transfers to firms.

In the third case (increasing returns with a strictly quasi-concave production function) the welfare program must be used to determine output levels q_j. As before interventions are needed to realize these output levels: firms must minimize cost, set price equal to marginal cost and satisfy demand. Their losses reduce the income of the consumers who own the firms so that additional conditions are needed to ensure that incomes of these consumers remain positive.

Again, one can consider an equilibrium, independently of welfare maximization, where firms minimize cost, set price equal to marginal cost and satisfy demand, under the restriction that competition allows only the producers which set the lowest price to sell. This is called a marginal pricing equilibrium [see Cornet (1988)]. The main problem with this approach is that under nonconvexities there may be many solutions to the first-order conditions of the welfare program. The marginal pricing equilibrium only verifies these conditions with the additional requirement that the transfers be zero. This would only be Pareto-efficient by coincidence.

An equilibrium solution with given δ_j or q_j (as determined in the welfare program) can be interpreted as being supported by efficient rationing. Firms then face binding constraints on production but (in contrast to the rationing that supports price rigidities, as discussed in Section 4.1.1) the equilibrium is Pareto-efficient.[88]

Finally, there is the case of a nonconvexity at the level of the economy. An equilibrium (without transfers) will exist in which all agents take prices as given, as long as the non-rival input (for example, experience gained with a particular production process) is not priced. Obviously, such an equilibrium, which is common in the endogenous growth literature, is inefficient [see Romer (1991)]. When one insists on efficiency, decentralization of equilibrium is quite

---

[88] In Section 4.2.3 we have encountered a case with nonconcavity of the efficiency wage relation which also led to efficient rationing.

problematic: it requires transfers between consumers and firms and rationing of the non-rival input.

In applied models as discussed in Section 3.2 either markups and a fixed number of firms are used or the marginal pricing rule is employed (negative markup). In neither case is Pareto-efficiency ensured.

5. Dynamics, assets and expectations

5.1. Finite horizon

So far time has entered only through recursive dynamics. Savings and investment were represented through behavioral equations in which either expectations did not appear or they were static. We now consider perfect foresight, postponing the discussion of uncertainty until Section 5.3.2. We start with a finite horizon model. This section mainly serves as an introduction to the treatment of infinite horizons and constraints on transactions.

We consider discrete time periods, indexed $t = 1, \ldots, T$. First we obtain the dynamic model in the usual Arrow–Debreu fashion by merely relabelling commodities of the static model. All markets are assumed to exist for all periods. Consumers and producers take all their decisions prior to period 1 and express their net demands for each period taking (present value) prices $p_1, \ldots, p_T$ as given. Consumers are not subject to a budget constraint for each period but to an aggregate one called wealth constraint. Similarly firms maximize a capitalized stream of profits. All prices reflect valuations at one moment, namely the moment of decision.

The consumer problem then reads:

$$\max u_i(x_{i1}, \ldots, x_{iT})$$
$$x_{it} \geq 0, t = 1, \ldots, T$$

subject to

$$\sum_t p_t x_{it} \leq h_i \tag{44}$$

given

$$h_i = \sum_t p_t \omega_{it} + \sum_j \theta_{ij} \, \pi_j(p_1, \ldots, p_T)$$

The profit of the firm is:

$$\pi_j(p_1, \ldots, p_T) = \max_{y_{jt}} \left(\sum_t p_t y_{jt} \mid (y_{j1}, \ldots, y_{jT}) \in Y_j \right) \tag{45}$$

and commodity balances are also disaggregated by period:

$$\sum_i x_{it} - \sum_j y_{jt} - \sum_i \omega_{it} \leq 0 \perp p_t \geq 0, \quad t = 1, \ldots, T$$

Clearly, all the properties of the competitive equilibrium and all the extensions of the static model apply. Since all markets exist, the welfare theorems continue to hold.

Equations (44), (45) can be regarded as a reduced form of a more elaborate formulation with a budget constraint for each period. It is convenient to use the more elaborate form as a point of departure for the introduction of financial assets (and taxes).

The consumer problem is then:

$$\max u_i(x_{i1}, \ldots, x_{iT})$$
$$x_{it} \geq 0, S_{it}, V_{i,t+1}, t = 1, \ldots, T$$

subject to

$$p_t x_{it} + S_{it} = h_{it}$$
$$V_{i,t+1} = V_{it} + S_{it} \tag{46}$$
$$V_{i,T+1} \geq 0$$
$$V_{i1} = 0$$

given

$$h_{it} = p_t \omega_{it} + \sum_j \theta_{ij} \pi_{jt}$$

where S_{it} is savings, V_{it} net worth, π_{jt} the dividend payments in period t. Similarly the producer problem is:

$$\max \pi_j$$
$$S_{jt}, V_{j,t+1}, y_{jt}, \pi_{jt}, \pi_j, t = 1, \ldots, T$$

subject to

$$\pi_j = \sum_t p_t y_{jt}$$
$$(y_{j1}, \ldots, y_{jT}) \in Y_j$$
$$\pi_{jt} = \sigma_{jt} \pi_j$$
$$\pi_{jt} + S_{jt} = p_t y_{jt}$$
$$V_{j,t+1} = V_{jt} + S_{jt} \tag{47}$$

$$V_{j,T+1} \geq 0$$

$$V_{j1} = 0$$

where σ_{jt} is the given[89] share of capitalized profits paid out as dividend in period t and V_{jt} and S_{jt} are net worth and savings.

It may be verified that in equilibrium net worth adds up to zero over consumers and producers in each period. Savings add up to zero as well. Hence there is no need for an additional equilibrating variable like an interest rate. This shows again that as long as Walras Law is respected and all future markets exist, there is no need for closure rules.

The obvious disadvantage of the finite horizon model is that the world "ends" at T. Hence the choice of T may dominate the results. This may even happen when T is relatively large (a point to which we return below) and has motivated the formulation of models with infinite horizon. Since infinite horizon models are in fact implemented as finite horizon models, applications of the two will be discussed together in the next section.

5.2. Infinite horizon

Infinite horizon models are important in economic theory, particularly, of course, in capital theory. In applied work one cannot simulate over an infinite horizon and therefore modellers use finite horizon approximations. We first discuss the theoretical models with infinite horizon, in order to assess the validity of finite horizon approximations. This digression is necessary because these approximations turn out to be quite problematic.

A natural way to extend the formulation (46), (47) and the commodity balances to an infinite horizon is to take T infinite while dropping nonnegativity conditions on terminal net worth.[90] The utility function would then have a domain of infinite dimensions. The production set would also become of infinite dimension. A more tractable formulation uses a time-recursive specification of technology and utility.

There are two types of infinite horizon models, those with a finite number of infinitely lived consumers and those with an infinite number of finitely lived consumers. These are called dynastic and overlapping generation models respectively. We consider the two models in turn.

---

[89] The value can be chosen arbitrarily without affecting prices and real allocations.
[90] Ponzi games are impossible because of the commodity balances.

5.2.1. Dynastic models

Specification. Dynastic models are best analyzed in the Negishi-format. This is because while the number of commodities becomes infinite, the number of consumers remains finite. We write the Negishi-program as:

$$v(k_1, \alpha^*) = \max \sum_i \alpha_i^* \sum_{t=1}^{\infty} (\beta)^{t-1} u_i(x_{it})$$

$$x_{it}, k_{t+1} \geq 0, i = 1, \ldots, m, t = 1, 2, \ldots$$

subject to

$$\sum_i x_{it} + G(k_{t+1}) \leq k_t \qquad\qquad (p_t) \qquad\qquad (49)$$

k_1 given

where the welfare weights are chosen so that:

$$\sum_{t=1}^{\infty} p_t^* x_{it}^* = p_1^* k_{i1} ,$$

with given individual capital ownership k_{i1} such that

$$\sum_i k_{i1} = k_1 . \qquad\qquad (50)$$

The program uses an intertemporally additive utility function where the discount factor β is positive, less than one and the same for all consumers.[91] The production technology is described by the function $G(k_{t+1})$ which specifies the use of commodities in the current period needed to make k_{t+1} units available in the next period.[92] The function should be convex and non-decreasing in k_{t+1} (when the optimal k_{t+1} depends only on k_t, as will be the case for trends, this requirement can be relaxed).

We will discuss the problem (49), (50) in two parts, starting with the welfare

---

[91] It can be obtained from the recursive utility function $w_i(x_i, u_i)$ as introduced by Koopmans et al. (1964), which is similar to the one discussed in Section 4.2.2 under empathy. Here it is the own utility in the next period that enters rather than the utility of the other consumers and the "selfishness" becomes discounting: $0 < \partial w_i/\partial u_i < 1$. When w_i is linear in u_i and the discount factor β is the same for all consumers, the intertemporally additive specification results. This specification is widely used but it is known to be restrictive because the intertemporal time preference is fixed and therefore independent of the level of consumption. As a result in a steady state only the consumer with the lowest rate of time preference will have positive consumption. For a further discussion of the dynastic model with recursive utility see Lucas and Stokey (1984).

[92] Exogenous changes in endowments, for example according to given growth rates, or other model parameters can also be described by the function G, as long as the number of parameters involved is finite. The present formulation is quite restrictive, as it rules out substitution, but the commodity balance can easily be replaced by the more general transformation constraint $F(\Sigma_i x_{it}, k_{t+1}, k_t) \leq 0$.

optimum (49) for given welfare weights and then turning to the Negishi-problem.[93] A similar case is discussed by Stokey and Lucas (1989, Chapter 4). They show that (49) reduces to the dynamic program:

$$v(k_t, \alpha) = \max_i \sum_i \alpha_i u_i(x_{it}) + \beta v(k_{t+1}, \alpha)$$

$$x_{it}, k_{t+1} \geq 0, i = 1, \ldots, m$$

subject to

$$\sum_i x_{it} + G(k_{t+1}) \leq k_t \qquad\qquad (p_t) \qquad\qquad (51)$$

for given k_t and welfare weights α_i (α is the vector of α_i's).

Solving (51) for all $t = 1, 2, \ldots$ yields a solution of (49). Hence the infinite horizon program can be analyzed as a sequence of single-period programs where the term $v(k_{t+1}, \alpha)$ in the objective serves as end-valuation of each period's stocks. The conversion is analytically convenient because standard results of convex programming can now be applied. For example, program (51) implies that if the concavity of u_i is strict, then x_i will be uniquely determined. If, in addition, utility is differentiable, then p_t will also be unique. Finally, if convexity of G is strict (with respect to elements of k_{t+1} which are not determined by trends only), then k_{t+1} will be unique. If all these conditions are satisfied these variables will be continuous functions of the parameters (k_t, α) and the value function $v(k_t, \alpha)$ will be continuously differentiable.[94] Moreover, $\partial v(k_1, \alpha)/\partial k_1$ is the value of initial stocks and $\partial v(k_1, \alpha)/\partial \alpha_i$ is the intertemporal utility $\sum_{t=1}^{\infty} (\beta)^{t-1} u_i(x_{it})$ of consumer i. Hence $\partial v(k_1, \alpha)/\partial \alpha_i \alpha_i$ is his full expenditure, as defined in Section 2.2.5.

We can now turn to the full Negishi-problem. In program (51) the welfare weights α are fixed but they have to be adjusted to satisfy (50), i.e. to ensure that budget deficits are zero. The computation of these budget deficits is not trivial since consumer expenditures involve an infinite number of terms, so that continuity of total expenditures as a function of α is not obvious. Kehoe (1991)

---

[93] The formulation (49) assumes that a maximum exists (i.e. the objective is bounded and the supremum attained). For this it is sufficient that $\sum_i x_{it}$ is bounded at all t, which will be the case if some necessary input (like land or labour) follows an exogenous trend that remains bounded and grows at a rate less than $(1/\beta - 1)$. Then, given the assumption on β the objective will remain bounded. Carlson and Haurie (1987) discuss the optimality concepts to be used when this condition is not satisfied. When the path is known to converge to a steady state it is for example possible to minimize deviations from the steady state [as in the regulator problem, see Wonham (1979)], otherwise more complex comparisons, like overtaking optimality, have to be used.

[94] The dynamic programming format requires knowledge of the function v. Of course one may try to obtain it iteratively, starting from some polynomial approximation $v(k_{t+1}, \alpha)$ in the objective, deriving the corresponding value function which is then entered into the objective and so on. Unfortunately as reported by Kehoe (1991) this procedure, while convergent, is inefficient. In fact the more efficient algorithms do not use the dynamic programming format but linear-quadratic approximations.

avoids this difficulty by computing expenditures as the difference between full income and consumer surplus, as we did in Section 2.2.5. This is done by treating the number n_i of consumers in group i explicitly, as follows.

Let i denote classes of consumers, each with a single member $(n_i = 1)$. Define the extended utility function $\tilde{u}_i(x_i, n_i) = n_i u_i(x_i/n_i)$ which clearly is homogeneous of degree one in (x_i, n_i) for nonnegative x_i and at $n_i = 1$. The objective of (51) may now be rewritten as:

$$v(k_t, \alpha, n) = \max \sum_i \alpha_i \tilde{u}_i(x_{it}, n_i) + \beta v(k_{t+1}, \alpha, n)$$

where n is the vector of n_i's. The budget deficit b_i may now be calculated as:

$$b_i = \partial v(k_1, \alpha, n)/\partial \alpha_i \, \alpha_i - \partial v(k_1, \alpha, n)/\partial n_i n_i - \partial v(k_1, \alpha, n)/\partial k_1 k_{i1}$$

The first term on the right hand side is the full expenditure of consumer i. The third term is the income from initial stocks. The second term is the consumer surplus. Like in Section 2.2.5 deducting consumer surplus from full expenditure yields actual expenditure. This may be seen as follows. For a continuously differentiable $u_i(x_i)$ one can apply Euler's rule to obtain, for each t:

$$\tilde{u}_i(x_{it}, n_i) = \partial \tilde{u}_i(x_{it}, n_i)/\partial x_{it} \, x_{it} + \partial \tilde{u}_i(x_{it}, n_i)/\partial n_i n_i$$

Using the definition $\tilde{u}_i(x_{it}, n_i) = n_i u_i(x_{it}/n_i)$, $n_i = 1$, and premultiplying by α_i:

$$\alpha_i \tilde{u}_i(x_{it}, n_i) = \alpha_i \partial u_i(x_i)/\partial x_{it} \, x_{it} + \alpha_i \partial \tilde{u}_i(x_{it}, n_i)/\partial n_i$$

The first term on the right hand side of this equation is equal to expenditure of group i in period t. Summing over t, with discounting, yields actual discounted expenditure as the difference between full expenditure and consumer surplus, which corresponds to the first and second right-hand side terms in the budget deficit equation. Hence budget deficits b_i are continuous functions of α and this makes it possible to adjust welfare weights like in the standard Negishi approach. This leads to a finite-dimensional fixed point problem so that an equilibrium exists. Moreover, the number of equilibria is (generically) finite.[95]

---

[95] Kehoe also applies the Negishi-format to show that the number of equilibria may become infinite whenever price distortions are introduced that are not fixed in nominal terms. This is commonly referred as the problem of indeterminacy. The reason for this indeterminacy is that there will be an infinite number of such distortions each represented through one term in the objective, one for each commodity for each period. This creates a potential indeterminacy when these terms have to be adjusted to satisfy a system of equations in which they also enter on a right-hand side. The equilibrium is a fixed point of such a mapping, which is now infinite-dimensional. Then theorems like Sard's theorem or the implicit function theorem can no longer be invoked to establish (generic) determinacy [see also Mas-Colell and Zame (1991)]. Ryan and Bean (1989) give several examples of indeterminacy in infinite horizon models.

Convergence to a steady state

In applications the steady state of this model plays a prominent role. The first-order conditions of the dynamic program (51) may be used to derive the steady state (if it exists) as a fixed-point of the mapping $k_{t+1}(k_t)$, i.e. the conditions under which $k_t = k_{t+1}$. Arrow and Kurz (1980) have studied the conditions under which in the Ramsey–Koopmans–Cass model (which has a single consumer, a single commodity and which is in continuous time) the optimal path converges to a steady state.[96] They find that for positive discount rates the optimal path is unique and converges to a unique steady state. It is important to stress that under more general conditions the steady state is not necessarily unique and the optimal path need not lead to any steady state. McKenzie (1987) provides a survey of so-called turnpike theorems, that is of conditions under which the dynamic path converges to a steady state. These theorems are specified for models with continuous time. However, Boldrin and Montrucchio (1986) show that, in discrete time, for any continuous policy function with compact domain, $k_{t+1}(k_t)$, one can find a dynamic program which generates this policy function. Hence nothing can be said in general on the global stability of the optimal path: it may converge, cycle or be chaotic.

Even locally around the steady state the path may be nonunique (to test this one may compute the eigenvalues of the difference equations) but even if it is unique this may only be so around one of several steady states.

Applications. Dynastic models have been used mainly to study investment in the energy and industry sectors, particularly in relation to environmental taxes (see Section 3.1) and to capital taxation (see Section 5.3 below). These are typically areas where dynamics of gestation lags in investment and intertemporal efficiency investment decisions matter. In recursively dynamic simulation one can only run scenarios, so that investment is either exogenous or it is specified according to a rule which is not derived from intertemporal optimization. In dynastic models intertemporal time-consistency can be maintained.

However, only finite horizon allocations can be represented on the computer. Therefore, any representation of a non-trivial infinite horizon model involves truncation of the time horizon and simulation over a finite time-horizon. Here we discuss how this is done.

Applied models are usually not written in a Negishi-format but in a Debreu-format with individual agents optimizing under perfect foresight over an

---

[96] This has led to applications in macroeconomics [see for example Lipton et al. (1982)].

infinite horizon. There are distortions[97] and exogenous variables which are kept constant beyond a given year. A solution consists of prices and allocations such that all markets are cleared. Usually one computes three solutions: an initial steady state prior to some shift in exogenous variables, a steady state after this shift[98] and a transition path from one steady state to the other. One is mainly interested in the transition path, toward the end of which all exogenous variables are kept fixed to allow the model to settle to a steady state.

The transition path is commonly obtained as follows. For given initial price expectations over the whole (infinite) period, one moves forward in time, accumulating capital and computing in each year the prices that clear the market of that year. Calculation proceeds over a T-period horizon using the steady state prices as end-valuation for the expectations beyond T. The computed prices serve as the expectations of a new round of calculations. One concludes that a solution has been found when no further price adjustments are needed and there is a convergence to a steady state towards the end of the simulation period.

The rationale for the approach is that if one succeeds in obtaining a path which converges to a steady state, one has a solution of the Euler and transversality conditions and therefore also a solution to the original model (49)–(50) [see e.g. Stokey and Lucas (1989), p. 98]. Hence while accepting that the solution is to (49)–(50) does not have to converge to a steady state, one only looks for convergent paths and is satisfied if one finds one.

However, the studies do not provide any criterion to check whether the finite horizon solution in fact lies on the infinite horizon path.

Shifting the end-date may lead to different solutions and we have seen that at infinity the solution may be indeterminate. Indeterminacy of a particular steady state can be tested via eigenvalues and some authors perform this test, although this is only a local test and results are rarely reported.[99] Since model descriptions are almost always vague on how the convergence to a steady state was obtained, it is difficult to conclude to what extent the truncation has affected the results: most authors [e.g. Jorgenson and Wilcoxen (1993), Goulder (1991), Mercenier and de Souza (1994) and Bovenberg and Goulder (1991)] suggest that the truncation has little effect but do not provide evidence. For a more formal assessment of the quality of the approximation one may use

---

[97] Some of the distortions are unintended: many models contain behavioural constraints on portfolio choice [Bovenberg and Goulder (1991)] and parameter estimates are obtained from continuous-time optimization (e.g. the Hayashi rule [Hayashi (1982)] which assume that the initial (pre-reform) conditions are at their intertemporal equilibrium level.

[98] Since exogenous variables may grow at different rates even in the long-run it may be unrealistic to work with a model that has a steady state.

[99] If the test is passed, the steady state has the saddlepoint property: only a single path (the stable branch) leads to it. In this case it is remarkable that an algorithm as simple the one described (Jacobi-method) seems to converge in practice.

measures based on the maximum post-T welfare [see e.g. Flam and Wets (1987) and Keyzer (1991)]. Even when the approximation is good, several steady states (with different welfare weights in (49)) may exist and one would like to compare alternative choices.

In summary, there still remain serious unresolved problems in assessing whether a computed transition path is a good approximation of the infinite horizon solution. Therefore, at the present stage there still is scope for using simpler tools and in fact in applications for developing countries this is also the practice: among the studies cited only the model by Mercenier and de Souza refers to a developing country (Brazil).

If perfect foresight and intertemporal efficiency are considered essential a finite horizon model with some end-stock valuation may be appropriate. For example Codsi et al. (1992) use a finite horizon model with explicit terminal conditions, without any requirement of convergence to a steady state. The model is linearly approximated and linear methods are applied to solve for a finite horizon equilibrium. Blitzer et al. (1986, 1994) solve a finite horizon model for Mexico and Egypt with particular reference to the energy sector discussed in Section 3.1.2 [see also Manne (1985)].

If perfect foresight and intertemporal efficiency are not required, recursively dynamic simulation can be used. It may then still be desirable to perform welfare comparisons over an infinite horizon. To achieve this Levy and van Wijnbergen (1991) introduce a valuation of end-stocks and debts in a post-T steady state. Although this is not a dynastic model (because investment and savings rates are exogenous) the approach allows to compare scenarios in a better way than would be possible with a single finite horizon measure.

5.2.2. Overlapping generations (OLG) models

Specification

Overlapping generations models date back to Allais (1947) and Samuelson (1958). Typically they describe two generations where the "young" work and save for old age and the "old" do not work but live on their savings. There is an infinite succession of such generations.

In applied work OLG models distinguish many generations. They have two attractions. First, they allow a more realistic treatment of savings by taking into account the life cycle of consumers. Since the generations overlap there will be no consumption spree in the aggregate: dissaving by the old is in each period offset by savings of the young. Secondly, OLG models can easily accommodate demographic variables. These variables are exogenous and are (unlike in recursive dynamic models) anticipated by consumers. This makes it possible for example to study how fertility rates affect savings and growth and it may be an important field of application for developing countries.

The model is most easily presented with two generations and without production. The generation born in t (denoted by the superscript t) solves:

$$\max u^t(x_t^t, x_{t+1}^t)$$

$$x_t^t, x_{t+1}^t \geq 0$$

subject to

$$p_t x_t^t + p_{t+1} x_{t+1}^t \leq p_t \omega_t^t + p_{t+1} \omega_{t+1}^t$$

Consumption x_1^0 of the old generation in the first period is given.[100] Commodity balances are imposed for every period $t = 1, 2, \ldots$:

$$x_t^{t-1} + x_t^t \leq \omega_t^{t-1} + \omega_t^t \perp p_t \geq 0$$

Balasko et al. (1980) have shown that it is possible to transform any model with a finite number of generations into a two-generation model. They also prove existence of equilibrium in a Debreu-format using excess demands. The OLG model can also be written in the Full format of Section 2.3.2, introducing budget constraints into the welfare program. One of the advantages of using this format is that it makes it possible to use weaker assumptions on utility functions.[101]

$$\max \sum_{t=1}^{\infty} (\beta)^{t-1} u^t(x_t^t, x_{t+1}^t)$$

$$x_t^t, x_{t+1}^t \geq 0, t = 1, 2 \ldots$$

subject to

$$x_t^{t-1} + x_t^t \leq \omega_t^{t-1} + \omega_t^t \qquad\qquad (p_t)$$

$$\bar{p}_t^t x_t^t + \bar{p}_{t+1}^t x_{t+1}^t \leq \bar{p}_t^t \omega_t^t + \bar{p}_{t+1}^t \omega_{t+1}^t \qquad\qquad (\rho^t) \qquad\qquad (52)$$

$$x_1^0 \text{ given}$$

where β is positive and less than one, $(t - 1$ is an exponent in the expression $(\beta)^{t-1}$). Note that $(\beta)^{t-1}$ is the fixed welfare weight of the generation born in t.[102] This weight is kept fixed to ensure boundedness of the objective.

---

[100] The consumption x_1^0 is a consumption claim which is assumed to be feasible. In some OLG-models this generation has an income claim fixed either in real or in nominal terms.

[101] Production can be introduced like in (49) but the solution to (52) will then not imply profit maximization, since the objective of the firm will be affected by the shadow prices ρ_t.

[102] Each consumer has a finite and nonzero lifetime endowment; each consumer owns a positive endowment of a commodity for which his utility function or the utility function of a consumer with whom he overlaps is increasing. This ensures that in (52) dual prices p_t will be nonzero in each period and that all consumers have positive income in equilibrium.

Prices $\bar{p}$ are given, nonnegative parameters determined in a feedback relation through rescaling of p_t such that the sum of absolute values is equal to $(\beta)^{t-1}$: $\|\bar{p}_t^t\|_1 + \|\bar{p}_{t+1}^t\|_1 = (\beta)^{t-1}$ for all t.

The usual (and rather technical) way of setting up a finite horizon version of this model is to take a T-period horizon in (52) and to add the restriction that the generation born in T gives a transfer to the generation that dies in $t = 1$ equal to the value of its consumption claim in $t = 1$ and spends the income remaining after the transfer according to a single-period utility function. The resulting model is an Arrow–Debreu model with imposed transfers for the last agent. The infinite horizon model can be viewed as a limiting case.[103] The finite horizon construction is clearly artificial and this is one of the reasons for the attraction of infinite horizon OLG models.

The finite horizon version makes clear that the first and the last agent are constrained in their transactions. For the first agent this is unavoidable. His past necessarily constrains him.[104] Since the last agent has to pay the first agent this suggests in the limit that there are imposed transfers and demands at infinity, so that the outcome may not be Pareto-efficient [see Geanakoplos and Polemarchakis (1991) for an advanced survey on this issue].

Letting T go to infinity leads to a second problem, the problem of indeterminacy of equilibrium, as the fixed point problem of (52) with feedback of normalized prices becomes infinite-dimensional, as in the case of the dynastic model with distortions. Like for dynastic models the convergence to a steady state is not ensured theoretically but it is commonly claimed in applications. Kehoe (1991) shows how sensitive the outcomes in early periods may be for small variations in the neighbourhood of the same steady state. He therefore suggests either to linearize the model or to use a finite horizon version. Alternatively, one may stop imposition of the budget constraints after T, assuming that transfers may be nonzero thereafter; this leads back to a dynastic model, which in the absence of distortions will have no indeterminacy.

Applications. Infinite horizon applications are so far restricted to developed countries. A famous one is Auerbach and Kotlikoff's analysis of fiscal policy for the United States. They describe a single-commodity economy but distinguish as many as fiftyfive age-cohorts, all with the same homothetic utility function. Because of this homotheticity, distributional changes do not affect

---

[103] Program (52) yields for each generation a pair of normalized prices. By construction the norm of these prices goes to zero for later generations. Using the same reasoning as in Balasko et al. (1980) one can prove the limit property. The Full format representation permits to avoid the more restrictive assumptions made by them which ensure that not all prices are zero in some period.

[104] Obviously, this can be captured by weaker forms than in (52), for example by only imposing the value of first period consumption.

aggregate demand and prices. As a result they can analytically solve many subproblems, such as the computation of a steady state solution. In addition uniqueness of the steady state can be ensured. The simulation experiments are designed as a transition path from an initial steady state to a new one over a finite horizon. Our earlier remarks on convergence to a steady state and determinacy apply and the authors themselves identify many of these problems [Auerbach and Kotlikoff (1987), p. 49, see also the discussion in Kehoe (1991), pp. 2122–2123].

Davies et al. (1991) have constructed a two-commodity version of the model, distinguishing a capital good from a consumption good. They find that such disaggregation significantly affects the results. Deaton (1991) has found little evidence in support of life cycle savings behaviour and argues that this is due to borrowing constraints.

The demographic aspects of fertility, mortality and migration have received attention in Kelley and Williamson (1984), who deal with them in a recursively dynamic model.

5.3. Cash-in-advance and incomplete asset markets

We previously considered money and financial assets in Section 3.3.3 as static extensions of the CGE-model. Here we consider them through explicit constraints on transactions.

In Section 2.3.2 we presented the basic CGE-model in Full format. There the budget constraints were seen to be nonrestrictive for appropriate welfare weights. This can be interpreted as follows. Consider a two-period model without uncertainty. The "Full format Negishi-planner" solves for an equilibrium and decentralizes his plan by communicating prices to the agents. The solution will involve some agents saving and others dissaving in period one. The planner will issue "paper money" which enables the agents who dissave to cover their first period budget deficit.[105] At the start of period two the savers will hold the money. Hence money serves as a store of value but it does not carry any rent. Since it has no other function it is a financial asset. Obviously in this setup the financial system does not constrain welfare. This easily extends to *T*-period models.

This story implicitly assumes that period one is so short, say one hour, that the only reason for holding money is as a store of value. However, in applications this period is much longer (one year or more) so that it necessarily

---

[105] Since there is no uncertainty and everyone remains on his intertemporal budget constraint the same could be obtained by having all debtors issue their own IOUs.

involves aggregation over "hours". In the aggregate money will be required to pay for consumption and inputs within the same period. This is the transactions demand for money. Hence transactions demand is only the result of un-avoidable aggregation over time. We shall now consider specifications where the "technology" of transactions may reduce welfare. This technology is characterized by the set of possible transaction activities and the availability of a medium of transaction. This is very similar to models with transport in which a road network and the availability of "trucks" define the transport possi-bilities.

We will now discuss two models, one with transactions demand for money only (the cash-in-advance model), the other with demand for money and other financial assets (the model with incomplete asset markets). The former will contain restrictions on availability (trucks), the latter on the network (roads). We maintain the assumption of certainty for the cash-in-advance model; uncertainty will be introduced in the model with incomplete asset markets. Cash-in-advance models have been applied but there are no applied general equilibrium models with incomplete asset markets.

5.3.1. A single period model with cash-in-advance

In the version of the cash-in-advance model to be discussed, money is needed for all purchases, that is not just for net purchases. The model describes a single period (a Hicksian week) at the beginning of which payments for inputs and consumption are paid to a "bank" which pays agents their receipts at the end of the period. In order to finance expenditure agents borrow money from the bank for a single period. For this they pay interest, the proceeds of which are redistributed to consumers by the bank in proportion to the initial ownership.

If the money supply at the beginning of the period is fixed in nominal terms (fiat money), the price level can adjust to support a zero rate of interest and one is back in the Arrow–Debreu situation, so that money is merely a veil.

However, if money is expressed in terms of commodities, the money supply can be constraining and a positive interest rate will result. With constant returns to scale the model can be written in Full format as follows.

$$\max \sum_i \bar{\alpha}_i u_i(x_i)$$

$$m_i, m_j \geq 0, x_i, y_j^+, y_j^- \geq 0, i = 1, \ldots, m, j = 1, \ldots, n$$

subject to

$$\sum_i x_i \leq \sum_j (y_j^+ - y_j^-) + \sum_i \omega_i \qquad (p)$$

$$(y_j^+ - y_j^-) \in Y_j$$

$$\bar{p}x_i \le (\bar{p}\omega_i + \sigma_i\overline{\mu m})/(1 + \bar{\mu}) \qquad\qquad (\rho_i) \qquad\qquad (53)$$

$$\bar{p}x_i = m_i$$

$$\bar{p}y_j^- = m_j$$

$$\sum_i m_i + \sum_j m_j \le \bar{m} \qquad\qquad (\mu)$$

with a feedback in which (1) $(\bar{p}, \bar{\mu})$ are normalized values of (p, μ) and $\bar{m}$ is a function of $\bar{p}$ which is continuous and homogeneous of degree one and (2) $\bar{\alpha}_i$ is adjusted to have $\rho_i = 0$ at equilibrium. Here outputs and inputs of firms are denoted by y_j^+, y_j^-, ownership shares of money by σ_i and $\bar{\mu}$ is the interest rate. The consumer's income $(\bar{p}\omega_i + \sigma_i\overline{\mu m})/(1 + \bar{\mu})$ is the discounted value of endowments plus the discounted value of interest receipts.

An equilibrium can be shown to exist [see Ginsburgh and Keyzer (forthcoming)] which amounts to having the consumer maximize utility subject to the budget constraint which appears in the program while the producer maximizes discounted revenue minus current cost.

The model assumes a unitary velocity with respect to total expenditure. Obviously the unitary value depends only on the choice of units. The velocity could be differentiated by category of expenditure or by agent. It is also possible that different groups of agents use different monies or that different monies are required for different transactions. In addition the model could be modified to represent only net marketed demands (one does not need money to buy one's own endowments).

In applied general equilibrium models the Hicksian week is at least a year long. Therefore, a significant part of the interest payments will have to be represented through transactions demand, as opposed to the theoretically more satisfactory borrowing between periods.

It is an empirical question whether money should be modelled as commodity money. Typically, under a gold standard there will be commodity money but even under fiat money the representation may be appropriate if the monetary authorities adjust the money supply $\bar{m}$ in proportion to prices. Then, since $\bar{m}$ is a function of $\bar{p}$ a falling price level cannot eliminate excess demand for money.

In some applied models the classical dichotomy holds. Money is then merely introduced as a matter of accounting. The dichotomy no longer holds when one introduces the cost of working capital discussed in Section 3.3.3. This may be interpreted as the interest charge on transaction money. Indeed working capital requirements can have no real effects unless transaction money is scarce. To represent stores of value between periods an asset representation is needed.

5.3.2. A two-period model with incomplete asset markets

Specification. We consider a two period model with financial assets. Uncertainty is represented by having S states of nature indexed $s = 1, \ldots, S$ for the second period. The first period is denoted by the subscript 0. The utility function is written as $u_i(x_{i0}, x_{i1}, \ldots, x_{iS})^{106}$ (obviously an expected utility formulation is a special case). This formulation is general in the sense that consumers need not agree on the probability of states of nature but they do have to agree on the list of states. For simplicity we assume that each consumer owns a firm and that there is no firm owned by more than one consumer and only represent production as the activity of consumers: this shifts the financing problem of the firm to the consumer and avoids having to deal with the financing problems of the firms. More elaborate specifications can be found in Magill and Shafer (1991).

Consumers buy inputs v_{i0} in the first period which affect their endowments in the second period according to a decreasing returns, multiple output production function $\omega_{is}(v_{i0})$.[107] There is a given number of financial assets. In the first period the consumer buys a portfolio a_i at given prices $\bar{\phi}$; a_i can have negative elements. There is no borrowing constraint. In the second period asset c generates receipts $\bar{p}_s D_{sc}(\bar{p}_0, \bar{p}_1, \ldots, \bar{p}_S, \bar{\phi})$ where the vector-function D_{sc} has to be nonnegative, nonzero, continuous and homogeneous of degree zero. It has one element for each commodity and is expressed as real returns but since it is a function of all prices it can also be used to represent returns which are not expressed in real terms. This enables the modeller to specify the characteristics of various financial assets. For example, a store of fiat money will give a return $\bar{\phi}$ in all states. Commodity money will yield a return that only depends on prices $\bar{p}_s$ in state s. In terms of the transport analogy the function D_{sc} imposes network restrictions. However, the number of "trucks" is unconstrained.

The model can be written in Full format as:[108]

---

[106] We maintain the assumption that consumer 1 has a utility function which is increasing and assume that his endowments are positive in period 0 and in all states of period 1. This ensures existence of equilibrium and positiveness of equilibrium prices. For a discussion of possible non-existence see Geanakoplos (1990).

[107] Production decisions are therefore taken before uncertainty is resolved. An alternative is a model in which recourse is allowed, that is the consumer can adjust inputs in period 1. The production function is then: $\omega_{is}(v_{i0}, v_{is})$.

[108] Note that the value function of this program is bounded due to the commodity balances. In the Debreu-format the problem may be unbounded for the individual consumer, since he can borrow without limit. This greatly complicates the existence proof in the Debreu format, see for example Magill and Quinzii (1991).

$$\max \sum_i \alpha_i u_i(x_{i0}, x_{i1}, \ldots, x_{iS})$$

$$v_{i0}, x_{i0}, x_{is} \geq 0, a_i, i = 1, \ldots, m, s = 1, \ldots, S$$

subject to

$$\sum_i (x_{i0} + v_{i0}) \leq \sum_i \omega_{i0} \qquad\qquad (p_0)$$

$$\sum_i x_{is} \leq \sum_i \omega_{is}(v_{i0}) + D_s(\bar{p}_0, \bar{p}_1, \ldots, \bar{p}_S, \bar{\phi}) \sum_i a_i \qquad (p_s)$$

$$\bar{p}_0 x_{i0} + \bar{p}_0 v_{i0} + \bar{\phi} a_i \leq \bar{p}_0 \omega_{i0} \qquad\qquad (\rho_{i0}) \qquad\qquad (54)$$

$$\bar{p}_s x_{is} \leq \bar{p}_s \omega_{is}(v_{i0}) + \bar{p}_s D_s(\bar{p}_0, \bar{p}_1, \ldots, \bar{p}_S, \bar{\phi}) a_i \qquad (\rho_{is})$$

$$\sum_i a_i \leq 0 \quad (\phi)$$

with a feedback in which (1) $(\bar{p}_0, \bar{p}_1, \ldots, \bar{p}_S, \bar{\phi})$ are normalized values of $(p_0, p_1, \ldots, p_S, \phi)$ and (2) α_i is adjusted to have $\rho_{i0} = 0$ in equilibrium.

The optimality conditions imply that normalized asset prices satisfy in equilibrium:

$$\bar{\phi} = \sum_{s \neq 0} (1 + \bar{\rho}_{is}) \bar{p}_s D_s, \text{ for all } i$$

where $\bar{\rho}_{is}$ are normalized values of ρ_{is}, using the normalization factor applied to $(p_0, p_1, \ldots, p_S, \phi)$.

As a consequence the well-known nonarbitrage condition follows which says that there exists no initial portfolio a with value $\bar{\phi}a < 0$ such that $\bar{p}_s D_s a \geq 0$ for all $s \neq 0$.

If the equilibrium values of $\bar{\rho}_{is}$ are equal across consumers, the financial markets are said to be effectively complete. The equilibrium is then competitive and therefore Pareto-efficient, so that the classical dichotomy holds. A sufficient condition for effective completeness is that the submatrix consisting of the rows of $\bar{p}_s D_s$ for which $\bar{\rho}_{is}$ is nonzero for at least one consumer has full row rank. When the financial markets are not effectively complete they constrain welfare. Pareto-efficiency will hold locally in the sense that there is no Pareto-superior allocation supported by the prevailing asset and commodity prices.

In the present formulation there are no firms owned by more than one consumer, so that there are no dividend payments and the consumer can be viewed as maximizing profits valuing his returns using his individual $\bar{\rho}_{is}$. When a firm is owned by more than one consumer, there must be (possibly negative) dividend payments and each consumer will value these according to his own

$\bar{\rho}_{is}$. When these valuations differ the firm will not maximize profits [for a further discussion see Magill and Quinzii (1991)].[109]

The formulation can readily be extended to represent further constraints on transactions, like transactions demand or bounds on borrowing. Physical assets like buffer stocks can be introduced which also provide a return but require a commodity input.

The model with incomplete asset markets is attractive for applications, particularly when it is written in the Full format because it can accommodate a large variety of financial assets in a theoretically satisfactory way. It can also be extended to incorporate other constraints on transactions than asset market incompleteness. In its application the main problem is to characterize the states of nature s adequately e.g. because this would involve specifying joint distributions of all the stochastic events as well as the consumer specific valuation of these events. As yet there have been no applications in general equilibrium.

Applications. In practice modellers try to capture uncertainty in a different way which may be interpreted as a simplification of (54). In such applications uncertainty does not appear explicitly and portfolio diversification is obtained by introducing additional constraints on the substitutability between assets in the two-period model (46)–(47) without uncertainty. Transactions demand is then introduced also. Feltenstein (1986) also specifies a borrowing constraint and Feltenstein et al. (1988) represent foreign and domestic bonds. In Bovenberg and Goulder (1989) the portfolio diversification constraints are thought to represent not only consequences of uncertainty but also preferences and habits of the consumers. Introduction of such constraints in a single-period recursively dynamic model leads to the specifications discussed in Section 3.3.3.

6. Conclusion

Applied general equilibrium models have been used to analyze a wide variety of policy issues. Trade liberalization was an early field of application. New developments in this area include the modelling of increasing returns to scale, imperfect competition and trade in new commodities such as emission rights. Also the effects of international migration have been studied. Unlike in the earlier studies the new applications suggest that the welfare gains from liberalization can be substantial. Applications which focus on agriculture often find that price reform needs to be supplemented with public investments in

---

[109] This is the case in models with constraints on transaction and nonzero profits.

infrastructure and irrigation: growth performance cannot be explained from price policies alone. Models developed for evaluating energy policies have recently been amended. They are now designed to approximate infinite horizon trajectories and have been extended to deal with environmental problems, in particular emission taxes.

Recently, many of these applications have given a more satisfactory treatment of dynamic issues including money, financial assets and demography. The models now often incorporate perfect foresight as well as constraints on short-run adjustment. This has made them suitable for the analysis of phasing issues in policy reform. For example, equilibrium models have been used to compare abrupt and gradualist forms of structural adjustment [Bourguignon and Morrisson (1992) and de Janvry et al. (1991)]. The dynamic models have the advantage that they show how resource allocation changes over time: as stressed by Powell and Snape (1992) it often is obvious in which sectors jobs will disappear as a result of trade liberalization measures, but not where new jobs will be created.

Hence the domain of applied general equilibrium modelling has expanded. In spite of this success the approach remains in some ways problematic. First, the empirical basis is often weak in two respects: the database is incomplete and many of the parameters have not been estimated by formal econometric methods or the estimation methods are very crude. This may restrict the operational usefulness of a model but obviously this cannot be judged in a survey such as this one, since it would involve detailed descriptions of country specific circumstances.

Secondly, there are problems in the application of theoretical models. The use of the equilibrium concept in applications remains controversial, for example by ruling out false trading. Applied work in the areas of imperfect competition, non-convexities, infinite horizons and financial assets is quite vulnerable to theoretical criticism. In addition in some cases the theoretical models themselves are still weak (e.g. when they assume perfect foresight).

Nevertheless, the field is promising: theoretical general equilibrium analysis is an active field of research and increasingly applied modellers have shown their ability to incorporate advances in theory. The resulting alternative specifications have been discussed in Sections 4 and 5 and are contrasted with the standard practice in Table 35.2 (the numbers indicate sections).

It may be noted that there is no entry for imperfect competition in this table. This is because, while we have been critical in Section 3.2 of the markup representation for imperfect competition, as yet there is no satisfactory alternative.

The potential for incorporating features of particular relevance to developing countries has only partly been exploited. There is scope for important

Table 35.2
Standard practice and alternative

Standard practice	Alternative
Fixed regime	Regime switches 4.1
Tax functions 2.4.5	External effects 4.2
Government as a consumer 2.4.2	Nonrivalness, empathy 4.2.1, 4.2.2
Labour endowments given	Efficiency wage relation 4.2.3
Convex production set	Nonconvexity 4.3
Closure rules 2.4.7	Dynamics 5.
Saving/investment function 2.4.6	Intertemporal decision 5.1, 5.2
Transaction demand for money 3.3	Cash-in-advance 5.3.1
Money and financial asset demand 3.3.3	Incomplete asset market 5.3.2

applications in the areas of external effects, nonconvexities and incomplete asset markets.

References

Adelman, I. and Robinson, S. (1978) *Income distribution policy in developing countries: A case study of Korea*. Stanford, CA: Stanford University Press.

Allais, M. (1947) *Economie et interêt*. Paris: Imprimerie Nationale.

Arrow, K.J. and Kurz, M. (1980) 'Optimization in the one-sector model: Application of the Pontryagin Maximum Principle', Chapter 3 in: *Public investment, the rate of return and optimal fiscal policy*. Baltimore: Johns Hopkins University Press.

Arrow, K.J. and Hahn, F. (1971) *General competitive analysis*. Edinburgh: Holden Day.

Arrow, K.J. (1981) 'Optimal and voluntary income distribution', in: *Collected papers*, volume I, Oxford: Basil Blackwell.

Auerbach, A. and Kotlikoff, L. (1987) *Dynamic fiscal policy*. Cambridge, MA: Cambridge University Press.

Avriel, M. (1976) *Nonlinear Programming*. Englewood Cliffs, N.J.: Prentice Hall.

Balasko, Y., Cass, D. and Shell, K. (1980) 'Existence of competitive equilibrium in a general overlapping generations model', *Journal of Economic Theory*, 23:307–322.

Barnett, W., Geweke, J. and Wolfe, M. (1991) 'Semi-nonparametric Bayesian estimation of consumer and factor demand models', Chapter 19 in: W.A. Barnett et al., eds., *Equilibrium theory and applications*. Cambridge: Cambridge University Press.

Behrman, J. and Deolalikar, A.B. (1989) 'Health and nutrition', Chapter 13 in: H. Chenery and T.N. Srinivasan, eds., *Handbook of development economics*, Vol. II. Amsterdam: North-Holland.

Benassy, J.P. (1982) *The economics of market disequilibrium*. New York: Academic Press.

Berthélémy, J.C. and Bourguignon, F. (1994) 'North-South-OPEC trade relations in an intertemporal applied general equilibrium model', in: J. Mercenier and T.N. Srinivasan, eds., *Applied general equilibrium and economic development*. Ann Arbor: University of Michigan Press.

Bevan, D.L., Collier, P. and Gunning, J.W. (1990) *Controlled open economies*. Oxford: Oxford University Press.

Bhagwati, J.N., Brecher, R.A. and Hatta, T. (1983) 'The generalized theory of transfers and welfare: Bilateral transfers in a multilateral world', *American Economic Review*, 73:606–618.

Blitzer, C.R. and Eckaus, R. (1986) 'Energy-economy interactions in Mexico: A multiperiod general equilibrium model', *Journal of Development Economics*, 21:259–282.

Blitzer, C.R., Eckaus, R.S., Lahiri, S. and Meeraus, A. (1994) 'A general equilibrium analysis of the effects of carbon emissions restrictions on economic growth in a developing country', in: J. Mercenier and T.N. Srinivasan, eds., *Applied general equilibrium and economic development.* Ann Arbor: University of Michigan Press.

Boldrin, M. and Montrucchio, L. (1986) 'On the indeterminacy of capital accumulation paths', *Journal of Economic Theory*, 40:26–39.

Bourguignon, F. and Morrisson, C. (1992) *Adjustment and equity in developing countries: A new approach.* Paris: OECD Development Centre.

Bourguignon, F., Branson, W. and de Melo, J. (1992) 'Adjustment and income distribution: A micro-macro model for counterfactual analysis', *Journal of Development Economics*, 38:17–39.

Bovenberg, A.L. and Goulder, L.H. (1989) 'Promoting international capital mobility: An international general equilibrium analysis', NBER Working Paper no. 3139.

Bovenberg, A.L. and Goulder, L.H. (1991) 'Introducing intertemporal and open economy features in applied general equilibrium models', Chapter 4 in: H. Don, Th. van de Klundert and J. van Sinderen, eds., *Applied general equilibrium modelling.* Dordrecht: Kluwer Academic Publishers.

Brooke, A., Kendrick, D. and Meeraus, A. (1988) *GAMS: A user's guide.* San Francisco, CA: The Scientific Press.

Burniaux, J.-M. and van der Mensbrugghe, D. (1990) 'The RUNS-model: A rural–urban, North–South general equilibrium model for agricultural policy analysis', OECD Development Centre Technical Paper 33. Paris: OECD.

Burniaux, J.-M., Martin, J. and Nicoletti, G. (1991) 'GREEN: A multi-sector, multi-region general equilibrium model for quantifying the cost of curbing CO_2 emissions: A technical manual', Economics and Statistics Department. Paris: OECD.

Burniaux, J.-M. and Waelbroeck, J. (1992) 'Preliminary results of two experimental models of general equilibrium with imperfect competition', *Journal of Policy Modeling*, 14:65–92.

Carlson, D.A. and Haurie, A. (1987) *Infinite horizon optimal control.* Berlin: Springer.

Chenery, H., Lewis, J., de Melo, J. and Robinson, S. (1986) 'Alternative routes to development', Chapter 11 in: H. Chenery, S. Robinson and M. Syrquin, eds., *Industrialization and growth, a comparative study.* Oxford: Oxford University Press.

Clarete, R.L. and Roumasset, J.A. (1990) 'The relative welfare cost of industrial and agricultural policy distortions: A Philippine illustration', *Oxford Economic Papers*, 42:462–472.

Codsi, G., Pearson, K.R. and Wilcoxen, P.J. (1992) *General purpose software for intertemporal economic models.* Amsterdam: Kluwer.

Collier, P. and Gunning, J.W. (1992), 'Aid and exchange rate adjustment in African trade liberalisations', *Economic Journal*, 102:925–939.

Condon, T., Corbo, V. and de Melo, J. (1990) 'Exchange rate based disinflation, wage rigidity and capital inflows', *Journal of Development Economics*, 32:113–131.

Cornet, B. (1988) 'General equilibrium theory and increasing returns: Presentation', *Journal of Mathematical Economics*, 17:103–118.

Cornielje, O.J.C. and van der Laan, G. (1986) 'The computation of quantity constraints equilibria with virtual taxes', *Economics Letters*, 22:1–6.

Dasgupta, P. and Ray, D. (1986) 'Inequality as determinant of malnutrition and unemployment: theory', *Economic Journal*, 96:1011–1034.

Davies, J., Whalley, J. and Hamilton, B. (1989) 'Capital income taxation in a two commodities lifecycle model: The role of factor intensities and asset capitalization effects', *Journal of Public Economics*, 39:109–126.

Deardorff, A.V. and Stern, R.M. (1986) 'The structure and sample results of the Michigan computational model of world production and trade', in: T.N. Srinivasan and J. Whalley, eds., *General equilibrium trade policy modelling*, pp. 151–188. Cambridge, MA: MIT Press.

Deaton, A. (1991) 'Saving and liquidity constraints', *Econometrica*, 59:1221–1248.

Debreu, G. (1959) *Theory of value.* New York: Wiley.

Decaluwé, B. and Martens, A. (1989) 'Developing countries and GE models: A review of the empirical literature', IDRC Report No MR 155e. Ottawa: International Development Research Center.

de Janvry, A., Sadoulet, E. and Fargeix, A. (1991) 'Politically feasible and equitable adjustment: some alternatives for Ecuador', *World Development*, 19:1577–1595.

Delorme, F. and van der Mensbrugghe, D. (1990) 'Assessing the role of scale economies and imperfect competition in the context of agricultural trade liberalization: A Canadian case study', OECD Economic Studies No 13, Paris: OECD Development Centre.

de Melo, J. (1988) 'Computable general equilibrium models for trade policy analysis in developing countries: A survey', *Journal of Policy Modeling*, 10:469–503.

de Melo, J. and Tarr, D. (1991) 'VER's under imperfect competition and foreign direct investment: A case study of the US auto-VER', PRE Working paper series no. 667. Washington, DC: The World Bank.

de Melo, J. and Roland-Holst, D.W. (1994) 'Tariffs and export subsidies when domestic markets are oligopolistic', in: J. Mercenier and T.N. Srinivasan, eds., *Applied general equilibrium and economic development*. Ann Arbor: University of Michigan Press.

Dervis, K., de Melo, J. and Robinson, S. (1982) *General equilibrium models for development policy*. Cambridge: Cambridge University Press.

Devarajan, S., Lewis, J.D. and Robinson, S. (1986) 'A bibliography of computable general equilibrium (CGE) models applied to developing countries', Department of Agricultural and Resource Economics, University of California at Berkeley, mimeo.

Devarajan, S., Jones, C. and Roemer, M. (1989) 'Markets under price controls in partial and general equilibrium', *World Development*, 17:1881–1893.

Devarajan, S. (1990) 'Can computable general equilibrium models shed light on the environmental problems of developing countries?', Harvard University, John F. Kennedy School of Government, mimeo.

Devarajan, S. and Rodrik, D. (1991) 'Pro-competitive effects of trade reform: Results from a CGE-model of Cameroon', *European Economic Review*, 35:1157–1184.

Dewatripont, M. and Michel, G. (1987) 'On closure rules, homogeneity, and dynamics in applied general equilibrium models', *Journal of Development Economics*, 26:65–76.

Dierker, E. (1972) 'Two remarks on the number of equilibria of an economy', *Econometrica*, 40:951–953.

Diewert, W.E. and Wales, T.J. (1987) 'Flexible functional forms and global curvature conditions', *Econometrica*, 55:43–68.

Dixon, P.B. (1990) 'A general equilibrium approach to public utility pricing: Determining prices for a water authority', *Journal of Policy Modeling*, 12:745–767.

Dixon, P.B., Parmenter, B.R. and Horridge, J.M. (1987) 'Forecasting versus policy analysis with the ORANI-model', in: H. Motamen, ed., *Economic modelling in the OECD countries*. London: Chapman and Hall.

Dixon, P.B., Parmenter, B.R., Powell, A.A. and Wilcoxen, P.J. (1992) *Notes and problems in applied general equilibrium economics*. Amsterdam: North-Holland.

Drèze, J. (1975) 'Existence of an exchange equilibrium under price rigidities', *International Economic Review*, 16:301–320.

Easterly, W. (1990) 'Portfolio effects in a CGE model: Devaluation in a dollarized economy', Chapter 1 in: L. Taylor, ed., *Socially relevant policy analysis*. Cambridge, MA: MIT Press.

Elbers, C.T.M. (1992) *Spatial disaggregation in general equilibrium models, with an application to the Nepalese economy*. Amsterdam: VU University Press.

Feltenstein, A. (1992) 'Oil prices and rural migration: The Dutch disease going south', *Journal of International Money and Finance*, 11:273–291.

Feltenstein, A. and Morris, S. (1990) 'Fiscal stabilization and exchange rate instability: A theoretical approach and some policy conclusions using Mexican data', *Journal of Public Economics*, 42:329–356.

Feltenstein, A., Lebow, D. and Sibert, A. (1988) 'An analysis of the welfare implications of alternative exchange rate regimes: An intertemporal model with an application to Australia', *Journal of Policy Modeling*, 10:611–629.

Feltenstein, A. (1986) 'An intertemporal general equilibrium analysis of financial crowding out: A policy model and an application to Australia', *Journal of Public Economics*, 31:79–104.

Fischer, G.K., Frohberg, K., Keyzer, M.A. and Parikh, K.S. (1988) *The basic linked system: A tool for international food policy analysis.* Amsterdam: Kluwer.

Fischer G.K., Frohberg, K., Keyzer, M.A., Parikh, K.S. and Tims, W. (1991) 'Hunger: Beyond the reach of the invisible hand', IIASA Research Report 91-15. Laxenburg, Austria: International Institute for Applied Systems Analysis.

Flam, S.D. and Wets, R.J.B. (1987) 'Existence results and finite horizon approximation of infinite horizon optimization problems', *Econometrica*, 55:1187–1209.

Gabzewicz, J.J. and Michel, P. (1992) 'Oligopoly equilibrium in exchange economies', CORE discussion paper 9247, Université Catholique de Louvain.

Garcia, C.B. and Zangwill, W.I. (1981) *Pathways to solutions, fixed points, and equilibria.* Englewood Cliffs: Prentice Hall.

Geanakoplos, J. (1990) 'An introduction to general equilibrium with incomplete asset markets', *Journal of Mathematical Economics*, 19:1–38.

Geanakoplos, J.D. and Polemarchakis, H.M. (1991) 'Overlapping generations', Chapter 35 in: W. Hildenbrand and H. Sonnenschein, eds., *Handbook of mathematical economics*, volume IV. Amsterdam: North-Holland.

Ginsburgh, V. and van der Heyden, L. (1985) 'General equilibrium with wage rigidities: An application to Belgium', in: *Mathematical Programming Study 23*, Amsterdam: North Holland.

Ginsburgh, V. and Waelbroeck, J. (1981) *Activity analysis and general equilibrium modelling.* Amsterdam: North-Holland.

Ginsburgh, V. and Keyzer, M.A. (forthcoming) *Applied general equilibrium: The theory.* Cambridge, MA: MIT Press.

Goldin, I. and Knudsen, O. eds. (1990) *Agricultural trade liberalization.* Paris: OECD Development Centre and Washington: World Bank.

Goldin, I. and Winters, A. eds. (1992) *Open economies: Adjustment and agriculture.* Cambridge: Cambridge University Press.

Goulder, L. (1991) 'Effect of carbon taxes in an economy with prior tax distortions: An intertemporal general equilibrium analysis for the U.S.', mimeo.

Grais, W., de Melo, J. and Urata, S. (1986) 'A general equilibrium estimation of the effects of reductions in tariffs and quantitative restrictions in Turkey in 1978', in: T.N. Srinivasan and J. Whalley, eds., *General equilibrium trade policy modelling*, pp. 61–88. Cambridge, MA: MIT Press.

Gunning, J.W., Carrin, G. and Waelbroeck, J. (with Burniaux, J.M. and Mercenier, J.) (1982) 'Growth and trade of developing countries: A general equilibrium analysis', Discussion Paper 8210, CEME, Université Libre de Bruxelles.

Hamilton, B. and Whalley, J. (1984) 'Efficiency and distributional implications of global restrictions on labour mobility: Calculations and policy implications', *Journal of Development Economics*, 14:61–75.

Harris, R. (1984) 'Applied general equilibrium analysis of small open economies with scale economies and imperfect competition', *American Economic Review*, 74:1016–1032.

Hayashi, F. (1982) 'Tobin's marginal q and average q: A neo-classical interpretation', *Econometrica*, 50:213–224.

Jorgenson, D.W. and Slesnick, D.T. (1985) General equilibrium analysis of economic policy, in: J. Pigott and J. Whalley, eds., *New developments in applied general equilibrium analysis.* Cambridge: Cambridge University Press.

Jorgenson, D.W. and Wilcoxen, P.J. (1990) 'Environmental regulation and U.S. economic growth', *Rand Journal of Economics*, 21:314–340.

Jorgenson, D.W., Slesnick, D.T. and Wilcoxen, P.J. (1992) 'Carbon taxes and economic welfare', *Brookings papers: Microeconomics*, pp. 393–431.

Jorgenson, D.W. and Wilcoxen, P.J. (forthcoming, 1993) 'Energy, the environment and economic growth', Chapter 27 in: A.V. Kneese and J.L. Sweeney, eds., *Handbook of natural resource and energy economics*, Vol. III. Amsterdam: North-Holland.

Kehoe, T.J. (1991) 'Computation and multiplicity of equilibria', Chapter 36 in: W. Hildenbrand and H. Sonnenschein, eds., *Handbook of mathematical economics*, Vol. IV. Amsterdam: North-Holland.

Keller, W.J. (1980) *Tax incidence: A general equilibrium approach.* Amsterdam: North-Holland.

Kelley, A.C. and Williamson, J.G. (1984) *What drives third world city growth? A dynamic general equilibrium approach.* Princeton, NJ: Princeton University Press.

Keyzer, M.A. (1987) 'Consequences of increased foodgrain production on the economy of Bangladesh', Chapter 3 in: G. van der Laan and A. Talman, eds., *The computation and modelling of economic equilibria.* Amsterdam: North-Holland.

Keyzer, M.A. (1991) 'On the approximation of infinite horizon allocations', Chapter 5 in: H. Don, Th. van de Klundert and J. van Sinderen, eds., *Applied general equilibrium modelling.* Amsterdam: Kluwer.

Keyzer, M.A., van Veen, W. and Tims, W. (1992) 'The SOW applied general equilibrium model', Chapter 5 in: E. Thorbecke, ed., *Adjustment and equity in Indonesia.* Paris: OECD Development Centre.

Kirman, A.P. (1992) 'Whom or what does the representative individual represent?', *Journal of Economic Perspectives,* 6:117–136.

Kooiman, P. (1984) 'Smoothing the aggregate fix-price model and the use of business survey data', *Economic Journal,* 94:899–913.

Koopmans, T.C., Diamond, P.A. and Williamson, R.E. (1964) 'Stationary utility and time perspective', *Econometrica,* 32:82–100.

Levy, S. and van Wijnbergen, S. (1991) 'Transition problems in economic reform: Agriculture in the Mexico–U.S. free trade agreement', Development Centre Research Paper. Paris: OECD Development Centre.

Lewis, J.D. (1994) 'Macroeconomic stabilization and adjustment policies in a general equilibrium model with financial markets', in: J. Mercenier and T.N. Srinivasan, eds., *Applied general equilibrium and economic development.* Ann Arbor: University of Michigan Press.

Lipton, D., Poterba, J., Sachs, J. and Summers, L. (1982) 'Multiple shooting in rational expectations models', *Econometrica,* 50:1329–1333.

Lucas, R.E. and Stokey, N.L. (1984) 'Optimal growth with many consumers', *Journal of Economic Theory,* 32:139–171.

Maasland, A. (1990) 'Continuing the tradition of equity in Sri Lanka: policy options in a CGE model', Chapter 7 in: L. Taylor, ed., *Socially relevant policy analysis.* Cambridge, MA: MIT Press.

Magill, M. and Shafer, W. (1991) 'Incomplete markets', Chapter 30 in: W. Hildenbrand and H. Sonnenschein, eds., *Handbook of mathematical economics,* Vol. IV. Amsterdam: North-Holland.

Magill, M. and Quinzii, M. (1991) 'The nonneutrality of money in a production economy with nominal assets', Chapter 3 in: W.A. Barnett, ed., *Equilibrium theory and applications.* New York: Cambridge University Press.

Manne, A.S. (1985) 'On the formulation and solution of economic equilibrium models', *Mathematical Programming Study,* 23:1–22.

Manne, A.S. and Richels, R.G. (1990) 'CO_2 emission limits: An economic analysis for the U.S.A', *Energy Journal,* 11:51–85.

Mas-Colell, A. and Zame, W.R. (1991) 'Equilibrium theory in infinite dimensional spaces', Chapter 34 in: W. Hildenbrand and H. Sonnenschein, eds., *Handbook of mathematical economics,* Vol. IV. Amsterdam: North-Holland.

McKenzie, L. (1987) 'Turnpike theory', in: J. Eatwell, M. Milgate and P. Newman, eds., *The new Palgrave: A dictionary of economics.* New York: Stockton Press.

McMahon, G. (1989) 'The income distribution effects of the Kenyan coffee marketing system', *Journal of Development Economics,* 31:297–326.

McMahon, G. (1990) 'Financial computable general equilibrium models of developing countries: A critical assessment', International Development Research Centre, Ottawa, Canada, mimeo.

Mercenier, J. (1992) 'Completing the European internal market: A general equilibrium evaluation under alternative market structure assumptions', Cahier 0892, CRDE, Université de Montréal, Canada.

Mercenier, J. and Schmitt, N. (1992) 'Sunk costs, free-entry equilibrium, and trade liberalization in applied general equilibrium: Implications for 'Europe 1992', CRDE, Université de Montréal, Canada.

Mercenier, J. and Sampaio de Souza, M. (1994) 'Structural adjustment and growth in a highly indebted market economy: Brazil', in: J. Mercenier and T.N. Srinivasan, eds., *Applied general equilibrium and economic development*. Ann Arbor: University of Michigan Press.

Mirrlees, J.A. (1975) 'A pure theory of underdeveloped economies', in: L. Reynolds, ed., *Agriculture and development theory*. New Haven: Yale University Press.

Mitra, P.K. (1992) 'Tariff design and reform in revenue-constrained economy: Theory and an illustration from India', *Journal of Public Economics*, 47:227–251.

Morrisson, C. (1991) *Adjustment and equity in Morocco*. Paris: OECD Development Centre.

Narayana, N.S.S., Parikh, K.S. and Srinivasan, T.N. (1990) *Agriculture, growth and redistribution of income: Policy analysis with a general equilibrium model of India*. Amsterdam: North-Holland.

Neary, J.P. and Roberts, K. (1980) 'The theory of household behaviour under rationing', *European Economic Review*, 13:25–42.

Negishi, T. (1972) *General equilibrium theory and international trade*. Amsterdam: North-Holland.

Nguyen, T. and Whalley, J. (1985) 'Equilibrium with price controls under endogenous transaction costs', *Journal of Economic Theory*, 29:290–300.

Norman, V.D. (1990) 'A comparison of alternative approaches to CGE-modeling with imperfect competition', *European Economic Review*, 34:725–751.

Nsengiyumva, F. and Decaluwé, B. (1992): 'Impact of economic policies in a credit rationed economy: Illustration with a real and financial CGE model applied to Rwanda', Department of Economics, Laval University, Canada.

Parikh, K.S., Fischer, G.K., Frohberg, K. and Gulbrandsen, O. (1987) *Towards free trade in agriculture*. Dordrecht: Martinus Nijhoff.

Powell, A.A. and Snape, R.H. (1992) 'The contribution of applied general equilibrium analysis to policy reform in Australia', Impact Project General Paper G98, Impact Research Centre, Monash University, Australia.

Rattsø, J. (1989) 'Macrodynamic adjustment in a dual semi-industrialized economy', *Journal of Development Economics*, 30:47–69.

Robinson, S. (1989) 'Multisectoral models', Chapter 18 in: H. Chenery and T.N. Srinivasan, eds., *Handbook of development economics, Volume 2*, Amsterdam: North-Holland.

Robinson, S. (1991) 'Macroeconomics, financial variables and computable general equilibrium models', *World Development*, 19:1509–1525.

Romer, P. (1991) 'Increasing returns and new developments in the theory of growth', in: W.A. Barnett, et al., eds., *Equilibrium theory and applications*. Cambridge: Cambridge University Press.

Rosensweig, J.A. and Taylor, L. (1990) 'Devaluation, capital flows, and crowding out: A CGE model with portfolio choice for Thailand', Chapter 11 in: L. Taylor, ed., *Socially relevant policy analysis*. Cambridge, MA: MIT Press.

Ryan, S.M. and Bean, J.C. (1989) 'Degeneracy in infinite horizon optimization', *Mathematical Programming*, 43:305–315.

Salauddin A., van der Geest, W., Keyzer, M.A. and Mujeri, M.K. (1986) 'The applied general equilibrium model for the third five-year plan of Bangladesh', *Bangladesh Journal of Political Economy*, 7:35–99.

Samuelson, P. (1958) 'An exact consumption-loan model of interest with or without the social contrivance of money', *Journal of Political Economy*, 66:467–482.

Sen, A.K. (1963) 'Neo-classical and neo-Keynesian theories of distribution', *Economic Record*, 39:53–64.

Shoven, J.B. and Whalley, J. (1984) 'Applied general equilibrium models of taxation and international trade', *Journal of Economic Literature*, 22:1007–1051.

Shoven, J. and Whalley, J. (1992) *Applying general equilibrium*. New York: Cambridge University Press.

Srinivasan, T.N. (1989) 'Food aid: A cause of development failure or instrument for success?', *World Bank Economic Review*, 3:39–65.

Stiglitz, J. (1976) 'The efficiency wage hypothesis, surplus labour and the distribution of income in LDC's', *Oxford Economic Papers*, 28:185–207.

Stokey, N.L. and Lucas, R.E. with Prescott, E.C. (1989) *Recursive methods in economic dynamics*, Cambridge, MA: Harvard University Press.

Strauss, S. and Thomas, D. (1994) 'Human resources: household decisions and markets', in this volume.

Taylor, L. and Lysy, F.J. (1979) 'Vanishing income redistributions: Keynesian clues about model surprises in the short-run', *Journal of Development Economics*, 6:11–30.

Taylor, L. (1990) 'Structuralist CGE models', Chapter 1 in: L. Taylor, ed., *Socially relevant policy analysis*. Cambridge, MA: MIT Press.

Thorbecke, E., in collaboration with Kim, B., Roland-Holst, D. and Berrian. D. (1992) 'A computable general equilibrium model integrating real and financial transactions', Chapter 4 in: Thorbecke, E. ed., *Adjustment and equity in Indonesia*. Paris: OECD Development Centre.

van Wijnbergen, S. (1982) 'Stagflationary effects of monetary stabilization policies: A quantitative analysis of South Korea', *Journal of Development Economics*, 10:133–169.

Varian, H. (1982) 'The non-parametric approach to demand analysis', *Econometrica*, 30:945–973.

Varian, H.R. (1984) *Microeconomic Analysis*, second edition. New York: Norton.

Whalley, J. (1985) *Trade liberalization among major world trading areas*. Cambridge, MA: MIT Press.

Whalley, J. (1986) 'Impact of a 50 percent tariff in an eight-region global trade model', in: T.N. Srinivasan and J. Whalley, eds., *General equilibrium trade policy modelling*, pp. 189–214. Cambridge, MA: MIT Press.

Whalley, J. and Wigle, R. (1991) 'Cutting CO_2 emissions: The effects of alternative policy approaches', *The Energy Journal*, 12:109–124.

Wonham, M. (1979) *Linear multivariate control: A geometric approach*, New York: Springer.

PART 8

RESOURCES, TECHNOLOGY, AND INSTITUTIONS

INTRODUCTION TO PART 8

Economic development often is described as an expansion of an economy's production possibility set. This set depends on the primary factor endowments, technology and institutions of the economy. The existence and functioning of institutions including markets determine how close the economy operates to the efficiency frontier of its production possibility set at any point in time. If for simplicity population growth is viewed as exogenous, this characterization implies that growth in per capita output depends on the growth in primary inputs per capita, technological change and institutional change. Growth accounting exercises in the tradition of Denison explicitly adopt such a framework. Critical questions for understanding the development process from this perspective are what determines the accumulation of capital stock and other produced means and what determines technological and institutional change. Because such concerns are viewed as so basic, a number of chapters in the first two volumes of the Handbook deal with them, including Chapter 5 by Joseph E. Stiglitz, Chapter 7 by Moshe Syrquin, Chapter 10 by Mark Gersovitz, Chapter 16 by Clive Bell, and Chapter 21 by Lyn Squire. For the same reason, there has continued to be further work on these questions subsequent to the publications of volumes I and II. Part 8 of the *Handbook* includes four chapters that are concerned primarily with savings that might permit physical capital stock accumulation (Chapter 36) and technology (Chapter 37) and institutions in developing countries (Chapters 38 and 39):

Chapter 36. Timothy Besley, "Savings, Credit and Insurance"
Chapter 37. Robert E. Evenson and Larry E. Westphal, "Technological Change and Technology Strategy"
Chapter 38. Justin Yifu Lin and Jeffrey B. Nugent, "Institutions and Economic Development"
Chapter 39. Partha Dasgupta and Karl-Goran Mäler, "Poverty, Institutions, and the Environmental-Resource Base"

In addition to these four chapters in Part 8, Chapter 34 in Part 7 deals with household demand determinants of the accumulation of human resources and Chapter 40 in Part 9 considers important aspects of the supply of public services related to both human and physical infrastructure.

Handbook of Development Economics, Volume III, Edited by J. Behrman and T.N. Srinivasan
© *Elsevier Science B.V., 1995*

In the early post-Second World War development literature, increased savings were viewed as a major means to increase rate of growth. In the simplest Harrod–Domar model, for example, the equilibrium growth rate that equals the growth in production capacity with the growth in demand is equal to the savings rate divided by the incremental capital output ratio. In a well-known analogy in his influential "Stages of Economic Growth", Rostow (1960) suggested that "take-off" to self-sustained growth occurred when an economy increased its savings rate above 10 percent. Sir Arthur Lewis, in his celebrated paper on economic development with unlimited supplies of labor, argued that the "central problem of economic development is to understand the process by which a community which was previously saving and investing 4 or 5 percent of its national income or less converts itself into an economy where voluntary saving is running at about 12 to 15 percent of national income or more. This is the central problem because the central fact of economic development is rapid capital accumulation (including knowledge and skills with capital)" (Lewis, 1954, p. 155). Except for Lewis, most other analysts assumed primacy of physical capital accumulation, often to the exclusion of other factors that might affect development, including human capital accumulation and the inducements created by changing institutions for dynamic efficiency and technological adoption. Therefore it is not surprising that such a view of the development process now appears simplistic, and that many countries that have much more than satisfied the Lewis–Rostow criterion do not appear to have taken off. For instance the mean gross domestic savings rate out of GDP reported for 1991 for all countries classified as low-income by the World Bank (1978, 1993) is 27 percent (up from 20 percent in 1970 for the same countries, and 12 percent in 1960 for another set of low income countries), but most commentators would agree that many of these economies have not entered into a period of sustained development.

Capital accumulation (particularly in the form of equipment) was, and still is, viewed as a major component of the development process (see De Long and Summers (1991) for a reiteration of Mahalanobis (1955)). But recently there has been a shift towards focus on the role of saving in performing smoothing and insurance functions from the perspective of micro entities in developing countries. Conceptually savings transfer resources across time and insurance transfers resources across states of nature. With a complete set of markets for assets and insurance, the decision to save can be separated from the decision to insure. For example, one can transfer resources across time without at the same time transferring resources across states of nature or vice versa. But with incomplete markets, the savings and insurance functions interact. Besley (Chapter 36) reviews much of the recent literature on the savings-credit-insurance nexus in developing countries, with focus on the possible role of financial markets in allowing the exploitation of gains from intertemporal and inter-state-of-nature trade. This literature has burgeoned because of significant theoretical advances in understanding financial contracts in the context of incomplete market structure and in the presence of imperfect information and limited enforcement and because of increased availability of micro data that permits formulation and testing of well-defined hypothesis. Much of this interest has centered on developing countries because of the relatively large shocks and the wide variety of non-market informal institutions (but limited development of formal credit and insurance institutions) in these economies. Because of the rapidly growing literature, Besley's chapter both complements and updates some of the material on savings in Volume I of the Handbook in chapters by Mark Gersovitz (Chapter 10) and Clive Bell (Chapter 16).

Besley explicitly adopts a trade theoretic approach, asking what gains might be obtained by trading across time or across states of nature (because of technological opportunities, taste differences, timing of income inflows, and increasing returns to scale in production) what limits such possibilities for trade, and what roles might governments have to improve such trade. He begins by studying self-insurance, i.e. saving in 'good' states of nature to augment consumption in 'bad' states, which points to the possible importance of liquidity constraints. He also reviews the theory and village level tests for the opposite extreme of efficient risk sharing in which households experiencing 'good' states transfer resources to augment the consumption of those experiencing 'bad' states. Then the experience with formal insurance schemes, such as crop insurance and commodity price insurance, and with informal insurance is reviewed. Limited enforcement and imperfect information have constrained the development of these insurance mechanisms. Recent literature has emphasized the possible advantages of combining aspects of informal credit – in particular monitoring through group lending programs – with the formal sector. Finally it also emphasizes the role of government in regulating the operation and development of credit and savings markets for prudential reasons because of imperfect information, the need for enforcement arrangements, protection for depositors, market power of money lenders and others, and for infant industry reasons.

This chapter points to the considerable shift in the focus on savings in the recent development literature and to the considerable progress in modeling and testing propositions related to smoothing and insurance functions of savings in the context of developing countries, with a wide range of institutions that serve such functions. While there has been considerable progress, there remains much to be learned regarding the savings-credit-insurance nexus. Progress is likely to be attained by further work integrating modeling of the particular institutions that have developed for this nexus in developing countries with careful empirical tests.

The process of development, of course, does not consist only in resource accumulation. Technological change often is emphasized as a critical means for increasing productivity of, and thus the income from, given resources.

A basic question regarding technology is whether there exists a shelf of available technologies produced in other economies that can be adapted by developing countries at relatively low cost. If so, technology policy is relatively straightforward. From the perspective of efficiency, policy-makers should consider the present discounted value of expected gains versus costs from policies designed to offset market failures. Perhaps the most compelling case for such policies is to assure the efficient distribution of information about the technological options, which is not likely to occur through markets because of public goods characteristics of information. There may also be a case for other interventions if there are other market failures, for example due to market power of technology providers. But the analysis is quite straightforward, with the considerations for technology just the same as for static efficiency considerations for a tradeable service.

Evenson and Westphal, in Chapter 37 on "Technological Change and Technology Strategy," stress that there is not simply a stock of available technologies that entities in developing countries can implement at very low cost. Instead they emphasize that technology generally is "tacit" and "circumstantial sensitive." By "tacit" they mean that technology is not "completely expressed by the sum of the reproducible elements in which it is partially contained; that is, in the codified information about it and the material inputs that provide physical means for its accomplishment" (pp. 2212–2213). By "circumstantial sensitive" they mean that qualities of ostensibly identical production inputs differ across locations in ways that affect the possible output from a given technique. There may be differences among sectors in the relative importance of technologies being tacit versus being circumstantial sensitive. For instance, for manufacturing technologies tacitness is more likely to be relatively important and for agricultural technologies circumstantial sensitivity (e.g., because of variations in soil quality, sunlight, water availability, temperature) is more likely to be greater. But all technologies have some degree of tacitness and circumstantial sensitivity. Evenson and Westphal summarize several studies that attempt to characterize the extent of these characteristics of technology across sectors, regions, and countries.

There are at least five major implications of the characterization of technology as shaped importantly by tacitness and circumstantial sensitivity for its adoption and adaptation.

First, investments are required to adopt new technologies in the developing countries. Because technology is tacit, investments are required to learn about the properties of a new technique. Because technology is circumstantially sensitive, investments are required to adapt technology to specific local conditions. "Technological distances" (in the sense of suitability of technology developed in one location to another) may vary substantially among locations. As Evenson and Westphal emphasize, because of the investment aspects of technological adoptions, rapid economic growth that is importantly based on technological change cannot be realized without supporting technological infrastructure and investments. There are important economic questions regarding what determines these investments that have only begun to be examined in systematic studies for developing countries, with most of the existing research on agriculture, a little on manufacturing and very little on services.

Second, for most applied purposes very little understanding can be gained from considering technology on a general abstract level. There are critical differences in the details both regarding tacitness and circumstantial sensitivity that mean that general abstractions or analyses are not very informative. Evenson and Westphal emphasize that, as a result, relatively few insights regarding how technology is generated, adopted and maintained have been provided by theoretical models and aggregate analyses such as in the "endogenous growth" literature. They argue that to progress in our understanding, instead, attention has to be paid to much more disaggregate behavior in the presence of considerable heterogeneities some of which may be difficult or impossible to observe by analysts.

Third, empirical research regarding the determinants of and the impact of technology is very difficult. Persuasive systematic research requires explicit recognition of and control for critical unobserved characteristics of adopters and potential adopters and of conditions in which adoption decisions are made. The estimation problems that are discussed in Chapters 33 and 34 are pervasive in considering the determinants of and the impact of technology adoption. Studies of associations between, for example, schooling and adoption decisions may be very misleading if there is no control for unobserved heterogeneity in other characteristics such as management capabilities or soil quality. The credibility of estimates in the literature of the high returns to technology adoption more generally depend critically on whether they persuasively identify and isolate the impact of the technological adoption from unobserved characteristics of the adopters. Yet most of the available empirical studies do not adequately address these difficult estimation issues.

Fourth, on a priori grounds the importance of learning about and adapting technology would seem to imply a critical role for complementary investments such as schooling that facilitate such processes. The implication would seem to be that, in the spirit of Welch (1970), Schultz (1975) and others, there would be high returns to schooling if there are new technological possibilities that are suitable to local conditions for which learning and adaptation are important, but that the returns to schooling would be much lower in the absence of such options. Thus the technological change questions would seem to be intimately related to the education investment determinants and returns issues that are considered in Chapters 13 by T.Paul Schultz and Chapter 34 by Strauss and Thomas. Nevertheless most related empirical studies do not consider explicitly the interaction between human resources and technological changes that are tacit and circumstantially sensitive within a dynamic framework, but merely examine cross-sectional associations between technology adoptions and education within a static framework. Some recent studies on the impact of the Green Revolution in India, however, do adopt a dynamic perspective and find that schooling returns were high in locations in which the new circumstantial-sensitive technologies were appropriate (e.g., Karnataka, Maharastra, the Punjab), areas in which these technologies were not appropriate for local conditions had low returns to schooling even if schooling and other human resources were relatively rich as in Kerala (Behrman, Rosenzweig and Vashishtha 1994, Foster and Rosenzweig 1994). But understanding of the empirical aspects of such processes is in its infancy.

Fifth, the efficiency arguments for policy interventions seem to vary considerably across the major production sectors, in part because of the different degrees to which the returns to technologically-related investments can be reaped by those who make the investments, which in turn reflects in part differentials in tacitness and circumstantial sensitivities of technologies. A related long-standing question is to what extent to balance off the private incentives for investments in forms of transferable technological innovations with the social gains from wider and earlier dissemination of such innovations through policies regarding intellectual property rights. The differentials in tacitness and circumstantial sensitivities of technologies also mean that policy-makers are not likely to be able to micro-manage well technological development and adoption processes, though there may be good efficiency reasons for helping to develop a technological infrastructure that supports technological development and adoption on a general level. Elements of this infrastructure are likely to include a stable macroeconomic environment that is conducive to all sorts of investments (including those in technology development and adoption), competitive markets (domestic and international), effective systems to protect intellectual property rights, and support for some forms of technological development, adoption and dissemination.

Institutions, like technology, often have been taken as given for economic analysis and are claimed to affect importantly the development process. Yet institutions, also like technology, respond to market and other incentives and involve constant small adaptations as well as less-frequent substantial innovations. The last two chapters in Part 8 consider some important dimensions of economic institutions and development. Lin and Nugent (Chapter 38) consider broad issues pertaining to institutions and economic development and Dasgupta and Mäler (Chapter 39) consider the interaction among poverty, institutions, and the environmental-resource base.

The importance of institutions – such as firms, families, contracts, markets, rules and regulations and social norms – to the process of economic development was emphasized by many classical, Marxian and early development economists. But during the half century or so after about 1930, mainstream economists in general – including development economists – shifted increasingly towards emphasis on more quantitatively tractable dimensions of economics. More recently, however, there has being growing (re-) recognition that institutions differ over time and across economies, that much economic activity takes place within institutions such as families and firms and governments rather than only in arms-length transactions in markets, and that institutions both affect and respond to the evolving economies in which they are embedded. The revived interest in and efforts at analyzing the development, behavior and impact of institutions is sometimes characterized as the "New Institutional Economics" (NIE). Those engaged in the NIE consider a broad range of topics and have a number of overlapping approaches, but often use as the core of their analysis focus on transaction costs and/or collective action.

Lin and Nugent (Chapter 38) consider institutions and economic development. They focus on two general propositions: (1) that institutions matter and (2) that the determinants of institutions are subject to economic analysis. They claim that "the theory of transaction and information costs and the theory of collective action can take us a long way toward giving us a set of testable hypotheses for explaining the choice and nature of particular institutions and predicting the likelihood of success in achieving such choice or changes therein over time in specific settings." (p. 2362) Transactions costs include the direct costs of obtaining information, negotiating among the parties to an agreement, and communicating all relevant provisions to the parties, as well as the indirect costs arising from the opportunistic behavior of economic entities in light of imperfect information and risks. The nature of these transactions costs in the context of alternative arrangements may shape what institutions are developed to deal with them and how such institutions evolve. There has been a considerable literature based on "stylized facts" regarding the role of different institutions and their evolution due to transactions costs and to changing market and political alternatives. The theory of collective action relates to the question of under what conditions it is advantageous for individual entities to participate in the collective action for the development of new or modified institutions given the distribution of expected costs and benefits to the individual innovators and the possible externality and/or free rider problems. The government might intervene to improve efficiency in light of externality and free rider problems, but the government itself is an institution that reflects the interests of particular entities ("interest groups") and whose operation may have externality and free rider problems.

Lin and Nugent use transaction costs and the theory of collective action as a basis to discuss what appear to be some systematic changes in the relative importance of various institutions in the process of development: the rise and subsequent fall of extended families, the expansion of markets, the expansion of governments and the substitution of the state for smaller groups in the provision of public goods and services. They discuss institutional adoptions and, in the terms used by Evenson and Westphal in Chapter 37, institutions are tacit and circumstantially sensitive, so that – like other forms of innovation and technological change – they usually are not transferable from one context to another at no or very low cost. They further emphasize that institutions interact, and that institutional inertia due to the cost of restructuring institutions de novo with great frequency and the difference between private and social returns to institutional reforms may result in inefficient institutional arrangements persisting over long periods of time.

But, as they observe, their two general propositions about institutions at this point are hypotheses for which very little systematic empirical evidence has been provided. A review of existing studies points more to methodological problems than to persuasive evidence. Lin and Nugent suggest that the shortage of systematic empirical research on institutions in developing countries reflects two inter-related shortcomings in developing countries: "the lack of data and the lack of interest in explaining institutions for economists working in developed economies" (wherein most economic researchers receive their advanced training). They suggest that data shortcomings reflect that institutions often are complex, difficult to quantify, and in many cases slow to change – and that such data shortcomings in themselves have limited the interest in empirical testing of hypothesis regarding institutions among mainstream economists. They also express the hope that these problems will become less serious with increasing data availability, increasingly rapid institutional changes in many developing economies, and increasing recognition of the possible importance of institutions and institutional change in the development process. They summarize a few recent studies primarily regarding land contracts and other arrangements in agriculture that make some progress in analyzing various institutions in developing countries. These studies also illustrate that it is critical to integrate the empirical analysis with the underlying modeling and to be sensitive to measurement problems and unobserved variables that both may affect the determination of institutions (e.g., the size and soil quality of farms) and may affect outcomes that are hypothesized to be affected by institutions.

Some of the other chapters in volume 3 of the *Handbook* also give some serious consideration to institutions and development that complements this chapter by Lin and Nugent. A number of studies of the institutions of households and labor markets, for example, are surveyed by Strauss and Thomas in Chapter 34. Their discussion supplements the survey by Lin and Nugent and points explicitly to some of the difficult issues in undertaking empirical research in this area. Besley in Chapter 36 also discusses models and empirical tests of some institutions that are distinctive in some developing countries such as ROSCOs (rotating savings and credit organizations). Evenson and Westphal in Chapter 37 further discuss some particular institutions related to intellectual property rights. Because of increasing data about institutions, ongoing efforts to model systematically their operations, and increasing appreciation of their possible importance in the development process, it seems probable that the coming years will witness an expansion of efforts to understand exactly in what ways institutions do indeed matter (rather then just proxy for other unobserved characteristics) and what determines which institutions exists in specific contexts. Lin and Nugent's chapter provides a valuable survey with insights on both theoretical modeling and empirical estimation. It is a useful foundation on which future studies of institutions and development can build.

Dasgupta and Mäler in Chapter 39 consider institutions and the environmental resource-base, with particular emphasis on the relation to poverty. They begin with the observation that the majority of the poor live in rural, resource-based economies, but that – until recently – the environmental resource base of the poor was practically ignored by mainstream economists. The resilience (to recover from perturbations, shock and surprises) of this resource base is critical, and there may be multiple equilibria relating the resource base to the number of poor people and of their livestock dependent on it that have very different welfare and productivity implications. The steady-state resource base is a capital asset that is affected directly and indirectly by market failures. While the direct effects of market failures often are emphasized (e.g., with respect to allocation of rights to resources in commons), some of the indirect effects also may be substantial. For example, limited credit, insurance and capital markets may encourage the poor to keep more livestock than they otherwise would as insurance, which places added burden on the carrying capacity of the local resource-base. While market failures are an important aspect of institutional failures that lead to environmental degradation, policy failures also often contribute to such degradation. Poverty, further, may be both a cause and a result of such degradation.

The environmental resource-base analytically is a multicomponent capital stock that can be augmented by investment or lessened by use and degradation. Such a characterization adds clarity to some environmental topics that have been muddled, in part because many commentators have ignored intertemporal welfare economics and the theory of optimal development. For example, some characterizations of "sustainable development" suggest that all capital stocks (e.g., soil and soil quality, ground and surface water and their quality) ought to be preserved at their initial levels, not that future generations enjoy no less welfare than that enjoyed by the present – which would be consistent with substitution among various capital stocks rather than the maintenance of all of them. Likewise some characterizations of intertemporal justice confuse positive discount rates due to diminishing marginal utility of consumption in a growing economy with weighing future generations less than the present one (or vice versa if future generations might have less consumption due to environmental developments such as global warming). Moreover such analysis ignores the possibly important option values in an uncertain world that may be lost if there are irreversible environmental changes (e.g., loss of genetic pools through species losses). One example is in the valuation of real net national product (NNP), over which there has been some controversy related to the inclusion of environmental effects. Dasgupta and Mäler argue that in a closed economy the correct notion of NNP to reflect social well-being is consumption plus the value of the net changes in physical, human and environmental capital, with valuation at shadow prices that include both use value and option value. The failure to include the option value in accounting prices would cause biases in the evaluation of NNP, as well as of particular projects.

Market failures occur because of environmental externalities that arise from incomplete property rights and information and transaction costs. Externalities may be unidirectional (e.g., the impact of upstream foresters on farmers in the downstream watershed) or reciprocal (e.g., common property resources).

In unidirectional cases Coase's well-known theorem states that the assignment of initial property rights is neutral in its effects on allocative efficiency under certain assumptions: (i) the pay-offs are common knowledge among participants, (ii) transaction costs are nil, (iii) the game is convex, and (iv) there are only two participants. If any of these assumptions are violated, whether or not the resulting allocation is efficient depends on the nature of the violation and the nature of the institutions. For example, Dasgupta and Mäler discuss an upstream-downstream case with non-convexities in which competitive prices for upstream pollution externalities do not exist if private property rights are well-defined and enforceable (i.e., the downstream community would define infinite quantities at positive prices and zero quantities at nonpositive prices). But if markets for upstream pollution externalities are prohibited there exists an optimal state-imposed equilibrium tax on upstream production. Of course implementing such a tax is difficult indeed since it requires information that is hard to obtain, including information about possible states of affairs that may be far removed from the economy's current position. Such tensions between the weakness of market solutions and the weakness of governmental interventions occur repeatedly in environmental economics.

In cases of reciprocal externalities Dasgupta and Mäler emphasize that, though such a distinction often is not made, it is critical to distinguish between global commons (open seas, the atmosphere) and local commons (e.g., village ponds and forests). For global commons, there are not in place effective monitoring and sanctioning arrangements. Therefore efficiency is likely to be obtained only through new co-operative schemes with institutions such as tradeable emissions rights.

Local commons, in contrast, have membership that usually is open only to those having historic rights-of-use (i.e., through community membership or kinship ties), and are often managed and monitored effectively by community norms and procedures. Changing these arrangements through privatizing the commons usually seems to cause destitution among the poorer members of the community who previously had access (typically particularly women given gender divisions of labor). In the words of Dasgupta and Mäler, "privatization of village commons and forest lands, while hallowed at the altar of efficiency, can have disastrous distributional consequences, disfranchising entire classes of people from economic citizenship." (p. 2428) They further argue that lessening access to such local common property may initiate a downward spiral of poverty by increasing the returns to parents of having more children for obtaining water and fuel, with the expanded population placing more stress on available resources. They also argue that local users are most knowledgeable about heterogeneities in such resources. Thus they conclude that as a general rule there are important distributional and efficiency reasons to protect local commons as commons with decisions regarding these commons left in the hands of the users themselves.

Thus the chapters in Part 8 on a general level address some traditional concerns of economic development regarding savings for physical resource accumulation, increases in resource productivity through technological change, and institutional developments. But they do in a manner that is based increasingly on micro theoretic models to explain an increasing range of individual and collective behavior which causes the chapters to be substantially different than they would have been had they been written a decade or two earlier. They also share an emphasis on the heterogeneity of unobserved attributes and information problems that have important implications not only for the limitations of policy, but for the difficulties of assembling persuasive empirical evidence. Finally they also share some tensions regarding the extent of market improvements to facilitate development (because of second-best problems in the absence of a complete set of markets, nonconvexities, externalities, and distributional concerns) versus policy interventions (because of policy-induced distortions, limited information about underlying heterogeneities, difficulties in monitoring, and the creation of rents for interest groups). As a result they are considerably less confident, but probably more realistic, in their policy prescriptions regarding the respective roles of the market and the state than would have been surveys on similar topics a decade or two ago. While the faith in markets as efficient institutions is tempered because of second-best problems in the absence of a complete set of markets, nonconvexities, externalities, and distributional concerns, the faith in government interventions to correct market failures is tempered as well because of informational problems and, more importantly, the ubiquitousness of lobbying and rent seeking to which governments are subject.

JERE BEHRMAN

T.N. SRINIVASAN

References

Behrman, J.R., Rosenzweig, M.R. and Vashishtha, P. (1994) 'Location, technical change and human capital: Consequences of the green revolution,' Philadelphia: University of Pennsylvania, mimeo.

De Long, J.B. and Summers, L.H. (1991) 'Equipment, investment, relative prices, and economic growth,' *Quarterly Journal of Economics* 106:2 (May), 445–502.

Foster, A. and Rosenzweig, M.R. (1994) 'Technical change and human returns and investments: Consequences of the green revolution,' Philadelphia, PA: University of Pennsylvania, mimeo.

Lewis, W.A., 1954, 'Economic development with unlimited supplies of labour,' *The Manchester School* 22, 139–191.

Mahalanobis, P.C. (1955) 'The approach of operational research to planning in India,' *Sankhya: The Indian Journal of Statistics*, Vol. 16, Parts 1 and 2, 3–62.

Rostow, W.W. (1960) *Stages of economic growth: A non communist manifesto*, Cambridge: Cambridge University Press.

Schultz, T.W. (1975) 'The value of the ability to deal with disequilibria,' *Journal of Economic Literature* 13:3, 827–846.

Welch, F. (1970) 'Education in production,' *Journal of Political Economy* 78:1 (January/February), 35–59.

World Bank (1978) *World development report*, Washington, D.C.: The World Bank.

World Bank (1993) *World development report*, Oxford: Oxford University Press for the World Bank.

Chapter 36

SAVINGS, CREDIT AND INSURANCE

TIMOTHY BESLEY*

Princeton University

Contents

*The Lynde and Harry Bradley foundation provided me with valuable support while the first draft of this chapter was prepared. I am grateful to Harold Alderman, Abhijit Banerjee, Jere Behrman, Kristin Butcher, Michael Carter, Shubham Chaudhuri, Steve Coate, Angus Deaton, Franque Grimard, Tim Guinnane, Jan Gunning, John Hoddinott, Karla Hoff, Sanjay Jain, Alec Levenson, Michael Lipton, Jonathan Morduch, Gillian Paull, Christina Paxson, Indira Rajaraman, Paul Seabright, Ammar Siamwalla, T.N. Srinivasan, Robert Townsend, Christopher Udry, Hal Varian and participants in the First ADB Conference on Development Economics for helpful advice, comments and discussions on the material covered here. I am solely responsible for the final product.

Handbook of Development Economics, Volume III, Edited by J. Behrman and T.N. Srinivasan

Contents (continued)

1. Introduction

To say that savings, credit and insurance are central to the functioning of an economy is a platitude. However, only relatively recently have applied economists begun seriously to confront many of the complex and interesting phenomena which are peculiar to the savings/credit/insurance nexus in developing countries. Burgeoning interest in such issues has perhaps three main roots. The first is the increased availability of data that permits formulation and testing of well-defined hypotheses. The second is the significant theoretical advances in understanding financial contracts, appreciating the importance of imperfect information and limited enforcement. The third is the re-orientation of development studies towards the view that poverty and rationality are not inconsistent and that there is much that can be learned by using the tools of neoclassical economics to study choice problems faced by those with few resources.

The aim of this chapter is to survey and synthesize the literature on these issues for developing economies. In so doing it will have to respect two main constraints. The first is shortage of space. While the chapter will cover the main ideas, there is insufficient space to do proper justice to every idea or author. In addition, there is almost no attempt to give a complete coverage of more technical aspects of the work; for this readers will have to return to the original sources. The second constraint respects the fact that the two earlier volumes in the series each had a contribution bearing directly on the issues treated in this chapter. In chapter ten Mark Gersovitz surveyed issues under the broad heading of savings and development. Inevitably, he touched on many of the issues raised here. A significant difference between Gersovitz's chapter and this one is the greater attention that I will pay to financial intermediation issues. In chapter sixteen, Clive Bell discussed credit markets in his survey on interlinkage. Consequently, there will be almost no discussion of such issues here. We will however, focus on many other institutions that are important in the provision of credit that Bell did not discuss. In both cases, the earlier chapters are complements with the present one and the reader of this chapter is encouraged to read them too. I have made a conscious effort to avoid repetition of material available in these chapters wherever possible.

Why is financial intermediation so important for economic development? Two immediate answers come to mind. First, if individuals live in risky environments then savings, insurance and consumption credit yield direct benefits in coping with risk. Second, the development of credit and insurance should enhance an economy's investment efficiency and, possibly, growth.[1]

---

[1] This view was argued for, long ago, in Schumpeter (1934).

Since efficiency requires that funds flow towards individuals who have the most productive investment opportunities, then failures of intermediation are intimately linked with misallocation of capital. Below I discuss some of the limits to intermediation.

The approach I adopt is explicitly *trade theoretic*, where the central idea is that credit and insurance respond to gains from trade. An act of saving is *intertemporal* trade (of current consumption for future consumption). Credit is, by definition, also intertemporal trade, since the act of receiving (extending) credit at a point in time is against a future repayment obligation (claim). Finally, insurance is trade across states of nature. Thinking about impediments to trade may also be helpful in understanding the institutional framework that we observe and defining the function of government. Thus for any institution providing credit and/or insurance, we might begin by asking what gains from trade are being sought. Not all such gains can, however, be successfully exploited and recent work in financial economics has emphasized certain impediments to trade due, for example, to imperfect information. Thus arises a second set of questions concerning what sustains trade. Finally, there are important questions about efficiency that might drive policy intervention. Are the mechanisms that sustain trade efficient and, if not, what can be done to remedy this? Much of the existing work, theoretical and empirical, give answers (implicitly or explicitly) to some of these questions. We will attempt to unify existing knowledge and indicate gaps in it by placing it within this framework.

The functions of savings, credit and insurance are intimately connected with one another in most developing economies. However, at first sight, there ought to a be a division of roles between transactions that transfer resources across time, as with savings and credit, and those that transfer resources across states of the world, as with insurance. Moreover, decisions about how to allocate resources over time and states ought to be separable in the sense that the consumer's decision about how much to borrow and save is independent of uncertainty about future events. This view turns out to be correct only under the most restrictive of circumstances, when we are in a competitive economy with a complete set of Arrow-Debreu securities and no externalities. As we shall see in what follows, this separation of the functions of insurance and saving/borrowing no longer holds when markets are incomplete. Thus the familiar idea that people should save for a rainy day[2] embodies the notion that *because* insurance markets work imperfectly, it is necessary to set aside some

---

[2] This is a curious expression for many LDCs where "saving for a dry day" might seem more fitting.

income for future times.[3] In this example, it appears to be the *absence* of an insurance possibility that motivates the savings opportunity. It is limitations on insurance possibilities that make it essential to treat savings, credit and insurance in a unified way.

Two features of developing economies are particularly germane to the link between savings and insurance. First, the absence of markets for trading in risks is particularly noticeable. Many types of insurance possibilities, taken for granted in developed countries, are simply not traded. This is especially striking given the relative importance of risk in the lives of many inhabitants of LDCs, such as the risk of suffering certain infectious diseases. Second, a large fraction of the population is typically dependent on agricultural income for their livelihood. The latter may be subject to drastic weather shocks and commodity prices fluctuations. It is thus not surprising to find that the majority of empirical studies investigating savings and insurance in LDCs use evidence from farm households. To reinforce the relative importance of risk in developing country agriculture, the reader might consider the following comparison taken from Rosenzweig and Binswanger (1993). They find that the coefficient of variation of income in their data from south India is 137. For white males aged 25–29 surveyed in the Longitudinal Survey of Youth in the U.S. in 1971, the number is just 39. These numbers are only illustrative but they help, perhaps, to set the context for the material of this chapter.

Although we will use theory as a way of organizing the issues, our main focus is not on theoretical models or concerns. Its twin objectives are to explore what we know based on existing empirical work and to consider, perhaps more importantly, what we do not know but is ripe for future investigations. We will also spend some time looking at the purpose and success of government intervention in credit and insurance markets. For better or worse governments, and other development agencies, have made the development of credit markets a focus for policy intervention. Among the many attempts to make credit markets work, there is a whole spectrum of performance relative to stated and other objectives. It is now common to regard the record on intervention as a poor one [see, for example, Adams et al. (1984)]. The lessons from the post war experience with intervention will also be discussed here. It should, however, be made clear that the purpose is to offer a unified framework for thinking about policy and practice in the credit-savings-insurance nexus based on thinking about the gains from trade.

---

[3] That is not to say that buying Arrow-Debreu securities is not also saving due to uncertainty about future events. The real issue is with the restrictions on asset portfolios that make individuals save in the form of non-contingent assets.

As such, some conceptual background material will be necessary to preface the discussion.

The organization of the remainder of this chapter is as follows. The next section discusses some further background material, identifying the different possible motivations for intertemporal trade and giving some background discussion of government policy and responses to it. We also discuss how we might judge whether the market system is operating efficiently in terms of the credit and insurance opportunities that it offers as well as some special features of the economies of LDCs in providing credit and insurance. Section 3 discusses autarky. We will study life-cycle/permanent income models that incorporate precautionary savings and liquidity constraints. We also discuss the evidence on the forward looking behavior by small farmers in LDCs. Section 4 considers trade, as well as formal credit and insurance possibilities. We also discuss informal institutions and their importance. In section 5 we attempt to tie some of the themes explored here into long-run development issues. Section 6 delves briefly into the implications for policy from the preceding discussion. Section 7 offers some concluding remarks.

2. Background

We will classify models of savings, credit and insurance according to how each treats individual behavior in relation to others. In a purely *autarkic* model, the savings decision is made in isolation. While in a developed country we might naturally think of saving using demand deposits that earn interest, this is not necessarily a good model for LDCs. There is evidence that because of high transaction costs, low levels of literacy and numeracy, and mistrust of financial institutions, individuals will often accumulate savings in forms other than demand deposits. They may also use informal deposit institutions such as the *susu* men of West Africa[4] and *shroffs* in India that we discuss below. In addition, there is a good deal of direct investment in assets.[5]

Alternatively, the savings decision can be modeled in a market context, with individuals having the possibility of placing funds on deposit for a given return. A good deal of the literature on savings [e.g., Deaton (1990)], adopts this perspective. We will also present a model of saving in this spirit. Since this does

---

[4] Susu men are informal bankers used by market women in Africa. They collect funds from them and return them at the end of the month, less a commission. The savings earn a negative rate of interest in exchange for safe keeping.

[5] The national accounts statistics of India, for example, report that in 1987–1988 more than 80 percent of gross domestic savings was accounted for by households and less than 52 percent of household savings was in the form of financial assets, the rest being direct saving in physical assets. [Bevan, Collier and Gunning (1989)] also discusses the importance of accumulation in non-financial assets after the Kenyan coffee boom in the late 1970's.

not involve considering the operation of the deposit institutions that pay the return on assets, we will classify this situation as one of autarky too.[6]

If savings are put to work to earn a return for savers, then we have to think about financial intermediation. Issuing productive loans is one way of putting savings to work. Intermediaries seek productive opportunities, pool risk and provide a means for individuals to sort themselves into savers and borrowers according to their needs and opportunities, i.e., to exploit the *gains from intertemporal trade*.

Even if gains from trade exist, realizing them may not be straightforward. For example, individuals must be assured about the safety of their savings and for this they need to worry about the behavior of intermediaries and the borrowers to whom they lend. Below we discuss impediments to trade due, for example, to limited enforcement and imperfect information. The actual institutions that exist and function effectively reflect what can be sustained and one of the key questions for policy makers is whether there exist gains from trade that could be realized under appropriate policies. Hence, we also initiate a discussion of the function of government in affecting the operation of savings, credit and insurance.

2.1. The gains from intertemporal trade

This section discusses the sources of gains from intertemporal trade under four main headings:[7] differences in technological opportunities, tastes and timing of endowments, and increasing returns to scale in technologies.

2.1.1. Technological opportunities

Individuals may wish to lend to others who have a better technological advantage for transferring resources over time. Thus if one individual has a better investment opportunity on her land than another, it would pay for *both* to invest in the higher yielding project. Indeed, it should be possible in theory for the individuals to write a contract that made both individuals better off than the autarkic solution in which they invest only in their own land. In agriculture, gains from trade based on technological comparative advantage can easily be

---

[6] Strictly speaking, we might want to draw a distinction between self-insurance through savings (as when an individual accumulates cash in a bank) and self insurance through *autarkic* savings (when the savings are in the form of grain or cattle). For most analytical purposes, this distinction is unimportant.

[7] In the standard international trade literature [see, for example, Dixit and Norman (1980)], it is argued that trade between economies can be based on differences in tastes, technologies, and factor endowments. Increasing returns to scale can also motivate trade. This is quite similar to the classification of the gains from intertemporal trade suggested here.

envisaged. For example, some land may be particularly suited to irrigation or fencing. An *efficient* financial system will be one that directs funds towards those projects whose technological possibilities are best.

2.1.2. Tastes

Differences in tastes may also mean that individuals will achieve a Pareto superior outcome by trading. Consider, for example, the possibility that some individuals differ in their patience, i.e., the relative weights that they attach to present and future consumption. In this case, gains from trade are possible when the impatient borrow from the patient consumers. Such trades may be important when it is realized that differences in patience can be induced by life cycle considerations (e.g., fertility patterns). Models in which taste differences over the timing of consumption drive gains from trade, are available in the literature on financial markets, e.g., the model of Diamond and Dybvig (1983) that examines bank runs.

2.1.3. Timing of endowments (synchronization)

A significant source of gains from intertemporal trade arises from differences in the timing of endowments between individuals. A straightforward example of this is in agriculture in which resource availability is highest immediately after a harvest (the seasonality problem). Individuals whose harvests occur at different times of the year would be able to gain by agreeing to a contract that had one individual lending to another for certain periods. Uncertainty in incomes also gives rise to gains from trade this way. Consider two individuals with identical preferences that are concave in current consumption and whose incomes fluctuate over time in a predictable way (with the same mean). Then, these individuals could both gain by agreeing to a contract that gave one of them a loan when one individual had a low income, to be repaid at some future date. The gains from such trades are based on differences in the timing of their endowments. Inter-generational trades in which the old lend to the young may also exploit gains of this kind.

2.1.4. Increasing returns to scale in production

Individuals can also gain from trade if there are increasing returns to scale in production technologies. The following example makes this clear. Suppose that there are two possible investment opportunities. The first yields r (>1) units of output tomorrow for one unit of foregone consumption today. The second yields $R > r$ units of output tomorrow for one unit of capital, but only if at least F (>1) units of capital are provided. Otherwise it yields nothing. Evidently, the second technology has increasing returns to scale. Even if no single individual has F units of capital available, there can be gains from intertemporal trade if individuals get together and invest using the increasing returns technology. There are no such gains in the absence of increasing returns; the autarkic solution would be perfectly efficient.

We have given four examples of how inter-temporal trade between individuals can be beneficial. When we begin to discuss the kinds of institutions that exist to take advantage of such gains, it will be useful to consider which of the above four reasons can be used to motivate their existence. It will also be a useful framework to think about identifying unexploited gains from trade. Our next focus is on how gains can be sustained and, in particular, what impediments exist to effectively exploiting trading opportunities.

2.2. Mechanisms for sustaining trade

The problems faced in sustaining trade can be divided into two main categories. First, there are problems arising from the asymmetries of information that may characterize the environment in which intertemporal trade occurs. This has many facets: lenders or insurers may be unable to observe the actions that their borrowers/insurers take (*moral hazard*). They may also be unable to observe certain characteristics that affect the ex ante profitability of contracting (*adverse selection*). These are well understood to limit the kinds of trade that are possible [see, for example, Stiglitz and Weiss (1981)].

The second set of difficulties concerns the enforcement of obligations in financial markets. By their nature, contracts written for intertemporal trade are *contingent* and rely on *future obligations* being met. An insurance contract is a promise by one party (the insurer) to pay another (the insured) a certain amount if an uncertain future event occurs. The ability of the parties to write such contracts presupposes a legal framework capable of ensuring that all contingencies and obligations are met. Thus, if the insurer reneges on the obligation, the insured will be entitled to certain remedies for breach of contract. In reality, there are limits on how this can work in any environment; for example, it is simply infeasible to write contracts that specify what will happen under all possible circumstances. This is partly the function of the sophistication of the contracting parties, and also of the legal framework. Possibilities for writing contracts for implementing intertemporal trade will be circumscribed by the abilities of the contracting parties to specify and enforce contracts. This may, however, have real economic consequences, for decisions to invest. Indeed, it is now well understood that incompleteness of contracts does reduce investment inefficiencies, [see, for example, Hart and Moore

(1988)]. While aspects of asymmetric information have been extensively analyzed, incomplete contracting approaches to financial markets are less well developed, both in theory and in applications to real world situations. They are, however, extremely relevant in LDCs where the formal legal infrastructure in which agents operate is quite poorly developed.

While both of the limitations on intertemporal trade may have serious consequences, there are ways of trying to circumvent some of the difficulties to which they give rise. Our next task is to discuss these and to consider how they function in developing economies.

2.2.1. Collateral

This may serve an important role in mitigating default problems in financial markets. To be functional, it should be appropriable by the lender at reasonable cost in the event of default, thus bounding the lenders' losses and encouraging the borrower to take care to avoid default. Collateral may also serve as a screening device, i.e., to overcome an adverse selection problem, as in Stiglitz and Weiss (1986) where the safer borrowers are willing to put up more collateral than the riskier ones. Common forms of collateral are fixed assets such as land and buildings.

In LDC credit markets, good sources of collateral are typically scarce. This may be because the individuals to whom one is considering lending have very few assets that could be collateralized. This is certainly the case for the extremely poor. However, of further concern is the institutional and legal framework in which collateral is used. Land rights are not always well formed enough so that individuals can use their land as collateral.[8] Other activities such as pledging, which is also a form of collateralization, may work very imperfectly [see the discussion of pledging cocoa trees in a Nigerian context by Adegboye (1972)].

In LDCs the use of peer pressure may serve a role in fostering repayment incentives in group lending programs: Besley and Coate (1995) refer to this as *social collateral*. For example, one individual might serve as another's guarantor and pledge her own collateral for another, thus extending the domain of appropriable collateral. However, social collateral may also just take the form of peer group punishments which are not an asset that is appropriable by the lender in the event of default. It is just a device for making default more costly to the borrowers.

---

[8] Atwood (1990) and Feder and Feeney (1990) discuss general land rights issues. For specific studies of links between land and credit, see Feder et al. (1988) on Thailand and Migot-Adholla et al. (1990) for Ghana, Kenya and Rwanda.

2.2.2. Reputation

Individuals may build reputations in financial markets that sustain trade. Borrower reputations, studied in Diamond (1989), can facilitate repayment incentives. By tying future loan terms and access to credit markets to past behavior, borrowers may be encouraged to take more care to repay the loan than in a one-shot relationship. This is quite important in practice. For example, the success of the BKK in Indonesia, studied in Patten and Rosengard (1991), is often attributed to its use of a reputation mechanism. Lender reputations may also be important, especially to depositors. Lenders may acquire reputations for selecting good projects to lend to and pursuing the best interests of depositors.

Because much of the basic infrastructure that supports credit market performance in developed countries is missing, it is quite difficult for reputation based mechanisms to function effectively in LDCs, at least on an economy wide basis. It is more difficult to facilitate the flow of information necessary to assemble individual credit histories as lenders become more geographically separated from borrowers, thus limiting the use of certain reputational mechanisms. Where reputation works in developing economies, it is thus usually on a very local basis.[9]

2.2.3. Social enforcement

This is an important source of contract enforcement in many economic transactions in LDCs, especially in the context of credit and insurance. Social enforcement mechanisms have their root in the social codes that affect individual behavior in a group setting. Norms of honesty, reciprocity and the like color human experience and interaction. Adherence to certain religious principles also prohibits certain kinds of behavior and encourages others. These are basic facets of social life. Of course, there is a question of whether economists can actually explain these things rather than taking them as given. As far as economic behavior goes, the existence of social mechanisms can provide a basis for trade. The relative ease with which individuals may borrow from their family and local community is indicative of this. Of course, information is part of the story here too, but so too is the type of enforcement sanctions for non-repayment that are available. The anthropological literature is replete with examples indicative of the importance of social structure for credit markets [see, for example, Ardener (1964)'s discussion of social

---

[9] The exception may be traders who make frequent visits to villages but who are not actually resident in the village. Long distance trader reputations are an important historical phenomenon, recently studied in Greif (1989).

enforcement of obligations in rotating savings and credit associations]. Among economists, Udry's (1990, 1993) studies of informal credit in Northern Nigeria indicate the great importance of social sanctions in understanding how credit transactions function.

2.2.4. Multilateral trading relations

This view encompasses elements of reputation and social enforcement. Most economic models of reputation work by denying access to future trades to anyone who "cheats" at any time. Enforcement may also be aided if individuals trade in a number of different activities and use the threat of withdrawing from all aspects of trade with each other if there is cheating in any one dimension. This is likely to be important in more traditional societies that typically involve individuals trading with one another in many different dimensions. It is also the basis of many of the interlinkages of credit with other activities such as rental of land reviewed by Bell in chapter sixteen. Below, we discuss the role of trader-lenders in some detail. The role of trade-credit linkages goes beyond reputation and social enforcement. It encompasses the transmission of information to the trader-lender about the potential borrower's productivity and the timing of his output. Trader-lenders may also collude in the collection of debt.

2.2.5. Information generation

Trades are also sustained under imperfect information by building institutions that can directly circumvent such problems. If an individual applies for a loan in a developed country, then there is often a check of their credit history. It might be thought difficult for such institutions to emerge spontaneously because of difficulties in keeping such information private. However, the evidence suggests a contrary perspective. The United States has loan evaluation companies dating back to the early nineteenth century. Pagano and Jappelli (1990) review the contemporary and historical experience with such institutions. Again because of the lack of infrastructure which is complementary with credit market functioning, this type of information generation and retrieval is not widespread in LDCs.

2.3. Characteristics of financial markets in LDCs

A central theme of this chapter is that developing countries rely much more on informal mechanisms for credit and insurance than do developed countries. This is quite consonant with the comparative advantage of informal mechanisms for enforcing contract performance due, for example, to the lack of collateral. It is also consonant with the lack of institutions that can be used to overcome information problems and of informal institutions to overcome information problems (discussed in section 4.6 below). To get an idea of the importance of the informal credit sector, consider the figures from Ghate (1992). He presents evidence that two-fifths of rural credit in India and Thailand is from informal sources, one- to two-thirds in Bangladesh and more than two-thirds in the Philippines. Informal finance is prevalent in both rural or urban areas. It is also not a sector specific phenomenon; it is prevalent in the industrial sector, especially in funding working capital [see, for example, Cole and Park's (1983) account of Korea].

A consequence of the large role played by the informal sector in the provision of credit and insurance in developing countries is the large degree of market segmentation. One key dimension of this is geographic, e.g., lending is predominantly local. However, this is reduced as capital markets develop. Davis (1971) gives an illuminating account of the breakdown of geographic segmentation in the USA during the nineteenth century. Segmentation need not be solely geographic, however, and credit and insurance may be available only within certain kinship groups living in the same area.

Whether segmentation implies an inefficiency in the allocation of credit is moot. Suppose, for example, that there are two regions, one of which has experienced a drought and wishes to borrow money for consumption smoothing purposes. The result is variation in the shadow price of credit across the regions. Theoretically, there is then a gain from trade by transferring resources spatially and if we do not observe this happening, it is tempting to conclude that the market is operating inefficiently. However, as we discuss in the next section, a more subtle discussion is necessary recognizing that there may be good economic reasons, based on information imperfections and limited enforcement, why funds do not flow between groups who could apparently gain from trading with one another.

Substantial gains from extending the scope of financial intermediation (especially over space) arise because of the covariance among farmers' risks. Weather fluctuations and changes in commodity prices may affect a whole group of farmers in a particular location. This has important implications for thinking about segmented informal credit and insurance arrangements. It may imply that a large fraction of borrowers are unable to repay their loans at a point in time, thus threatening the integrity of the financial system. This would not be a problem if lenders were able to hold a portfolio of loans that are not highly correlated. However, this is often not the case. Such considerations underpin the possibility that there are increasing returns to scale from spatially diversified financial intermediation.[10]

---

[10] A number of interesting discussions of financial intermediation over space can be found in Townsend (1990).

2.4. *Efficiency in economies with missing and imperfect markets*

The above discussion raises the issue of how we might judge whether the system of credit and insurance in a particular economy is functioning well. Thus, this section investigates appropriate notions for deciding whether the economy is efficient. This sets the stage for our discussion of the role of government in regulating the financial sector that we cover in greater detail below. Of course, the fact that there is a considerable degree of inequity in resource allocation might also be the basis for government intervention and we shall return to this in due course.

A central proposition from neo-classical welfare economics tells us that a perfectly competitive equilibrium without externalities is Pareto efficient. Arrow and Debreu showed that this result continues to hold if risk is introduced so long as there is a complete set of markets for contingent claims. Once the latter assumption is relaxed, as seems reasonable in light of all of the reasons why there is difficulty in sustaining trades discussed above, one needs a more general notion of efficiency as a benchmark for the allocations achieved. The notion commonly used is *constrained* Pareto efficiency. An allocation is constrained Pareto efficient if there is no way to bring about a Pareto improvement given all feasibility and other constraints on implementing trades, such as ability to enforce outcomes and collect appropriate information about various parties. It is also important to consider the costs of actually setting up and operating some kinds of markets. This may be a partial explanation of the absence of futures exchanges in many developing countries. The high costs of running markets often reflects the high cost of communication in low-income economies.

Respecting information constraints is a serious issue and may significantly affect conclusions about efficiency. A good example is the argument that tariffs may be efficient when markets for insurance are incomplete. Eaton and Grossman (1985) argued that if insurance is unavailable, there may be a case for using tariffs to protect certain risk-prone industries. They assumed that markets were *exogenously* incomplete, i.e., they did not model the underlying features of the economy which result in market incompleteness. If the reasons for market incompleteness are moral hazard and adverse selection, then it can sometimes make a difference to model these phenomena explicitly in considering the case for government intervention. In this spirit, Dixit (1987) examined the case for tariffs as insurance when markets are limited by moral hazard and the incentive constraints due to moral hazard are explicitly modeled. He emphasized that in some cases there is no argument for intervention, the market is constrained Pareto efficient if the social planner is constrained by the same moral hazard incentive constraints as the private sector. This illustrates the importance of providing a level playing field between governments and the market in examining the case for government intervention. In considering what allocations can be achieved by a benevolent social planner, it is important to confront her with the same constraints faced by private traders unless there is a good reason to relax them.

Even when all constraints on transactions are recognized, we are not likely to find that markets are constrained efficient. This point is made forcefully by Greenwald and Stiglitz (1986), who show that economies with imperfect information almost always have important externalities that are not taken into account by existing institutions and which a social planner could conceivably have a comparative advantage in confronting. The following examples illustrate this idea in relevant contexts:

Example 1. Credit and insurance: Credit and insurance markets are linked in a number of ways. Individuals with insurance are potentially more likely to repay their loans since they face a lower probability of defaulting. This may imply a positive externality between the workings of credit and insurance markets.[11] There is also the possibility of negative externalities if individuals reduce their effort committed to projects once they are insured. This raises the possibility that some attempts by a government to oversee the externalities when deciding on a strategy for developing credit and insurance markets may be beneficial.

Example 2. Formal and informal credit markets: Externalities between formal and informal credit markets may also be important. Suppose that we parameterize individuals in terms of two characteristics, the quality of their investment opportunities and their *perceived* riskiness, and suppose that these are positively correlated. The formal sector will tend to exclude those who are perceived to be risky. If interest rates are set so that each risk class breaks even, then individuals will sort themselves into groups, those who use the formal and those who use the informal sector. Suppose furthermore that information about the borrower's project is known in the informal sector. Then individuals will select between the sectors. The question arises whether this division will be efficient. The answer is typically negative because the informal lenders do not take into account the effects that the terms they offer have on the equilibrium interest rates in the formal sector through the effect on the composition of formal sector borrowers. If the informal sector "takes" borrowers who have more efficient projects, then the formal sector works less efficiently, assuming that because of better access to diversification, it is better

---

[11] Private lenders, such as the Grameen Bank, who lend to groups have been able to internalize this kind of externality by requiring that groups create savings pools that function as insurance funds for the members. But banks that extend loans on a purely individualized basis are usually not well positioned to internalize this externality.

to have a larger formal sector. In this sense, informal markets can be dysfunctional.[12]

The upshot of this is there are good reasons to think that there may be externalities preventing efficient financial intermediation. There may also be sufficiently many parallel market failures to think that some kind of government action is warranted. However, the theoretical importance of using constrained efficiency in assessing the achievements of financial structures in developing countries, should be weighed against the fact that identifying such cases empirically is a very tall order. That is why the tests for first best efficiency discussed below are an interesting first step. The main value of constrained efficiency is to prevent naive policy conclusions based on how the world would look if information and enforcement problems were non-existent.

2.5. Government policy

Governments intervene to affect individuals' abilities and incentives to engage in intertemporal trade. Many aspects of tax/expenditure policies impact on this. There are, for example, explicit attempts to stabilize commodity markets, thereby reducing risk and the need by households to rely on savings and credit. We discuss such programs in greater detail below. Second, there is a host of interventions regulating the financial sector ranging from legislated state monopolies for banks to more standard regulations via disclosure laws and reserve requirements.

Policy towards capital markets in developing countries has, like so many other aspects of development policy, recently undergone a considerable amount of rethinking. In the state-managed development policies characteristic of the first three decades after the Second World War, the financial sector was regarded as a tool for manipulation by government. Thus credit programs were controlled as part of more general planning procedures. One pair of policies which together became known as the policies of *financial repression* [see, for example, McKinnon (1973)] was the use of interest rate ceilings for borrowers and depositors, coupled with selective allocation of credit to favored sectors. More recently, there has been a move towards financial liberalization, a movement that essentially advocates lifting many of the old controls.

An intermediate position based more directly on recent thinking in mainstream economics might be called the *market failure* view. From this perspective the government should justify all attempts to intervene in financial markets by clear reference to a market failure that is being confronted. One should also

---

[12] Arnott and Stiglitz (1991) have considered related arguments in the context of formal and informal insurance markets.

establish that the intervention will genuinely provide an improvement over the initial state of affairs. This is intermediate between the old *etatist* view that governments should intervene as an integral part of achieving the aims of planned development, and a view that government intervention should not attempt to influence market forces, a more overtly libertarian view. It is also important to weigh up the possibility of government failures, due either to bureaucratic efficiency or the possibility that programs can be captured and re-oriented by certain political groups. Whether the market failure perspective on policy will actually change policy in the long run is too early to predict, but it certainly suggests that many of the old policies that were symptomatic of financial repression can be given little economic justification.

3. Models of autarkic savings behavior under uncertainty

This section investigates savings in an autarkic world when individuals lack opportunities to diversify risk. The two categories of savings that are most relevant here are usually referred to as permanent income/life-cycle savings and precautionary savings, although there are likely to be important interactions between uncertainty and asset accumulation to which we will return in section 6 below. The models in this section are referred to as *autarkic* because trades among individuals are not modeled. Hence, we assume in this section that any positive return earned on assets in this section comes entirely from autarkic investment opportunities.

Pure permanent income/life-cycle savings are possible without uncertainty if individuals' income profiles are not coincident with their first best consumption profile.[13] With income uncertainty, a good deal of income smoothing can be motivated similarly if individuals' marginal valuations of consumption are declining, i.e., their utility functions are concave. It will then be optimal to put something aside out of windfall gains. *Precautionary* savings are relevant if the marginal utility of income function is both decreasing and convex. It can explain why an increase in income uncertainty increases savings. As we shall see shortly, the source of the convexity in the marginal utility of income function can be either tastes or constraints. In particular, future liquidity constraints can result in a convex marginal utility of income function so that individuals save more if income uncertainty increases.

The whole of this analysis can be set against the folk "wisdom" of some older contributions in development economics that poor people are

---

[13] With additive and concave preferences, this will be that path of consumption that keeps the current value of the marginal utility of income equal to the discounted expected future marginal utility of income.

spendthrifts and do not provide for any future contingencies. A typical view, expressed by Bauer and Paish (1952) concerns the behavior of risk-prone farmers: "Small producers are unlikely to have the self-restraint and foresight in good times to build sufficient reserves to cushion the effects of worse ones, or even if they have, may be debarred from doing so by social customs and obligations" (p. 766). Recent interest in savings behavior in LDCs has to a significant degree been motivated by researchers who reject this "wisdom" on a priori grounds.

There are broadly two approaches to the link between savings and income uncertainty, although operationally the distinction may be less important than is suggested here. The first looks for conditions on individuals' *preferences* which imply that increased income uncertainty increases savings. A complementary approach is to examine the impact on savings of *constraints* that individuals may face, chiefly if they are unable to borrow. We will investigate whether there is a positive link between savings and uncertainty induced by liquidity constraints.

In the model that we consider here, an individual earns a fixed rate of return on every unit of postponed consumption, i.e., the return to saving is not contingent on any risks that the individual faces. We will analyze three models: We begin with a two-period model with convex marginal utility of income. Then we consider a three-period model with liquidity constraints but quadratic preferences. Finally, we present a model with general preferences, liquidity constraints and infinite lifetimes.

3.1. A two-period model

The canonical savings model can be represented by individuals who live for two periods and have current wealth of y_1 with a stochastic future income y_2. There is only one asset which earns a gross return of r between the first and second period, and the discount factor is δ. The per period utility function is $u(\cdot)$ and is assumed to be strictly increasing and strictly concave. The choice of savings, denoted s, solves

$$\text{Max}_s \; \{u(y_1 - s) + \delta E\{u(y_2 + sr)\} | s \geq l) , \tag{3.1}$$

where $E\{\cdot\}$ denotes the expectations operator taken with respect to income. We impose a constraint that $s \geq l$ to represent the possibility of a limit on borrowing equal to l. The case where $l = 0$ is a situation where individuals have no access to outside funds. Let us denote the solution to (3.1) as s^*. One interesting question concerns how the choice of s relates to income uncertainty.[14] To answer this, suppose that we represent increased uncertainty by a mean preserving spread in the distribution of y_2. Then a well known result [Leland (1968)] says that $s*$ will be higher if $u'''(\cdot) > 0$, i.e., the marginal utility of income function is convex.[15] This gives us a link between uncertainty and saving; *greater uncertainty about future income increases current saving.* This has nothing to do per se with the borrowing constraint l. Even if there were no such constraint and $s* < 0$, i.e., it were optimal for an individual to borrow, it would still be true that desired dissaving would be less after a mean preserving spread in future income.

3.2. A three period model: the importance of liquidity constraints

We now investigate the importance of liquidity constraints on savings behavior. Suppose that an individual may face a future income shock and that she cannot borrow above some limit, then does *this* imply that she will save more today? To investigate this, we use a three-period model in which $u''' = 0$, so that Leland's argument does not apply.[16]

We parameterize the utility function as $u(y) = \alpha y - (\beta/2)y^2$. The distribution of income is assumed to be iid and to vary continuously on the bounded interval $[\underline{y}, \bar{y}]$ with cdf $G(y)$ and mean μ. Savings is now denoted s_i, where the subscript refers to the time period. Realized income levels, y_i, are also subscripted in this way. The problem solved by a representative individual is now

$$\underset{s_1,s_2}{\text{Max}} \{u(y_1 - s_1) + \delta E\{u(y_2 + s_1 r - s_2) + \delta^2 E\{u(y_3 + s_2 r)\}\}$$

subject to

$$s_1 \geq l, s_2 \geq l.$$

There is now a constraint on borrowing in both periods, which again is denoted by l. To solve the optimal savings problem we proceed recursively, solving

---

[14] The argument is easily generalized to cope with many different sources of risk, such as on the interest rate and future tastes. In a multi-period world (see below), it is increases in the riskiness of future consumption rather than income which matter.

[15] To see this, use the well known result [see Rothschild and Stiglitz (1970)] that $\int \psi(x) \, dF(x) \leq \int \psi(x) \, dG(x)$ for all $\psi(\cdot)$ increasing and convex if $F(x)$ dominates $G(x)$ in the sense of second order stochastic dominance. Moreover, a mean preserving spread is a special case of second order stochastic dominance. To apply this result, observe that the first order condition associated with (3.1) is $-u'(y_1 - s*) + E\{u'(y_2 + s*r)\}\delta r \geq 0$ (with equality if $s* > l$). Since $u'(\cdot)$ is convex, a mean preserving spread in y raises $E\{u'(y_2 + s*r)\}\delta r$ and given the second order condition, $s*$ must be no lower than before the change.

[16] If $l = -\infty$, then this is the standard permanent income model.

from period 2 backwards. In the second period, it is easy to show (assuming quadratic preferences) that we have the following first order condition for the choice of s_2:

$$-[\alpha - \beta(y_2 + s_1 r - s_2)] + \delta r[\alpha - \beta(\mu + s_2 r)] \geq 0, \tag{3.2}$$

with equality if $s_2 > l$. This defines a savings function, $s_2(y)$, whose form is:

$$s_2 = \begin{cases} \phi(y_2 - \hat{y}) & \text{for } y_2 - \hat{y} > l/\phi \\ l & \text{otherwise} \end{cases}, \tag{3.3}$$

where $\phi \equiv 1/(1 + \delta r^2)$ and $\hat{y} \equiv \alpha(1 - \delta r)/\beta + r\delta\mu - s_1 r.^{17}$ Thus in period two, an individual will save only if he has a high enough income draw. The implications of (3.3) for savings behavior are easiest to see for $l = 0$. In this case, there is a critical income level, $\hat{y}$, such that the individual will save a fraction $\phi(<1)$ of her income above that level. Below it, the borrowing constraint binds and the individual saves nothing. Equation (3.3) has only the mean of future income in it. Hence, *a change in the variance of future income has no effect on period 2 savings*, just as we would have predicted from the Leland model with quadratic preferences.

Moving back to the first period, the first order condition for the choice of s_1, given first period income y_1, is:

$$-[\alpha - \beta(y_1 - s_1)] + \delta r \left[\alpha - \beta(\mu + s_1 r) \right.$$

$$\left. + \beta \left\{ G\left(\frac{l}{\phi} + \hat{y}\right) l + \phi \int_{(l+\phi)+\hat{y}}^{\bar{y}} (y_2 - \hat{y}) \, dG(y_2) \right\} \right] \geq 0, \tag{3.4}$$

with equality if $s_1 > l$. We make two observations on (3.4). First, compared to the last period, we have an extra term affecting the incentive to save [the third term in (3.4)]. More significantly, this term depends upon properties of the distribution of y other than its mean. It is now interesting to ask whether a mean preserving spread in the distribution of future income raises savings, as in the Leland model above. To say that it does, we need only observe that the savings function described in (3.3) is convex on $[\underline{y}, \bar{y}]$. This is illustrated in Figure 36.1. We can then use the result in footnote 15, that a mean preserving spread in income raises the expected value of any convex function of income, to conclude that expected period-two savings increases as period-one income becomes more uncertain. Thus, the final term, and hence the whole expres-

---

[17] Note that the second order condition holds since $1 + \delta r^2 > 0$.

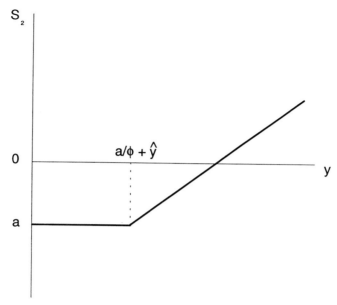

Figure 36.1.

sion, in (3.4) is increasing in income uncertainty implying that *saving (that is s_1) is positively related to uncertainty*. This is true even though we have assumed that $u''' = 0$.

A second observation on (3.4) is that period-two savings are increasing in l, the liquidity constraint, i.e., $\partial/\partial l\{G[(l/\phi) + \hat{y}]l + \phi\int_{(l/\phi)+\hat{y}}^{\bar{y}} (y - \hat{y}_2)\,dG(y_2)\} = G(l/\phi + \hat{y}) > 0$. This, in turn, increases period-one savings. This also squares with the idea that it is potential liquidity constraints that make saving worthwhile. Note also that as l becomes large and negative, then $\hat{y}$ tends to $\underline{y}$ and the extra term representing precautionary savings would depend only upon mean income as in (3.2).

There are two ways of understanding these results. First, one might observe that the marginal utility of income function in period 2 has a kink in it at $y = l/\phi + \hat{y}$. This makes the marginal utility of income convex, i.e., as if the third derivative of the utility function were positive just as in the Leland model. Second, one might consider the intuitive argument that there is a level of period 2 income such that for all incomes below this level, an individual would want to borrow. She is, however, prevented from doing so by the liquidity constraint. By saving more in period 1, it is less likely that an individual will encounter this constraint. Again, the potential of facing a liquidity constraint boosts the incentive to save.

3.3. An infinite horizon model

The issues discussed above have been explored in greater detail and sophistication in Deaton (1989, 1991). His investigations use an infinite horizon model.
The framework is as follows. Consider an individual with a single period utility
function $u(\cdot)$, that satisfies $u'(\cdot) >$, $u''(\cdot) < 0$ and $u'''(\cdot) \geq 0$. Thus lifetime utility
is

$$\sum_{t=0}^{\infty} \delta^t u(c_t) , \tag{3.5}$$

where c_t is consumption in period t. Assets, which we denote by A_t, evolve
according to the equation:

$$A_t = A_{t-1} r + y_t - c_t , \tag{3.6}$$

where we are explicitly assuming that there is a known, time invariant return
on assets. Equation (3.6) just says that current assets equals last period's
assets, multiplied by the gross interest rate, plus current savings. Given an
initial condition on assets (A_0), a transversality condition and a no Ponzi
scheme condition,[18] the solution to maximizing the expectation of (3.5) subject
to (3.6) can be characterized straightforwardly. In order to make the problem
more relevant for LDCs, Deaton imposes the further constraint that $A_t \geq 0$.
Hence, analogously to the analysis above, there is a liquidity constraint. He
also assumes that $\delta r < 1$. This implies that, without uncertainty, individuals
would not wish to save at all.

The maximization problem obtained under the liquidity constraint is a little
trickier to analyze. Since we have an infinite horizon, it makes sense to study
the stationary solutions to the problem, i.e., those where the optimal savings
policy depends only on cash on hand (current assets plus current income).
Formally, this can be expressed in the form of a policy function $c = h(A + y)$. It
is the absence of a time subscript on the function $h(\cdot)$ that is the essence of
stationarity. A stationary solution can be shown to exist for this model under
the assumptions laid out [see Deaton and Laroque (1992) for details]. The
optimal policy function can be derived from the solution to[19]:

$$u'(c_t) = \max\{u'(A_t + y_t), E_t\{\delta r u'(c_{t+1})\}\} , \tag{3.7}$$

where $E_t\{\cdot\}$ is the expectations operator taken over income at time t.[20]

---

[18] These are standard considerations in problems of this kind. See, for example, [Blanchard and
Fischer (1989)], Chapter 6.
[19] See Deaton (1990) pages 64–68 for details.
[20] The fact that expectations are time dependent represents the possibility of there being a
non-stationary income process.

Equation (3.7) says that this period's marginal utility of income is either that obtained from consuming all income and assets at time t $(A_t + y_t)$, or is equal to the expected, discounted marginal utility from consumption next period. The liquidity constraint binds when the first of these cases is relevant. Using (3.7), it can be shown that the consumption function (equivalently the savings function) has a kink in it around the zero asset point. If income is so low that individuals run their assets to zero (i.e., the liquidity constraint is binding), then individuals must just consume their incomes. Above this point, they save some fraction of their incomes, i.e., the marginal propensity to save lies between zero and one. Note that this resembles our finding in equation (3.3). Formally, the dynamic program solved here is known as a renewable problem; whenever the constraint $A_t \geq 0$ binds, the decision problem faced by a representative consumer begins anew.

Beyond this, analytical characterizations of the policy function and its implications are hard to discern. Deaton has, therefore, proposed computing solutions under various assumptions about preferences and the income process. Here, we present his results where $u'(c) = c^{-\rho}$ and income is identically and independently distributed in each period. Perhaps the main issue is whether an individual is able to obtain much insurance by saving according to the optimal policy function. This can be investigated by comparing the variability of income and consumption when the consumption path is chosen optimally. Figure 36.2

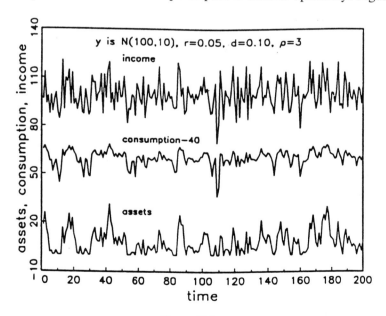

Figure 36.2.

is reproduced from Deaton (1991). It is notable from the figure how autarkic saving can cushion a significant number of the troughs in income, when it is optimal for the individual to "stock out", i.e., to spend all cash on hand. The drawback with autarkic saving is that it makes an individual immediately susceptible to further low income shocks. However with the income process being iid, this is less of an issue than with positive correlation in income. Deaton (1991) investigates other income processes, looking at whether positive correlation in income through time tends to reduce the effectiveness of autarkic solutions. He finds broadly that it does, since the strategy of stocking out occasionally looks much riskier if income shocks are correlated through time.

The latter, in particular, suggests that the kinds of savings schemes investigated here are probably best at handling shocks that are close to iid processes, rather than large persistent shocks such as a fire that damages an individual's tree crops. The model also ignores the possibility that the stock of savings may be in the form of productive assets. If I sell my land to get food this year, then this may reduce my ability to earn next period. Thus stocking out may have serious long run consequences even if I survive today. This again would tend to reduce the attractiveness of using dissaving as an insurance substitute.[21]

3.4. Empirical evidence

There is a huge literature that studies savings behavior. The aim here is not to provide a comprehensive review, but to highlight a few interesting studies. Any test of the savings behavior is limited by data availability; reliable savings data are typically difficult to obtain. Nonetheless, there are some important studies that try to test directly whether individuals save out of windfall income and use savings as an insurance substitute. The first type of study tests the permanent income model, rather than focusing directly on precautionary savings or borrowing constraints. Other studies have tried to test the Euler equation from intertemporal optimization by consumers, incorporating explicitly the possibility of liquidity constraints. Most such studies take the income process as given. A couple of recent studies have, however, looked at the links between portfolio choice and investment where consumers also care about income smoothing. We also review these here.

One strand of work, beginning with Wolpin (1982), uses weather data to separate permanent and transitory components of income. This allows the researcher to test whether, as theory would predict, there is greater saving out

---

[21] Rosenzweig and Wolpin's (1993) study of bullocks in India, discussed below, begins to get at some of these issues.

of transitory income.[22] The exposition of this idea here follows Paxson (1992)'s study of Thailand. She uses deviations of rainfall from their historical means for each region as a correlate of the transitory income shock experienced by a household. Thus she estimates a savings equation of the form:

$$S_{irt} = \gamma_t + \gamma_{or} + X_{irt}^P \gamma_1 + X_{rt}^T \gamma_2 + v_{irt} ,$$
(3.8)

to explain savings of household i in region r at time t, X_{irt}^P is a vector of characteristics of household i in region r at time t that are determinants of permanent income, such as amount of land owned. X_t is a set of region-specific variables that affect transitory income, in this instance deviations from average values of regional rainfall in each of four seasons. The variable γ_{or} is a region specific effect. To test whether there is saving from transitory income, one can focus on the coefficient γ_2. It reflects two things — the extent to which income shocks are transitory, and the marginal propensity to save out of transitory income. To get a measure of the former, one can estimate an equation of the form

$$Y_{irt} = \beta_t + \beta_{or} + X_{irt}^P \beta_1 + X_{rt}^T \beta_2 + \varepsilon_{irt} ,$$
(3.9)

where Y_{irt} is a measure of household income. Thus γ_2/β_2 is a measure of the marginal propensity to save out of transitory income. She finds that estimated propensities out of transitory income for rice farmers in Thailand range between 0.73 and 0.83. In the process of deriving these, she also deals with issues of measurement error which should concern any researcher dealing with income data from farmers in LDCs.

Bevan, Collier and Gunning (1989) have examined the evidence on saving after the Kenyan coffee boom in the late 1970s brought on by a frost in Brazil. This is a significant idiosyncratic event that individuals should have realized was transitory. They claim to find savings rates of close to 65 percent out of transitory income in this instance, which again is evidence consistent with the view that small farmers are forward looking.

Morduch (1990), who uses the ICRISAT data from southern India, studies consumption behavior exploiting information about credit explicitly. This begins to address some of the questions concerning the link between savings and liquidity constraints discussed above. He also considers a model in which households make both production and consumption decisions. His approach, which essentially follows Zeldes (1989), is to estimate an Euler equation for an optimally chosen intertemporal consumption path. With $u(\cdot)$ as usual denoting

---

[22] For other empirical implementations of the permanent income model of developing country data, see Bhalla (1979), (1980).

the utility function, A_{ht} being total assets of household h, δ the discount factor, and r the interest rate, he sets out to estimate the following model of consumption

$$u'(c_{ht}) = E_t\{\delta ru'(c_{ht+1})\} + \lambda_{ht}, \quad \text{with } A_{ht} - c_{ht} \geq 0 \text{ if and only if } \lambda_{ht} = 0.$$

The interpretation of λ_{ht} is as a Lagrange multiplier that is positive only if the constraint that assets be non-negative binds. Morduch divides the population into those whom he suspects might be liquidity constrained on a priori grounds, such as those with small amounts of land, and those whom he suspects not to be so constrained. His approach involves parameterizing the utility function with constant relative risk aversion and then deriving an equation for $\log\{c_{ht+1}/c_{ht}\}$. The test for liquidity constraints is whether the log of current income is significant in explaining $\log\{c_{ht+1}/c_{ht}\}$. He finds some evidence for this indicating that liquidity constraints could be important in these data. He also tests whether those farmers who appear to be liquidity constrained are those who also appear to be engaging in risk-averting behavior. In favor of this, he finds that there is a greater crop diversification among the farmers who appear to be liquidity constrained.

The value of this methodology, i.e., using the consumer's Euler equation to characterize liquidity constrained behavior, has been questioned in Deaton (1992c, chapter 6). First, there is an issue of how the approach relates to the results developed in Deaton (1989) which solves for the globally optimal consumption function under liquidity constraints, rather than using Euler equations. Deaton (1989, 1991) finds that consumption patterns are quite different with liquidity constraints than without, even though cases where the liquidity constraint actually binds [$\lambda_{ht} > 0$ in (3.10)] are very rare. Thus solutions to (3.10) may be misleading. Deaton (1992c) has also observed that it is possible to get results which are quite similar to those exhibited by estimating (3.10) without liquidity constraints, by allowing for precautionary savings.

Most models of savings behavior make the strong assumption that the income process is given. Yet individuals have many ways of affecting the riskiness of their income stream, e.g., via choice of a crop portfolio or investments in irrigation. Morduch's study, cited above, does look at the effect of liquidity constraints on production behavior in his work. A significant step in integrating production decisions with risk choices is also taken in Rosenzweig and Binswanger (1993). They estimate how weather risk affects a farmer's choice of investments using the ICRISAT panel data. Their work supports the hypothesis that the composition of asset portfolios is influenced significantly by the degree of rainfall variability. They find that the *timing* of rainfall, in particular the monsoon, has a significant effect on crop profits. They estimate the effect of the variance of the monsoon date on different investments, finding significant effects.

Rosenzweig and Wolpin (1993) also tries to integrate production choices with uncertainty and consumption smoothing motives. They build a structural dynamic model to investigate whether bullocks serve a role in consumption smoothing. In doing so, they recognize that non-cash savings may be important in an LDC context. In their model, bullocks are productive as well as providing a means of consumption smoothing. Thus an individual who is thinking of selling a bullock must weigh up the loss of future income if he sells a bullock in addition to the concerns about managing his stock of assets that we modeled above.[23] They estimate a model that allows explicitly for concerns about the future in buying and selling bullocks in response to shocks, finding evidence that bullock transactions are motivated by consumption smoothing goals.

3.5. Uncharted territory

There are still many questions concerning savings and uncertainty that have not been addressed in the literature to date, in spite of the recent increase in interest. I will conclude this section by outlining a few of them.

All savings in the models discussed so far are in the form of cash or interest-earning demand deposits. Conceptually speaking, nothing precludes other assets, even some with negative rates of return. However, the model is not particularly realistic and does not do justice to the rich array of assets that are accumulated in practice, many of which have uncertain returns. Ideally, one would like to further integrate savings models with models of portfolio choice in order to reflect these concerns.

While cash savings have the advantage of fungibility, their returns tend to be poorly indexed to some prices that matter, such as those of staple foods. Hence, some saving in the form of grain stocks is often worthwhile even if there is some spoilage through time and the expected return is negative. Other important forms of asset accumulation in poor countries are jewelry, land and livestock. To model the accumulation of these assets satisfactorily, however, one would need to supplement the savings model with one of equilibrium in the market for such assets. Thus if risks are covariant, land may function badly as an insurance device since the price of land will tend to be low when most individuals want to sell it. Rosenzweig and Wolpin (1993), discussed above, is one of the few studies that takes such issues seriously. Unfortunately, there are not yet any studies that have integrated different sources of saving. Future work in this area will likely begin to address the links between markets for fixed assets and the availability of credit and insurance. This will probably

---

[23] Formally, this would be like allowing the distribution of future incomes to depend upon the stock of assets owned.

require taking a more sophisticated approach to asset market equilibrium than in the savings literature to date.

A second issue for future work concerns the fact that we know very little about how individuals' savings respond differently according to the persistence of the income shock that they experience. There is much scope for more work that looks at the effect on such things as permanent disablement and/or fires and floods that wipe out significant amounts of a household's productive capital. The theoretical models that we discussed above suggested that use of savings as a buffer against risk is likely to be most effective for income fluctuations that display relatively little persistence and it would be good to have more empirical evidence on this.

A third issue, not addressed in the literature to date, concerns constraints on savings opportunities. In defense of Bauer and Paish (1952), their quotation above spoke of social constraints on savings. In understanding the social context of savings in LDCs this is certainly a factor worth considering. A good example to illustrate this is the Susu men who operate in African markets to "safeguard" the savings of market women. A frequently heard rationale for the existence of this institution is that there are difficulties for those who have a stock of liquid assets in resisting the claims of their friends and relatives (or even spouses). This reflects the social organization of societies in which mutual assistance is an important ethic. A similar difficulty may arise for governments who try to save when they have to resist political claims. This influence on savings behavior in developing countries deserves to be taken more seriously than it has to date. There may actually be some *illiquidity* preference on the part of savers in order to resist the claims of others.

4. Credit and insurance

The above models of savings behavior study individuals apart from their interactions with other individuals in markets or other trading institutions. While neglecting some types of credit and insurance markets might be defended based on their limited importance in credit and insurance provision for large segments of the population in LDCs, ignoring institutions altogether cannot. The aim of this section is therefore to initiate a discussion of credit and insurance institutions, and the way in which they exploit gains from trade. The following simple example is intended to motivate some of the ideas developed below.

Consider a world populated by just two individuals, denoted A and B, who live for two periods and have uncertain incomes. Each individual is assumed to have identical tastes and expected incomes. However, in each period each receives an income draw that may differ between the individuals. We assume, furthermore, that each individual expects the same mean income next period. We consider the possibility that individual A can make a transfer to individual B denoted by θ. This involves a "repayment" in period 2 of R. Thus period 1 expected utilities, after period one incomes are realized, are

$$V_A(\theta, R) = u(y_A - \theta) + \delta E\{u(Y + R)\}$$

and

$$V_B(\theta, R) = u(y_B + \theta) + \delta E\{u(Y - R)\}, \tag{4.1}$$

where $u(\cdot)$ is an increasing, concave utility function and $E\{\cdot\}$ is the expectations operator. We are interested in the case where there exists a contract $\{\theta, R\}$ to which both individuals agree. To investigate this, consider each individual's offer curve, denoted $\theta_i(R, y_i)$ for $i = A, B$. These are illustrated in Figure 36.3 for the case where $y_A > y_B$ so that individual A is willing to make a transfer to individual B. The shaded area gives the set of contracts that yield

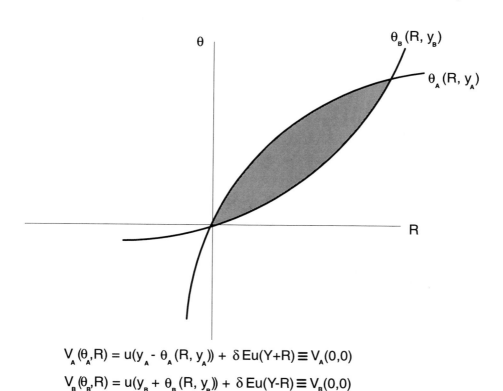

$$V_A(\theta_A, R) = u(y_A - \theta_A(R, y_A)) + \delta Eu(Y+R) \equiv V_A(0,0)$$

$$V_B(\theta_B, R) = u(y_B + \theta_B(R, y_B)) + \delta Eu(Y-R) \equiv V_B(0,0)$$

Figure 36.3.

Pareto improvements over autarky. Note that with $y_A < y_B$, the shaded interval would be in the bottom left hand corner of the diagram. Only in the case where $y_A = y_B$ would there be no region in which a $\{\theta, R\}$ contract could be reached.

This example illustrates how two risk averse individuals can potentially strike a deal that dominates autarky. The contract was deliberately set up to look like a credit contract. However, as we discuss below, there are more general possibilities that could be considered where the insurance element is clearer.

4.1. Efficient risk sharing: theory and tests

At the opposite extreme from an autarkic model is the Arrow–Debreu paradigm of perfect and complete insurance. The starting point for this model is the observation that all of the ideas of competitive equilibrium can be extended to economies with uncertainty by imagining that a whole array of contingent commodities is available; these are commodities whose returns are indexed to the state of nature. The existence of markets for a complete set of contingent commodities preserves the link between perfect planning and the market allocation. Moreover, any efficient allocation of the economy can be supported by redistribution of its endowments under suitable convexity assumptions.

The Arrow–Debreu picture is far removed from casual empirical analysis of the economies of LDCs. Most individuals face few opportunities, in markets at least, to buy securities whose returns are indexed to anything significant. This will be particularly apparent in our discussion of formal insurance possibilities in LDCs below. Even most basic forms of insurance, e.g., for fire or theft, taken for granted in developed countries, are absent in LDCs. Thus the paradigm of efficient risk sharing would hardly seem worthy of mention in any study of risk sharing in LDCs. However, a recent literature has sparked renewed interest. While it seems highly implausible to suggest that economies should result in fully efficient allocations of risk, given the absence of markets and/or perfect planning, it may not appear to be such a bad characterization of village economies, where there appear to be relatively rich opportunities at a village level for making state-contingent transfers and/or trades.

While nobody has actually suggested that full efficiency might be achieved, a large number of anthropological and more informal economic studies have suggested that institutions exist to pool and share risk in developing countries [see Platteau (1991)]. The idea that village economies are efficient at risk sharing cannot, however, be taken to represent the idea that there is literally a complete set of contingent commodities. Rather the aim is to test how close observed institutions might come to yielding an efficient outcome.

Our next task is to discuss some recent studies of complete risk sharing using consumption data suggested by Townsend (1991), and also the basis of work on US data by Altonji et al. (1992), Hayashi et al. (1991), Cochrane (1991) and Mace (1991). The basic idea is as follows.[24] Suppose that consumption decisions are made by a benevolent social planner whose objective is to efficiently allocate consumption across H households at each date over some horizon $t = 1, \ldots, T$. Household h's per-period utility function depends upon its consumption at time t, c_{ht}, and on its (possibly random) characteristics at date t, denoted by ε_{ht}. Thus $u_{ht} = u(c_{ht}, \epsilon_{ht})$, which is assumed to be increasing and concave in its first argument. The lifetime utility function is assumed to be additively separable through time and across states (represented by possible values of ε_{ht}). Thus, defining $c_h \equiv (c_{h1}, \ldots, c_{hT})$, we have

$$V_h(c_h) = E\left\{ \sum_{t=1}^{T} \delta^t u(c_{ht}, \varepsilon_{ht}) \right\},$$

(4.2)

where $E\{\cdot\}$ denotes the expectations operator taken with respect to ε_{ht}, and other things that determine consumption, such as income. At each date, each individual earns a (stochastic) income y_{ht}. We use $Y_t = \sum_{h=1}^{H} y_{th}$ to denote aggregate income. We will suppose that all shocks are visible to the planner who is able to index consumption on any shocks that take place. We will simplify the problem by supposing that the planner does not save or borrow, i.e., all resources generated in any period must be consumed in that period. An efficient consumption vector, $\{c_{th}\}_{h=1}^{H}$, solves the following problem, for some vector $(V_2, \ldots, V_H)$:

$$\underset{\{c_{th}\}_{h=1}^{H}}{\text{Max}} \ V_1(c_1)$$

$$\text{subject to: } V_h(c_h) \geq V_h, \quad \text{for } h = 2, \ldots, H$$

$$\text{and } \sum_{h=1}^{H} c_{th} = Y_t,$$

(4.3)

where Y_t is the total stock of resources on hand at date t (which may be a random variable). This is the standard characterization of Pareto efficiency [see, for example, Varian (1992) page 330] which says that we maximize utility of one individual subject to constraints on the utility levels of all others and resource constraints. The latter says that the first order condition for the choice of c_{th} is

$$\partial u_h(c_{th}, \varepsilon_{th})/\partial c_{th} = \lambda_t/\theta_h, \quad \text{for all } t = 1, \ldots, T \ \& \ h = 1, \ldots, H.$$

(4.4)

---

[24] See Townsend (1991) for a more detailed account of this. He, for example, allows income to be generated by labor allocation decisions. The results of the case that we develop are robust in the face of this provided that preferences between consumption and leisure are additively separable.

where λ_t is the multiplier on the aggregate resource constraint at time t and θ_h is the multiplier on the expected utility constraint for household h. Equation (4.4) immediately reveals a feature of the optimum, *that individual income is irrelevant to the determination of individual consumption conditional on* λ_t. All that matters in determining c_{th} is the aggregate consumption and shocks ε_{th}. To see this, note that (4.4) enables us to write $c_{th} = f(\lambda_t/\theta_h, \varepsilon_{th})$. Now using the resource constraint, we have $\Sigma_{h=1}^{H} f(\lambda_t/\theta_h, \varepsilon_{th}) = Y_t$. This can be used to solve for λ_t. But it is clear that λ_t depends only on Y_t, not on the individual y's, thus proving the result.

The essence of Townsend's empirical test for efficiency is that individual consumption should depend only on Y_t and *not* y_{ht}. This is a general result. However, since θ_h and ε_{ht} also enter the picture, more work is necessary to get something that can tractably be estimated. Specifically, Townsend makes the further simplifying assumption that household preferences fall into one of two classes: constant absolute or constant relative risk aversion. Consider the first of these cases, where $u(c_{ht}, \varepsilon_{ht}) = -\exp[-A\{c_{ht} - \varepsilon_{ht}\}]$, so that if ε_{ht} is a scalar, then

$$c_{ht} = y_t + (\varepsilon_{ht} - \bar{\varepsilon}_t) + \psi_h , \qquad (4.5)$$

where $y_t = Y_t/H$, $\bar{\varepsilon}_t \equiv \Sigma_{j=1}^{H} \varepsilon_{jt}/H$, $\psi_h \equiv 1/A\{ln(\theta_h) - \Sigma_{j=1}^{H} ln(\theta_j)/H\}$. Thus consumption depends upon mean income in the group of households,[25] how household characteristics differ from the mean of the group and a time-invariant household shift variable which sums to zero across the group and can be thought of as a measure of the aggregate lifetime resources available to the household. An implication of the full insurance hypothesis is that if we were to put *individual* income into an equation like (4.5), then we would not expect to find it being significant. More specifically if we were to estimate:

$$c_{ht} = \alpha_h + \beta y_t + \gamma y_{ht} + \delta z_{ht} + \eta_{ht} \qquad (4.6)$$

for some vector of household characteristics z_{ht}, then we should find that $\beta = 1$ and $\gamma = 0$.

Tests along these lines have been performed by Townsend on household level survey data for three villages in the ICRISAT panel for southern India.[26] His specific goal is to test whether there appears to be perfect within village sharing of income. Thus households are grouped into villages and he uses the test of whether mean village income/consumption explains individual con-

---

[25] Relaxing the assumption that there is no saving in the aggregate would suggest putting aggregate consumption rather than income here. In fact this is what is done in empirical applications of the model.
[26] He puts the mean of consumption of households other than h on the right hand side to proxy for y_t.

sumption. He uses a fixed effect for ψ_h and other variables in the data set to control for ε_{ht}. Townsend finds that own incomes matter statistically for own consumption so that the hypothesis of complete markets is rejected. However, "the effect of (own) incomes on consumptions is not high" (p. 36). Mace (1991) performs a similar test for US data, as does Cochrane (1991). The first of these studies is supportive of efficiency while Cochrane finds that ill-health and job loss appear not to be efficiently insured against.

Given the rejection of efficiency, it is tempting to move on to other things immediately. However, there are certain questions about the methodology of testing for full insurance as suggested here that bear mention. In particular, there is the issue of measurement error. Alderman and Paxson (1992) point to two effects that may work in opposite directions. If risk is not fully pooled, and if household income is measured with error, then estimates of γ in (4.6) will suffer from attenuation bias, which biases γ towards zero. The second source of error arises from remembering that farm households typically produce for own consumption in a way that it is difficult for even the most carefully collected household data to measure accurately. This implies that both income and consumption are mismeasured and may induce a spurious positive correlation between them. This will then tend to bias γ upwards. The overall direction of bias is thus uncertain a priori.[27] Apart from the issue of measurement error, there is the question of whether the type of test performed by Townsend and others has any power against the alternative hypothesis that individuals are saving autarkically. If the latter provided quite good protection against income risk, then it would also imply a weak relation between own income and consumption. Moreover, an individual's income could appear significantly related to village income if individuals within a village face covariant risk. Such issues are currently under investigation.

Townsend's tests of efficiency are important because they take significant theoretical ideas to the data and attempt to test them. The findings that they seek, that institutions exist that can provide for efficient risk sharing in village economies, do not square well with theoretical expectations or the anthropological evidence. It is therefore comforting to find that efficiency is rejected by most tests.

A slightly different test for within village risk sharing is suggested and implemented by Deaton (1992a) on data from the Côte D'Ivoire. He supposes that households' consumptions in village v depend in part on their own income y_{hvt} and on some measure of aggregate per capita village resources y_{vt}. Deaton uses the following equation to explain households' consumption:

$$c_{hvt} = \beta y_{hvt} + (1 - \beta)y_{vt} + \eta_{hvt}, \tag{4.7}$$

---

[27] In more recent work, Townsend has experimented with some different ways of dealing with measurement error, finding little change in his results.

where β characterizes the "sharing rule" that the village uses. One way to proceed is via estimating (4.7) directly. But that would raise many of the issues that we discussed in the context of Townsend's work above. Instead Deaton proposes estimating the relationship between consumption and income with and without village dummies, which is a way of providing a proxy for aggregate consumption. If there were significant within-village risk sharing, then putting in the dummies, which proxy for y_{vt} should *reduce* the sensitivity of consumption to own income. This also serves as a test of partial risk sharing at a village level. Deaton is also careful to deal with the correlated measurement error that might arise because much consumption for poor farm households comes from own production. Even so, his empirical evidence is mixed, finding some evidence of risk sharing for some villages but not all.[28]

These ideas have been taken further on the same data set by Grimard (1992). He follows the anthropological literature on Côte d'Ivoire to suggest that risk sharing could be important across ethnic lines, rather than geographically as suggested by using village dummies. By putting in ethnic dummies instead, he finds evidence in favor of a partial insurance function being served by ethnic groups.

Using consumption data to test for efficient risk sharing has become a cottage industry and deserves to be taken seriously. It is also a natural direction away from autarkic savings models in light of the considerable anthropological evidence that such informal risk sharing schemes are important. It seems likely, however, that future work will focus more directly on the partial insurance available for specific risk sharing schemes rather than trying to test for efficiency. We will review evidence on particular risk sharing schemes in section 4.4.

4.2. Formal insurance

There are enough examples of formal insurance schemes in LDCs to make discussion of them relevant. Working examples will also help the reader to appreciate the kinds of practical difficulties that have been faced in getting insurance arrangements to function in LDCs. Insurance markets are explicit attempts to trade in risks. An individual with ability to diversify risk typically offers to buy another individual's risks at a premium. It is this difference in attitudes towards risks (perhaps driven by differences in ability to bear risk) that generates beneficial gains from trade.

---

[28] This is, of course consistent with the idea that village level variation in village organizations is important. Although from a different context, Townsend (1992)'s study of Thailand finds considerable differences in the kinds of risk sharing institutions found in different villages.

The presence of significant risk in agricultural production has made the design and performance of insurance possibilities in LDCs an issue of key concern. Especially significant is the idea that there could be inefficiencies in private markets and non-market arrangements and thus scope for beneficial government intervention. The latter focus is especially appropriate in light of the fact that most attempts at providing formal insurance arrangements in developing countries have involved some direct government involvement.

Most insurance schemes that have been attempted in LDCs are partial; they either cover particular types of risks, e.g., price fluctuations in certain crops, or else are only effective under extreme conditions, e.g., drought, fire or flood. We begin this section with a brief discussion of the theory of demand for partial insurance against risks. Our next step is to review the types of insurance arrangements observed in LDCs and practical experience with them.

A formal insurance contract can be thought of as a security that offers an indexed return in exchange for a fee (the premium), the variables on which the indexation takes place and the nature of this dependence being specified in the contract.

Example 1: Crop insurance: pays a farmer according to how much the yield on a particular crop (or set of crops) falls below some level. Such schemes may be contributory, i.e., rely on farmer premia to finance them, or else be provided from government funds.

Example 2: Commodity price stabilization: smooths out the price profile faced by a farmer for the commodity in question. This is effectively an insurance scheme that is indexed to the price of the commodity.

Example 3: Health insurance: typically pays a sum of money indexed to an individual's consumption of medical care.

The theory of complete income insurance is simple and well understood [see Arrow (1963)]. Any individual who is risk averse will wish to purchase complete actuarially fair protection against income risk above some deductible limit. This is one of the most fundamental results in the theory of insurance, yet is of limited applicability when studying the kinds of insurance schemes that actually operate in developing countries. For these one needs to appeal to the generalizations that are necessary to study situations in which income insurance is not the issue and/or there is some background risk.

The basic results for such situations go somewhat against the view that pure risk aversion is enough to characterize the demand for insurance. Consider the following scenario. An individual faces two sources of income uncertainty. Concretely, these can be thought of as the price and quantity of a crop that she

T. Besley

grows, or amounts of income from two different crops grown on different parcels of land. Then suppose that insurance for one of these risks is available, e.g., price variability is reduced or else it is possible to reduce the income fluctuation due to yield variation in one of the crops. Then, under what conditions will an individual wish to purchase this kind of partial insurance? The simple answer is that risk aversion is insufficient to characterize the demand for partial insurance in this way. The reason is that it is *income* risk that matters and partial insurance of some component of income may not serve the ultimate objective of lowering income risk. Either some stronger characterization of risk aversion [see, for example, Ross (1981), or Kihlstrom, Romer and Williams (1981)] or else some restriction on the structure of asset returns, e.g., the covariance between the two sources of risk, is needed to generate an unambiguous demand for partial insurance.

The latter is seen most easily in the following example. Suppose that a farmer grows two types of crops with perfectly negatively correlated returns, which also have the same mean. Then if he sows half of his land to each crop, he faces no income risk. It is then clear that actuarially fair insurance on the return to one of the crops *increases* the riskiness of his income and is undesirable. This example is simple and extreme, but illustrates the central point in dealing with partial insurance with many sources of risk.

That assumptions on preferences may also be necessary to generate a demand for partial insurance can be seen by thinking of the case where an individual's income is made up of two components that are independently distributed, i.e., $y = x + w$. The means are denoted by capitals (Y, X, W). Suppose that an individual is able to insure the variability generated by x but not w. Then we are interested in cases where

$$E_w v(w + X) > E_{X,w} v(w + x),\qquad(4.8)$$

where $v(\cdot)$ is increasing and concave. Kihlstrom, Romer and Williams (1981) show that this is the case if we make the assumption that $v(\cdot)$ displays decreasing absolute risk aversion and w and x are independent.

The issues just discussed are of more than academic interest given that the kinds of insurance schemes that are typically suggested for LDCs are partial in nature, e.g., insurance of yields on particular crops and/or price insurance schemes. The value of such schemes is dependent on the extent of the demand for insurance, an issue that will depend upon the concerns raised above.

A large portion of the recent literature on insurance concerns the implications of information problems for the performance of contracts, given that individuals differ in the extent to which they face risk (*adverse selection*) and their private behavior may change once they are insured (*moral hazard*). Both pose threats to the effective implementation of insurance contracts and are often cited as the Achilles heels of attempts to provide large-scale insurance services in developing countries. The existence of moral hazard and adverse selection problems motivates the fact that insurance will be incomplete. Agents must be faced with residual risk in order to preserve incentives to take effort that reduces the prospects of having to draw on insurance support [see Mirrlees (1976) and Holmstrom (1979) for standard treatments of this issue]. It will also be necessary to structure insurance contracts so that different risk classes self-select into different insurance groups [see Stiglitz (1977) for an analysis of this]. A typical result from this literature is that the less risk-prone individuals end up with less insurance, but pay a lower premium. A vast literature has developed that discusses these issues in detail and this is not the place to offer a complete review. The interested reader is referred to Laffont (1989) for further discussion. Below we will consider whether failure to account for information problems can account for the poor performance of some kinds of insurance arrangements in practice.

Practical experience with insurance is reasonably widespread in LDCs although there have been relatively few attempts to study it systematically. We will discuss three main types of insurance: crop insurance in developed and developing countries; price insurance via commodity price stabilization schemes; and health insurance.

4.2.1. Crop insurance

The scope of crop insurance schemes provided in LDCs has been quite varied. At one extreme are attempts to insure only when there are severe life-threatening events such as droughts or floods. At the other, are schemes designed to deal with year-to-year and day-to-day fluctuations in individuals' incomes. It should be noted that very often attempts at providing insurance in predominantly agricultural areas of LDCs are not easily separable from other kinds of intervention. A case in point is schemes more explicitly aimed at income maintenance. Thus rural public works[29] projects that may play an important role in providing income support for the long term poor may also provide an important insurance function in helping the temporarily poor. Indeed, for dealing with idiosyncratic shocks to farm incomes, little modification is needed to such schemes in their insurance mode as in their more general income support mode. For more general region-wide shocks, the insurance function of rural public works would be enhanced were the availabili-

---

[29] These are discussed in Ravallion (1991), Dreze and Sen (1992). For a formal model and some discussion in relation to historical and contemporary debates about welfare reform, see Besley and Coate (1992). For an analysis of rural works with an applied general equilibrium model for India, see Narayana et al. (1991).

ty of employment in such settings tied to the performance of the regional economy.

More explicit crop insurance schemes are also observed. These can involve insuring many different aspects of farm incomes. Crop insurance schemes are most often targeted at insuring *yields* on specified crops. The magnitude of administrative work involved in doing this should not be underestimated and some regard this as a major impediment to developing such schemes in LDCs. In general the performance of publicly provided crop insurance has not been impressive, in part because political expediency rather than principles of insurance have been allowed to dictate the mode of operation. Successful operation of self-financing crop insurance has tended to coincide with schemes that are restricted to narrowly defined perils for specific crops with compulsory enrollment to avoid adverse selection. A good example is the Mauritius Sugar Insurance Fund (MSIF), in operation since 1947, which insures only against windstorm, fire and excessive rain [see Roberts and Dick (1991)]. Those schemes that have focused on yield insurance, as in India or the Philippines, have tended to need significant subsidies to survive.[30]

When crop insurance was introduced in the U.S., there was an attempt to use previous years' farm yields to create a reasonable measure of "normal" yield used as the basis of insurance. Even with this level of sophistication, early crop insurance schemes had only limited success and ultimately required significant levels of government subsidies to keep going [see Gardner and Kramer (1986)]. In the U.S. only a fifth of farmers are covered by crop insurance schemes but the level of subsidy is considerable: the cost is estimated at $1.40 for every premium dollar. The total cost to the government, including administrative costs and subsidies, between 1981 and 1986 amounted to $20 per hectare insured [see FCIC (1986)].

The reasons for the poor performance of crop insurance involve failures of both supply and demand. Since crop insurance is available only to cover limited risks and neglects other kinds of more significant risks such as price, the demand for it may be rather meager. Along these lines, it might also be argued that individuals may already have enough insurance coverage through other means, e.g., precautionary savings and informal insurance, so that yield risk insurance is not very valuable. A third argument suggests that private insurance for certain risk is unavailable precisely *because* the government is unable to commit not to provide certain kinds of insurance. Thus, farmers know that if there is a drought or flood, then the government will step in to help them out. Insurance provided by private companies to supplement this guaranteed catastrophic insurance may then have relatively little value.

---

[30] Indian crop insurance arrangements have been intimately tied to insuring loan repayment especially of cooperatives; see Dandekar (1976) and Prabhu and Ramachandram (1986).

Problems with crop insurance may also be on the supply side. Binswanger (1986) blames the problems of moral hazard and adverse selection: the monitoring needed to overcome the information problems in crop insurance is prohibitively expensive. In support of this Binswanger notes that one of the few successful examples of privately provided crop insurance is for hail damage to fruit, an easily monitored condition.

A further important variant of crop insurance is loan guarantee insurance in rural areas. Under such schemes, the government insures either the loan portfolios of agricultural development banks or else insures the farmer's ability to repay loans. For example, Mexico's BANRURAL compulsorily insured all loans with ANAGSA, a government owned insurer. The incentive effects of such schemes have made such activities very costly to the government and, in particular, have undermined banks' incentives to sanction delinquent borrowers.

One important empirical issue with crop insurance, which seems not yet to be properly understood, is its general equilibrium implications. The focus of standard insurance concerns is on the individuals who actually buy the insurance and the benefits that they receive. Yet landless agricultural laborers are part of the group affected by insurance, for example, if their wages and how they respond to fluctuations in the environment is changed. It seems important to understand such market-mediated links in properly evaluating the costs and benefits of crop insurance and the social benefits of subsidies to it.

4.2.2. Commodity price stabilization

Providing ways of reducing the price risk faced by farmers has been an issue of long standing concern and has spawned a large number of proposals for insurance schemes. Typical scenarios have been schemes set up and run by governments. However there have also been grander proposals, e.g., by UNCTAD in the 1970s, that have considered commodity price stabilization on a world scale.[31]

In terms of the framework discussed above, note that price insurance is partial, only insuring one dimension of the many risks to which farm households are subject. This may devalue proposals to stabilize commodity prices right away. Imagine, for example, that an individual faces price and quantity risk and that outputs are correlated across individual producers. Selling to a market will bring a kind of insurance with it: the price will fall when outputs are high, and will rise when outputs are low. This is desirable, in

---

[31] It was this proposal which spawned the leading book in the field by Newbery and Stiglitz (1981). The interested reader is referred there for much interesting material related to this chapter at a general level as well as of commodity price stabilization in particular.

an insurance sense, since it smooths fluctuations in an individual's income. If the government acts to stabilize the commodity price, then the farmer no longer has insurance via the market and it is possible that his income risk could actually be *increased*.

Thinking about such examples also reinforces the idea that a preferred solution to stabilizing prices is to allow farmers to choose their own level of price insurance. One way of doing this is by allowing trade in futures markets [see, for example, Newbery and Stiglitz (1981), chapter 13] . Such markets do exist in a number of LDCs but are relatively rare and, for good reasons such as high transactions costs, are not accessible to many farmers.[32] In addition, they require some background infrastructure to function. The possibility of building futures markets is, however, an important caveat to some of what follows.

We will consider a commodity price stabilization scheme run by the government. The model developed here is based on Mirrlees (1988). Suppose that producers face some risk from production and price risk from selling to the world market. Production is represented by a variable x and output is θx, where θ is a random variable with a mean of one. The cost of undertaking activity x is denoted by $c(x)$, which is assumed to be increasing and convex. The commodity price is q. Hence, the producer's problem is

$$\underset{x}{\text{Max }} E\{u(q\theta x - c(x))\} . \tag{4.9}$$

A number of timing assumptions are possible. Mirrlees supposes that q is announced and known to the farmer at the time of planting. We will not assume this here. A pricing policy for the government is described by a function $\psi(p)$ where p is the world price. Hence $q = \psi(p)$. Assuming that it buys the crop from farmers and sells it to the world market, the revenues received/required are

$$(\psi(p) - p)X . \tag{4.10}$$

If we assume that there is a large group of identical farmers and all production risk is idiosyncratic, then $X = x_\psi$, where x_ψ is the production plan that maximizes (4.9) under pricing policy $\psi(\cdot)$. We assume that farmers know p and the policy function $\psi(\cdot)$ that is chosen in equilibrium. An optimal commodity pricing policy is a function $\psi(\cdot)$ which maximizes (4.9) subject to any constraints on the government's ability to finance the scheme. If the government is able to smooth its "trading profits" perfectly, then one candidate constraint for the government is that $E\{(\psi(p) - p)x_\psi\} = 0$, i.e., that ex ante trading profits are zero. This represents an extreme case in which the

---

[32] Other countries, such as India, prohibit the creation of futures markets on the grounds that they encourage "harmful" speculation.

government can perfectly smooth while farmers cannot. Moreover, the price stabilization scheme is actuarially fair. In light of the credit worthiness problems of many countries in the 1980s, this assumption may not seem very realistic. It would however be possible to introduce alternative constraints which reflect plausible limits on governments' abilities to run deficits or even surpluses in such programs. It is, however, an interesting benchmark case.

The first order condition for choice of $\psi(\cdot)$ in this problem is

$$
E_\theta \{ u'(\psi(p)\theta x - c(x))\theta x | p \} + \lambda \left\{ x + (\psi(p) - p) \frac{\partial x}{\partial \psi(p)} \right\} = 0 , \qquad (4.11)
$$

where λ is the Lagrange multiplier on the government's budget constraint.[33] There are basically two terms to consider. The first represents the expected marginal utility of income from an increase in price, while the second represents the impact on the government budget constraint, in part because of a change in production of the commodity. Equation (4.11) reveals two main reasons why it may not be optimal to perfectly stabilize prices. First, there is the issue of how price and quantity risk are correlated. Second, there are incentive effects. To see this, observe that if there were no output risk, i.e., $\theta = 1$ always, and $\partial x/\partial \psi(p) = 0$ for all p, then the solution described above would reduce to the familiar optimal insurance condition: $u'(\psi(p)x - c(x)) = \lambda$. It is also clear from thinking about equation (4.11) that the extent to which individuals can obtain insurance elsewhere either through precautionary saving or informal insurance will be important since that determines how $u'(\cdot)$ varies with changes in either q or θ.

Note furthermore that there is an analogy between this model and optimal taxation. The model views the commodity price stabilization problem as being one of optimal compensatory taxation.[34] This contrasts with commodity price stabilization schemes that involve the government buying and selling the commodity to stabilize the market. Hence, the framework suggested here is most appropriate for thinking about a government selling a good to a world market. In cases, such as maize or rice, where a good fraction of production and consumption is domestic, price stabilization can involve government storage if there is no way of opening the country to trade and then using the kind of compensatory taxation discussed above. One of the difficulties with buffer stock schemes is the possibility of speculative attack, an idea that is discussed in Salant (1982) and Newbery and Stiglitz (1981).

The model laid out above also enables us to think about political economy

---

[33] Equation (4.11) maximizes pointwise by differentiating under the integral sign. Thus $\partial x/\partial \psi(p)$ is the effect on farmers' effort of a change in the policy function for the state where the world price is p.

[34] A further analysis of related issues can be found in Newbery (1990).

constraints in commodity price stabilization. We assumed above that the government is committed to a pricing scheme that involves it accumulating revenues after a sequence of high prices and running a deficit after a sequence of bad shocks. One issue concerns the political sustainability of this. Governments who care about their political survival may be tempted to spend buffer stock surpluses on staying in power rather than using them to stabilize prices. Thus the kind of policy described above might violate a time consistency constraint if governments need a minimum amount of revenue to survive in office. If their other revenue base takes a shock then they may raid the stabilization scheme and cut prices to farmers. This problem is compounded when the farmers' choice problem is over a long horizon as with tree crops, since the government may be tempted to offer high prices early on and then renege at some future date.[35] Such political economy of commodity price stabilization has received very little attention in the economics literature, although Bates (1981) has an interesting discussion of the politics of certain schemes in Africa. Further recent discussion of the political economy of commodity pricing can be found in Deaton (1992b).

4.2.3. Health insurance

An area in which there has been a great deal of attention is health insurance. There is much interest in the question of how better access to medical care can be achieved and, to the extent that market-based access to medical care is considered, the provision of insurance schemes is very important. The move towards charging user fees for public sector medical care, discussed in the chapter by Jimenez, has also heightened interest in these issues.

Provision for ill health is an area in which informal insurance of the kind discussed below has traditionally been important. Formal insurance has generally been the preserve of wealthy urban dwellers and is generally part of the social security system. Evidence from Latin America is given in World Bank (1987) (see especially table 8). As of 1977, the higher middle income countries were covering as much as 80 percent of the population, while a typical figure for lower middle income countries was 10 percent . Extending schemes into the rural areas is an important challenge for the future. There are a few instances of such schemes being used to deliver basic medical care. A good example is the program implemented in Malaysia discussed in Myers (1988). Two other examples of semi-formalized health insurance include projects in China [see Hu (1984)] and Nepal [see Donaldson (1982)].

Since health risk is important in developing countries, there is much work to be done in looking at the impact of improved health insurance on many aspects

---

[35] A model of this phenomenon is developed in Besley (1992).

of the household economy. For example, health insurance may be complementary with farm innovations if a reduction in health risk enables a farmer to invest in riskier but higher yielding technologies. Whether such links are observed empirically is not yet known, but this is an important issue in understanding the social returns to health insurance that will doubtlessly receive attention in future.

4.3. Informal insurance

Informal institutions aimed at providing insurance are especially important in light of the limitations of formal insurance markets. These have existed historically in many countries. A good example is the institution of Friendly Societies which were so prevalent in the nineteenth century, especially in England. These societies operated primarily as self-help groups among working classes to cope with risks of illness or unemployment [see, for example, Johnson (1985)]. Some British friendly societies claimed a lineage dating back to Roman times.[36] A typical function of such societies was to accumulate a common fund that paid out in times of sickness. There was, however, great diversity in rules of operation and function. Such societies catered predominantly to the skilled working classes and not to agricultural laborers and unskilled workers.[37]

There are two broad perspectives on such institutions, neither of which need predominate. The first says that their existence is best motivated by altruistic feelings between members of a neighborhood or social class. This was argued, perhaps most famously, in Thompson (1971), in his discussion of the eighteenth century British working classes. He coined the term "moral economy" to describe the network of altruistically motivated institutions for self-help.

Motivating transfers of resources between individuals need not rest, however, on altruism; there is an alternative tradition that appeals instead to reciprocity in sustaining risk sharing arrangements between individuals who are essentially self-interested. For example, they may have an interest in trading with one another because their income flows are not synchronized. An individual is supposed to be willing to make transfers to another, if she expects reciprocal behavior by that individual in future.

These two perspectives on social interaction in traditional societies have led

---

[36] Friendly societies have rather colorful names, such as the "Independent Order of Oddfellows", the "Royal Antediluvian Order of Buffaloes" and the "Ancient Order of Forresters".

[37] This perhaps reflects the need for a certain amount of organizational capital in order to build a friendly society. In addition, the relatively certain income streams of the skilled may have made it easier to organize in this way.

to greater antagonism outside of economics than within. A celebrated proponent of the moral economy view is Scott (1976), whose account of southeast-asian peasant culture emphasized the institutional basis of support sustained by an ethic of mutual assistance. Popkin (1979) develops a contrary perspective in his study of Vietnam, arguing that Scott presents an excessively romanticized picture of village life.[38] We discuss some differences between these two approaches below. However, the root of this debate lies in the philosophical underpinnings of the two approaches, their perspectives on the nature of man and his relationships. These are things about which economists are apt to disagree very little.

The reciprocal approach to income transfers has recently been formalized by Coate and Ravallion (1993) and it is their approach that we will follow here. In the context of the example with which we began Section 4, they recognize that an individual cannot be relied upon to honor his/her commitment to pay R in the second period. This suggests that the enforcement mechanism used to sustain informal risk sharing needs further investigation.

They consider a model where preferences are individualistic but the interactions between individuals are repeated through time. In fact, because of intergenerational links, they consider an infinitely repeated interaction. At any date individuals receive incomes and must decide how much to transfer to each other. The enforcement problem arises because one individual cannot formally commit to reciprocate at some future date, i.e., the contract is incomplete. Thus if one individual gets a particularly poor income draw at some date and receives a transfer from the other individual, then rather than helping out his partner at some later date, he may prefer to end the arrangement while he is ahead. Coate and Ravallion argue persuasively that an arrangement that has the property that an individual will want to default on the arrangement at some later date should not be admissible. Thus they are interested in solving for the best transfer scheme that does not have this property.

The idea that no one should wish to deviate at some later date can be formalized in the form of an incentive constraint. Before doing this, however, it is necessary to stipulate what will happen if one individual does decide to renege. They suppose that an individual will be unable to form another alliance for risk sharing purposes after a defection. Thus he is forced into autarky. This is a very strong restriction, but it serves to illustrate the main ideas.[39] They also make the strong assumption that no saving is possible either within the transfer arrangement or outside of it, i.e., under autarky. Thus if an individual defects, she will be bound to consume her income for ever more. Assume that the

---

[38] One should, however, note that Scott acknowledges that the moral economy is no egalitarian Utopia.
[39] More generally, the greater the severity of the punishments on defaulters, the larger the set of transfer arrangements that can be sustained.

transfer arrangement is a function only of the current income draws (y_A, y_B) and is described by a function $\theta(\cdot, \cdot)$ denoting resources transferred from A to B. We use V^a to be an individual's future expected utility after defaulting, and $\bar{V}$ to be her future expected utility under the proposed scheme. The scheme is then said to be implementable if and only if:

$$v(y_A) - v(y_A - \theta(y_A, y_B)) \leq \delta\{\bar{V} - V_A^a\} \tag{4.12.A}$$

$$v(y_B) - v(y_B + \theta(y_B, y_A)) \leq \delta\{\bar{V} - V_B^a\} \tag{4.12.B}$$

for all (y_A, y_B) in the support of the income distribution. The right hand side of these equations represents the *future* gain from sticking with the risk sharing scheme for each individual, while the left hand side gives the gain from an immediate deviation from the scheme, by not honoring the commitment to transfer $\theta(y_A, y_B)$. In equilibrium $\bar{V} \equiv E\{v(y_A - \theta(y_A, y_B))\} = E\{v(y_B + \theta(y_B, y_A))\}$ (since the individuals are identical) and $V^a \equiv E\{v(y)\}$. Only schemes that satisfy (4.12) are sustainable.

Coate and Ravallion consider the properties of the *optimal* informal transfer scheme that solves the problem of maximizing the sum of the two individuals' utilities subject to it not violating the incentive constraints in (4.12). It is interesting to compare this with the benchmark of perfect insurance. An unconstrained optimum would equalize the marginal utilities of income of the two individuals, i.e., $u'(y_A - \theta(y_A, y_B)) = u'(y_B + \theta(y_B, y_A))$, for all income levels: (y_A, y_B). This is the efficient risk sharing solution of the Townsend model laid out above. For values of (y_A, y_B) such that (4.12) holds, this is also the incentive compatible outcome. This will typically be true, for example, where income differences are small, since $\theta(y_A, y_B)$ (and therefore the left hand sides of (4.12)) will tend to be small. The model predicts that the incentive constraint will have its greatest effect if individuals in the scheme face large differences in their incomes, for it is then that they need to transfer large sums to equalize their marginal utilities of income. Individuals who receive large transfers will be inclined to renege on the agreement under such conditions. The model therefore predicts that there will be under-insurance for large income differences due to inability to commit. Thus this model explains why there could be incomplete risk sharing in an informal setting, even if information between group members is quite good.

The model's prediction contrasts sharply with the idea that individuals should help each other out *only* when income levels are very different, i.e., that individuals share large windfalls and help those with very poor income draws. Consumption smoothing is very effective for incomes that are very close in this model. In reality one imagines that such income fluctuations are largely smoothed using accumulated savings. One extension which could change the results, however, would be to consider imperfect information, especially moral hazard. If individuals' incomes depend upon effort and luck, but effort is hard to observe, then under certain conditions, it will be reasonable to infer that very bad draws are due to bad luck and good ones due to good luck. The incentive consequences of helping individuals in the tails of the income distribution will thus not be as severe as helping out around the mean.

Another important issue concerns the determination of the size of risk sharing groups. Ideally, transfer schemes would be organized across large groups of individuals to spread the idiosyncratic risks as far as possible. There are a number of difficulties in organizing this effectively. First, there may be adverse selection problems. The model set out above assumed that the individuals were identical. There is no problem in having the individuals being different provided that they both know this and can tailor the scheme so that the "better off" individual is willing to participate. It is when individuals' income profiles are unobservable that difficulties can arise. It seems reasonable to suppose that as the size of the group grows, the information that existing members have about new members will tend to decrease. Increasing the group size may also increase monitoring difficulties in two dimensions. First, because of increased free-riding in monitoring intended to overcome moral hazard and second, because it may be more difficult to organize collective punishments in larger groups.[40]

As we argued above, most economists would regard a model in which agents enforce trade using using reciprocity as a somewhat more natural way of modeling informal transfer schemes. An interesting twist on this might, however, be to point out that altruism brings its own set of problems that could actually make the successful operation of transfer schemes more difficult. A general class of such cases are called *Samaritans' Dilemmas*. In certain situations altruistic individuals can be taken advantage of due to the fact that they are unable to commit not to make transfers to others. Thus, if I know that others will not be able to refuse me assistance in future, then this reduces my incentives to make the investments necessary to avoid having to draw on their support. The result is that altruistically linked individuals may actually do worse than if they were selfish. Some examples of this are studied in Bernheim and Stark (1988).

The model discussed here is potentially applicable in a wide variety of contexts where informal insurance operates, i.e., where there is no formal

---

[40] A further issue with this model is the fact that it does not allow for renegotiation between the two parties following a default. This is allowed by Kletzer and Wright (1992) in their analysis of sovereign debt which has a large number of similarities with Coate and Ravallion, but more especially with Thomas and Worrall (1988) who examine non-stationary solutions to a risk sharing problem without commitment. Renegotiation possibilities will tend to lead to even greater deviations from first best insurance, since it reduces the severity of the penalties that are imposed on deviators ex post.

contractual mechanism to enforce trades. It can thus be thought of as a theoretical underpinning for models where intra-family transfers are observed, such as from migrant workers. The element of reciprocity is not always as straightforward as it is above. In that case, for example, it may be the desire of the migrant to return to the farm at some future date. A number of these issues are discussed in Hoddinott (1992) who uses Bernheim, Shleifer and Summers' (1985) model of strategic bequests as a possible example of a reciprocal mechanism for enforcement of trade between generations. Here transfers from children are supported self-interestedly because parents can reduce their bequest otherwise.

4.4. Empirical studies of informal risk sharing

This section discusses studies that examine informal mechanisms for risk sharing and tries to find evidence that they serve the functions that the theory suggests. There are broadly two approaches. One is to compare the "smoothness" of the consumption paths of individuals or households who participate in informal risk sharing and compare these with non-participants.[41] Alternatively, researchers have looked at the actual transfers in such schemes and tried to relate them to features of the environment such as whether an individual is sick or has a poor harvest.

Rosenzweig and Stark (1989) relate the possibility of risk sharing to marriage patterns in southern India, again using the ICRISAT panel. They observe that 94 percent of married women in three of the villages report having been married outside the village[42] and hypothesize that selecting a bride from a greater distance would be worthwhile if a larger distance implied reduced covariation between your own household income and that of your bride's family. Thus distance marriages might represent a desire to diversify risk. They test this using the time series component of the data to generate individual variances for crop income and consumption for each household. They then regress variance of consumption on the variance of crop income interacted with variables such as number of women and average distance of women's birthplaces, finding that both appear to reduce the variability of household consumption.

Udry (1994) also investigates insurance using data that he collected in northern Nigeria. He does not, however, use consumption data in his

---

[41] In general, one needs to be careful of selection bias in such analyses, since individuals with the riskiest income streams have the greatest incentive to join in informal risk sharing arrangements.

[42] In some contexts, other social constraints limit this. In south India, the custom of cross-cousin marriages restricts many marriages to being within the village. In his field work in southern India, Paul Seabright found that 95 percent of marriages are still to cross cousins.

investigations. Instead he collects data on individuals' credit transactions. He tests the idea that loans serve as state contingent commodities and that the amount that a borrowing household has to repay will be indexed according to his or her income draw. He specifies an empirical model which determines the amount that a household borrows during a cropping season as a function of individual wealth, age and other household characteristics. His test of full income pooling is whether the amount borrowed or lent depends only on aggregate village and not individual income. A second test is whether the shocks received by transaction partners affect loan repayments. With complete income pooling, only aggregate and not individual income shocks should affect loan repayments. In his data, the hypothesis of full income pooling is rejected, which is consistent with the majority of the consumption based studies discussed above.

Udry (1994) also examines the role of loans as state contingent commodities in risk sharing in greater detail. He investigates the idea that loans to individuals who have a shock beyond their control will tend to be forgiven, and that if the lender receives a greater shock, then he is paid back more. Both of these regularities are supported in his data, thus giving credence to the idea that loan transactions may play an important role in sharing risk. This is formally like a situation described in the opening example of this section where R is made contingent on the second period income draw.

There are a number of studies of transfers between family members. Many of these examine remittances by migrants, particularly from urban to rural areas in LDCs. For example, Johnson and Whitelaw's (1974) study of Kenya suggests that 21 percent of wage income in the urban sector is remitted. Rosenzweig and Stark (1989)'s evidence on marriage patterns in India also bears on this issue. There is as yet, however, relatively little good empirical evidence on the determination of remittances. The empirical literature seems to favor models based on some kind of self-interested behavior. Thus Collier and Lal (1986) argue that remittances are a way for migrants to enhance the value of their family farms to which they will eventually return. Their view is explicitly based on credit constraints; remittances enable credit-constrained households to innovate. A self-interested model is also suggested by Lucas and Stark (1985)'s examination of Botswanan evidence. If remittances can flow in both directions, then a model of informal risk *sharing* may seem appropriate. Lucas and Stark take the fact that they find a *positive* relationship between remittances and the income of the recipient household as evidence against the altruistic view which would give a negative relationship. One might be concerned that the Lucas and Stark result could be explained by selection bias, i.e., the richer households having a greater propensity to have migrants. While we have no way of knowing whether this would be true in Botswana, Hoddinott (1994) finds that using Heckman's (1979) procedure to correct for selectivity bias does change the results significantly, using data from western Kenya. The coefficient on income from regressing remittances on income falls after the correction, although it does remain positive and significant. Studies such as that by Lucas and Stark (1985) remind us, above all, that studying the economic circumstances of *both* the recipient and the sender is probably essential to gaining a proper understanding of the motives to remit.

Rosenzweig (1988) also examines transfer schemes directly using the IC-RISAT panel data, which reports net transfers (amount paid less amount received) by households as well as the amount that they borrowed. Most of the borrowing comes from moneylenders and local merchants. In the raw data, both net transfers and borrowing are negatively correlated with income. This is consistent with using loans and transfers as part of a consumption smoothing strategy. His analysis also reveals that transfers respond to own and village income, as does indebtedness. Wealthier households seem to rely less on credit than poorer ones, suggesting that they are more likely to self-insure. He also suggests a trade-off in which Rs. 1 of transfer income reduces borrowing by Rs. 5.

Examining specific institutional contexts in which risk sharing takes place is a valuable exercise and the empirical studies that we have reviewed here all make serious attempts to examine how family and community links serve to provide insurance. It seems quite likely that such studies will continue in the future if more and better data on the mechanics of institutions become available. One particular theme suggested by some of the anthropological evidence hinges on the exact nature of risk sharing schemes. Some of the studies discussed here look for evidence of schemes where individuals above their mean transfer to those below it. An alternative model, however, is that individuals only really make transfers in the tails, organizing a feast if they have a large windfall gain or helping someone out after a serious shock. If most activity is in the tails then such events will tend to be rare in the data and may lead econometric researchers to find very little evidence of transfers; this may happen even though, for significant idiosyncratic events, community insurance is important.

A further issue for future empirical investigations concerns the exact nature of transfers between individuals. Hours spent working for other individuals may be an important means of supporting them, e.g., if they are sick.[43] Movement of individuals between households, as suggested by the anthropological evidence from Côte D'Ivoire, may also be an important part of community-based support schemes. Thus children may be transferred either seasonally or after household shocks. Ainsworth (1990) investigates child fostering and Butcher (1992) more general movements of household members

---

[43] Platteau (1991) surveys the huge diversity of ways in which transfers are made.

in response to economic conditions using data from Côte D'Ivoire. Such things are intriguing and, if better data on household formation and composition becomes available, further insights into these issues will doubtless be forthcoming.

4.5. Formal credit

In most developing countries there is significant reliance on formal banks that serve the main banking functions of taking deposits and making loans. An immediately notable feature, however, is the extent of state ownership in formal sector banking in the developing world. Indeed, many countries prohibit private banks from operating in many sectors of the economy. While not particularly surprising in the broader context of development policies that have been pursued in LDCs, it is important, in appraising experience with formal banking, to realize that the paradigm of a profit-making, private sector banking system may not be very helpful. This is borne out in the evidence of banks that concentrate their loan activities in areas dictated by government and do not enforce repayment in many circumstances. Banks are also forced to hold government bonds to a much greater extent than profit maximization would suggest.

The formal sector in developing countries covers a relatively small part of the population, especially in rural areas. Those who are covered tend on the whole to be wealthier and more politically influential. The history of financial institutions, especially in the rural areas of developing countries is now widely agreed to have been only of limited success using standard economic criteria. Overviews of the issues and an outline of the historical experience are available in Adams and Vogel (1986) and Braverman and Guasch (1986). The main symptom of the poor performance of formal banks in many developing countries is the high rate of non-repayment of loans. Aleem (1990), for example, reports formal sector default rates of 30 percent for Pakistan.[44] Reasons for this can be divided broadly into two categories: *inability* and *unwillingness* to repay. We discuss possible theoretical reasons for each and how well they can explain the history.

(i) Inability to repay: Inability to repay a loan could simply reflect a failure of the project that a borrower has undertaken. For default to be widespread, then we might invoke economy (or region) wide shocks such as poor weather or a change in commodity prices. The high default rate that has been experienced in formal banking could then simply be explained by the inherently risky environment in which loans are made. While there are good reasons to

---

[44] This contrasts with rates of 15 percent in the informal sector.

believe that lending to agriculture is quite risky, there is enough experience of doing so with fairly high repayment rates, as in most of the history of the US farm credit program, not to regard the link between agricultural lending and low repayment as axiomatic. There are however, episodes, such as the US agricultural depression of the 1890s where large scale default on agricultural loans has been an issue.

In seeking an explanation of the poor repayment rates, some commentators, including Braverman and Guasch (1986) have turned to imperfect information arguments. Lenders may be unable to identify good projects (giving rise to a kind of adverse selection problem) and find it too costly to monitor their implementation (leading to moral hazard). This is partly related to the limited infrastructure available for information gathering to which we referred above. While problems of this kind are real for many formal sector lenders, their existence cannot alone explain the historically poor performance of formal lending. If lenders faced appropriate incentives and lent only to projects that they could monitor and knew were ex ante profitable given all available information, then we might observe a low level of lending to certain sectors (especially small farm agriculture), but not necessarily a large amount of default. To explain the latter, one needs to understand better the incentives that lenders have faced to offer loans *without* undertaking appropriate monitoring and *without* screening the projects first. It also seems unlikely that ex ante profitability has a been a dominant criterion in making loans. To understand this, one needs to appreciate the political economy of lending, where predominantly state owned banks have been encouraged to lend to certain sectors and activities as an end in itself, irrespective of any clearly defined social or private profitability criteria. Thus the information environment seems to be at best a proximate cause of the difficulties in the area of inability to repay.

(ii) Unwillingness to repay: Even if individuals have the resources to repay, it may not be straightforward to enforce repayment. In part this reflects the difficulties of getting bank officials to make the effort to sanction borrowers, when they may have little incentive to do so. Bank officials are agents of their depositors or the government and need to be given appropriate incentives. Second, the government may not be committed to loan repayment for political reasons. This idea is expressed succinctly by Harriss (1991) in his study of the North Arcott district in India. He observes that "It is widely believed by people in the villages that if they hold out long enough, debts incurred as a result of failure to repay these loans will eventually be canceled, as they have been in the past (as they were, for example, after the state legislative assembly elections in (1980)" (p. 79). Thus the political environment fuels borrowers' expectations that they will not have to repay loans and, in addition, undermines their incentives to use their funds wisely, worsening the problem of

ability to repay. Third, there are costs of getting loans repaid by seizing collateral or using other sanctions. This reflects the widespread lack of usable forms of collateral to which we referred above.

Again this begs the question of why loan programs subject to such difficulties can persist, and the political economy of lending programs needs once again to be invoked. With low levels of repayments, many programs resemble grants rather than loans. They thus become means of making transfers that further political rather than economic goals. Viewed in this way, moribund loan programs might be regarded as relatively efficient ways of servicing political constituencies. However, it may not be without some economic cost, especially if the kinds of expectations that are generated by such schemes prevent the operation of genuine credit programs along side. Governments also seem to be anxious to maintain their monopoly on the formal financial sector, which may also stunt genuine financial development.

All of these problems are illustrated in the experience of specific credit programs. One particular feature of many formal programs, that can be tied into the above discussion, is the concentration of lending among the relatively wealthy farmers. This is illustrated, for example, by Sayad's (1984) study of Brazil. He found that farmers with more than 10,000 hectares received loans in value equal to 75 percent of their agricultural output, while those with less than 10,000 hectares received loans in value equal to only 6 percent of their agricultural output. The disproportionate benefits to large farmers are similarly documented in Vogel's (1984) study of Costa Rica. This observation is consistent with both a politically motivated view of much formal credit and the view that we observe greater lending to large farmers because they are easier to monitor than small ones. It is interesting to note that Carter and Weibe (1990) find significant differences in the marginal productivity of credit over farms of different sizes, with the marginal productivity being highest for small farmers. However, this is consistent with a world in which monitoring costs decrease with size as well as a non-economic view of farm credit allocation. Perhaps the best evidence that the allocation of credit serves an important political function is the evidence that a disproportionate number of large farmers are defaulters. This is illustrated by Khan's (1979) study of Bangladesh. While this could reflect the pattern of foreclosure costs or adverse shocks affecting inability to repay, the straightforward explanation of political influence seems like a strong contender to explain this.

In discussing the poor record with formal sector banking, we have emphasized the importance of agency problems. In banking there is a dual agency problem. Shareholders (in joint stock banks) and depositors (equals the government in many LDC contexts) are principals, while borrowers and bank employees are agents. Designing optimal banking arrangements involves providing incentives for both sets of agents, i.e., so that borrowers use loans wisely and bank employees monitor and apply sanctions in the interests of depositors and shareholders. Much of the above discussion suggests that the higher tier agency problem between bank employees and their principals is key in understanding how formal sector lending has worked in LDCs.

Although in the past there has been relatively little concern to develop organizational forms to implement effective lending programs, there has been greater recent interest in the question of how formal sector banking institutions can be reformed to improve their performance according to economic criteria. In such discussions, there seems to be an increased appreciation of the fact that institution design matters. Debates about the success of the Grameen Bank in Bangladesh and the BKK in Indonesia are indicative of this. Below, we review what we know about how organizational forms, such as group lending, can improve the operation of formal banking. In particular, how they are able to overcome the agency problems discussed above.

The importance of informal sector financial institutions in developing countries comes in large part from their comparative advantage in overcoming agency problems in lending. Money lenders, for example, often lend their own funds, thus eliminating the separation of ownership of funds from control. In the early history of banking, local family-run banks were often also able to circumvent the agency problem between depositors and bank managers, by having only a few large depositors, all of whom were well known to the banking family [see, for example, Lamoreux (1986)].

To conclude, the experience of government owned or sponsored banking in developing countries is the product of political as much as economic factors. This is especially true in agriculture. To understand this, it is important also to appreciate the incentives of lenders who have rarely been encouraged to operate on anything resembling a commercial basis.

4.6. Informal credit

Informal credit institutions are very important in LDCs and have been widely studied. The huge diversity across space of institutional forms is well illustrated in an Asian context, by Ghate (1992), which presents survey evidence from Bangladesh, India, Indonesia, Philippines and Thailand. However, in much discussion of informal finance, there has been a tendency to focus on some very specific institutional forms. Thus Bouman (1989) observes that "Informal finance is usually equated with the 'evil' village money lender". (p. 33). There is an increasing realization that this focus is not altogether helpful and that a broader array of institutions merits attention. Among the main sources of informal credit discussed here are: loans from friends, relatives and community members; rotating savings and credit associations; money lenders and informal banks; tied credit and pawning.

4.6.1. Loans from friends, relatives and community members

This is frequently found to be a quantitatively significant source of rural finance. For example, Onchan (1992) reports this as accounting for between one fifth to a half of all credit in Thailand depending upon the year and region (see p. 107, Table 2). Graham (1992) reports such finance to be the majority loan source in Niger. Udry's (1990, 1994) studies of Northern Nigeria are based largely on this type of informal finance.

Such finance performs a whole array of functions. Udry (as noted above) focuses on the risk-sharing function of loans, with repayments being indexed to the borrowers' and lenders' economic circumstances. Educational loans between family members may also be important with repayment appearing as urban-to-rural remittances. The main enforcement mechanisms for such loans tend to be informal social sanctions.

4.6.2. Rotating savings and credit associations (roscas)

Roscas are a remarkably widespread informal financial institution that travel under many different names, including *Chit Funds* (India),[45] *Susu* (Ghana, Gambia), *Kye* (Korea), *Hui* (China) and *Tontines* (Senegal).[46] They operate by having a group of individuals committing to putting a certain sum of money into a pot which each period is allocated to one member of the group by a system of drawing lots (a random rosca) or by bidding (a bidding rosca). Each period the process repeats itself, with past winners excluded, until the last member has received the pot. There is a huge informal literature on roscas, beginning with anthropological studies by Geertz (1962) and Ardener (1964). Our discussion of roscas will follow that developed by Besley, Coate and Loury (1993).

Roscas should not be confused with general informal credit. Two important operating rules, characteristic of many roscas, are:
(a)   Each individual in the rosca wins the pot once and only once.

---

[45] It should be noted that in India many Chit Funds are now part of the formal sector and fall under government regulatory policy. This seems to be a common pattern over time. The U.S. Savings and Loans Associations began life, in many instances, as roscas.

[46] Bouman (1977) reports that 60 percent of the population in Addis Ababa belongs to a rosca. Radhakrishnan et al. (1975) reports that in 1967, there were 12491 registered chit funds in Kerala alone. Studies of roscas in specific countries include Adams and Canavesi de Sahonero (1989), Anderson (1966) and Begashaw (1978).

(b) There are no demand deposits.

Property (a) sets random roscas apart from a pure gambling scheme. Roscas provide ways of rationing access to a pot of funds, but each individual will get the pot at some point in the rotation. Note, however, that this limits the potential for roscas to serve as a risk sharing device. This is especially true of a rosca that randomly allocates access to the pot. The many anthropological studies do, however, emphasize that members of roscas are treated leniently by their fellow members if they fail to make their contributions due to some significant misfortune such as ill-health. Roscas may also serve a function in financing significant life-cycle events, such as a wedding, if access to the pot can be ensured at the relevant time, or the timing of the wedding can be altered to coincide with winning the pot. One advantage of rule (a) in operating a rosca is that members are unable to run up large debts to the rosca over a long period. Property (b) distinguishes a rosca from an informal bank. Apart from reducing the vulnerability of the rosca to dishonest book-keeping and management, it also prevents the roscas being susceptible to runs on deposits.

The existence of roscas is best explained as facilitating small scale capital accumulation.[47] In particular, it can be argued that they exploit gains from trade due to indivisibilities. As we shall see, this rationalizes the two properties (a) and (b) above. This can be seen quite clearly using the simple model of roscas developed in Besley, Coate and Loury (1993). Imagine a world in which n individuals wish to acquire a durable good that costs B. Each has additive preferences over durable and non-durable consumption: $v(c)$ without the durable and $v(c) + \xi$ with it. Ignoring discounting and supposing that each individual has a fixed income flow of y over a life of length T, an individual can save up for the durable under autarky and solves the following problem in doing so:

$$\underset{c,t}{\text{Max}}\ (T - t)(v(y) + \xi) + tv(c) \quad \text{subject to } t(y - c) = B , \qquad (4.13)$$

where t is the acquisition date for the durable and c is consumption during the accumulation phase. The first term in the maximand refers to the period after time t when the durable has been acquired, while the second term is utility during the period of accumulation. The constraint just says that enough saving must have been done before t to buy the durable. By re-arranging the

---

[47] This may be an overstatement. Some bidding roscas, by providing funds to members at opportune times, are able to provide an important source of liquidity. This still leaves a puzzle, however, for if this were the main purpose of roscas one would expect to observe an institution with a more flexible rule for access to the pot, where some members can share in the pot more than once. This may indeed be the case in reality and deserves attention. The distinction between a rosca and simple loan market would however become blurred in such a case.

maximand and substituting in the constraint, it is straightforward to see that the value of the autarky program can be written as:

$$T(v(y) + \xi) - B\mu(\xi),\tag{4.14}$$

where $\mu(\xi) \equiv \text{Min}_c \{v(y) + \xi - v(c)/(y - c)\}$. The interpretation of this is clear. The first term represents maximal lifetime utility were the durable a free good, i.e., an individual could own it for his whole life without having to forego any current consumption. The second represents the utility cost of saving up.

The operation of roscas can be examined using this framework. We focus on the example of a random rosca that allocates the pot of funds accumulated by drawing lots. Besley, Coate and Loury (1993) also consider bidding. A random rosca gives each member of the group of n individuals a $1/n$ chance of winning the pot at each of the rosca's meeting dates. Thus viewed ex ante, the rosca gives uniformly distributed acquisition dates on the set $[1, 2, \ldots, n]$. An individual who joins the rosca and wins the pot at time $(i/n)t$ has life-time utility of $(T - t)(v(y) + \xi) + t(v(c) + (i/n)\xi)$. His lifetime expected utility is thus

$$(T - t)(v(y) + \xi) + t\left(v(c) + \frac{n - 1}{2n}\xi\right).\tag{4.15}$$

Supposing that the rosca aims to maximize the expected utility of its representative member, it maximizes this subject to the budget constraint $t(y - c) = B$, which says that there are enough funds in the pot at each meeting date to buy the durable. Maximized lifetime utility in a rosca can be written as:

$$T(v(y) + \xi) - B\mu((n - 1)\xi/2n),\tag{4.16}$$

where the function $\mu(\cdot)$ is as defined above. It is easy to prove using the envelope theorem that $\mu'(\cdot) > 0$ and hence that, since $(n - 1)/2n < 1$, the random rosca lowers the utility cost of saving up to acquire the durable. The reason is, of course, plain to see. Even if it maintained the same saving pattern as under autarky, the rosca gives each of its members a chance of winning the pot early by drawing lots. In fact, all but the last member of the rosca is better off holding savings fixed.[48] The rosca will however choose a lower savings rate than under autarky.

This simple model demonstrates some basic features about roscas. First, despite lot drawing being a widespread form of allocation for the accumulated funds, it has very little to do with tastes for gambling. A rosca has to find some

---

[48] In fact Besley, Coate and Loury (1993) show that the optimally designed random rosca will make the last individual to receive the pot strictly worse off than under autarky.

way of rationing access to its accumulated funds; it is this function that drawing lots fulfills. Roscas rely on social sanctions to ensure that an individual continues to contribute after he/she has won the pot. A typical social group from which members of a rosca are drawn is an office block, a village community or a neighborhood. In each of these cases, the rosca members have every chance of being able to sanction delinquent members. Although systematic evidence on the frequency of default in roscas does not appear to be available, most anecdotal evidence suggests that it is rare. Indeed, the anthropological literature on roscas is replete with examples of extreme aversion to default. For example, Ardener (1964) observes that "a member may go to great lengths, such as stealing or selling a daughter into prostitution in order to fulfill his obligation to his association; failure to meet obligations can even lead to suicide" (p. 216).[49]

Local knowledge is brought to bear in selecting rosca members. Default may also be diminished in roscas by having an organizer who volunteers to receive the pot last and whose job it is to monitor other members.

4.6.3. Money lenders and informal banks

Finance from local money lenders is also a significant component of informal finance. Most finance from such sources appears to be reasonably short term. There are also stock anecdotes concerning the very high annual interest rates that are implied on short term loans given by money lenders; see, for example, Basu (1989) and Bouman (1989, p. 96), who reports interest rates of 5–10 percent per month. Although one is loath to generalize, money lenders seem to lend mostly their own capital (not using loans from elsewhere).[50] They circumvent the information problems faced by formal banks by knowing their clients well and typically have access to sanctions not available to the bank. The gains from trade reaped by money lenders stem from the fact that they have access to superior information and better enforcement technologies than formal lenders. This view of money lenders is expressed succinctly by the

---

[49] To examine the incentive to default one might consider the decision of the first individual to win the pot, since he has the greatest incentive (i.e., avoids making the largest number of rosca contributions). By avoiding his remaining $(n-1)$ payments, he gains an amount $\{(n-1)/n\}B\{v(y) + \xi - v(c)/y - c\}$. Whatever sanctions are available to the rosca must give an individual enough incentive to forego the gain above. Note that as n increases, this increases the gain from defaulting and as c goes down, the default gain also falls. Thus default constraints are likely to mean operating smaller roscas which last for a shorter time. Default may also increase with n because of limitations in enforcement capability. Thus merging two roscas from adjacent office blocks may not make sense because of the reductions in the sanctions available after default.

[50] Bell (1990) gives evidence from the Reserve Bank of India's 1951 All India Rural Credit survey that only about 4 percent of money lenders borrowed from commercial banks. Unfortunately, later rounds of the survey did not collect such information and we do not know how this has changed over time.

Reserve Bank of India: "There is little that escapes his eye in the circumstances of his debtors. What cooperatives merely postulate, he actually possesses, namely, a local knowledge of the 'character and repaying capacity' of those he has to deal with". (RBI, 1954, vol. 2, p. 171).[51] Lenders earn better returns by exploiting their local knowledge than they would by depositing their money with a financial intermediary or investing in the capital market. An abiding concern with money lenders as providers of rural finance has been market power. This is natural: lenders typically lend to those who have no other source of funds or, at least limited access to funds elsewhere.[52] We discuss some policy implications of this below.

Informal banking systems such as the *shroffs* of Western India are a further interesting example of an informal institution, in this case a kind of indigenous banking scheme.[53] They provide trade credit, hold deposits, make loans and perform many services similar to formal banks at lower cost and with greater flexibility [see Ghate (1992)]. Again their existence can be motivated by the use of local knowledge and enforcement.

4.6.4. Tied credit

There are many types of informal credit under this broad heading. The essential feature here is that the individual or institution who grants the loan deals with the borrower in a non-lending capacity, e.g., as a landlord or a merchant. This other capacity is often the basis of an information or enforcement advantage over the formal sector. The kinds of interlinked credit transactions between landlords and tenants reviewed by Bell in Chapter 16 fall into this category. Another widespread example of tied credit is that given by shopkeepers, where the availability of a loan is tied to purchases at a particular store. This is documented, for example, in Sanderatne (1992)'s study of informal finance in Sri Lanka. A related phenomenon is the institution of trader-lenders, whom we discuss in greater detail below. A typical arrangement has an individual being granted a loan that is tied to future crop sales. Since traders typically receive funds from the formal sector, this is also seen as a way of building links between the formal and informal sectors. This aspect of such arrangements is discussed further in Section 4.7.3.

---

[51] Cited by Bell (1990) p. 312.

[52] Both Bell (1990) (Table 8) and Siamwalla et al. (1990) report that a significant number of borrowers use both the formal and the informal sector in a given year.

[53] In Pakistan, such institutions are called "bisi". This comes from the Urdu word for twenty which is the typical membership of such institutions.

4.6.5. Pawning

Pawning is another important institution for providing credit. It most often works via a broker, who takes some asset in exchange for a loan. The pawned item can then be redeemed at a later date provided that the contractual terms of the loan are fulfilled. Otherwise, the pawned item becomes the property of the pawnbroker. Bouman (1989) found pawning of jewelry to be a significant source of seasonal rural finance. He cites a study of Malaysia by Wells (1979) in which pawnbroking constitutes 18 percent of total borrowings in 1980, coming second only to shop-keeper finance. The 1986 national Malaysian rural credit survey of 1986 found that 54 percent of paddy farmers who borrowed informally took their loans from pawnbrokers. In India, Bouman also reports findings that loans from pawn brokers are important for loans of Rs 50–100 among relatively poor farmers (p. 77).

Pawning provides a way of increasing the liquidity of fixed assets. It may thus rationalize why even poor individuals may find it attractive to buy an asset like jewelry. It is easy to transport, and is easily valued and sold by a pawnbroker. Johnson's (1985) historical study of working class savings patterns in 19th century England also found that "workers bought durable goods in periods of full employment with deliberate intention of pawning them when jobs were scarce and money short, or when some other crisis hit the family" (p. 177). This again emphasizes the seasonal basis of this kind of finance.

Some productive assets may also be pawned. Doing so with land is known as *pledging* in West Africa, and is described in detail in Hill (1956). An individual secures a loan on a piece of land that is then either farmed by the creditor, or sometimes share-cropped, until the agreed repayment has been made. In other parts of the world this is known as a *usufructuary mortgage* or *land pawning*. Such contracts seem mostly to be individualized, rather than working through a broker. This arrangement may provide an attractive alternative to land sales for many farmers and as a good substitute for using land as collateral, as is suggested by Nagarajan, David and Meyer (1992) in their study of land pawning in the Philippines. Siamwalla et al. (1990) discuss the importance of this type of arrangement in backing loans for workers to migrate to foreign countries from Thailand.

There are, however, limits to what pawning can achieve. One sees mainly pawning of assets whose value is easy to appraise and which cannot easily be harmed while in the custody of the creditor. Livestock would be a poor asset for the latter reason.[54] Furthermore, Hill (1956) reported concerns about the

---

[54] Bliss and Stern (1982) find that rental markets in bullocks are thin in Palanpur because of such concerns.

lack of incentives to invest to improve pledged land in Ghana. Hence, while pawning does provide a vital function, there are limits to its use as a credit instrument.

4.7. Combining the advantages of the formal and informal sectors

In recent discussions of financial markets in LDCs there has been increased interest in trying to combine the advantages of the formal and informal sectors. While the formal sector appears to have a comparative advantage over the informal sector in intermediating funds over space and reaping scale economies, it seems to fare worse in solving enforcement and information problems. The latter is the comparative advantage of the informal sector. This has provoked interest in finding institutional solutions that combine the best of both sectors. This general idea is not new as is brought out in Guinnane's (1992a) investigations of the 19th century German cooperative movement. The latter was motivated by idea that local knowledge could be exploited in the design of credit institutions and the founder of many of the coops, Friedrich Raiffeisen, built a network of them based on the principles of local enforcement and information collection. In addition, he recognized the importance of building a network of "Centrals", a kind of central banking system aimed at intermediating funds between coops to reflect shocks to the local economies. Credit cooperatives are important in developing countries. In addition, there has been a revival of interest in group loans as a device for using local knowledge and enforcement to improve repayment. Both aspects have been modeled in the literature. Stiglitz (1990) and Varian (1989) discuss information and peer monitoring advantages of credit coops and group lending. The enforcement advantages are analyzed in Besley and Coate (1995).

We develop these ideas here using a simplified version of Stiglitz's (1990) peer monitoring model. A risk averse individual has the possibility of a safe or risky project. The former yields Y_s if it is successful while a risky project yields $Y_r (>Y_s)$. Both projects yield nothing if unsuccessful. The probabilities of success of each project are p_s and p_r with $p_s > p_r$. Each project costs one unit of capital to undertake. If the project fails, then the borrower defaults and individuals get utility of $\bar{u}$, which we normalize to be zero. An individual's utility level, if the (gross) interest rate is R, is:

$$v(R) = \max\{p_s u(Y_s - R), \ p_r u(Y_r - R)\}, \tag{4.17}$$

where we have assumed that the loan is repaid if the project succeeds for the range of R's being considered. The project selection choice is displayed in Figure 36.4, where we have used the fact that $p_s u'(Y_s - R) - p_r u'(Y_r - R) \geq 0$,

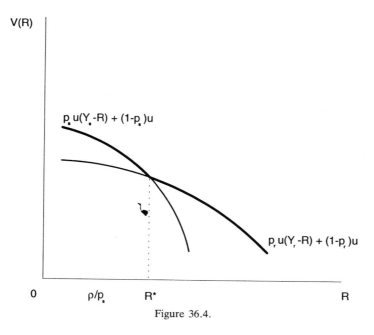

Figure 36.4.

for the relevant range of R's. Thus there is a critical interest rate such that the risky project is chosen for all greater interest rates. If we call this interest rate R^* and assume that lending is a free-entry activity so that lenders make zero expected profits ex ante, then if $R^* \leq \rho/p_s$, where ρ is the lender's opportunity cost of funds, the risky project will be chosen in equilibrium.

To introduce peer monitoring, suppose that there are two borrowers each of whom has the choice between the two projects specified above. They are neighbors and are able to tell which project each is undertaking. The lender may now assign some liability to an individual for the project that his neighbor undertakes. This implies that if the individual's project is successful and his neighbor's fails, then he has to repay some extra amount denoted here by l. Suppose also that individuals jointly decide whether to both implement the risky or the safe project. Then the utility function of a typical individual becomes:

$$v(R, l) = \max\{ p_s^2 u(Y_s - R) + p_s(1 - p_s)u(Y_s - R - l),$$
$$p_r^2 u(Y_r - R) + p_r(1 - p_r)u(Y_r - R - l)\} \tag{4.18}$$

This expression reflects the fact that there are now basically four states of the world depending upon whether each of the individual's project succeeds or fails. We now ask whether the safe project is implementable with peer monitoring. The key observation is that an increase in l increases the utility of undertaking the safe project relative to the risky one if $p_s(1 - p_s)u'(Y_s - R - l) - p_r(1 - p_r)u'(Y_r - R - l) \leq 0$. This will tend to hold if the variance of the two projects differs greatly and utility functions are not too concave, other things being equal. Thus the effect of introducing liability for the other individual's project may be to encourage both individuals to undertake the safer project.[55] This is the essence of the idea that peer monitoring can be important. Clearly this is not always true, although given our hypothesized parameter values, it is not possible to do worse with peer monitoring than without.

4.7.1. Credit cooperatives

These institutions, which are also called credit unions, are found in many parts of the world. In some respects they work like formal sector banks, raising deposits from and making loans to their members. They are often set up with some government involvement, either as a catalyst or as a lender. This is true, for example, in India where they have been actively promoted as an alternative to village money lenders [see Bell (1990) for further discussion]. In developed countries, credit unions are most often attached to places of employment and can benefit from access to employee information and are guaranteed repayment of loans through individuals' pay packets as long as they are employed. Agricultural credit cooperatives are intended to provide a closer structure of monitoring of borrowers than do conventional banks. While in a large scale bank, an individual may wish to monitor those who have been loaned money and on whose performance the return to his savings depends, it is usually prohibitively costly to do so. In a credit cooperative, this may be possible, given his local knowledge of borrowers and the relatively small size of the membership. This may reduce both kinds of agency problems experienced in banking.

Incentive problems in credit cooperatives can be considered using the model of credit cooperatives developed in Banerjee, Besley and Guinnane (1994). Credit cooperatives typically borrow funds from inside sources (their members) and outside funds (a bank or the government). Borrowing members of the cooperative undertake projects about which they have some private information. If there is a moral hazard problem, the other coop members have to be induced to monitor. There are thus two agency problems in a coop: the borrower's and the monitor's. Banerjee, Besley and Guinnane consider three

---

[55] That is not to say that we always want to encourage safer investments (see Section 5 below). The idea of the example is simply to illustrate how peer monitoring can affect project choice.

ways of providing incentives to both agents. First, to encourage monitoring, the non-borrowing member can be made liable for the debts of the coop. In effect he serves as a guarantor for the coop. The outside creditor can then appeal to non-borrowing members of the coop in the event of default on loans from non-members. Second, incentives to monitor can be fostered by making the non-borrowing member a creditor. Herein lies the importance of raising some funds internally and explains why generating internal funds is such a central part of the cooperative ideal. Finally, the terms of the loan contract can be altered. If the interest rate on internal funds depends on the success of the borrower's project, then this enhances the incentive to monitor.

An optimally designed credit cooperative might choose values of these three parameters to maximize its ex ante surplus. Banerjee, Besley and Guinnane give a picture of the optimal use of different aspects of cooperative design and relate their findings to the nineteenth century German experience. They show that providing incentives via liability rules and via using internally generated funds are substitutes. Some German cooperatives were founded with limited liability for non-borrowing members, while others had unlimited liability. Each system can be optimal under some parameter configurations.

There are two important problems with cooperatives, both in theory and practice. The first concerns the fact that there may be a large number of non-borrowers within a cooperative and each will be required to play some monitoring role according to the type of structure discussed above. In practice, there may be free-rider problems in monitoring where no non-borrower wishes to put in the effort required to get the optimal level of monitoring. An additional problem arises with the possibility of collusion between borrowers and non-borrowers who may be better off by not repaying their loan to the lender. There is an interesting irony here from the peer monitoring perspective. Cooperatives are likely to be more effective from a monitoring point of view if individuals have good information about each other. However individuals with good information are also likely to know each other well enough for the possibilities of collusion to be real. Designing cooperatives that are collusion proof is potentially important and the failure to do so in the past may explain why the practical performance of cooperatives falls short of hopes. Guinnane's (1992b) discussion of the failure of German-style credit cooperatives in Ireland makes plain the collusion problem in a practical context. Further evidence on this can be found in Huppi and Feder (1990).

4.7.2. Group lending programs

Group lending programs have also recently gained much popularity as a way of improving the quality of loans from formal sector institutions to poor individuals. In particular, the Grameen Bank in Bangladesh has received a good deal of attention, often being cited as a paragon of institutional design.[56] It was set up in 1976 and by 1987 had 300 branches covering more than 5400 villages. Even before the Grameen bank, the idea of group lending received enthusiastic support, with the World Bank (1975) arguing that "the best prospects in future will lie in some form of group responsibility for individual loans". A group lending program differs from a credit cooperative in one essential way: it is a method for managing credit rather than raising deposits. Also, unlike the model of credit cooperatives discussed in the previous section, all members are simultaneously in debt. Thus a bank makes a loan to a group of individuals, each of whom is liable for repayment of the loan and will be sanctioned by the borrower if any one individual defaults. The idea, as in the case of a credit cooperative, is to take advantage of the fact that members of the group provide information and enforcement functions.[57] Individuals may also repay each other's loans. Indeed a central function of the Grameen Bank is to encourage mutual assistance. Thus Hossein (1988) observes that "Other members of the group also extend financial support to a member in times of genuine difficulty" (p. 26).

A careful examination of incentives under group lending reveals that it is not the obvious paragon that some proponents have suggested. There are at least two effects that must be weighed in judging these programs.[58] First, bad borrowers can inflict negative externalities on good ones; a good borrower might be prepared to repay his own loan but will be sanctioned anyway if a partner in his group does not repay. He may therefore choose not to repay himself.[59] There are however, positive effects. For example, one individual whose project is successful may repay another's loan and thereby reduce the default risk faced by a bank. It has also been argued that group lending might serve as a catalyst for risk sharing. In the Stiglitz peer monitoring model laid out above, the joint liability affected incentives precisely because individuals were given a stake in each other's projects. Although this forces the lenders to bear some of the risk that was previously borne by the bank, it also leads to some pooling of idiosyncratic risk.

Reviewing the evidence on group lending, as in Huppi and Feder (1990), reveals a mixed performance. As a generalization it would be hard to support

---

[56] For an overview and description of how Grameen operates and some basic data on its early performance, see Hossein (1988).

[57] This is put nicely in Desai (1984) who argues that "Neither the clear and inheritable land title, the hypothecation of reasonably assured crop harvest nor the guarantee of the reputable third party could be available from the rural poor. The joint liability principle, peer pressure and collective responsibility implied by group lending were considered to act as a substitute for the conventional collateral", pp. 23–24.

[58] The following argument is formalized in Besley and Coate (1995).

[59] As argued in Varian (1989), such effects may be mitigated if group members exclude potentially bad borrowers.

the view that group lending yields higher rates of loan repayment than conventional lending programs. This bears out the idea that there may be a trade-off between positive and negative effects from group lending, where the net effects are ambiguous a priori. Even the performance of the highly touted Grameen Bank leaves unresolved issues. The Grameen Bank does relatively little lending to agriculture, with all its uncertainties. Moreover, there is very little detailed quantitative research on the performance of its group lending programs. Thus we know very little about how defaults are actually handled and what forms of group selection and management have been successful in practice. This is strange given that one often hears attempts to promote the Grameen Bank as a model for other countries. It would seem that much more ought to be known about how it actually operates (and why other group lending programs have had such mixed success) before advocating a much wider use of group lending in other contexts.[60] One should also note that recent work by Yaron (1992) has shown that the Grameen Bank's current operations are also heavily dependent on government subsidies.

There is also the question of whether it is actually the group function of Grameen Bank that has led to its very good performance record. An additional incentive mechanism comes from the fact that individuals who do not repay are not given access to funds in future. Moreover, as far as can be discerned, this sanction seems actually to be imposed in practice. This kind of dynamic reputation device may also serve to enhance repayment. Elsewhere, such as in the case of the BKK in Indonesia, this alone has served to enhance repayment quite apart from the adoption of the group principle.[61]

One issue that has received insufficient attention in the literature on informal groups such as roscas, credit cooperatives and group lending is endogenous group formation. In understanding well how different schemes function, it would seem essential to model and investigate empirically who joins in groups with whom. Varian (1989) provides an interesting introductory discussion of this, but certainly more work in this area is warranted.

4.7.3. Credit from trader-lenders

The importance of trader-lenders in the provision of credit has also motivated interest in using the informal sector as a means of funneling funds from the formal sector to borrowers who would normally use the informal sector. This differs from the previous two examples in this section in that the aim is to use the informal sector directly as intermediaries. Nonetheless, the motivation is

---

[60] This is equally true of credit cooperatives. Guinnane (1992b) documents the failure of German model credit cooperatives in Ireland.

[61] For discussion of the BKK, see Patten and Rosengard (1991).

similar in spirit; the informal sector is deemed to have a comparative advantage in information and enforcement which can be harnessed. A typical scenario here is of a trader who markets a farmer's crops and extends an advance, i.e., a loan, secured on future crop sales. The loan is repaid after the harvest is realized. If the trader uses the formal financial sector as his source of finance, then this provides a link between the formal sector and certain kinds of borrower. The analytics of such arrangements have recently been examined by Floro and Ray (1992)[62] and Hoff and Stiglitz (1992). Both remark that, despite the prevalence of this type of credit, there is relatively little conceptual or empirical analysis that has examined the consequences of such links between the formal and informal sector. A good example of this type of arrangement in practice is that of rice trader-millers in the Philippines [see Floro and Ray (1992)]. They provide credit to farmers as well as marketing their rice crop. Moreover, the government has made specific attempts to channel funds to farmers via credit to the millers, taking advantage of the fact that the traders have ways of enforcing repayment from rice growers that are not available to formal lenders.

Hoff and Stiglitz (1992) build a model of monopolistic competition in the credit market to understand the general phenomenon of trader-lender credit. They are particularly interested in the incidence of expanding formal sector credit to traders on those who borrow from the traders. Their comparative statics are sometimes surprising, suggesting the possibility of perverse effects on interest rates; an increase in the availability of credit can actually *increase* the interest rate paid by small farmers. Such apparently perverse results are due to new entry of new trader-lenders into the credit market. Such theoretical findings only reinforce the importance of having a good empirical understanding in order to understand the effects of certain policies. In general, looking at the effect of indirectly mediated funds from the formal sector is important. If the benefits of government provided credit are through equilibrium effects on informal markets, then the kinds of models that are used to evaluate these interventions should certainly reflect this.

To conclude, the idea of better appreciating links between the formal sector and informal ties is important. It is not however a panacea for financial development. There are very few good empirical studies that permit us to appreciate the conditions under which different arrangements succeed or fail. However, research on these issues is still unfolding and it is likely to remain an active area of interest for some time to come.

---

[62] Floro and Yotopoulos (1991) provides further evidence on this in their detailed study of the Philippines.

5. Credit, insurance and long run development

The discussion so far has focused largely on the micro-economics of credit and insurance provision; with a particular emphasis on risky agricultural environments. This section broadens this perspective and develops the bigger picture, focusing on credit, insurance and long-run development and growth. A significant part of this link works via the role of intermediaries in providing finance for industrialization and, consequently, much lending of this sort occurs in an environment that is, arguably, not very special to developing countries.[63] Nonetheless these issues are important and we will examine a number of them here.

A central link between credit, insurance and long run growth is via aggregate capital accumulation. There is a vast literature, reviewed by Gersovitz in Chapter 10 of this Handbook, on aggregate savings and its link to growth. For any given aggregate level of savings, the quality of financial intermediation is a crucial determinant of the efficiency of investment choices, i.e., in ensuring that savings find their way into the most productive opportunities. Insurance may also be important, especially in relation to incentives to adopt new, riskier technologies. Both of these themes will be discussed in greater detail below.

5.1. An historical overview

One way of investigating the link between credit, insurance and long-run development is to consider their function in the broad sweep of history. Perhaps the most famous discussion of the link between growth and the development of financial intermediaries was initiated by the economic historian Alexander Gerschenkron. His ideas were rooted in empiricism. He put forward the hypothesis that banks played an essential role in the economic development of countries, after they have attained a particular level of economic development. In his celebrated essay on "economic backwardness in historical perspective" [Gerschenkron (1962)], he contrasted the experience of three countries in this regard: England, Germany and Russia.

England, he argued, had managed to develop largely without the use of banks, the reason being that at the point at which it industrialized, capital requirements were low. Most finance was raised by re-investing profits and borrowing from friends and relatives. This was an example, therefore, where

---

[63] Space precludes us from dealing with the special questions concerning the provision of credit in Eastern Europe.

informal finance had provided the necessary capital to be an engine of growth. The fact that England had also developed a dynamic trade and agricultural sector before industrialization was also helpful. In understanding the experience of Germany, Gerschenkron argued that the role of banks is much more critical. The large German banks accompanied "an industrial enterprise from the cradle to the grave, from establishment to liquidation", [Gerschenkron (1962, p. 14)]. Banks were key not only in providing the large blocks of capital necessary to reap scale economies, but they also provided entrepreneurship. This picture is somewhat consonant with the model of corporate control that seems to apply to Germany and Japan even today. The history of Russia was of a country, according to Gerschenkron, that was too backward to use banks at the time that it began its industrialization. Partly this reflected a history in which investors had little confidence in the banking industry. Russia therefore relied on the state for the provision of the capital needed for industrialization.

The validity of Gerschenkron's hypothesis has been widely debated among historians. Perhaps English banking was more important than he suggests and to the extent that it was not, this may be due to the legal structure that prohibited joint stock banks until 1826 [see, for example, Cameron (1967)]. The importance of banks in the German context may also have been exaggerated, with a significant amount of industrialization preceding the rise of the large banks. Conceding all of this, however, the systematic analysis of where banks fit into the development process historically is something from which modern development economics can learn.

A second important theme in the relationship between credit markets and long-run development concerns financial integration. A characteristic of financial markets in developing countries today, and many now developed countries historically, was a lack of institutions for funds to flow to where capital could be most productively used. For example, Davis (1971) notes the slow speed with which funds flowed to the Southern U.S. in the late nineteenth century and Matthias (1973) remarks on the geographical gap in inter-regional capital transfers between the industrializing North and Midlands in England and the predominantly agricultural East, South and West during the Industrial Revolution. Both accounts emphasize that the evolution of financial institutions can be understood in large part as trying to overcome this, leading to a more efficient allocation of capital throughout the economy. This view is based on realizing gains from trade from differences in technologies. This discussion also seems relevant to modern day developing countries where, as we remarked above, market segmentation is significant. Davis emphasizes the importance of learning and the increased sophistication of savers as ways of overcoming this in the US. Improvements in infrastructure and communications, more generally, also plays a central role in improving market integration.

Goldsmith's (1969) pioneering work provides, perhaps, the most detailed descriptive overview of the relationship between the growth of intermediation and per capita income on a world-wide basis. He defines a country's financial interrelations ratio as the quotient of the aggregate market value of all financial instruments, at a given date, to the value of its "tangible net national wealth". Below we discuss the use of this type of indicator in econometric studies. Goldsmith observes that the ratio tends to increase in the course of economic development, although it seems to level off after a point (at a value between one and one and a half). He also shows that developing countries and the nineteenth century US and Western Europe had ratios between one and two thirds. In addition, he studies the concomitant development of banking and other financial institutions as income per capita increases. In line with the themes of this chapter, Goldsmith recognizes that the relative size of the financial superstructure is a measure of the extent to which the economy is able to exploit gains from trade arguing that the main determinant of the financial interrelations ratio is "the separation of the function of savings and investment among different economic units" (p. 45). He also recognizes the importance of learning in building a financial superstructure. The policy implications of such infant industry concerns are discussed below.

5.2. Theoretical models and econometric evidence

A number of formal models have recently been proposed to represent the microeconomic mechanism that leads to an association between financial intermediation and growth. Those in Bencevinga and Smith (1991) and Greenwood and Jovanovic (1990) both emphasize the gains from risk bearing that accompany financial intermediation, thus fitting closely with the themes of this chapter. In Bencevinga and Smith, there is a link between financial intermediation and growth because the banking system permits individuals to invest in technologies that yield higher long-run returns. They consider a world in which individuals have uncertain consumption horizons: they may wish to consume one or two periods in the future, but are uncertain. Under autarky, this would imply that they would have to invest only in short-run projects to insure against needing to consume next period. With a financial intermediary, society is able to invest in some longer run projects, i.e., it needs only to finance enough short run projects to satisfy period one consumption needs, which in the aggregate are more certain. Intermediaries in this world reap gains from trade because individuals have non-synchronized consumption needs.

In Greenwood and Jovanovic (1990), the gains from trade are also from risk sharing. Individuals in intermediaries pool their resources and are thus willing to undertake some high-risk/high-return projects. They assume that there is a lump sum cost to using an intermediary so that only those with large amounts of capital use it. This results in the rich getting richer at first, because of their access to intermediation, providing a micro-foundation for Kuznet's infamous inverted "U" relationship between development and inequality. As income levels rise in this model, more individuals use intermediaries and this leads to more high-risk/high-return projects being undertaken. It is the latter that provides a link between financial intermediation and growth.

Both of the above models that link financial intermediation to growth emphasize the insurance function of intermediaries and the inefficiency of autarkic saving. In an LDC context Eswaran and Kotwal (1989) have discussed how access to credit may affect technology adoption decisions. Townsend's (1992) study of northern Thai villages attributes the non-adoption of new rice varieties to the absence of insurance possibilities. This view is also suggested in Feder, Just and Zilberman's (1985) review of the technology adoption literature. A simple model along these lines can be developed as follows.

Suppose that an individual is able to invest in one of two technologies: a safe low return technology that always yields μ and a new technology that is risky for one period, i.e., an individual will learn after one period whether or not it is better than the old one. This new technology yields y_h with probability p and y_l with probability $(1-p)$. We assume that $y_l < \mu$ so that individuals abandon the new technology if it turns out to yield y_l. Suppose that individuals live for three periods, do not discount and have utility functions that are increasing and concave. Then the utility from adopting the new technology in period one is

$$V(l) \equiv p2v(y_h) + (1-p)\left(\underset{b}{\text{Max}} \ \{v(y_1 + b) + v(\mu - br)|b \le l\}\right), \qquad (5.1)$$

where l represents any borrowing constraint that an individual faces and b the level of borrowing. The first term represents the case where the technology is successful. In this case individuals receive y_h in periods 2 and 3. The second represents the case where it is not successful. In this case individuals will wish to borrow in anticipation of the higher income on returning to the old technology in the final period. To decide whether to adopt the new technology the individual needs to compare $v(\mu - c) + V(l)$ with $3v(\mu)$.[64] A central observation is that $V'(l) > 0$ if the individual faces a binding borrowing constraint in period 2, which says that an individual would be better off adopting the new technology if he is not liquidity constrained in the event that the technology is no good. Thus the inability to smooth consumption will tend to reduce the incentive to innovate. Thus we have a theoretical link between

---

[64] Note that we ignore the possibility that an individual will borrow in period one to finance the adoption of the technology. Clearly if she were able to do this then this would make it more likely that the technology would be adopted.

innovation and ability to smooth consumption. Of course, if the individual had accumulated a stock of savings as insurance, then this could be done without borrowing. However, this solution fails to secure some potential gains from trade. It would be better for a group of individuals to get together and for some to commit to lend to one of them if he tries out the new technology and is not successful.

The model developed is very simple. However, the main ideas underlying it are important for a number of the discussions above. A proper appreciation of the importance of the savings/credit/insurance nexus must look at the dynamic implications of achieving better gains from intertemporal trade. Many of the inefficiencies that arise because insurance possibilities are lacking may take the form of a failure to adopt new technologies and appropriate investments.[65]

Another link between financial intermediation and growth suggested by Gerschenkron's hypothesis is that intermediaries serve a function in the implementation of increasing returns to scale technologies. Theoretically, this can be modeled using Besley, Coate and Loury's (1993) model of roscas which emphasized the importance of indivisibilities. The idea here is that improvements in the scope of intermediation across space will make larger scale projects implementable and thus lead to an improvement in investment efficiency.

The above discussion suggests that a reduced form way of thinking about improvements in financial intermediation is as a kind technological progress that raises the return to capital, thus stimulating aggregate investment. This is quite consonant with Davis's (1971) discussion of financial integration in the US; technological progress in that sector translates into increased efficiency in the use of a given stock of capital and, in turn, raises aggregate accumulation.

Given the strong theoretical reasons for linking financial intermediation with growth, it is interesting to investigate whether evidence of a link between the two can be found econometrically. This question has recently been addressed using aggregate data in King and Levine (1993). They consider a sample of 80 countries to investigate whether measures of financial intermediation seem to be positively related to growth. They consider four measures of the extent of intermediation: the ratio of liquid liabilities to GDP; the ratio of deposit money bank domestic assets to deposit money bank domestic assets plus central bank domestic assets; the proportion of credit allocated to private enterprises; the ratio of claims on the non-financial private sector to GDP. Each is found to be robustly positively correlated with growth, providing some evidence in favor of the view that intermediation can be important to growth.

---

[65] It should be remembered, however, that nothing we have described here suggests that the decision not to adopt the new technology is inefficient, although there are good reasons to think that it might be. The next section returns to some of the main arguments why we might suspect inefficiency in the market outcome.

As the authors acknowledge, there is the question of whether financial intermediation measures are really exogenous. To assuage such concerns, they point out that similar results on the importance of measures of financial intermediation are obtained, if only beginning of sample values of the financial indicators are used on the right hand side.

The discussion so far has focused mainly on the link between financial development and growth. However, inequality, and its persistence through time, are also influenced by individuals' access to capital markets. These themes have recently been explored in a series of papers by Aghion and Bolton (1993), Banerjee and Newman (1991, 1993, 1994), Galor and Zeira (1993), and Piketty (1992). Their main contribution is to make capital market imperfections central to understanding the dynamics of inequality. Here, we present a simple example to illustrate some of their ideas, based on Banerjee and Newman (1994).

Suppose that each individual in the economy has access to the same production technology $f(k)$, where k stands for capital, which is consumed in the production process. Individuals differ in their initial wealth, w, which they can use as collateral for raising capital. We assume that lenders charge an interest rate of r (which is also the return on collateral) and can catch a defaulting borrower with probability π, whereupon they seize his collateral and any returns to investments that he has made. The lender will lend any amount for which repayment is guaranteed, i.e., any amount k such that

$$f(k) - r(k - w) \geq (1 - \pi)f(k) . \qquad (5.2)$$

Equality in (5.2) can be thought of as defining a $k(w)$ schedule denoting how much an individual can borrow as a function of their initial wealth. Under reasonable assumptions this will be increasing in w.

To derive implications of the model for the dynamics of inequality, suppose that there is an optimal amount of capital k^* which maximizes $f(k) - rk$ and yields a profit of $Y^*(\equiv f(k^*) - rk^*)$. For levels of capital below that, profits are denoted by $Y(k)$. Being able to operate the technology at the optimal scale will correspond to owning an initial capital level of w^* defined by $k(w^*) = k^*$. Now supposing that each generation (denoted by t) bequeaths an exogenously given amount σ of its wealth to the next. We then have the following equation governing the dynamics of inequality.

$$w_{t+1} = \begin{cases} \sigma(rw_t + Y(k^*)) & \text{for } w_t \geq w^* \\ \sigma(rw_t + Y(k(w_t))) & \text{otherwise} \end{cases} \qquad (5.3)$$

This equation succinctly captures the idea that wealth begets wealth. Having reached the cutoff level of w^* wealth accumulation is the same for all dynasties in absolute terms. However, the poorer individuals accumulate more slowly than the richer ones (with inequality widening through time).

By building in a minimum level of k that is needed to operate the technology at all, an even more dire prediction is reached, that some individuals with very low wealth never use the technology at all, since they cannot get enough wealth to borrow the smallest amount of capital necessary to operate it. In this case, the model displays a clear cut "poverty trap" for which capital market imperfections are responsible.[66]

This type of model can also be used to demonstrate how aggregate economic activity depends upon the distribution of wealth in society. For instance, it is straightforward to make labor demand, and therefore the equilibrium wage rate, depend upon the wealth distribution in this framework. This will lead to further interesting links between credit markets and the evolution of inequality, which can quickly turn out to be quite complex [see, for example, Banerjee and Newman (1993)]. Such models then give an alternative mechanism linking growth, development and credit market imperfections.

There are sound theoretical reasons to believe that there are links between the financial intermediation and long-run development. Moreover, the aggregate evidence seems to support this as far as growth is the issue. However, while it is key in much policy discussion, we know very little about the relative importance of different mechanisms that are driving the link in practice. Future work directed towards remedying this will therefore be immensely valuable.

6. Policy issues

This section discusses some specific issues of policy towards the development of credit and insurance institutions in developing countries. There are broadly two normative criteria that can be applied to motivate policy. The first is based on concerns about equity. Poor people are most likely to be excluded from trade in formal financial markets. There is a plethora of reasons for this. They tend to lack reliable forms of collateral, are less likely to be literate and numerate, may face higher transactions costs and lack the influence needed to gain subsidized loans. This suggests that interventions that genuinely broaden the scope of financial intermediation may have a major impact on the poor. While acknowledging this, however, there remains the question of whether interventions in financial markets are themselves an appropriate policy response. This raises the large subject of what are appropriate policy interventions to deal with poverty, surveyed in detail by Lipton and Ravallion in Chapter 42 of this

---

[66] Although as Piketty (1992) and Banerjee and Newman (1993) have shown, it is quite possible to get a poverty trap through aggregate effects even when there is no fixed cost.

Handbook. Credit programs directed towards the poor or groups that are discriminated against are commonplace in developing countries. These are motivated directly on equity grounds. A complete review of the issues involved in targeting credit can be found in Rashid and Townsend (1992).

Interventions to affect the working of credit and insurance may also be motivated by considerations of efficiency. One of the questions to be addressed in this section is how easily such interventions can be motivated in practice. Space precludes a detailed investigation of all aspects of these issues. There are five principal ways in which government intervention to improve the working of financial markets might be justified on efficiency grounds.[67]

6.1. Imperfect information arguments

We have referred to the importance of imperfect information in understanding the workings of financial markets. Both moral hazard and adverse selection can be used to justify intervention in financial markets. The main question for this section, however, is the type of inefficiency to which this gives rise. One of the most important models of credit markets under imperfect information is due to Stiglitz and Weiss (1981). They consider models with both adverse selection and moral hazard. Their analysis is most often remembered for its observation that credit may be rationed and that there is a presumption in favor of there being too little lending in equilibrium. This result is not, however, robust to respecification of the model, as deMeza and Webb (1987) have observed. In their model, which is a variant of Stiglitz and Weiss's but which supposes that the mean return of a project, not its riskiness, is the borrower's private information, there is too much lending in equilibrium relative to the social optimum. Neither model, however, predicts that lending will be efficient. The implication for interventions is unfortunately not robust to changes in the information problem facing lenders.

Multiple indebtedness also creates inefficiencies in credit markets with imperfect information.[68] Consider, for example, a model of moral hazard to which lenders respond by monitoring borrowers. It may be difficult for lenders to prevent each other from getting benefits from their monitoring and there will be under-provision of monitoring in equilibrium. Externalities may also be important because there is a common agency problem in that lenders affect the probability that *others'* loans are repaid when they change the terms and

---

[67] These arguments are developed in greater detail in Besley (1992a).

[68] Multiple indebtedness, especially between formal and informal lenders, is common in practice. For an analysis that recognizes this, see Bell, Srinivasan and Udry (1988).

conditions of their own loan contracts. A priori, it is difficult to predict the direction of the inefficiency and it is also difficult to imagine direct interventions for these inefficiencies. Moreover, there is almost no evidence on the empirical significance of such things, and most interventions motivated from this point of view would be empirically blind.

One interesting type of policy aimed at trying to promote lending to individuals who might be rationed out of the credit market is transaction cost subsidies. On one hand, these are attractive because they are targeted at the problem of imperfect information. On the other hand, it is not clear that transactions costs are excessive from some social point of view without some argument to the effect that there is misallocation of a resource, such as human capital, that needs to be used in project appraisal. It is however an interesting avenue for further investigation just because it focuses directly on the potential source of inefficiency in the financial market in question.

6.2. Enforcement arguments

One obvious way for the government to improve enforcement conditions for credit markets is to improve the possibilities for usable sources of collateral. One good example of this is the implementation of land registration programs, as have been undertaken in some countries, a good example being Kenya. The link between credit market performance and land rights is studied in detail by Feder et al. (1988) for Thailand and Migot-Adholla et al. (1990) for Ghana, Kenya and Rwanda. The former find results that are broadly supportive of the idea that better land rights improve access to credit markets. However, the latter fail to find any significant link.

In certain important respects the government is part of the enforcement problem. As we discussed above, the government has often failed to enforce loan repayment in schemes that it has set up and run, in part due to the agency problem of finding individuals to run such schemes who will carry out the necessary sanctions. Another interpretation is in terms of the political economy of credit markets, that have typically concentrated loans in the hands of the richer and more politically influential farmers. Governments have also occasionally engaged in debt forgiveness programs. Whatever the distributional merits served by such schemes, there can be little doubt that they diminish incentives of farmers to put in effort to make their projects successful.

There is little doubt that governments can undertake tasks that improve the possibilities for enforcement in credit markets. However, much of this is a question of having a better understanding of the political economy of intervention and trying to reorient credit programs away from redistributing wealth towards politically favored groups.

6.3. Protecting the depositor

Much regulation in credit markets is geared towards protecting the depositor. Individuals who deposit their funds with a bank need to be convinced that they will get the return that they are promised and better still, will not lose their money. Banks may face a number of problems in courting depositor confidence. Returns may be low just because of shocks to fundamentals in the economy, e.g., due to a weather shock that makes it difficult for farmers to repay their loans. Agency problems may also be an issue as we have argued throughout. Banks face an agency problem since intermediaries must monitor borrowers and make wise investment choices. This makes lender reputations important in financial markets. Finally, confidence in banks can be undermined for no good reason at all as in the bank run model of Diamond and Dybvig (1981). In similar spirit, any individual who decided to sell insurance would have to convince borrowers that she will deliver on the contract that is promised in the event that the insured has a need to claim.

In practice, all of these reasons have motivated government regulation. Of particular concern is the need to reduce the susceptibility of banks to failure. There are broadly two different views of bank runs in the literature that reach quite different conclusions about the motives for government regulation in this context. In Diamond and Dybvig's (1983) model, bank failures can be caused by losses in confidence that have little or nothing to do with fundamentals. Runs may occur simply because all depositors believe that they will, i.e., a run can be a self-fulfilling prophecy. Attempts by governments to institute a means of reducing an economy's susceptibility to bank runs, e.g., via deposit insurance, is efficiency enhancing in this framework.

An alternative view of bank runs put forward by Calomiris and Kahn (1991) inter alia says that bank runs are the natural consequence of the monitoring activities of depositors. It is the possibility of bank runs that leads more diligent depositors to desire to withdraw funds early and therefore to monitor the activities of banks. On this view an institution such as deposit insurance blunts depositors' incentives and may thereby reduce the efficiency of the banking sector.

In light of the possibly negative consequences of attempts to protect the depositor, there is renewed interest in finding ways of improving the flow of funds across space to deal with different fundamental shocks to regions as seem common in agricultural economies.

6.4. Market power

One of the main features of some kinds of financial institutions is monopoly power on the part of lenders. This may also create a rationale for government intervention. A good example is the case of local money lenders that we discussed above. The usual economic argument that it is efficient to regulate firms with market power is just that monopolists will reduce their output in order to earn greater rents. This is the usual "social costs of monopoly" argument. Recently Basu (1989) has questioned how appropriate a model this is of money lenders. To see this, one needs to consider the basis of their monopoly power. One perspective is that it is rooted in informational superiority compared to formal lenders. However, if this is so, then a better model of rural money lenders may be as discriminating monopolists. In this case, they may be efficiently transferring rents from borrowers to lenders and not actually inducing any inefficiency in the process. This means that the justification for intervention is based on distributional rather than efficiency concerns.

Even if Basu is right and a pure surplus extracting view has greater merit, there may still be an inefficiency loss in rural credit markets if lenders are unable to commit to future actions. A frequently-heard anecdote about village economies, where monopoly power in the credit markets is important, is that borrowers are worried about losing their land and are thus afraid of going into debt. This view is found, for example, in Bliss and Stern's (1982) study of an Indian village. One way of rationalizing this is to say that lenders may foreclose on loans backed by land as collateral and will thus force a distress sale of the land. This concern makes sense only if the borrower cannot borrow elsewhere to repay another lender who forecloses, i.e., it is a symptom of monopoly power in the credit market. Ideally a lender should be able to commit not to foreclose. Thus the real cost of monopoly power, even with a surplus extracting monopolist, may be that individuals do not borrow to finance some investments for fear that lenders will foreclose at an inopportune time. This view suggests that monopoly can be socially costly for quite different reasons from those suggested above and is consistent with Basu's (1989) idea that the conventional efficiency loss due to monopoly may not be important. It is also consistent with some of the anecdotal evidence. The role of competition in this case is to provide a "second source" in the sense of Farrell and Gallini (1989).

In practice, there has been a good deal of intervention intended to reduce the market power of village moneylenders. One example is India, where the credit cooperatives were explicitly motivated as an alternative to the money-lenders. This is quite consistent with a distributional- rather than an efficiency-based motive for intervention. Many commentators, e.g., Bell (1990), have doubted the efficacy of such strategies: "Casual observation .. suggests that their cooperatives are enfeebled or dormant and that those who staff the few branches of commercial banks settle for a quiet, or even venal, life, thus leaving the private lender's power unchallenged". (p. 325).[69]

6.5. Infant industry arguments

Infant industry arguments may also be an important source of justification for interventions in financial markets. The current state of financial markets in developed countries is the product of many centuries of experience and such economies have accumulated a wealth of organizational capital. The development of financial institutions thus requires a learning process. Government intervention can be motivated in two ways. First by asymmetric information, where the government is assumed to know more, for example, about what institutional structures have proved successful, than would-be bankers. Arguably, governments have access to a wider experience with how financial institutions work. A second role for government intervention arises if there are gains to experimentation in organizational structure. In that context, experimenters can create an externality in the form of increased knowledge about what financial structures work. Such learning externalities can support a case for government intervention since we would expect a sub-optimal amount of experimentation and a rate of growth of knowledge below the social optimum.

Neither of these arguments for intervention is special to the financial sector. They could apply equally in almost any context where the government has access to a better information set than its citizens, or there are learning externalities in technological diffusion. In the first case, the best intervention is provision of information to citizens. However, this can be costly and some kinds of demonstration programs could be justified. In the second case, the kind of intervention required is less clear cut. Some attempts to sponsor experiments in institutional design, as has occurred in the case of the Grameen Bank, for example, seem appropriate.

The question of sequencing interventions is particularly difficult, given that attempts to sponsor the set-up of new industries often creates vested interests that make removing subsidies difficult. It should be noted, however, that if infant industry arguments for government intervention are taken seriously, they seem not to justify many of the government interventions observed in practice. Moreover, the role of government historically has often made it harder to build viable financial institutions. Running credit programs where

---

[69] It should, however, be noted that money lenders and other financial institutions may be serving somewhat different functions.

delinquents go unpunished for political reasons may have induced individuals to learn that default often goes unpunished.

A final argument that is related to, although distinct from, the infant industry argument is the issue of general investment in infrastructure. As we argued at the outset, the ability to operate an effective financial superstructure hinges on the development of infrastructure. Thus implications for the development of financial markets might figure as a consideration in the decision to invest in the latter.

7. Concluding remarks

The aim of this chapter has been to examine aspects of the savings/insurance/ credit nexus in developing countries. We have considered a large number of theoretical and empirical issues. While there has been much progress in this area, there is still much to be done in understanding how this nexus operates. The above review suggests a number of messages. Chief among them is that institutions matter. The huge diversity in insurance and credit arrangements in developing countries is quite bewildering. Understanding the limits and potential of these is an important step towards a better appreciation of the factors that influence financial development. The approach that we have suggested is two-pronged. First one can ask what gains from trade are being exploited by a particular institutional structure and second, one can inquire into how trade is being sustained. This may help in moving towards theoretical and empirical models that are tailored towards the institutional context being investigated. Many of the best contributions reviewed above distinguished themselves in the way that they brought theory and data together. The challenge presented by this transcends the subject matter of this paper, although the value of doing it in the area under review here is surely as great as anywhere.

References

Adams, D.W., et al. (1984) *Undermining Rural Development with Cheap Credit*. Boulder, CO: Westview Press.

Adams, D.W., and Canavesi de Sahonero, M.L. (1989) 'Rotating savings and credit associations in Bolivia', *Savings and Development*, 13:219–236.

Adams, D.W., and Vogel, R.C. (1986) 'Rural financial markets in low-income countries: Recent controversies and lessons', *World Development*, 14(4):477–487.

Adegboye, R.O. (1972) 'Procuring loans by pledging cocoa trees', in: J.D. Von Pischke, D. Adams and G. Donald, eds., *Rural financial markets in developing countries*. Baltimore: Johns Hopkins University Press.

Aghion, P. and Bolton, P. (1993) 'A trickle down theory of growth and development with debt overhang', typescript.

Ainsworth, M. (1990) 'Economic aspects of child fostering in the Côte D'Ivoire', Washington D.C.: Africa Technical Department, The World Bank.

Alderman, H. and Paxson, C. (1992) 'Do the poor insure? A synthesis of the literature on risk reduction in developing countries', typescript.

Aleem, I. (1990) 'Imperfect information, screening, and the costs of informal lending: A study of a rural credit market in Pakistan', *World Bank Economic Review*, 4(3):329–350.

Altonji, J., Hayashi, F. and Kotlikoff, L. (1992) 'Is the extended family altruistically linked? Direct tests using micro-data', *American Economic Review*, 82(5):1171–1198.

Anderson, R.T. (1966) 'Rotating credit associations in India', *Economic Development and Cultural Change*, 14:334–339.

Ardener, S. (1964), 'The comparative study of rotating credit Associations', *Journal of the Royal Anthropological Society of Great Britain and Ireland*, 94(2):201–229.

Arnott, R. and Stiglitz, J.E. (1991) 'Moral hazard and nonmarket institutions: Dysfunctional crowding out or peer monitoring', *American Economic Review*, 81(1):179–190.

Arrow, K. (1963) 'Uncertainty and the welfare economics of medical care', *American Economic Review*, 53:941–973.

Atwood, D. (1990) 'Land registration in Africa: The impact on agricultural production', *World Development*, 18:659–671.

Banerjee, A. and Newman, A.F. (1994) 'Poverty and well-being in developing countries', *American Economic Review (Papers and Proceedings)*, 84(2):211–215.

Banerjee, A. and Newman, A.F. (1993) 'Occupational choice and the process of development', *Journal of Political Economy*, 101(2):274–298.

Banerjee, A. and Newman, A.F. (1991) 'Risk-bearing and the theory of income distribution', *The Review of Economic Studies*, 58(194):211–235.

Banerjee, A., Besley, T. and Guinnane, T. (1994) 'Thy neighbor's keeper: The design of a credit cooperative with theory and a test', *Quarterly Journal of Economics*, May: 491–515.

Basu, K. (1989) 'Rural credit markets: The structure of interest rates, exploitation and efficiency', in: P. Bardhan, ed., *The Economic Theory of Agrarian Institutions*. Oxford: Oxford University Press.

Bates, R.H. (1981), *Markets and states in tropical Africa: The political basis of agricultural policies*. Berkeley: University of California Press.

Bauer, P. and Paish, F. (1952) 'The reduction of fluctuations in the incomes of primary producers', *Economic Journal*, 62:750–780.

Begashaw, G.E. (1978) 'The economic role of traditional savings institutions in Ethiopia', *Savings and Development*, 2:249–262.

Bell, C. (1987) 'Credit markets and interlinked transactions', Chapter 16 in: H. Chenery and T.N. Srinivasan, eds., *Handbook of Development Economics, Volume 1*, Amsterdam: North-Holland.

Bell, C. (1990) 'Interactions between institutional and informal credit agencies in rural India', *World Bank Economic Review*, 4:297–328.

Bell, C., Srinivasan, T.N. and Udry, C. (1988) 'Agricultural credit markets in the Punjab: Segmentation, rationing and spillover', typescript.

Bencevinga, V.R. and Smith, B.D. (1991) 'Financial intermediation and endogenous growth', *Review of Economic Studies*, 58(2):195–210.

Bernheim, B.D. and Stark, O. (1988) 'Altruism within the family reconsidered: Do nice guys finish last?', *American Economic Review*, 78:1034–1045.

Bernheim, B.D., Shleifer, A. and Summers, L. (1985) 'The strategic bequest motive', *Journal of Political Economy*, 93:1045–1076.

Besley, T. (1992) 'Monopsony and time-consistency: sustainable pricing policies for perennial crops', typescript.

Besley, T. (1994) 'How do market failure arguments justify interventions in rural credit markets', *World Bank Research Observer*, 9(1):27–47.

Besley, T., and Coate, S. (1995) 'Group lending, repayment incentives and social collateral', *Journal of Development Economics*.

Besley, T., and Coate, S. (1992) 'Workfare vs. Welfare: Incentive arguments for work requirements in poverty alleviation programs', *American Economic Review*, 82(1):249–261.

Besley, T., Coate, S. and Loury, G. (1993) 'The economics of rotating savings and credit associations', *American Economic Review*, 83(4):792–810.

Bevan, D., Collier, P. and Gunning, J.W. (with Bigsten, A. and Horsnell, P.) (1989) *Peasants and government: An economic analysis*. Oxford: Clarendon Press.

Bhalla, S.S. (1979) 'Measurement errors and the permanent income hypothesis: Evidence from India', *American Economic Review*, 63:295–307.

Bhalla, S.S. (1980) 'The measurement of permanent income and its application to savings behavior', *Journal of Political Economy*, 88:722–744.

Binswanger, H. (1986) 'Risk aversion, collateral requirements, and the markets for credit and insurance in rural areas', in: P. Hazell, C. Pomerada, and A. Valdes, eds., *Crop insurance for agricultural development*. Baltimore: Johns Hopkins University Press.

Bliss, C.J. and Stern, N.H. (1982) *Palanpur: The economy of an Indian village*. Oxford: Clarendon Press.

Blanchard, O. and Fischer, S. (1989) *Lectures on macroeconomics*. Cambridge, MA: MIT Press.

Bouman, F.J.A. (1977) 'Indigenous savings and credit societies in the third world: A message', *Savings and Development*, 1:181–218.

Bouman, F.J.A. (1989) *Small, short and unsecured: Informal rural finance in India*. Delhi: Oxford University Press.

Braverman, A. and Guasch, J.L. (1986) 'Rural credit markets and institutions in developing countries: Lessons for policy analysis from practice and modern theory', *World Development*, 14(10/11):1253–1267.

Butcher, K. (1992) 'Household size, changes in household size, and household responses to economic conditions: Evidence from the Côte D'Ivoire', typescript.

Calomiris, C. (1989) 'Deposit insurance: Lessons from the record', *Federal Reserve Bank of Chicago Economic Perspectives*, May–June.

Calomiris, C. and Kahn, C. (1991) 'The role of demandable debt in structuring optimal banking arrangements', *American Economic Review*, 81(3):497–513.

Cameron, R. (1967) *Banking in the early stages of industrialization*. New York: Oxford University Press.

Carter, M.R. and Weibe, K.D. (1990) 'Access to capital and its impact on agrarian structure and productivity in Kenya', *American Journal of Agricultural Economics*, December: 1146–1150.

Coate, S. and Ravallion, M. (1993) 'Reciprocity without commitment: Characterization and performance of informal insurance arrangements', *Journal of Development Economics*, 40:1–24.

Cochrane, J. (1991) 'A simple test of consumption insurance', *Journal of Political Economy*, 99(5):957–976.

Cole, D.C. and Park, Y.C. (1983) *Financial development in Korea 1945–1978*. Cambridge, MA: Harvard University.

Collier, P. and Lal, D. (1986) *Labour and poverty in Kenya 1900–1980*. Oxford: Clarendon Press.

Dandekar, V.M. (1976) 'Crop insurance in India', *Economic and Political Weekly*, 11(26):A61–80.

Davis, L. (1971) 'Capital mobility and American growth', in: R.W. Fogel and S.L. Engerman, eds., *The reinterpretation of American economic history*. New York: Harper and Row.

Deaton, A.S. (1990) 'Saving in developing countries: Theory and review', *World Bank Economic Review (Proceedings of the World Bank Annual Conference on Development Economics, 1989)*, 61–96.

Deaton, A.S. (1991) 'Saving and liquidity constraints', *Econometrica*, 59:1221–1248.

Deaton, A.S. (1992a) 'Saving and income smoothing in Côte D'Ivoire', *Journal of African Economies*, 1(1):1–24.

Deaton, A.S. (1992b) 'Commodity prices, stabilization and growth in Africa', typescript.

Deaton, A.S. (1992c) *Understanding Consumption*. Oxford: Oxford University Press.

Deaton, A.S. and Laroque, G. (1992) 'On the behaviour of commodity prices', *Review of Economic Studies*, 59:1–24.

DeMeza, D. and Webb, D. (1987) 'Too much investment: A problem of asymmetric information', *Quarterly Journal of Economics*, 102:281–292.

Desai B.M. (1984) 'Group based savings and credit programs in rural India', in: *International Labor Organization: Group based savings and credit for the rural poor*. Geneva: ILO.

Diamond, D.W. (1989) 'Reputation acquisition in debt markets', *Journal of Political Economy*, 97(4):828–862.

Diamond D.W. and Dybvig, P. (1983) 'Bank runs, deposit insurance, and liquidity', *Journal of Political Economy*, 91:401–419.

Dixit, A. (1987) 'Trade and insurance with moral hazard', *Journal of International Economics*, 23:201–220.

Dixit, A. and Norman, V. (1980) *Theory of international trade*. Cambridge: Cambridge University Press.

Donaldson, D.S. (1982) 'An analysis of health insurance schemes in the Lalitpur district Nepal', typescript.

Dreze J. and Sen, A.K. (1992) *Hunger and public action*. Oxford: Oxford University Press.

Eaton, J. and Grossman, G. (1985) 'Tariffs as insurance: Optimal commercial policy when domestic markets are incomplete', *Canadian Journal of Economics*, 18:258–272.

Eswaran, M. and Kotwal, A. (1989) 'Credit as insurance in agrarian economies', *Journal of Development Economics*, 31 (1):37–53.

Farrell J. and Gallini, N. (1989) 'Second sourcing as a commitment: Monopoly incentives to attract competition', *Quarterly Journal of Economics*, 103:673–694.

FCIC (1986). *Annual report to Congress, 1981–1986*. FCIC, Washington, D.C.

Feder, G. and Feeney, D. (1990) 'Land tenure and property rights: Theory and implications for development policy', *World Bank Economic Review*, 5 (1):135–154.

Feder, G., Onchan, T., Chalamwong, Y. and Hongladarom, C. (1988) *Land policies and productivity in Thailand*. Baltimore: Johns Hopkins University Press.

Feder, G., Just, R. and Zilberman, D. (1985), 'Adoption of agricultural innovations in developing countries: A survey', *Economic Development and Cultural Change*, 33(2):255–298.

Floro, M.S. and Ray, D. (1992) 'Direct and indirect linkages between formal and informal financial institutions: An analytical approach', typescript.

Floro, S. and Yotopoulos, P. (1991) *Informal credit markets and the new institutional economics: The case of Philippine agriculture*. Boulder, San Francisco and Oxford: Westview Press.

Galor, O. and Zeira, J. (1993) 'Income distribution and macroeconomics', *Review of Economic Studies*, 60(1):35–52.

Gardner, B.L. and Kramer, R.A. (1986) 'Experience with crop insurance programs in the United States', in: P. Hazell, C. Pomerada and A. Valdes, eds., *Crop insurance for agricultural development*. Baltimore: Johns Hopkins University Press.

Geertz, C. (1962) 'The rotating credit association: A "middle rung" in development', *Economic Development and Cultural Change*, 10:241–263.

Gerschenkron, A. (1962) 'Agricultural backwardness in historical perspective', Chapter 1 in: *Agricultural backwardness in historical perspective*. Cambridge, Mass: Harvard University Press.

Gersovitz, M. (1988) 'Savings and development', Chapter 10 in: H. Chenery, and T.N. Srinivasan, eds., *Handbook of Development Economics, Volume 1*, Amsterdam: North-Holland.

Ghate, P. (1992) *Informal finance: Some findings from Asia*. Manila: Oxford University Press for the Asian Development Bank.

Gilbert, C.L. (1991) 'Domestic price stabilization policies for developing countries', Queen Mary and Westfield College, University of London, Economics Department Discussion Paper No. 231.

Goldsmith, R.W. (1969), *Financial structure and development*. New Haven, CT: Yale University Press.

Graham, D.H. (1992) 'Informal rural finance in Niger: Lessons for building formal institutions', in: D.W. Adams and D.A. Fitchett, eds., *Informal finance in low-income countries*. Boulder, Oxford: Westview Press, 71–83.

Greenwald, B. and Stiglitz, J.E. (1986) 'Externalities in economies with imperfect information and incomplete markets', *Quarterly Journal of Economics*, 101(2):229–264.

Greenwood, J. and Jovanovic, B. (1990) 'Financial development, growth and the distribution of income', *Journal of Political Economy*, 98:1076–1107.

Greif, A. (1989) 'Reputation and coalitions in medieval trade: Evidence on the Maghribi traders', *Journal of Economic History* 44(4):857–882.

Grimard, F. (1992) 'Consumption smoothing within ethnic groups in Côte d'Ivoire', typescript, Department of Economics, Princeton University.

Guinnane, T. (1992a) 'Financial intermediation for poor borrowers: The case of German credit cooperatives, 1850–1914', typescript.

Guinnane, T. (1992b) 'A failed institutional transplant: Raiffeisen's credit cooperatives in Ireland, 1894–1914', forthcoming in *Explorations in economic history*.

Harriss, J. (1991) 'The green revolution in North Arcot: Economic trends, household mobility and the politics of an 'awkward class'', in: P.B.R. Hazell and C. Ramasamy, eds., *The green revolution reconsidered*. Baltimore, MD: Johns Hopkins University Press.

Hart, O. and Moore, J.H. (1988), 'Incomplete contracts and renegotiation', *Econometrica*, 56(4):755–786.

Hayashi, F., Altonji, J. and Kotlikoff, L. (1991) 'Risk sharing, altruism and the factor structure of consumption', typescript.

Heckman, J.J. (1979), 'Sample selection bias as a specification error', *Econometrica*, 47:153–161.

Hill, P. (1956) *The gold coast cocoa farmer*. London: Oxford University Press.

Hoddinott, J. (1992) 'Rotten kids or manipulative parents: Are children old age security in Western Kenya?', *Economic development and cultural change*, 40:545–565.

Hoddinott, J. (1994) 'A model of migration and remittances applied to Western Kenya', *Oxford Economic Papers*, 46(3):459–476.

Hoff, K. and Stiglitz, J.E. (1992) 'A theory of rural credit markets with costly enforcement', typescript.

Holmstrom B. (1979) 'Moral hazard and observability', *Bell Journal of Economics and Management Science*, 10(1):74–91.

Hossein, M. (1988) *Credit for alleviation of rural poverty: The Grameen Bank in Bangladesh*, International Food Policy Research, Washington, D.C.

Hu, T.W. (1984) 'Health services in the People's Republic of China', in: M.W. Raffel, ed., *Comparative health care systems: Descriptive analyses of fourteen national health systems*. University Park, PA: Pennsylvania State University Press.

Huppi, M. and Feder, G. (1990) 'The role of groups and credit cooperatives in rural lending', *World Bank Research Observer*, 5(2):187–204.

Johnson, G.E. and Whitelaw, W.E. (1974) 'Urban-rural income transfers in Kenya: An estimated remittances function', *Economic Development and Cultural Change*, 22(3):473–479.

Johnson, P. (1985) *Saving and spending: The working class economy in Britain 1870–1939*. Oxford: Oxford University Press.

Khan, A. (1979) 'The comilla model and the integrated rural development programme in Bangladesh: An experiment in 'cooperative capitalism', *World Development*, 7:397–422.

Kihlstrom, R.E., Romer, D. and Williams, S. (1981) 'Risk aversion with random initial wealth', *Econometrica*, 49:911–920.

King R. and Levine, R. (1993) 'Finance and growth: Schumpeter might be right', *Quarterly Journal of Economics*, 108(3):717–737.

Kletzer, K. and Wright, B. (1992) 'Sovereign debt renegotiation in a consumption smoothing model', typescript.

Laffont, J.-J. (1989) *The economics of uncertainty and information*. Cambridge, MA: MIT Press.

Lamoreux, N.R. (1986) 'Banks, kinship and economic development: The New England case', *Journal of Economic History*, 46:657–667.

Leland, H. (1968) 'Saving and uncertainty: The precautionary demand for saving', *Quarterly Journal of Economics*, 82:465–473.

Levhari, D. and Srinivasan, T.N. (1969) 'Optimal savings under uncertainty', *Review of Economic Studies*, 36(2):153–163.

Lucas, R. and Stark, O. (1985) 'Motivations to remit: Evidence from rural Botswana', *Journal of Political Economy*, 93(5):901–918.

Mace, B. (1991) 'Full insurance in the presence of aggregate insurance', *Journal of Political Economy*, 99(5):121–154.

Matthias, P. (1973) 'Capital, credit and enterprise in the industrial revolution', *Economic History Review*, 121–143.

McKinnon, R. (1973) *Money and capital in economic development*. Washington, D.C.: The Brookings Institution.

Migot-Adholla, S., Hazell, P. and Place, F. (1990) 'Indigenous land rights systems in sub-Saharan Africa: A constraint on productivity?', *World Bank Economic Review*, 5(1):155–175.

Mirrlees, J.A. (1976) 'The optimal structure of incentives and authority within an Organization', *Bell Journal of Economics and Management Science*, 7(1):105–131.

Mirrlees, J.A. (1988) 'Optimal commodity price intervention', typescript, Nuffield College, Oxford, England.

Morduch, J. (1990) 'Risk, production and savings: Theory and evidence from Indian households', typescript.

Myers, C. (1988) 'Thailand's community finance experiments: Experience and prospects', *Health Care Financing Review*,

Nagrajan, G., David, C.C. and Meyer, R.L. (1992) 'Informal finance through land pawning contracts: Evidence from the Philippines', *Journal of Development Studies*, 29(1):93–107.

Narayana, N.S.S., Parikh, K. and Srinivasan, T.N. (1991) *Agriculture, growth and redistribution of income: Policy analysis with a general equilibrium model of India*. Amsterdam and Bombay: North-Holland and Allied Publishers.

Newbery, D.M.G. (1989) 'The theory of food price stabilisation', *Economic Journal*, 99(398):1065–1082.

Newbery, D.M.G. and Stiglitz, J.E. (1981) *The theory of commodity price stabilization: A study in the economics of risk*. Oxford: Oxford University Press.

Onchan, T. (1992) 'Informal rural finance in Thailand', in: D.W. Adams and D.A. Fitchett, eds., *Informal finance in low-income countries*. Boulder, Oxford: Westview Press, 103–117.

Pagano, M. and Jappelli, T. (1992) 'Information and sharing in the market for consumer credit', typescript.

Patten R.H. and Rosengard, J.K. (1991) *Progress with profits: The development of rural banking in Indonesia*. San Francisco, CA: ICS Press.

Paxson, C. (1992) 'Using weather variability to estimate the response of savings to transitory income in Thailand', *American Economic Review*, 82(1):15–33.

Pischke, J.D. (1983) 'A penny saved: Kenya's cooperative savings scheme', in: J.D. Von Pischke, D.W. Adams and G. Donald, eds., *Rural financial markets in developing countries*. Baltimore: Johns Hopkins University Press.

Piketty, T. (1992) 'Imperfect capital markets and persistence of initial wealth inequalities', typescript, Massachusetts Institute of Technology.

Platteau, J.-P. (1991) 'Traditional systems of social security and hunger insurance: Some lessons from the evidence pertaining to third world village societies', in: E. Ahmad, J. Dreze, J. Hills and A.K. Sen, eds., *Social security in developing countries*. Oxford: Oxford University Press.

Popkin, S. (1979) *The rational peasant: The political economy of rural society in Vietnam*. Berkeley: University of California Press.

Prabhu, K. and Ramachandram, S. (1986) 'Crop-credit insurance: Some disturbing features', *Economic and Political Weekly*, 21(42):1866–1869.

Radhakrishnan, S., et al. (1975) *Chit funds*. Madras: Institute for Financial Management and Research.

Rashid, M. and Townsend, R. (1992) 'Targeting credit and insurance: Efficiency, mechanism design and program evaluation', typescript, World Bank, Washington, DC.

Ravallion, M. (1991) 'Reaching the poor through rural public works: Arguments, evidence and lessons from South Asia', *World Bank Research Observer*, 6:153–175.

Roberts, R.A.J. and Dick, W.J.A. eds. (1991) *Strategies for crop insurance planning*, FAO Agricultural Series Bulletin, No. 86, FAO, Rome.

Rosenzweig, M. (1988) 'Risk, implicit contracts and the family in rural areas of low income countries', *Economic Journal*, 98(4):1148–1170.

Rosenzweig, M. and Binswanger, H. (1993) 'Wealth, weather risk and the composition and profitability of agricultural investments', forthcoming in the *Economic Journal*.

Rosenzweig, M. and Stark, O. (1989) 'Consumption smoothing, migration and marriage: Evidence from rural India', *Journal of Political Economy*, 97(4):905–927.

Rosenzweig, M. and Wolpin, K. (1993) 'Credit market constraints, consumption smoothing and the accumulation of durable production assets in low income countries: Investment in bullocks in India', forthcoming in *Journal of Political Economy*.

Ross, S. (1981) 'Some stronger measures of risk aversion in the small and in the large', *Econometrica*, 49:621–638.

Rothschild, M. and Stiglitz, J.E. (1970) 'Increasing risk I: A definition', *Journal of Economic Theory*, 2:225–243.

Salant, S.W. (1982) 'The vulnerability of commodity price stabilization schemes to speculative attack', *Journal of Political Economy*, 91:1–38.

Sanderatne, N. (1992) 'Informal finance in Sri Lanka', in: D.W. Adams and D.A. Fitchett, eds., *Informal finance in low-income countries*, Boulder, San Francisco and Oxford: Westview Press.

Sayad, J. (1984) 'Rural credit and positive real rates of interest: Brazil's experience with rapid inflation' in: Adams et al., 146–160.

Schumpeter, J.A. (1934) *The theory of economic development* (1968 edition translated by R. Opie, with an introduction by J.E. Elliott) New Brunswick and London: Transactions Books.

Scott, J. (1976) *The moral economy of the peasant: Rebellion and subsistence in Southeast-Asia.* New Haven, CT: Yale University Press.

Siamwalla, A., Pinthong, C., Poapongsakorn, N., Sarsanguan, P., Nettayarak, P., Ming-maneenakin, W. and Tubpin, Y. (1990) 'The Thai rural credit system: Public subsidies, private information and segmented markets', *World Bank Economic Review*, 4(3):271–296.

Stiglitz, J.E. and Weiss, A. (1981) 'Credit rationing in markets with imperfect information', *American Economic Review*, 71(3):393–419.

Stiglitz, J.E. and Weiss, A. (1986) 'Credit rationing and collateral', in: J. Edwards and C. Mayer, eds., *Recent developments in corporate finance.* Cambridge: Cambridge University Press.

Stiglitz, J.E. (1977) 'Monopoly, non-linear pricing and imperfect information: The insurance market', *Review of Economic Studies*, 44:407–430.

Stiglitz, J.E. (1990) 'Peer monitoring and credit markets', *World Bank Economic Review*, 4(3):351–366.

Thomas, J. and Worrall, T. (1988) 'Self-enforcing wage contracts', *Review of Economic Studies*, 55:541–554.

Thompson, E.P. (1971) 'The moral economy of the English crowd in the eighteenth century', *Past and Present*, 50:76–136.

Townsend, R. (1990) *Financial structure and economic organization*, Oxford: Basil Blackwell.

Townsend, R. (1991) 'Risk and insurance in village India', typescript.

Townsend, R. (1992) 'Financial systems in Northern Thai villages', typescript.

Udry, C. (1990) 'Credit markets in Northern Nigeria: Credit as insurance in a rural economy', *World Bank Economic Review*, 3:251–271.

Udry, C. (1994) 'Risk and insurance in a rural credit market: An emprical investigation in North Nigeria', *Review of Economic Studies*, 61:495–526.

Varian, H. (1992) *Microeconomic Analysis*, New York: W.W. Norton & Co.

Varian, H. (1989) 'Monitoring agents with other agents', *Journal of Institutional and Theoretical Economics*, 146:153–174.

Vogel, R.C. (1984) 'The effect of subsidized agricultural credit on income distribution in Costa Rica', in: Adams et al., 133–145.

Von Pischke, J.D. (1983) 'A penny saved: Kenya's cooperative savings scheme', in: J.D. Von Pischke, D. Adams and G. Donald, eds., *Rural financial markets in developing countries.* Baltimore: Johns Hopkins University Press.

Wells, R.J.G. (1979) 'Sources and utilization of rural credit in Mukim Langgar', *Malayan Economic Review*, 3:89–97.

Wolpin, K.I. (1982) 'A new test of the permanent income hypothesis: The impact of weather on the income and consumption of farm households in India', *International Economic Review*, 23:583–594.

World Bank (1975) *The assault on world poverty.* Washington, DC: World Bank.

World Bank (1987) *Financing health services in developing countries: An agenda for reform*, Washington, DC: World Bank.

Yaron, J. (1992) *Successful rural financial institutions*, World bank discussion papers No. 150., Washington, DC: The World Bank.

Zeldes, S. (1989) 'Consumption and liquidity constraints: An empirical investigation', *Journal of Political Economy*, 97(2):305–346.

Chapter 37

TECHNOLOGICAL CHANGE AND TECHNOLOGY STRATEGY

ROBERT E. EVENSON

Yale University

LARRY E. WESTPHAL*

Swarthmore College and United Nations University

Contents

* Useful comments on drafts were received from John Enos, Brian Fikkert, Jeffrey James, Wolfgang Keller, and Howard Pack. T.N. Srinivasan and Jere Behrman provided necessary prodding tempered with graciously offered criticism and insight. Evenson received support in undertaking this survey from the Economic Growth Center at Yale University; Westphal, from the United Nations University, Institute for New Technologies, in Maastricht, The Netherlands.

Handbook of Development Economics, Volume III, Edited by J. Behrman and T.N. Srinivasan
© *Elsevier Science B.V., 1995*

Contents (continued)

1. Introduction

Except with respect to agriculture, investments in technological change by less developed countries (LDCs) have not been emphasized in economic thought about the general design of development policy. Development textbooks do devote considerable attention to technological topics in nonagricultural sectors, such as the choice of techniques and technology transfer through direct foreign investment. And international institutions do engage in technological projects beyond the agricultural sector; supporting activities in the industrial sector to disseminate technical information and to upgrade production, for instance. But neither the topics nor the projects are generally perceived in relation to technological investments. Typically they are seen from other perspectives – choice of techniques, in terms of generating appropriately remunerative employment; technology upgrading, in terms of assistance to structural adjustment following market opening; and so on. They are seldom brought together in a unified discussion of technology and development or in some nodal point within bureaucratic structures. Why are the technological aspects of development usually considered as disparate elements? We suspect that part of the answer lies in the absence of a common conception of the role and nature of technological change in the context of economic development. Thus, in attempting to provide a more unified treatment, we find it necessary to devote some space at the outset to conceptual matters.

1.1. Concepts of technological change

In the past, many development economists have approached technological change from the vantage of structural change and technique choice. "Technological change" has meant the first appearance in local production of any novel process or product. It has been considered the result of an endogenous process; the demand for new techniques is induced by other changes within the economy. And it was often thought that the supply of techniques was readily available from the "shelf" of techniques produced in developed countries. Perhaps most common has been the conception of dynamic comparative advantage, grounded in the tradition of Heckscher–Ohlin–Samuelson trade theory [Chenery (1967)]. New products are introduced into local production as the structure of production evolves in response to changes in the composition of domestic demand as well as in the balance of factor supplies and demands. And new processes are adopted as the allocation of resources adjusts to changes in relative factor prices. But, apart from the costs of searching for and acquiring new technical information, investments in technological change have had no meaningful role in this view.

The policy implications of this approach are straightforward. Technological-ly, it is sufficient if the policy regime simply insures the timely initial adoption of economically warranted techniques and their appropriate diffusion through the economy. Accordingly, the requisite policies are those required to achieve an efficient allocation of resources in the context of exogenously determined technological alternatives. Among these policies, the only ones explicitly focused on technology per se are those that address inefficiencies that may result where techniques are not freely available. One such commonly employed technology policy, justified as providing a public good, is government sponsor-ship of institutes that collect, process, and disseminate technical information. But technology policies per se are of secondary importance relative to the other kinds of policies that are conventionally associated with achieving efficient resource allocation in a static setting.

Two assumptions taken together would justify this inattention to endogenous elements on the supply side of technological change in the development process. One is an assumption that technology consists simply of a set of discrete techniques, each wholly described by its "blueprint". The other is that all techniques are created in the developed countries, from whence they flow to the technologically backward LDCs. On these assumptions, there is no place in development for investments in creating technology, in the form of either assimilating imported techniques or developing new techniques through adap-tive invention. The first assumption implies that assimilation is costless. The second implies that there is little scope for LDCs to make useful adaptive modifications in technology.

If technology is perceived in more complex terms, consistent with empirical evidence, one is led to conclusions quite different from those based on the assumptions noted above. Most obvious is the evidence, reviewed later in this survey, that technology is in fact created in the LDCs. This and other important aspects of technological reality can only be fully comprehended by recognizing that technology is, most fundamentally, knowledge about how to do things. Techniques, defined as singular ways of doing particular things, are the result of choices made when applying technology in specific circumstances with respect to economic, physical, and social conditions. In effect, a technique is a solution to a problem of constrained maximization in which technology and circumstances form the constraints.

1.1.1. Tacitness and circumstantial sensitivity

No existing technique is completely expressed by the sum of the reproducible elements in which it is partially contained; that is, in the codified information about it and the material inputs that provide the physical means for its accomplishment. This is because much of the knowledge about how to perform elementary processes and about how to combine them in efficient systems is tacit, not feasibly embodied and neither codifiable nor readily transferable. Thus, though two producers in the same circumstances may use identical material inputs in conjunction with equal information, they may nonetheless employ what are really two distinct techniques owing to differences in understanding of the tacit elements. In turn, currently existing techniques do not necessarily exhaust the potentially beneficial applications of technology. Even supposing that they represent optimal solutions for the circumstances in which they are respectively used, it does not follow that they must necessarily be optimal with respect to different circumstances where they have not been previously tested.

Tacitness and circumstantial sensitivity in the application of technology are often disregarded, being obscured by the tendency to think about techniques and circumstances in terms that are general rather than specific. Techniques are customarily identified in generic terms, typically with reference to key physical inputs – variety of seed, for example. But technologies in use that are based on the same seed variety differ a great deal; planting and harvesting dates differ among locations, as do the optimal amounts of water and fertilizer used. In industry, machines can be calibrated to operate in different ways and can be used with distinct kinds of ancillary fixtures to achieve various effects. Circumstances are ordinarily identified with economic variables, which are frequently summarized very simply in terms of the wage–rental ratio, neglecting not only other economic variables but also physical and social conditions. Nontradeable inputs – land, labor, utilities, and services – vary greatly in characteristics and quality.

Similarly, ostensibly identical material inputs – natural resources in particular – are characterized by widely differing precise specifications. Among social institutions, labor-management relations are particularly variable.

1.1.2. Investments in technological change

Once technology is understood in these more complex terms, it is quite obvious that investments in technology are made whenever it is newly applied, regardless of the novelty of the application. Learning about technology and problem solving using the knowledge acquired in mastering technology are not costless, even if the choices made in realizing the technique to be used are identical in generic terms to choices previously made elsewhere. The magnitude of the warranted investment depends crucially on the circumstantial sensitivity of existing reproducible elements of technology. As will be discussed in detail later, there are pronounced sectoral differences in the circumstantial sensitivity of generic techniques and, correspondingly, in the scale of problem solving investments across sectors.

A stream of investments over time is typically required to overcome tacitness and thus achieve mastery. Not only is much technology tacit, so too is much knowledge about the specifics of local circumstances and about the ways that differences in circumstances affect the productivity of particular techniques. Tacit knowledge can only be acquired through investments in learning – learning that is importantly grounded in purposeful analysis of information gained through practical experience. With learning comes increased under- standing of technology and of circumstances, which typically results in changes away from the original solution, as techniques are adapted to local circum- stances or otherwise modified to achieve higher productivity. Learning is generally a sequential process, so that alterations in techniques usually take place through a progression of problem reformulations leading to new solu- tions.

Investments in learning lead either to assimilation, duplicating understanding that exists elsewhere without adding to the stock of reproducible technology, or to invention and innovation, adaptive or otherwise, creating novel elements of reproducible technology that yield higher productivity under local conditions.[1] To determine the relative frequencies of these outcomes in the experience of even one LDC would be an enormous undertaking because of the detailed firm-level information that would be required. Patent statistics and similar indicators, supplemented by case study research, clearly indicate that invention does occur in most LDCs, and that the advanced LDCs may be about on a par with developed countries in this regard. Moreover, case study research strongly suggests that internationally competitive levels of productivity are seldom if ever achieved through simple assimilation. It also suggests that the conventional measures fail to capture a great deal of the technological effort that underlies the attainment of competitive productivity levels.

Simple models of learning-by-doing [e.g. Arrow (1962b)] do not capture the essential elements of technological development even at the level of an individual firm that is pioneering the local introduction of some new technology [Bell (1984)]. They are not at all suited to comprehending the complexities of technological development among many interacting entities forming an economy. The essential elements are those that have been stressed by economic historians [Landes (1969), David (1975), Rosenberg (1976, 1982), among others] in writing about technological development in the now advanced countries. Technological efforts to overcome tacitness and to adapt technology

---

[1] The Schumpeterian (1934) definitions of "invention" and "innovation" are used throughout this survey; the terms refer to the creation and commercialization, respectively, of new technology. Many authors in the field use "innovation" to mean both things.

to local circumstances have figured importantly whenever technological follow-ers have succeeded in effectively utilizing leaders' technology. From them have come many of the fundamental institutional and organizational innovations that have helped to make technological change an integral part of economic activity in the advanced countries.

The investment required to accomplish a particular technological change depends critically on two things: 1) the degree of external participation in its accomplishment; and 2) the internal technological capability (ability to make effective use of technology) that has been acquired through previous invest-ments in technology. By substituting for internal technological capability through providing various technological services, external agents can substitute for current investment.[2] Accordingly, the management of technological change involves choices of both the changes to be made and the investments to be undertaken. The latter are essentially "make-buy" choices in which the decision to make results in the creation of technological capital. These choices raise important policy issues with regard to the sequencing of an LDC's investments in technological capital and to their phasing relative to other processes of economic development.

1.2. The catchup concept

The concept of catchup economic growth has been in the development literature for many years [Landes (1990)]. From Gerschenkron's (1962) discussion of the advantages of backwardness to the contemporary literature dealing with convergence [Barro and Sala-i-Martin (1992)], the proposition that technological followers benefit from the technology created by technologi-cal leaders has been accepted as an empirical truth. A strong version of this proposition is that the scope for catchup growth is proportional to the difference in technological capabilities between a follower and the leaders. This version predicts an inverse relationship between technological capabilities at any point in time and subsequent productivity (as well as economic) growth.

The mechanism generally specified as underlying this process can be described as technology transfer. Followers, with appropriate policies and investments, are expected to learn about the leaders' technology, choose the best techniques for particular purposes, and then implement them. As previously indicated, the policies required for transfer are usually not seen to differ from those required for achieving economic efficiency. The investments entailed are usually thought to be investments in education, physical capital, and general management capability. In particular, R&D (research and de-

---

[2] Their effectiveness in doing so is, however, constrained by the tacitness of local circumstances.

velopment) and related activities that are considered essential to the maintenance of technological leadership are often not deemed to be important for
success by follower countries.

Studies of economic growth in the post-World War II era have shown that
general convergence of income or productivity levels has not occurred [Easter-
lin (1981), Landes (1990), Barro (1991), Williamson (1991)]. True, several
former LDCs, now typically classified as newly industrialized countries (NICs),
have grown at very rapid rates and have, in fact, converged on the leading
industrialized countries. And there has been convergence among the OECD
countries. But most LDCs are not on a path of convergence toward the
industrial countries.

Few studies have attempted to document carefully the sources of initial
divergence in levels of economic development. "Uneven development" studies
[e.g. Hymer and Resnick (1970), Hymer (1972)] generally attribute it to
political factors; economic historians [e.g. Ayres (1944), Landes (1969), Morris
and Adelman (1989), Rosenberg et al. (1992)], to a broader constellation of
institutional and social factors. But it appears to be generally accepted that
adverse institutions and deficient policy regimes are responsible for the failure
by most LDCs to achieve catchup growth over the past four decades. This
survey will conclude in addition that specific investments in technology over
sustained periods are essential to the realization of technological catchup by
followers. Institutions and policy regimes may explain why the investments
have not been made, or why the investments made have been ineffective in
many cases. But the investments are essential [Dahlman and Nelson (1991)].
No LDC has to date achieved rapid economic growth without continued
technological investment.

1.3. Readers guide

This chapter addresses questions that are primarily microeconomic in nature:
What are the relevant varieties of technological investments? How large are
the associated net returns? What factors motivate their being undertaken? Do
private agents allocate adequate resources to the right kinds of technological
changes? How can governments overcome likely market failures? What can be
learned about probable government failures from the record of the past?
Answers to these questions would provide the basis for gauging whether past
technological investment has been insufficient or misdirected and, if so, for
probing the causes and consequences.

As will be seen, answers are more nearly complete for agriculture than for
other sectors. This reflects the disparity in the attention and funding given by

public authorities to promote technological change in different sectors. (The agricultural sector, while often penalized by price policy, is favored by technology policy.) In turn, this survey includes work on developed countries where answers are at least partially available for them but not for LDCs. This is not done to imply that the issues and answers for both kinds of countries are necessarily the same, but instead to provide a meaningfully comprehensive overview of the topic at hand.

Relatively little is said here about technological change in the provision of services, for several reasons. Though there is an extensive body of careful empirical research relating to this topic in developed countries, there does not appear to be much parallel work for LDCs. Severe conceptual and empirical problems are faced in doing research on productivity in service activities [see the editor's introduction in Griliches (1992)]. To have dealt with them adequately in the context of what literature does exist for the LDCs would have enlarged an already lengthy survey. But it should not go unnoticed that much of this survey is in fact concerned with the provision of services related to the transfer, assimilation, and adaptation of technology. As is discussed throughout, a good deal of technological development occurs through changes in the services provided and the means by which they are provided.

A number of major themes pervade this survey. Several that build on the tacitness and circumstantial sensitivity of technology are critical to an understanding of processes of technological change. These themes come primarily from empirical – econometric and case study – investigations of LDC experience. As will be argued in Section 2, where pertinent theoretical work is reviewed, relatively few insights have been provided by theorists, most of whose work neglects key features of empirical reality in the LDCs. The themes are developed in Sections 3 through 5, which collectively summarize the useful analytical structures that have been derived from empirical studies in the field.

The first theme is developed in Sections 3 and 4: rapid economic growth that is importantly based on technological change can not be realized without technological development in the sense of creating technological infrastructure in the form of specialized institutions and capital stocks. And there are wide differences in levels of technological development among LDCs. Sections 4 and 5 articulate a second theme: technology flows from countries that are technological leaders to those that are followers in two distinct ways. One is through the direct transfer of techniques which are then typically adapted to local circumstances. The other is through the transfer of knowledge that is then used by the follower country to generate new techniques. A follower's technological capabilities are critical for both modes of transfer, but in different ways. Section 5 also adds a related theme: differences in economic, physical, and social conditions coupled with the sensitivity of technology to these differences creates "technological distance" between any two locations.

Distances are large in many fields of technology and critically affect the technological make–buy choices that confront entities in LDCs.

The final major theme, present throughout the chapter, is that effective technology transfer requires distinct activities and investments to minimize the cost of implementing the new technology and to maximize its productivity once in place. The optimal package depends on the field of technology as well as on the technological distance involved. It further depends on the behavior of technology suppliers and on the recipient's level of technological development. Policies affecting resource allocation and the availability of supporting infrastructure play a major role in determining whether the optimal package is actually chosen.

Sections 6 and 7 review the evidence from empirical studies of, first, the factors affecting the accumulation of technological assets in LDCs and, second, the returns to investments in such assets, including the growth and distributional implications of technological change. Policy issues are dealt with in Section 8. It argues that the policy options faced by individual LDCs are significantly conditioned by technological development levels and, that for most countries, the building of technological capabilities should be a central objective of overall development strategy. Section 9 concludes the survey with a brief discussion of research priorities.

2. Theoretical contributions

Economic development has been the focus of a large part of economic growth theory. Much research was done in the 1950s and 1960s in the context of long-run equilibrium growth to model economies characterized by labor surplus and other conditions thought relevant to LDCs [Lewis (1954), Fei and Ranis (1964), Jorgenson (1966)]. This research produced a heightened appreciation for the important role of technological change in sustaining the development process and generated greater comprehension of the significance of sectoral differences in rates of technological change. But it contributed practically nothing to understanding how technological change is generated and maintained. The models simply treated technological change as an exogenous process, one occurring at a steady rate over time.

Techniques of development planning that evolved in symbiosis with growth theory embodied simple views of the sources of technological change. The most extreme view was that derived from socialist planning theory and practice. The capital goods sector, drawing on R&D performed in specialized institutes, was thought to be the singular driving force of technological change. Inspired by Mahalanobis (1955), India was one of several countries which put this view into practice through development planning in the 1950s and 1960s.

As will be discussed in further detail below, the priority given to indigenous technology creation in the socialist approach proved to be highly counter-productive. So did the disregard for product innovation, which was thought merely to cater to frivolous tastes.[3]

A less extreme view, held by many Western advocates of development planning, saw technological change as being concentrated in the design and implementation of investment projects. It was thought to emanate from the activities of engineers who were responsible for selecting the best available techniques and plant designs as well as for seeing to their effective implementation. As in the socialist approach, hardly any systematic attention was given to assuring continual processes of technological change within existing enterprises. Nonetheless, formal planning models often incorporated exogenous technological change parameters, yielding projections which generally turned out to be unrealistic. Regardless of its ideological underpinnings, the planning mentality of the 1950s and 1960s had a serious consequence. It stifled consideration of many forms of investment in productivity enhancement.

In this section we review those few bodies of theoretical analysis that do at least meaningfully incorporate some aspect of the processes of technological change. Included are the recently emerged body of endogenous growth theory, models of invention and discovery, as well as older models of induced innovation and technology diffusion. Our own conclusion is that the work in these areas has contributed useful insights to the analytical structures that we will later bring to bear on the analysis of technological change, but that most of our understanding of technological change comes from empirical studies.

2.1. Endogenous growth models

Endogenous growth theory [e.g. Romer (1986, 1990), Lucas (1988), Murphy et al. (1989), Grossman and Helpman (1991), Barro and Sala-i-Martin (1992)] differs from its precursor in the explicit introduction of activities which can affect the long-run growth rate. Human capital formation and/or R&D investment are modeled as being subject to increasing returns, with various arguments being given about the source of the non-convexity, which is generally found in some form of externality or spillover phenomenon.[4] The

---

[3] A prime example is the Indian Ambassador automobile. The original model remained unchanged for 30 years, this in spite of global advances in engine efficiency, braking systems, and the like.

[4] The arguments are built on micro foundations provided by previous theoretical research on the generation of new technology and the formation of human capital which demonstrated that R&D and schooling are not conventional factors of production, both being characterized by important positive externalities. On R&D, see Arrow (1962a), Mansfield, et al. (1977b), Scherer (1986), Griliches (1991); on schooling, Denison (1962), Becker (1964).

presence of increasing returns (or, more accurately, a lower bound on diminishing returns to capital) is responsible for the possibility of per capita income growth in the long run (asymptotically). By exploring the implications of the properties of technology as knowledge, the theory has increased the general understanding of the importance of technological investment.[5]

To date, endogenous growth theory has achieved few robust policy generalizations. Moreover, development economists who grew up arguing about the merits of Rosenstein-Rodan's (1943) "big push" and debating balanced versus unbalanced growth are prone to find much that is not really new in endogenous growth theory. The vocabulary is new, but many of the insights that are today considered novel were the staple of development economics in the 1950s and 1960s. Indeed, as is relatively well known, the basic insights on which much endogenous growth theory is built are present in Adam Smith's (1776) discussion of pin making technology.

Translation of the theory into empirically testable models is confounded by using steady-state conditions as guides to specification. While these conditions do offer insight, it is not at all clear that they provide directly applicable guides for empirical work. Economies may require long periods to reach steady-state, particularly if the incentives for appropriate investments are not in place or are endogenously established. Moreover, technology spillovers are not well specified in these models, and indivisibilities in processes of technology creation are not fully captured. Additionally, the available data have grave limitations which severely constrain attempts at discriminating empirical inquiry [Srinivasan (1994)].

Most efforts to test insights derived from endogenous growth theory have in fact focused on implications of the older, neoclassical growth theory [Pack (1994)]. Nonetheless, the empirical work [e.g. Lichtenberg (1991), Kortum (1992), Mankiw et al. (1992)] so far spawned by the theory has produced some findings of consequence for attempting to understand technological development. Particularly noteworthy in this respect is Lichtenberg's (1991) work demonstrating the importance of distinguishing among different asset accumulation processes; in particular, R&D versus schooling. Also promising is work like that done by Coe and Helpman (1993), which investigates the relationship between total factor productivity (TFP) growth in OECD countries and domestic as well as foreign R&D expenditures, with the latter being included to capture international technology spillovers. Additional research of this kind is discussed in Sections 5 through 7.

Endogenous growth theory has made a significant contribution through the

---

[5] Rodrik (Chapter 45 of this Handbook) discusses endogenous growth theory in relation to issues of policy reform. In turn, for general discussion of endogenous growth theory, see the symposium on new growth theory in the Winter 1994 issue of the *Journal of Economic Perspectives*.

disciplined rigor that it has introduced into the analysis of the technological underpinnings of long-run growth. No less important, it has brought issues of long-run growth back into mainstream discussion, making development again a matter of interest to many economists. Additionally, the incorporation of endogenous growth considerations into international trade theory has greatly increased its relevance in the context of technological development. The most important work here is that of Grossman and Helpman (1991). Their models treat inventive activity and related investments in a systematic fashion to derive a number of new insights centered on the distinctive roles of these investments in generating trade between technological leaders and followers. But the comments made above in relation to endogenous growth theory generally apply here as well. Moreover, these models do not fully come to grips with the disparities in technological capabilities among countries at widely different levels of technological development.

2.2. Models of invention

Growth theory is concerned with the implications of particular properties of technological activity rather than with comprehending the activities per se. Early work on invention did not consider international dimensions but it did establish the basic rationale for intellectual property rights (IPRs) and clarified their value. Machlup (1958) reviewed the effectiveness of existing IPR systems. Arrow (1962a) and Nordhaus (1969) developed the basic model for analyzing the incentives to engage in R&D that are afforded by IPRs. In later studies within the industrial organization tradition, Barzel (1968), Dasgupta and Stiglitz (1980), Gilbert and Newbery (1982) and Dasgupta (1986) developed models of patent races which demonstrated the possibility of excessive duplication of R&D activity (due to overfishing in the pool of latent inventions).

None of these studies paid attention to the peculiar circumstances of LDCs, nor did they foster much work to verify their propositions empirically. Even so, some theorists consider that this work has weakened what was once an overwhelming case for IPRs. In the realm of developed country policy, however, there is a clear trend toward stronger IPR protection, both in case law and in legislation. This trend has an obvious international thrust, with trade law increasingly being used to achieve IPR compliance by other countries. The just concluded GATT negotiations attest to the importance that is attached to IPRs by the developed countries.[6]

---

[6] We review the limited empirical work regarding IPR impacts on R&D investment in Section 6.4.

2.2.1. Search models

The invention process differs considerably across fields of technology. In each field, the pre-invention sciences (see Section 3.2) have devised procedures for discovery and invention – a kind of technology for the discovery of technology. Scientific instruments, for example, are part of this technology. Well developed experimental design structures are another. Animal and plant improvement sciences rely on models of genetic improvement. Industrial engineering uses design principles grounded in both theory and practical experience. And so on.

Thus it is incorrect to say that the invention process is not amply understood by the researchers working in most technological fields. Models of genetic selection, for example, can explain animal and plant improvement quite well. Nonetheless, each invention entails an "inventive step" that goes beyond the known and conventional. Trial and error, or search, along with an element of boldness and risk-taking is involved. Important pioneering, or "macro" [Mokyr (1990)], inventions are characterized by large inventive steps. They are typically followed by commonplace, or "run-of-the-mill" [Nordhaus (1969)], inventions that come in a reasonably obvious (to those familiar with invention in the field) sequence. Lower down the scale are the frequent minor, adaptive sub-inventions characterized by a low inventive step.[7] These are the predominant inventions in LDCs, which rarely produce pioneering inventions and, except for the more advanced among them, contribute relatively few commonplace follow-on inventions.

Several authors have applied search concepts to examine the general nature of the invention process [Schmookler (1966), Nordhaus (1969), Scherer (1972), Evenson and Kislev (1975, 1976), Binswanger and Ruttan (1978), Lee (1982)].[8] The basic search model has two elements that are particularly relevant to the invention of improved technology for LDCs. It provides for changes over time in the pool of knowledge from which inventions are drawn (invention potential). Such changes do not only flow from upstream, basic research; they come as well from the search process itself and from similar research activities elsewhere.[9] The model also provides for diminishing returns within a period of research while allowing for diminishing, constant, or increasing returns over periods depending on changes in the pool of potential inventions.

The search process is modeled as a sequence of experiments, each composed

---

[7] Patents apply to the first two kinds of invention; utility models, to the third. More is said about these forms of IPRs in Section 3.1.

[8] Nelson and Winter (1982) built an evolutionary theory of what would now be termed endogenous growth on the basis of a somewhat different search model.

[9] As will be seen in Section 5.2, research results obtained elsewhere and transferred in the form of germplasm are the dominant mode of biological technology transfer in agriculture.

of n trials or draws. A single draw can be a new crop variety, a certain dose of fertilizers, an alternative planting date, etcetera. At the beginning of a research period, a distribution of potential inventions exists. This distribution is determined by factors which are importantly influenced by the country's level of technological development within a particular field: the design of the research project, the skills and inventiveness of the R&D personnel, the results of research in previous periods, and the stock of inventive "germplasm" available from science and from practical experience. In the case of biological inventions, germplasm applies literally in the form of biological parent material. But the concept of parental material applies to other fields of invention as well, since inventions tend to build on inventions in what Rosenberg [(1976), Chapter 6] has termed "compulsive sequences"; in other words, inventions tend to be the progeny of prior inventions, with important pioneering inventions being an exception.

The search model treats the uncertain outcome of a research project as a random draw from the distribution of potential inventions. Evenson and Kislev (1975) employ the exponential density function in their model, which yields the result that research within a single period is subject to diminishing returns – the expected value of the research objective changes in proportion to the log of the number of trials.[10] The optimal extent of search is given by the condition that the expected value of the marginal gross benefit should be equal to the marginal cost of extending the search by one trial. Associated with the optimal search are an expected maximum value and, at the end of the period, a realized maximum value.

In the following period the research system faces a new set of conditions. If the preceding research was successful, the way to achieve a better than previously realized outcome has been discovered. But the last period's research findings will generally also enable the researchers to identify avenues of search that should no longer be considered promising, leading to a rightward shift in the mean, though not necessarily in the all important righthand tail, of the distribution of outcomes relative to the previous distribution. However, the entire distribution may be shifted to the right by the introduction of new elements. New skills, methods, and knowledge may have been discovered by additional activities undertaken in the previous period, including the monitoring of developments in science and in other R&D programs in the same field. New germplasm in the form of new materials or potentially adaptable inventions from domestic or foreign sources may also have become available.

Thus in the following period the researchers face a greater challenge insofar

---

[10] Kortum (1992) demonstrates diminishing returns under more general specifications of the density function. Only "fat-tailed" Cauchy-type distributions do not yield diminishing returns in this type of model. See Nordhaus (1969) for applications.

as they must improve on their previous success. But they also confront a changed distribution of potential discoveries. Continued search is optimal only if the new distribution offers sufficient additional inventive potential relative to the result of the preceding period's research. Absent the introduction of new elements that go beyond the results of the formal search process, there will quickly be insufficient additional potential to justify continued search. Thus the introduction of new elements leading to sufficiently large rightward shifts in the distribution over time is the necessary condition for sustained inventive search. Without these elements, there will be falling R&D activity and invention as the corresponding field of technology becomes subject to exhaustion.[11]

Within any given field, advanced countries are more dependent on scientific progress to avoid exhaustion than are their technological followers. There are several reasons for this. The germplasm available to a follower is effectively increased or renewed as more is learned about its peculiar circumstances. In turn, a follower's technological development within any field enables additional elements of technology to be effectively transferred to serve as germplasm for new avenues of adaptive invention. Moreover, individual followers can benefit from inventions and research results emanating from other followers' technological efforts. The search model not only embraces these means of overcoming local exhaustion, it more importantly highlights their critical importance, which is supported by ample empirical evidence.

2.3. Induced innovation models

Models of induced innovation are less concerned with the search process per se than with the determinants of the direction of search; for example, whether the search is for more labor-intensive or for more capital-intensive techniques. These models posit what is essentially a transformation frontier – or "invention cum innovation possibilities frontier" (IPF) – among factor augmenting and/or saving reductions in cost:

$$I(\mathrm{d}L, \mathrm{d}K, E) = 0, \tag{1}$$

where $\mathrm{d}L$ ($\mathrm{d}K$) is labor (capital) augmenting or saving productivity or technological change relative to the unit isoquant and E is R&D expenditure. Thus, for a given R&D budget, various combinations of $\mathrm{d}L$ and $\mathrm{d}K$ can be achieved. Relative factor prices determine the combination yielding the largest cost reduction. Binswanger [Chapters 4 and 5 in Binswanger and Ruttan

---

[11] Empirical evidence of exhaustion in some fields is reported in Evenson and Kislev (1975) and Evenson (1992).

(1978)] discusses the specification of an IPF based on search processes. His model overcomes the seriously objectionable characterization of invention as a deterministic process that is found in other IPF models.

Applied to the advanced countries, to technological change at the global frontier, induced innovation models suffer from a lack of evidence about the character of the IPF. In this context, the most complete evidence supporting the induced innovation hypothesis, assembled in Binswanger and Ruttan (1978), is drawn from agriculture. Applied to LDCs, the hypothesis that expected factor prices affect the direction of search activity has greater plausibility insofar as there is less uncertainty about outcomes behind the global frontier. There is, in fact, a good deal of case study research that is at least consistent with the hypothesis. This research generally supports the view that "getting factor prices right" is important not only for choice of technique reasons but also in relation to incentives affecting the nature of technological activity. But there is an important respect in which induced innovation models are fundamentally misleading, particularly in the LDC context. These models take the exploitation of invention potential for granted. However, cross-country evidence (discussed in Section 4.3) clearly indicates that the mere existence of potential inventions is insufficient to motivate investments to realize them. In most countries, the fundamental problem concerns the absence of invention, not its direction.

2.4. Diffusion models

Diffusion models focus on the spread of innovations across firms engaged in similar activities. They relate to the evaluation and adoption of a well specified technology by individual producers operating in relatively homogeneous production conditions. The classic statements of the diffusion model are given by Griliches (1957) for agriculture and by Mansfield (1961) for industry.

The general diffusion model assumes that the probability of a particular firm's deciding to adopt an innovation at a particular point in time depends on three things: the proportion of the firms in the industry that have already adopted the innovation; the benefits from adopting it; and the costs of its adoption.[12] In the standard implementation of the model, the derived functional form is a logistic equation:

$$p(t) = 1/[1 + ae^{-bt}] \tag{2}$$

---

[12] The dependence of one firm's adoption decision on prior decisions by other firms has been variously interpreted in terms of information costs, risk reduction, and competitive pressure.

where $p(t)$ is the proportion of firms that have adopted the innovation by time t, a is a constant, and b is a coefficient expressing the dependence of the diffusion rate on the benefits and costs of adoption.[13] The model has traditionally been applied to analyze the determinants of differences in diffusion rates across distinct innovations or groups of firms.

Results from applying the diffusion model are generally interpreted to signify that adoption decisions are economically motivated.[14] That is, empirical tests of economic behavior with respect to diffusion demonstrate that the profitability of new technology is what matters when its adoption is being considered. Inventions that have higher costs and lower benefits diffuse more slowly; conversely, lower costs and higher benefits lead to faster diffusion. Some studies have found that skills related to adoption also matter. In agriculture, diffusion rates are higher among educated farmers and are accelerated by extension programs.[15] In industry, higher diffusion rates are found in industries that spend proportionately more on R&D. Market structure is also sometimes found to exert a significant influence.

The basic insights of the diffusion model are supported by empirical research in both developed and less developed economies. But the standard empirical specification has not been successfully applied to the spread of technology across widely differing conditions of production, either within or between countries. This is because it does not provide a straightforward means to incorporate the circumstantial sensitivity of technology, which often acts as a barrier to the simple diffusion of well specified techniques. Other approaches that embody the basic insights in a framework that directly accommodates circumstantial differences have proven more fruitful. Vernon's (1966) model characterizing the international product cycle is the seminal case in point for manufacturing activities. Recent work, discussed at length later in this survey, has used econometric methods to measure and incorporate technological distance in models of technology transfer.

2.5. Growth accounting

The development of growth accounting methods and their application to developed countries has had a profound effect on economists' thinking about development. Following the discovery [Solow (1957), among others] in the 1950s of the large "residual" in the growth of per capita output that could not

---

[13] Plotted against time, the estimated value of p(t) appears as a forward falling S; the proportion of adopters first grows slowly, then rapidly, and then again slowly.

[14] See, for example, Mansfield et al. [(1977b), Chapters 6 and 7].

[15] On the roles of education and extension in agriculture, see Griliches (1957), Birkhauser et al. (1991), and Jamison et al. (1991).

be attributed to the growth of per capita capital service flows, economists embarked on two related lines of empirical research to comprehend its basic nature. Both lines of research have been relevant to understanding technological development.

The first, starting with Griliches (1957, 1963) and Denison (1962), sought to explain the residual by more carefully and properly measuring inputs. Capital, labor, and output measures were disaggregated into distinct types to take account of changes in their quality. Early work on labor quality, adjusting for increases in schooling and changes in occupational composition, "explained" a considerable part of the residual. Denison, in particular, made further adjustments to account for changes in such things as the composition of economic activity, market structures, and public infrastructure. Encouraged by the initial work, Jorgenson and Griliches (1967) attempted a full explanation. But the attempt was not generally considered to be persuasive [see Denison (1969)]. In subsequent work, Jorgenson and his colleagues [Jorgenson et al. (1987)] have continued refining the measurement of input quality and the estimation of substitution parameters, leading to the identification of a residual "cleansed" of the impact of quality changes.

The second line of research has used statistical methods derived from hedonic regression approaches to identify sources of economic and TFP growth. Many studies in this tradition first compute TFP measures and then examine their statistical association with various forms of investment and different policy variables. In this work, Griliches and others have directly focused on the variables that determine input and output qualities as well as contribute to the cleansed residual, variables like R&D, schooling, infrastructure, and the policy regime. Much of their work has been concentrated on developing measures of the determining variables, distinguishing between investments in stocks and flows of services. Section 7.1 of this chapter surveys research within this vein to estimate returns to R&D and to investigate spillovers of the results of research in one location to other locations.

3. Technological infrastructure

Developing countries have not realized rapid economic growth without also having experienced significant technological development. Technological development involves both institutions and organizations which together constitute a country's technological infrastructure. The principal institutions take the form of IPRs and contract laws that provide incentives to develop technology and facilitate its exchange among economic agents. The organizations are those where the scientific and technical competence of significant numbers of people are combined to achieve the advantages of specialization and exchange. Such organizations may be private or public; they may exist as separate bodies or as constituent elements of larger entities. In them resides a substantial share of any society's accumulated stock of technological investment.[16]

3.1. Intellectual property rights

IPRs are generally considered to be elements of a social contract rather than "natural" rights. The United States and some European countries have long experience with them, while international agreements (or conventions) providing IPRs for foreigners have been respected in most developed countries for more than a century. Many LDCs possess operating IPR systems and have subscribed to the international conventions. But there is a good deal of controversy about the effectiveness of IPRs and their role in technological development. In the 1970s IPRs became part of the North-South debate over the terms of technology transfers. LDCs saw IPRs as primarily protecting advanced country interests and as being partially responsible for what was perceived as "unfair", or at least inappropriate, pricing of technology. Most LDCs actually weakened their IPR systems during this period. The debate shifted sharply in the 1980s as the North, led by the United States, began to use trade law to push for stronger IPRs for technology originating in the North.

Several major kinds of intellectual property are distinguished in laws governing the rights to them.[17]

- patents, for conventional inventions;
- utility models, for minor or "petty" inventions;
- plant breeders rights, for new plant varieties;
- copyrights, for creative works (writing and music, for example);
- trademarks, for identifying names or symbols;
- trade secrets, for proprietary information; and,
- industrial designs, for designs and shapes.

The laws of most relevance to technological development pertain to patents, utility models, and plant breeders rights, all of which relate to inventions broadly conceived. However, copyrights have been used to protect inventions in the form of computer software. Trademarks and industrial designs protect products, which may or may not embody new technology. Trade secrecy law

---

[16] Nelson (1993) provides extensive descriptions of the technological infrastructure that has been established in Argentina, Brazil, Israel, Korea and Taiwan.

[17] See Siebeck et al. (1990) for a review.

provides a distinct form of protection because it does not require the disclosure of proprietary information. But not all privately held information is eligible for such protection.

In these laws, the term "protection" essentially means "a limited right to exclude" others from making or using the designated property without the permission of the holder of the right. The right is limited to a fixed term of years (17 to 20 years for patents, 4 to 7 years for utility models, and so forth) and by its scope of coverage, discussed below. Moreover, the right applies only in the country granting the right. However, international agreements provide "national treatment" to foreigners from signatory countries. The major such agreements are the Paris Convention for patents and the Berne Convention for copyrights.

The scope of protection is implicitly defined by the accepted standard for obtaining the particular right. For patents these standards include:

- novelty: the invention must be new in prescribed terms;
- usefulness: it must be useful and practical or operational in form;
- inventive step: it must not be obvious to a person skilled in the art.

The patent document must also provide an "enabling disclosure" that serves to reveal the true nature of the invention to the public. Weaker standards, designed to protect minor national inventions, are applied in the case of utility models. Novelty is sometimes judged against a national standard – the invention need only be new in the country in question. Additionally, the inventive step may be lower than is required for a patent. When properly administered, utility models (the term utility refers to usefulness) provide protection for adaptive inventions of a minor nature. In this regard they are similar to industrial designs.

Multicellular plants and animals have in the past been excluded from the scope of patent protection because they are naturally occurring and, as with concepts, are considered to be the common heritage of mankind [see, e.g., Persley (1990)]. Plant breeders rights were developed as an alternative to patents to provide incentives to private plant breeding activities. With the emergence of biotechnology has come renewed controversy over the protection that should be afforded to living organisms. In the United States, patent protection has for some time been provided to new plant varieties; more recently, administrative decisions by the U.S. Patent and Trade Mark office have extended patent protection to multicellular animals.[18]

In granting property rights to inventors, societies give legal sanction to

---

[18] The movement toward stronger IPRs in all developed countries is likely to bring these changes to more countries.

monopolies that might otherwise be sustained through de facto (not de jure) trade secrecy. But this is done in exchange for public disclosure, which is important in providing germplasm for subsequent inventions. An offsetting cost is associated with the monopoly power that is bestowed by IPRs, but this cost has to be assessed as well in relation to the likelihood that inventive activity is stimulated by the presence of IPR protection.[19] In principle, the scope – breadth and length – of the monopoly right can be adjusted to maximize the expected net benefits provided by a country's IPR system.[20]

The economic case for international agreements to recognize the rights of foreigners by treating them on a par with nationals is clear for countries at similar levels of technological development. Such agreements broaden the markets for inventions and strengthen the incentives to inventive activity in the subscribing countries. They also provide protection for direct foreign investment and incentives to sell technology abroad. The experience of recent decades has shown that international conventions, which do not include enforcement sanctions, work effectively among countries which both buy and sell technology. But they do not work well between industrialized countries and others that are primarily buyers of technology, as are most LDCs. This point is elaborated in the concluding section on policy, in the context of a more general discussion of the LDCs' failure to use IPRs to their advantage.[21]

3.2. The structure of knowledge generating activities

Agricultural research and extension systems adhere to a common design and afford the most transparent example of the structure of technological activities. For this reason, and because of agriculture's importance in the economies of the poorest countries, the general design of these systems is worthy of particular attention.

The agricultural sector is subject to three phenomena that differentiate it from most other sectors:

- the predominance of small family farm units in producing most agricultural products in most countries;
- the limited scope for intellectual property protection for biological technology, particularly for plant varieties and animal types; and,
- the high degree of sensitivity to the physical environment for much agricultural technology.[22]

---

[19] The evidence regarding IPRs as stimulants to invention is discussed in Section 6.4.
[20] Nordhaus (1969) gives the standard treatment.
[21] See also Evenson (1990).
[22] See Timmer, Chapter 8 in Volume 1 of this Handbook, for additional discussion.

These conditions have led the public sector to take on the principal re-sponsibility for developing agricultural technology in most countries, even in highly market-oriented economies.

They have additionally motivated a hierarchical structure of specialized R&D organizations, with regionally focused experiment stations at their base and various supporting laboratories at supra-regional levels.[23] This structure extends globally to a number of international agricultural research centers which operate under the aegis of the Consultative Group for International Agricultural Research (CGIAR). The hierarchical structure is loosely paral-leled by the boundaries that define the many interlinked fields of specialized knowledge that contribute, directly or indirectly, to the development of agricultural technology. These boundaries are the result of institutional evolution over many decades.

Figure 37.1 identifies the specialized fields of knowledge in a hierarchical ordering that depicts the flows of knowledge among fields and the relationships to various agricultural activities and branches. It is based on the present-day agricultural research system in the United States, one of the world's most advanced. The primary objective of the system is to yield innovations at level IV. These are the products of R&D taking place at level III, which is conducted in both private firms and public sector programs. Three vertically interrelated levels of R&D activity are present in the figure. Upstream from inventive activity at level III are the pre-technology sciences (level II), which are differentiated in their objectives and incentive structures from the general sciences (level I), but which employ the same language and scientific methods. The general sciences (more often referred to as basic sciences) do science for scientists. In contrast, the pre-technology sciences do science for inventors; that is, they anticipate or perceive inventors' demands and respond according-ly, just as inventors anticipate or perceive users' demands for their inventions. Downstream from levels III and IV are extension activities (level V) which support the implementation of new technology by the users of inventions. Public agricultural extension programs serving farmers are an integral part of the system of research, teaching, and extension among the American "land grant" institutions. Private firms supplying farm technology also invest in extension to aid them in their testing and experimental activities as well as to inform farmers about the use of their products.

Extension services are located spatially close to the users. In the United States, each county (jurisdiction below the state level) has an extension program whose agents are supported by specialists working in agricultural experiment stations (level III applied R&D units). Typically, a number of such

---

[23] Huffman and Evenson (1993) provide extensive descriptions of archetypal hierarchical structures.

THE R&D SYSTEM

Layer/Activity	Mathematical Sciences	Physical Sciences	Biological Sciences		Social Sciences
I. GENERAL SCIENCES (University and public agency research primarily)	Mathematics Probability & Statistics	Atmospherical & Meteorological Sciences Chemistry Geological Sciences Physics	Bacteriology Biochemistry Botany Ecology	Genetics Microbiology Molecular Biology Zoology	Economics Psychology
II. PRE-TECHNOLOGY SCIENCES (University and public agency research primarily)	Applied Math Applied Physics Engineering Computer Science	Climatology Soil Physics & Chemistry Hydrology & Water Resources Environmental Sciences	Plant Physiology Plant Genetics Phytopathology	Animal & Human Physiology Animal & Human Genetics Animal Pathology Nutrition	Applied Economics Statistics & Econometrics Political Science Sociology
III. TECHNOLOGY INVENTION (Public and private research)	Agricultural Engineering & Design Mechanics Computer Design	Agricultural Chemistry Soils & Soil Sciences Irrigation & Water Methods Integrated Pest Management	Agronomy Horticulture Plant Breeding Applied Plant Pathology	Animal & Poultry Science Animal Breeding Animal & Human Nutrition Veterinary Medicine	Farm Management Marketing Resource Economics Rural Sociology Public Policy Studies Human Ecology
IV. PRODUCTS FROM INNOVATION (Agro-industrial development)	Farm Machinery & Equipment Farm Buildings Computer Equipment/Software	Commercial Fertilizers Agricultural Chemicals Irrigation Systems Pest Control Systems	Crop/Plant Varieties Horticultural/Nursery Species Livestock Feed	Animal Breeds Animal Health Products Food Products	Management Systems Marketing Systems Institutional Innovations Health Care Child Care
V. EXTENSION (Public and private)	Resources & Environment <-->	Commodity Oriented	Management & Marketing		Public Policy <-->
VI. FINAL USERS/SOURCES (Clientele problems)	Producers	Governments			Consumers

Source: Huffman and Evenson (1993)

Figure 37.1.   Hierarchical specialization in R&D systems for agriculture.

stations are distributed geographically throughout a state, with a central unit at the apex, most often located at a state university where it is closely integrated with teaching. The federal government also operates a number of separate, specialized experiment stations, some of which have close ties to state universities. Level II pre-technology sciences are well developed only in the larger university systems (Cornell, Minnesota and Wisconsin, among others). In the course of doing science for inventors, they serve as the training ground for most agricultural scientists (especially those who will be engaged in invention).

The structure of scientific and technological effort in agriculture is rather unique insofar as it is organized around the public sector's large role in invention and extension, though it does have a reasonably close counterpart in medicine and public health in most countries. But not all biological research for agriculture is public. Private firms have long been active in those areas where the biological technology provides inherent protection to inventors, as it does for hybrid crops such as corn and sorghum.[24] With rice becoming a hybrid crop in some regions, private firms have begun to undertake rice research as well. More generally, the private sector is growing in importance as a supplier of technology to farmers in both developed countries and more advanced LDCs. In part this follows the strengthening of IPRs for plant varieties (and, to some extent, animal breeds), which has led to an expansion of plant breeding programs in the seed industry [Pray (1987)].

There are very few extensive systems of public sector invention for the industrial sector; among LDCs, India has had the largest – the network of laboratories associated with India's Council for Scientific and Industrial Research. More generally, most LDCs invest very little in level III activities regardless of sectoral orientation; they publicly invest virtually nothing in extension outside of agriculture. In the developed countries, except in agriculture, most level III efforts are carried out by private firms with the encouragement of well developed incentive systems. Private firms also engage in extension through various consulting and engineering activities as well as though services related to the sales of producer goods, but these activities are seldom referred to in terms of extension.

3.2.1. Empirical evidence of structural linkages

Evidence for the hierarchical structuring of related scientific and technological activity comes from studies of citations in journal articles as well as in patents.

---

[24] Unlike seeds for open pollinated crops, hybrid seeds can not be obtained from the previous year's harvest. Instead, they must be produced continually through a sequence of inbreeding and crossing. This creates a market for improved seed varieties, since new seeds must be purchased from seed producers annually.

To examine article citations within and between fields, Huffman and Evenson (1993) classified some 300 journals dealing with research on animals, crops, forestry, nutrition, and agriculturally-related social science according to their levels. For the first two of these areas, they found that articles pertaining to the pre-invention sciences formed the link between the general sciences and technology invention. In relative terms, few citations were found directly linking levels I and III, while many were found in both directions between levels I and II as well as between levels II and III. Moreover, from examining the impact of agricultural research on American farm productivity, they concluded that the pre-invention sciences yielded the highest social returns per dollar spent on research.[25] Their findings are consistent with the view that research at level II plays a vital role in some technological fields through augmenting the pools of knowledge from which level III inventions are drawn. Further evidence of the importance of knowledge upstream from level III comes from cross-country comparative research by Evenson (1993c) that examined factors responsible for differences among LDCs in the productivity of agricultural research.

Patent documents in many countries, including the United States, give citations of relevant precursors, which often include scientific publications. It does not necessarily follow in such cases that a scientific discovery was the initiating factor behind the invention. In fact, there is a good deal of research to show that inventions are primarily motivated by demand factors [Rosenberg (1974)]. Nonetheless, the citation of a scientific reference does signify its importance as a facilitating factor. Correspondingly, such references can be used to identify differences among technological fields with respect to their dependence on scientific knowledge as opposed to the results of practical experimentation. Evenson (1990) studied patent citations in six fields: dentistry, animal husbandry, general medicine, genetic engineering, molecular biology, and plant agriculture (patents here largely pertain to chemical and mechanical technology). Molecular biology exhibited the highest linkage to science, with 70 percent of the sampled patents citing one or more scientific publications. Next were animal husbandry and genetic engineering, with citation ratios of 61 and 50 percent respectively. Inventions in plant agriculture, general medicine, and dentistry had the least linkage to science, having citation ratios of between 15 and 8 percent. For most mechanical invention, the linkages to science would be even less.

---

[25] Huffman and Evenson (1993) also discuss the historical evolution of the pre-technology sciences, observing that they were not developed until invention oriented researchers at level III expressed a demand for more science of a distinct kind to enhance their inventive activities.

3.3. *Intersectoral interdependencies*

Just as there are multiple and variable linkages between scientific areas and technological fields, so too there are technological interdependencies among sectors of economic activity, such that no sector is wholly self-sufficient in generating its own technology. Inventions generated in one industry may be used in the same industry or in other industries. Typically, apart from those embodied in machinery, process inventions have the same industry of manufacture (IOM) and sector of use (SOU).[26] But for most product inventions, IOM and SOU differ. Thus, distinct from a conventional input-output matrix of product flows, there is an implicit technological input-output matrix mapping invention flows from IOM to SOU. This technology matrix is critical to measuring and understanding the relationship between R&D, inventions, and productivity change.

Evenson et al. (1989) used information generated by the Canadian Patent Office to develop an IOM-SOU concordance, which gives the frequency distributions of IOMs and SOUs for each of more than six thousand (aggregated) International Patent Classification (IPC) categories; that is, technological fields. Canada's Patent Office has assigned IPC categories along with IOM and SOU categories (4-digit level) to all patents granted since 1972. By 1990, more than two hundred thousand patents had been so assigned, yielding a large sample from which to determine the concordance frequency distributions. Since most of the world's important inventions are patented in Canada (only 12 percent of the patents are to Canadian inventors), the concordance is a plausible estimate of its global counterpart.

Using the concordance, any set of patents can be distributed into IOMs and SOUs to obtain an estimate of the corresponding technology matrix.[27, 28] Figure 37.2 demonstrates the basic nature of inter-industry technology flows. Based on all patents registered in Canada between 1972 and 1990, for each 2-digit SIC industry, it shows the percentages of total inventions originating in (vertically) other industries and utilized by (horizontally) other industries respectively. Industries above the diagonal are net users in proportionate terms; those below, net suppliers. The dashed lines in the figure show the

---

[26] "Manufacture" here refers to the sector in which the patented input is produced, which need not be – but often is – the same as the sector from which the patent originated.

[27] Tables 37.2 and 37.3, discussed in Sections 4.3 and 5.4, respectively, show applications to Indian and Korean data as well as to international data used to determine a measure of technological distance.

[28] One can also apply the concordance to data on R&D expenditures or scientists and engineers engaged in R&D to get some idea, for example, of how much R&D within the manufacturing sector is for the benefit of the agricultural sector, or of how much R&D attention is given elsewhere to sectors that perform little or no R&D.

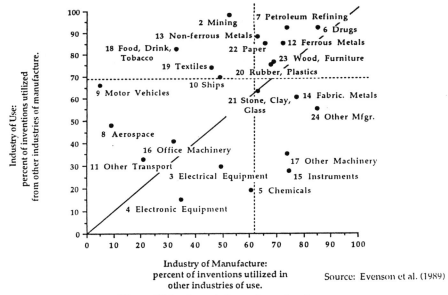

Figure 37.2.   Inter-industry invention flows.

sample means. Industries in the southwest quadrant with respect to these lines are correspondingly self-sufficient in relative terms, while those in the north-east quadrant exhibit relatively high interdependence. Consider the drug industry as one example. Most of the inventions used by it originate in the chemicals sector; most of its inventions are used in the health sector.

It is clear from Figure 37.2 that manufacturing industries are substantially dependent on one another for technology. Not obvious from the figure is the fact that most non-manufacturing sectors – including agriculture, forestry, fishing, construction, communications, health, finance and trade – depend on manufacturing for much, in some cases most, of their technology.[29]

4. Technological assets and development

Most technological development in LDCs in some way or another starts with and builds on transfers – of various kinds, including spillovers – of technology

---

[29] This is clearly demonstrated in Table 37.2, as is discussed in Section 4.3.

from technologically more advanced countries.[30] Indeed, technological development can not be understood apart from various forms of international trade that importantly involve technology. Consider the two extremes by which a particular sector can be established in an LDC. One is the virtually autarchic creation (or re-creation) of technology by locally providing all of the necessary elements through developing the corresponding technological capabilities. This approach is likely to be very costly and time consuming even if extensive use is made of readily available foreign knowledge that spills over through documentary sources and imported "protypes". But it does guarantee the achievement of at least rudimentary proficiency in the associated capabilities. The opposite extreme is the establishment and operation of an industry using only foreign capabilities with no local technological development whatsoever. This sometimes happens, for example, with direct foreign investment in an enclave when indigenous involvement is limited to the employment of unskilled labor. It can be an effective way of generating employment and foreign exchange, at least over the short to medium term, but in the absence of appropriate policies it need not contribute to the development of local capabilities.

As the foregoing extremes illustrate, trade possibilities involving technology are such that there is no necessary relationship between the sectoral composition of a country's economic activity and the extent of its technological development sector-by-sector. Individual sectors can be created and developed through many alternative combinations of local and foreign capabilities. Thus various paths of technological development can be followed to reach the same level of economic development. To comprehend technological development in these terms, one needs an analytical framework that integrates investment choices among technological assets with trade choices among transactions involving elements of technology. This section develops such a framework and then examines differences in levels of technological development among LDCs.

4.1. Technological assets

The critical technological assets are human and organizational capital, the latter being the knowhow used to combine human skills and physical capital into systems for producing and delivering want-satisfying products. Corresponding to the wide variety of technological fields and elemental activities

---

[30] The term "spillovers" generally refers to benefits of any kind conveyed in the form of externalities derived from invention. In this survey, "spillovers" refer to benefits derived from the transmission of knowledge used either directly or indirectly (as inventive germplasm) by other units.

through which knowledge is applied, there are a vast number of differentiated technological capabilities. They can be classified in various ways, each of which corresponds to a different approach to distinguishing among the aspects of technological knowledge and its practical application.[31] For analyzing technological development in general terms, it is most useful to separate technological capabilities into three broad categories according to whether they are related to production, investment, or invention:

- Production capabilities: pertain to the operation of productive facilities; they encompass various activities involved in product design, production management and engineering, repair cum maintenance, input sourcing and output marketing, and so forth.
- Investment capabilities: relate to the expansion of existing capacity and to the establishment of new production facilities; they embrace the many activities related to project selection, design cum engineering, and execution as well as extension services and manpower training.
- Invention capabilities: concern indigenous efforts to adapt, improve, and develop technology.

The grounding of proficiency in experience limits the scope for transferring capability gained in one activity to other activities. The highly differentiated nature of technological knowledge also establishes a strong association between capabilities and activities. The boundaries created by experience and knowledge differentiation are often fuzzy, but their existence nonetheless means that specific investments are required to develop distinct capabilities. One shouldn't, however, think that all capabilities are specific to particular sectors. Some, like the ability to mix iron ores to achieve the best blast furnace charge, are highly sector specific. But many, such as the basic knowhow involved in the adhesive properties of different materials, are more generally applicable. Others – such as those related to information and control systems or to aspects of project execution – find even more widespread application.

Investments in technological capabilities, whether to strengthen existing ones or to add new ones, are often associated with changes that alter patterns of specialization and exchange. These changes occur through investments embodied in organizational structures, codified knowledge and procedures, and less formalized customs that govern behavior within and among entities. They are fundamentally important because they are the means by which transactional modes involving technology are changed. Indeed, technological change can

---

[31] Westphal et al. (1985), Fransman (1986), Lall (1990), and Enos (1991) discuss the capability concept at some length. Westphal et al. (1990) discuss a systematic, quantitative application.

occur solely as the result of such changes, as when the creation of new modes of distributing products leads to lower transactions costs.

The potential benefits of technological development can often not be fully realized without changes in transactional forms. The changes are typically in the direction of increasing specialization on the basis of technological capability, either through the creation of new units within existing entities or the establishment of new entities. For example: In manufacturing, young firms often carry out activities like quality control, project engineering, and R&D in a generalized production management cum engineering department; but as the capabilities and their uses increase over time, these activities are separated into specialized departments, which sometimes then evolve into separate entities [see, for example, Katz (1987)].

4.2. Trade and technological development

With specialization and exchange, technological capabilities are deployed across entities through market transactions involving elements of technology. These transactions occur between countries as well as within them and take many forms which involve – singly or in combination – goods, services, and information. In terms of broad categories, the transactional elements of technology include:

- Information: about physical processes and social arrangements that underlies and is given operational expression in technology.
- R&D: activities of generating new knowledge or inventive germplasm with the ultimate objective of practical use.
- Technical services: activities, such as engineering, of translating technological knowledge into the detailed information required to establish or operate a productive facility in a specific set of circumstances.
- Embodiment activity: activities of forming physical capital in accord with given and complete design specification.
- Training services: activities of imparting the skills and abilities that are used in economic activity.
- Management services: activities of organizing and managing the operation of productive facilities, the implementation of investment projects, and the development of process and product innovations.
- Marketing services: activities of matching the capacity of productive facilities to existing and latent market demands.

Trade involving elements of technology has many transactional modes that serve numerous objectives.[32] Licensing, subcontracting, technical agreements, management contracts, marketing arrangements, turnkey project contracts, direct foreign investment, and trade in capital goods are only a few of them.[33] Some of these modes provide complementary services without any real flow of technology. Marketing services provided under international subcontracting are an example, but they are often combined with technical services which do provide technology. Other modes bundle information together with services required to translate it into useable form. Direct foreign investment, turnkey project contracts, and trade in capital goods are obvious examples.

Technology trade can be used to supplement – as a substitute for or a complement to – local capabilities as well as to augment them.[34] Implicit in the import of any technological element is a decision to rely on foreign rather than local capabilities. Where the capabilities do not exist locally, the decision is a choice not to develop them through means that involve indigenous effort. A great deal of technological development is import substitution to replace foreign capabilities with indigenous ones. The benefits extend beyond simple import replacement to include dynamic economies of various forms. But technological development can not reasonably be seen as having the objective of progressive import substitution for all of the elements of technology. Even the most advanced countries are far from technological autarchy. Notions of efficiency and comparative advantage are as important to technological development as they are to other kinds of development.

It is economically appropriate to develop the capability to supply some elements of technology – or to make rather than buy it – only if the net benefit of doing so is positive. The difficulty here lies not in the principle of make–buy decisions but in the practice. Costs of developing a capability can often be determined with some precision; they are the investment expenditures needed to create the capability, including the higher expenses and greater risks relative to imports which may be incurred as initial experience applying the capability is acquired. Benefits can not so readily be determined. The direct benefit of import replacement in terms of foreign exchange savings is no harder to determine for technological development projects than for those of other kinds. The problem is in assessing the other, indirect but potentially more

---

[32] Cortes and Bocock (1984) provide an illuminating description of alternative modes, and of factors on both sides of the market that affect choices among them, in the case of petrochemical technology.

[33] In a turnkey project, a local owner contracts with a foreign agent to provide all the elements needed to design and establish a facility as well as to initiate production. Among the elements is enough training to impart the rudimentary mastery needed to operate a well maintained facility under assumed conditions relating to such things as material input availability and specifications.

[34] As discussed in Section 5.3, transfers of new biological material from international agricultural research programs substitute for absent fundamental R&D capabilities and thereby complement local experimental and extension capabilities.

important, benefits. Technological development is a cumulative process in which capabilities acquired during the present can provide important foundations for making technological changes of acquiring other capabilities in the future. It is difficult at best to foresee all of the consequences that may follow from foundations presently being laid, and to evaluate the corresponding benefits.

Technology trade contributes to technological development when it augments local capabilities. But, sometimes overlooked is a simple fact – trade involving elements of technology is meant to provide the elements, not the capabilities to supply them, certainly not as a direct or immediate consequence of their being provided. Nonetheless, the relationship of elements involved to capabilities enhanced is complicated because capabilities that are ostensibly meant to be developed are often not. Plants established under turnkey projects, for example, often continue years later to produce well under their design capacity owing to insufficient local effort to develop the requisite production capabilities. But just as intended results are often not achieved owing to insufficient effort, so too others can be achieved on the basis of atypical effort. Trade of any form can provide wherewithal for at least some forms of learning given sufficient will and capacity to learn.

4.3. Indicators of technological development

In analyzing technological development, one ideally wants to know how much has been invested in what kinds of capital with what rates of return. Unfortunately, such information is not generally available and is exceedingly difficult to obtain on an aggregate basis for some important forms of capability acquisition, like those which occur in connection with initial efforts to attain increased mastery over newly acquainted industrial technology. Available instead are data for various indicators related to distinct aspects of technological capability. These indicators offer a limited, but meaningful for the corresponding aspects, way of gauging levels of technological development across countries. Together with indices of overall economic performance, Table 37.1 displays several indicators for eight levels of technological development.

The typology of levels shown in Table 37.1 is taken from Weiss (1990), which may be consulted for qualitative details about the various attributes of each level. The concern here is with a few illustrative quantitative indicators.[35] In

---

[35] Lall (1990) provides data for a more comprehensive set of indicators relating to technological development in the manufacturing sector for level 2 countries. The range of possible indicators is quite extensive, as may be seen from those given in National Science Board (1991) and OECD (1993). Similar compilations are available for several of the more advanced developing countries.

Table 37.1
Selected technological capability indicators for eight synthesized levels of technological development

Indicators	Level 1 Developing countries			Level 2 Developing countries			Recently industrialized	OECD industrialized
	1a Traditional technology	1b First emergence	1c Islands of modernization	2a Mastery of conventional technology	2b Transition to NIC-hood	2c NIC-hood		
I. Real Growth (1965–1990)								
GDP per capita	.5	.5	1.5	2.4	2.5	7.1	2.8	2.5
GDP: Aggregate	2.5	2.6	2.8	4.7	5.3	8.1	4.0	3.5
Agriculture	2.5	2.5	2.6	3.8	3.0	3.1	2.5	1.5
Industry	5.0	5.0	4.5	5.1	6.0	9.1	3.1	3.1
Services	5.0	5.0	4.8	5.0	6.0	10.0	3.5	3.5
II. R&D intensity								
R&D/GDP (1990)								
Aggregate:								
Public	.2	.2	.3	.4	.6	.6	.7	.7
Private	0	0	.02	.05	.2	1.0	1.2	2.3
Agriculture:								
Public	.4	.4	.5	.6	.7	.8	.8	1.5
Private	0	0	0.01	0.05	.1	.2	.5	1.5
Industry:								
Public	.05	.05	.1	.2	.4	.3	.3	.3
Private	0	0	.02	.05	.05	1.0	1.2	2.3

Services:								
Public	0	0	0	.01	.05	.05	.1	.3
Private	0	0	0	0	.05	.1	.2	.5
Science/GDP (1990):								
Public	.02	.02	.03	.04	.10	.20	.25	.40
Private	0	0	0	0	0	.02	.04	.05
III. S&E intensity								
S&E/GDP (index)	.2	.2	.4	.6	.8	1.3	1.0	1.0
IV. Invention indicators								
Inventions/S&E*	0	0	0	.05	.1	.5	.3	.2
Invention import share	0	0	.9	.95	.81	.64	.80	.31
Invention export share	0	0	0	0	.05	.10	.20	1.70
V. Intellectual property rights								
International recognition	0	0	1	2–3	2–3	2–3	4–5	5
Domestic use	0	0	0	1	2	4	4	5

* Number of inventions per scientist and engineer engaged in R&D, in 1989.

Typical Countries:
1a: Yemen, Laos; 1b: Nepal, Ethiopia; 1c: Sri Lanka, Kenya; 2a: Malaysia, Turkey, Colombia; 2b: India, Thiland, Mexico; 2c: Korea, Taiwan. Recently industrialized Greece, Portugal, Spain.

Source: Authors' estimates

general terms: Level 1 countries have not yet achieved what might be considered "basic" levels of technological capabilities in at least some important sectors. Basic capabilities are possessed by all of the level 2 countries, but not all have been expanding and improving their capabilities.

Level 1 includes 75 countries having a combined population of one billion persons. One tenth of them reside in 16 level 1a countries (all small, except Zaire), which have little or no technological infrastructure. Roughly 20 percent live in 19 level 1b countries, where there is some research capacity in agriculture but virtually none in other sectors. Countries at level 1c, which account for the rest, have good agricultural research capacity and undertake some industrial research in the public sector. But they, like the other level 1 countries, have no industrial R&D capacity in producing firms.

Twenty countries are found at level 2. Among them, only four [Hong Kong, (in truth, a colony), Korea, Taiwan, and Singapore] achieved full NIC (newly industrialized country) status by the 1980s. Several more countries [China, Indonesia, Malaysia, and Thailand (plus, possibly, Chile)] are currently experiencing development sufficient, if maintained, to qualify as NICs in the near future. All of these countries have adopted the macro and micro economic policies that are required to achieve rapid, technologically driven growth. In most of them, public policy explicitly promotes technological development through the accumulation and utilization of technological infrastructure.

The figures in the table illuminate several aspects of technological development; this is notwithstanding various caveats, that go unstated here, regarding the comparability of such indicators across countries. Consider first the aggregate figures. Public sector investment in applied R&D as a percent of GDP increases roughly threefold from level 1a (reliance on traditional technology) to level 2c (NIC-hood). Private sector R&D investment is effectively nil in level 1 countries; it is quite substantial in the NICs, though well below the OECD country standard. The availability of scientists and engineers (S&E) relative to GDP rises in an even more dramatic fashion across the levels, being greater in the NICs than in countries more developed than they. Expenditures on science relative to GDP show an even more pronounced change, as does the domestic patent indicator.

Patent indicators are used to express cross-country differences in the extent of inventive activity, but they also indirectly reflect differences in laws governing IPRs. The IPR indicators appearing at the bottom of the table are qualitative indexes (using a scale of 0 to 5) developed by Evenson (1990). Countries at levels 1a and 1b do not have functioning IPR systems; moreover, many of them lack legal systems that would support an IPR system. Level 2 developing countries generally have IPR systems of intermediate strength from the perspective of foreign inventors. Most of these countries have been accused of pirating inventions patented abroad, with the NICs having been regarded as the most serious offenders. The domestic use indicator demonstrates the failure of most LDCs to give adequate support to domestic inventive activity. Only the NICs use IPRs aggressively as a means of encouraging domestic R&D.

Virtually no patents are awarded to domestic inventions in level 1 countries; in the NICs, more patents are awarded to domestic inventions relative to the number of scientists and engineers than in the more advanced countries. Nonetheless, as shown by the invention import share figures, which give ratios of patents granted to foreigners relative to total patents granted, patents awarded to foreign inventions exceed those granted to domestic inventions in all LDCs, NICs included. In turn, the invention export share data, which give ratios of patents obtained abroad to total patents awarded domestically, indicate that exports of inventions from LDCs are practically nil until they come close to achieving NIC status, and that only the industrialized countries are net exporters of inventions.

The magnitude of the difference in indicators between the lowest and the highest levels of LDC technological development, particularly in industry, suggests that a great deal of investment in technological development is required to achieve NIC-hood. Much other evidence, some direct and some indirect, confirms that this is so. As the NICs' (and, before them, Japan's) track record reveals, LDCs can grow faster than the advanced countries. Being able to use modern technology without having to expend resources creating it from scratch, LDCs can – it appears – catch up to advanced country levels of economic development. But convergence through catchup growth can not happen in the absence of substantial investment in technological development. It is simply not the case, therefore, that LDCs can enjoy a technological free ride on the road to NIC-dom.

It can be seen from Table 37.1 that technological development is quite different in the agricultural and industrial sectors. There is a rather sizeable amount of agricultural R&D (in proportion to agricultural GDP) in the level 1 countries, most of it in public sector experiment stations that develop new seed varieties and the like. These research units, which also exist in the level 2 countries, are linked in a two-way exchange of biological materials, new knowledge, and R&D personnel to a network of international research centers; R&D expenditures by the international centers for the benefit of LDCs (not shown in the table) amount to roughly ten percent of national expenditures. Private sector agricultural research is of some importance in level 2 countries, although it is only in the advanced OECD countries that private sector R&D is as important as public sector R&D.

In comparison with public sector spending on agricultural R&D, public expenditure on industrial R&D is low, being greatest – roughly half as much (relative to industrial GDP) – in level 2b countries.[36] Private sector industrial R&D assumes significant proportions in level 2 countries; among the NICs, it is roughly three times the value of public sector expenditure – the difference is sevenfold in the advanced OECD countries. However, as will be discussed below, data on industrial R&D do not capture many related kinds of technological effort that are disproportionately important at lower levels of technological development. Comparatively little R&D is performed in the service sector at all levels, though industrialized countries do engage in considerable health sector R&D.

Table 37.2 provides data on industrial R&D and IPR utilization in India and Korea to portray some typical patterns in technologically advanced LDCs. Korea (level 2c) performs more R&D in relation to sales than does India (2b), but both countries exhibit a roughly similar structure of relative R&D intensities across industries. There is little difference between the countries in their reliance on foreign patents (IOMF, by industry of manufacture), which are 65 percent of total patents granted in India and 62 percent in Korea. The number of patents granted to domestic investors (IOMD, by industry of manufacture) in different sectors demonstrates the relative strength of chemical and machinery sector research in India; in Korea, it is the electronic sector that stands out.

Industry of manufacture-sector of use (IOM-SOU) comparisons show that more than 20 percent of domestic patents in both countries, and more than 48 percent of utility models in Korea, are used in non-manufacturing sectors where little R&D is performed and few inventions are generated. This is especially noteworthy owing to the great technological distances that characterize many activities in these sectors (see Section 5.4). The chemicals and machinery industries contribute disproportionately to other sectors. Utility model protection, not available in India, is widely used in Korea, with the number of utility models being 3.7 times the overall total of patents. Very few utility models are granted to foreigners in Korea, as in other countries where they exist. Utility models are extensively used by the electronics and machinery industries, but are comparatively little used by the chemical and drug industries.

4.4. Sectoral trajectories

The substantial difference in patterns of R&D expenditures between agriculture and industry across levels of technological development reflects inherent

---

[36] India, which has long had an atypically extensive system of public industrial R&D institutes, is a level 2b country.

Table 37.2
Industrial R&D and patents in India and Korea

Sector	R&D/Sales*		Inventions (1986–1988)**						Utility models Korea (1986–1988)	
	India (1989)	Korea (1989)	India			Korea				
			IOMF	IOMD	SOUD	IOMF	IOMD	SOUD	IOMD	SOUD
Agriculture	na	2.16	–	–	46	–	–	73	–	763
Food and beverage	.50	.52	53	42	91	46	165	227	116	411
Pulp and paper	.35	.77	31	14	38	28	24	65	145	199
Textiles	.35	.99	56	31	85	121	130	299	458	655
Chemicals	.97	1.37	877	559	352	1309	504	227	137	155
Drugs	1.60	2.19	73	40	118	180	75	174	21	27
Basic metals	.39	1.11	401	213	171	213	165	193	1590	615
Electronics and Computers	1.01	4.80	721	284	194	975	682	569	3294	2491
Machinery	.25	2.36	1174	658	308	1002	634	245	3012	1600
Construction	.25	.51	–	–	129	–	–	100	–	1041
Utilities	na	.34	–	–	131	–	–	101	–	590
Trade and finance	na	na	–	–	47	–	–	81	–	652
Health	na	na	–	–	108	–	–	86	–	358
Government and education	na	na	–	–	55	–	–	67	–	852

* Ratio times 100.
** IOMF: industry of manufacture, foreign inventors; IOMD: industry of manufacture, domestic inventors; SOUD: sector of use, domestic inventions.
Source: Computerized patent data base, International Patent Documentation Center, Vienna.

differences in the underlying logic of technological development in the two sectors. As indicated previously, two fundamental phenomena lie behind the empirical observation that catchup economic growth can not be achieved without the simultaneous development of technological capabilities. The first is the circumstantial sensitivity of much technology, which provides the rationale for the spatial organization of technological effort in agriculture. The second phenomenon is the tacitness of much technology. Agricultural and industrial technology are alike in being characterized by both circumstantial sensitivity and tacitness. But the dominant feature, the one which has exerted the greatest influence in shaping the course of technological development in the LDCs over the past four decades, has differed between the two sectors.

Circumstantial sensitivity has played the major role in agriculture. Strong interaction between the environment and biological material makes the productivity of agricultural techniques, which are largely embodied in re-producible material inputs, highly dependent on local soil, climatic, and ecological characteristics. Industrial technology is not circumstantially sensitive in the same way as agricultural technology. Nonetheless, industrial processes must nearly always be specifically tailored to the particular circumstances in which they are being used to achieve economic levels of productivity. This is readily comprehensible in cases where the chemical and physical properties of inputs vary across alternative sources, or where product characteristics differ owing to differences in finely-grained preferences. Other, not so obvious but still significant, circumstantial differences relate to matters of scale and scope as well as to established labor and management conventions. Investments to adapt technology to local circumstances are therefore just as warranted in industry as in agriculture. But industrial adaptation largely involve changes in the design and operation of capital goods or in ancillary processes rather than changes in primary material inputs.

The archetypal adaptive efforts in agriculture are undertaken by scientists using established R&D principles to fashion new inputs; those in industry are performed by engineers carrying out conventional measurements and computa-tions to customize new processes and products. Newly engineered processes and products in industry are no less inherently "new" than newly developed inputs in agriculture. Moreover, the distinct locations of adaptive effort – closer to science in agriculture; to engineering in industry – are largely a reflection of the language used in the respective sectors. The efforts entailed are neither more nor less inherently routine in one sector than the other. The significant differences between the sectors as regards adaptive efforts are found elsewhere; in the first instance, in the scale of the circumstantially specific effort and in the scope of its application.

Important forms of adaptive agricultural R&D require a substantial commit-ment of resources dedicated to developing techniques for a particular set of agronomic conditions. The users of the newly developed techniques are as numerous as the farmers who work subject to those conditions. In contrast, adaptive industrial engineering can be accomplished using resources that are not circumstantially dedicated. Furthermore, it is a commonplace activity in any well executed project to establish industrial facilities. And most, if not virtually all, of the adaptations made in the course of designing a project are highly specific to that project.

Seen comparatively, industrial technology is readily transferable but not so easily mastered. Thus tacitness has been the principal factor conditioning the trajectory of technological progress in industry. None of the indicators shown in Table 37.1 captures the kinds of technological investments that dominate in the early stages of an industry's development, when the tacitness of production technology is initially being overcome. Even in the technologically most advanced countries, many important innovations come from sources other than what is formally classified as R&D; the system of "just-in-time" production scheduling is a notable example. In other words, R&D is only one form of technological effort, or activity to improve technology. Other forms of technological effort leading to technological change are the crucial ones as newly established industries begin to progress beyond rudimentary levels of mastery.

Case study research on infant industries reveals that significant increases in productivity, where they occur, come initially from technological efforts related to raw material control, product and process quality control, production scheduling, repair and maintenance, changes in product mix, as well as others including episodic trouble-shooting to overcome problems encountered in the course of operations. Additional sources of productivity change are found in many of the distinct tasks related to investment; that is, related to expanding existing production facilities and establishing new ones. Infant industries rarely achieve international competitiveness without having realized productivity gains from such technological efforts [Bell et al. (1984)].

Even though the returns to these forms of effort often appear – from qualitative, case study evidence – to be quite large, they seldom are associated with inventions that are patentable abroad. They do not yield improvements that are sufficiently inventive relative to the known state of the art. Nonetheless, the improvements are not infrequently sufficiently novel and useful to qualify for petty patent (or utility model) protection in countries having this form of IPR. In turn, formal R&D activities typically commence only after a substantial degree of capability has been acquired in production and in at least some aspects of investment. This is in large part because of their differentiated nature, but it also reflects some redefinition of pre-existing technological activities when they are incorporated into the R&D departments that emerge from the increasing division of labor within firms among specialized units.

A great deal of costly and purposeful effort must be expended to master any newly acquired technology, and therefore to achieve its potential productivity. This fact is equally relevant in agriculture and in industry. But the central locus of effort differs in the two sectors: in industry, it is found within individual firms; in agriculture, it resides in the complex of institutions that are engaged in research and extension. This follows from the difference between the sectors in what is directly transferable; production methods in the former, and R&D and extension methods in the latter. Effective mastery of transferred agricultural R&D methods has entailed substantial costs and has been no less problem ridden than have been the ventures to establish large scale, sophisticated plants in the industrial sector.

5. International flows of technology

It is important to distinguish between the fact that technology developed for one location can generally be employed, given enough resources, in another location and the fact that its relative economic value in another location may not be the same as in its original location. Few models of technological discovery and diffusion incorporate this distinction, in part because few are internationally focused. Models of discovery do recognize knowledge as a form of inventive germplasm, but they typically fail to include any meaningfully specified form of knowledge transmission. Diffusion models recognize knowledge transmission but generally incorporate little insight into the adaptive process. This section examines how technological distances in agriculture and industry condition the international flow of technology.

5.1. Factors determining technological distance

As noted above, a given technique or technical change does not have the same relative value in every circumstance. This is generally understood insofar as the effects of factor price differences on the choice of technology are concerned. Less generally understood, at least outside of agriculture, is the effect of physical and social differences across circumstances. These differences can also reduce the value of technology as it flows from one location to others. Two factors are relevant when assessing disparities in the value of a technique (or a particular element of knowledge) between locations. One is the circumstantial difference between the locations. The other is the sensitivity of the technique to circumstantial differences. Together they determine the technological distance between locations.[37]

Circumstantial differences include those in physical (soil, climate, and length of day, for instance), economic (relative prices, infrastructure, and so on), and social (legal systems, transactions costs, and the like) factors. Disparate fields of technology exhibit distinct sensitivity gradients with respect to these factors. Biological technologies are perhaps the most highly sensitive to physical factors; crop agriculture is particularly affected, with some crops (corn, or maize) being more sensitive than others (wheat). Mechanical technologies in agriculture exhibit similar sensitivity, which is reflected, for example, in the existence of myriad types of plows, cultivators, and harvesting equipment, each suited to a particular set of soil conditions.

Nearly all technologies are sensitive to relative factor prices, with the degree of sensitivity being greater the higher is the elasticity of substitution between capital and labor. Peripheral activities in manufacturing, activities such as packaging and in-plant materials conveyance, are particularly sensitive to the wage–rental ratio. Most technologies are also sensitive to what is available from the existing infrastructure, though infrastructural deficiencies can often be overcome by complementary investments to alter circumstances, as when manufacturers invest in auxiliary power generators to offset frequent disruptions in electricity distribution. Some technologies, construction methods for example, are particularly sensitive to social factors [see, for example, Sud et al. (1976) or Green and Brown (1976)]. Technology requiring delicate maintenance will perform differently in different institutional and infrastructural environments. In short, most technology is circumstantially sensitive in some way.

It is, therefore, fundamentally important to consider both circumstantial difference and technological sensitivity when considering whether and how technology may flow from one location to another. Little adaptation is required if circumstantial differences are small or the sensitivity gradients are flat, but there is still need for investments in technology in order to accomplish the transfer and master the technology. If circumstantial differences are considerable and the sensitivity gradients are steep, there may be no effective transferability. In intermediate cases, where transfers require adaptation to be realized effectively, investments in creating technology are necessary. In these cases, foreign technology serves as parental germplasm which has value only insofar as there is the capability to invent appropriate offspring and the incentives (IPRs and otherwise) to do so.

Positive technological distance between advanced and developing countries is often optimally overcome by adaptive technological effort. Two distinct

---

[37] An empirical measure of technological distance is discussed in Section 5.3.

forms of adaptation can be distinguished. Minor adaptations involve changes in the technique but leave its core unaffected; for example, running a loom at higher speed, or replacing an automatic filling mechanism with hand labor. In turn, inventive adaptations make use not of the technique but of the knowledge that underlies it. Here knowledge from the source serves as inventive germplasm. Producers are often observed to undertake minor adaptations without formal R&D activity. But inventive adaptations typically require some kind of formalized R&D capabilities. As a general rule, minor adaptation can not overcome great technological distances, only inventive adaptation has the potential of doing so.[38]

National research programs in the public sector, in research institutes as well as in universities, have recognized knowledge spillovers in the form of nonrival public goods. Programs in non-defense related areas, for example those in agricultural experiment stations, do not seek to withhold proprietary information. On the contrary, they usually endeavor to "extend" research findings to as many users as possible. Moreover, in agriculture, research findings – new plant varieties, for instance – developed in one location are freely transmitted to researchers in other locations, nationally and often internationally as well. The international agricultural research centers were established to facilitate international spillovers of germplasm and of results from pre-technology science more generally. In recent years, scholars have increasingly recognized that R&D conducted by private firms may have significant spillovers. Jaffe (1986), Romer (1986, 1990), Grossman and Helpman (1991) and others distinguish between firm-specific proprietary knowledge and public good information that is not proprietary and is valuable to other firms because it provides inventive germplasm.

5.2. Inventive adaptation in agriculture

Technological distance in biological technology can often be surmounted only through inventive adaptation. Griliches (1957), in his pioneering study of the diffusion of hybrid corn in the United States, made this point forcefully. He noted that long after farmers in Iowa and Illinois had adopted hybrid varieties suited to these Corn Belt states, farmers in Alabama (outside of the Corn Belt) had not yet adopted any hybrid varieties. This had little to do with the farmers' capabilities. Rather, differences in climate and soil between the Corn Belt and

---

[38] Implicit throughout this survey is the belief that there is no general justification for LDCs to go beyond inventive adaptation in undertaking R&D. Some authors, Stewart (1977) for example, have argued – using the induced innovation hypothesis – that there is ample justification, on the grounds that invention in the advanced countries is increasingly irrelevant to the developing countries owing to growing divergence between them in key circumstantial factors.

Alabama, along with the sensitivity of hybrid corn to these differences, resulted in there being a large technological distance between these areas. Thus, as Griliches noted, Alabama farmers could not benefit from hybrid varieties until hybrid research took place in Alabama, using knowledge acquired in the Corn Belt as inventive germplasm. The same lesson applies to most LDCs. Corn farmers in the Philippines got no direct benefit from the 75 years of American hybrid corn research that produced a tripling of U.S. corn yields. They indirectly benefited from previous hybrid research in the U.S. only after the capacity to undertake inventive adaptation was created in the Philippines.

Technological distance in biological technology is related to Darwinian processes of natural selection. Animals and plants evolved into numerous variegations of species, each suited to a particular environmental "niche". The domestication of some animal and plant types led to centuries of selection by farmers, producing further differentiation within species. In rice, for example, more than one hundred thousand "landrace" types within the O. Sativa species have been selected by farmers since rice was first cultivated for food. Each of these landraces had some form of comparative advantage in the particular niche where it was selected. Modern plant breeding has consisted of crossing and selection programs to find improved genetic combinations. In rice, virtually all of this work has been undertaken in publicly supported experiment stations.

The earliest rice improvement research activities were in Japan, where major gains were made early in this century through improving Japonica landraces suited to subtropical regions. It was not until after World War II that concerted efforts were made to improve the Indica landraces. As of that time, rice producers in Japan, Korea, Taiwan, and parts of mainland China had achieved a 50 year technological lead over the tropical rice producing areas. In the 1950s, an Indica-Japonica crossing program sponsored by the Food and Agricultural Organization of the United Nations, coupled with the creation of the International Rice Research Institute (IRRI) in the Philippines, gave major impetus to rice improvement for tropical conditions. By 1965, many national rice breeding programs had been established in tropical countries. India, for example, had 23 programs in various locations. Around 200 rice breeding programs existed in some 40 countries by 1970. Most had, and have maintained, a close association with IRRI, which has served as a nodal point in the transfer of inventive germplasm.

IRRI achieved a breakthrough in 1964 leading to the release of the semi-dwarf variety IR-8 which, along with other modern varieties (C4-63, Masuri, TN-1), ushered in the "green revolution" in rice [Hargrove (1979)]. IRRI's IR-8 variety was widely planted after its release in 1966, but by 1970 its yields were severely diminished owing to Darwinian processes of disease and pest evolution in reaction to its introduction. The various breeding programs led by IRRI were able quickly to develop new varieties, comparable in yields to IR-8's initial levels, but having genetic resistance to the then common diseases and pests. By 1975, high yielding semi-dwarf varieties were planted in 30 percent of Asia's rice area. Continued varietal development to incorporate additional pest and disease resistance, cold tolerance, and other improvements have, in effect, produced a second green revolution leading to further diffusion of the high yielding varieties, so that they were planted in roughly 70 percent of Asia's rice area in 1990. Rice varieties suited to upland conditions (where irrigation is absent) and to deep water conditions (prevalent in parts of Southeast Asia) have not yet been developed [Chang (1989)].

A recent study of varietal development in rice by Gollin and Evenson (1991) analyzes more than 90 percent of the varietal releases (that is, successful inventions of improved varieties) of Indica rices since 1965. It shows that IRRI has played a relatively small role as a producer of varieties – it accounts directly for only some 17 percent of the varieties released. Roughly 10 percent of the varieties that were developed in national programs were released in other countries. Of more policy relevance are the findings in regard to parent varieties (the germplasm from which planted varieties are derived). IRRI contributed 65 percent of all parent varieties. National programs (particularly India's) have also contributed parent material that has crossed borders.

Studies of wheat technology, where a similar green revolution has occurred, show a very similar history to that of rice. Maize (corn) technology exhibits greater circumstantial specificity than either rice or wheat. Most other crops are similar in this regard. Fewer studies have been undertaken on livestock. Huffman and Evenson (1993) report evidence that circumstantial sensitivity for livestock is less than for crops.

5.3. Measuring the effects of technological distance in agriculture

We are aware of only one attempt to measure technological distance directly in order to show its impact on the value of technology transfers. Evenson (1992) used the following measure of technological distance between locations i and j with respect to all of the techniques that may be used individually to conduct some given activity:

$$D_{ij} = C_{j*/i}/C_{i*/i} \tag{3}$$

where the denominator, $C_{i*/i}$, is the unit cost of carrying out the activity in location i using technique $i*$, the optimal choice of technique for that location; and the numerator, $C_{j*/i}$, is the unit cost in location i using the technique that is optimal for location j.[39] This distance measure reflects both differences in circumstances and sensitivity to those differences. If circumstances were identical, or if technology were insensitive to differences in circumstances, the optimal choice of technique in both locations would be the same, and D_{ij} would equal one. Values greater than one indicate a positive technological distance.

This measure is based on existing technology and reflects prior technological development in the two locations. But it may also serve as an indicator of the proximity of their future technological development. Thus, it may show the value in location i of research conducted in location j, since new technology developed for location j must overcome the existing distance if it is to be useful in location i. If D_{ij} equals one, it may be considered highly likely that inventions in location j will have immediate application in location i. More generally, it may be expected that higher values of D_{ij} imply lower probabilities of direct transfer and lesser gains from any indirect transfers that might take place. However, the use of the measure in this way may be confounded if research in either location is circumstantially specific, causing D_{ij} to increase over time. But even with such divergence, inventions in one location may serve as parental germplasm to others as illustrated above in the discussion of rice technology.

Evenson (1992) applied the measure to data generated from rice yield trials in India. In such trials, common sets of cultivars are planted in each of many locations, with all varieties being subject to the same experimentally controlled production conditions in each production location. The values for rice across regions of India range from 1.05 to 1.67.[40] They exceed one entirely because of differences in soil and climate conditions. They reflect the fact that farmers may choose among many rice varieties, each having a comparative advantage in a distinct set of soil and climate conditions.

The distance measures just discussed were used to estimate the relative value of rice research conducted elsewhere within India. The basic specification was as follows:

$$T_i = \sum_j D_{ij}^\alpha R_j + \gamma Z_i \qquad (4)$$

where T_i is a TFP index for district i, D_{ij} is the distance measure, R_j is the depreciated stock of research expenditure in district j, and Z_i is a vector of

[39] Note that D_{ji} need not equal D_{ij} owing to the impact of differences in circumstances between locations i and j.
[40] These values relate to average yields in location i for the three crop varieties that have the highest yields in location j relative to the three varieties that have the highest yields in location i. To obtain the distance measure, the not unreasonable assumption was made that unit costs vary in direct but inverse proportion to yields.

other productivity affecting variables, including irrigation, weather conditions, and the like. The estimated value of the alpha parameter is -5.0. For D_{ij} equal to 1.1, the benefit to region i of one dollar's worth of research in region j is 0.62 times the benefit of spending a dollar in region i's own research program; for D_{ij} equal to 1.5, the relative benefit of research in region j drops to 0.13. Thus, even when knowledge spillovers are considered, technological distance greatly affects technology transfer possibilities.

As will be discussed further below, a number of studies – in both agriculture and industry – have attempted to incorporate technological distance by utilizing various circumstantial variables when investigating the value of spillovers [Jaffe (1986), Griliches (1991)]. One line of empirical research relates productivity measures to, among other variables, separate research stock variables, one for the region's own R&D and the other for R&D conducted in regions that are circumstantially close neighbors. Another line of research utilizes patent statistics in place of R&D expenditures. These studies have shown that individual regions generally do benefit from research in other regions that are circumstantially not too far distant. But they have equally demonstrated that local research capacity is required in order to gain spillover benefits from research done elsewhere.

5.4. Technology transfer in industry

In substantial contrast to policy makers dealing with agricultural technology, many policy makers concerned with industrial technology appear to believe that technological distance depends solely on economic circumstances; that is, that industrial technology is not sensitive to physical and social circumstances.[41] Following from this belief is their view that the only issues of consequence with respect to industrial technology relate to the dependence of choice of technique on factor prices. Often implicit is the corollary notion that LDCs can simply free-ride on industrial technology created in the advanced countries, thereby avoiding the cost of creating technological capabilities. But, as argued previously, developing countries do not obtain industrial technology as "manna from advanced countries" even if the technology is insensitive to circumstances. Owing to the tacitness of technology, substantial investments in acquiring production capability are always required to master a new technology.

There are, as yet, no direct estimates of technological distances for industrial technologies. Nonetheless, there is a great deal of evidence that product and

[41] For analysis and evidence indicating that this is not so even in the developed countries, see Cohen and Levinthal (1989).

process designs alike are sensitive to differences in circumstances in virtually all industries. For example, observers of invention in India conclude that much of it consists of adapting foreign technology to local circumstances [see, for example, NCAER (1971), Bhagwati and Srinivasan (1975), Desai (1984), and Lall (1987)]. Such adaptation is motivated by differences between developed and developing countries in things like income levels, consumer preferences, factor costs, climatic conditions, and material input characteristics. Sometimes these differences are artificially created by import-substitution policy regimes, which force producers to purchase particular inputs from domestic sources that supply inputs of inferior quality relative to their foreign counterparts. To make the most effective use of such inputs, firms are often forced to undertake a form of policy-induced technological effort, with low social returns [Teitel (1987)].

Important evidence of adaptation in response to significant circumstantial differences comes from the engineering activity that occurs whenever new production facilities (or additions to existing facilities) are being established. It is hidden from casual observation which fails to recognize that engineering design involves tailoring technology to local circumstances. Additional evidence comes from case studies of the use of industrial technology in LDCs. As noted previously (Section 4.4), these studies demonstrate that production capability is in large part acquired through a variety of technological efforts which lead to productivity enhancing technological changes. Many of the numerous changes uncovered can only be described as having been intended to adapt the technology to local circumstances [see, for example, Mikkelsen (1984)]. Not always clear from the information provided is whether the adaptations are motivated by differences in physical, social, or economic circumstances. Some of them are obviously related to differences in relative prices. Otsuka et al. (1988) provide a notable study of adaptations to economic circumstances in the development of Japan's textile industry. But there are also obvious cases of adaptations to differences in physical circumstances. For instance, producers of cement, steel and other natural resource-intensive products have often been found to alter their processes to adapt them to peculiar raw material characteristics [Dahlman (1979)].

Dahab's (1986) study of farm machinery producers in Brazil is instructive in this regard. The industry was established by multinational firms that progressively lost market share to indigenous producers who first imitated and subsequently adapted the multinationals' models, making them better suited to local circumstances. Within 20 years the indigenous producers dominated the markets for all but the most complex models.[42]

---

[42] However, owing to changes in macroeconomic policy, they suffered a serious loss of market share in the 1980s.

Patent and utility model protection appears to have given the indigenous producers important incentives in this process.

There is very little direct evidence about sensitivity to social circumstances. In some cases it is thought that they can preclude the use of labor-intensive methods that would otherwise be the optimal choice. Pack (1987), for example, argues that labor-intensive weaving techniques which were used effectively in Korea can not be used in some African settings because of social factors which preclude sustained accumulation of the necessary skills.

Indirect evidence of sensitivity to circumstantial differences comes from international patent data. If technological distances were nil, one would not observe much domestic invention in LDCs, since they could simply free-ride. But, as reported in Evenson (1990) and reflected in data provided for India and Korea in Table 37.2 (in Section 4.3), there is domestic invention in a number of LDCs. Reflecting perceived invention opportunities, ratios of R&D to sales differ among performing industries in a roughly similar pattern in India and Korea. In turn, reflecting inherent differentials in technological distance, proportions of patented inventions having foreign and domestic origins also differ among industries in both countries. If there were no differences in technological distances across industries, one would expect to find similar ratios of imported to total inventions in all industries.

Table 37.3 provides complementary evidence of sectoral differences in technological distance. The indices reported there are average ratios, inverted, among eight OECD countries, of patents obtained by domestic inventors in their home country to patents obtained by them in the other countries. A value of 7.0, for example, would indicate that inventions originating in any one country were patented in all eight countries. This could only happen if all inventions were equally valuable across the range of diverse circumstances present in all eight countries, which would mean that technological distances were nil. No index has a value higher than 4.5, while most are well below 3.0. This is consistent with the notion that most inventions are adaptive modifications to local circumstances of other inventions having more extensive application. But it also appears that industries differ considerably in the potential for direct technology transfer owing to intrinsic differences in technological distance.

The table shows index values both by industry of manufacture and by sector of use. The highest ratios for industry of manufacture are found in drugs, chemicals, and office machinery, which also have high ratios of foreign to domestic inventions in both Korea and India. These industries are characterized by relatively low technological distances. The ratios for sector of use afford a comparison of technological distances in the agricultural sector with those in other sectors. While technological distance in agriculture is indeed comparatively large (i.e., the inter-country patenting index has a relatively low value), agriculture does not exhibit the greatest technological distance on this measure. Several manufacturing sectors appear to be characterized by larger

Table 37.3
Sectoral inter-country patenting indices
(Eight OECD countries 1969–1987)

	Inter-country patenting indices	
	Industry of manufacture	Sector of use
Finance – business	–	1.687
Wood & furniture	1.620	1.705
Construction	–	1.735
Transportation services	–	1.767
Ships	1.664	1.779
Other manufacturing	1.719	1.814
Other services	–	1.866
Fabricated metals	1.806	1.887
Mining	1.842	1.903
Aerospace	1.876	1.929
Other transport	1.642	1.961
Agriculture	–	1.966
Communication – utilities	–	2.002
Health services	–	2.031
Motor vehicles	2.009	2.044
Other machinery	2.060	2.084
Food, drink & tobacco	2.271	2.106
Electrical machinery	2.122	2.185
Electronic equipment	2.199	2.201
Ferrous metals	2.195	2.217
Instruments	2.015	2.239
Stone, clay & glass	2.093	2.260
Petroleum refineries	2.179	2.264
Rubber and plastics	1.952	2.381
Paper and printing	1.900	2.470
Non-ferrous metals	2.548	2.483
Textiles and clothing	2.019	2.488
Chemicals	2.788	2.788
Drugs	2.696	3.039
Office machinery	2.071	4.345

Note: Sectors are arrayed in ascending order of using sector indices.
Source: Evenson (1993a).

technological distances, as do most service sectors.[43] Reference to Table 37.2 shows that the non-manufacturing sectors in India and Korea also utilize inventions from other sectors, and that, in Korea, the utility model particularly benefits these sectors.

Further evidence that technological distance matters for industrial sectors is found in recent research by Englander and Evenson (1993). Their study examines the relationship between domestic as well as foreign R&D expenditures and TFP growth in 11 industries across 11 OECD countries. Foreign expenditures include only those by technologically more advanced countries, aggregated using labor productivity differentials to weight expenditure values. In a cross-industry analysis incorporating the technology distance indices, they found that foreign R&D expenditure by technological leaders is associated with increasingly higher domestic TFP growth as technological distance diminishes. No less important, they also found that domestic R&D expenditure appears to be increasingly more productive in TFP growth terms as technological distance increases.

In sum, industrial technology is circumstantially sensitive, but this is manifested in a different way than in the case of agricultural technology. In industry, differences in circumstances do not generally preclude the direct transfer of techniques (appropriately engineered) as they typically do in agriculture. But once the techniques are transferred, and given sufficient attention to the acquisition of appropriate capabilities, further adaptive technological changes occur in response to evolving perceptions of local circumstances. In agriculture, inventive capabilities are required to accomplish most transfers; in industry, the transfer of techniques, when effective, triggers a process of simultaneous capability acquisition and technology adaptation, leading ultimately to patenting.

The adaptation of industrial technology to LDC circumstances has, however, to be seen in historical perspective to be completely understood. Technology developed in advanced countries may cascade through several circumstantially specific stages of adaptation before it reaches the poorest countries, with each successive stage making the technology less suited to advanced countries but more suited to less developed ones. By adopting the appropriate choice of technology, LDCs that are today at a particular stage of development can benefit from adaptations made by countries that have previously passed through the same stage. For example, some of the adaptations in textile machinery made by the Japanese in the early 1900s still remain in use

---

[43] Measurement at lower levels of aggregation would show considerable variation among technologies within sectors. Evenson (1993c), for example, has found that the use of imported patents among advanced countries is proportionately much greater in the manufacture of agricultural chemicals than in the production of harvesting machinery, which reflects the relative variability of soil characteristics.

elsewhere. Thus, assuming that knowledge of previous adaptations has not been lost, the need for adaptive effort with respect to economic circumstances is less. More generally, different vintages of technology, if not obsolete, may offer alternatives tailored to a variety of circumstances.

Nonetheless, adaptation is sometimes necessary before transfer. Mikkelsen (1984) showed that the key activity enabling Philippine rice producers to benefit from rice threshing technology developed in Japan was the adaptive invention of a prototype thresher at IRRI. Using this prototype, local inventors made the specific adaptations required to enable the economic use of threshers in the many different circumstances in which they are now used in the Philippines. Mikkelsen concluded that utility model protection was an important factor stimulating the post-IRRI inventive activity. What is particularly notable in this example is the implication that the available IPR protection was insufficient to elicit the initial transfer. Had a private producer played IRRI's role, it would have been unable to appropriate sufficient returns owing to the rapid entry of niche-specific competitors. In different circumstances, absent widely diffused metal working abilities, a private producer might have been able to appropriate sufficient returns.

But it is not always the older vintages that are the most appropriate (either directly or indirectly) for LDCs. Vernon's (1966) product cycle model has exactly the opposite implication; technologies are not transferred (or transferable) to LDCs until they have matured to the point where processes have been invented that enable the use of unskilled labor in mass production. But Vernon's model relates to a different phenomenon, namely the evolution of frontier technology. Moreover, it is not the complete process which is transferred, but only those parts which are amenable to labor intensive production; assembly activity rather than component production, for example.

6. Technological investment in the private sector

Studies of various forms of investment (or the lack thereof) in technology are important for policy purposes because of the need to understand the factors that normally stimulate such investment. There are many issues, including matters of appropriability, that must be addressed. Public sector choices are important as well as private sector decisions. Unfortunately, we have relatively little evidence from LDCs about the determinants of investment activities by private firms.[44]

---

[44] Cohen and Levin (1989), in their survey of the evidence from developed countries, make many general observations that are of relevance in the LDC context as well.

6.1. Capability acquisition and technological change

Case studies of technological development in industry at the firm level clearly indicate that many important forms of investment in technology are not captured in conventional measures. This is especially true of investments that are made in the course of mastering newly acquired technology. As was previously indicated, most of these investments do not count as formal R&D. Nonetheless, they simultaneously lead to productivity-enhancing technological changes and to the accumulation of technological capability. In both respects, they are the means whereby the tacitness of technology and of local circumstances is overcome through experience-based learning and complementary additions of technological elements from outside the firm. Moreover, they contribute the foundations from which the capability effectively to undertake formal R&D evolves. In short, without them there can be no meaningful technological development.

One of the few generalizations about technology that has no known exceptions is the observation that no newly acquired technology is initially operated at its potential productivity. No less generally true is the principle that the initial level of productivity as well as the time and resources required to achieve the potential productivity depend on the starting level of mastery. Three factors appear to be most important among those responsible for these phenomena. First, labor can not effectively be trained apart from experience in the activity, while labor training is an art that improves in effectiveness with practice that is consciously monitored. Second, technologies are typically systems of elements that can be integrated in various ways. Achieving the proper integration in the operation of technology requires experimentation, which in turn is an art based on experience. Third, as stressed throughout this survey, technologies are circumstantially sensitive and much of the requisite knowledge about local circumstances and how technology responds to them in its operation can only be acquired through experimentation.

Achievement of mastery in the senses just discussed is by no means automatic; it requires systematic attention to the lessons of experience and often entails the search for elements of technology that were initially neglected out of ignorance of their importance [Dahlman et al. (1987)]. Thus the body of case study research and anecdotal evidence includes numerous cases of failure to achieve the minimum mastery needed to attain the levels of productivity expected when the physical investment was undertaken. It also includes numerous cases of unforeseen success in achieving sufficient mastery to exceed the expected levels of productivity. In the former cases there is no technological development to benefit subsequent investments in implementing the same or similar technology. In the latter cases there is technological development so that subsequent investments are implemented with increasing efficiency due to spillovers from previous experience.

In truth, the degree of mastery that is required to achieve the expected productivity depends on the choices made at the stage of engineering design and the care with which those choices are embodied in the productive facility. It is much easier to master the operation of a well designed and executed project than to overcome the deficiencies of a poorly engineered and executed one. But the ability to make effective choices and to oversee their implementation requires considerable mastery of the technology.[45] Indeed, it requires mastery well beyond that needed for efficient startup under the best possible conditions. This is why it is frequently the case that significant adaptations of the technology are required to realize the expected productivity. These adaptions are not unlike those often found to be necessary in order to respond effectively to changes in market conditions or to enable higher than expected productivity levels, which is typically accomplished by making changes that exploit local circumstances.

Included among the enormous variety of adaptive changes that have been observed are various means of capacity stretching, bottleneck breaking, improved by-product utilization, alterations in raw material sources, modifications in product design, and expansions of product mix. It is from these kinds of changes that the complex of production and investment capabilities that is needed to achieve sustained productivity increases is derived. Without sustained productivity increases, international competitiveness can neither be achieved nor maintained in the face of the continual productivity improvements by firms at the leading edge of global competitiveness. Very few of the kinds of changes just enumerated take place in the context of formal R&D or yield inventions that can be patented abroad. Some of them are amenable to utility model protection, but most are simply improvements in various aspects of operation or engineering practice. It is generally only after the achievement of higher levels of mastery acquired through making these kinds of changes that firms go on to establish formal R&D and then begin to engage in inventive activities which may ultimately lead to patenting. But very important is the fact that mastery achieved in relation to these kinds of changes is what enables the efficient acquisition of technology through means other than formal purchase.

It is a striking fact that formal purchase of technology in complete packages through such means as turnkey plant contracts and licensing, plus their functional equivalent – direct foreign investment, accounts for only a modest

---

[45] A high level of mastery is not sufficient by itself to insure an efficient outcome. See, for example, Desai (1972) for a case study illustrating some of the many things that can go wrong in a complex industrial undertaking over which local control is lacking due to financial exigencies.

share of the technology that has been mastered in Korea, to cite a particularly revealing case about which relatively much is known [Westphal et al. (1984)]. In many instances formal purchase contributed the seed from which were developed the capabilities to acquire vastly more additional technology through means other than formal purchase. Sometimes the process of acquiring additional elements of technology was akin to apprenticeship – participation with foreigners in project execution and startup provided the initial learning. Other times the process was one of imitation through sequential reverse engineering leading to the emergence of new processes and products. But regardless of how one might characterize the underlying processes, the basic principle was successively to master individual elements in a progression running from the simpler to the more complex. It would therefore be incorrect to characterize the process as one of reinvention; it is rather one of step-by-step mastery, though the successive steps can often be so rapidly achieved as to seem to have been undertaken simultaneously.

Thus it is that an effective process of technological development through the focused acquisition of production and investment capabilities can provide the means to assimilate and then adapt a great deal of foreign technology on the basis of selectively importing some of the elements while developing the others locally. The process is externally constrained only insofar as key elements of the technology are proprietary and not available through arms-length purchase. In the past, judging by the experience of the successful export-led economies, relatively little of the technology required for rapid industrialization has been proprietary. In turn, again judging by their experience, purchases of imported capital goods play a vitally important role in the overall process. First has come learning how to use imported equipment; learning how to produce equipment has taken place more slowly. Additionally, a good deal of the information needed to augment basic capabilities has come from the buyers of exports who freely provided product designs and offered technical assistance to improve process technology in the context of their sourcing activities. Some part of the efficacy of export-led development must therefore be attributed to externalities derived from exporting.

In sum, much – perhaps most – of the investment required by firms to achieve the NICs' level of private sector technological development can not be inferred from conventional statistical sources relating either to technology purchase or invention. The more readily observable investments are but the tip of an iceberg. But this analogy, while descriptively evocative, is analytically misleading because one can not infer the extent of hidden investment simply on the basis of knowing the magnitude of the visible investment. The fact remains that most LDCs have so far failed to achieve a sufficient volume of investment in acquiring technological capabilities. The analogy is additionally misleading insofar as the warranted mix of technological investments shifts with the progress of technological development toward the more readily observable forms. But this consideration is as yet of little real consequence for most LDCs.

6.2. *Direct foreign investment*

The effects of direct foreign investment on the accumulation of domestic technological assets are complex and not easily disentangled. As a means of technology transfer, direct foreign investment is, in the first instance, a substitute for the development of indigenous capabilities. But foreign firms are no less affected by the circumstantial sensitivity of technology and the tacitness of local circumstances than are domestic firms. Thus they may generally be expected to invest in the accumulation of specific technological assets and to undertake adaptive technological changes. But this does not mean that they necessarily make the same choices that would be made by domestic firms acting in their place. In some respects they may be expected, at least initially, to make better choices, because they can rely on capabilities developed through previous experience elsewhere and because they face lower costs of searching for and evaluating technology. But in other respects they may make worse choices, because they lack experience in the local circumstances and because their objectives are to varying degrees externally determined.

Possible differences in behavior between domestic and foreign firms have in fact been a central issue in the literature on direct foreign investment. Helleiner's survey (Chapter 28 in Volume 2 of this Handbook) of this literature largely focuses on behavior with respect to technology choice and concludes that, if anything, it appears that foreign firms may typically make superior choices. As Helleiner implies, there is much less evidence about behavior with respect to the accumulation of technological assets over time; what evidence there is does not appear to support any particular generalization apart from the statement that ill-advised policies can lead both domestic and foreign firms to the wrong kinds of behavior. Indeed, there may be no valid generalization beyond this one. Consider Korea and Singapore, two countries that have achieved spectacular development success. One, Korea, is an outlier in having relied relatively little on foreign firms for technology transfer. The other, Singapore, is an outlier in the opposite direction, having continually and extensively relied on foreign firms for its technological development.

Considerable attention has recently been given to the possibility that foreign firms may contribute importantly to technological development through spillovers to indigenous firms. The most obvious form of possible externality occurs through the mobility of labor trained by foreign firms. Other externalities may result from the transfer of technology to their local suppliers. Foreign firms often appear to have important indirect, demonstration effects as well; for example, opening avenues of profitable activities which are soon travelled by local imitators. Several attempts have been made to test for spillover effects using firm-level data that distinguish among sectors as well as between domestic and foreign ownership.[46] Spillovers are inferred if the productivity performance of domestic firms is related to some measure of the extent of participation by foreign firms. Results from these studies have been mixed. Moreover, such studies can at best show that the evidence is consistent with the notion of spillovers. But case study research, like that reported in Rhee and Belot (1990), does demonstrate that real spillovers do sometimes occur. In turn, other forms of technology transfer, for example construction of turnkey plants, may have externalities of equal or greater significance for productivity growth in domestic firms.

6.3. Foreign and domestic technology: Complements or substitutes

Several studies have investigated the relationship between domestic R&D and the purchase of disembodied foreign technology. The typical methodology has been to use data at the level of firms or industries to regress formal R&D expenditures or some other measure of domestic inventive effort on technology purchase and other explanatory variables such as sales [Lall (1983), Katrak (1985, 1990), Kumar (1987), Braga and Willmore (1991)]. Blumenthal (1979) followed the converse approach, regressing technology purchases per employee on R&D expenditures per employed. In a similar vein, Katrak (1991) performed a probit estimation of the probability that technology is imported as a function of the R&D expenditures of firms. Mohnen and Lepine (1991) used Canadian data to estimate a factor demand system in which technology purchase is one of the variable factors and R&D is treated as a fixed input.

Studies of the foregoing kind are not conclusive owing to specification errors of several types. First, either R&D or technology purchase is taken to be exogenous, making the estimates subject to simultaneity bias [Arora (1991)]. Second, there is a selection bias in most of these studies because firms are sampled on the basis that they perform R&D, purchase technology, or do both [on the general subject of selection bias, see Maddala (1983)].

Deolalikar and Evenson (1989) used Indian industry level data to estimate a factor demand system in which both inventive effort (proxied by patents granted during the period) and foreign technology purchase are treated endogenously. They found that both variables are significantly and positively

---

[46] See, for example, Blomstrom and Persson (1983) or Haddad and Harrison (1991).

related to stocks of U.S. patents in the same industries, but they were unable to identify the relationship between domestic patenting and foreign technology purchase in the absence of prices for each. Fikkert (1993) tackled both problems using Indian firm level data. His sample includes firms that do no R&D and/or no technology purchasing and a maximum likelihood estimation technique is used to take account of corner solutions in these respects. Domestic R&D and foreign technology purchases were found to be substitutes. In other words, a lower effective price for technology purchases induces an increase in technology licensing and a reduction in local R&D and vice versa. Basant (1993), using a different approach based on multinomial logit analysis, came to a similar conclusion.

Case studies of technological effort show that technology purchase and local R&D are in some cases complements and in others substitutes. They are complements when R&D is used in the process of assimilating and adapting purchased technology. They are substitutes when R&D is used to develop some element of technology that could otherwise have been purchased. Basant and Fikkert interpret their estimates as demonstrating the preponderance of the latter case in India, which they take to be evidence that the Indian government succeeded in its objective of stimulating domestic technological development through regulating the import of technology. However, neither study was able to determine how the relationship between technology purchase and local R&D would have been changed if alternative policies had been followed. If only for this reason, their finding that domestic R&D and technology purchase are substitutes can not be generalized to other LDCs following different policies.

But their findings in other respects may be of greater immediate relevance. They found strong evidence of spillover effects from domestic and foreign invention, with increases in the stock of either being a stimulus to increased local R&D. Moreover, both found that increases in the stock of foreign inventions were associated with greater expenditures on technology purchase. In subsequent joint work [Basant and Fikkert, (1993)], they determined that the private rate of return to domestic R&D in India was at least as high as that found in developed countries, while the private rate of return to technology purchases was much higher still.[47] Taken together, these results imply that increases in domestic R&D and technology purchase expenditures would have been highly profitable in private terms, and – at least in the case of R&D – even more so in social terms. The Indian policy regime over the period examined by these authors was characterized by relatively weak patent protection and regulations that discouraged technology purchases. On both

---

[47] Specific rates of return are not given here because estimates for India, as for developed countries, are highly sensitive to the specification employed.

counts it appears that India's policies did not stimulate as much technological effort as could have been productively undertaken.

Case study evidence clearly implies that accessing foreign elements of technology and investing in technology creation are complements in the fundamental sense that firms which are found to have the most effective approaches to managing their technological development do both [see, for example, Bell et al. (1984) or Dahlman et al. (1987)]. But not all access to elements of foreign technology is through formal purchase; nor are all investments in technology creation done in the context of formal R&D activity. Thus the relationship between formal purchase and formal R&D is a quite separate matter. Nonetheless, there is an obvious reason for thinking that these expenditures must effectively be substitutes over at least some range of technological development. As was discussed in Section 4, much of technological development involves substituting for imports of technology and related technological services. One result, as was seen in Table 37.1, is an increase in the share of domestic relative to imported inventions, which suggests that "make" does effectively substitute for "buy".

But, in truth, the simple make versus buy characterization is fundamentally misguided. This is not merely because the choice to buy is limited by the existing stock of purchasable technology. More importantly, absent this limitation, it is because effective decisions to make typically come after basic elements of technology have been bought by one means or another.[48] Efforts to make technology are rarely successful in economic terms if not founded on domestic experience using elements of the technology, experience which leads naturally to minor adaptive changes and, ultimately, to patentable inventions. Thus decision making is more aptly characterized in terms of "buy, then decide about make", with the fundamental make choices being related to particular elements of the technology.

More generally, efficient technological effort builds on both the cumulation of domestic capabilities and the evolution of global technology. Thus indigenous adaptations to local circumstances and the incorporation of continuing foreign technological advances are importantly complementary activities. In the past, countries that have sought technological self-sufficiency have sacrificed efficiency gains that can be had by directing technological efforts to derive the greatest advantage from the utilizing global technology. Once created, their R&D establishments typically became locked into programs that focused on improving outmoded technologies introduced at their inception. The Indian automotive, fertilizer, and textile industries, for example, have suffered greatly from the resulting technological isolation, as did the industries of most socialist regimes. In other countries, many in Latin America for

---

[48] For example, through machinery imports.

example, technological isolation was not so much associated with the early creation of R&D establishments as with later efforts to generate R&D by restricting access to foreign technology.

6.4. IPR protection and investment behavior

Studies that attempt to determine the incentive effects of IPR protection on decisions to invent and imitate fall into two categories: studies of behavior, either of firms holding patents or of firms that conduct systematic R&D and may choose patenting as one option for appropriating returns; and studies – such as that by Pakes and Schankerman (1986) – that try to establish for different sectors the intrinsic value of a patent in comparison to the value of other incentives driving private R&D activity. The following discussion focuses on the former studies.

A number of surveys rank patents as being relatively unimportant among the determinants of R&D investments [Scherer (1986) and Nogues (1990) provide reviews]. However, a 1981 survey of American firms in the chemical, drug, electronics, and machinery industries found that these firms would not have introduced about one-half of the patented inventions that composed the sample without the benefit of patent protection [Mansfield et al. (1981)]. A survey in Canada, a major technology importer, also concluded that patents were not the dominant factor in decisions by American firms to invest in establishing Canadian subsidiaries [Firestone (1971, Chapters 7 and 10)]. Watanabe (1985, pp. 217, 250) reports on a survey of over two thousand Japanese firms conducted in 1979–1980. In this survey, nearly 30 percent of the firms cited the patent system as being the most important incentive to industrial innovation; considered next most important were tax and other financial incentives, with roughly 13 percent of the firms citing each respectively. But patent protection ranked third in importance in the motivation of individual researchers, of whom only some 12 percent considered it the most important incentive to them as individuals. More important in their eyes were competition with other firms (23 percent) and academic or technical interest (17 percent). Greif (1987), however, shows that R&D investments and patent applications are closely correlated in the Federal Republic of Germany, suggesting that patents have a stimulative impact.

The survey evidence on the stimulus effect of patents suggests that the benefits of a patent system vary across industries. Industry studies show that patents are important for some industries, particularly for pharmaceuticals. For example, in their effort to simulate the effects of weaker patent protection in the United Kingdom, Taylor and Silberton (1973, Chapter 14) found that the most affected industries would be pharmaceuticals and specialty chemicals, the two industries that use patents most intensively. Similar findings were obtained by Levin et al. (1987) when they interviewed over 600 R&D managers in major U.S. firms. In most of the lines of business covered by that survey, patents were rated as being less effective than trade secrets or sales and service activities as means for securing returns from R&D; the notable exceptions were pharmaceuticals and scientific instruments.

The foregoing evidence seemingly gives only weak support to the proposition that patent protection stimulates R&D. But it must be recognized that much of it is attitudinal evidence comparing patents with other incentives in settings where patent protection has typically been available for long periods. It is not uncommon for respondents in such surveys to understate the importance of institutions that have long been commonplace. Furthermore, the evidence does not generally address the question of what would happen if the patent system were eliminated. Clearer, stronger evidence of its importance is found in the fact that all developed countries have been strengthening their own patent systems over time.

In turn, there is strong evidence that patents do not effectively deter imitation by rivals for very long.[49] This is in part because patents carry the means for their own destruction in the sense that they disclose to rivals the information needed to reproduce the invention. Mansfield (1985) conducted a random survey of 100 U.S. firms in 13 major manufacturing groups that yielded an estimate of the average time period between a firm's decision to commit to a new process or product and the point at which the detailed nature of the new process or product was known to its rivals. The period was roughly one year for product inventions and less than 10 months for process inventions. Patents were indicated to be a chief conduit through which the knowledge spread.

Moreover, it does not appear from this research that patent protection prevented competitors from entering the market. Firms participating in Mansfield's survey believed that patent protection postponed rival entry for only a matter of months in the case of about one-half of the sample innovations. For only 15 percent of the sampled inventions was it thought that patent protection delayed imitation by more than four years. Though patents were considered to increase the costs of rival imitation, the additional cost was not considered sufficient to markedly affect the speed of entry by rivals. The survey by Levin et al. (1987) also found that imitation, even in the presence of a patent, occurs rapidly, in part because of the information that patents convey to competitors. But the fact that imitation takes place rapidly does not necessarily mean that patents have little effect on inventors' revenues, either during the period before imitation or after.

---

[49] Except in certain chemicals-related areas, it is generally rather easy to devise a functional substitute for a successful new product that does not actually infringe the original inventor's patent.

The studies discussed to this point do not allow one to draw any direct conclusions about the behavior of firms in LDCs. But there are very few studies of firms in LDCs that are directly pertinent. One study is that conducted jointly in Brazil by the Action Center for Small and Medium Sized Companies, the Ministry of Industrial Development and Commerce, and the American Chamber of Commerce, cited by Sherwood (1990, pp. 115–116). Approximately eighty percent of the 377 firms responding declared that they would invest more in internal R&D and in labor training if better legal protection were available. In turn, we know of no studies that have rigorously demonstrated losses or damages in any country from strong IPRs. Even for those few level 2b and 2c countries (in Table 37.1) with pirating capacity, there is little evidence that stronger IPRs would have resulted in higher net payments for technology from abroad. But there is evidence that suppliers of technology respond to weak IPRs and piracy by withholding technology, often going to considerable trouble in the process [Mansfield (1993)]. Thus countries with weak IPR systems may suffer a double loss, offering insufficient incentives for domestic inventive effort while also experiencing a diminished flow of foreign inventions that would further stimulate local efforts.

7. Returns to technological activities

The direct approach to the study of technological development is to evaluate technological efforts as "projects" and to apply standard economic evaluation methods. In principle, one should be able to estimate productivity conse-quences (benefits) as well as costs, thereby to assess the economic growth consequences of technology investments. In addition, one should be in a position to evaluate distributional consequences. The evaluation methods for such studies, while complex and technical, do not necessarily depend on a detailed technical understanding of the research activities themselves. These types of evaluations, along with case study evidence, constitute the bulk of the empirical foundations on which our understanding of technological develop-ment in both developed and developing countries is based.

This section reviews studies of the returns to investments in both the agricultural and industrial sectors; it also considers the conclusions from studies of distributional impacts. For agriculture, we have a large number of studies evaluating research and extension programs in both developed and developing countries. For industry, we are less well situated. We have very few studies for LDCs. We are well aware of the limited relevance of the empirical studies undertaken in developed countries for developing countries, but we believe a discussion of the developed country evidence is useful nonetheless.

7.1. Benefit-cost studies for agriculture

Two methodological approaches to project and program evaluation have been followed in the literature. Both of them are based on TFP growth accounting principles (discussed in Section 2.5). The first is based on direct imputation and is an application of project evaluation methods. The second approach is statistical and entails construction of variables derived from investments in research, extension, schooling, infrastructure, and other TFP enhancing activities. These variables are typically expressed in "stock-service flow" terms, with appropriate temporal and spatial weights to reflect time lags, depreciation, and spillovers. These variables are sometimes termed "meta" variables to distinguish them from conventional input variables. Statistical frameworks used have included:

- TFP decompositions using hedonic regression specifications, where TFP measures are regressed on meta variables of the kind just discussed;
- production function specifications where meta variables are included together with conventional inputs in a production function framework that is usually Cobb–Douglas in form; and,
- profit functions or output-supply, input-demand systems which include meta variables and rely on duality theory plus the assumption of competitive markets to obtain estimates of production function parameters.

    The key issue in the direct imputation studies is typically the identification of an appropriately matched sample of before-and-after or with-and-without observations relating to technology or program use. Once this has been accomplished and any remaining issues of selectivity bias have been properly dealt with, productivity differences can be attributed to program use and the benefits measured in relation to costs. The classic study by Griliches (1957) demonstrated the basic methodology.[50] Griliches utilized data on the first generation of hybrid corn varieties developed by both private firms and public experiment station systems. The costs of developing these varieties began to accrue around 1905. Experiment station and farm level data enabled Griliches to estimate the yield advantage of hybrid corn varieties over the older varieties in each state. These data were used along with adoption data to compute year-by-year benefit values, given by the change in producer plus consumer surplus. The resulting cost and benefit time series were used to compute benefit-cost and rate of return measures.
    The statistical studies employing meta variables have in some cases estimated

---

[50] Some of the results from this study are discussed in Section 5.2.

both the temporal and spatial spillover weights utilized in constructing these variables. Temporal weights estimated for agricultural research programs indicate that TFP responses generally begin one or two years following expenditures, rising to reach a peak after 7 to 10 years and then declining as pests and diseases begin increasingly to erode the value of the technology. Agricultural extension programs have faster and shorter-lived impacts. Studies for industry usually do not attempt to estimate temporal weights; rather, weights (typically non-increasing with time) are simply assumed.

Spillover weights are designed to capture the value contributed by research programs outside of the region. Often they are combined with technological distance measures of the kind discussed in Section 5. Earlier studies used climatic indicators as simple proxies for technological distance. Industrial studies typically specify that a firm benefits from R&D undertaken by other firms in the same industry. Griliches (1991) provides a review of studies that have examined spillover effects.

The estimated coefficients on the meta variables in these studies are used to compute the economic impacts from an increment in investment. The marginal benefits from the increments have temporal and spatial dimensions which are taken into account in deriving benefit-cost and rate of return measures. In turn, some studies provide parameter estimates which can be used in computable general equilibrium models to examine the distributional consequences of technological investments.

7.1.1. Returns to R&D

Table 37.4 summarizes results of 156 studies estimating returns to agricultural research programs and 40 studies of industrial R&D. Most of the agricultural studies surveyed utilized secondary data (district-level data by year in India, for instance) and were to some degree based on cross-section variation in the meta variables. Cross-section variability in research and extension inputs has been quite important in permitting the identification of their impacts; very few studies based on simple time series have been able to identify their impact. (It should be noted that cross-section studies are subject to a number of statistical problems and that these have not been uniformly dealt with in all studies.) The TFP determining variables include measures of research, extension, schooling, roads, markets, prices, and related variables. In principle, the included variables should encompass the full range of TFP enhancing activities, but not all studies have succeeded in this respect.

Several of the studies estimated the separate contributions of pre-technology scientific research and of downstream applied research. Several also estimated the contributions to agricultural TFP growth of private sector R&D by firms supplying inputs to the agricultural sector. This contribution constitutes a

Table 37.4
Estimated rates of return to R&D

	Number of studies	Estimate not significant	Range of estimates				Mean
			1–24	25–49	50–75	75+	
Public sector							
Agricultural research							
Africa	10	1	2	3	3	1	41
Latin America	36	2	14	22	13	13	46
Asia	35	2	7	20	23	25	56
All developing countries*	85	5	23	45	40	44	80
All developed countries	71	5	21	54	26	29	48
Private sector							
Industrial research							
Developing countries	5	0	0	3	3	2	58
Developed countries	35	0	10	20	10	5	44
Public sector							
Agricultural extension							
Developing countries	17	1	4	2	4	6	50
Developed countries	6	0	1	0	3	2	63

* Includes international agricultural research centers.
Note: Rates of return are in percent.
Source: Evenson (1993b).

pecuniary spillover from industry to agriculture, one which occurs because supplying firms capture only part of the return to their R&D through higher prices for improved inputs. Of the 292 reported rates of return to public agricultural research summarized in Table 37.4, 139 were above 50 percent; only 11 fell below 10 percent. The distribution of estimated returns shows higher estimated rates for programs in developing countries compared to those in developed countries. The few studies reporting rates of return to private sector R&D used in agriculture also showed high returns.

Fifty three of the 156 studies gave estimates pertaining to entire agricultural research systems rather than to individual commodity research programs. The distribution of estimated rates of return in these studies did not differ from that for studies focused on specific commodities. The similarity between the distributions of system-wide and commodity-specific programs suggests that the latter studies do not suffer from a serious selectivity bias; that is, that they have not focused only on the best programs. Nonetheless, as in other types of studies, it remains possible that there has been some failure to report estimates that are not deemed "high enough" to report.

One way to test the likely validity of the estimates is to examine the growth of output or productivity that is implied by the rates of return when considered in relation to the amounts invested. Unfortunately, few studies have made the relevant calculation. One that did is the study by Rosegrant et al. (1993), which provides a full accounting for Indian TFP growth in agriculture over the 1956–1988 period. Public sector research and extension were found to account for approximately 60 percent of TFP growth. R&D in the private sector, domestic plus foreign spillovers, accounts for 30 percent, with infrastructural improvement accounting for the remainder.

A number of observers have been puzzled by the result that agricultural research programs in LDCs appear to be generally as productive as similar programs in developed countries. They argue that LDC programs suffer from lower skill levels and poor organization cum management, implying that the comparative deficiencies should lead to lower returns. Two counter arguments are pertinent. If a country is underinvesting in these activities, marginal and average rates of return may be relatively high. Thus, an appeal to diminishing returns can explain why a low quality system subject to under-investment could have a marginal impact as large or even larger than a higher quality system with less under-investment. (It should be noted that investments in agricultural research did grow rapidly in the 1960s and 1970s in response to perceived high returns, but that this response was not sufficient to bring returns down to normal levels.)

Alternatively, large returns to LDC research may reflect their receipt of greater spillovers from developed country research than can be realized among developed countries. Indeed, LDC systems, in concentrating on adaptive invention, do rely on the international agricultural research centers (IARCs) and developed country systems for pioneering invention and pre-technology science. At least in principle, this ought to enable them to generate equal returns with lower skill levels. Moreover, it does in fact appear that most IARCs are enabling significant spillovers to LDCs. Several of the studies reviewed by Evenson (1993b) found high rates of return to the IARCs' research programs. For example, one of these studies [da Cruz and Evenson (1989)] examined the role of a program for the Southern Cone countries in Latin America that has made particularly concerted efforts in facilitating international exchanges of technology and found high returns to this activity. Another, recent study of genetic resources in rice [Gollin and Evenson (1991)] reported high returns to the International Rice Research Institute's (IRRI) international system to maintain genetic material. In turn, the Rosegrant et al. (1993) study, discussed above, found substantial spillovers from foreign private as well as public sector R&D.

7.1.2. Returns to extension

Investment in agricultural extension has been seen as an attractive policy option in LDCs for several reasons. Among the valid reasons is the fact that the real costs of extension services in LDCs are comparatively low relative to the costs of research activities. LDCs spend only one fifteenth as much per extension worker as is spent in the advanced countries; in agricultural R&D, they spend half as much per researcher. Less valid is the often encountered twofold presumption that technology invented in the advanced countries is immediately transferable to developing countries and that extension services play the major role in transfer.

Experience in Asia and Latin America in the 1950s and 1960s ran counter to both notions. Large investments in extension and rural development programs had relatively small impacts in many countries. T.W. Schultz (1965), in his classic monograph on traditional agriculture, argued from this and other, micro evidence that traditional peasants were "poor but efficient", having exhausted the potential of the best suited technology. He, of course, noted the importance of education and skills, but he argued that in a setting where little new technology was being made available to farmers, even the least skilled farmers would learn to do the best that could be done given the available technology. Thus it was generally accepted in the 1970s that the gap between the average and the best productivity levels was much smaller than earlier thought, so that extension could be productive only after local research programs generated new, circumstantially tailored technology. This perception was greatly re-inforced by the development of the high yielding rice and wheat varieties that came to be associated with the green revolution. It was easy to identify the associated productivity gains with the widespread adaptation of these varieties to different local circumstances, which only strengthened the view that extension programs were of secondary importance and could not generate significant results.

Perceptions have changed somewhat in recent years. A new approach to extension, the Training and Visit (T&V) System, was developed in World Bank projects in the late 1970s [see Benor and Baxter (1984)]. This system imposes a formal structure linking extension workers to technical specialists and entails a fixed schedule of extension worker visits to farmers and farm groups. In its initial applications, the T&V approach proved successful in overcoming the frequently criticized absence of sufficient extension worker skills and disciplined management in previous approaches. Thus it has been introduced into a large number of Bank funded programs and has, in fact, become the principal program in the Bank's lending for agriculture in Africa, which has generally not yet benefited from invention of new technology. In some cases the introduction of the T&V system in Sub-Saharan Africa has led to a reduction in extension and related personnel, but in the majority of cases expenditures on extension are higher than under previous systems.

Some of the early studies to investigate the return to extension relied on variables measuring extension worker contact with farmers as indicators of extension provision. Since extension contact is at least partly determined by farmers' behavior, such variables are endogenous and positive correlations between them and farm productivity can not be used to claim the existence of a causal link between extension and productivity. Later studies have overcome the problem of endogeneity by using extension supply variables. Technological and price information is diffused to farmers through a broad range of channels, with farmer-to-farmer communication being especially important.

Birkhauser et al. (1991) reviewed 40 studies of returns to agricultural extension programs. Few of the early studies showed significant returns. But, of the more recent studies, 15 of the 26 that provide estimates of rates of return report values in excess of 50 percent (see Table 37.4). These include two recent studies [Bindlish and Evenson (1993) and Bindlish et al. (1993)] of T&V extension in Kenya and Burkino Faso, suggesting that countries in Africa still have considerable scope for reducing inefficiency even when new technology is not being made available to farmers.

7.2. Returns to industrial R&D

Surveys of returns to private R&D in developed countries show that investments in R&D, when evaluated ex post, yield private returns that are at least as high as returns to other investments [Mohnen (1990)]. Mansfield et al. (1977a) report on 17 case studies of innovation for which the median private rate of return was 25 percent. Griliches (1980) reports rates of returns for large U.S. industrial firms ranging from 30 to 50 percent. Mairesse and Sassenou (1991), on reviewing a number of studies giving statistical estimates of the impact of research expenditure on firm-level productivity covering several advanced countries (France, Japan, and the U.S.), found that all implied positive and highly significant elasticities, with approximate rates of return ranging from 14 to 24 percent. They found corroborating evidence in another set of firm-level studies that gave direct estimates of rates of return, leading them to conclude that, for the countries covered, private rates of return to R&D were no less than those for other forms of investment. Significantly, in the case of Japan, the estimates, and thus the conclusion, relate to the 1960s when it was largely engaged in adaptive R&D using imported technology as germplasm.

Social rates of return should exceed the private rates owing to the individual firm's inability to appropriate, or capture, the full benefits from conducting

R&D. Even in the presence of strong IPR protection, a private firm's rents from licensing or product sales generally represent only a fraction of the real value of the invention to the economy; that is, of the invention's social return. Indeed, according to the previously cited study by Mansfield et al. (1977a), social rates of return (median, 56 percent) were in most cases more than double the private rates. Griliches (1991) and Nadiri (1993) have reviewed a number of empirical studies and conclude that R&D spillovers are of substantial importance, which provides additional evidence that social returns are considerably in excess of private returns.

Very few studies have estimated returns to industrial R&D in LDCs. The study by Basant and Fikkert (1993) is seemingly unique in providing soundly based econometric estimates derived from firm-level data covering a wide range of manufacturing activities. As was discussed in Section 6.4, their estimates of the private returns to R&D in India are no less than comparable estimates obtained for developed countries. They also find evidence that social returns exceed private returns. Two studies of industrial R&D in industries supplying agriculture have reported high rates of return as measured by the impact on agricultural productivity [see Rosegrant et al. (1993)]. Pack (1987, 1990) computed potential returns from productivity enhancing expenditures that would both accomplish adaptive modifications and elevate levels of mastery over disembodied aspects in a sample of Philippine textile firms. He concluded that more than 80 percent of the firms in the industry would realize higher returns from such expenditures than from alternative investments.

Pack's estimates pertain to investments designed to reduce the dispersion of TFP levels across firms within the industry by moving the inefficient firms closer to the best practice frontier. To understand their full significance, they must be considered in relation to the fact that all studies of firm-level productivity differences within LDC industries find high variance in TFP levels across firms.[51] Most LDC firms are well behind the local production frontier and even further behind the frontier of international best practice. Given this evidence, Pack's estimates suggest that there is tremendous potential for realizing high returns from investments that would enable the achievement of best practice.

It is exceedingly difficult to measure directly the overall volume of technological effort related to technological change in the industrial sector.[52] Generally, one can at most infer the results of such activity from estimates of productivity growth. It appears that very few LDCs have experienced discernible TFP growth in industry over the past three decades [Pack (Chapter 9 in Volume 1 of this Handbook)]. Korea and Taiwan are notable exceptions,

---

[51] Pack (Chapter 9 in Volume 1 of this Handbook) surveys these studies.
[52] Mikkelsen (1984) demonstrates one approach to the problem.

where recent research indicates that TFP in the industrial sector has grown at an average annual rate of roughly five percent, considerably more than can reasonably be attributed to sources external to the technological efforts of individual firms, and sufficient to have contributed a sizeable share of the growth of real value added.[53]

A comparative historical study of the textile industry in India and Japan by Otsuka et al. (1988) gives strong evidence about the gains that can be derived from investments in mastery acquisition and adaptive change. During the late 19th and early 20th centuries, Japanese firms invested much while Indian firms invested little. The consequence was that Japan displaced India in world markets and became a leading exporter of textiles. The authors trace the source of the difference in performance to Japanese policies which both removed price distortions and encouraged technology transfer and adaptive investment.

Indirect evidence also suggests that there are high returns to technological investments. Consider: given what is known about the high volume of technological effort in Korea and Taiwan, one can only conclude from the apparent absence of significant TFP growth in most other countries that they have either failed to invest sufficient amounts in technological change or that their technological investments have been seriously misdirected. Inward looking trade policies and restrictions placed on international flows of technology are undeniably important sources of misdirection, as discussed elsewhere in this chapter.

Very few LDCs have managed to establish coherent and aggressive technological development strategies for the industrial sector, comparable to those that have been implemented in most countries for the agricultural sector. The evidence about the returns to technological efforts of various kinds, while limited, does not suggest that the reason is a lack of high payoff investment opportunities. It is more likely that there has simply been a failure to recognize that such opportunities do exist and to provide incentives and support for them.

7.3. Distributional impacts

A number of studies have attempted in different ways to evaluate the consequences of technological change for income distribution. Many authors have followed Kuznets in examining the relationship between income growth

---

[53] The recent studies are summarized in World Bank (1993, Chapter 6). Notable studies for Taiwan and Korea include Pack (1992) and Pilat (1993), respectively. Lau and Kim (1993) and Young (1993) provide dissenting opinions, arguing that rapid growth in Korea and Taiwan was more the result of rapid factor accumulation than of atypical TFP growth.

and income distribution. Their work can be regarded as indirectly concerned with the distributional impact of technological change insofar as technological change is what produced the underlying productivity changes. This literature will not be reviewed here, except to note its general conclusion that the distributional consequences of productivity growth are largely determined by a host of non-technological factors.[54] Two kinds of study are especially germane to this survey – studies employing computable general equilibrium (CGE) models and studies of micro-empirical evidence.

Careful attention to product mix and regional disaggregation is important in the specification of CGE models to evaluate distributional consequences in agriculture.[55] Product disaggregation is required to capture the fact that a research induced change in the production function for a single product has an effect on the supply functions for all products competing for the same resources as well as on the demand functions for variable factors. Indeed, the availability of improved rice and wheat varieties had a major impact reducing the supply of other cereals and pulses, something generally overlooked in the literature appraising the green revolution [Evenson (1992)]. Also too frequently neglected is the impact of the circumstantial sensitivity of the new technology, which makes it suitable for adoption only in regions having the requisite circumstances (for example, the possibility of controlled irrigation). Many micro studies, conducted for regions where the new technology was adopted, have concluded that employment and incomes were increased by its adoption. However, they have failed to recognize that there were negative distributional impacts in regions that were unable to adopt it.

A principal result from nearly all CGE and micro studies is that the major gainers from new agricultural technology are the consumers of agricultural products. For urban consumers, improved agricultural technology leading to lower prices is an unmitigated blessing no matter where or how the gains are realized. Farmers and rural workers also gain as consumers, but may lose as workers and owners of rural assets. The central parameter of concern in this regard is the demand elasticity for the product. With inelastic demand, total farm revenues and demands for variable inputs fall. This can result in a decline in the incomes of small farmers and rural workers. Subsistence farmers tend to be insulated from such changes because they consume most of what they produce [Barker and Herdt (1985)]. In an open economy facing a highly elastic world demand for the product, total farm revenues increase and farmers as well as workers gain.

---

[54] General literature surveys are given by Taylor and Arida as well as by Adelman and Robinson in Chapters 6 (Volume 1) and 19 (Volume 2), respectively, of this Handbook.
[55] Among the relevant CGE models are those constructed for the Philippines by Quisumbing et al. (1993) and for India by Quizon et al. (1991).

Many of the micro studies were motivated by a concern that advances in agricultural technology harmed the poorest rural families, small farmers and landless peasants. There appears to be a consensus that this is generally not true and that losses, where they have occurred, have accrued to landowners in areas that were circumstantially unsuited to adopt the new varieties. Barker and Herdt (1985) review studies for rice showing that small rice farmers adopt new technology about as rapidly as do larger farmers and thus share in the gains to early adopters. In turn, a recent study for rice at IRRI examined wage differentials within seven countries across regions which are differently endowed with respect to the ability to adopt the new varieties and found that they have been largely eroded by labor mobility. Instead of wage differentials, land rent differentials have emerged [David and Otsuka (1990)].

Thus the empirical evidence, at least for agriculture, is consistent with the basic analytical implications of general equilibrium theory. Improved technology enables more production from given resources. Various equilibrating mechanisms, labor mobility being one of them, insure that any losses ultimately accrue to fixed factors that are disadvantageously located relative to the technological change.

We are unaware of any studies that have systematically addressed distributional issues in relation to industrial technological change in LDCs. The studies of Becker et al. (1992) for urbanization in India do show impacts on regional employment and migration, but generalizations are difficult to make. Virtually all improved technology, when implemented, changes the demand for factors in spatially specific ways. With sufficient mobility, both locationally and occupationally, gains become widely dispersed. Ranis (1990) found that such mobility has been an important factor in maintaining, and indeed improving, Taiwan's relatively equitable income distribution. High degrees of mobility are also found in other countries; what evidence there is suggests that it has generally insured favorable distributional outcomes over time from technological change.

8. Policy issues

Technology policy is made by public bodies at the international, national, and regional levels. Private enterprises and individuals also make policy, largely by responding to incentive systems established by public policy makers. This section discusses policy options for international and multilateral agencies as well as for national (and, to some degree, sub-national) governments.

8.1. International policies

Until recently, IPRs were administered on an international level through international "conventions" or agreements – the Paris Convention for patents, the Berne Convention for copyrights, and so on. As noted previously and discussed in a number of studies, the mechanism for administration and enforcement of IPRs has recently shifted to trade law. The United States has pursued this shift most vigorously by treating weak or absent enforcement of IPRs in LDCs as forms of "unfair" trade practice, subject to sanctions under Section 301 of U.S. trade law. With the conclusion of the Uruguay Round of the GATT, a new and powerful enforcement mechanism is in place to facilitate the harmonization of IPR laws and their administration throughout the world.

This development has two important implications for LDCs. First, it ostensibly provides a mechanism under which they might seek compensation for opening their markets to foreign technology. Such compensation can be in the form of trade concessions, but these will be granted only if the governments seeking them are effectively able to negotiate them. The second and more immediate implication is that most LDCs no longer have the option of seeking to pirate technology under systems of weak IPR protection to foreigners.

These changes will affect different countries in different ways. For level 1a and 1b countries (see Table 37.1), the stress will be on developing effective IPR systems were they do not now exist. Emphasis in the level 1c countries will be placed on building more effective IPR systems. Level 2 countries are likely to find that defiance and laggard efforts on full harmonization of IPR systems will be very costly in terms of restricted market access and technology withholding. An important issue in IPR policy for all national governments is that they not let policy be determined or dominated by the interests of the developed countries who have pressed for the new GATT agreement. As discussed below, it is crucially important that domestic inventions be given adequate incentives in national IPR policies.

There is considerable evidence of the effectiveness of international research and information centers as well as training efforts directed toward the agricultural sectors (and possibly also the health sector). The international agricultural research centers have clearly served to facilitate international exchange of technology and parental germplasm. Their effectiveness has been dependent on national agricultural research centers, extension services, and farmer schooling. There is little doubt that these programs in support of agricultural technological development warrant continued support.

Far fewer resources have been directed toward similar programs for the industrial sector. Past initiatives to establish organizations that would roughly parallel those for agriculture have been stifled. This may in part be due to the unwillingness of private firms to share knowledge and technology openly. Trade secrecy is much more a part of industry than of agriculture.[56] But, even adjusting for this, we do not observe the same effectiveness in programs of research and information exchange for industry as for agriculture. But there is sufficient promise in this domain to warrant further experiments seeking more effective international programs in support of technological development in industry. The same conclusion would appear to hold for the service sector as well.

8.2. National policies

The policies of national governments are constrained by international policies. But the constraints do not hinder the formulation of appropriate national policies that would be sufficient to achieve rapid technological development in tandem with meaningful economic progress. Indeed, international policies, even in the realm of IPRs, are actually supportive of and complementary to adequate national policies.

The public sector has two roles to play in technological development.[57] One is to provide an appropriate policy environment for private-sector investments in technology. Policies that directly affect private sector technological development include regulations on trade in technology (for example, on technology purchase agreements) and in goods that significantly embody technology (capital goods, for instance) as well as tariffs on the latter. They also include subsidies and taxes that affect technological efforts of various kinds along with domestic IPRs. The public sector's other role is to be the investor in areas where the private sector can not effectively operate. Public investments include expenditures on R&D and technology dissemination as well as support for training and related activities. There are important policy issues with respect to both roles as well as in relation to the proper boundary between them. In the following, boundary issues will be dealt with where most appropriate in the course of a discussion that focuses first on promotional policies and then on public investments.

---

[56] There are several reasons for this. One of the more important is that technology in the form of practical methods ["routines" in the parlance of Nelson and Winter (1982)] embodied in complex organizations – more typical outside of agriculture than within it – is more readily maintained as proprietary than is technology in other forms that are principally embodied in particular inputs.
[57] See Ergas (1987) for a general discussion of technology policy.

8.2.1. Trade policy

Protectionist policies to foster import substitution have historically been the principal tool for attempting to stimulate private-sector technological development. The fundamental rationale for protection is found in the tacitness of technology, which implies that internationally competitive levels of productivity can not be reached without experience-based learning which entails comparatively high costs that must in some way be financed. But, as is well recognized, tacitness per se is not a sufficient grounds for granting protection, since an efficient capital market would provide the financing to cover any losses from warranted learning. In this respect the first best policy is to promote the development of an efficient capital market. In fact, financial institutions in most LDCs appear to lack effective capability in relation to financing technological investments of all kinds [Stiglitz (1989a, 1989b)]. Thus the importance of capital market development for technological development can not be denied, but there are no quick fixes in this realm just as there are none in the technological realm. The gains from improvements in the financial sector will be largest for countries at higher levels of technological development; capital market development alone will achieve little in the level 1a and 1b countries owing to their lack of basic production capabilities.

Externalities that preclude the complete appropriation of returns to technological investments provide the most general and compelling rationale for promoting technological development [Pack and Westphal (1986)]. This has long been recognized with respect to related investments in labor training.[58] But the recognition that externalities pervade the process of technological development has been slow in coming. Externalities related to the nonrivalrous nature of technology have their source not in its tacitness but rather in its circumstantial sensitivity and in the tacitness of local circumstances. Additional sources of externalities are found in the increasing returns that characterize many forms of technological investment and in the savings in transactions costs that result from technological development.[59] Some of the externalities are real or "technological" [Scitovsky (1954)]; many are Marshallian externalities – pecuniary insofar as they are transmitted through market transactions, but

---

[58] Labor training confers no externalities if workers bear training costs through acceptance of lower wages, as they have an incentive to do for training that is generally useful. It is often argued that workers' choices in this regard result in inefficient outcomes due to capital market failures in LDCs [for example, see Corden (1974, pp. 260-262)]. There appears to have been no empirical research to test this argument, which is undoubtedly the unfortunate result of the absence of requisite panel data.

[59] Stewart and Ghani (1991) provide a detailed discussion of the forms of many relevant externalities.

nonetheless "real" in their allocative implications because they are associated with investments characterized by significant indivisibilities; others take the form of spillovers, including demonstration effects.

The foregoing forms of externality would not be sufficient grounds for government intervention if they could somehow be rapidly internalized within market institutions. But this is improbable in the case of externalities that are widely diffused and incompletely understood without experience [Stiglitz (1989a)]. Even so, none of these externalities constitute a sufficient reason for protectionist policies. Apart from considerations of strategic trade policy – which, if relevant, would apply only to the most advanced LDCs (level 2c), protection is never the first-best policy on theoretical grounds; subsidies to technological investment are first-best, as is well known. Thus the only case that can be made for protection is one based on pragmatic grounds [see, for example, Pack and Westphal (1986)]. That said, the evidence overwhelmingly indicates that protectionist policies have not fostered successful technological development except, perhaps, in those few countries where they have been coupled with additional policies that effectively insure the rapid achievement of internationally competitive levels of capability, so that protection is indeed a temporary "necessity". The only policies so far known to possibly qualify in the latter respect are those that make the rapid growth of exports profitable. Export activity also has the additional benefit of greatly facilitating spillovers from foreign entities.[60]

The foregoing discussion applies equally to all forms of protectionist policy including those aimed at various kinds of technology import. Temporary protection against technology imports, through such means as restrictive licensing of purchases of capital goods and disembodied technology or domestic content regulations for project engineering, might appear – on pragmatic grounds – to offer a strong means for encouraging technological development. However, such policies can more easily have the effect of severely retarding technological development by blocking access to critical elements of foreign technology. Like all protectionist policies, but even more so, their potential effectiveness depends entirely on whether they are administered with adequate enforcement mechanisms to insure that they are indeed promoting meaningful technological development.[61]

Consider that both India and Korea have used similar, albeit differently administered, protectionist policies to restrict technology imports. There can

---

[60] Pack (1992, 1993) explores externalities that may be associated with export activity. The linkage between export-led industrialization and rapid TFP growth is examined in a CGE modeling framework in de Melo and Robinson (1992).

[61] Stewart's (1979) survey of technology licensing policies makes this point forcefully.

be no doubt that, coupled with an inward-looking policy regime, they had disastrous consequences in India.[62] But in Korea they may well have been generally effective. The most apparent and undoubtedly consequential difference between the Indian and the Korean implementation of the policies was one of timing. They were seriously applied in Korea only at a relatively late stage of technological development, after the achievement of high levels in a wide range of production capabilities and in some investment capabilities. The Indian strategy was more nearly one of attempting to acquire the full range of capabilities through efforts, that were initially centered in the capital goods industries, to reinvent technology. Among other effects, these efforts had the unintended consequence of locking producers in many sectors into the use of outmoded technologies. Another important difference in the implementation of protectionist policies in these countries may be found in the distinct structures of their bureaucracies. The Indian bureaucracy was seemingly incapable of accomplishing the high volume of administrative processing that would have been required to enable rapid growth.

8.2.2. Domestic policies

Given the factors that constrain public policy in all LDCs, the pragmatic argument for protection is an ex post rationalization of its possibly successful use, not an ex ante justification in its favor. Other kinds of incentive policies offer a seemingly more straightforward means of stimulating technological investments. Direct subsidies and tax preferences have theoretical justification but are of limited relevance insofar as some important kinds of technological investment, particularly some of those related to the achievement of mastery, are not readily separable activities. Formal R&D activity, purchases of technology, and related labor training are the only readily identifiable investments. Many countries, particularly those at level 2 where formal R&D becomes increasingly more relevant, provide subsidies for R&D activity. As with subsidies for other activities, they do not always achieve the desired results, sometimes leading only to the relabeling of activities anyway undertaken. Nonetheless, they are a means to achieve more R&D by producers.

The inherent difficulty of directly subsidizing many relevant forms of technological investment would seem to imply that IPRs and indirect measures must be the principal means, apart from institution building, of promoting private-sector technological development. IPRs are discussed at some length below. Among the indirect measures, most important are the assurance of a stable macro environment, the enforcement of competitive market behavior,

---

[62] Lall (1987) provides a detailed discussion of Indian performance in technological development.

and an open-economy strategy with respect to trade of all forms.[63] No country has achieved sustained technological development without continual attention to these policy imperatives.

Institutional development in capital and insurance markets is also fundamentally important. Returns to investments in technological assets are sometimes highly uncertain, leading to substantial risk which may often preclude efficient allocation due to the incompleteness of markets that would enable entrepreneurs to exercise their risk aversion by means that do not yield underinvestment in social terms. The consequences must be particularly severe in the case of innovators, who face the greatest uncertainty, but provide information (whether or not they succeed) of real social value by reducing uncertainty for potential followers. Direct incentive measures that effectively spread some of the risk to the public undoubtedly have some effect in mitigating underinvestment, but they would appear to be a poor substitute for adequate institutions.[64] The government's appropriate role in fostering institutional development in this respect is highly controversial [see, for example, Stiglitz (1989b)]. Sufficient empirical evidence is simply not available.

Of the other indirect measures that have been discussed in the literature, four merit brief mention here. One is the use of public enterprises to transfer and develop technology. More often than not, the pursuit of non-market objectives by these enterprises retards rather than promotes technological development. However, there are some notable exceptions, such as the USIMINAS steel firm in Brazil [Dahlman (1979)]. A closely related measure is the selective promotion of certain industries on the grounds that they are the drivers of technological development; the contemporary favorites include the familiar "hightech" industries such as "informatics". At some levels of technological development there clearly are certain activities that merit priority; metal working and simple machinery repair at levels 1a and 1b, for example [see, for example, Pack and Todaro (1969)]. But there are few such obvious cases, and even with respect to them there is too often little attention paid to performance monitoring and enforcement.

Also closely related in its apparent rationale to the promotion of public enterprises is the promotion of large scale, conglomerate firms, such as the chaebol in Korea. Here the comparison between Korea and Taiwan is telling. Taiwan's industrial structure is as much dominated by small and medium enterprises as is Korea's by super-large ones. Yet the two countries have comparable records of technological development. This suggests, as does other comparative evidence, that large firms have no inherent advantages in relation

---

[63] On the importance of indirect policies more generally, see Sagasti (1978) and Stewart (1987).
[64] Tax measures are typically such that the public shares in positive returns but not in losses. Removal of this asymmetry is an obvious direct incentive that could have a significant impact.

to technological development [see, for example, Levy (1991) and Levy and Kuo (1991)]. The final indirect measure is the promotion of direct foreign investment. It is indirect because of the need for complementary measures to realize the full gains from the operations of foreign firms. In Singapore, for example, foreign investment promotion has been coupled with extensive public support to technical education and training in order to insure continued technological development through the attraction of a rapidly changing mix of foreign firms. Except in some industries, direct foreign investment is neither a necessary nor an obviously superior means of technology transfer. But it may be the only effective means to initiate a process of sustained technological development in the level 1a and some level 1b countries. Here its potency will depend on the use of complementary policies to insure spillovers through labor mobility into local small and medium enterprises.

8.3. IPR policy

Developing countries have an obvious incentive to pirate foreign inventions unless there are effective penalties against doing so. Penalties are both overt in the form of sanctions imposed by foreign governments and covert in the form of supplier reluctance to sell technology of any kind. As discussed previously, the imposition of sufficient penalties in the case of the level 2 countries can now seemingly be considered a fact of life. If these countries do not recognize the IPRs of foreigners, they will suffer from retaliation in their export markets and will be unable to obtain elements of technology needed to fuel their technological development. But the recognition of foreign IPRs is only half of what is needed. Strong domestic IPRs are also needed to stimulate adaptive cum imitative invention, in part as a legitimate counter to the recognition of foreign IPRs. Existing and prospective international arrangements do not place any barriers to the implementation of strong domestic IPRs.

Strong IPRs can be a powerful instrument for encouraging many forms of investment at all levels of technological development if they are sufficiently focused on promoting those forms of investment which are respectively important at each level. More imagination than has previously been given to their design is clearly in order. Breeders rights and utility models exemplify the gains to creativity in this area. Utility model protection, for example, is actively sought in the few countries, like Korea, that grant it. Moreover, the evidence suggests that it stimulates the kinds of minor, adaptive inventions that are important in the early to middle phases of technological development.

The development of improved IPR systems in the level 1a and 1b countries is, however, probably not feasible; other activities, particularly the establish-

ment of a legal infrastructure for property rights enforcement, take prece-
dence. The level 1c countries need to evaluate their existing IPR systems,
which are in most cases colonial legacies, in order to develop systems better
suited to their own needs. Given their level of technological development, the
use of IPRs to facilitate imports of technology through formal means is an
important consideration. Level 2a and 2b countries typically have weak IPR
systems reflecting the previous dominance of international concerns to the
detriment of domestic interests. They need to recognize the importance of
IPRs in stimulating domestic inventive effort and refashion their IPR systems
accordingly.

8.4. Public sector investment

The issues relating to public sector investments in technological development
are neither easily summarized nor readily resolved. Where there is sufficient
justification, such investments can yield high returns. This is evident from
public sector investments in R&D and extension relating to biological (agricultural and medical) technology. Unfortunately, the rationale for public sector
investment is nowhere else so clear-cut.[65] But rationale alone is not enough;
adequate management is also required. The principal difficulty in managing
public sector investment is insuring that it meets the real needs of its clients. A
workable model for doing so exists in agriculture. The absence of comparable
models for investments in other areas imposes additional costs and uncertainties of undeniable significance. From the scanty, largely anecdotal, evidence
that is available, one has to conclude that various forms of public sector
investment in other areas have in some places and at some times yielded high
returns. One can only guess at the average returns on a global basis for any of
the modes; the best guess is that the returns have been quite low. But more
often than not it would appear that the reasons for low returns have as much, if
not more, to do with poor management than with inadequate potential returns
to the activity if properly directed.

Of the more specific lessons that may be drawn from past experience, those
in two areas stand out. The first relates to industrial R&D undertaken by
public sector research institutes. R&D to reinvent technology simply does not
pay unless it is conducted to overcome absolute restrictions on supply, a
consideration that is relevant only to the level 2c countries attempting to enter
certain industries. Otherwise, seemingly successful cases of reinvention turn
out on closer inspection to be instead well managed cases of adaptive transfer;

---

[65] Justman and Teubal (1986, 1991) demonstrate the elements of a rigorous justification for
public investment in technological infrastructure to benefit the industrial sector.

notable examples of this kind of research have been undertaken by Taiwan's Industrial Technology Research Institute. In turn, the obstacles to achieving high returns from adaptive public sector research on technologies already well established in production are nearly insurmountable. To be productive, industrial research must be conducted in close proximity to experience gained in production. Simply stated, the good ideas for implementable adaptive invention come largely from production experience and are not easily communicated beyond the plant perimeter. Ways around the obstacles to adaptive research can be found, but few institutes appear to have discovered them.

The second area where important lessons have been learned relates more generally to the fact that the public sector's role as a direct investor is too much taken for granted by those concerned about the promotion of technological development. Consider public sector extension services to serve industry. The most obvious point to be made here is that the returns to promoting the development of private sector suppliers of technology may well exceed those to investing in public sector extension. But seldom are such private sector alternatives even recognized. In turn, diffusion of best practice technology has in some countries been effectively performed by industry associations acting on behalf of their private members. As a rule, too little attention is paid to stimulating such private institutional means of providing what are essentially club goods. These observations are not intended to suggest that private sector solutions are necessarily best; in truth they are often infeasible. Rather, possible private sector solutions merit attention because such solutions can be expected to accelerate technological development.

8.5. Complementary investments

Some final comments about investments in science and in human capital formation are in order lest it be thought that inattention implies unimportance. Evidence of high returns indicates that investments in pre-technology sciences are important for adaptive invention in areas where technological distances are large. In turn, comparative human capital data strongly imply that the NICs could not have succeeded without investing heavily in technical and scientific education through the college years and in vocational training. But in nearly all LDCs the problem has been on the demand side, not on the supply side. It makes no sense to invest more in high-level technical human capital formation until sufficient progress is achieved in realizing technological development.[66]

---

[66] Enos (1991) provides a comprehensive discussion of the relationship between technological development and human capital formation.

9. Research directions

There are many studies, both analytical and empirical, that are being undertaken with some success at present. On the analytic front, endogenous growth and dynamic trade models are offering more to the field than much earlier theory. Further contributions and insights will undoubtedly be forthcoming. The specifications of imitation and spillover in models to date are clearly not yet capturing the full richness of real world phenomena; distinct levels of technological development need to be incorporated into this work more clearly. The same can be said with respect to important distinctions among modes of technology transfer ranging from direct foreign investment through informal apprenticeship. Without capturing significant differentiations in these respects there is likely to be little progress in adequately distinguishing between cases of success and failure in catchup growth.

It goes almost without saying that theory, at least as regards technology, unsupported by empirical work deservedly has a rather short life. Also that more than simply stylized facts are needed. Theorists must develop testable propositions, and empiricists must devise ways to do the kind of testing required to discriminate between alternative hypotheses. This is not to say that carefully conducted case studies are unimportant. But in the future case studies will need to be conducted with more attention to analytical rigor and careful quantification of costs and benefits than has been true in past; that is, they will have to do so if they are to contribute useful results that go beyond suggestive interpretations. Case studies of seemingly successful public sector investment programs outside of agriculture are especially needed.

This survey makes clear that there are many significant gaps in the body of pragmatic empirical studies as between developing and developed countries. There can be no question about the need for many more studies estimating rates of return and examining relationships between domestic investment and foreign technology in the industrial sector. Here future studies should be guided by the methods and specifications now being used in state-of-the-art research on developed countries. A methodology for addressing issues concerning externalities and spillover is at hand and should be widely applied. Another important branch of pragmatic studies employs direct questioning of managers to obtain insights regarding decisions and decision making processes. Such studies of foreign suppliers and domestic purchasers of technology can add importantly to the understanding of motivation and behavior.

The relative neglect of service activities in this survey in part reflects a parallel disregard in the literature. If only because of their importance in the overall economy, they require much greater attention in future research on technological change. But there are other, no less substantial reasons for focusing considerable research on services. Many service sectors have recently been experiencing rapid technological change with seemingly profound consequences in markets for goods and for labor. Changes in information technology directly affect possibilities for institutional development (related to export marketing, for example) and for improved management of various aspects of economic development [regarding the latter, see Hanna and Boyson (1993)]. In turn, a number of the smaller LDCs are largely service economies. Commercial and financial services have recently been the leading sectors in two of the more dynamic NICs, Hong Kong and Singapore. Our understanding of the changing nature and role of services in relation to development is inadequate. Indeed, many important questions undoubtedly remain even to be articulated in operational terms.

Suggestions for a complete research agenda are not made here. In particular, studies of factor bias and distributional impact are not considered. This is not because such studies are without value, it is rather because the first order of business in a large part of the developing world must be the improvement of productivity through policy reform and investment in technology. Distributional problems can usually be dealt with (when they occur) using policy instruments that do not affect the overall pace of technological development.

References

Arora, A. (1991) 'Indigenous technological efforts and imports of technology: Complements or substitutes?', unpublished manuscript. Pittsburgh, Pennsylvania: Carnegie Mellon University.
Arrow, K.J. (1962a) 'Economic welfare and the allocation of resources for inventions', in: R.R. Nelson, ed., *The rate and direction of inventive activity*. Princeton: Princeton University Press.
Arrow, K.J. (1962b) 'The economic implications of learning by doing', *Review of Economic Studies*, 29:155–173.
Ayres, C.E. (1944) *The theory of economic progress*, 1st edition. Chapel Hill, North Carolina: University Press. [Second edition, New York: Schocken Book, 1962 and reprinted with a new and important 'Foreword' in 1965.]
Barker, R. and Herdt, R.W. (1985) *The rice economy of Asia*. Washington, DC: Resources for the future.
Barro, R. (1991) 'Economic growth in a cross-section of countries', *Quarterly Journal of Economics*, 106:407–443.
Barro, R. and Sala-i-Martin, X. (1992) 'Economic growth', unpublished manuscript. New Haven, Connecticut: Yale University.
Barzel, Y. (1968) 'Optimal timing of innovations', *Review of Economics and Statistics*, 50:348–355.
Basant, R. (1993) 'R&D, foreign technology purchase, and technology spillovers in Indian industry: Some explorations', mimeo. Maastricht, The Netherlands: United Nations University Institute for New Technologies.
Basant, R. and Fikkert, B. (1993) 'Impact of R&D, foreign technology purchase and technology spillovers on Indian industrial productivity: Some estimates', mimeo. Maastricht, The Netherlands: United Nations University Institute for New Technologies.
Becker, C.M., Williamson, J.G. and Mills, E.S. (1992) *Indian urbanization and economic growth since 1960*. Baltimore: Johns Hopkins University Press.
Becker, G. (1964) *Human capital*. New York: Columbia University Press.

Bell, M. (1984) 'Learning and the accumulation of industrial capacity in developing countries', in: M. Fransman and K. King, eds., *Technological capability in the third world.* London: Macmillan.

Bell, M., Ross-Larson, B. and Westphal, L.E. (1984) 'Assessing the performance of infant industries', *Journal of Development Economics*, 16:101–128.

Benor, D. and Baxter, M. (1984) *Training and visit extension.* Washington, DC: The World Bank.

Bhagwati, J. and Srinivasan, T.N. (1975) *Foreign trade regimes and economic development: India.* New York: Columbia University Press.

Bindlish, V. and Evenson, R.E. (1993) 'Evaluation of the performance of T&V extension in Kenya', Agriculture and Rural Development Series No. 7. Washington, DC: The World Bank.

Bindlish, V., Evenson, R.E. and Gbebitibou, M. (1993) 'Evaluation of the performance of T&V based extension in Burkina Faso', mimeo. Washington, DC: The World Bank, African Region Technical Department.

Binswanger, H.P. and Ruttan, V.W., eds. (1978) *Induced innovation: Technology, institutions and development.* Baltimore, Maryland: Johns Hopkins University Press.

Birkhauser, D., Evenson, R.E. and Feder, G. (1991) 'The economic impact of agricultural extension: A review', *Economic Development and Cultural Change*, 39:607–650.

Blomstrom, M. and Persson, H. (1983) 'Foreign investment and spillover efficiency in an underdeveloped economy: Evidence from the Mexican manufacturing industry', *World Development*, 11:493–501.

Blumenthal, T. (1979) 'A note on the relationship between domestic research and development and imports of technology', *Economic Development and Cultural Change*, 27:303–306.

Braga, H. and Willmore, L. (1991) 'Technological imports and technological effort: An analysis of their determinants in Brazilian firms', *Journal of Industrial Economics*, 39:421–432.

Chang, T.T. (1989) 'Domestication and spread of the cultivated rices', in D.R. Harris and G.G. Hillman, eds., *Foraging and farming: The evaluation of plant exploitation.* Cambridge: Cambridge University Press.

Chenery, H. (1967) 'Comparative advantage and development policy', in: E.A. Robinson, ed., *Surveys in economic theory, II.* New York: St. Martins Press.

Cohen, W.M. and Levin, R.C. (1989) 'Empirical studies of innovation and market structure', in: R. Schmalensee and R.D. Willig, eds., *Handbook of industrial organization*, 2. Amsterdam: Elsevier.

Cohen, W.M. and Levinthal, D.A. (1989) 'Innovation and learning: The two faces of R&D', *Economic Journal*, 99:569–596.

Coe, D.T. and Helpman, E. (1993) 'International R&D spillover', NBER Working Paper No. 4463. Cambridge, Massachusetts: National Bureau of Economic Research.

Corden, W.M. (1974) *Trade policy and economic welfare.* Oxford: Clarendon Press.

Cortes, M. and Bocock, P. (1984) *North-south technology transfer: A case study of petrochemicals in Latin America.* Baltimore: Johns Hopkins University Press.

da Cruz, E. and Evenson, R.E. (1989) 'The economic impact of the PROCISAR program', Discussion Paper. New Haven, Connecticut: Yale University, Economic Growth Center.

Dahab, S. (1986) 'Technological change in the Brazilian agricultural implements industry', unpublished Ph.D. dissertation. New Haven, Connecticut: Yale University.

Dahlman, C.J. (1979) 'A microeconomic approach to technical change: The evolution of the USIMINAS steel firm in Brazil', unpublished Ph.D. dissertation. New Haven, Connecticut: Yale University.

Dahlman, C.J. and Nelson, R. (1991) 'Social absorption capability, national innovation systems and economic development', mimeo. Washington, DC: The World Bank.

Dahlman, C., Ross-Larson, B. and Westphal, L.E. (1987) 'Managing technological development: Lessons from the newly industrializing countries', *World Development*, 15:759–775.

Dasgupta, P. (1986) 'The theory of technological competition', in: J.E. Stiglitz and G. F. Mathewson, eds., *New developments in the analysis of market structure.* Cambridge: M.I.T. Press.

Dasgupta, P. and Stiglitz, J. (1980) 'Industrial structure and the nature of innovative activity', *Economic Journal*, 90:266–293.

David, P.A. (1975) *Technical choice, innovation and economic growth: Essays on American and British experience in the nineteenth century.* London: Cambridge University Press.

David, C.C. and Otsuka, K. (1990) 'Differential impact of modern rice technology across production environments in Asia', mimeo. Los Banos, Laguna, Philippines: International Rice Research Institute.

de Melo, J. and Robinson, S. (1992) 'Productivity and externalities: Models of export-led growth', *Journal of International Trade & Economic Development*, 1:41–68.

Denison, E.F. (1962) *Sources of economic growth in the United States and the alternatives before us*. New York: Committee for Economic Development.

Denison, E.F. (1969) 'Some major issues in productivity analysis: An examination of estimates by Jorgenson and Griliches', *Survey of Current Business*, 49:1–27.

Deolalikar, A. and Evenson, R. (1989) 'Technology production and technology purchase in Indian industry: An econometric analysis', *Review of Economics and Statistics*, 71:689–692.

Desai, A. (1984) 'India's technological capability: An analysis of its achievements and limits', *Research Policy*, 13:303–310.

Desai, P. (1972) *The Bokaro steel plant: A study of Soviet economic assistance*. Amsterdam: North-Holland.

Easterlin, R.A. (1981) 'Why isn't the whole world developed', *Journal of Economic History*, 41:1–19.

Englander, A.S. and Evenson, R.E. (1993) 'International growth linkages between OECD countries: An industry study', mimeo. New Haven, Connecticut: Yale University, Economic Growth Center.

Enos, J. (1991) *The creation of technological capability in developing countries*. London: Pinter.

Ergas, H. (1987). 'Does technology policy matter?', in: B. Guile and H. Brooks, eds., *Technology in global industry*. Washington, DC: National Academy Press.

Evenson, R.E. (1990) 'Intellectual property rights, R&D, inventions, technology purchase, and piracy in economic development: An international comparative study', in: R.E. Evenson and G. Ranis, eds., *Science and technology: Lessons for development policy*. Boulder, Colorado: Westview.

Evenson, R.E. (1992) 'Research and extension in agricultural development', ICEG Occasional Paper No. 25. San Francisco, California: ICS Press.

Evenson, R.E. (1993a) 'Human resources and technological development', in C.D. Goodwin, ed., *International investment in human capital*. New York: International Institute for Education.

Evenson, R.E. (1993b) 'Estimated returns to research and extension: A review', unpublished manuscript. New Haven, Connecticut: Yale University, Economic Growth Center.

Evenson, R.E. (1993c) 'Science for agriculture: International perspectives', unpublished manuscript. New Haven, Connecticut: Yale University, Economic Growth Center.

Evenson, R.E. and Kislev, Y. (1975) *Agricultural research and productivity*. New Haven, Connecticut: Yale University Press.

Evenson, R.E. and Kislev, Y. (1976) 'A stochastic model of applied research', *Journal of Political Economy*, 84:265–281.

Evenson, R.E., Putnam, J., and Kortum, S. (1989) 'Invention by industry', unpublished manuscript. New Haven, Connecticut: Yale University.

Fei, J.C.H. and Ranis, G. (1964) *Development of the labor surplus economy*. Homewood, Illinois: Irwin.

Fikkert, B. (1993) 'An open or closed technology policy? The effects of technology licensing, foreign direct investment, and technology spillovers on R&D in Indian industrial sector firms', unpublished Ph.D. dissertation. New Haven, Connecticut: Yale University.

Firestone, O.J. (1971) *Economic implications of patents*. Ottawa: University of Ottawa Press.

Fransman, M. (1986) *Technology and economic development*. Boulder, Colorado: Westview Press.

Gerschenkron, A. (1962) *Economic backwardness in historical perspective: A book of essays*. Cambridge: Harvard University Press.

Gilbert, R.J. and Newbery, D. (1982) 'Pre-emptive patenting and the persistence of monopoly', *American Economic Review*, 72:514–526.

Gollin, D. and Evenson, R.E. (1991) 'The economic impact of the International Rice Germplasm Center (IRGC) and the International Network for the Genetic Evaluations of Rice (INGER)', mimeo. Los Banos, Laguna, Philippines: International Rice Research Institute.

Green, P.A. and Brown, P.D. (1976) 'Some aspects of the use of labour-intensive methods for road construction', Papers for Panel Discussion, Indian Roads Congress, 37th Annual Session. New Delhi: Indian Roads Congress.

Greif, S. (1987) 'Patents and economic growth', *International Review of Industrial Property and Copyright Law*, 18:191–213.

Griliches, Z. (1957) 'Hybrid corn: An exploration in the economics of technological change', *Econometrica*, 25:501–522.

Griliches, Z. (1963) 'The sources of measured productivity growth: United States agriculture 1940–1960', *Journal of Political Economy*, 71:331–346.

Griliches, Z. (1980) 'Returns to research and development expenditure in the private sector', in: J.W. Kendrick and B.N. Vaccara, eds., *New developments in productivity measurement and analysis*, Studies in income and wealth, volume 44. Chicago: University of Chicago Press.

Griliches, Z. (1991) 'The search for R&D spillovers', NBER Working Paper No. 3768. Cambridge, Massachusetts: National Bureau of Economic Research.

Griliches, Z., ed. (1992) *Output measurement in the service sectors*, Studies in income and wealth, volume 56. Chicago: University of Chicago Press.

Grossman, G. and Helpman, E. (1991) *Innovation and growth in the global economy*. Cambridge: M.I.T. Press.

Haddad, M. and Harrison, A. (1991) 'Are there dynamic externalities from direct foreign investment? Evidence for Morocco', Industry and Energy Department Working Paper, Industry Series Paper No. 48. Washington, DC: The World Bank.

Hanna, N. and Boyson, S. (1993) 'Information technology in World Bank lending: Increasing the developmental impact', World Bank Discussion Paper No. 206. Washington, DC: The World Bank.

Hargrove, T.R. (1979) 'Diffusion and adoption of semi-dwarf rice cultivars as parents in Asian rice breeding programs', *Crop Science*, 19:571–574.

Huffman, W.E. and Evenson, R.E. (1993) *Science for agriculture*. Ames, Iowa: Iowa State University Press.

Hymer, S.H. (1972) 'The multinational corporation and the law of uneven development', in: J.N. Bhagwati, ed., *Economics and world order from the 1970s to the 1990s*. New York: Macmillan.

Hymer, S.H. and Resnick, S.A. (1970) 'International trade and uneven development', in: J.N. Bhagwati, R.W. Jones, R.A. Mundell, and J. Vanek, eds., *Trade, Balance of Payments and Growth*. New York: North-Holland.

Jaffe, A.B. (1986) 'Technological opportunity and spillovers of R&D: Evidence from firms' patents, profits, and market value', *American Economic Review*, 76:984–1001.

Jamison, D.T., Lau, L.J., Lockwood, M.E., and Evenson, R.E. (1991) 'Education, extension and farmer productivity', in *Encyclopedia of educational research*, 6th ed. New York: Macmillan.

Jorgenson, D.W. (1966) 'Testing alternative theories of the development of a dual economy', in: I. Adelman and E. Thorbecke, eds., *The theory and design of economic development*. Baltimore: Johns Hopkins University Press.

Jorgenson, D.W., Gallop, F. and Fraumeni, B. (1987) *Productivity and US economic growth*. Cambridge: Harvard University Press.

Jorgenson, D.W. and Griliches, Z. (1967) 'The explanation of productivity change', *Review of Economic Studies*, 34:249–280.

Justman, M. and Teubal, M. (1986) 'Innovation policy in an open economy: A normative framework for strategic and tactical issues', *Research Policy*, 15:121–138.

Justman, M. and Teubal, M. (1991) 'A structuralist perspective on the role of technology in economic growth and development', *World Development*, 19:1167–1183.

Katrak, H. (1985) 'Imported technology, enterprise size and R&D in a newly industrializing country: The Indian experience', *Oxford Bulletin of Economics and Statistics*, 47:213–229.

Katrak, H. (1990) 'Imports of technology and the technological effort of Indian enterprises', *World Development*, 18:371–381.

Katrak, H. (1991) 'In-house technological effort, imports of technology and enterprise characteristics in a newly industrializing country: The Indian experience', *Journal of International Development*, 3:263–276.

Katz, J.M. (1987) 'Domestic technology generation in LDCs: A review of research findings', in:

J.M. Katz, ed., *Technology generation in Latin American manufacturing industries*. London: Macmillan.

Kortum, S. (1992) 'Inventions, R&D and industry growth', unpublished Ph.D. dissertation. New Haven, Connecticut: Yale University.

Kumar, N. (1987) 'Technology imports and local research and development in Indian manufacturing', *The Developing Economies*, 30:220–233.

Lall, S. (1983) 'Determinants of R&D in an LDC: The Indian engineering industry', *Economic Letters*, 13:379–383.

Lall, S. (1987) *Learning to industrialize: The acquisition of technological capability in India*. London: Macmillan.

Lall, S. (1990) *Building industrial competitiveness in developing countries*. Paris: OECD Development Centre.

Landes, D.S. (1969) *The unbound prometheus: Technological change and industrial development in Western Europe from 1750 to the present*. Cambridge: Cambridge University Press.

Landes, D.S. (1990) 'Why are we so rich and they so poor', *American Economic Review*, 80:1–13.

Lau, L.J. and Kim, J.-I. (1993) 'The sources of economic growth of the East Asian newly industrialized countries', unpublished manuscript. Stanford, California: Stanford University, Department of Economics.

Lee, T.K. (1982) 'A nonsequential R&D search model', *Management Science*, 28:900–909.

Levin, R.C., Klevorick, A.K., Nelson, R.R. and Winter, S.G. (1987) 'Appropriating the returns from industrial R&D', *Brookings Papers on Economic Activity*, 3 (Special Issue on Microeconomics):783–820.

Levy, B. (1991) 'Transactions costs, the size of firms and industrial policy: Lessons from a comparative case study of the footwear industry in Korea and Taiwan', *Journal of Development Economics*, 34:151–178.

Levy, B. and Kuo, W.J. (1991) 'The strategic orientations of firms and the performance of Korea and Taiwan in frontier industries: Lessons from comparative case studies of keyboard and personal computer assembly', *World Development*, 19:363–374.

Lewis, W.A. (1954) 'Economic development with unlimited supplies of labor', *Manchester School*, 22:139–191.

Lichtenberg, F.R. (1991) 'R&D investment and international productivity differences', NBER Working Paper No. 4161. Cambridge, Massachusetts: National Bureau of Economic Research.

Lucas, R.E. (1988) 'On the mechanics of economic development', *Journal of Monetary Economics*, 22:3–42.

Machlup, F. (1958) *An economic review of the patent system*. Study number 15 of the Subcommittee on Patents, Trademarks, and Copyrights of the Committee on the Judiciary, United States Senate, 85th Congress, Second Session. Washington, DC: U.S. Government Printing Office.

Maddala, G. (1983) *Limited-dependent and qualitative variables in econometrics*. Cambridge: Cambridge University Press.

Mahalanobis, P.C. (1955) 'The approach of operational research to planning in India', in: P.C. Mahalanobis, ed., *Sankhya: The Indian Journal of Statistics*, 16, parts 1 and 2.

Mairesse, J. and Sassenou, M. (1991) 'R&D and productivity: A survey of econometric studies at the firm level', *STI Review*, 8:9–43.

Mankiw, N.G., Romer, D., and Weil, D.N. (1992) 'A contribution to the empirics of economic growth', *Quarterly Journal of Economics*, 107:407–438.

Mansfield, E. (1961) 'Technical change and the rate of imitation', *Econometrica*, 29:741–766.

Mansfield, E. (1985) 'How rapidly does industrial technology leak out', *Journal of Industrial Economics*, 34:217–223.

Mansfield, E. (1993) 'Unauthorized use of intellectual property: Effects on investment, technology transfer, and innovation', mimeo. Washington, DC: National Research Council.

Mansfield, E., et al. [Rapoport, J., Romeo, A., Wagner, S. and Beardsley, G.] (1977a) 'Social and private rates of return from industrial innovations', *Quarterly Journal of Economics*, 77:221–240.

Mansfield, E., et al. [Rapoport, J., Romeo, A., Villani, E., Wagner, S. and Husic, F.] (1977b) *The production and application of new industrial technology*. New York: Norton.

Mansfield, E., Schwartz, M. and Wagner, S. (1981) 'Imitation costs and patents: An empirical study', *The Economic Journal*, 91:907–918.

Mikkelsen, K.W. (1984) 'Inventive activity in Philippine industry', unpublished Ph.D. dissertation. New Haven, Connecticut: Yale University.

Mohnen, P. (1990) 'R&D and productivity growth: A survey of literature', mimeo. Montreal: University of Quebec at Montreal.

Mohnen, P. and Lepine, N. (1991) 'R&D, R&D spillovers and payments for technology: Canadian evidence', *Structural Change and Economic Dynamics*, 2:213–228.

Mokyr, J. (1990) *The lever of riches: Technological creativity and economic progress*. New York: Oxford University Press.

Morris, C.T. and Adelman, I. (1989) 'Nineteenth-century development experience and lessons for today', *World Development*, 17:1417–1432.

Murphy, K., Shleifer, A. and Vishny, R. (1989) 'Industrialization and the big push', *Journal of Political Economy*, 97:1003–1026.

Nadiri, M.I. (1993) 'Innovations and technological spillovers', NBER Working Paper No. 4423. Cambridge, Massachusetts: National Bureau of Economic Research.

National Science Board (1991) *Science and engineering indicators–1991*. Washington, DC: U.S. Government Printing Office.

NCAER (1971) *Foreign technology and investment*. New Delhi: National Council of Applied Economic Research.

Nelson, R.R., ed. (1993) *National innovation systems: A comparative analysis*. New York: Oxford University Press.

Nelson, R.R. and Winter, S.G. (1982) *An evolutionary theory of economic change*. Cambridge: Harvard University Press.

Nogues, J. (1990) 'Patents, distortions, and development', PRE Working Paper Series No. 315. Washington, DC: The World Bank.

Nordhaus, W.D. (1969) *Invention, growth and wealth*. Cambridge: M.I.T. Press.

OECD (1993) *OECD basic science and technology statistics*. Paris: Organization for Economic Cooperation and Development.

Otsuka, K., Ranis, G. and Saxonhouse, G. (1988) *Comparative technology choices: The Indian and Japanese cotton textile industries*. London: Macmillan.

Pack, H. (1987) *Productivity, technology, and industrial development*. New York: Oxford University Press.

Pack, H. (1990) 'Industrial efficiency and technology choice', in: R.E. Evenson and G. Ranis, eds., *Science and technology: lessons for development policy*. Boulder, Colorado: Westview.

Pack, H. (1992) 'New perspectives on industrial growth in Taiwan', in G. Ranis, ed., *Taiwan: from developing to mature economy*. Boulder, Colorado: Westview.

Pack, H. (1993) 'Technology gaps between industrial and developing countries: Are there dividends for latecomers?', in: L.H. Summers and S. Shah, eds., *Proceedings of the World Bank Annual Conference on Development Economics, 1992*. Washington, DC: The World Bank.

Pack, H. (1994) 'Endogenous growth theory: Intellectual appeal and empirical shortcomings', *Journal of Economic Perspectives*, 8:55–72.

Pack, H. and Todaro, M. (1969) 'Technological change, labour absorption and economic development', *Oxford Economic Papers*, 21:395–403.

Pack, H. and Westphal, L.E. (1986) 'Industrial strategy and technological change: Theory versus reality', *Journal of Development Economics*, 22:87–128.

Pakes, A. and Schankerman, M. (1986) 'Estimates of the value of patent rights in European countries during the post-1950 period', *Economic Journal*, 96:1052–1076.

Persley, G.J., ed. (1990) *Agricultural biotechnology: Opportunities for international development*. Wellingford, U.K.: C.A.B. International.

Pilat, D. (1993) *The economics of catch-up: The experience of Japan and Korea*. Groningen Growth and Development Centre Monograph Series, No. 2. Groningen, The Netherlands: University of Groningen.

Pray, C.E. (1987) 'Private sector agricultural research in Asia', in: V.W. Ruttan and C.E. Pray, eds., *Policy for agricultural research*. Boulder, Colorado: Westview.

Quisumbing, A., Bantilon, C.L., and Evenson, R.E. (1993) 'Population, technology and rural poverty in the Philippines: Rural income implications from a CGE impact multiplier model', in: A. Balisacan, ed., *Rural poverty in the Philippines*. Manila: University of Manila Press.

Quizon, J., Binswanger, H.P., and Gupta, D. (1991) 'The distribution of income in India's northern wheat region', in: R.E. Evenson and C.E. Pray, eds., *Research and productivity in Asian agriculture*. Ithaca: Cornell University Press.

Ranis, G. (1990) 'Science and technology policy: Lessons from Japan and the East Asian NICs', in: R.E. Evenson and G. Ranis, eds., *Science and technology: Lessons for development policy*. Boulder, Colorado: Westview.

Rhee, Y. and Belot, T. (1990) 'Export catalysts in low-income countries: A review of eleven success stories', World Bank Discussion Papers No. 72. Washington, DC: The World Bank.

Romer, P.M. (1986) 'Increasing returns and long-run growth', *Journal of Political Economy*, 94:1002–1037.

Romer, P.M. (1990) 'Endogenous technological change', *Journal of Political Economy*, 98:S71–S102.

Rosegrant, M., Evenson, R.E. and Pray, C.E. (1993) 'Sources of agricultural productivity growth in India', Research Report. Washington, DC: International Food Policy Research Institute.

Rosenberg, N. (1974) 'Science, invention and economic growth', *Economic Journal*, 84:90–108.

Rosenberg, N. (1976) *Perspectives on technology*. Cambridge: Cambridge University Press.

Rosenberg, N. (1982) *Inside the black box: Technology and economics*. Cambridge: Cambridge University Press.

Rosenberg, N., Landau, R. and Mowery, D.C. (1992) *Technology and the wealth of nations*. Stanford: Stanford University Press.

Rosenstein-Rodan, P.N. (1943) 'Problems of industrialization of Eastern and South-Eastern Europe', *Economic Journal*, 53:202–211.

Sagasti, F. (1978) *Science and technology for development: Main comparative report on the STPI project*. Ottawa, Canada: International Development Research Center.

Scherer, F.M. (1972) 'Nordhaus's theory of optimal patent life: A geometric reinterpretation', *American Economic Review*, 62:422–427.

Scherer, F.M. (1986) *Innovation and growth: Schumpeterian perspectives*. Cambridge: M.I.T. Press.

Schmookler, J. (1966) *Invention and economic growth*. Cambridge: Harvard University Press.

Schultz, T.W. (1965) *Transforming traditional agriculture*. New Haven, Connecticut: Yale University Press.

Schumpeter, J.A. (1934) *The theory of economic development*. Cambridge: Harvard University Press.

Scitovsky, T. (1954) 'Two concepts of external economies', *Journal of Political Economy*, 62:143–151.

Sherwood, R.M. (1990) *Intellectual property and economic development*. Boulder, Colorado: Westview.

Siebeck, W., Evenson, R.E., Lesser, W. and Braga, C.P. (1990) 'Strengthening protection of intellectual property in developing countries: A survey of the literature', World Bank Discussion Paper No. 112. Washington, DC: The World Bank.

Smith, A. (1776) *An inquiry into the nature and causes of the wealth of nations*. [Two volume publication, Oxford: Clarendon Press, 1976. R.H. Campell and A.S. Skinner, general editors; W.B. Todd, textual editor.]

Solow, R.M. (1957) 'Technical change and the aggregate production function', *Review of Economics and Statistics*, 39:312–320.

Srinivasan, T.N. (1994) 'Data base for development analysis: An overview', *Journal of Development Economics*, 44:3–27.

Stewart, F. (1977) *Technology and underdevelopment*. Boulder, Colorado: Westview.

Stewart, F. (1979) 'International technology transfer: Issues and policy options', World Bank Staff Working Paper No. 344. Washington, DC: The World Bank.

Stewart, F., ed. (1987) *Macro-policies for appropriate technology in developing countries*. Boulder, Colorado: Westview.

Stewart, F. and Ghani, E. (1991) 'How significant are externalities for development', *World Development*, 19:569–594.

Stiglitz, J.E. (1989a) 'Markets, market failures, and development', *American Economic Review, Papers and Proceedings*, 79:197–203.

Stiglitz, J.E. (1989b) 'Financial markets and development', *Oxford Review of Economic Policy*, 5:55–68.

Sud, I.K., Harral, C.G. and Coukis, B.P. (1976) 'Scope for the substitution of labour and equipment in civil construction: A progress report', Papers for Panel Discussion, Indian Roads Congress, 37th Annual Session. New Delhi: Indian Roads Congress.

Taylor, C.T. and Silberton, Z.A. (1973) *The economic impact of the patent system*. Cambridge: Cambridge University Press.

Teitel, S. (1987) 'Towards an understanding of technical change in semi-industrialized countries', in: J.M. Katz, ed., *Technology generation in Latin American manufacturing industries*. London: Macmillan.

Vernon, R. (1966) 'International investment and international trade in the product cycle', *Quarterly Journal of Economics*, 80:190–207.

Watanabe, S. (1985) 'The patent system and indigenous technology development in the third world', in: J. James and S. Watanabe, eds., *Technology, institutions and government policies*. London: Macmillan.

Weiss, C. (1990) 'Scientific and technological constraints to economic growth and equity', in: R.E. Evenson and G. Ranis, eds., *Science and technology: Lessons for development policy*. Boulder, Colorado: Westview.

Westphal, L.E., Kim, L. and Dahlman, C.J. (1985) 'Reflections on Korea's acquisition of technological capability', in: N. Rosenberg and C. Frischtak, eds., *International technology transfer: Concepts, measures, and comparisons*. New York: Praeger.

Westphal, L.E., Kritayakirana, K., Petchsuwan, K., Sutabutr, H. and Yuthavong, Y. (1990) 'The development of technological capability in manufacturing: A macroscopic approach to policy research', in: R.E. Evenson and G. Ranis, eds., *Science and technology: Lessons for development policy*. Boulder, Colorado: Westview.

Westphal, L.E., Rhee, Y.W. and Pursell G. (1984) 'Sources of technological capability in South Korea', in: M. Fransman and K. King, eds., *Technological capability in developing countries*. London: Pinter.

Williamson, J.G. (1991) 'Productivity and American leadership: A review article', *Journal of Economic Literature*, 19:51–68.

World Bank (1993) *The East Asian miracle: Economic growth and public policy*. Oxford: Oxford University Press.

Young, A. (1993) 'Lessons from the East Asian NICs: A contrarian view', NBER Working Paper No. 4482. Cambridge, Massachusetts: National Bureau of Economic Research.

Chapter 38

INSTITUTIONS AND ECONOMIC DEVELOPMENT*

JUSTIN YIFU LIN

Peking University, Australian National University and Duke University

JEFFREY B. NUGENT*

University of Southern California

Contents

* The authors are grateful to Samar Datta, Timur Kuran and Mustapha Nabli for contributions in the formative stage in some of the research on which this chapter is based, to Thrainn Eggertsson, Robert Evenson, Michiel Keyzer and other participants at the First Asian Development Bank Conference on Development Economics and especially Jere R. Behrman and T.N. Srinivasan for helpful comments on earlier drafts.

Handbook of Development Economics, Volume III, Edited by J. Behrman and T.N. Srinivasan
© *Elsevier Science B.V., 1995*

Contents (continued)

1. Introduction

It is well-known that developing countries (LDCs) have startlingly different productivity of various kinds and very different institutions than DCs. Much less well-known are answers to the following types of questions:
* Why are the institutions so different?
* Why are they the way they are and how did they get that way?
* How and to what extent do they explain the differences in productivity?
* Why and how do inefficient institutions sometimes get locked in?
* Of all the institutional differences that exist, which ones really matter?
* How and to what extent can institutions be changed in desirable directions?

These are among the many interesting and challenging questions taken up in analyses of the relationship between institutions and economic development. The relationship between institutions and economic development is clearly two-way: On the one hand, institutions can influence both the level and pace of economic development; on the other hand, economic development can and frequently does trigger institutional change.

Until recently at least, standard textbooks were of little help in answering any of the above questions because, in much of the standard analysis, institutions were either ignored or taken as given. In neoclassical analyses, transactions were often assumed to be costless, relevant information freely available, and governments ready and willing to undertake socially beneficial projects that take advantage of economies of scale and internalize existing externalities. In Marxian analyses, classes were assumed to exist and act in prescribed ways.

Take, for example, some of the key welfare propositions of neoclassical analysis. With some assumptions about the characteristics in a market economy of production and utility functions constituting the "classical environment", the two well-known optimality theorems of welfare economics are derived: first, if there is perfect competition, the resource allocation is Pareto-optimal; second, any specified Pareto-optimal resource allocation that is technically feasible can be achieved by establishing free markets and an appropriate pattern of factor ownership. Moreover, the static versions of these theorems were extended by Arrow and Debreu to deal with resource allocations in time, space, and uncertain states of nature. The essential ingredient in such extensions is the existence of a particular institution, namely, a complete set of markets for the purchase or sale of goods contingent on each possible combination of time, space, and state of nature. With such an institution, a firm is reduced to a production function to which a profit maximization objective has been ascribed

(Williamson, 1980). Since these theorems are, of course, only characterization theorems in that they say nothing about actual processes in time, they should not mask the need to explain just how such markets are developed and why they work the way they do. Even more important, they should prevent us neither from examining alternative institutions for accomplishing the same objectives nor from considering government intervention in cases other than those in which the "classical" environment is violated.

Indeed, it must be realized that, in fact, different non-market institutions coexist with markets even in the most advanced economies. Large, modern hierarchical business enterprises and government policy makers compete with markets in coordinating production and allocating resources. Market and non-market institutions are also highly complementary to one another. Indeed, it is because of such competition and complementarity among different institutions that institutions matter. For this reason, to continue taking existing market and other institutions as given would critically limit the applicability of economics to deal with a wide variety of economic issues of relevance to the relation between institutions and economic development.

Admittedly, and indeed most fortunately, the importance of institutions, such as firms, families, contracts, markets, rules and regulations, and social norms to economic development was realized in the writings of classic economists such as David Hume (1948), Adam Smith (1776), John Stuart Mill (1847), and others. Lewis (1955), Kuznets (1966, 1973), Myrdal (1968), and other modern development economists have also provided additional insights on the way institutions affect economic development. However, despite these important insights and increasing modeling sophistication, until recently much of the attention (except for lip service) had turned away from institutions so as to focus on more mathematically tractable topics. As a result, not long ago a leading economist could still state that "it cannot hide the fact that, in thinking about institutions, the analytical cupboard is bare..". [Schultz (1968)].

Similar shortcomings in the ability to analyze institutions could also be attributed to Marxists who, for example, simply assumed the existence of classes and class consciousness [Bardhan (1988)], thereby failing to explain how classes managed to overcome the free-rider problems inherent in class formation and action. This is, of course, despite the fact that Marx may have been the first both to raise the question of how and why institutions (production relations in his terminology) develop and to incorporate them into economic theory.

Fortunately, there is growing realization of the need to drop the assumption of given institutions and thereby to return to some themes of classical economics. In particular, there is growing appreciation of the potential for endogenizing institutions within a broadened framework in which both the actions that agents take and the constraints within which they must operate in maximizing over their lifetimes with respect to their defined objectives can be political and social as well as economic. Recent attempts to accomplish this constitute important contributions to the analysis of the relationship between institutions and economic development and to the New Institutional Economics (NIE).

Like other fields of analysis, the NIE has been built upon earlier ideas. In addition to the above-mentioned classical and modern development economists, other important forerunners to and motivators of NIE were members of the Institutionalist School, including such eloquent contributors as Thorstein Veblen, John R. Commons, Wesley Mitchell, and Clarence Ayres. Indeed, the NIE resembles the "old" Institutionalist School in several important respects. Both are extremely broad in scope and replete with many interesting and diverse perspectives.

Although essentially microeconomic in perspective, the NIE includes several distinctive approaches to the analysis of institutions, each with its own techniques, concepts, advantages and disadvantages. While there is as yet no consensus on the confines of the NIE, two broad but overlapping approaches are salient, namely, those of transaction costs and collective action.

The transaction cost approach has proved particularly useful in analyzing the comparative demand for alternative institutional arrangements. On the other hand, with its emphasis on free-rider problems (themselves the consequence of transaction costs), the collective action approach, has been especially useful in analyzing the supply of alternative institutional arrangements. While these two general approaches have developed quite separately, they are by no means independent of each other and, as demonstrated below, are in many ways complementary.

Because of the field's rapid and multidimensional growth, a synthesis of the entire field is far beyond the scope of this chapter.[1] Our present purpose, therefore, is the more modest one of relating some of the most important strands of institutional analysis to the economics of development. Because, as in the older analysis, the Achilles heel of the NIE is the difficulty of empirical testing, considerable attention in this chapter is given to empirical studies and to the problems in carrying out tests.

The structure of this chapter is as follows: Section 2 discusses the definition, functions, and interdependence of institutions and demonstrates that institutions matter. Section 3 presents the theory of transaction costs and its application to the demand for institutions and institutional change. Section 4 develops the theory of collective action and applies it to the supply of institutions and of institutional change. Section 5 identifies and briefly explains some of the most important and general institutional changes that occur in the process of economic development. Section 6 focuses on empirical applications

---

[1] The most complete existing survey of the field is Eggertsson (1990).

and their problems in a variety of LDCs. Some concluding remarks are provided in Section 7.

2. The logic of institutions

It is instructive to begin our analysis of institutions with the frequently told story of Robinson Crusoe. In the absence of contact with the outside world, Robinson makes his decisions about what to produce based on his decisions about what to consume, but in isolation of what anyone else in the world is doing. There is no need for institutions in this setting. One could easily contemplate, however, the effect of linking Robinson with the outside world. In that case, his production and consumption decisions would depend on the type of institutions which surround him. For example, if he faced a competitive product market, Crusoe's production decisions would be entirely separated from his consumption decisions. Moreover, with knowledge of a set of commodity prices alone, his actions would be closely coordinated with those in the rest of the world. The outcome would be consistent with the afore-mentioned fundamental welfare theorems. This simple experiment illustrates how the demand for institutions arises and how an institution can significantly affect welfare not only in the rest of the world but also on Crusoe's island. The product market, of course, is but one,[2] and perhaps not the most important, institution, but it amply illustrates how much institutions can matter.

One should realize, however, that markets and other institutions do not just automatically appear. There may exist a variety of obstacles to their develop-ment that are difficult to overcome. Even when such institutions emerge, they may do so only after the prior development of various other complementary institutions[3] and still be quite imperfect. Of course, some of these other institutions may make sense only if there are markets. Institutions may therefore need to occur in complexes.

2.1. The definition of institutions

But, what are institutions? Although, like other terms, in common parlance the term institution is used in a variety of ways, for the purpose at hand, an institution is defined as a set of humanly devised behavioral rules that govern

---

[2] For example, another might be a rule which encourages both Crusoe and Friday to spend part of their time in activities designed to increase the productivity not only of themselves but also of their island.

[3] Among these are those protecting markets, defining and enforcing the property rights over the items transacted, collecting and transmitting information about prices, and developing means of settling disputes.

and shape the interactions of human beings, in part by helping them to form expectations of what other people will do. In so constraining behavior, institutions may be reflected in the appearance of certain behavioral regularities or norms.

It is clear from this definition why institutions can consist of both formal entities like laws, constitutions, written contracts, market exchanges and organizational by-laws and informal ones like shared values, norms, customs, ethics, and ideology. In short, all such institutions involve rules that can constrain behavior over a certain domain and give rise to behavioral regularities. For any institution, it must be clear to whom and when the rules apply. For example, the rules that apply to specific officers of organizations need to be distinguished from those that apply to the membership at large, and the kinds of situations to which these rules apply (e.g. to activities among members) need to be distinguished from those to which they do not (e.g. to activities between members and non-members).

Some common confusions in terminology can be avoided by distinguishing between "institutional arrangements" and "institutional structure". An "institutional arrangement" is a set of behavioral rules that govern behavior in a specified domain. "Institutional structure", on the other hand, is the totality of institutional arrangements in an economy, including its organizations, laws, customs, and ideology. When the term "institution" is used by economists, it generally refers to an institutional arrangement. Likewise, "institutional change" usually refers to a change in one institutional arrangement, not to a change in all arrangements in the structure.[4] For convenience of exposition, we use the terms institutions and institutional arrangements interchangeably and institutional change to represent a change in an institutional arrangement (not a change in institutional structure).

2.2. The functions of institutions

Why are institutions indispensable? Since institutions are rules governing behavioral relations among individuals, it is the functions that the rules perform that make institutions matter.

The most basic function is to economize, i.e. to allow one or more of the agents to improve their welfare without making others worse off, or to allow them to attain a higher level of their objectives within their constraints.[5]

---

[4] The failure to distinguish between an institutional arrangement and the institutional structure has caused some controversy in the literature about the possibility of endogenizing institutional change [Field (1981), Grabowski (1988), Basu, Jones, and Schlicht (1987)].

[5] This is not to say that institutions always or even generally have such a pure (efficiency) motive. To the contrary, such a motive may often be mixed up with the desire to make one party better off at the expense of another, i.e. the redistribution motive to be discussed below.

Neither their objectives, nor their constraints or even their alternative actions need be strictly material or economic.

There may be several important and quite distinct means of achieving this basic economizing function of institutions. One of these is by taking advantage of potential economies of scale, specialization, and/or external economies. Numerous different institutions, both market institutions (such as contracts and commodity and factor markets) and non-market institutions (such as firms and communities), can serve these functions (though in many cases with rather different distributional consequences). This suggests the potential for competition among alternative institutional arrangements.

Another means of improving welfare is to prevent individuals and groups from making mistakes. One important institutional mechanism for avoiding mistakes is collecting more and better information and making that information available to decision makers. Of course, information is not costless, and the costs as well as the benefits of new or better information need to be carefully considered. Information is relevant not only for present decisions but, because of the effects of the evaluations of present decisions on future decisions, also for future decisions. In other words, one of the institutional mechanisms for avoiding future mistakes may be a better information system that allows mistakes to be discovered quickly and alerts decision-makers not to repeat their mistakes. However, since the appropriate decision-making framework is that of maximizing the present value of present and future decisions, the prevention of either present or future mistakes is not conceptually distinct from the basic economizing function of an institution.

Various aspects of informational deficiencies need to be distinguished. First, as already mentioned, since information is costly, there may be nothing nonoptimal about the existence of incomplete or imperfect information. Second, the effects of such informational deficiencies vary with the type of information which is incomplete or missing.[6] Second, one needs to consider the distribution of information across the relevant agents. In some cases, all the relevant agents are equally constrained by incompleteness or imperfections in information. In others, however, one party, for example the possessor-seller of a durable good, may have inherently better information about the good's quality than another, e.g. a potential buyer of the good. This is a case of "asymmetric information". Institutional solutions to informational deficiencies may well differ substantially depending on whether or not informational asymmetries exist since where they do exist, one party may be able to take advantage of another through opportunistic behavior.

---

[6] For example, the effects of being wrong about the way the physical world works may be much broader and more costly than those of a mere observation error about one instance of its application.

By the same token, because risk aversion is ordinarily a basic component of the preference function of the individual or group, risk reduction should not be considered a separate function but rather as still another concomitance of the basic economizing function of institutions. The importance of risk and uncertainty reduction depends, of course, on (1) the preferences themselves, (2) the characteristics of alternative institutional arrangements and (3) the sources and magnitudes of risk and uncertainty.

Since in LDCs the sources of risk and their magnitudes are sufficiently varied and large and the relevant probability distributions of alternative outcomes unknown (implying that the problems are more of uncertainty than of risk), and insurance markets against such risks are less well developed,[7] risk and uncertainty problems are likely to be very important. Also, the degree of risk aversion may well be larger in LDCs than elsewhere, in part because incomes are nearer to the minimal subsistence level [Binswanger (1980), Binswanger and Rosenzweig (1986)], and in part because these risks are more interrelated to other problems. For example, with weather fluctuations, it may be more difficult with the available information to distinguish among the following alternative explanations for an observed production shortfall: (1) the direct effects of bad weather on output, (2) the indirect effects of bad weather on output via the effects on health and the effective labor supply, (3) producer mistakes in resource allocation, and/or (4) shirking of the workers.[8]

If it becomes more difficult to distinguish among the various possible sources of production shortfalls, agents may feel they can get away with being less careful in their resource allocation decisions, and with more shirking at the expense of other parties. In other words, the interaction of production risks with information asymmetries may increase opportunistic behavior and hence reduce production. As a result, there may be special opportunities for institutions, such as laws, courts, various kinds of bonding mechanisms, social norms, and the structure of incentives in future contracts, that can better limit the practice of opportunistic behavior by the different agents.

Hence, in many cases the contribution of the particular institutional arrangement to the economizing function may be very indirect. For example, the adoption of judicial rules inducing judges to be more conscientious and objective in their legal decisions may influence primarily by inducing more accurate and careful monitoring and enforcement of exchange contracts.

---

[7] For a recent study which seems to suggest that risk markets are in fact better developed than generally believed, see Townsend (1991).

[8] See, for example, Binswanger and Rosenzweig (1986). Rural institutions like inter-village marriage [Rosenzweig and Stark (1989)], remittance from migrated members [Lucas and Stark (1985)], and transhumance in arid and semiarid areas [Binswanger, McIntire and Udry (1988), Nugent and Sanchez (1993)] have the implicit function of insuring against income and consumption fluctuations.

Prominent among economizing institutions are property-rights institutions which internalize externalities [Alchian (1959, 1965), Demsetz (1967)]. Property rights are the formal or informal rules that delimit an individual's or group's rights over the assets (including one's own labor) that they possess, including the rights to consume, obtain income from, and alienate the assets. The gains of exchange of goods, services, and assets among different agents resulting from such property rights can both improve resource allocation and smooth consumption patterns.

While property rights may be a crucial ingredient in the economizing function of institutional change, they also illustrate the importance of the other basic function of an institution, namely that of redistribution. This is because, even if they economize, property rights are seldom neutral with respect to the distribution of the gains of specialization and exchange, i.e. of the economizing function. Because the distributional stakes are likely to be high, and the attributes of assets difficult to measure and costly to enforce, the costs of creating and maintaining property rights may also be high. As a result, irrespective of the specific nature of the property rights, property rights will never be perfectly defined and enforced [Barzel (1989)]. Therefore, how well a property-rights institution performs its function may depend heavily on the existence and comparative efficiency of other auxiliary institutions, such as law, ideology, and morality.

In any case, improving one's own position at the expense of others, i.e. the redistributive function, may be a primary function or motive for many institutional arrangements. Where the relative powers to impose rules on others are very unequally distributed and the competition among alternative institutional arrangements especially weak, it is entirely possible that the redistributive function of institutions may well be dominant, implying that the value of resources may not be maximized.

2.3. The interdependence of institutions

In illustrating the definition and functions of institutions, some of the above examples clearly underscore two kinds of interdependencies, namely, those among different functions of a single institutional arrangement and those among different institutional arrangements within the overall institutional structure.

With respect to the first type of interdependence, the two functions of institutions are likely to operate hand-in-hand. For example, property rights institutions perform both economizing and redistributive functions at the same time. Indeed, they may not succeed in one function without also succeeding in the other since any change in property rights implies both winners and losers.

Since the efficacy of any institutional arrangement depends on how well it copes with opportunism of the relevant agents, it can also be affected by the existence and strength of the surrounding auxiliary institutions whose economizing functions are only indirect. For example, the opportunism arising from the discretionary behavior of managers in modern corporations can be greatly mitigated by the existence of competitive managerial labor markets and stock markets but also by loyalty, team spirit, morality and other non-market institutions [Alchian and Demsetz (1972), Arrow (1974), Simon (1991)]. A firm will also perform differently if it has a soft budget constraint [Kornai 1986)].

Therefore, dramatic differences in the efficiency of a specific form of an economizing institution may arise from subtle differences in the surrounding, auxiliary institutions, some of which may prove difficult to observe directly. For example, in Section 2.4 we present evidence suggesting that a collective farming system is less efficient than a household farming system. A collective farm is likely to face a serious shirking problem of its members due to the difficulty of monitoring the labor effort of agricultural workers by a third party.[9] Nevertheless, if the collective members could reach a self-enforcing agreement in which each member promises to honor his obligations but, if others do not, has the right to exit or withdraw, collective farms could be more efficient than household farms due to the economies of scale in production and risk sharing. This is because in self-enforcing contracts in which some parties default on their commitments, the only recourse may be the ability to terminate the contract [Telser (1980)]. Hence, in such circumstances, it may be important to protect the right to exit.

As an illustration of the importance of the right to exit in collective institutions, consider the Chinese experience of the 1950s. In the early 1950s, the right to exit from China's collectives was respected and productivity remained fairly high. When in 1958 the right to withdraw from the collective was removed, however, immediately thereafter the productivity of Chinese agriculture collapsed. Indeed, the collapse resulted in the severe famine of 1959–61 in which 30 million human lives are thought to have been lost, and from which productivity did not recover until the reintroduction of the household system in 1979. Similar collapses in productivity were also observed in the former Soviet Union when membership in its collectives became mandatory and imposed by force.[10]

---

[9] Dong and Dow (1993) provide an estimate of between 10 and 20 percent of labor time as a lower bound on the cost of monitoring in teams on collective farms.

[10] See Lin (1990, 1993) and "the Symposium on Theoretical and Historical Perspectives on Chinese Agricultural Cooperatives" in the Journal of Comparative Economics, vol. 17, no. 2, June 1993.

In other cases, it is found that limitations on the ability of one party to penalize another for breach of contract can reduce not only the efficiency of resource use but also resource accumulation. For example, if a firm cannot dismiss or otherwise discipline a worker for poor performance, it may invest less in training of that worker. Similarly, if loan defaulters cannot be penalized, it may prove difficult to induce individuals or financial institutions to make loans.[11] Also, because of the importance of collateral and access to it to the functioning of credit markets, the absence of well-defined and enforced private property rights in land may effectively prohibit the successful operation of formal credit markets in rural areas [Binswanger and Rosenzweig (1986), Feder et al. (1988), Feder and Feeny (1991)].

The effectiveness of institutions like constitutions, laws, property rights, and political systems also depends on the effective functioning of other arrangements in the institutional structure. For example, the Constitution of the United States is generally credited with facilitating economic development in that country. Although similar constitutions were adopted in many Latin American countries after their independence in the nineteenth century, they have been less effective due to less effective enforcement mechanisms, and both norms of behavior and world views that are less conducive to innovation and growth [North (1990), Chapter 11]. Likewise, although many LDCs have adopted similar systems of property rights as in DCs, for similar reasons seldom have these adoptions been successful.

Because of the possible dominance of the redistributive function of institutions over the economizing one, the extent of economizing may depend on various other elements in the institutional structure which serve to insulate a country's economic management from redistributive demands. Such an insulation may be difficult to provide and is a fairly complex issue to be taken up in Section 4 below. What can be said with confidence here is that, even where the rules of institutions are the same, the enforcement mechanisms, the behavioral norms, and the ideology of the actors involved in these institutions may well differ in subtle but important ways, making for considerable variation in the effectiveness of the institutions.

The understandable significance of interdependencies among various institutions, however, gives rise to the following important methodological problem. Namely, the very interdependence of institutions implies that it is necessarily that much more difficult to assess the determinants and effects of institutions.

---

[11] According to Fry (1974), Afghanistan represented a rather extreme case of where these conditions were not fulfilled and hence where credit markets remained extremely underdeveloped.

As demonstrated in Section 6 below, this has caused problems in numerous empirical applications of NIE.

2.4. Institutions matter

As already noted, institutions perform several different valuable functions. Not surprisingly, and as demonstrated in Section 4, the relative importance of these different functions is likely to change substantially over time. For example, in the very early stages of economic development, where income levels hover around the subsistence level, the risk-reduction element of the basic economizing function may be the dominant one. It is this element, therefore, which may provide the basic rationale for some of the most important institutions, such as the family, the tribe, or the kin group. In such contexts, institutions, such as the need to offer hospitality to everyone in the village and to allow every individual to obtain much knowledge about each other, may be very efficient. This is especially true where production techniques are simple and most exchanges are personal and repeating. Opportunistic behavior is rare because the aforementioned institutions make for its easy detection.[12]

As an economy develops, however, production and exchange become increasingly complex, and the institutional structure of the economy changes accordingly. Each arrangement tends to be more well-defined and to perform more specialized functions and hence traditional institutions may no longer be optimal. Since the same function may be performed by several different institutional arrangements which vary in their abilities both to fit local circumstances and to perform their respective tasks, different arrangements may have different implications for efficiency, economic growth, and distribution.

The efficiency of any particular economizing arrangement depends on many factors: some pertaining to the technical nature of the production process and others to the existence and efficiency of other auxiliary institutions, such as those attempting to mitigate the effects of opportunism.

The successful experience of China with decollectivization of agriculture in the early 1980s (to which we return in more detail in Section 6.2 below) has quite naturally received considerable attention in demonstrating the relevance of institutions and the incentives derived from them to economic efficiency. Gaynor and Putterman (1993) develop a model for assessing the efficacy of the

---

[12] This is what Otsuka, Kikuchi and Hayami (1986) call the "efficient community".

very means used by the Chinese in redistributing land to households in this process. Their model of monocrop (grain) agriculture shows that, in the absence of markets for land and labor, total factor productivity would be higher if land were distributed among households according to both the household labor force and household size than could be obtained by any other means of distribution. In other words, under these assumptions there is no inconsistency between the equality in distribution and efficiency. Since the absence of land and labor markets and other uses of agricultural land is necessary to the results obtained, in other circumstances no such conclusion would hold.

They then go on to provide evidence from a township in northern China in the early 1980s where these conditions were alleged to be fairly realistic to support this conclusion. In particular, they show that, in practice, the land distributions in the township studied were consistent with the optimal rule. The distributional rule used would not have been an efficient or optimal one, had land and labor markets existed, hence providing a clear demonstration that institutions matter.

Some economists ("functionalists") assume that competition – actual or potential – among alternative arrangements would assure the emergence of efficient institutions, in turn implying that the existing institutions in an economy must be the efficient institutions. Although there is some empirical support for some such propositions, such as the alleged equality of land productivity on each of the alternative forms of land ownership in Sub-Saharan Africa (Migot-Adholla et al. 1991), they would be true only if the following conditions were satisfied: (1) at the beginning of every production cycle, the institutions would have to be adjusted anew according to the changes in technology, factor endowments, and so on; and (2) any resulting changes in institutions are costless. Yet, if these two conditions were met, as Matthews (1986) has pointed out, the institutions would be continuously adapted to changing circumstances, making institutional change a mere concomitance, rather than an independent "determinant", of economic growth.

Another more likely scenario is that institutions may not always evolve "efficiently". Indeed, institutional rigidity and inertia may set in, thereby preventing, even for long periods of time, institutional adaptations to environmental changes and causing institutions to be inefficient. Basu, Jones and Schlicht (1987) have suggested that it is quite possible that some institutional alternatives are eliminated from the feasible set by historical precedent. Since efficient institutions may not be known, or even if known, may be ruled out by the idiosyncrasies of a society's historical "endowment", there is no reason to believe that such an assumption of institutional efficiency is generally justified. Moreover, inefficiencies of some existing institutions may be known to their members, and yet these same members may have insufficient motivation to do anything about it.[13]

If institutional inertia can persist even when no member of society benefits from the institution, clearly they can persist when only some members of society are disadvantaged by it. Even if the benefits of institutional change are sufficiently large, that, at least potentially, those who would benefit from it could compensate those who would be hurt by it, it does not mean that they will necessarily do so. They may be impeded in doing so by: (1) the difficulty of identifying and obtaining agreement on the best among all possible means of accomplishing such compensation, (2) any possible conflict with social convention and (3) difficulties in measuring the potential benefits and costs and their distribution (which would be expected to be more substantial in LDCs). Quite conceivably, frustrated groups may eventually be induced to resort to physical force in either promoting or impeding institutional change. All such actions would, of course, have the effect of further adding to the social costs of institutional change and lowering the likelihood that existing institutions would be efficient.

Last, but by no means least, an efficient institutional arrangement may be excluded from the individual agents' choice set by the restrictive government policies, e.g. the suppression of markets after a socialist government's adoption of a planned system. While government subsidies may allow an inefficient arrangement to survive in the face of competition, once such subsidies are suspected of being non-sustainable, promises of their continuance may lose their credibility.

3. The demand for institutions and changes therein: The role of transaction costs

As noted above, institutions provide valuable services but are costly to establish and operate. The costs, broadly defined as transaction costs, include those of organizing, maintaining, and enforcing the rules of an institutional arrangement. Since there are always alternative institutional arrangements that can perform a particular institutional function, with given transaction costs, one institutional arrangement may provide more services and hence be more

---

[13] For example, this may arise if each member of a society fears being penalized (by ostracism or otherwise) for not adhering to the institutional rules [Akerlof (1976)]. A frequently cited example is the caste system in India which is almost universally rejected as undesirable but nevertheless maintained by society as a whole. Kuran (1987) shows that preference falsification (wherein one reveals not one's true preferences but only those which one wants others to know about or think they will want) can play a large part in such situations.

efficient than another. Alternatively, for a given amount of service, one may have lower transaction costs than another. Economic rationality predicts that a more efficient institution should be preferred over less efficient alternatives. The purpose of this section is to provide a survey of literature on the transaction cost approach to institutional analysis.[14]

3.1. The origins of transaction costs

Because the concept of transaction costs provides the basis for analyzing institutional choice, it is important to understand the origins of such costs. We have argued that institutions exist to exploit the gains from trade, specialization, and external economies. Such gains are obtained through the exchange of goods and services based on explicit or implicit contracts which necessarily involve the following types of costs, the relative importance of which may vary from one context to another.

First, there are the direct costs of (a) obtaining the information that the various parties to the contract need in order to assess both the relevant quantities and qualities of what is exchanged and the benefits and costs of the contract (visa-vis the relevant alternatives), (b) negotiating among the parties to reach agreement on the provisions of the contract, and (c) communicating all such provisions to all the relevant agents.

More importantly, contracting costs also include the indirect costs arising from the opportunistic behavior induced by the involvement of multiple agents in contexts in which various sources of risk are present. Among these indirect costs are those of monitoring and enforcing the terms and conditions of the contracts and the output lost due to contractual default.

Some of these costs occur before the transaction takes place (the ex ante costs) and some are incurred only after the transaction (the ex post transaction costs). Among the former are the direct and indirect costs arising from the contract selection process, including those of generating the relevant information and of drafting, negotiating, and safeguarding the agreement. The ex ante costs also include those arising from "adverse selection", the principle (from the literature on insurance) wherein, for any given insurance program

---

[14] The transaction cost approach is stimulated by the celebrated work of Coase (1937, 1960) and championed by Williamson (1975, 1979, 1985). However, we will also include in this approach the work on property rights [Alchian (1959, 1965), Demsetz (1967), Barzel (1989)], the information problem (see Stiglitz 1988–Chapter 5 in volume 1 of the Handbook), and the agency problem (Jensen and Meckling 1976). The work on incomplete information and asymmetries in information has been developed quite separately from the work by Williamson and is more mathematically oriented. However, information costs are closely related to transaction costs. It is possible to define transaction costs in a sufficiently broad way for the theory of transaction costs to serve as a unifying framework for analyzing the institutional choice studied in each of the above strands of research.

and specified premium, those with the incentive to accept it would be primarily those with insurance risks exceeding the stated premium. Adverse selection can therefore add to costs and undermine viability.

The ex post transaction costs arise because contracts are incomplete, incompletely self-enforcing and incapable of dealing with all possible aspects of human action and contingencies. These costs include the costs of (a) dispute resolution and the establishment and operation of governance procedures; (b) dealing with the maladaptation of the actual provisions of the contract, including its renegotiation; (c) monitoring the contract; and (d) bonding the contractual parties to continue to work together. Even more importantly, the ex post transaction costs include efficiency losses arising from distortions induced by the terms of contract, i.e. "moral hazard".

3.2. Transaction costs and contractual choice

An important application of transaction cost analysis is to provide a framework for analyzing contractual choices. For example, consider an agrarian setting in which there are only two inputs, land and labor. First, assume that land and labor are equally distributed among all households in a community. There are two possible institutional arrangements: either each household produces independently, or all households pool their resources and produce collectively. In the first arrangement, there are no monitoring and incentive problems because each household is a residual claimant, but this arrangement sacrifices possible gains from economies of scale and risk sharing. In the collective arrangement, the gains and losses are just the opposite of those of the individual household arrangement.

In the real world the inputs may well be distributed unequally among the households in a community. For simplicity of exposition, assume that the households can be classified into two polar classes: owners of land and owners of labor. Then, in addition to the collective arrangement, three basic types of arrangements can exist between the owners of land and the owners of labor: fixed wage, fixed rent, or share contracts. An owner of land can rent the land out to an owner of labor at a fixed rent (the fixed rent contract), lease it out for a share of output (the share contract), or hold it but hire labor at a fixed wage rate (the wage contract).

The rights and obligations of the owners of land and labor differ among these arrangements. For a fixed wage contract, the owner of land is the residual claimant and unlikely to shirk but the worker may shirk because his benefit is unrelated to his effort. Therefore, the owner of land has to spend time and resources to monitor the worker to guarantee that he works to the extent agreed upon and indeed may have an incentive for labor misuse [Pagano (1985)].

Under a fixed rent contract, however, the worker is the residual claimant and hence is not expected to shirk in his supply of labor effort. On the other hand, and especially if the fixed rent contract were only for a short period of time, both the landowner and especially the worker have an incentive to shirk on maintenance activities and/or to over- or mis-use the land so as to get more output in the short run (at the cost of less future output). In addition, the owner of land may not have an incentive to share with the worker specific knowledge of the land he possesses.

In a share contract, the residual is shared by both parties, and the incentive structure lies between the fixed wage and fixed rent arrangements. There would be some incentive for the worker to undersupply labor effort (or the landowner to misuse labor) and some incentive for land mismanagement (though in both cases to a lesser extent than in the case of the polar contracts). There would also arise an incentive for one of the parties to underreport the output to the other party. The incentives of the landowner and worker to invest in acquiring new information and new technology also may vary with the type of contract.[15]

Although outside of the simple agrarian economy the complexity of technology may increase exponentially, the alternative contractual arrangements are similar. For example, in industry the most important inputs are generally labor and capital instead of labor and land. Nevertheless, the institutional arrangements can be classified first into state- or collective-owned firms, on the one hand, and private-owned firms, on the other hand. Then, among the private arrangements, there are several forms: (1) labor hires capital by paying for it at a fixed interest rate, (2) capital hires labor at a fixed wage rate, or (3) both agree to share the output.

Certainly, no matter whether in agriculture or industry, rented assets can be misused; labor may shirk with respect to effort; both effort and output may be unobservable or imperfectly measured. The relative severity of these different problems depends on both environmental conditions and the production process. Although one type of contractual arrangement may prevail over others in one production process and environment, it may not do so in others. For example, in addition to the mean value of their income streams, labor and asset owners may also value the stability of their income streams. If the insurance markets in the economy are absent or imperfect, the relevant agents will likely attach more value to risk sharing in the selection of a contract.

---

[15] Specifically, in rather different circumstances, Zouteweij (1956) and Newbery (1977) have suggested that the incentives for investment might well be lower under share contracts than other contracts, though the evidence for this in either agriculture or fishing seems wanting [Besley (1993), Platteau and Nugent (1992)].

The basic proposition of transaction cost analysis is that, although the various components of transaction costs can be distinguished, what is generally relevant to a contractual choice is only their total (and therefore cost minimization in general). Therefore, for convenience, rather than dealing separately with the costs of information, negotiation, bonding, and so on, the analysis can be in terms of aggregate transaction costs. In Section 5, we cite some empirical evidence supporting the proposition that transaction cost considerations can be important in explaining the choice of contractual forms.

3.3. Transaction costs and institutional changes

If the role of transaction costs in the choice of an institutional arrangement is granted, transaction costs can also be used to explain institutional changes. Given the level of a demanded institutional service, an arrangement is more efficient than other available options if it requires less total transaction costs than the other arrangements in the choice set (North 1984). Starting from an institutional equilibrium, a disequilibrium may result from exogenous shocks in: (1) the demand for institutional services; (2) the technologies related to transaction costs; and/or (3) the choice set of available institutional arrangements. Regardless of source, any such shock could render an existing institutional arrangement less efficient than one or more other arrangements in the choice set.

Since a change from an existing institutional arrangement to a new one is bound to be costly in itself (in part because the gainers from the change may need to compensate the losers), as noted above it is by no means certain that the less efficient arrangement will actually give way to the more efficient one. However, if the costs of change are smaller than the potential gains, an institutional innovation may be expected. Such a change is an "induced institutional innovation" [Davis and North (1970), Hayami and Ruttan (1985), and Binswanger and Ruttan (1978)]. As shown below, although analyses of induced institutional innovations focus on what one might call the demand for institutional change, supply considerations, the subject of Section 4, may also be relevant.

3.3.1. Shifts in the demand for an institutional service

Historically, the most important sources of shifts in the demand for institutional service have probably been those derived from long-term changes in the relative abundance of factors of production. Such changes have had profound impacts on the emergence of property rights institutions. If a certain factor is not in scarce supply, its price will be zero and open access to that factor may be

efficient. When a factor becomes scarce, its price becomes positive and there
will exist a demand for an ownership arrangement whereby the factor's use can
be allocated. In their long processes of development, many countries have
experienced a gradual evolution from conditions characterized by plentiful land
and scarce labor to conditions of scarce land and plentiful labor. Boserup
(1965), North and Thomas (1971, 1973), Hayami and Kikuchi (1982), Ruttan
and Hayami (1984), Jodha (1985), Salehi-Isfahani (1988) and Alston, Libecap
and Schneider (1993) have all pointed to cases in which such changes have
induced the establishment of private property rights to land.[16] Likewise, a
relative price rise of a product should raise the value of exclusive use of factors
used in its production. The rise of private property rights among the Montag-
nais Indians of Labrador is a classic example [Demsetz (1967)]. Before arrival
of the Europeans, the price of beaver pelts was low, and the beaver habitat was
held in common. With access to the European market where these pelts were
highly valued, beaver habitats were converted to private property. The
experience in Africa and elsewhere appears to have been similar.[17]

Likewise, mineral rights have often evolved in contemporary LDCs as they
did with gold and silver in the American West of the 19th century when
high-valued deposits were discovered. At discovery, seldom do mining laws
exist. The discoveries, however, bring dramatic increases in land values,
thereby triggering the development of legal procedures for assigning rights.
Even before that, private arrangements for establishing and mutually respecting such rights may develop, as they did in the American West [Hallagan
(1978), Libecap (1978 a,b; 1979), McCurdy (1976), and Umbeck (1977,
1981)].

Similarly, for nineteenth century Thailand, Feeny (1982, 1989) has shown
that the increasing importance of international trade raised the price of rice,
which induced changes in the relative prices of land. Compounded with other
domestic and international political motives, as well as ideological and
normative factors, the traditional property rights in man were replaced by
private property rights in land. Likewise, Hawaii's shift to private property
rights in land was induced by the increased value of land arising from an
increased foreign demand for sugar production [La Croix and Roumasset
(1990)],[18] land registration in Brazil's Parana State by increasing markets for
coffee [Alston, Libecap and Schneider (1993)] and the enclosures of open

---

[16] For further discussion of the land-labor linkage and the evolution of property rights to land,
see Binswanger, Deininger, and Feder (Chapter 45 of this volume).

[17] The increase in the relative price of a factor or product will increase the incentive to steal,
which raises the costs of policing [Barzel (1989), p. 67; Umbeck (1981)]. Therefore, there will be a
better delineation of rights only when the net gains are positive.

[18] Another reason for the transformation in Hawaii was the government's desire to increase tax
revenues.

fields in England by increases in the price of wool and population size [Baack (1979), McCloskey (1972)].

Notably also, it was upon the discovery of large oil and gas reserves in the North Sea that ownership rights to that sea were created and allocated among the countries bordering it in the 1958 Convention on the Continental Shelf [Barzel (1989, pp. 72–73)]. Similarly, the increased scarcity value of fish would seem to have been the most important factor behind the establishment of the International Law of the Sea creating exclusive economic zones extending 200 nautical miles from each country's seacoast [Hannesson (1991)].

Since as noted above the functions of different institutional arrangements are interdependent, a change in one particular arrangement may result in corresponding changes in the demand for the services of other arrangements. As Lewis observes, "Once institutions begin to change, they change in ways which are self-enforcing. The old beliefs and institutions are altered, and the new beliefs and institutions gradually become more consistent with each other and with further change in the same direction" [Lewis (1955), p. 146]. For example, North and Thomas (1971) trace the evolution of medieval European property rights, especially the system of labor dues and its ultimate replacement by a fixed-rent arrangement. In the early stages of this evolution they hypothesize that the general absence of goods markets, combined with only the most rudimentary market for labor, justified input-sharing as a low transaction cost contractual arrangement. As population grew, a goods market developed to capture the gains from specialization and trade. This in turn made it possible to negotiate and specify the peasants' consumption bundle in money terms. As a result, fixed wage and fixed rent contracts gradually replaced input-sharing contracts, which involved higher monitoring and enforcement costs.

A most important change in an institutional arrangement which can trigger other institutional changes is the emergence of the state. In a primitive society without a state-enforced law and order, Posner (1980) points out the importance of individual and family honor. Honor is important because it induces people to trust and cooperate with its possessor and to behave in ways that might be regarded as predictable and lawful despite the absence of formal laws. To maintain one's honor in such a situation requires retaliation. Credible threats of retaliation, of course, can act as an important incentive for behaving in such a way that retaliation is unnecessary. Although honor may still be highly valued in modern states, the state itself often becomes the sole institutional instrument for preserving social order. It prohibits retaliation and duels, and as a result honor becomes both less necessary and more difficult to maintain.

Pre-industrial, low productivity societies are also often permeated with important patron-client relationships. These relationships may reduce aggregate transaction costs by reducing the need for various different specialized markets, such as those for labor, land, credit, insurance, and so on, each of which involves transaction costs [Hayami and Kikuchi (1982), Chapter 2]. Conversely, the expansion of such markets lessens the need for mutual help and patron-client relationships [Polanyi (1944)]. For example, Lin (1989b, 1992b) shows that the rural factor markets in land, labor, and capital, which did not exist under the collective farming system, have reemerged in rural China after the shift to the household system.

Finally, changes in the demand for institutional service may also have their origin in production technology. New institutional arrangements may be required in order to take advantage of, or treat, externalities arising from the new technology or to modify the partitioning of income streams among factor owners. The rise of modern firms relative to traditional family workshops in manufacturing may result from the need to take advantage of the scale economies of new capital- and scale- intensive production and distribution techniques [Brewster (1950), Chandler (1973, 1977) Jones (1987)]. Along the same lines, the introduction of modern high-yield varieties of rice and increased labor supplies in the Philippines have resulted in the replacement of the traditional hunusan contract, in which all villagers have the right to participate in harvesting and to receive one-sixth of the yield, by the gama contract, which gives an exclusive right of harvesting for the same share to the workers who weed but without receiving a wage [Hayami and Kikuchi (1982), Chapter 5]. Clearly, the innovation of the gama system was induced by the desire to modify the new income stream between landowners and laborers.

3.3.2. Exogenous changes in transaction costs

As mentioned above, an exogenous shock in transaction costs can shift the supply curve of an institutional service, thereby constituting another source of institutional change. The changes in transaction costs may come from changes in technology, ideology, law, or other institutional arrangements.

One indicator of the critical role of transaction costs in the rise and fall of markets throughout history is that, when trade routes were relatively unhindered by piracy, wars, insurrections, taxation, and so on, markets have developed, the specialization of labor and other activities increased, incomes grown, and civilizations flourished. Conversely, when trade routes are rendered increasingly risky and/or less profitable because of one or more of the above-mentioned sources of high transaction costs, market activities tend to decline in favor of non-market ones. This results in decreased specialization and often lower levels of development.

In particular, as the rule of Roman law and the use of Roman roads yielded to political and military turmoil in the twilight of the Roman Empire, markets declined in favor of feudal autonomy.[19] Subsequently, however, with the greater peace and tranquility of the European renaissance, markets reemerged, and feudal institutions gave way to market institutions. Notably, the first merchants in the reemerging European market economy were itinerant merchants who came to trade fairs in groups, thereby providing each other with protection. The trade fairs were at first only sporadic; by concentrating all the transactions into a short period of time, they mitigated the problems associated with "thin" markets.[20] Gradually, however, as trade developed, these markets became more permanent [Braudel (1979)]. A somewhat similar rise and fall of market institutions in contemporary Africa is identified by Sahn and Sarris (1993).

The decline of the Roman Empire also left a mark on property-rights institutions. In particular, the collapse of the Roman Empire and disintegration of its legal system raised the cost of excluding outsiders from one's private property. As a result, private property was replaced by the open field system, in which land was shared by a larger group of individuals and protected by the weaker feudal lords [Pejovich (1972), Field (1989), Hoffman (1975), Thirsk (1964), Blum (1971)].

The experience of the nineteenth century American West provides another interesting example of the role of exogenous changes in transaction costs on property rights institutions. In the early part of the century, in the absence of state-provided law and order, low population density, and prohibitively high costs of fencing in semi-arid lands, exclusion costs were higher for private property than for common property, individual ranchers joined together in common cattle pools and common property rights dominated over private property rights in land. Nevertheless, as barbed wire was discovered and introduced and law and order spread throughout the region in the last decades of the century, there was a significant shift away from common property in land to private property [Anderson and Hill (1975), Dennen (1976), Libecap (1979) and Nugent and Sanchez (1993)]. Similar changes were observed for similar reasons in animal husbandry in Africa, Asia, Australia and Latin America [Nugent and Sanchez (1993), Giberti (1988)].

---

[19] The feudal economy may be interpreted as a simple "coalition economy" [Townsend (1984)]. Even in simple coalition economies, however, a considerable amount of hierarchy and supervision may be necessary in order to monitor the performance of the different agents with respect to the responsibilities with which they are charged. For evidence see Bennett (1937).

[20] For similar reasons, in sparsely populated rural areas the markets operate but once every week or two and in urban areas the operating hours of infant stock exchanges may be confined to but a few hours a week.

3.3.3. Changes in the institutional choice set

Just as the set of feasible production technologies is a function of the stock of knowledge in physics, chemistry, other natural sciences and engineering, the set of feasible institutional arrangements for a particular institutional service may depend on the relevant stock of social science knowledge. Ruttan (1984, 1986) has argued forcefully that the demand for knowledge in economics and the other social sciences is derived primarily from the demand for institutional change and improvements in institutional performance. Advances in social science (and learning from past mistakes as well as successes) improve understanding of how societies function and increase not only individual abilities to manage existing institutions but also society's knowledge of alternative institutional arrangements. Ruttan (1986) cites the absence of quantitative knowledge on the costs and benefits of price supports and of income payments for the delay in the shift from more distortionary and inefficiency-inducing price support programs to income supplement programs for farmers in the United States and other countries. Krueger (1988) points to the relevance of knowledge concerning the reaction of markets, politicians, and other actors, and the consequences thereof, for group interests in determining how sugar markets are regulated. In the same spirit, detailed studies of some of the undesirable (including inequality-increasing) effects of income redistribution programs and of government regulations are alleged to have contributed to the current trend toward the dismantling of welfare programs, deregulation and privatization in LDCs.[21]

Just as contacts with other economies may increase the available technological choice set, so too they may enlarge the institutional choice set. As a result of such contacts, an originally efficient arrangement may become obsolete. Bauer (1984, p. 12) emphasizes the role of individual traders in bringing in new technology and institutional arrangements and, as a result, in encouraging people to question existing habits which delay the erosion of attitudes and customs uncongenial to material progress. Further, he attributes the unfavorable development record of post-independence Africa to purposeful suppression of this useful link (traders) to institutional and technological change.

The possibility of institutional change through borrowing another society's institutional arrangements may reduce the need for costly investments in basic social science research. Yet, since research may still be needed on how to adapt them to local conditions, the need for such social science research is by no

---

[21] It is worth emphasizing that knowledge about the dysfunctional state of an institutional arrangement is a necessary condition but not a sufficient condition for institutional change. Due to institutional inertia, which Akerlof emphasized (1976), even when everyone in a society is fully aware that a particular institutional arrangement is dysfunctional, it may still continue for an extended period of time.

means eliminated. This is particularly true since the efficiency of an institutional arrangement depends so heavily on the existence of other complementary institutional arrangements, making its direct transfer especially difficult.[22] Finally, the institutional choice set can also be enlarged or contracted by a change in government policies. For reasons discussed in the next section, if governments exclude some useful institutional arrangements from the choice set, the removal of such restrictions can have the beneficial effect of enlarging the choice set. For example, prior to the late 1970s China's government prohibited household farming arrangements; as a result, the only acceptable mode was collective farming. With the simple removal of such restrictions by the Chinese government, about 95 percent of households in China converted to household-based farming between 1980 and 1983 [Lin (1987)]. Conversely, if the government institutes a new and binding constraint, an initially less efficient arrangement may become a dominant one in the restricted choice set. The recent emergence of permanent labor contracts in Philippine villages is an inefficient substitute for tenancy contracts under legal restrictions on the choice of tenancy [Otsuka, Chuma, and Hayami (1992)].

4. The supply of institutions and of changes therein: The role of collective action and the state

The transaction cost theory discussed in the previous section suggests that, when institutional disequilibria exist, profitable opportunities for new institutional arrangements will arise, and if the transaction costs of change are not excessive, institutional change, perhaps even a change in the whole institutional structure, may eventually result. Yet, because of information and transaction costs, there is no guarantee that an institutional disequilibrium will trigger an immediate move to the new equilibrium structure. When, under what conditions, and to what extent will such institutional change take place are questions posed by the theory of collective action.

Numerous factors may stand in the way of the movement to a new equilibrium. Among these are the information and transaction costs of identifying, designing and implementing the new arrangements. These are complicated by the fact that individuals with different experiences and roles in the structure may have different perceptions of the degree and source of disequilibrium and may also try to partition the gains from the change in different ways. Therefore, when institutional disequilibrium occurs, the process

---

[22] Recall the examples discussed in Section 2.4, wherein the transplantation of the U.S. constitution to Latin American countries after their independence in the nineteenth century and land reform programs did not result in the same effectiveness as in the United States and other developed countries with better auxiliary institutions.

of institutional change may commence with a change in but one arrangement in an historically determined structure and only gradually spread to the other arrangements. Institutional change is thus conditioned by the existing structure and is "path-dependent" [North (1990), Chapter 11]. Consequently, some arrangements – favorable from an abstract theoretical point of view – may be non-viable because of incompatibility with other existing arrangements in the structure. Although the fundamental properties of an institutional structure may be altered only when the accumulative changes of individual arrangements reach a certain critical point, the process of institutional change may appear evolutionary [Alchian (1950), Nelson and Winter (1982)].

As explained in Section 3.3, society as a whole gains from an institutional innovation that captures a profitable opportunity arising in institutional disequilibrium. Yet, whether or not this innovation takes place depends on the expected gains and costs to the individual innovators, their distribution, and the possibility of externality and/or free-rider problems.

Once in place, most institutions are like public goods in that the benefits thereof are jointly consumable and exclusion is very costly. Because of this, efforts to introduce them (time and money) will often be subject to free-rider problems. (If the benefits leak out to those who do not contribute to their creation, why contribute?)

Not all institutions and institutional innovations, however, are like this. For example, in principle, an institution might be patentable or due to a monopoly in political, economic or military power, the individual responsible for introducing it might be able (through taxation) to capture all the benefits arising from it. In such cases, institutional change is like producing a private good which can be carried out by one or more individuals without need for collective action.

A similar situation may arise when an existing institution, such as a social norm underscoring the need to provide charity to others when asked, can be taken advantage of by an outsider or by a deviant from the social norm. In the absence of insurance markets, the "giving charity to others is good when one can" norm may be very beneficial for the mutual insurance it provides. Yet, the deviant who deliberately demands charity from others without ever providing it may be able to reap tremendous personal benefits without ever having to work. Since his success may undermine the existing norm, he could be said to be the innovator of a new institutional arrangement, the benefits of which would have accrued largely to him.[23]

---

[23] For an interesting discussion of these possibilities in the context of norm evolution see Basu (1992).

More typically, with social norms, individual innovators may be considered by others to be violating the existing rules and hence are likely to pay a heavy price (e.g. social ostracism) for such violations.[24] The new institutional arrangement will become a new socially sanctioned rule only when the majority of the individuals in the society abandon the original arrangement and adopt the new one. An externality problem arises in this case because the institutional arrangement is not patentable in that, when a new behavioral norm is adopted by one individual, others can imitate it and benefit from it. Therefore, the returns to the innovator are less than those to the society as a whole. Because of the externality, the intensity and frequency of institutional innovation may be less than socially optimal and result in the persistence of institutional disequilibria.[25]

Some institutions have the property of a club good: namely, although (because of economies of scale in production or consumption) the good is jointly consumable, outsiders may be excluded from its benefits. For example, the innovation of a periodic market in a certain locality, which may be beneficial to everyone in the locality quite naturally excludes those from distant communities. Yet, its introduction requires at least several relevant parties – buyers and sellers – to show up at the same place and time and bear the costs of creating the market. Club-like institutions face both externality and free-rider problems but often manage to control them.

In other cases, however, institutional innovations may more closely resemble pure public goods in which the free rider problems are more severe. Because of the incentive to free ride, even very beneficial institutional innovations may be left unexploited. Whereas the literature on transaction costs is relatively silent on free-rider issues, that on collective action, discussed throughout this section, concentrates on these issues. In the process of solving free-rider problems, however, collective action theory identifies a new problem associated with institutional change, namely that a new arrangement may be created by a small group of people for their own benefit but at the cost of the economy as a whole. The purpose of Section 4.1 is to review the principles relevant to the analysis of collective action and to examine their application to institutional change. For the externality problem, welfare economics suggests that govern-

---

[24] See the numerous examples in Bauer and Yamey (1957) and the discussion of Akerlof (1980).
[25] However, in some cases it may be optimal for an individual, having observed the actions of those ahead of him, to follow the behavior of the preceding individuals without regard to his own information; an information cascade, discussed by Bikhchandani, Hirshleifer, and Welch (1992), may occur. In these cases, if a few people start to deviate from the conventional behavioral patterns, suggesting that a different course of action is optimal, the population may adopt the new norm, custom, or fad with surprising rapidity.

ment intervention is potentially desirable. Yet, before being able to know whether or not the government has the incentive and capacity to intervene in an appropriate way, a theory of the state (Section 4.2) is required.

4.1. Collective action and institutional change[26]

The main contributions to the theory of collective action by Olson (1965, 1982), R. Hardin (1982) and their followers have focused on the identification of group characteristics favorable to success in achieving collective action. Olson's theoretical analysis deals primarily with a static game framework in which non-cooperative solutions are dominant strategies. His contribution lies in the identification of restrictions on individual behavior and the interactions among group members that may allow the free-rider problem to be overcome. In particular, Olson and his followers have argued that collective action is likely to be more feasible (a) the smaller the group,[27] (b) the more homogeneous the origin of the group, (c) the longer the members of the group have been associated with one another or the group has been in existence, (d) the closer the social and physical proximity among group members,[28] (e) the more differentiated (in a complementary way) the goals of different members (or subgroups) of the group,[29] (f) the greater the sensitivity of the group to a threatened loss arising from inaction, and (g) the more unequal the distribution of wealth or power among group members.[30] What makes these principles

[26] Different authors have used different terms for interest groups, such as "distributional coalitions". Although in some cases, the different terms may have slightly different interpretations, in the subsequent discussion the terms "interest groups", "collective action groups", and "distributional coalitions" are used interchangeably. Whereas interest groups and organizations are clearly distinguishable, not all interest groups have organizations and not all organizations are interest groups, in fact (as we shall see), the two tend to go hand in hand. Once interest groups form, usually they develop organizations that are relatively permanent, hence justifying the application of collective action theory to both in the same section. The most important connection between interest groups and organizations is that organizations facilitate collective action on the part of interest groups by reducing start-up costs and/or long-run average costs.

[27] Small size is alleged to be advantageous for collective action not only because communication among members is facilitated but also because the incentive for free-riding is diminished. However, as we shall see below, there are also reasons for believing that a "critical mass" of numbers or resources may be necessary in certain situations.

[28] Characteristics (b), (c), and (d) facilitate communication among members and make it easier for them to agree on methods and objectives. They may also lead to greater altruism among group members, increase the sense of responsibility among them, and make it more difficult for individual members to refuse to go along with the wishes of the majority.

[29] Characteristic (e) makes the objectives more additive rather than competitive to one another, thereby raising the prospects for "logrolling" and other means of satisfying the different objectives of different subgroups at the same time. This raises the prospect that these subgroups will support each other and then join in collective action benefiting all groups.

[30] This characteristic makes it likely that the critical minimum of support for the collective action can be achieved even in the event that some smaller, less wealthy, and less powerful members choose to free-ride.

(hypotheses) relevant and potentially important is that most of them can be operationalized relatively easily. For example, characteristic (a) can be measured by membership size,[31] (b) by commonality of place or class of birth of group members, (c) by the length of time the group has been in existence, (d) by geographic or sectoral concentration, (e) by differences in stated objectives among group members, and (g) by inequality in the distribution of wealth among group members.

Although, as suggested above, Olson's theoretical framework is that of a static game, the reason why characteristics (c) and (d) are favorable to collective action could be attributed alternatively to the greater likelihood of cooperative solutions when group members interact repeatedly.

In situations where the obstacles to collective action would otherwise seem formidable, the prospects for collective action may be enhanced by the availability of "political entrepreneurs". As Hardin (1982, p. 35) defined them, "political entrepreneurs are people who, for their own career reasons, find it in their private interest to work to provide collective benefits to relevant groups". Thus, political entrepreneurship can help explain why certain groups may become engaged in successful collective action even if, on other bases one would think that these groups would be likely to remain "latent".[32] Indeed, since large numbers and geographical dispersion may be attractive characteristics to political entrepreneurs, this can be an important offset to the Olsonian hypotheses suggested above.

Success in collective action by a particular group, e.g. Group A, may also be affected by whether or not other groups, such as B, C, D, etc., engage in collective action [Becker (1983)]. Specifically, Group A may be deemed more likely to succeed in such collective action the more one of these other groups has been successful in engaging in an action that is harmful or threatening to the interests of A. Moreover, even if A is not directly affected by the other groups, other groups' success may affect A's success through a demonstration effect.

The environmental circumstances in which group members find themselves, such as the available alternatives to collective action, may also play an important role in group actions. For example, Hirschman (1970, 1981) has focused on the possibilities for "exit" solutions (rather than "voice" or collective action solutions) to a given group facing unfavorable circumstances. Specifically, he hypothesized that the easier it is to exit and the more attractive

---

[31] As Hardin (1982) and Ostrom (1990) have indicated, however, the measurement of size is by no means unambiguous. For example, it can mean the number of members, the amount of resources, or some combination thereof.

[32] We use the terms latent, dormant, passive and inactive interchangeably to identify groups that are neither organized nor actively engaged in collective action. As pointed out below, however, even latent groups can be forced to take collective action if they are sufficiently threatened. Generally, however, such action is temporary. After the action, successful or not, the group returns to its latent state.

are the alternatives to remaining in the group, the lower is the possibility for successful collective action. For example, collective action may be less likely the easier it is to substitute private goods for public ones. However, among those who choose not to exit, those for whom exit is most attractive may well have the most influence. In a similar vein, Iannaccone (1992) hypothesizes that the apparently unproductive costs, such as dietary restrictions, painful initiations, and other sacrifices or stigma required by some religious groups, fraternities, communes, political parties, and other social groups, are rational measures for overcoming free-rider problems. They screen out only marginally committed members while at the same time increasing participation among those who remain by raising the relative costs of alternative activities.

Because of the importance of group perceptions, the communication, organizational skill, and knowledge of the technology of collective action on the part of group members, especially those in leadership positions, may also contribute to success in collective action. For example, the prospects of success may be enhanced by the ability of the proponents of the action to conceal from all parties the magnitude of the costs and to exaggerate the benefits. One way in which this might be accomplished is by suggesting an analogy between the action under consideration and previously successful, apparently similar actions, even if the analogy is actually false [Hirschman (1967)].[33] Success in collective action can be enhanced by the clarity of the logic connecting the action with its intended benefits and by the extent to which that logic is communicated to all group members [Nelson (1984)]. Organizational ability can be of considerable use. For example, the advantages of group characteristics (a) through (e) in the above list of factors favorable to collective action may be strengthened by organizing local, homogeneous groups into national (or even international) federations [Olson (1965)]. Since expectations of the ability to execute and enforce collective action may affect an individual's willingness to participate, the prestige, elite status, and power of group leaders may also be highly conducive to success in collective action [Wade (1987)]. Likewise, any actual improvement in the technology of collective action that increases the expected benefits relative to the expected costs may increase the likelihood of collective action.[34]

Collective action theory may also help explain the character, size, and breadth of interest groups and thereby affect economic efficiency and long-term development. In particular, a "narrow/special-interest" group which is

---

[33] Naturally, this does not mean that deliberate deception is necessarily going to lead to success. Indeed, to be persuasive in this respect the claimant has to have credibility, something that gross misrepresentation is hardly likely to generate.

[34] Closely related influences are changes in social values concerning the benefits of the public goods produced by the collective action [North (1986)] and changes in knowledge about the effects [Ruttan and Hayami (1984), Ruttan (1986)].

small in relation to the total size of the society, tends to have homogeneous but narrowly focused objectives. On the other hand, an encompassing interest group is larger and more heterogeneous. Hence, the former may be easier to organize than the latter.

The prospects for success in collective action may also be enhanced by the practice of selective incentives,[35] both positive and negative. For example, positive incentives such as the prestige and honor accorded to those making especially large or well-sustained gifts as part of an organization's fund-raising appeals, are often useful for encouraging large and regular financial donations. Likewise, negative incentives, such as penalties in the form of fines or even physical punishment, have often been found to be effective in reducing free-riding and, accordingly, in increasing the prospects of success in collective action, at least in some circumstances [Olson (1965), Chapter 6, R. Hardin (1982), pp. 31–34].[36]

Given the importance of organizations in reducing the cost of collective action and the difficulty of determining the existence of organization-less interest groups, collective action theory is probably more directly applicable to the creation of interest group organizations than to the creation of the interest groups themselves.[37] Because encompassing groups are far more difficult to organize, selective incentives are likely to prove more important in analyzing their effectiveness. In particular, positive selective incentives may be necessary to encourage active participation and leadership, and negative selective incentives to prevent members from violating group decisions.[38] Organizations may also be useful in serving the interests of political entrepreneurs [R. Hardin (1982), p. 36] and for monitoring the activities of opposing or partner groups whose efforts may affect the results of the collective action.

The structure of organizations and the rules by which they function may well be determined by transaction costs. Indeed, organizations would be expected to adopt governance structures designed to minimize the long-run transaction costs (including the costs of the selective incentives) of collective action. When

---

[35] The use of selective incentives implies that the goods involved are not strictly or completely public goods of non-exclusionary character and jointness of supply. As Ostrom (1990) points out, in practice public goods may conform to one of these criteria more than to the another, with possible differences in the likelihood of collective action.

[36] An important shortcoming of the theory in this respect, however, is that it does not explain which selective incentives would be most conducive to success in different situations.

[37] Note that our position in this respect, though close to that of Uphoff (1986), is quite different than that of R. Hardin who states unequivocally: "The logic of collective action is not a theory about interest group organizations. Rather, it is a theory about whether there will be interest group or any kind of collective action" [R. Hardin (1982), pp. 14–15].

[38] Indeed, the importance of selective incentives for the emergence and long-run success of encompassing groups may account for why some analysts identify the implementation of selective incentives as an important objective of the organization of interest groups [R. Hardin (1982), p. 34, and Olson (1982), pp. 38–40].

exogenous shocks occur, well-managed organizations may institute appropriate changes in group objectives so as to avoid the start-up costs of organizing a new collective action group.

Although groups and organizations may undertake "private actions" to provide directly for their own club goods, more typically they do so indirectly by means of the state. In fact, an important means of increasing the technical efficiency of collective action is by gaining access to the state and its ability not only to impose regulations but also to monitor and enforce them [R. Hardin (1982)]. Since the state can also affect the degree to which groups can practice selective incentives, it can influence the likelihood of success in collective action indirectly. Among the means by which the state can do so are (a) changing the level, breadth of distribution, and composition of the benefits it provides free-of-charge to the public; (b) passing judgement on the legality of imposing negative incentives upon those not participating in group activities; and (c) insisting on certain voting procedures, such as the secret ballot, that may affect the feasibility of imposing selective incentives on those supporting or opposing collective action.

Because of the state's natural interest in demonstrating its responsiveness to the desires of its constituents, the barriers to indirect collective action by way of the state may well be considerably weaker than those to direct collective action without the involvement of the state. Another important advantage of collective action by way of the state is the stamp of legitimacy that state acceptance or tacit authorization can give to such action, at least in the case of a state whose legitimacy is generally accepted [Baumol (1952), Chapter 12].

If the state plays only a mediating role in collective action, responding only passively to interest group pressures, then the principles of collective action discussed in the previous section can be directly applied to the determination of the relative influence of different interest groups over policy.[39] Yet, because the state, according to Max Weber's definition, has a monopoly over the legitimate use of coercion in a given region, it can impede a desirable institutional innovation. This brings us to the theory of the state and political economy.

4.2. Political economy and the state

Since the state provides a framework of order on which the rest of the economy is built, the importance of the state and its policy for economic growth cannot be over-emphasized. Moreover, due to incomplete markets,

---

[39] The state will not just act passively in response to the influence of the pressure groups. Indeed the state can itself influence the tastes and constraints of pressure groups. See the discussions in Section 4.2.

imperfect information, transaction costs, and imperfect competition, potentially the state can play a major role in facilitating economic development [Stiglitz (1989), World Bank (1991)]. After surveying more than 100 years of comparative development experience in 40 LDCs, Reynolds (1983, p. 976) states that "the single most important explanatory variable is political organization and the administrative competence of government". The fact that there is a potentially important role for the state in facilitating development-promoting institutional changes, however, implies neither that the state will inevitably take the initiative nor that its policies are bound to succeed. The state can fail not only if it does the wrong thing but also if it does too little or too much about the right thing. Unless we can explain the behavior of the state, we cannot fully explain the process of economic development.

4.2.1. Economic approaches to the state

The basic functions of the state are to provide law and order and to protect property rights. Such services are generally exchanged in return for tax payments. Since there are large economies of scale in using coercive power, the state may belong to the category of natural monopolies. Moreover, as the single group in society to which all belong and from which exit may be least possible, the state may also solve a variety of coordination problems and overcome externalities plaguing other institutions. If so, the existence of the state may be considered a precondition for economic progress. No matter how exploitative a state might be, it may be better than anarchy [North (1979)]. Normatively, the most desirable state might be the minimal state that is "limited to the narrow functions of protection against force, theft, fraud, enforcement of contracts, and so on" [Nozick (1974), p. ix]. However, in reality, being monopolists in the legitimate use of coercive power, states can extend their spheres of influence well beyond those of a minimal state. Although the state cannot determine how an institution will work, it has "the power of deciding what institutions shall exist" [Mill (1848), p. 21]. A more interesting question is whether the state has the incentive and ability to design and institute a suitable arrangement, which the induced innovation process fails to provide due to the externality or/and free-rider problems.

The analogy of the state to a natural monopoly, however, is often far from realistic in the sense that there may be different levels of government, i.e. local and state as well as national, and different functional agencies at any given level, competing for turf. Nevertheless, many of the same issues which arise at the national level apply also at lower levels and even in non-state institutions like tribes and religious or ethnic groups.

Several approaches have been proposed for studying decision making by the state. The first approach views the state as a personalized organic entity with its own values, motivations, and objectives that are independent of the individuals of whom the state is composed. As an integrated cell of the state, an individual loses his own identity. The state acts to maximize its own welfare or utility.

According to the second approach, the state consists of a multitude of agents: politicians who must seek political support from various groups, bureaucrats and technocrats. Each agent has his/her own interests, and as in the literature of public choice and rent seeking, the state is viewed as an instrument of achieving collective action. It is merely a set of processes, a machine through which individuals can satisfy some of their interests. The policies of the state are endogenously determined by the competing powers of the various interest groups.

The third approach, advocated by a wide range of social scientists including Marxists, is similar to the second but views the state as the agency of a particular group or class. As such, its function is to ensure the legal, institutional, and ideological hegemony of the dominant class over subordinate classes. The state will institute property rights that maximize the revenue of the ruling class regardless of its impact on the wealth of the nation as a whole.

The latter two approaches are incomplete in that they fail to explain how the powers of interest groups or classes come about and are sustained. Moreover, if all policy instruments are endogenously determined by the competing powers, it is impossible to ask normative questions about the effects of alternative policies [Srinivasan (1992)].

A fourth approach, suggested by Downs (1957), is where decision making by the state is seen from the point of view of a single political party (or set of political elites [Grindle and Thomas (1991)]. The party is a multi-person team seeking to control the governing apparatus by legal means. Since its members are assumed to agree on all (not simply some of) their goals, it can be viewed as a single person with a consistent preference ordering. As Downs (1957, p. 26) himself admits, this approach is also unrealistic since "In reality not even the key officials of any government have exactly the same goals".

Most theories discussed above have postulated the political institutions and behavioral characteristics of the advanced industrial countries. However, LDC states display greater variation in their institutional arrangements than their DC counterparts. According to the classification by Findlay (1990), the states which currently exist in the LDCs of Asia, Africa, and Latin America range from traditional monarchies, through traditional dictatorships, to right-wing and left-wing authoritarian states, and finally to democratic states. Each type of state has its unique ideology and political organization. Today, almost all LDC states, however, share the characteristics that they tend to dominate civil society and have a substantial degree of autonomy in policy making. Accordingly, they are by no means only the passive agents of various interest groups or the executive committees of the ruling classes.

A more appropriate framework for studying the behavior of the state in LDCs, therefore, is the multi-level, principal-agent framework. At the first level of such a framework, the head of the state – the ruler – can be treated as the agent of either the people, as in Locke or Rousseau, or the ruling class, as in the Marxian variants. The ruler – king, dictator, president, prime minister, or behind-the-scenes supreme leader – is a rational person.

Within such a framework the principal has the problem of monitoring the activities of the ruler to see whether or not the ruler is adhering to the implicit social contract. The conventional principal-agent problem is compounded by the fact that the ruler is empowered with a legal monopoly in the use of force, leaving the ruler with a substantial degree of autonomy in pursuing his (her) own preferences in policy decisions although within the constraints determined by the ruler's legitimacy, the legal tradition of the society, and other cultural endowments.[40]

Within the constraints, a ruler can do whatever best satisfies his (her) own preferences. However, since the power, prestige, and wealth of the ruler ultimately depend on the wealth of the state and its members, a rational ruler has an incentive to maintain a set of institutions including (a) property rights institutions that facilitate production and trade, (b) a judicial system for settling disputes and enforcing contracts, and (c) a system of weights and measures to reduce measurement costs and the potential for rent dissipation [Barzel (1974), Cheung (1974)]. Since the compliance costs of the political system depend on the ruler's perceived legitimacy, the ruler will invest in ideological education to convince constituents of the legitimacy of his (her) authority.

At the second level of the principal-agent problem, the ruler has to employ bureaucrats as agents to assist him (her) in implementing law and order, collecting taxes, inflicting punishment, securing national sovereignty, and providing other public services. An efficient bureaucracy enables the ruler to govern. Nevertheless, bureaucrats are rational individuals whose interests will not completely coincide with those of their principal – the ruler. Hence, bureaucrats attempt to use the authority delegated to them by the ruler to benefit themselves, possibly at the expense of the ruler (state). Since the costs of supervising a bureaucrat's discretionary behavior are likely to be convex, the ruler may reduce the costs of supervision by implementing a reward system

---

[40] Even a monopolistic ruler, however, may face potential competition as in the theory of contestable markets. An interesting example of the importance of control by the principal (the people) over the ruler and his bureaucrats is that of American Indian reservations whose ruler has been in large part the U.S. Bureau of Indian Affairs. Krepps and Caves (forthcoming) show that, at least with respect to their forest resources, once the tribes themselves obtained control over the use of these resources (the result of a 1975 act of the U.S. Congress), the efficiency of resource management and the benefits to the Indians increased substantially [see also Haddock (1994)].

that promotes loyalty to the ruler and by inculcating an ideology that encourages honest and unselfish commitment to one's office.[41] Nevertheless, since discretionary behavior by bureaucrats cannot be completely eliminated, even in totalitarian states the power of ruling the state may be shared between ruler and bureaucrats.

The constraints on the ruler's decision making and the bureaucrat's discretion vary with the nature of the state, often becoming more restrictive as the nature of the state shifts from traditional monarchy, to traditional dictatorship, to authoritarian state and, finally, to democratic state. However, it may not be possible to determine a priori which type of state is more congenial to economic development. If the ruler and bureaucrats in a dictatorship/authoritarian state are enlightened and growth-minded, the economy may perform better than a democratic state whose policies are more likely to be endogenously determined by pork-barrel politics. However, if the opposite holds, the ruler and his bureaucrats may use the effective monopoly of force to repress the mass of the people in the interests of the ruler and his few supporters. Such an economy will perform more poorly than a democratic state. Theoretically, the mean performance of a dictatorship or an authoritarian state may differ little from that of a democratic state, but its variance in performance may be larger [Sah (1991)]. The available empirical evidence supports such a prediction [World Bank (1991), Chapter 7, Przeworski and Limongi (1993)].

However, a dictatorship or authoritarian regime may not be compatible with long-run economic growth. The more successful is such a state in achieving economic development, the more likely it is that the state will face a legitimacy crisis. This is because both a financially independent middle class and the integration of the domestic economy with the world economy are at the same time both necessary conditions for and natural effects of economic success in the modern world. As a result, democratic ideology of DCs may penetrate the middle class and undermine the legitimacy of the regime. These pressures may also force the state to cut its own power of intervention in order to make credible its commitment to such reforms. Thus, authoritarian states may gradually be transformed into democratic states, as seems to be happening in Korea, Taiwan, and Chile.

4.2.2. Why institutional reforms often go astray

As the economy develops, the existing property rights, laws, norms and other institutions may become inefficient. Although some of the disequilibria will be

---

[41] In the modern Third World, the rewards that rulers give to their bureaucrats typically take the form of high paying jobs, import licenses, or contracts assigned by the ruler [Findlay (1990)].

removed by private initiatives, some will persist because of the divergence between private and social benefits and costs and the free-rider problems. The state can play an essential role in restoring institutional equilibrium. Most politicians also see institutional change as a source of economic development because that is the source of change that they have a comparative advantage in bringing about [Matthews (1986)]. Examples assembled by a World Bank study show that "in many instances, the state has stimulated growth by restructuring institutions: the abolition of feudal arrangements and the standardization of currency, taxes, weights and measures, and internal tariffs in revolutionary France in the 1790s; patent laws in nineteenth-century Europe and the United States; the integration of customs, commercial, and civil and commercial law in both Germany and Italy in the nineteenth century; the modernization of Meiji Japan in the second half of the 1800s, and that of Turkey in the early part of this century; Brazil's company-law reforms in the early 1970s; the creation of stock exchanges in East Asia and the economic integration of Western Europe after 1945. All of these depended on state action" [World Bank (1991), p. 135]. However, relatively few LDC states have yet instituted and fully implemented serious institutional reforms resulting in sustained economic growth. The above principal-agent model of autonomous states suggests several alternative explanations for such a failure: discretionary authority of the ruler, ideological rigidity, bureaucracy problems, interest group conflicts, and limitations in social science knowledge.

Discretionary authority and preference of the ruler

The efficiency of an institutional arrangement is defined, in part, by its effects on economic growth. In traditional monarchies, like those in Saudi Arabia and the Gulf oil sheikdoms, the distinction between the public treasury and the private purse of the monarch is blurred [Findlay (1990)]. If the ruler is a wealth maximizer and the treasury is proportional to the national income, within the limit of his authority, the ruler would have an incentive to institute the arrangement that is most efficient. However, although a more efficient property-rights institution may bring higher income to the nation, it may also raise the costs of monitoring, metering and collecting taxes, thereby lowering the ruler's net tax revenues, and lowering the ruler's incentive for creating property rights institutions [North (1979)]. Indeed, the weaker is the linkage between the ruler's wealth and the growth of national income, the more likely a myopic wealth-maximizing ruler bestowed with absolute personal power, (e.g. Marcos in the Philippines), might be tempted to eschew property rights in favor of maximum surplus extraction. Rulers may be especially inclined to predatory taxation and other conditions unfavorable to economic growth when threatened [North and Weingast (1989)].

Furthermore, even if rulers are not deliberately opportunistic, wealth may be only one element of their utility function. If they should be more concerned about their prestige abroad, as perhaps Cuba's Castro and Iraq's Hussain, they may institute arrangements that strengthen military power at the cost of economic growth. Utility maximization in such a case implies that rulers would pay more attention to their own prestige the greater are their wealth, absolute power, and tenure security.[42]

Although rulers who commit to national welfare rather than to personal indulgence and wealth is more likely to initiate growth-enhancing institutional reforms,[43] even with political will, they may still fail to undertake such reforms if the information required to recognize and comprehend the institutional disequilibria and to design and institute appropriate new arrangements are too complex or difficult. The reform failures of the former Soviet Union, Eastern Europe, Castro's Cuba and Sandinista Nicaragua ably demonstrate that good intentions are not sufficient conditions for successful reforms. There are indeed no simple rules, check lists, or optimal sequencing that reform-minded rulers in the Third World can follow so as to improve institutional efficiency. To initiate effective institutional reforms, rulers have to proceed in a step-by-step and trial and error way to distinguish the feasible from the infeasible within existing institutional structures and to introduce viable institutional innovations.

Ideological rigidity

Inasmuch as it becomes difficult and costly to maintain order once the will to obey breaks down, state rule relies on the obedience of its citizens. The transaction costs of state rule are reduced if the constituents strongly believe in the legitimacy of the ruler's authority and the fairness of existing institutional arrangements. Ideology can be perceived as a form of acquired social capital that endows members of the society with feelings of legitimacy concerning the ruler and the existing institutional structure (Lin 1989a). Most LDC states are still ruled by military juntas or one-party dictatorships whose rulers promote ideologies legitimizing their authoritarian rule and inculcate their constituents with such ideologies.

With the passing of time, however, institutional disequilibria may emerge, increasing the gap between the authoritarian ideology and reality due to changes in economic conditions and/or increasing contact with DCs and other

---

[42] That is, as the wealth of the ruler increases, the marginal utility of the wealth declines, and the marginal utilities of other commodities, such as prestige, position in history, and so on, increase. Therefore, the ruler will substitute away from pursuing the enlargement of wealth to pursue prestige and other commodities.

[43] Perkins' (1991) comparison of President Park Chung Hee in South Korea and President Marcos in the Philippines is a good example.

sources of information about democratic ideology. Giving up the old official ideology, however, is likely to undermine the legitimacy of the ruler's authority, as demonstrated during the fall of communist regimes in Eastern Europe and the former Soviet Union. Therefore, instead of reforming the institutional arrangements, LDC rulers may maintain old, inefficient arrangements and battle to purify the ideology for fear that their authority may otherwise be shaken. Hence, institutional reforms are often possible only after the old rulers are replaced by new ones unassociated with the promotion of the old ideology (e.g. as in the case of Spain after the death of Franco). The success of institutional reforms depends very much on the ability of the new rulers to articulate new ideologies that mobilize their nations and unite all factions of power in a new course. However, even if the new ideology is successful, as the economy develops, and the old institutional disequilibria are replaced by new ones, the new ideology could again fetter further reforms in the future.

Bureaucratic discretion

As discussed above, the power of ruling a state is shared by the ruler and his bureaucrats. Institutional development requires not only enlightened rulers but also effective administrative bureaucrats responsive to changing needs. However, as agents of the ruler, bureaucrats have personal interests that differ from both those of the ruler and those of the ruler's principal, the people. A policy promulgated by the ruler is bound to be distorted so as to favor the bureaucrats. In some cases, there is collusion between bureaucrats and others so as to divide up the revenue of the state by bribe-taking and rent-seeking.[44] In other cases, the bureaucrats may undermine or sabotage the policies of their rulers in order to safeguard their own interests. For example, many rulers in the former socialist economies of Eastern Europe had been aware of the weaknesses of central planning and introduced various reforms to decentralize management in the state sectors, but with little or no success. Winiecki (1990) argues that the reforms failed primarily because of sabotage by middle-level agents of the party and the bureaucracy who (with the reforms) would have had to forgo the rents that they enjoyed under the existing system.

---

[44] Indeed, such collusion may partially explain the following puzzle posed by Srinivasan (1992): Why do governments often choose policies that, from an economist's perspective, impose avoidable welfare costs on society? For example, although the least costly way to encourage domestic production of an importable is via direct production subsidies rather than by imposing tariffs or quotas on imports, in practice governments often choose tariffs and quotas. This is probably due to the facts that subsidies are likely to give rise to conflicts among the various producers and that bureaucrats find tariffs and quotas easier to implement and may generate for them opportunities of bribe-taking. Similarly, tariffs and quotas (rather than direct taxes) are used as measures to discourage luxury consumption of importable.

An efficient bureaucracy does not in itself guarantee success in institutional reform. Indeed, it can even retard the necessary changes. Yet, if the rulers can restrain bureaucratic discretion and if the polity can ensure the functioning of efficient bureaucracies, then the likelihood of success in implementing institutional reforms will be greatly increased.

Interest group conflicts

As noted above, since changes in institutional arrangements often redistribute wealth, income, and political power among various groups of constituents, if the losers from such changes are not compensated, they are likely to oppose them. Even uncertainty about the distribution of gains and losses from a given reform may cause the ex post gainers to oppose it and carry the day ex ante [Fernandez and Rodrik (1991)]. Also, if the opponents of the institutional reform are reliable supporters, the ruler will be reluctant to institute a change for fear of eroding his own political support.

Feeny (1982, Chapter 7) finds for Thailand that, because the elite stood to gain little from socially desirable public investments in irrigation, such investments were not made by the government; as a result, Thai agricultural development was retarded. Similarly, in Old-Regime France of the eighteenth century, although the advantages of consolidating scattered land strips by enclosure were known, this was not done and, as a result, French agriculture failed to attain English levels of productivity. The reason for this failure was because although, in principle, the rights to graze animals on the land were the property of the entire village, in practice they were the property of the wealthy peasants and others who controlled the village governments. Enclosing the fields and eliminating the strips would have removed the grazing rights of the wealthy and powerful. While the French king was personally favorable to such enclosures, he failed to bring it about because of the opposition of the wealthy animal owners [Hoffman (1989)]. For similar reasons, profitable irrigation systems were not constructed until after the revolution that wiped out the power of the local elites (Rosenthal 1991). In a similar vein, de Janvry and Sadoulet (1989) argue that the very limited redistribution of land in Latin America during the 1960s and 1970s, in spite of the widespread implementation of land reform, is attributable to the fact that the medium and large farmers used their hegemony to secure two advantages from the state: (1) a credible promise of nonexpropriation of modernized operations and (2) subsidized credit to externalize part of the cost of modernization. With its budget tied up in providing subsidized credit for modernization, the state found itself unable to purchase even the agreed upon non-modernized lands for land reform.

The monopoly power of the ruler is constrained by potential rivals – inside or outside the state – who can provide the same services. Those constituents with easy access to the rivals of the ruler should have strong bargaining power and hence should receive more and better services from the ruler. A change will not be instituted if such a change would drive such groups to the ruler's rivals and if the benefits that the ruler gains from the remaining constituents would not compensate for the ruler's loss of support of the former groups [North (1981), Chapter 3]. Furthermore, as discussed in Section 4.1.2, a ruler may not be able to resist the requests from powerful groups to institute institutional changes that redistribute income to this group, even though such changes would be detrimental to the growth of the economy.

Limitations of social science knowledge

As in Section 3.3 concerning transaction costs, the choice set of institutional arrangements is bounded by the stock of social science knowledge. Even if it has the intention to initiate a correct institutional reform, the state may fail to institute the reform because of inadequate knowledge either of it or of how to bring it about. Many LDCs adopted Soviet-type central planning in the early fifties as an institution for rapid industrialization. Although it is hard to determine how much of this policy was a direct result of the prevailing social knowledge at that time as opposed to past experience and other factors, Bauer (1984), Lal (1985) and Krueger (1994) have demonstrated that such policy was validated by the then-prevailing theory of economic development.

Drawing on the history of the last three centuries of English and other Western economies, Schultz (1977) finds that the alteration and establishment of various distinct political – economic institutional arrangements in various societies were induced or shaped by the dominant – though not necessarily correct – social ideas of those times. Even more fundamentally, appropriate policy solutions are ruled out by the limited availability of information and experience.

The limitation of social science knowledge is especially acute with respect to the design of institutional reforms in LDCs. The defect lies in ignorance of not only the identity of the optimal institutions but also how to institute them. Both issues reflect the failures of social scientists to unite general theory with the specific institutional structures of LDCs. Most modern social science has been developed in DCs and assumes their legal, political and economic institutions to be ones essential for the economic, political, and social development of LDCs [Trubek (1972)]. However, since the institutional structures of LDCs are different from those of DCs, some institutions regarded as inefficient in DCs may turn out to be efficient given the specific institutional structures of LDCs.

For example, notions from contemporary DC conditions and outdated economic theorizing that share-cropping, interlinked credit markets, and other agrarian institutions are inefficient and inequality-increasing have permeated many land reforms in LDCs. More realistic (for LDCs) theoretical work, based on costly information and incomplete markets, has begun to question this notion [Binswanger and Rosenzweig (1986), Stiglitz (1988)]. Likewise, tribal institutions, such as chiefs and communal ownership of land, can perform the important functions of reducing externality and free-rider problems in scarcely populated, arid and semi-arid LDCs where conditions are quite different than in Europe and North America [Binswanger and McIntire (1987), Binswanger, McIntire and Udry (1988), Nugent and Sanchez, (1988, 1993), Nugent (1993)]. Such institutions are often regarded as inefficient and barriers to economic development. Many African countries have practiced various policies designed to eliminate these institutions. While some of these policies have been well motivated, often they were based on faulty understanding of local conditions (e.g. aridity) in general and of the special problems of certain activities (like transhumance) in particular. Not surprisingly, therefore, the results of those policies have often been rather disastrous [Nugent and Sanchez (1993)].

Yet, correct social science knowledge, by itself at least, is not a sufficient condition for successful reforms. Even if there were no question as to the identity of the optimal institutions, there would still exist the question of how to bring these institutions about. Institutional reforms inevitably result in redistributions of income and power among various economic groups and may require political reforms as well. Therefore, questions such as "Should the strategy of reforms be gradual or big bang?" and "Should political reforms precede economic reforms?" are likely to arise. What is the appropriate constitutional regime for guiding the recontracting process which is clearly so important for the attainment of institutions befitting their environments.

Yet, clearly, such questions can be answered only with a good grasp of the delicate balance of power between various groups, the legitimacy of the government, the political skill of the ruler, the capacity of the bureaucracy, and so forth. Only recently, especially after the dramatic events in Eastern Europe and the former Soviet Union, has research on dynamic and country-specific issues of reforms started to appear [Dewatripont and Roland (1992a, 1992b), Sachs (1992), Kornai (1990), McMillan and Naughton, (1992), Lin, Cai, and Li (1993)]. However, the development of the link between theory in general and country-specific knowledge in particular has lagged far behind the demand. Therefore, institutional reform in a country very often has to proceed on a "trial and error" basis and success remains heavily dependent on the luck and ingenuity of the political leaders.

5. Important institutional changes in the process of development

If the aforementioned principles of institutional analysis are to be considered useful and to serve as a guide in future research, they will have to demonstrate:

(1) that they can help explain some of the major institutional changes that take place in the process of development and (2) that they can be operationalized and hence facilitate hypothesis testing as in the other more standard areas of economic research. The purpose of this section is to illustrate some applications in which the first of these abilities is demonstrated. The second of these abilities and the rather formidable problems involved in them are the subjects of Section 6.

In the five subsections of this section institutional explanations are outlined for the following important changes: the rise and decline of families, the rise of money, credit and other instruments for conducting transactions over long distances, changes in contractual forms, the substitution of state services for those supplied by communities and kinship groups, changes in political economy and public policy, and the development of property rights.[45] Admittedly, the proposed applications of the analysis to the explanation of some major institutional changes are illustrative; they are not based on carefully constructed tests with reliable data and clear-cut outcomes.

5.1. The rise and fall of families and households

The available historical evidence indicates that many developing countries were originally (and some still are) dominated by tribal societies in which the tribe, clan or community was (is) the basic unit of society.[46] In such societies, land and other resources were (are) held in common, and many activities, such as hunting and gathering and some forms of animal husbandry, were (are) undertaken collectively. Cooperation among members is crucial to both success in economic activity and the minimization of risks, including those threatening to very survival.

Nevertheless, as land and natural resources become relatively scarcer, the nature of economic activity changes and family households become dominant as the basic unit of society within which the bulk of economic activity takes place.[47] At a later stage, however, firms and markets grow in importance and size, thereby eclipsing the role of households in several important respects. How can the insights of institutional economics help explain this pattern of the rise and fall of households, especially in production?

As agricultural and other more labor-intensive activities replace hunting, gathering and animal husbandry, but without appreciable reductions in pro-

---

[45] Since the latter receives considerable attention both in Chapter 45 of this volume and some attention in other sections of this chapter, our focus is on the other institutional changes.

[46] See, e.g. Lee (1968), Posner (1980) and Smith (1991) and the references therein.

[47] This may well occur even though the members of different households remain related to one another through kinship and kinship relations remain strong.

duction risk, opportunism in the form of labor shirking becomes a more serious threat to success in collective activities. As a result, it becomes economic to encourage self-supervision. This can better be accomplished within smaller and more spatially concentrated family households than within larger and more dispersed tribes or bands. Therefore, by making the household the residual claimant in the proceeds of its activities and the members thereof shareholders in those claims, and by giving the head rather strong powers over resource allocation, coordination and the application of selective incentives, the transaction costs of labor shirking can be reduced. Naturally, the transaction cost saving in moving from the tribe or community to the household would be the determining factor only in the absence of economies of scale in production and risk reduction.

Since agricultural technologies are generally characterized by constant or even decreasing returns to scale,[48] this part of the condition is generally fulfilled and accounts for why the family farm has become so pervasive in agriculture throughout the world. The risk-reduction benefits of the greater scale and scope offered by tribes and regions are less easily overcome. Nevertheless, households have adopted various ingenious strategies for dealing with the problem, thereby gaining the transaction cost reductions without substantially increasing production cost or risk.

When transport costs are high (as they often are in less developed and sparsely settled regions) and guarantees of quality are limited to the local community (where personal reputations are highly valued, easily checked, and impacted by performance), product markets may remain relatively undeveloped. As a result, production in most agricultural households is largely limited to self-consumption.

At the same time, the importance of risk and the absence of insurance leads most agricultural households to adopt a crop diversification production strategy. Household units often attempt to further reduce their risks (which in addition to those of production and price include also vulnerability to theft, disability and death) by making the households rather large in size and diverse in composition by including members of different age, gender, and generations through vertical and/or horizontal extension. They also attempt to build bridges with both wealthier households in the same community, as in patron – client relations, and more distant households, e.g. by sending children to relatives and/or by marrying daughters or sons into other households with implicit contracts for mutual help provision between households.[49] Hence, principles of transaction costs can go a long way toward explaining the rise of family households.

[48] See, for example, Yotopoulos and Nugent (1976).
[49] See especially Rosenzweig (1988).

As incomes rise with development, however, consumption patterns move away from basic goods toward luxuries and manufactures in which production technologies are characterized by greater (a) division of labor, (b) capital-intensity, (c) economies of scale, and (d) economies of scope (in coordinating the larger number of more specialized agents). These changes also imply (a) the growing importance of new forms of opportunism (e.g. asset misuse and failure to cooperate) and hence also (b) economies of scope in supervision. As a result, the locus of production shifts to hierarchical firms that both provide the capital and hire, train, supervise, and coordinate the laborers and other inputs purchased from households and markets. Consequently, households become less important as units of production.

To mitigate agency costs, early firms are often family firms. Eventually, however, family firms give way to non-family firms when the specialization, scale, and economies of scope in supervision advantages of larger firms with more highly differentiated tasks within them outweigh the transaction cost disadvantages of greater size and asset specificity.[50] In short, the comparative rise and fall of family households in the process of development can be attributed to a combination of changes in consumption patterns, technology, and transaction costs.

5.2. The rise of markets and related institutions

For local transactions involving products, factors, credit, and insurance, barter arrangements within and among families or between households within communities may be adequate. Indeed, the intimate mutual knowledge and observability that is possible within families (and to a lesser extent within communities), and the ability of household heads (or community heads and elders) to impose penalties on those failing to live up to what was expected of them, imply that the transaction costs of contract monitoring and enforcement would be lower within households (and to a lesser extent within communities) than between households and communities, especially those far apart from one another.[51]

As the importance of capital continues to increase, it becomes necessary to attract capital from beyond the bounds of both individual households (even

---

[50] Nabli, Nugent, and Doghri (1989) use these principles to explain variations in the organizational form and size of manufacturing firms in Tunisia both across sectors and over time. Particular attention is given to an organizational form of the partnership variety, which combines the advantages of the individual family firm with the limited liability and capital accumulation benefits of the corporate form.

[51] This explains why lower-valued types of labor such as child and female labor may not be transacted between households and why wage and price differentials may be quite large between different villages. For evidence of the latter see Bardhan and Rudra (1986).

very wealthy ones) and individual communities. Since the traditional sanctions for default on credit or the concealing of profit shares by social ostracism or the withdrawal of future borrowing privileges are no longer sufficient, different kinds of credit and risk-reducing institutions are needed, such as credit bureaus, loans based on collateral, futures markets for commodities and money, and bond and equity markets. Likewise, the right to reciprocal credit is no longer a sufficient inducement to the supply of interest-free or low-interest loans. Hence, new forms of ownership, such as the infinitely lived and limited liability corporation, new forms of credit, such as those requiring the deposit of valuable collateral, and complementary facilitating institutions, like letters of credit, notary publics, and courts capable of imposing harsh penalties on defaulters, are all developed.

In small, closed communities, quality control and effective delivery can be accomplished at low cost by the abilities to transmit information about product quality from one consumer to another and to penalize suppliers of low quality goods by withholding future purchases or forcing severe price discounting.[52] In larger and more open communities, and with products that are more sophisticated and less frequently purchased but also traded across longer distances, however, such means of assuring quality become either more costly or less effective (or both). For example, as the distance of transactions and the risk of loss in shipment or trans-shipment increase, naturally the more expensive it is to have the seller guarantee security in all such phases by personally accompanying the goods. A lower cost alternative is for each person (firm) in the shipment process to take responsibility for delivery to the next person (firm) in the link.

As a result, instruments, like the issuance of guarantees of various kinds (e.g. of refunds to non-satisfied customers), trademarks, the registration of signed contracts, bills of lading, letters of credit, contract law with stipulated penalties for non-performance, and product liability suits, are developed. These instruments, at least when used together and backed up by the complementary legal environment of laws and courts, can operate effectively even over long distances.[53]

Another not always easily satisfied requirement for long-distance trade, either domestic or international, is security over markets and transport routes and hence of safe delivery of the goods. In the absence of states with their

---

[52] Kuran (1989) provides a fascinating and still observable example of a quality guarantee institution, namely the "amin", a knowledgeable, respected, and objective individual to whom consumers had access for purposes of testing sellers' claims concerning the authenticity and quality of the goods in question.

[53] Greif (1992) develops a model for dealing with opportunism with respect to non-reimbursement of sellers for exported goods and identifies these institutional innovations as not necessarily unique solutions to the problem.

police powers or international police forces to provide such security, from collective action theory one could hypothesize that such security would be more likely to be provided the fewer and more concentrated are the agents capable of providing such security. An interesting historical example in Africa that would seem to be consistent with this hypothesis is that of the Touareg of the Sahara and Sahel regions of Africa. The hierarchical structure of this tribe implied that very few members were capable of providing adequate protection to caravans across the region. Since these same people also dominated the trade itself, they had maximum incentive to provide security (the incentive to free-ride on the activities of others being minimal).[54]

Naturally, different societies have different cultural and legal environments, and the character of the environments within which economic activities and transactions take place also affects the relative transaction costs of different institutional arrangements. As a result, these environmental differences can affect both the nature of the institutions at any point in time and their evolution over time.[55]

Long-distance trading, credit, and other transactions also require means of payment that are either accepted internationally or convertible to an international standard. This in turn may require exchange rate stability or some means of coping with exchange risk, such as forward exchange rate markets and convertibility guarantees.

The benefits relative to costs of all these instruments or institutional arrangements are likely to be unequally distributed among the various social groups in any given society. As a result, there are bound to be some losers (even for socially desirable changes in institutional arrangements), and the losers may be capable of resisting socially desirable institutional changes. For this reason, the mere growth in the relative importance of long-distance

---

[54] North (1990, 1991), however, argues that, because Tuareg success and leadership in the caravan trade relies on the value of their personal reputation (i.e. in situations where they are known personally to their customers), their leaders would have little incentive to develop new and potentially competing institutions capable of facilitating anonymous long-distance transactions. He claims this to be the reason why further institutional development did not take place in that region. While North has a point, the principles of collective action would suggest that the same Tuareg could have been just as successful in bringing about the new institutions as the old ones, if (contrary to fact) there had been sufficient demand for such trade and hence for the institutions to support it.

[55] For example, Greif (1992) argues that the information system of the Maghrebi traders of North Africa was much better than that of Genoese traders of the Middle Ages inasmuch as the culturally "collectivist" characteristics of the former gave everyone – not only the direct parties to a contract – the incentive to provide relevant information on contract fulfillment, whereas the individualist character of the latter gave no one except the direct parties to the contract incentives to provide such information. This difference is used to explain why the former traders continued to use the same system based on personal reputation and informal enforcement mechanisms, whereas the latter introduced the various institutional innovations mentioned in the text.

exchange may be no guarantee that the aforementioned transaction-cost-reducing institutional changes may be undertaken.

As a result, the supply of institutional change becomes relevant, implying potential for explaining the adoption or nonadoption of institutional change in terms of the theory of collective action. The transaction cost advantages of international convertibility and other related institutional changes should be expected to rise with income and decline with size of country, and, from collective action theory, the barriers to collective action in the support of such changes should be weaker in sectors and countries dominated by small numbers of geographically concentrated individuals. These expectations are consistent with the fact that it is primarily small and relatively high-income developing economies like Taiwan, Uruguay, Hong Kong, Singapore, Bahrain, Costa Rica, pre-civil war Lebanon, and Panama that have most consistently and successfully maintained currency convertibility and financial liberalism.

5.3. Changes in contractual forms

In the case of simple contracts among relatively few agents, changes in contractual form may require, instead of collective action, only the leadership of one party to the contract (or consensus among the various parties) to bring them about. Hence, for the most part, such changes should be explicable in terms of transaction costs.

The aforementioned increases in capital intensity, economies of scale and complexity, and the division of labor, all associated with the process of economic development, could be expected to raise the costs of both asset misuse and the failure to coordinate. As a result, according to the principles of transaction costs articulated in Section 3 above, one would expect the choice among contracts to shift from rent[56] and share contracts to fixed wage contracts. That this has been the case in mining, manufacturing, and transportation, is well established.[57] The pattern in agriculture is less clear since local environmental circumstances (including the availability of reliable supervisory personnel and the specific crop and its technology) tend to make quite a difference. Fishing is something of an exception in that both teamwork and various kinds of risk remain very important. Also, working in close proximity aboard a fishing boat facilitates mutual monitoring and makes for economies of scope in monitoring the various sources of opportunistic behavior to which

---

[56] Frequently, however, rental contracts are ruled out by greater risk aversion by the potential tenant than by the asset owner and/or by insufficient ability to pay in advance.

[57] A short but relatively broad survey of these sectors is provided by Datta and Nugent (1989).

share contracts are vulnerable. As a result, share contracts remain dominant in most types of fishing.[58]

Let us consider a less frequently treated, but nevertheless important, activity, namely, tax collection. In many developing countries from North and West Africa to China, taxes were for long periods of their history collected by "tax farmers", i.e. individuals or firms to whom the right to collect a certain kind of tax in a certain area for a certain period of time was rented out, generally for a specified fixed payment in kind or cash.

Collecting taxes with this method can be advantageous in the following conditions: (a) the quantity or value of the item to be taxed is difficult to measure or the tax payment difficult to extract from the taxed agent (i.e. the transaction costs are relatively high); (b) in the absence of an insurance market and with considerable uncertainty as to the amount of tax revenue that can be collected in any given year, the government to whom the tax is owed is more risk-averse than the agent who collects it; (c) the technology of tax collection is labor intensive, implying that labor shirking in tax collection is the primary source of opportunistic behavior (as opposed to overexploitation of the party who pays the tax); and (d) there are economies of scope in the various stages of the tax collection process (identification of taxable activities, assessment, collection, enforcement, and appeal) so that all can be done by a single agent rather than separately by different specialized agents. In such circumstances, tax farming can be advantageous because, being a residual claimant to his own efforts, the tax farmer has the maximum incentive to collect the taxes. Azabou and Nugent (1988) demonstrate (a) that the rise and fall of tax farming over time and space more or less coincide with environmental and institutional changes that would be expected to trigger such changes and (b) that tax farming continues to be practiced with reasonably satisfactory results in the taxation of periodic markets in Tunisia and other LDCs. Such taxation is an important source of income for local government in rural areas.[59]

5.4. The substitution of the state for smaller groups in the provision of public goods and services

In Section 4 above, it was explained why groups may find it advantageous to get the state to produce the public goods they need or desire rather than doing

---

[58] For more details see Platteau and Nugent (1992).

[59] In particular, since these local communities are not able to borrow and have relatively fixed payments for their employees, they are more risk-averse than the tax farmers, who at any given time generally have a diversified portfolio of different tax farms. As a result, they arrange a competitive auction and auction off the right to a certain tax farm for one year to the highest bidder.

so themselves. As this happens over time, it contributes to the explanation of the growing relative importance of the state in public goods production. Moreover, some of the principles of institutional analysis identified in preceding sections can contribute to the explanation of the rising importance of the state.

One factor leading to this result is the aforementioned notion of interest group competition [Becker (1983)]. When those on one side of an issue pressure the state to do something for them, those on the other side may have to get the state to do the same for them.

An even more important element in the explanation may lie in the fact that various traditional norms that underpin the efficient functioning of informal institutions of the community, ethnic, tribal, kinship, religious, and other groups are systematically undermined by various characteristics of the development process. Consider the example of the norm that children have the responsibility to care for their elderly parents. As urban labor markets grow in size, scope, and attraction, adult children from rural areas may have greater incentive to exit from the community, quite possibly abandoning their traditional responsibilities in the process. Once they have left, the traditional means of sanctioning them for norm violation may no longer be effective. As a result, sooner or later, such norms may begin to break down even among those remaining in the community. So, too, through its regulatory and tax powers, and production of public goods, the state itself may be the source that undermines traditional norms. State supply of public goods may crowd out their supply from informal (non-state) sources.

No matter what the source of undermining traditional norms, once they have been undermined, the public may demand that care to the elderly and other services be supplied by the state through more formal mechanisms. Because small, highly concentrated groups (like government and unionized workers) are likely to be more successful in this than larger, more dispersed ones (like farmers), it is likely that the availability of such services will at first be limited to the much more well-off urban residents. Their appearance, of course, further undermines the viability of the traditional, informal systems. As indicated in Section 5.2 above, among the prerequisites for these more formal mechanisms are laws (and hence legislatures), agencies to monitor compliance with and implementation of such laws, and judges and courts to review the relevant evidence of law violation, decide upon the degree of guilt, and choose and enforce the appropriate penalties. These are all activities over which, thanks to their superior compulsion power, states have typically been abrogating more exclusive rights and powers and now enjoy a distinct comparative advantage relative to tribal and community groups.[60]

---

[60] See especially Stiglitz (1989).

Another reason, again implicit from the preceding sections, is that, as the geographic scope of exchange expands, so too does the scope of market externalities (technology, information and marketing activities all having characteristics of public goods). Such externalities can be better internalized by the state than by local government or other institutions and states often enjoy easier and lower cost access to the resources used in producing public goods. This access is attributable partly to the dominance of state-to-state capital flows in official development assistance, but also, and certainly more importantly, to the tax power of the state, which in turn derives from its greater power of compulsion.

What lies behind the compulsion power of the state? Even here the principles of collective action would seem applicable in that this power is inversely related to the ability to exit. Tribes and local governments are normally weaker than the state in that it is easier to exit from them and hence to avoid being taxed by them than in the case of states.

Finally, there is growing realization of the importance of credibility to the effectiveness of state intervention. Credibility, in turn, depends on factors such as (a) the absolute amount of resources available for backing up a certain intervention (such as the stocks of commodities or foreign exchange available for intervening in such markets), (b) past experience and (c) the ability to conduct international treaties that bind the state's future actions (as in the case of Mexican participation in NAFTA). Because of the importance of critical mass with respect to factor (a) and the state's exclusive power to conduct the treaties relevant to factor (c), both of these considerations favor the state relative to lower level groups.

5.5. Changes in political economy and policy orientation

As is well known, the most characteristic feature of state policy in LDCs is the distinct tilt in such policy in favor of urban interests and against the relatively poor rural interests.[61] Especially sharp in such countries is the sizable difference in the relative influence exerted over policy between farmers and industrialists. These biases appear in many kinds of policy, ranging from the allocation of credit and tariff rates on inputs and outputs to the provision of government services and so on.[62] In virtually all respects, farmers (excluding large plantation owners) are disadvantaged [Landsberger and Hewitt (1970), Bates (1981), Lipton (1977)] relative to industrialists.

Numerous elements of the theory of collective action identified in Section 4.1

---

[61] This is what Lipton (1977) calls the "urban bias". See also Bates (1981).
[62] For evidence, see Balassa and Associates (1971) and Lutz and Scandizzo (1980).

contribute to the explanation of these biases. Compared with farmers, industrialists are usually fewer in number, have more differentiated goals (some being more demanding of credit, others of subsidized interest rates, imports, or electricity), and are likely to be more highly concentrated geographically and sectorally, thereby making it easier for them to plan and execute collective action, including the monitoring of free-riding.[63] Frequently also, the industrial sector is characterized by greater inequality in the distribution of assets and size than the agricultural sector, thereby reducing the incentives for free-riding. In the early stages of industrial development, because their wage rates and hence incomes are relatively low, industrial workers are likely to spend large fractions of their disposable incomes on food, making them especially sensitive, and hence resistant, to higher food prices. By contrast, for agriculturalists, and especially for small landowners and (landless) agricultural laborers, exit in the form of migration to the cities may constitute a relatively attractive and easy alternative to the use of "voice", i.e. remaining in agriculture to fight for better conditions [Bates (1981)].

Another generally recognized pattern of relative influence is that the direction of the policy bias among sectors tends to be reversed in countries at higher levels of development.[64] Once again, this seeming anomaly can be explained in terms of the theory of collective action. As development proceeds and massive rural-urban migration takes place, most of the effects described above are reversed. For instance, the industrial sector becomes larger, less geographically concentrated, more heterogeneous, and thus more difficult to organize. At the same time, as agriculturalists become fewer in number, more concentrated in cultivating specific commercial crops, more dependent on the ability to market their agricultural surplus, and better endowed with capital, transport and communications as to make exit a less viable possibility, both their need for collective action and their ability to bring it about are greatly enhanced. Also, because of the smaller size of the agricultural sector, the cost burden of agricultural subsidies is less threatening to other potential coalition partners as it would have been before [Bates and Rogerson (1980), Balisacan and Roumasset (1987)].

Another potentially fruitful application of the theory of collective action is in distinguishing success from failure in the formation, maintenance, and improvement of squatter communities. For example, homogeneity of origin, the high cost of exit once their living quarters have been erected, and the actual or

---

[63] Naturally, the bias would be reversed when the situation is characterized by only a few large, commercially oriented landholders and many small, dispersed industrial producers such as in some Latin American countries.

[64] This is demonstrated in the studies of Balassa and Associates (1971), Guttman (1978), Krueger (1978), Binswanger and Scandizzo (1983), Anderson and Hayami (1986), and Balisacan and Roumasset (1987).

perceived threat from the actions of opposing groups, such as the state and its instruments (the military or police), have been found to be extremely important factors in determining the strength of collective action in squatter communities [Hirschman (1984)]. Squatting is more common on public land than on private land precisely since squatters believe the chances of ouster to be less likely. Since the strength and likelihood of collective action on the part of squatters rise with the extent of the threatened loss arising from inaction, it is easy to understand why collective action is at a peak when the threat of eviction is greatest, but then, once the threat of eviction falls, even the most collectively active squatter groups return to their original state of latency [Gilbert and Ward (1985)].

6. Empirical problems and applications

The purpose of this section is to illustrate in more detail the methodological problems faced in empirical studies of the determinants and effects of institutions. Section 6.1 reviews a number of empirical studies of sharecropping in a number of different countries. It identifies both problems and the advantages and disadvantages of different approaches to these problems. Section 6.2 provides a more detailed demonstration of testing an application of the induced institutional change hypothesis to the decollectivization of Chinese agriculture between 1979 and 1982. Section 6.3 provides an even more powerful demonstration of the important methodological problems facing institutional analyses in the context of assessments of the effect of property rights on investment. It also provides an appropriate note of caution on the validity of even some of the most widely cited findings of institutional analyses and the need for more and better data to permit more rigorous tests.

6.1. Empirical applications to sharecropping

As mentioned above, the most frequently performed empirical tests with respect to tenure type in general and sharecropping in particular have been for productivity differences of land under different forms of contract. Many – but certainly not all – such studies have demonstrated productivity to be higher under self-cultivation and fixed rent than under share contracts. Yet, most of these studies have simply *assumed* the tenure choice to be exogenous, something of dubious validity from the institutional economics perspective. This flaw could have serious consequences for the outcome of such productivity tests since for example a landowner might be more willing to lease-out land of lower quality (and hence less vulnerable to asset misuse) than higher quality land. In other words, the self-selectivity bias could be quite substantial in such studies.

The fact that so many studies[65] have shown land under sharecropping to be less productive than land under other types of tenure has called even more attention to the paradox of sharecropping: "if sharecropping is inefficient, why is it so widely practiced?" Yet, despite the persistence of the paradox, as noted in the preceding section, there has in fact been a trend away from share contracts in many activities, even including agriculture. Hence, of particular interest, are situations where the incidence of sharecropping is high or even on the rise.

As reported in Matoussi and Nugent (1989), one place where such a trend in favor of sharecropping (from both wage and rent contracts) is evident is one of Tunisia's best agricultural areas near the town of Medjez-el-Bab. In this area, located on the bank of Tunisia's only important river (the Medjerda), the incidence of sharecropping increased sharply between 1970 and 1985.[66] Whereas prior to 1970 over 75 percent of the contracts[67] were in the form of wage contracts and the remainder relatively evenly split between rent and share contracts, by 1985 almost 75 percent of the contracts were share contracts and the remaining 25 percent split between wage and to a lesser extent rent contracts.

Naturally, over this fifteen year period the region had experienced quite a few environmental changes which could have contributed to the changes in contract. The most important of these were: (1) a rapid rise in real agricultural wage rates, (2) growing scarcity in supervisory labor (due to the outmigration of almost all the adult children of heads of household), (3) a sharp increase in irrigation, making it possible to grow two crops per year instead of one, and (4) as a result of both better farm-to-market transportation and irrigation, a shift in the cropping pattern in favor of high-valued, labor intensive crops in which know-how was also important. The higher real wage rates, labor intensity, and multiple cropping imply a substantial increase in the potential costs of labor shirking per unit of land. Yet, the outmigration of secondary workers in the landowning families implied a decreasing ability of such families to provide the necessary monitoring. At the same time, the increased importance of irrigation equipment (increasing the potential importance of asset misuse) and know-how (to that point virtually exclusively possessed by

---

[65] See Shaban (1987) and Otsuka, Chuma and Hayami (1992).

[66] While this region is rather small and not necessarily representative of the country as a whole, research-wise, since one of the authors (Matoussi) was from this town, it offered the advantage of being able to collect high quality and easily checked information from all households in the area at various points in time. For a more recent study showing still another change in contractual form see Laffont and Matoussi (1993).

[67] Note the use of the contract instead of the household or land area as the unit of analysis.

the landowners) induced a switch away from rent contracts. The authors concluded that under the circumstances, the switch to share contracts reduced transaction costs by diminishing both the need for labor supervision (relative to wage contracts) and the vulnerability to asset misuse (relative to fixed rent contracts).[68]

As evidence in support of their conclusion the authors provided both the subjective and qualitative responses of the landowners who had switched from wage to share contracts and more quantitative evidence explaining variations in the choice of contracts in 1985. The qualitative evidence was based on the ranked responses to a question asking the landowners to rank by importance the various reasons listed for their switch to share contracts. The responses "permits increased productivity of the primary worker" and "alleviates the need for supervision" were ranked highest on a list of six alternatives, both entirely consistent with a transaction cost explanation.

For their quantitative evidence the authors construct simple measures and proxies (based on characteristics considered relevant to contractual choice) from both landowning and worker households. They then use these measures to explain the variation in the incidence of share contracts (the dummy variable ISHARE) across all contracts observed in the sample. Specifically, the explanatory variables were as follows: the landowner's endowments of (1) land (in hectares), (2) irrigated land, (3) hydraulic equipment, and (4) labor, dummy variables for the following alternative principal occupations of the landowner, (5) agriculturalist, (6) civil servant, and (7) emigrant (an absentee landowner), (8) the labor endowment of the working household, and (9) the supply of credit by the owner to the working household.

Since the dependent variable ISHARE is a dummy variable, the logistic form of the estimating equation is used. Since credit to the working household, quite conceivably, could be considered to be determined jointly with the type of contract, the logistic regression is estimated twice, once with the credit variable as an included exogenous variable and once with it excluded (as a reduced form equation for ISHARE in a simultaneous system).

Because of economies of scale in supervision, and that large farms in the region typically have land of lower quality, the effect of owner's acreage would be expected to be negative. Since irrigation increases the labor-intensity of

---

[68] The authors also explained how the disadvantage of share contracts, namely, their vulnerability to output underreporting, was avoided. In particular, the facts that the head of household was resident on the farm and that the farms were almost all very small, and subject to economies of scope in supervision made it possible for resident landowners to monitor labor, asset use and the quantity of output at the same time without a great deal of help. An entire field was planted with a single specialty crop (like tomatoes, lettuce or watermelon) for which the workers would have limited appetites. This combined with the fact that the entire crop ripened at the same time served to control the one remaining threat to output underreporting (consumption in the field by the workers).

production, both measures of irrigation would be expected to have positive effects on the incidence of share contracts (ISHARE). Because of economies of scope in supervision, if the landowner's primary occupation were agriculture (emigrant), it would be expected to have a positive (negative) influence on ISHARE. Since a larger endowment of labor by the landowning household would reduce the importance of substituting self-supervision for direct supervision, its effect would be expected to be negative. Since share contracts facilitate the use of nonmarketed labor, the effect of labor endowment of the working household would be expected to be positive. Finally, since the provision of credit by the landowner can make it easier for the share tenant to bear risks and afford to wait until harvest time to receive remuneration, its effect should be positive.

While conceivably still other explanatory variables could be jointly determined and some of the measures are far less than optimal, the results generally supported the above hypotheses.[69] In a subsequent study in the same region, Laffont and Matoussi (1993) explain the dominance of share contracts in a different way. They disregard opportunism in the form of output under reporting and asset misuse, thereby concentrating (as in much of the literature) on that of labor shirking. In such a context, rent contracts would be optimal, but according to Laffont and Matoussi, are largely ruled out (in the absence of a credit market) by financial constraints on the ability of working households to pay a fixed rent. Share contracts are thus a second best.

Some methodological advantages of this study are that it (1) makes more use of a formal economizing framework in deriving the relationships to be estimated empirically and (2) treats the share of output accruing to the tenant as a continuous variable (ranging from 0 for a wage contract to 1 for a rent contract with various shares in between) instead of only a dummy variable as in Matoussi and Nugent. Since the measures of the financial constraint variables, however, are largely the same as those in Matoussi and Nugent and are again highly significant, the difference between them is largely in the interpretation of their role (in the former case representing not financial capability but rather their vulnerability to asset misuse and non-marketability). This comparison of studies using largely the same data but deriving quite different conclusions reveals a common methodological problem in empirical analyses of institutional arrangements, namely that the same proxies may be interpreted so as to represent quite different variables and to yield different conclusions.

The final step in the Laffont and Matoussi analysis is a demonstration that efficiency in the use of various inputs varies significantly in ways predicted by the theory, being higher on rent contracts than under wage and share

---

[69] For further explanation, details on the measures, and qualifications, see Matoussi and Nugent (1989).

contracts.[70] No attempt is made either to account for variations in land quality across contract types (assumed to be quite important in the earlier study) or to distinguish between overuse of the land under rent contracts and higher productivity. Yet, unlike many of the other studies of productivity which merely *assume* the choice of contracts to be exogenous in the determination of productivity, these authors test for it (and find it supported).

At least two methodological problems in the aforementioned and many other similar studies are overcome in the study of Shaban (1987). This empirical study was based on ICRISAT data on farm households in several villages in semi-arid parts of India for different years between 1975 and 1982. Like the study of Laffont and Matoussi (1993), this study focuses on the under supply of inputs (primarily labor-shirking) as the primary source of moral hazard and hence on the Marshallian inefficiency of sharecropping vis a vis rent contracts and owner occupation. In particular, Shaban controls for differences in both unobserved factors which differ between farmers and land quality differences which vary among different parcels. The former is accomplished by using the convenient trick earlier used by Bell (1977) wherein owner cultivated land is distinguished from land cultivated under share contracts by the same farmer, hence holding the many other characteristics of the farmer constant. The latter is accomplished by taking advantage of land quality data for the sampled villages (irrigation, plot value, soil depth and soil quality).

The variables to be explained are the various inputs (family and hired labor of each sex, bullock labor, seed, fertilizer and other) per acre and output per acre. The variations in such input and output intensities across time and households are explained in terms of several factors, including village dummy variables (as proxies for cost-sharing and other differences between villages), and the land quality variables. Then, the differences in input and output intensities between those on the owned plots and sharecropped and fixed rent parcels are compared. The results show highly significant differences between owned and fixed rent land on the one hand and sharecropped land on the other.

Another possible source of estimation bias remaining in such studies of the determinants and effects of sharecropping and other contracts is systematic measurement error and the incompleteness of the relevant information. In large part, this is the natural result of the fact that the contracts involved concern a minimum of two parties, whereas the information used (usually from surveys with random sampling of either landowners or farm operators and workers) is almost invariably from only one of the parties to such contracts.[71]

---

[70] Interestingly, however, though the difference between them was found to be mitigated by the length of the relationship between them.

[71] Bell, Raha, and Srinivasan (1994) attempt to rectify that shortcoming by collecting information from both sides of randomly selected contracts.

Still another is that, even after endogenizing other variables assumed to be exogenous in the earlier studies of both the determinants and effects of contracts, some additional candidates remain. One such candidate is the size of the household because as noted above, for a given plot and disregarding other sources of opportunistic behavior than labor shirking, a landowner may expect to be much less disadvantaged by a share contract with a large family relative to a fixed rent contract than she would with a small family.[72]

One rather unfortunate side effect of the fascination with share contracts, has been insufficient attention to many other contractual issues not only within agriculture but in other industries. While there are many fewer applications to the determinants and effects of other types of contracts and institutions, it is clear that similar problems arise: conceptual problems in measuring the relevant variables, systematic measurement error, non-exogeneity of right-hand side variables, ambiguous interpretations of the role of the explanatory variables, self-selection and so on.[73]

6.2. Empirical application: Decollectivization of farming in China

The change in China from a collective farming system to a household-based system provides another opportunity for careful examination of the transaction-cost approach to institutional change. The independent family farm had been the traditional farming institution in rural China prior to the founding of the People's Republic in 1949. However, the government took measures to transform the household farming system to a collective system in 1953. Due to the difficulties of monitoring labor effort within a collective team, the collective members' incentives to work were low (Lin 1988). Empirical studies show that the total factor productivity in the collective system was about 20 to 30 percent lower than in the household system [McMillan, Wholly and Zhu (1989), Lin (1992a), Wen (1993), Tang (1984)]. Nevertheless, a real departure from the collective system was possible only after the death of Mao Zedong, who had personally promoted the collective system.

Decollectivization started in 1979. When Deng Xiaoping replaced Mao Zedong as the paramount leader, the government encouraged collectives to delegate the agricultural production to smaller groups in order to improve their management of labor but the household farming system remained prohibited. Nevertheless, near the end of 1978 a small number of collectives in a poverty-stricken province tried out a system of contracting out the collectively owned

---

[72] One study of contractual choice which has endogenized household size is Horowitz (1994).

[73] For some recent and highly competent tests of explanations for the theories concerning another form of tenancy, namely that of labor service tenancy, see Sadoulet (1992) and Horowitz (1994).

land to individual households, first secretly and later with the blessing of local authorities. A year later these collectives brought in yields far larger than those of other collectives in the same region. The central authorities later conceded to the existence of this new form of farming but required that it be restricted to poor agricultural areas. This restriction was ignored in most regions. Full official approval of the household system in agriculture was eventually given in late 1981. By that time, 45 percent of the collectives in China had already been dismantled and by the end of 1983, 98 percent of the collectives had adopted the household system.

The spontaneous nature of the decollectivization process provides an unique opportunity to test the induced institutional innovation hypothesis of Davis and North (1970) and Hayami and Ruttan (1985). The individual household farming system was precluded from peasants' institutional choice set by government dictate before 1978. The government's recognition of the losses attributable to the weak incentives for labor effort in the collective system softened the institutional rigidity and thus reduced the external costs of institutional innovation. The household system, therefore, entered the feasibility set of production modes. One can hypothesize that the diffusion of the household system would be faster in areas where (a) the gains in productivity were larger or (b) the costs of breaking up the collectives were smaller.

Lin (1987) uses provincial level data on the diffusion of the household farming system in the period 1981–1983 to test the above hypotheses. The average size of collectives (N) and the ratio of the value of gross production from crops to that of animal husbandry in a province (RATCH) are used as the proxies for the gains of shifting from the collective system to the household system. Other things being equal, the more members in a collective (N), the harder it would be to monitor and hence the greater the incentive for diffusion of the household system. Because of the extremely high costs of monitoring with respect to animal husbandry, even under the collective system, animal husbandry was carried out by individual households. Therefore, the greater the importance of crop cultivation relative to husbandry (RATCH), the more severe were the labor – management problems under the collective system and hence the greater would be the gains of adopting the household system. The degree of difficulty in breaking up a collective would be expected to rise with the degree of indivisibility of the inputs. Among all the agricultural inputs, capital goods are typically the least divisible. Two types of capital goods were of relevance and importance in this respect: (1) farm machinery and tractors which in regions where they were in use were generally very large and very expensive and (2) draft animals which in regions where they were relevant were quite numerous and inexpensive. Relative to the extremely small size of parcels distributed to the individual households under the household responsibility system, farm machinery was deemed poorly divisible but draft animals rather easily divisible. Since the two forms of capital are substitutes for one another, it is hypothesized that costs of breaking up the collectives would be positively related to the number of farm machines per collective (MACH) but negatively related to the number of draft animals per collective (DRAFT). Therefore, the ratio of collectives converting to the household system in year t to the total number of collectives (RT) is expected to be negatively related to MACH but positively related to DRAFT.

To be precise, the empirical equation that Lin estimated is

$$RT = C + a1N + a2RATCH + a3MACH + a4DRAFT + (a5Y1 + a6Y2) + u , \tag{1}$$

where C is a constant term, N, RATCH, MACH and DRAFT are as defined above, Y1 and Y2 are year dummies and u is the stochastic residual component.

The size of a collective, the numbers of machines and of draft animals in a collective are themselves choice variables. Hence, they may be correlated with the residual term. Consistent estimates of their parameters, however, can be obtained by the two-stage-least-squares regression. The instrumental variables that Lin used in the first-stage regression to estimate the endogenous regressors include cultivated land per worker, the ratio of irrigated land to total cultivated land, a multiple cropping index, the ratio of urban population to rural population, and population density, all of which are beyond the control of a collective.[74]

Table 38.1 reports the estimates by the 2SLS regression. From Column 2 Lin finds that all the hypothesized relations are confirmed.

6.3. Empirical assessments of the benefits of property rights

As noted above, one of the most frequently investigated issues in institutional economics pertains to the determinants and effects of property rights. While costs of creating property rights are conceded, the advantages of creating private property rights (Feder et al. 1988, Feder and Feeny 1991) are often argued strongly. Underdevelopment has sometimes been attributed to the lack of property rights and demonstrated empirically by comparing productivity of land with and without private property rights. Yet, some methodological problems inherent in some of these demonstrations are easy to identify: the assumed exogeneity of property rights, measurement problems with respect to

---

[74] The exogeneity of some of these variables could conceivably be questioned, again highlighting the problem in institutional analyses of avoiding various kinds of specification error.

Table 38.1
2SLS Estimates of the Diffusion of Household Farming System

	(1) Hypothesized Sign	(2) 1981–1983
Intercept		−0.58
		(.25)
N	+	0.43
		(.05)
RATCH	+	0.06
		(.001)
MACH	−	−0.31
		(.001)
DRAFT	+	0.02
		(.001)
Y1982		0.32
		(.001)
Y1983		0.55
		(.001)
$\bar{R}^2$		.70

Note: Figures in parentheses indicate the significance levels of the parameters immediately above them. In other words, .01 indicates that the coefficient is significantly different than zero at the 1 percent level.
Source: Lin, Justin Yifu (1987) 'The household responsibility system reform in China: A peasant's institutional choice'. *American Journal of Agricultural Economics*. 69:410–15.

property rights, (e.g. where careful distinctions need to be made between various types of property rights), insufficient controls for other differences.

In an interesting study Besley (1993) uses a detailed survey on property rights and investment in land from almost 400 households and over 2000 fields in two different regions of Ghana to test the relative importance of different types of property rights on investments in land over time. Whereas without considering endogeneity of the rights and other differences between households, the results showed that the number of different rights subject to approval by local authorities had a positive and significant effect on investment in both regions and the number of extra rights without having to have approval had a significant positive effect on investment in one of the regions. Yet once, the endogeneity of the existence of those right was recognized and treated with instrumental variables, the effects of property rights were no longer significant. Besley's conclusion is therefore noteworthy: (pp. 25–26) "the paper confirms the idea that there may be a link between these two (property rights and investment), but also cautions that issues of measurement error and endogeneity should not be neglected in such studies.... The results in this paper only reinforces the need for more data and careful empirical studies rather than regarding the consequences of conscious interventions to develop land rights as self-evident".

7. Concluding remarks

In this chapter, we attempt to establish two propositions: (1) institutions matter and (2) the determinants of institutions are susceptible to the tools of economic analysis. The subject of institutions is a rather new area in the mainstream neoclassical economics. The exposition in this chapter shows that the theory of transaction and information costs and the theory of collective action can take us a long way toward giving us a set of testable hypotheses for explaining the choice and nature of particular institutions and predicting the likelihood of success in achieving such choice or changes therein over time in specific settings. However, as commented by Matthews (1986) in his Presidential Address to the Royal Economic Society, "Theory has made an indispensable contribution in recent times to advances of understanding in this area. But ...in the economics of institutions theory is now outstripping empirical research to an excessive extent". This comment is particularly relevant to institutions and institutional changes in LDCs. Most of the empirical evidence reviewed in this chapter is anecdotal in nature. Rigorous empirical analyses are rare. The shortage of empirical research is probably the result of two shortcomings: the lack of data and the lack of interest in explaining institutions for economists working in developed countries. The first of these shortcomings is attributable to the facts that institutions are complex, difficult to quantify and in many cases changing only very slowly, thereby implying the difficulty of conducting ceteris paribus experiments. The second and more important shortcoming, probably as a result of the first, is the lack of interest among the mainstream economists. As Lewis (1984, p. 8) observes, many Ph.D students in economics come to think "that work on institutions will not count for distinction in Ph.D. exams". However, institutional change is an integrated component of economic development in LDCs. Without a tested theory of institutions and institutional change, economists will not be able to fully understand the process of economic development. Hopefully, both deficiencies will be overcome by increasing availability of data outpouring from the more rapid institutional transitions in many LDCs and former socialist economies and by the recent upsurge of interest in institutions.

For some LDCs, institutional reforms may be imperative as a means of breaking the low-level equilibrium traps in which they may be caught. The analysis in this chapter suggests that mere transplantations of successful institutions from DCs to LDCs is, at best, unlikely to have the expected positive effects on performance, and, at worst, may have rather disastrous effects. Where to start and how to bring out the reforms in a country are questions that can be answered only with serious consideration of the country's existing institutional structure and human and physical endowments.

Nevertheless, the motivation of behavior in LDCs is often subject to the same determinants as in the DCs. Moreover, as has been argued above, the analytical tools of modern economics are capable of shedding light on issues confronting the LDCs, narrowing down the desirable institutional choices, and outlining the requirements for a successful reform. Knowledge of the existing institutional structure in a country may further narrow the scope of feasible choices in that country. Research on institutions and institutional change in a country may contribute not only to the development of economic theory in general but also to that of institutional reforms in that country. This is one area that development economists, as Tullock (1984) says, "can do well while doing good".

References

Akerlof, G. (1976) 'The economics of caste and of the rat race and other woeful tales'. *Quarterly Journal of Economics*. 90:599–617.

Akerlof, G. (1980) 'A theory of social custom, of which unemployment may be one consequence'. *Quarterly Journal of Economics*. 94:749–775.

Alchian, A.A. (1950) 'Uncertainty, evolution, and economic theory'. *Journal of Political Economy*. 58:211–222.

Alchian, A.A. (1959) 'Private property and the relative cost of tenure'. in: P.D. Bradley ed. *The public stake in union power*. Charlottesville: University of Virginia Press.

Alchian, A.A. (1965) 'Some economics of property'. *Il Politico*. 30:816–829. (Originally published in 1961 by the Rand Corporation.) Reprinted in Alchian, A.A. (1977) *Economic forces at work*. Indianapolis: Liberty Press.

Alchian, A.A. and Demsetz, H. (1972) 'Production, information costs, and economic organization'. *American Economic Review*. 62:777–795.

Alston, L., Libecap, G.D. and Schneider, R. (1993) 'An analysis of property rights, land value, and agricultural investment on two frontiers in Brazil'. mimeo.

Anderson, K. and Hayami, Y. (1986) *The political economy of agricultural protection: East Asia in international perspective*. Sydney: Allen and Unwin.

Anderson, T.L. and Hill, P.J. (1975) 'The evolution of property rights: A study of the American west'. *Journal of Law and Economics*. 18:163–179.

Arrow, K.J. (1974) *The limits of organization*. New York: Norton.

Azabou, M. and Nugent, J.B. (1988) 'Contractual choice in tax collection activities: Some implications of the experience with tax farming'. *Journal of Institutional and Theoretical Economics*. 144:684–705.

Baack, B. (1979) 'The development of exclusive property rights to land in England: An exploratory essay'. *Economy and History*. 22:63–74.

Balassa, B. and Associates (1971) *The structure of protection in developing countries*. Baltimore: Johns Hopkins University Press.

Balisacan, A.M. and Roumasset, J.A. (1987) 'Public choice of economic policy: Growth of agricultural production'. *Weltwirtschaftliches Archiv*. 123, Heft 2:232–248.

Bardhan, P. (1988) 'Alternative approaches to development economics'. in: T.N. Srinivasan and H.B. Chenery, eds. *Handbook of Development Economics*, Vol. I, pp. 39–72.

Bardhan, P.K. and Rudra, A. (1986) 'Labor mobility and the boundaries of the village moral economy'. *Journal of Peasant Studies*. 14:90–115.

Barzel, Y. (1974) 'A theory of rationing by waiting'. *Journal of Law and Economics*. 17:73–96.

Barzel, Y. (1989) *Economic analysis of property rights*. Cambridge: Cambridge University Press.

Basu, K. (1992) 'Civil institutions and evolution'. Ithaca: Paper presented to the Conference on State, Market and Civil institutions, Cornell University.

Basu, K., Jones, E. and Schlicht, E. (1987) 'The growth and decay of custom: The role of the new institutional economics in economic history'. *Exploration in Economic History*. 24:1–21.

Bates, R.M. (1981) *Markets and states in tropical Africa: The political basis of agricultural policies*. Berkeley: University of California Press.

Bates, R.M. and Rogerson, W.P. (1980) 'Agriculture in development: A coalition analysis'. *Public Choice*. 32:513–527.

Baumol, W.J. (1952) *Welfare economics and the theory of the state*. Cambridge, Mass.: Harvard University Press.

Bauer, P.T. (1984) *Reality and rhetoric*. Cambridge, MA: Harvard University Press.

Bauer, P.T. and Yamey, B.S. (1957) *The economics of under-developed countries*. Chicago: University of Chicago Press.

Becker, G.S. (1983) 'A theory of competition among pressure groups for influence'. *Quarterly Journal of Economics*. 98:371–400.

Bell, C. (1977) 'Alternative theories of sharecropping: Some tests using evidence from Northeast India'. *Journal of Development Studies*. 13:317–346.

Bell, C., Raha, A. and Srinivasan, T.N. (1994) 'Matching and contractural performance: The case of tenancy in Northern India'. Paper presented at the allied social science meetings in Boston, Massachusetts, January 3–6, 1994.

Bennett, A.S. (1937) *Life on the English manor: A study of peasant conditions*. Cambridge: Cambridge University Press.

Besley, T. (1993) 'Property rights and investment incentives: Theory and micro-evidence from Ghana'. Princeton: Princeton University, Research program in development studies, Discussion Paper 170.

Bikhchamdani, S., Hirshleifer, D. and Welch, I. (1992) 'A theory of fads, fashion, custom, and cultural change in informational cascades'. *Journal of Political Economy*. 100 (5):992–1026.

Binswanger, H.P. (1980) 'Attitudes toward risk: Experimental measurement in rural India'. *American Journal of Agricultural Economics*. 62:395–407.

Binswanger, H., Deininger, K. and Feder, G. (1994) 'Power, distortions, revolt and reform in agricultural land relations'. in: T.N. Srinivasan, and J. Behrman, eds. Chapter 45, *Handbook of Development Economics*, Vol. III, Amsterdam: North Holland.

Binswanger, H. and McIntire, J. (1987) 'Behavioral and material determinants of production relations in land-abundant tropical agriculture'. *Economic Development and Cultural Change*. 36:73–99.

Binswanger, H., McIntire, J. and Udry, C. (1988) 'Production relations in semi-arid African agriculture'. in: P. Bardhan, ed. *The economic theory of agrarian institutions*. Oxford: Clarendon Press, 122–144.

Binswanger, H.P. and Rosenzweig, M.R. (1986) 'Behavioural and material determinants of production relations in agriculture'. *Journal of Development Studies*. 22:504–539.

Binswanger, H.P. and Ruttan, V.W. (1978) *Induced innovation: Technology, institutions, and development*. Baltimore: Johns Hopkins University Press.

Binswanger, H.P. and Scandizzo, P.L. (1983) *Patterns of agricultural protection*. World Bank, Agricultural Research Unit, Report No. 15.

Blum, J. (1971) 'The European village as community: Origins and functions'. *Agricultural History*. 45:157–178.

Boserup, E. (1965) *The conditions of agricultural growth*. Chicago: University of Chicago Press.

Braudel, F. (1979) *The wheels of commerce: Civilization and capitalism 15–18th centuries*, vol. 2. New York: Harper and Row.

Brewster, J.M. (1950) 'The machine process in agriculture and industry'. *Journal of Farm Economics*. 32:69–81.

Chandler, Jr., A.D. (1973) 'Decision making and modern institutional change'. *Journal of Economic History*. 33:1–15.

Chandler, Jr., A.D. (1977) *The visible hand: The managerial revolution in American business*. Cambridge: Harvard University Press.

Cheung, S.N.S. (1974) 'A theory of price control'. *Journal of Law and Economics*. 17:53–72.

Coase, R.H. (1937) 'The nature of the firm'. *Economica*. 3:386–405.

Coase, R.H. (1960) 'The problem of social cost'. *Journal of Law and Economics*. 3:1–44.

Datta, S.K. and Nugent, J.B. (1989) 'Transaction cost economics and contractual choice: Theory and evidence'. in: M.K. Nabli and J.B. Nugent, eds. *The new institutional economics and development: Theory and applications to Tunisia.* Amsterdam: North-Holland, 34–79.

Davis, L. and North, D.C. (1970) 'Institutional change and American economic growth: A first step toward a theory of institutional innovation'. *Journal of Economic History.* 30:131–149.

de Janvry, A. and Sadoulet, E. (1989) 'A study in resistance to institutional change: The lost game of Latin American land reform'. *World Development.* 17:1397–1407.

Demsetz, H. (1967) 'Toward a theory of property rights'. *American Economic Review.* 57:61–70.

Dennen, R.T. (1976) 'Cattlemen's associations and property rights in land in the American West'. *Explorations in Economic History.* 13:423–436.

Dewatripont, M. and Roland, G. (1992a) 'The virtues of gradualism and legitimacy in the transition to a market economy'. *The Economic Journal.* 102:291–300.

Dewatripont, M. and Roland, G. (1992b) 'Economic reform and dynamic political constraints'. *Review of Economic Studies.* 59 (4):703–730.

Dong, X.Y. and Dow, G.K. (1993) 'Monitoring costs in Chinese agricultural teams'. *Journal of Political Economy* 101:539–553.

Downs, A. (1957) *An economic theory of democracy.* New York: Harper & Row.

Eggertsson, Thrainn (1990) *Economic behavior and institutions.* Cambridge: Cambridge University Press.

Feder, G. and Feeny, D. (1991) 'Land tenure and property rights: Theory and implications for development policy'. *The World Bank Economic Review.* 5:135–153.

Feder, G., Onchan, T., Chalanwong, Y. and Hongladarom, C. (1988) *Land policies and farm productivity in Thailand.* Baltimore: Johns Hopkins University Press.

Feeny, D. (1989) 'The decline of property rights in man in Thailand, 1800–1913'. *Journal of Economic History.* 49:285–296.

Feeny, D. (1982) *The political economy of productivity.* Vancouver: University of British Columbia Press.

Fernandez, R. and Rodrik, D. (1991) 'Resistance to reform: Status quo in the presence of individual-specific uncertainty'. *American Economic Review.* 81:1146–1155.

Field, A.J. (1981) 'The problem with neoclassical institutional economics: A critique with special reference to the North/Thomas model of pre-1500 Europe'. *Explorations in economic history.* 18:174–198.

Field, B.C. (1989) 'The evolution of property rights'. *Kyklos.* 42:319–345.

Findlay, R. (1990) 'The new political economy: Its explanatory power for LDCs'. *Economics and Politics.* 2:191–221.

Fry, M.J. (1974) *The Afghan economy: Money, finance and the critical constraints to economic development.* Leiden: Brill.

Gaynor, M. and Putterman, L. (1993) 'Productivity consequences of alternative land division methods in China's decollectivization: An econometric analysis'. *Journal of Development Economics.* 42:357–386.

Gilbert, A. and Ward, P.M. (1985) *Housing the state and the poor.* Cambridge: Cambridge University Press.

Grabowski, R. (1988) 'The theory of induced institutional innovation: A critique'. *World Development.* 16:385–394.

Greif, A. (1992) 'Cultural beliefs and the organization of society: A historical and theoretical reflection on collectivist and individualist societies'. Palo Alto: Stanford University, Dept. of Economics (mimeo).

Grindle, S.M. and Thomas, J.W. (1991) 'Policymakers, policy choices, and policy outcomes: Political economy of reform in developing countries'. in: D.H. Perkins, and M. Roemer eds., *Reforming economic systems in developing countries.* Cambridge: Harvard University Press, 81–114.

Guttman, J. (1978) 'Interest groups and the demand for agricultural research'. *Journal of Political Economy.* 86:467–484.

Haddock, D.D. (1994) 'Foreseeing confiscation by the sovereign: Lessons from the American West' in T.L. Anderson and P.J. Hill, eds., *The political economy of the American West.* Latham, MD: Rowman and Littlefield.

Hallagan, W.S. (1978) 'Share contracting for California gold'. *Explorations in Economic History.* 15:196–210.

Hannesson, R. (1991) 'From common fish to rights based fishing: Fisheries management and the evolution of exclusive rights to fish'. *European Economic Review.* 35:397–407.

Hardin, R. (1982) *Collective action.* Washington, D.C., Resources for the Future.

Hayami, Y. and Kikuchi, M. (1982) *Asian village economy at the crossroads.* Baltimore: Johns Hopkins University Press.

Hayami, Y. and Ruttan, V.W. (1985) *Agricultural development: An international perspective.* (revised and expanded edition). Baltimore: Johns Hopkins University Press.

Hirschman, A.O. (1967) *Development projects observed.* Washington: Brookings Institution.

Hirschman, A.O. (1970) *Exit, voice and loyalty: Responses to decline in firms, organizations and states.* Cambridge: Harvard University Press.

Hirschman, A.O. (1981) *Essays in trespassing.* Cambridge: Cambridge University Press.

Hirschman, A.O. (1984) *Getting ahead collectively: Grassroots experiences in Latin America.* New York: Pergamon Press.

Hoffman, P.T. (1989) 'Institutions and agriculture in old-regime France'. *Journal of Institutional and Theoretical Economics.* 145:166–181.

Hoffman, R.C. (1975) 'Medieval origins of the common fields'. in: W.N. Parker and E.L. Jones. eds. *European peasants and their markets.* Princeton: Princeton University Press, pp. 23–71.

Horowitz, A.W. (1994) 'Dualism and family size in wage-homestead tenancies', Nashville: Vanderbilt University (mimeo).

Hume, D. (1948) *Hume's moral and political philosophy.* H.D. Aiken, ed. New York: Hafner.

Iannaccone, L.R. (1992) 'Sacrifice and stigma: Reducing free-riding in cults, communes, and other collectives'. *Journal of Political Economy.* 100:271–291.

Jensen, M.C. and Meckling, W.H. (1976) 'Theory of the firm: Managerial behavior, agency costs and ownership structure'. *Journal of Financial Economics.* 3:305–360.

Jodha, N.S. (1985) 'Population growth and the decline of common property resources in Rajasthan, India'. *Population and development review.* 11 (2):247–264.

Jones, S.R.H. (1987) 'Technology, transaction costs, and transition to factory production in the British silk industry, 1700–1870'. *Journal of Economic History.* 41:71–96.

Kornai, J. (1986) 'The soft budget constraint'. *Kyklos.* 39:3–30.

Kornai, J. (1990) *The road to a free economy.* New York: W.W. Norton.

Krepps, M.B. and Caves, R.E. (forthcoming) 'Bureaucrats and Indians: Principal-agent relations and efficient management of tribal forest resources' *Journal of Economic Behavior and Organization.*

Krueger, A.O. (1978) *Foreign trade regime and economic development: Liberalization attempts and consequences.* Cambridge: Ballinger Publishing Co., Vol. 10.

Krueger, A.O. (1988) 'The political economy of control: American sugar'. NBER Working Paper, No. 2504.

Krueger, A.O. (1994) 'Lessons from development experience since the second world war'. in: T.N. Srinivasan and J. Behrman, eds. *Handbook of Development Economics,* Vol. III, Chapter 34.

Kuran, T. (1987) 'Preference falsification, policy continuity and collective conservatism'. *Economic Journal.* 97:642–665.

Kuran, T. (1989) 'The craft guilds of Tunis and their Amins: A study in institutional atrophy'. in: M.K. Nabli and J.B. Nugent, ed. *The new institutional economics and development: Theory and applications to Tunisia.* Amsterdam: North Holland, 236–264.

Kuznets, S. (1966) *Modern economic growth: Rate, structure, and spread.* New Haven: Yale University Press.

Kuznets, S. (1973) 'Modern economic growth: Findings and reflections'. *American Economic Review,* 63:247–258.

La Croix, S. and Roumasset, J. (1990) 'The evolution of private property in nineteenth-century Hawaii'. *Journal of Economic History.* 50:829–852.

Laffont, J.-J, and Matoussi, M.S. (1993) 'Moral hazard, financial constraints and sharecropping in El Oulja' (mimeo).

Lal, D. (1985) 'The misconceptions of development economics'. *Finance and development.* 22:10–13.

Landsberger, H.A. and Hewitt, C.N. (1970) 'Ten sources of weakness and cleavage in Latin American peasant movements'. in: R. Stavenhagen, ed. *Agrarian problems and peasant movements in Latin America.* New York: Doubleday.

Lee, R.B., (1968) 'What hunters do for a living, or, How to make out on scarce resources'. in R.B. Lee and I. DeVore, eds., *Man the hunter.* Chicago: Aldine:30–48.

Lewis, W.A. (1984) 'The state of development theory'. *American Economic Review.* 74:1–10.

Lewis, W.A. (1955) *Theory of economic growth.* London: Harper & Row.

Libecap, G.D. (1978a) 'Economic variables and the development of law: The case of western mineral rights'. *Journal of Economic History.* 38:338–362.

Libecap, G.D. (1978b) *The evolution of private mineral rights: Nevada's Comstock Lode.* New York: Arno Press.

Libecap, G.D. (1979) 'Government support of private claims to public minerals: Western mineral rights'. *Business History Review.* 53:362–385.

Lin, J.Y. (1987) 'The household responsibility system reform in China: A peasant's institutional choice'. *American Journal of Agricultural Economics.* 69:410–415.

Lin, J.Y. (1988) 'The household responsibility system in China's agricultural reform'. *Economic development and cultural change.* 36, no. 3 (supplement): s199–s224.

Lin, J.Y. (1989a) 'An economic theory of institutional change: Induced and imposed change'. *Cato Journal.* 9:1–33.

Lin, J.Y. (1989b) 'Rural factor markets in China after the household responsibility reform'. in: B. Reynolds, ed. *Chinese Economic Policy.* New York: Paragon, pp. 157–192.

Lin, J.Y. (1990) 'Collectivization and China's agricultural crisis in 1959–1961'. *Journal of Political Economy.* 98:1228–1254.

Lin, J.Y. (1992a) 'Rural reforms and agricultural growth in china'. *American Economic Review.* 82:34–51.

Lin, J.Y. (1992b) 'Rural reforms, technological innovation, and nascent factor Mamkets in China: An empirical study of institutional change'. Beijing: Development research center (mimeo).

Lin, J.Y. (1993) 'Does free exit reduce shirking in production teams: A reply'. *Journal of Comparative Economics.* 17:504–520.

Lin, J.Y., Cai, F. and Li, Z. (1993) 'On China's gradual approach to economic reform'. *Jingji Yanjiu* (Economic Research, monthly). 1993 (September):3–11.

Lipton, M. (1977) *Why poor people stay poor: A study of urban bias in world development.* London: Temple Smith.

Lucas, R.E.B. and Stark, O. (1985) 'Motivations to remit: Evidence from Botswana'. *Journal of Political Economy.* 93:901–918.

Lutz, E. and Scandizzo, P.L. (1980) 'Price distortions in developing countries: A bias against agriculture'. *European Review of Agricultural Economics.* 7:5–27.

Matoussi, M.S. and Nugent, J.B. (1989) 'The switch to sharecropping in Medjez-el-Bab'. in: M. Nabli and J.B. Nugent, eds., *The New Institutional Economics and Development.* Amsterdam: North-Holland,140–157.

Matthews, R.C.O. (1986) 'The economics of institutions and the sources of growth'. *Economic Journal.* 96:903–918.

McCloskey, D.N. (1972) 'The enclosure of open fields: Preface to a study of its impact on the efficiency of English agriculture in the eighteenth century'. *Journal of Economic History.* 32:15–35.

McCurdy, C.W. (1976) 'Steven J. Field and public land law development in California, 1850–1866'. *Law and Society Review.* 10:235–266.

McMillan, J. and Naughton, B (1992) 'How to reform a planned economy: Lessons from China'. *Oxford Review of Economic Policy.* 8:130–143.

McMillan, J., Whally, J. and Zhu, L. (1989) 'The impact of China's economic reforms on agricultural productivity growth'. *Journal of Political Economy.* 97:781–807.

Migot-Adholla, S., Hazel, P., Blarel, B. and Place, F. (1991) 'Indigenous land rights systems in sub-Saharan Africa: A constraint on productivity'. *World Bank Economic Review.* 5:155–175.

Mill, J.S. (1847) *Principles of political economy.* 5th ed. New York: Appleton, 1895.

Mill, J.S. (1848) *Principles of political economy with some of their applications to social philosophy.* Reprinted. Clifton, N.J.: Augustus M. Kelly, 1973.

Myrdal, G. (1968) *Asian drama: An inquiry into the poverty of nations.* New York: Twentieth Century Fund.

Nabli, M., Nugent, J.B. and Doghri L. (1989) 'The size distribution and ownership type of firms in Tunisian manufacturing'. in M. Nabli and J.B. Nugent, eds. *The new institutional economics and development.* Amsterdam: North Holland, 200–232.

Nelson, J. (1984) 'The political economy of stabilization: commitment, capacity and public response'. *World Development.* 12:983–1006.

Nelson, R.R. and Winter, S.G. (1982) *An evolutionary theory of economic change.* Cambridge, MA: Belknap Press of Harvard University Press.

Newbery, D.M.G. (1977) 'Risk sharing, sharecropping and uncertain labor markets'. *Review of Economic Studies.* 44:585–594.

North, D.C. (1979) 'The state in economic history'. *Exploration in Economic History.* 16:249–259.

North, D.C. (1981) *Structure and change in economic history.* New York: Norton.

North, D.C. (1984) 'Transaction costs, institutions and economic history'. *Zeitschrift für die Gesamte Staatswissenschaft.* 140:7–17.

North, D.C. (1986), 'Institutions and economic growth: An historical introduction'. Ithaca: Cornell University, Conference on Institutions and Development.

North, D. C. (1990) *Institutions, institutional change and economic performance.* Cambridge: Cambridge University Press.

North, D.C. (1991) 'Institutions'. *Journal of Economic Perspectives.* 5:97–112.

North, D.C. and Thomas, R. (1971) 'The rise and fall of the manorial system: A theoretical model'. *Journal of Economic History.* 31:777–803.

North, D. C. and Thomas, R. (1973) *The rise of the western world: A new economic history.* Cambridge: Cambridge University Press.

North, D.C. and Weingast, B.R. (1989) 'Constitutions governing public choice in seventeenth century England'. *Journal of Economic History.* 49:803–832.

Nozick, R. (1974) *Anarchy, state, and utopia.* New York: Basic Books.

Nugent, J.B. (1993) 'From import substitution to outward orientation: Some institutional and political economy conditions for reform' in H. Handoussa, ed., *The new development economics and the global context* (forthcoming).

Nugent, J.B. and Sanchez, N. (1988) 'On the efficiency of the Mesta: A parable'. *Explorations in Economic History.* 26:261–284.

Nugent, J.B. and Sanchez, N. (1993) 'Tribes, chiefs and transhumance: A comparative institutional analysis'. *Economic Development and Cultural Change.* 42:87–113.

Olson, Jr., M. (1965) *The logic of collective action: Public goods and the theory of groups.* Cambridge: Harvard University Press.

Olson, Jr., M. (1982) *The rise and decline of nations: The political economy of economic growth, stagflation and social rigidities.* New York: Yale University Press.

Ostrom, E. (1990) *Governing the commons: The evolution of institutions for collective action.* Cambridge: Cambridge University Press.

Otsuka, K., Chuma, H. and Hayami, Y. (1992a) 'Land and labor contracts in Agrarian economies: Theories and facts'. *Journal of Economic Literature.* 30:1965–2018.

Otsuka, K., Kikuchi, M. and Hayami, Y. (1986) 'Community and market in contract choice: The Jeepney in the Philippines'. *Economic Development and Cultural Change.* 34:279–298.

Pagano, U. (1985) *Work and leisure in economic theory.* Oxford and New York: Basil Blackwell.

Pejovich, S. (1972) 'Toward an economic theory of the creation and specification of property rights'. *Review of Social Economy.* 30:309–325.

Perkins, D.H. (1991) 'Economic systems reform in developing countries'. in D.H. Perkins and M. Roemer, eds. *Reforming economic systems in developing countries.* Cambridge, MA: Harvard Institute for International Development distributed by Harvard University Press, pp. 11–54.

Platteau, J.-P. and Nugent, J.B. (1992) 'Share contracts and their rationale: Lessons from marine fishing'. *Journal of Development Studies.* 28:386–422.

Polanyi, K. (1944) *The great transformation: The political and economic origins of our time.* New York: Rinehart.

Posner, R.A. (1980) 'A theory of primitive society with special reference to law'. *Journal of Law and Economics*. 23:1–53.

Przeworski A. and Limongi, F. (1993) 'Political regimes and economic growth'. *Journal of Economic Perspective*. 7 (summer):51–69.

Reynolds, L.J. (1983) 'The spread of economic growth to the third world: 1850–1980'. *Journal of Economic Literature*. 21:941–980.

Rosenzweig, M.R. (1988) 'Risk, implicit contracts and the family in rural areas of low Income countries'. *Economic Journal*. 98:1148–1170.

Rosenzweig, M.R. and Stark, O. (1989) 'Consumption smoothing, migration and marriage: Evidence from rural India'. *Journal of Political Economy*. 97:905–926.

Rosenthal, J. (1991) *The fruit of revolution*. Cambridge: Cambridge University Press.

Ruttan, V.W. (1984) 'Social science knowledge and institutional change'. *American Journal of Agricultural Economics*. 39:549–559.

Ruttan, V.W. (1986), 'Institutional innovation and agricultural development'. Ithaca, Cornell University Conference on Institutions and Development.

Ruttan, V.W. and Hayami, Y. (1984) 'Toward a theory of induced institutional innovation'. *Journal Development Studies*. 20:203–223.

Sachs, J.D. (1992) 'Accelerating privatization in eastern europe: The case of Poland'. *The World Bank Economic Review: Proceeding of the World Bank annual conference on eevelopment economics 1991*. 6:15–31.

Sadoulet, E. (1992), 'Labor-service tenancy contracts in a latin american context'. *American Economic Review*. 82:1031–1042.

Sah, R.K. (1991) 'Fallibility in human organizations and political systems'. *Journal of Economic Perspectives*. 5:67–88.

Salehi-Isfahani, D. (1988) 'Technology and preferences in the Boserup model of agricultural growth'. *Journal of Development Economics*. 28:175–191.

Sahn, D.E. and Sarris, A. (1993) 'States, markets, and the emergence of new civil institutions in rural Africa'. Ithaca: Paper presented at the Conference on State, Market and Civil Institutions, Cornell University.

Schultz, T.W. (1968) 'Institutions and the rising economic value of man'. *American Journal of Agricultural Economics*. 50:1113–1122.

Schultz, T.W. (1977) 'Economics, agriculture, and the political economy'. in: P. Anderou, ed. *Agricultural and economic development of poor nations*. Nairobi: East African Literature Bureau, 1977.

Shaban, R.A. (1987) 'Testing between competing models of sharecropping'. *Journal of Political Economy* 95:893–920.

Simon, H.A. (1991) 'Markets and organisation'. *Journal of Economic Perspective*. 5:25–44.

Smith, A. (1776) *An inquiry into the nature and causes of the wealth of nations*. New York, 1937.

Smith, V.L. (1991) 'Economic principles in the emergence of humankind'. Tucson: University of Arizona, Dept. of Economics Discussion Paper 91–98.

Srinivasan, T.N. (1992) 'Bad advice: A comment'. *Economic and Political Weekly*, July 11, 1992.

Stiglitz, J.E. (1988) 'Economic organization, information, and development'. in: T.N. Srinivasan and H. Chenery, *Handbook of Development Economics*, Vol. I, pp. 93–160.

Stiglitz, J.E. (1989) 'On the economic role of the state'. in: A. Heertje, ed. *The Economic Role of the State*, Oxford: Blackwell.

Stone, A., Levy, B. and Paredes, R. (1992) 'Public institutions and private transactions: A comparative study of the legal and regulatory environment for business transactions in Brazil and Chile'. Washington, D.C.: World Bank Working Paper.

Tang, A.M. (1984) *An analytical and empirical investigation of agriculture in mainland China*. Taipei: Chung-Hua Institution of Economic Research, distributed in U.S. by University of Washington Press.

Telser, L.G. (1980) 'A theory of self-enforcing agreements'. *Journal of Business*. 53:27–44.

Thirsk, J. (1964) 'The common fields'. *Past and Present*. 29:3–25.

Townsend, R. M. (1984) 'Taking theory to history: Explaining financial structure and economic organization'. Working Paper, Carnegie-Mellon University.

Townsend, R.M. (1991) 'Risk and Insurance in village India' (mimeo).

Trubek, D.M. (1972) 'Toward a social theory of law: An essay on the study of law and development'. *Yale Law Journal*. 82:1–50.

Tullock, G. (1984) 'How to do well while doing good!' in: D.C. Colander. ed. *Neoclassical political economy: The analysis of rent-seeking and DUP activities*. Cambridge, MA: Harper & Row, Ballinger.

Umbeck, J. (1977) 'A theory of contract choice and the California gold rush'. *Journal of Law and Economics*. 20:421–437.

Umbeck, J. (1981) 'Might makes right: A theory of the formation and initial distribution of property rights'. *Economic Inquiry*. 19:38–59.

Uphoff, N. (1986) *Local institutional development*. West Hartford: Kumarian Press.

Wade, R. (1987) 'The management of common property resources: Finding a cooperative solution'. *World Bank Research Observer*. 2:219–234.

Wen, J.G. (1993) 'Total factor productivity change in China's farming sector: 1952–1989'. *Economic Development and Cultural Change*. 42:1–41.

Williamson, O.E. (1985) *The economic institutions of capitalism: Firms, markets, relational contracting*. New York: Free Press.

Williamson, O.E. (1980) 'The organization of work'. *Journal of Economic Behavior and Organization*. 1:5–38.

Williamson, O.E. (1975) *Markets and hierarchies: Analysis and antitrust implications*. New York: Free Press.

Williamson, O.E. (1979) 'Transaction-cost economics: The governance of contractual relations'. *Journal of Law and Economics*. 22:233–261.

Winiecki, J. (1990) 'Why economic reforms fail in the Soviet system: A property rights-based approach'. *Economic Inquiry*. 28:195–221.

World Bank (1991) *World development report 1991: The challenge of development*. Oxford: Oxford University Press published for the World Bank.

Yotopoulos, P.A. and J.B. Nugent (1976) *Economics of development: Empirical investigations*. New York: Harper and Row.

Zouteweij, H. (1956) 'Fishermen's remuneration'. in: R. Turvey and J. Wiseman, eds., *The Economics of Fisheries*. Rome: FAO.

Chapter 39

POVERTY, INSTITUTIONS, AND THE ENVIRONMENTAL RESOURCE-BASE

PARTHA DASGUPTA

University of Cambridge, and
Beijer International Institute of Ecological Economics

KARL-GÖRAN MÄLER

Beijer International Institute of Ecological Economics, and
Stockholm School of Economics

Contents

This article is based on a course of lectures delivered by us in November 1992 in Bombay at a workshop for senior civil servants from developing countries, sponsored jointly by the Swedish International Development Authority (SIDA), the Beijer International Institute of Ecological Economics, the UNU/World Institute for Development Economics Research (UNU/WIDER), and the Indira Gandhi Institute for Economic Development Research. These lectures were further developed at teaching workshops on environmental economics, sponsored by UNU/WIDER and held in Colombo in December 1992 and Gozo (Malta) in July 1993, for university teachers of economics from developing countries. We have learnt much from the comments of the participants of these workshops, and from discussions with our co-lecturers: Scott Barrett, John Dixon, Carl Folke, Mohan Munasinghe, Theo Panayotou and Kirit Parikh.
In preparing the final version of this article, we have benefited greatly from the comments of Jere Behrman, Lawrence Lau, T.N. Srinivasan and Stefano Zamagni.

Partha Dasgupta, University of Cambridge, Faculty of Economics, Sidgwick Avenue, Cambridge, England CB3 9DD.
Karl-Göran Mäler, University of Stockholm, Universitetsuvagen 10A, Stockholm S-10691, Sweden.

Handbook of Development Economics, Volume III, Edited by J. Behrman and T.N. Srinivasan
© *Elsevier Science B.V., 1995*

Contents (continued)

Part I: Basics

1. The resource basis of rural production

People in poor countries are for the most part agrarian and pastoral folk. In 1988, rural people accounted for about 65 percent of the population of what the World Bank classifies as low-income countries. The proportion of total labour force in agriculture was a bit in excess of this. The share of agriculture in gross domestic product in these countries was 30 percent. These figures should be contrasted with those from industrial market economies, which are 6 percent and 2 percent for the latter two statistics, respectively.[1]

Poor countries are for the most part *biomass-based subsistence economies*, in that their rural folk eke out a living from products obtained directly from plants and animals. For example, in their informative study of life in a microwatershed of the Alaknanda river in the central Himalayas in India, the (Indian) Centre for Science and Environment (C.S.E., 1990) reports that, of the total number of hours worked by the villagers sampled, 30 percent was devoted to cultivation, 20 percent to fodder collection, and about 25 percent was spread evenly between fuel collection, animal care, and grazing. Some 20 percent of time was spent on household chores, of which cooking took up the greatest portion, and the remaining 5 percent was involved in other activities, such as marketing (see also Sections 18–19). In their work on Central and West Africa, Falconer and Arnold (1989) and Falconer (1990) have shown how vital are forest products to the lives of rural folk. Poor countries, especially those in the Indian sub-continent and sub-Saharan Africa, can be expected to remain largely rural economies for some while yet.

The dependence of poor countries on their natural resources, such as soil and its cover, water, forests, animals, and fisheries should be self-evident: ignore the environmental resource-base, and we are bound to obtain a misleading picture of productive activity in rural communities there. Nevertheless, if there has been a single thread running through forty years of investigation into the poverty of poor countries, it has been the neglect of this resource base. Until very recently, environmental resources made but perfunc-

---

[1] International figures, such as these, are known to contain large margins of error. Nevertheless, they offer orders of magnitude. For this reason, we will allude to them. However, we will not make use of them for any other purpose.

tory appearances in government planning models, and they were cheerfully ignored in most of what goes by the name development economics.[2]

The situation is now different. As regards timing, the shift in attitude can probably be identified with the publication of the Brundtland Report (World Commission, 1987), and today no account of economic development would be regarded as adequate if the environmental resource-base were absent from it. This chapter, therefore, is about the environment and emerging development issues. Our intention is not to attempt a survey of articles and books on the subject. We will instead weave an account of a central aspect of the lives of the rural poor in poor countries on the basis of a wide-ranging analytical and empirical literature that has developed quite independently of the subject of development economics and the Brundtland Report.

2. Ecosystems: Functions and services[3]

The ecological services we rely upon are produced by *ecological systems* (or *ecosystems* for short). These services are generated by interactions among organisms, populations of organisms, communities of populations, and the physical and chemical environment in which they reside. Ecosystems are involved in a number of functions and offer a wide range of services. Many are indispensable, as they provide the underpinning for all human activities. So they are of fundamental value. Among other things, ecosystems are the sources of water, of animal and plant food and other renewable resources. They also maintain a genetic library, sustain the processes that preserve and regenerate soil, recycle nutrients, control floods, filter pollutants, assimilate waste, pollinate crops, operate the hydrological cycle, and maintain the gaseous composition of the atmosphere. The totality of all the ecosystems of the world represents a large part of what we may call our natural capital-base.[4] For vividness, we will often refer to it in what follows as the *environmental resource-base*. Environmental problems are thus almost always associated with resources that are regenerative, but that are in danger of exhaustion from

---

[2] There were exceptions of course (e.g. C.S.E., 1982, 1985; Dasgupta, 1982a). Moreover, agricultural and fisheries economists have routinely studied environmental matters. In the text, we are referring to a neglect of environmental matters in what could be called 'official' development economics.

[3] This section is based on Dasgupta (1994) and Dasgupta, Folke and Mäler (1994).

[4] The natural capital-base includes in addition minerals and ores underground.

excessive use. For this reason we may identify environmental resources with *renewable natural resources.*[5]

Resource economists typically view the natural environment through the lense of *population ecology*. Since the focus there is the dynamics of interacting populations of different species, it is customary to take the background environmental processes as exogenously given. The most well-known illustration of this viewpoint is the use of the logistic function for charting the time path of the population size of a single species of fish enjoying a constant flow of food. Predator-prey models (e.g that of Volterra) provide another class of examples; as do the May–MacArthur models[6] of competition among an arbitrary number of species.

Environmental economists, on the other hand, often find it useful to base their studies on *ecosystem ecology*. Here, the focus is on such objects as energy at different trophic levels and its rate of flow among them, the distribution and flows of bio-chemical substances in soils and bodies of water, and of gases and particulates in the atmosphere. The motivation here is to study the biotic and abiotic processes underlying the various functions that are performed by ecosystems. Holling's characterization of ecological processes as one of cycles of birth, growth, death, and renewal, is a particularly illuminating example of this viewpoint (Holling, 1987, 1992). In such settings, the central concern of the economist, qua economist, is the valuation of the services that are provided by ecosystems. Economic studies of global warming, eutrophication of lakes, the management of rangelands, and the pollution of estuaries are typical examples of such endeavour (e.g. Nordhaus, 1991; Costanza, 1991; Mäler et al., 1992; Walker, 1993).

Formally, population and ecosystem ecology differ by way of the state variables that are taken to characterize complex systems. In the former, the typical state variables are population sizes (or, alternatively, tonnage) of different species; in the latter, they are indices of the kinds of services mentioned above. It is often possible to summarize the latter in terms of indices of "quality", such as those for air, soil, or water. These ought all to be interpreted as summary statistics, reflecting as they do different forms of

---

[5] There are exceptions of course, such as perhaps the Ozone layer. But nothing is lost in our ignoring these exceptions here. We also recognize that minerals and fossil fuels are not renewable. For reasons of space, we will ignore non-renewable resources in this chapter. For an account of what resource allocation theory looks like when we include exhaustible resources in the production process, see Dasgupta and Heal (1979), Hartwick and Olewiler (1986), and Tietenberg (1988). For a non-technical account of the theory and the historical role that has been played by the substitution of new energy resources for old [see Dasgupta (1989)].

[6] See May (1972) and May and MacArthur (1972).

aggregation. Therein lies their virtue: they enable the analyst to study complex systems by means of a few strategically chosen variables.

The viewpoint just offered, that of distinguishing population and ecosystem ecology in terms of the state variables that summarize complex systems, permits us to integrate problems of resource management and those of environmental pollution and degradation [Dasgupta (1982a); Section 3 below]. In this way, insights from one field of study can be, and have been, used for gaining an understanding of others. The viewpoint also reminds us that environmental economics is concerned with the study of renewable natural resource systems when they are subject to human predation.

When described in such stark terms, both population and ecosystem ecology offer only partial viewpoints. For example, ecological processes are patently dependent on the composition of the biota, so implicit in ecosystem ecology is an account of population structures and the way they may be expected to alter over time through interactions both among themselves and with the abiotic processes at work. By the same token, population dynamics cannot be understood in the absence of knowledge of the relevant abiotic processes. Thus, the Clements–MacArthur proposal, if one may amalgamate the two perspectives, that species of organisms can be partitioned into those that are "r-strategists" (the pioneer, opportunistic species in recently disturbed habitats) and those that are "K-strategists" (the conservative, or climax, species possessing strong competitive abilities), can be seen as a direct use of the logistic growth function mentioned earlier for the construction of a theory of ecological succession.[7] It follows that unified ecological models have both quantity and "quality" indices as state variables. It follows also that viewing the environmental resource-base as a gigantic capital stock, as economists typically do, is a fruitful exercise.

Since the services this base provides us are essential for our survival, it would seem prudent to monitor it in much the way we routinely monitor our manufactured capital stocks, such as roads, buildings, and machinery. Unhappily, this has not been standard practice. It is even today not conducted in any systematic way. Instead, reliance is often placed on time trends in gross outputs of commodities (e.g. agricultural crops, fisheries, forest products) and trends in their prices for obtaining a sense of, for example, whether growth in the world's population has been imposing strains on the environmental resource-base. This is a mistake. Agricultural output could in principle display a rising trend even while the soils are being mined. Increasing production is consistent with unsustainable production. Growing and sustainable output are

---

[7] If X is the population size of a species, its dynamics, when growth can be characterized by the logistic function, is: $dX/dt = r(X - X^2/K)$, where r and K are positive constants. For small values of X, the first term dominates, and the population experiences exponential growth, at the rate r. However, the long run stable population size is K.

not the same and it is a fundamental error to think that they are. The environmental resource-base is a dynamic and complex living system, consisting as it does of biological communities that interact with the physical and chemical environment, in time and space. The interactions are often non-linear [e.g. Holling (1992)]. In particular, the state of a resource base can display threshold effects, which means that there can be discontinuities lying in wait in the flow of services that we enjoy.

The *carrying capacity* of an ecosystem is the maximum stress it is capable of absorbing without it flipping to a vastly different state. Ecosystems are endemically subject to natural shocks and surprises (e.g. fires, storms, droughts, and so on). This means that it would be incorrect to regard them as fixed stocks of capital, to be relied upon to provide us with a steady flow of resources. Our natural capital-base has evolved over millions of years. It has adapted to modifications and fluctuations in the background environment. The self-organizing ability of ecosystems determines its capacity to respond to the perturbations they are continually subjected to [Holling (1992), Wilson (1992), Perrings et al. (1994)].

The study of *biological diversity* (or *biodiversity* for short) is a testimony that population and ecosystem ecology are but partial lenses. Even today it is a popular belief among economists that the utilitarian value of biodiversity is to be located in the potential future uses of genetic material, say, for pharmaceutical purposes. Preserving biodiversity is seen as a way of holding a diverse portfolio of assets with uncertain payoffs. But ecologists have for years stressed a somewhat different reason for the importance of biodiversity, which is that it plays a central role in the evolution of ecosystems. Not only does biodiversity provide the units through which both energy and materials flow (thus giving the system its functional properties), it also provides an ecosystem with *resilience*. [Schultze and Mooney (1993), provide fine empirical confirmations of the latter.][8]

Resilience is the capacity of an ecosystem to recover from perturbations, shocks, and surprises. It is the capacity to absorb disturbances without undergoing fundamental changes. If a system loses its resilience, it can flip to a wholly new state when subjected to even a small perturbation. Thus, field studies suggest that an ecosystem that is diverse in its biota withstands stress (due, say, to the occurrence of violent events), in that it manages to sustain much of its functions even when the composition of species changes. (Resilience should, therefore, be thought of as functional, as opposed to structural, stability of complex systems.)[9] This is because there are species that are

---

[8] Weitzman (1992, 1993) has developed a quantitative measure of biodiversity. The appeal of his approach is that the measure he proposes is based on an axiomatic structure.
[9] The literature on the mathematics of complexity is now extensive. [See, for example, Stein (1989)].

"waiting in the wings" to take over the functions of those that are denuded or destroyed. Now this is reminiscent of the assumption of "substitutability" among inputs in commodity production, an assumption that is often made in economic models of technological processes. But resilience presupposes that there *are* species waiting in the wings. So, to invoke the idea of substitutability among natural resources in commodity production in order to play down the utilitarian importance of biodiversity, as economists frequently do, is to engage in muddled thinking.

This point deserves emphasis. The economist's panacea, the view that there are unending substitution possibilities among various resources, that society will be able smoothly to move from one resource base to another as each is degraded beyond usefulness, is internally contradictory, because it *presupposes* biodiversity.

As noted earlier, an ecosystem's carrying capacity does not remain constant, but is subject to change, usually in ways that are unpredictable. This is because ecosystems evolve continually. Economic policies that apply fixed rules so as to achieve constant yields (e.g. fixed sizes of cattle-herds or wildlife, or fixed sustainable yield of fish or wood) in general lead to a reduction in an ecosystem's resilience. Large reductions in resilience would mean that the system could break down in the face of disturbances that earlier would have been absorbed.

Grazing in the semi-arid grasslands of East and South Africa offers a good illustration of these observations. Under natural conditions, these grasslands are periodically subjected to intense grazing by large herbivores. The episodes are much like pulsations, and they lead to a dynamic balance between two functionally different groups of grasses. One group, which tolerates grazing and drought, has the capacity to hold soil and water. The other is productive in terms of plant biomass and enjoys a competitive advantage over the first group during those periods when grazing is not intensive. In this way, a diversity of grass species is maintained. This diversity serves two ecological functions: productivity and drought protection. Grazing by large herbivores that periodically shift from intense pulses to durations when recovery is permitted forms a part of the overall dynamics of the ecosystem. However, when fixed management rules are applied there (for example, the stocking of ranch cattle at a sustained and moderate level), it can mean a shift from the periodically-intense pulses of grazing to a more modest, but persistent, level of grazing. The latter mode, occasioned by deliberate economic policy, supports the competitive advantage of the productive, but drought-sensitive, grasses at the expense of the drought-resistant grasses. This in turn means that the functional diversity we spoke of earlier is reduced, and the grassland can flip and come to be dominated by woody shrubs that are of low value for grazing.

3. Classification of environmental resources

Thus far, we have stressed the role of ecosystems in our production and consumption economy. But we have not demonstrated that environmental resources can be identified with the resources that comprise ecosystems. In this section we will do so.

The earth's atmosphere is a paradigm of renewable natural resources. In the normal course of events, the atmosphere's composition regenerates itself. But the speed of regeneration depends upon, among other things, the current state of the atmosphere and the rate at which pollutants are deposited. It also depends upon the nature of the pollutants. (Smoke discharge is different from the release of chemicals or radioactive material). Before all else, we need a way of measuring such resources. In the foregoing example, we have to think of an atmospheric quality index. The net rate of regeneration of the stock is the rate at which this quality index changes over time. Regeneration rates of atmospheric quality are complex, often ill-understood matters. This is because there is a great deal of synergism associated with the interaction of different types of pollutants in the atmospheric sink, so that, for example, the underlying relationships are almost certainly non-linear, and, for certain compositions, perhaps greatly so. What are called "non-linear dose-response relationships" in the ecological literature, are instances of this.[10] But these are merely qualifications, and the analytical point we are making, that pollution problems involve the degradation of renewable natural resources, is both true and useful [see also Ehrlich, Ehrlich and Holdren (1977)].

Animal, bird, plant, and fish populations are other examples of renewable natural resources, and there are now a number of studies addressing the reproductive behaviour of different species under a variety of "environmental" conditions, including the presence of parasitic and symbiotic neighbours.[11] Land is also such a commodity, for the quality of arable and grazing land can be maintained only by careful use. Population pressures can result in an extended period of overuse. By overuse we mean not only an unsustainable shortening of fallow periods, but also deforestation, and the cultivation and grazing of marginal lands. This causes the quality of land to deteriorate, until it eventually becomes a wasteland.

The symbiotic relationship between soil quality and vegetation cover is central to the innumerable problems facing sub-Saharan Africa, most especially the Sahel.[12] The management of the drylands in general has to be sensitive to

---

[10] The economic issues arising from such non-linearities are analysed in Dasgupta (1982a). See also Section 15.

[11] Ehrlich and Roughgarden (1987) is an excellent treatise on these matters.

[12] Anderson (1987) contains an authoritative case study of this.

such relationships. It is, for example, useful to distinguish between, on the one hand, a reduction in soil nutrients and humus, and, on the other, the loss of soil due to wind and water runoff. The depletion of soil nutrients can be countered by fertilizers (which, however, can have adverse effects elsewhere in the ecological system), but in the drylands, a loss in topsoil cannot be made good. (In river valleys the alluvial topsoil is augmented annually by silt brought by the rivers from mountain slopes. This is the obverse of water runoff caused by a lack of vegetation cover.) Under natural conditions of vegetation cover, it can take anything between 100 and 500 years for the formation of 1 cm of topsoil. Admittedly, what we are calling "erosion" is a redistribution of soil. But even when the relocation is from one agricultural field to another, there are adjustment costs. Moreover, the relocation is often into the oceans and non-agricultural land. This amounts to erosion.[13]

Soil degradation can occur if the wrong crops are cultivated. Contrary to general belief, in sub-tropical conditions most export crops tend to be less damaging to soils than are cereals and root crops. (Groundnuts and cotton are exceptions.) Many export crops, such as coffee, cocoa, oil palm, and tea, grow on trees and bushes that enjoy a continuous root structure and provide continuous canopy cover. With grasses planted underneath, the rate of soil erosion that is associated with such crops is known to be substantially less than the rate of erosion associated with basic food crops [Repetto (1988), Table 2]. But problems are compounded upon problems in poor countries. In many cultures the men control cash income while the women control food. Studies in Nigeria, Kenya, India and Nepal suggest that, to the extent that women's incomes decline as the proportion of cash-cropping increases, the family's nutritional status (most especially the nutritional status of children) deteriorates [Gross and Underwood (1971), von Braun and Kennedy (1986), Kennedy and Oniang'o (1990)]. The indirect effects of public policy assume a bewildering variety in poor countries, where ecological and technological factors intermingle with norms of behaviour that respond only very slowly to changing circumstances.[14]

The link between irrigation and the process by which land becomes increasingly saline has also been much noted in the ecological literature [Ehrlich, Ehrlich and Holdren (1977)]. In the absence of adequate drainage,

---

[13] One notable, and controversial, estimate of worldwide productivity declines in livestock and agriculture in the drylands due to soil losses was offered in UNEP (1984). The figure was an annual loss of $26 bn. For a discussion of the UNEP estimate, see Gigengack et al. (1990). The estimate by Mabbut (1984), that approximately 40 percent of the productive drylands of the world are currently under threat from desertification, probably gives an idea of the magnitude of the problem. For accounts of the economics and ecology of drylands, see Falloux and Mukendi (1988) and Dixon, James and Sherman (1989, 1990). We will discuss the notion of environmental stress in Section 7.

[14] See Dasgupta (1993) for further discussion of these linkages.

continued irrigation slowly but remorselessly destroys agricultural land owing to the salts left behind by evaporating water. The surface area of agricultural land removed from cultivation worldwide through salinization is thought by some to equal the amount added by irrigation [United Nations (1990)]. Desalinization of agricultural land is even today an enormously expensive operation.

The environment is affected by the fact that the rural poor are particularly constrained in their access to credit, insurance and capital markets. Because of such constraints, domestic animals assume a singularly important role as an asset [Binswanger and Rosenzweig (1986), Rosenzweig and Wolpin (1985), Hoff and Stiglitz (1990), Dasgupta (1993)]. But they are prone to dying when rainfall is scarce. In sub-Saharan Africa farmers and nomads, therefore, carry extra cattle as an insurance against droughts. Herds are larger than they would be were capital and insurance markets open to the rural poor. This imposes an additional strain on grazing lands, most especially during periods of drought. That this link between capital and credit markets (or rather, their absence) and the degradation of the environmental resource base is quantitatively significant [World Bank (1992)] should come as no surprise. The environment is itself a gigantic capital asset. The portfolio of assets that a household manages depends on what is available to it. In fact, one can go beyond these rather obvious links and argue that even the fertility rate is related to the extent of the local environmental resource base, such as fuelwood and water sources. Later in this chapter (Section 18), we will see not only why we should expect this to be so, but we will also study its implications for public policy.

Underground basins of water have the characteristic of a renewable natural resource if they are recharged over the annual cycle. The required analysis is a bit more problematic though, in that we are interested in both its quality and its quantity. Under normal circumstances, an aquifer undergoes a self-cleansing process as pollutants are deposited into it. (Here, the symbiotic role of microbes, as in the case of soil, is important). But the effectiveness of the process depends on the nature of pollutants and the rate at which they are discharged. Moreover, the recharge rate depends not only on annual precipitation and the extent of underground flows, but also on the rate of evaporation. This in turn is a function of the extent of soil cover. In the drylands, reduced soil cover beyond a point lowers both soil moisture and the rate of recharge of underground basins, which in turn reduces the soil cover still more, which in turn implies a reduced rate of recharge, and so on.[15] With a lowered underground water table, the cost of water extraction rises.

In fact, aquifers display another characteristic. On occasion the issue is not

---

[15] See, for example, Falkenmark (1986, 1989), Olsen (1987), Nelson (1988), Reij, Mulder and Begemann (1988) and Falkenmark and Chapman (1989).

one of depositing pollutants into them. If, as a consequence of excessive extraction, the groundwater level is allowed to drop to too low a level, there can be saltwater intrusion in coastal aquifers, and this can result in the destruction of the basin.

Environmental resources, such as forests, the atmosphere, and the seas, have multiple competing uses. This accentuates management problems. Thus forests are a source of timber, bark, saps, and, more particularly, pharmaceuticals. Tropical forests also provide a habitat for a rich genetic pool. In addition, forests influence local and regional climate, preserve soil cover on site, and, in the case of watersheds, protect soil downstream from floods. Increased runoff of rainwater arising from deforestation helps strip soil away, depriving agriculture of nutrients and clogging water reservoirs and irrigation systems. The social value of a forest typically exceeds the value of its direct products, and on occasion exceeds it greatly [Ehrlich, Ehrlich and Holdren (1977), Dasgupta (1982a), Hamilton and King (1983), Anderson (1987)].

It is as well to remember that the kinds of resources we are thinking of here are on occasion of direct use in consumption (as with fisheries), on occasion indirectly, as inputs in production (as with plankton, which serves as food for fish species), and sometimes in both (as with drinking and irrigation water). The value may be utilitarian (e.g. as a source of food, or as a keystone species), it may be aesthetic, or it may be intrinsic; indeed, it may be all these things (Section 13). Their stock are measured in different ways, depending on the resource: in mass units (e.g. biomass units for forests, cowdung and crop residues), in quality indices (e.g. water and air quality indices), in volume units (e.g. acre-feet for aquifers), and so on. When we express concern about environmental matters, we in effect point to a decline in their stock. But a decline in their stock, on its own, is not a reason for concern. This is seen most clearly in the context of exhaustible resources, such as fossil fuels. To not reduce their stocks is to not use them at all, and this is unlikely to be the right thing to do. In Section 9 we will appeal to modern welfare economic theory to study the basis upon which their optimal patterns of use should be discussed. But even a casual reading of the foregoing examples suggests that a number of issues in environmental economics are "capital-theoretic". These issues will be the substance of Part II of this chapter.[16]

---

[16] There are added complications, among which is that the impact on the rate of regeneration of environmental resources of a wide variety of investment decisions is not fully reversible, and in some cases is quite irreversible. The capital-theoretic approach guides the exposition in Clark (1976), who, however, concentrates on fisheries. For an empirical application of the theory see, for example, Henderson and Tugwell (1979). Dasgupta (1982a) contains a unified capital-theoretic treatment of environmental management problems in the context of poor countries.

4. Institutional failure and poverty as causes of environmental degradation

If these were all, life would have been relatively simple. But these are not all. Admitting environmental resources into economic modelling ushers in a number of additional, potent complications for development policy. They occur for two reasons: institutional failure and poverty.

The early literature on the subject identified failure of market institutions as the underlying cause of environmental problems [e.g. Pigou (1920), Lindahl (1958), Meade (1973), Mäler (1974), Baumol and Oates (1975), Dasgupta and Heal (1979): see Section 14 below]. Indeed, more often than not, environmental economics is even today regarded as a branch of the economics of externalities. Recently, however, certain patterns of environmental deterioration have been traced to inappropriate government policies, not market failure [e.g. Feder (1977), Dasgupta (1982a), Mahar (1988), Repetto (1988), Binswanger (1991), Dasgupta and Mäler (1991), see Section 17 below]. Taken together, they reflect institutional failures. They will be the object of study in Part III of this chapter, where we will place these matters within the context of the thesis that environmental degradation is a cause of accentuated poverty among the rural poor in poor countries.

At the same time, poverty itself can be a cause of environmental degradation. This reverse causality stems from the fact that, for poor people in poor countries, a number of environmental resources are complementary in production and consumption to other goods and services, while a number of environmental resources supplement income, most especially in times of acute economic stress [Falconer and Arnold (1989), Falconer (1990)]. This can be a source of cumulative causation, where poverty, high fertility rates and environmental degradation feed upon one another. In fact, an erosion of the environmental resource base can make certain categories of people destitutes even while the economy on average grows [Dasgupta (1993), Chapter 16]. We will develop this idea informally in Sections 17–19.

These two causes of environmental degradation (namely, institutional failure and poverty) pull in different directions, and are together not unrelated to an intellectual tension between concerns about externalities (such as, for example, the increased greenhouse effect, acid rains, and the fear that the mix of resources and manufactured capital in aggregate production is inappropriate in advanced industrial countries) that sweep across regions, nations and continents; and about those matters (such as, for example, the decline in firewood or water availability) that are specific to the needs and concerns of poor people of as small a group as a village community. This tension should be borne in mind, and we will elaborate upon an aspect of it in the following section, when we come to evaluate an empirically-based suggestion by World Bank (1992) concerning the nature of a possible tradeoff faced by poor countries between national income per head and environmental quality.

Environmental problems present themselves differently to different people. In part it is a reflection of the tension we are speaking of here. Some people identify environmental problems with wrong sorts of economic growth, while others view them through the spectacles of poverty. We will argue that both visions are correct: there is no single environmental problem; rather, there is a large collection of them. Thus, for example, growth in industrial wastes has been allied to increased economic activity, and in industrialized countries (especially those in the former Socialist block), neither preventive nor curative measures have kept pace with their production. These observations loom large not only in environmental economics, but also in the more general writings of environmentalists in the West.

On the other hand, economic growth itself has brought with it improvements in the quality of a number of environmental resources. For example, the large-scale availability of potable water, and the increased protection of human populations against both water- and air-borne diseases in industrial countries, have in large measure come in the wake of the growth in national income that these countries have enjoyed over the past 200 years or so. Moreover, the physical environment inside the home has improved beyond measure with economic growth. (Cooking in South Asia continues to be a central route to respiratory illnesses among women). Such positive links between wealth and environmental quality have not been much noted by environmental economists, nor by environmentalists in general. We would guess that this lacuna is yet another reflection of the fact that it is all too easy to overlook the enormous heterogeneity of the earth's natural consumption and capital base, ranging as it does from landscapes of scenic beauty to watering holes and sources of fuelwood. This heterogeneity should constantly be kept in mind.

5. "Kuznets" curves: Economic growth and the environment

In its admirable document on development and the environment, [World Bank (1992) Chapter 1] suggests on empirical grounds that there is a relationship between gross domestic product (GDP) per head and concentration levels of industrial pollutants. Summarizing the historical experience of OECD countries, the document argues that concentrations of a number of atmospheric pollutants (e.g. sulfur dioxide) are increasing functions of gross domestic product (GDP) per head when GDP per head is low, and are decreasing functions when GDP per head is high. In short, the typical curve has the inverted-U shape (Figure 39.1). It will be recalled that the so-called "Kuznets" Curve relates indices of income inequality to real national income per head in

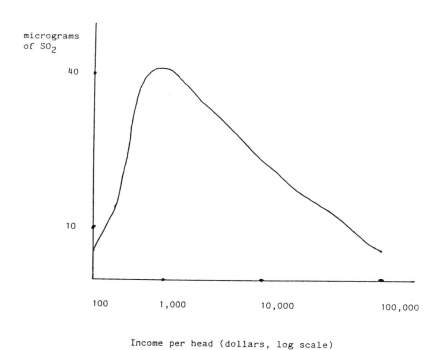

Figure 39.1.   Urban concentration of sulfur dioxide. *Source*: World Bank (1992, Figure 4).

much the same way. So we will call this putative empirical relationship between national income per head and concentration levels of industrial pollutants the Environmental "Kuznets" Curve.

Panayotou (1992) has observed the inverted-U shape in cross country data on deforestation, and emissions of SO_2, NO_x, and SPM (particulate matters). Sweden, for example, was found to lie on the downward part of the curve. Indeed, time series on timber stocks and sulfur and nitrogen emissions in Sweden, covering the decade of the 1980s, are consistent with this: timber stocks have increased, and the emission rates of sulfur and nitrogen have declined. [See also Grossman (1993)].

Like all broad generalizations in the social sciences, the Environmental "Kuznets" Curve is almost certainly something of a mirage. Nevertheless, the idea behind it has an intuitive appeal, since environmental commodities are often thought to be luxury goods. We suggested earlier that a number of them are in fact necessities; most especially for the poor. In fact, such evidence as has been accumulated [in Sweden and the United States; see Kanninen and Kriström (1993)] suggests that income elasticities of demand are less than 1 even for such goods as virgin forests and places of scenic beauty (i.e. even these goods are not luxuries). However, this finding is consistent with the thought that poor countries cannot afford clean technologies because they are expensive. The latter is in part reflected in the incontrovertible fact that citizens in poor countries absorb environmental risks that are not acceptable to their counterparts in rich nations (e.g. safety conditions at work). They do so not because they care less about their well-being, but because the cost of not accepting such risks is too high for them: it means not earning a living. We would therefore expect that the income elasticity of demand increases with income.

It is possible to provide an explanation of Environmental "Kuznets" Curves at a broader level. We begin by noting that the environmental impacts of economic activity in poor countries, being biomass-based subsistence economies, are limited to their resource bases and to biodegradable wastes. Now economic development has often been accelerated by means of an intensification of agriculture and resource extraction. In this phase, therefore, we would not only expect rates of resource depletion to exceed their rates of regeneration, but we would also expect the generation of wastes to increase in quantity and toxicity. At higher levels of economic development, however, matters should be expected to be different. Structural change towards in-formation-intensive industries and services, coupled with increased environ-mental awareness and expenditure (allied to stiffer enactments and enforce-ments of environmental regulations), would be expected to result in a gradual decline in deteriorations of the environment.

This is an intuitively plausible scenario. But we should be circumspect before using it to conclude that there are Environmental "Kuznets" Curves associated with all environmental resources. First of all, the observations are based on the assumption that environmental damages are reversible. This is true only for some resources, and is not a good approximation for many others (e.g. when investment is directed at hydro-electric power, or when the activity exting-uishes an entire species). More generally, environmental threshold effects (see Section 15) provide instances where reversibility of the impact of economic decisions is not a good assumption.

Second, if there really are quantifiable relationships between income per head and environmental quality to be discovered, they must surely depend on other factors as well; in particular, the characteristics of growth strategies pursued by countries. If economic growth were to be encouraged by means of an improved institutional structure (e.g. by a removal of large-scale distortions, see Sections 11–14 and 17), rather than by the decimation of forests and extractive ores, then it is not clear if poor countries would face a tradeoff between increased national income and environmental quality. Zylics (1990) has attributed the high levels of pollution in the former socialist countries of Europe to the adoption of inappropiate industrial technologies. He has argued, for example, that by setting artificially low prices for energy, these countries consumed (and continue to consume) much more energy than the rest of Europe.[17] In Sections 11–14 and 17 we will see analytically why an improvement in production efficiency could be expected to be beneficial to the environment, broadly defined, so that even while some resources deteriorate in quality (or reduce in quantity), others would show an improvement, at least in the long run. However, partial improvements in prevailing resource allocation mechanisms cannot be guaranteed to enhance environmental quality: if important distortions persist elsewhere in the economy, the elimination of market or policy failure in a given sector would not necessarily lead to an improvement in human well-being. This is the central message of the theory of the second-best in welfare economics.

All this has a bearing on structural and sectoral adjustment programmes. If they are carefully designed, such programmes should not be unfriendly towards the environment.[18] Furthermore, the elimination of price distortions would make economic analyses of environmental problems that much more transparent. In the presence of government-induced distortions, it is often very difficult to locate the ultimate causes of any particular environmental problem. In such situations, the temptation of governments is to enact ad hoc policies aimed at countering the problem in question. Over time this can result in a patchwork of taxes and subsidies, quotas, and regulations, so intricate, that it proves impossible to devise ways of sustaining anything like an optimal pattern of resource use.

Implicit in the Environmental "Kuznets" Curve depicted in Figure 39.1 are two key assumptions: (1) the variable measured along the horizontal axis is gross national product (GNP) per head, conventionally measured, and (2) the vertical axis measures industrial pollution. The nature of the tradeoff between poverty and environmental quality is conditional on both assumptions. In Sections 11–14 and the Appendices, we will focus on (1) and study why and how conventionally measured GNP ought to be replaced by an index of real net national product (NNP) that takes into account depreciation (or appreciation) of the natural-resource base. If living standards were to be assessed by a correct measure of NNP, then the nature of tradeoffs between human well-

---

[17] Poland's GNP represents about 3 percent of European GNP (excluding the former Soviet Union); but its energy consumption is about 8 percent of the corresponding European figure.
[18] World Bank (1992) offers a similar viewpoint.

being and environmental quality, even for poor countries, should be expected to be different from that implied by the Environmental "Kuznets" Curve. Or so we will argue. In Sections 15–19 we will focus on (2) and develop a point stressed earlier, that as regards local environmental resources (e.g. local forest products, grazing lands, water sources), the link between poverty and the environment is different from that suggested in the Environmental "Kuznets" Curve.

Part II: Environmental economics as capital theory

6. The balance of materials

Every elementary textbook in economics contains a figure illustrating the circular flow of goods and services across interdependent markets. Typically, though, the figure neglects the circular flow of goods and bads between human society and nature, a matter at the foundations of environmental economics. Figure 39.2 illustrates the flow of materials between the economy and its supporting ecosystems.

The arrow labelled "input" depicts those inputs into production that are drawn from the environment. They include mineral ores, oil, timber, fish, agricultural products, air, water, and so on. These goods are processed and are then either sold to households as consumer goods or converted into capital goods.[19] The box labelled "production" illustrates this.

In this connection, it is useful to recall the First Law of Thermodynamics, which states that neither matter nor energy can be created or destroyed, but that each can be transformed into a different form of itself.[20] This means that the mass of inputs entering the production box in Figure 39.2 must equal the mass of the outgoing flow. One component of this outgoing flow is the mass of final goods (i.e. consumption and production goods). The other component is the flow of residuals, or wastes, which is deposited into the environment.

The same argument can be applied to the box labelled "households". The flow of consumer goods entering this box must have a corresponding flow of residuals leaving it.[21] Some of these residuals are transported to waste-treatment and recycling plants. A key point to note is that waste treatment does not

---

[19] We are keeping consumption and production units separate here, because this is how the matter is typically presented. In subsistence economies, households are involved in both production and consumption. Our account would in fact be simpler for such systems.

[20] See especially Georgescu-Roegen (1971) for a critique of production models that neglect this Law.

[21] This equality is subject to the assumption that there are no consumer durables. The mass of inflows would exceed the mass of outflows if consumer durables were significant.

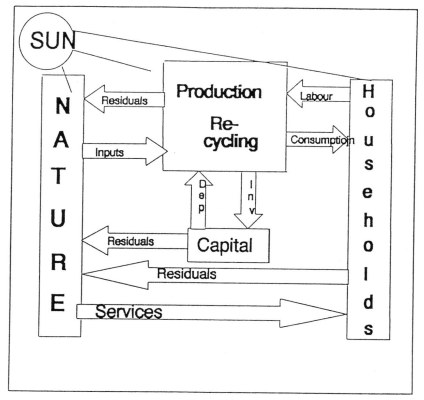

Figure 39.2.

reduce the mass of the outgoing stream; it transforms the stream into other forms of matter.

If the treatment is effective, the transformed matter is less damaging to the environment. But there is no getting away from the fact that the mass that enters production and consumption must eventually emerge as residuals. For this reason, the equality is called the "material balance principle".[22] In the box labelled "capital", the mass of inflows can exceed that of outflows by significant amounts. This is because matter is stored in real capital (e.g. buildings and machinery). There is a sense in which real capital can be considered as stored natural resources.[23]

---

[22] The principle was introduced into economics by Ayres and Kneese (1969), and was further developed by d'Arge, Ayres and Kneese (1970) and Mäler (1974). This section is based on Mäler (1974).

[23] In saying this, we are not subscribing to an environmental theory of value.

In addition to providing inputs for production, the environment also provides a broad category of services directly to households. They include life supporting services (e.g. clean air, water, climate control, food), as well as amenities. As a general rule, the discharge of residuals affects the quantity and quality of these services. It follows that the quality of these services depends upon the amount of matter we extricate from the environment. This forms a major concern of ecological economics.

Our entire ecosystem is driven by current and past solar radiation.[24] The concentrated solar energy is used by natural systems and humans, and is degraded in a manner that is governed by the Second Law of Thermodynamics. It is often suggested that modern resource allocation theory is innocent of the Second Law. But this is not so. The economics of exhaustible resources, for example, is built on the assumption that the integral over time of the flow of "consumption" that we derive from such a resource must be less than or equal to its total available stock. But this in turn assumes that recycling is not a possiblity – an example of the Second Law at work for such commodities as fossil fuels and natural gas. (On this, see Dasgupta and Heal, 1979.)

There are several lessons to be drawn from the exercise we have just conducted with the material balance principle, the most important of which is that an increase in the scale of production typically leads to an increase in the mass of inputs, and, thereby, to an increase in the load imposed on nature from the increased mass of residuals. If economic growth were instead to be associated with less material-intensive technologies (e.g. services, rather than mechanical engineering), then damages to the natural environment would be that much less. Admittedly, recycling offers a way of reducing the flow of residuals. But recycling requires energy, and if that energy were to be obtained from fossil fuels, we would be back full circle to the problem we started with; namely, an increase in the flow of residuals, and an eventual increase in the load borne by the environment.

The only sources of energy that could counter this problem are nuclear or solar energy. Nuclear energy, however, raises its own problems, and they have been much discussed in the environmental literature. There remains solar energy. If technological discoveries were to yield effective ways of harnessing solar energy (and ways of exporting the high entropy heat resulting from the use of that solar energy to outer space), then recycling would offer society a way of expanding the production base without causing damage to the environment. But these possibilities lie in an unpredictable future.

We may conclude that sustained and uniform growth in production and consumption would damage the environment. However, economic growth also

---

[24] There is an exception: the energy released from nuclear plants. But as this is negligible, we will ignore it.

brings in its wake a higher material standard of living. As noted earlier, the demand for a better environment would be expected to increase with growing wealth, and this would induce structural changes in the economy in a way that reduces the deleterious effects of living on the surrounding environment. The link between economic growth and environmental pollution is even today not well understood.

7. Needs, stress, and carrying capacity: Land and water

How much land does a man need?[25] Here we will provide some orders of magnitude in tropical subsistence economies, and for simplicity we will ignore uncertainty in production.[26]

Rice cultivation in the drylands using conventional techniques requires something like 130 person-days of labour time per hectare each year, and it yields about 15 billion joules (GJ), or 1000 kg of rice. If the average energy input in cultivation per working day is taken to be 3 million joules (MJ), total energy required for cultivation amounts to 390 MJ, or 0.39 GJ, per hectare over the year. Therefore, the net energy produced amounts to 14.61 GJ. Assuming an individual's energy requirements is 2,200 kcal per day, a family with five members would require 17 GJ of food energy per year.[27] This in turn means that the family would need approximately 1.2 ha of land to remain in energy balance. Inversely, a family of five would be the *carrying capacity* of 1.2 ha. Total work input on this amount of land is 0.39×1.2 GJ, or approximately 0.5 GJ. Therefore, the ratio of energy output to energy input in this form of cultivation is 34:1. This is quite high, and compares very favourably with the energy output-input ratios associated with the technologies available to hunter-gatherers, pastoralists and food-garden systems in fertile tropical coastal areas.[28]

Crude, but revealing, calculations of this kind can also be done for water requirements. While 70 percent of the earth's surface is covered by water, about 98 percent of this is salt-water. Most of the earth's fresh water is stored

[25] We are putting the question in the way Tolstoy did.

[26] The computation is taken from Payne (1985, p. 7). An original source of this kind of calculations is Leach (1975), who provided estimates of energy inputs and outputs per hectare for a variety of agricultural systems [see also Bayliss Smith (1981)]. Higgins et al. (1982) estimated the carrying capacity of different types of land in poor countries. This section is taken from Dasgupta (1993).

[27] 1 kcal (kilocalorie) equals approximately 4.184 kJ (kilojoules).

[28] The carrying capacity of land can be increased enormously by suitable investment. In irrigated rice cultivation a hectare can support as many as 15 people, provided fertilizers, pest controls, and improved seeds are used. See Norse (1985) for sample calculations of this sort. It may be noted that China averages only about 0.09 hectares of arable land per head, while Indonesia, India and the USA average 0.12, 0.20 and 0.55, respectively (see Clark, 1989).

as polar ice-caps and in underground reservoirs. (Only about 0.015 percent is available in rivers, lakes and streams). It is distributed most unevenly across regions.

The three sources of water for any given territory are trans-frontier aquifers, rivers from upstream locations, and rainfall. The water that is available from precipitation comes in two forms: soil moisture, and the annual recharge of terrestrial water systems (aquifers, ponds, lakes, and rivers). Rain-fed agriculture consumes an amount of water roughly proportional to the produced biomass (the water is returned to the atmosphere as plant evapotranspiration). Water can be recycled, and so the water utilization rate can be in excess of the water supply. (Israel, Libya, and Malta have utilization rates well in excess of annual water supplies.) The problem is that, in semi-arid and arid regions, losses due to evaporation from natural vegetation and wet surfaces are substantial, and not much effort is made in the poor drylands to develop technologies for reducing them (e.g. improved designs of tanks and reservoirs). The mean annual precipitation divided by mean annual potential evapotranspiration is less than 0.03 in hyper-arid regions (annual rainfall less than 10 cm); between 0.03 and 0.20 in arid regions (annual rainfall between 10 and 30 cm); between 0.20 and 0.50 in semi-arid regions (annual rainfall between 20 and 50 cm); and between 0.50 and 0.75 in sub-humid regions (annual rainfall between 50 and 80 cm). According to most classifications, this set of regions comprises the *drylands*. Within the drylands, rain-fed agriculture is suited only to sub-humid regions. Occupying about a third of the earth's land surface, the drylands are the home of some 850 million people (Dixon, James and Sherman, 1989, p. 3).

Losses due to evapotranspiration are dependent upon soil cover. It would appear to be at a maximum when the soil moisture is at full capacity (the so called "field capacity") and the soil is fully covered with vegetation. So a reduction in cover would lower evapotranspiration. But this would be so only upto a point: ecosystems are structurally stable only within limited regions of the space of their underlying parameters.[29] The idea of "thresholds effects" are an instance of this. Thus beyond a point, losses due to evaporation in the drylands are accelerated by disappearing biomass. For example, only about 10–20 percent of rainfall finds use in the production of vegetation in the Sahelian rangelands (where the annual rainfall is in the range 10–60cm). Some 60 percent is returned to the atmosphere as unproductive evaporation. Irrigation schemes in the drylands, bringing water from distant parts, is unlikely to be cost-effective. This is a solution more appropriate to temperate

[29] They must possess some structural stability, otherwise they would have been destroyed a long time ago. The much-discussed Gaia hypothesis concerns the structural stability of the global eco-system [see e.g. Ehrlich and Roughgarden (1987)].

zones. It has been argued that, the proportion of rainfall in the drylands that is productive can be increased to 50 percent if vegetation is allowed to grow, and if suitable catchments are constructed [Falkenmark (1986), Barghouti and Lallement (1988)].

Something like 1,250 cubic metres of water per person is required annually for the supply of habitats and for the production of subsistence crops in the drylands. This does not include the water that is required for municipal supplies, for industry, and for the production of cash crops. (Agriculture currently uses about 75 percent of the world's use of fresh water, industry about 20 percent, and domestic activities the remaining 5 percent). A community experiences *water stress* if, for every 1 million cubic metres of water available annually for use, there are 600–1,000 persons having to share it. When more than 1,000 persons are forced to share every 1 million cubic metres of water annually, the problem is one of severe shortage. Currently, well over 200 million people in Africa are suffering from water stress or worse [Falkenmark (1989)]. The tangled web of population growth, deforestation, water stress, and land degradation defines a good deal of the phenomenon of destitution in the world as we now know it.

8. Social objectives, 1: Sustainable development

World Commission (1987) popularized the phrase *sustainable development* in connection with the use of environmental resources, and it continues to be the focal point of much of the writings on the environment. Unfortunately, the emerging literature has in great measure been developed independently of both intertemporal welfare economics and the theory of optimal development, two subjects that have provided us for over twenty-five years a language in which we may usefully ask questions regarding intergenerational justice. In the event, most writings on sustainable development start from scratch and some proceed to get things hopelessly wrong. It would be difficult to find another field of research endeavour in the social sciences that has displayed such intellectual regress.

Much attention has been given to defining "sustainable development". Consider, for example, the following: "we can summarize the necessary conditions for sustainable development as constancy of the natural capital stock; more strictly, the requirement for non-negative changes in the stock of natural resources, such as soil and soil quality, ground and surface water and their quality, land biomass, water biomass, and the waste-assimilation capacity of the receiving environments" (Pearce, Barbier and Markandya, 1988, p. 6). Or consider instead the passage cited by Solow (1991) from a UNESCO document: "every generation should leave water, air and soil resources as pure and unpolluted as when it came on earth".

Both passages involve a category mistake, the mistake being to identify the determinants of well-being (e.g. the means of production of the means of production of well-being) with the constituents of well-being (e.g. health, welfare, and freedoms). But leaving that aside for the moment, the point is not that sustainable development, as it is defined by these authors, is an undesirable goal: rather, it is an impossible goal. In any event, the focus of concern should be present and future well-being, and methods of determining how well-being is affected by policy. History, introspection, and experience with analytical models since the early 1960s tell us that reasonable development paths would involve patterns of resource substitution over time.

To be sure, a number of authors writing on sustainable development have recognized that the starting point ought to be the realization of well-being over time. But the thought that, barring exhaustible resources, a just distribution of well-being implies that all capital stocks ought to be preserved, retains an emotional pull. For example, elaborating on the notion of sustainable development, von Amsberg (1993, pp. 15–16) writes: "Under (the) guidelines for intergenerational resource distribution, the endowment of every generation would include the sustainable yield of the earth's natural capital plus the benefits from resource depletion of natural capital if adequate compensation is made to future generations . . . owning land would only include the right to harvest the sustainable yield of the land while leaving the capital value intact . . . the guidelines for intergenerational resource distribution could be implemented through a sustainability constraint . . . The purpose of the sustainability constraint is to ensure some minimum level of welfare of future generations and a guarantee that a basic stock of natural capital is passed on to the next generation".

Two constraints? No doubt *some* index of natural capital would have to be preserved if a minimum level of welfare for the future is to be guaranteed. Why then introduce it as an additional constraint? Preservation of the index ought to be derivable from the optimization exercize.

A second weakness of the formulation is this: it offers no direct ethical argument for imposing either of the side constraints. A more general (and intellectually firmer) approach would be to allow future generations' well-beings to be reflected in a function that is defined over the well-beings of all generations. In other words, the idea is to appeal to an aggregate social well-being function. Such a tactic would enable us also to experiment with different degrees of substitutibility between different generations' levels of well-being. The demands on the present generation could well be stiffer in this framework than that it be required merely to ensure that some minimum level of well-being is guaranteed for future generations.[30] This point of view was adopted by the late Tjalling Koopmans in his formulation of the problem of intergenerational justice.

9. Social objectives, 2: Optimal development, discount rates and sustainability

In a remarkable set of contributions, Koopmans (1960, 1965, 1967, 1972a,b) conducted a series of thought-experiments on intertemporal choice so as to see the implications of alternative sets of ethical assumptions in plausible worlds.[31] Underlying Koopmans's programme of research was the premise that no ethical judgment in such abstract exercizes as those involving resource-use should be taken as being decisive. We should instead play off one set of ethical assumptions against another within plausible scenarios, see what their implications are for the distribution of well-being, and then appeal to our varied intuitive senses before arguing policy. For example, he showed [Koopmans (1965, 1967)] that we can have no direct intuition about the validity of discounting future well-beings, unless we know something concrete about feasible development paths. As the set of feasible paths in a world with an indefinite future is enormously complicated, the reasonable thing would be to work with alternative discount rates on well-being and see what they imply.[32] Although seemingly innocuous, this suggestion represents a radical break with a philosophical tradition, stretching from Ramsey (1928) to Parfit (1984), that has argued against discounting future well-beings without first having studied its distributional consequences across generations in plausible worlds. That this tradition is otiose was demonstrated by Mirrlees (1967) and Chakravarty (1969), who showed that in plausible economic models, not to discount future well-beings could imply that the present generation be asked to save and invest around 50 percent of gross national product. This is a stiff requirement when GNP is low.[33]

For simplicity of exposition, let us assume that population size is constant over time (t), and that generation t's well-being is an increasing function of its level of consumption (C_t), which we denote by $W(C_t)$. We assume time to be continuous. Let Γ_C be the set of feasible consumption paths – from the present to the indefinite future – and let Γ_W be the corresponding set of well-being

---

[30] This issue was the focus of Dasgupta and Heal (1974) and Solow (1974a). See Dasgupta and Heal (1979, Chapters 9–10) for an elaboration.

[31] For an account of this programme, see Dasgupta and Heal (1979, Chapters 9–10).

[32] Dasgupta and Heal (1974) and Solow (1974a) provide exercizes of this sort in economies with exhaustible resources.

[33] For a re-assertion of the Ramsey–Parfit viewpoint, see Broome (1992).

paths. We take it that there is no uncertainty, and that Γ_W is uniformly bounded. Imagine that there is an underlying ethical preference ordering defined over Γ_W. Alternative policies are therefore to be evaluated in terms of this ordering. Koopmans (1960) showed that under a plausible set of assumptions, this ordering can be represented by a numerical functional (which we may call _aggregate well-being_) possessing the "utilitarian" form:

$$\int_0^\infty W(C_t) \exp(-\delta t)\, dt, \text{ where } \delta > 0.\ ^{34} \tag{1}$$

Now (1) may look like classical utilitarianism, but it is not. There is nothing in the Koopmans axioms to force a utilitarian interpretation upon W. Moreover, (1) involves discounting future well-beings at a constant rate ($\delta > 0$). In short, positive discounting of well-being is seen to be an implication of a set of ethical axioms that, at face value at least, would appear to have nothing to do with discounting.

When conducting analytical experiments with alternative assumptions embedded in (1), it makes sense to go beyond the Koopmans axioms and allow for consideration the case where $\delta = 0$. It also makes sense to go beyond the axioms and to consider unbounded well-being functions. This way we are able to test models to see what all this implies for public policy and the choice of discount rates in social cost-benefit analysis. On the other hand, purposeless generality should be avoided. So we will assume that $W(C)$ is strictly concave, to give shape to the idea that intergenerational equity is valued as an ethical goal.[35]

It is as well to begin by noting that discount rates in use in social cost-benefit analysis (Sections 10–13) are "consumption discount rates". In first-best situations, they equal "income discount rates". (They are also sometimes, misleadingly, called "social discount rates", and are different from market interest rates in second-best situations; see below). If consumption is expected to grow, then the discount rate used in cost-benefit analysis would be positive even if δ were taken to be zero. This follows from the strict concavity of $W(C)$. To see this, recall that, in discrete time the consumption rate of discount at time t is the marginal social rate of indifferent substitution between consumption at times t and $t + 1$ minus 1. This means that it is the percentage rate of

---

[34] Koopmans's theorems were proved under the assumption that time is discrete. In Koopmans (1972a,b) the ethical axioms are imposed directly on Γ_C, and $W(.)$ is obtained as a numerical representation.
[35] For simplicity of exposition, we will begin by focussing on a full optimum. In Section 10, when commenting on cost-benefit analyses of policies to combat global warming, we will look at second-best situations. Social cost-benefit analysis in second-best circumstances was the subject of discussion in Dasgupta, Marglin and Sen (1972) and Little and Mirrlees (1974).

decline in discounted marginal well-being over the interval $(t, t+1)$. Let ρ_t denote this. Reverting to continuous time and the "utilitarian" form in (1), it is an easy matter to confirm that

$$\rho_t = \rho(C_t) = \delta + \alpha(C_t)[dC_t/dt]/C_t \tag{2}$$

where $\alpha(C_t) > 0$ is the elasticity of marginal well-being at t [see e.g. Arrow and Kurz (1970)]. Moreover, along a full optimum, the consumption rate of discount equals the productivity of capital (i.e. the social rate of return on investment). This is the famous Ramsey Rule.

Iso-elasticity offers a simple, flexible form of $W(.)$. So let us assume that

$$W(C) = -C^{-\alpha}, \text{ where } \alpha \text{ is a positive constant.} \tag{3}$$

In this case the optimality criterion reflected in (1) depends only upon two parameters: α and δ. They reflect different concerns. α is an index of the extent to which intergenerational equity in the distribution of consumption is valued (see below). δ is more directly interpretable: the larger is δ, the lower is the weight awarded to future generations' well-beings relative to that of the present generation. The moral of Mirrlees's (1967) computations was that introducing a bias in favour of earlier generations through suitable choice of δ would be a way of countering the advantages to be enjoyed by later generations, should the productivity of capital and technological progress prove to be powerful engines of growth in well-being.

Nevertheless, consider the case $\delta = 0$. As an example, let us assume that $\alpha = 2.5$ (a not implausible figure if $W(C)$ were to be based on revealed preferences). If the rate of growth of optimum consumption at t is, say, 2 percent, then $\rho_t = 5$ percent. It will be noticed that the larger is α, the more egalitarian is the optimal consumption path. As $\alpha \to \infty$, the well-being functional represented in (1) resembles more and more the Rawlsian maxi-min principle as applied to the intergenerational distribution of consumption (and thus well-being). This in turn means that, even in productive economies, optimal growth in consumption is slow if α is large. In the limit, as $\alpha \to \infty$, optimal growth is zero, a supremely egalitarian outcome. From equation (2), we can now see why the consumption rate of discount is bounded (and how it manages to equal the productivity of capital) even in these extreme parametric terrains. (On this, see Dasgupta and Heal, 1979, Chapters 9–10.)

Social discount rates are percentage rates of change of intertemporal shadow prices. It follows that, unless the optimizing economy is in a steady state, social discount rates typically depend upon the numeraire that has been adopted.[36]

---

[36] Therefore, unless the numeraire has been specified, the term "social discount rate" is devoid of meaning.

As equation (2) makes clear, the well-being discount rate differs from consumption rates of discount. This is not an obvious point, and it continues to be misunderstood in a good deal of the environmental literature that is critical of social cost-benefit analysis [e.g. Daly and Cobb (1991)]. Modern philosophers writing on the matter make the same mistake and conflate well-being and consumption rates of discount. They argue that δ should be zero and then criticize the practice of discounting future flows of consumption in social cost-benefit analysis [Parfit (1984), Cowen and Parfit (1992)].

Although simple, the Koopmans formulation spans a rich variety of ethical considerations. Among other things, it tells us that consumption rates of discount do not reflect primary value judgements: they are derived notions. They are essential when we try to implement optimal policies by means of cost-benefit analysis of projects.

Notice that in equation (3), $W(C)$ is unbounded below. If $\delta = 0$, this ensures that very low consumption rates are penalized by the optimality criterion reflected in (1). On the other hand, if δ were positive, low consumption rates by generations sufficiently far in the future would not be penalized by (1). This means that unless the economy is sufficiently productive, optimal consumption will tend to zero in the very long run. As an illustration of how critical δ can be, Dasgupta and Heal (1974) and Solow (1974a) showed in a model economy with exhaustible resources that optimal consumption declines to zero in the long run if $\delta > 0$, but that it increases to infinity if $\delta = 0$. It is in such examples that notions of sustainable development can offer some cutting power. If by sustainable development we wish to mean that the chosen consumption path should as a minimum never fall short of some stipulated, positive level, then the value of δ would need to be adjusted downward in a suitable manner to ensure that the optimal consumption path satisfies the requirement. (Alternatively, one could introduce the requirement as a side constraint). This was the substance of Solow's remark [Solow (1974b)] that, in the economics of exhaustible resources the choice of δ can be a matter of considerable moment. In any event, these analytical results confirm Koopmans' thesis that striking a fair balance between the claims of different generations would be no easy matter if we were to rely on the set of axioms that yield formula (1) as our overall ethical goal.[37]

A more plausible interpretation of the idea of sustainable development is

---

[37] Choice of a "high" value of δ does not necessarily imply an anti-conservationist stance. As we have observed in the text, ceteris paribus, a "high" value of δ implies a "low" growth rate of optimal consumption (and national product), which in turn means a "low" demand for environmental resources in the long run. Musu (1994) and Rowthorn and Brown (1994) have provided examples where an increase in δ implies an optimal policy that preserves greater biodiversity. Put another way, choosing a high value of δ is the same as giving a low weight to the well-being of future generations relative to the present. However, this on its own does not translate into a rapacious use of the environmental resource-base.

that well-being (and, therefore, consumption) must never be allowed to decline. One way of ensuring this would be to introduce the requirement as a side constraint in the Koopmans formulation. If δ is less than the productivity of capital, the valuation criterion reflected in (1) ensures that the optimal consumption path satisfies the requirement (this follows immediately from equation (2) and the Ramsey Rule), in which case the side constraint does not bite. If, on the other hand, δ is greater than the productivity of capital, then the side constraint would bite and prevent consumption from ever declining. But side constraints are an unattractive way of formulating ethical principles (see below). So we will explore other avenues.

To begin with, it is as well noting that the idea of unbounded consumption streams is based on science fiction. It ignores the environmental resource-base, which is very much finite in extent, and from which human societies are already drawing or eliminating some 40 percent of the basic energy supply from photosynthesis that is being harvested by all terrestrial animals [Vitousek et al. (1986)]. Indeed, no ecologist we know thinks that a population of some 10 billion (which is a reasonable projection for world population in the year 2,050) can support itself indefinitely at a standard of living of today's representative West-European.[38] So it makes sense to regard feasible consumption streams as being uniformly bounded. For the purposes of tractability, let us restrict ourselves to bounded well-being functions, so that feasible well-being streams are uniformly bounded as well.

As noted above, one way of trying to preserve something like a balance among the generations would be to maximize expression (1), subject to the constraint that the well-being of no generation falls below some acceptable level. The weakness of this approach is that side constraints do not admit tradeoffs between competing goals: the shadow price of a side constraint is nil when the constraint is non-binding, but is positive whenever it binds. For this reason, welfare economists typically avoid side constraints as a device for avoiding morally indefensible outcomes.

A more appealing alternative would be to weaken the Koopmans-axioms in some directions even while strengthening them in some others, so as to build in directly the idea that the dictates of intergenerational fairness prohibit zero or "near-zero" consumption level for any generation. One way of doing this would be to regard aggregate well-being as a weighted sum of expression (1) and average well-being over time. Formally, consider the aggregate well-being functional

$$\int_0^\infty W(C_t) \exp(-\delta t)\, dt + \liminf_{T \to \infty} \left[\int_0^T W(C_t)\, dt/T \right], \text{ with } \delta > 0. \tag{4}$$

---

[38] We discussed some illustrations of the notion of carrying capacity in Section 7.

This is linear in $W(.)$; that is, the ordering implied by expression (4) is independent, upto a positive affine transformation, of the well-being function $W(.)$. The second term in expression (4), called the "asymptotic part", gives prominence to the well-being of distant generations, something that is masked in the first term, called the "series part", due to the fact that δ is positive.

Expression (4) is not ad hoc. For consumption streams that possess a long-run average, (4) becomes

$$\int_0^\infty W(C_t) \exp(-\delta t)\, dt + \lim_{T \to \infty} \left[\int_0^\infty W(C_t)\, dt/T \right], \text{ with } \delta > 0. \tag{5}$$

Expression (5) is a member of the class of linear, continuous functionals that were identified in a classic paper by Radner (1967) as being the natural generalization of the notion of present discounted-value of intertemporally-efficient well-being streams.[39] Its underpinnings for intergenerational justice have been studied by Chichilnisky (1994).

In Sections 10–13 and Appendix 2 we will study the implications of this framework for social cost-benefit analysis and national income accounting, both of which are central to the evaluation and choice of public policies. However, for mathematical tractability, we will work with the simpler framework implied by expression (1), and not with expression (5).

10. Second-best optima, global warming, and risk

Analysing full optima (i.e. first-best allocations) helps fix ideas. In reality, a vast array of forward markets are missing (due to an absence of property rights, the presence of transaction costs, or whatever). It is a reason why, typically, market rates of interest ought not to be used in discounting future incomes in the social evaluation of projects and policies.

The phenomenon of global warming offers a good instance of what this can imply. As we noted in Section 3 (see also Sections 14 and 21), the atmosphere is a global commons par excellence, and greenhouse emissions are a byproduct of production and consumption activities. In short, there is "market failure". Social cost-benefit analysis needs to be undertaken with these failures in mind.

---

[39] We are deliberately being loose here. Radner worked on the space l_∞, which is a normed space of bounded sequences of real numbers. In contrast, we are working with continuous time, and so the well-being streams are not sequences.

Consider then that a number of simulation studies on the economics of global warming [e.g. Nordhaus (1991)] have indicated that the social costs of doing much to counter the phenomenon in the near future would far exceed the benefits, because the benefits (e.g. avoiding the submergence of fixed capital in low-lying areas, and declines in agricultural outputs) would appear only in the distant future (viz. a hundred years and more). In these studies future costs and benefits, when expressed in terms of income, are discounted at a positive rate over all future periods, even when doing nothing to combat global warming is among the options that are being considered.

These results, quite rightly, appear as something of a puzzle to many. They imagine that global warming will result eventually in declines and dislocations of incomes, production, and people; and yet they are informed that "economic logic" has been shown to cast a damper on the idea that anything really drastic needs to be done in the immediate future to counter it. Perhaps then, or so it is on occasion thought, when deliberating environmental matters, we ought to use social rates of discount that are different from those in use in the evaluation of other types of economic activity.

We have seen earlier why this would be a wrong thought. On the other hand, using a constant discount rate for the purposes of simulation in the economics of global warming is not sound either. If global warming is expected to lead to declines in (weighted) global consumption over some extended period in the distant future, then the logic underlying formula (2) would say that over this same extended period consumption rates of interest could well be *negative*. If this were so (and it would certainly be so if $\delta = 0$), then from our current viewpoint future losses due to global warming could well be amplified; they would not be reduced to negligible figures by the relentless application of a constant and positive discount rate. It is then entirely possible that far more aggressive policies than are implied by current simulation models to combat global warming are warranted.

Introducing risk into the theory of optimal development raises additional questions, and avoiding future disasters that could arise from global warming provides another reason why more aggressive current action may be called for. Here lies another weakness of most numerical models of global warming [e.g. Nordhaus (1991)]: all estimates are point estimates, and so the downside of risky situations do not get to play a role. The theory of rational choice under uncertainty (i.e. the von Neumann–Morgenstern–Savage theory) instructs us to expand the space of commodities and services by including in their description the event at which they are made available. It tells us that the appropriate generalization of (1) is the expected value of the sums of flows of (possibly discounted) well-being.

Optimal development when future technology is uncertain has been much studied within this framework [e.g. Phelps (1962), Mirrlees (1965, 1974), Levhari and Srinivasan (1969), Hahn (1970), Dasgupta and Heal (1974) Dasgupta, Heal and Mujumdar (1977)]. Risk of extinction of the human race provides an additional reason for discounting future well-beings. If the possibility of extinction is judged to be approximately a Poisson process, then the modification is especially simple: it involves increasing the well-being discount rate by the probability rate of extinction [Mirrlees (1967), Dasgupta (1969, 1982a)]. We will identify a number of the salient features of optimal development paths under uncertainty in Appendix 2 (Section A2.4).

Uncertainty about future possibilities and the fact that economic decisions can have irreversible impacts, together provide us with a reason to value flexibility [Arrow and Fisher (1974), Henry (1974)]. The underlying idea is that the present generation should choose its policies in a way that helps preserve future generations' options. Environmentalists have frequently interpreted the idea of sustainable development in this light.

One way of formulating the idea of keeping future options open is to study the structure of Γ_C (which, recall, is the set of feasible consumption paths, from the present to infinity) in terms of the resource and capital base a generation inherits from the past, and to consider only those actions on the part of the generation that, as a minimum, preserves Γ_C. Thus, writing by K and S the stocks of manufactured capital (including knowledge and skills) and environmental resources, respectively, let $\Gamma_C^{\,t}(K, S)$ denote the set of feasible consumption paths defined over $[t, \infty)$. To preserve future generations' options would be to insist that $\Gamma_C^{\,t} \subseteq \Gamma_C^{\,t+1}$ for $t \geq 0$. This idea was suggested by Dasgupta and Heal (1979, Chapter 9) and subsequently explored by Solow (1991).

There are two problems with it. First, but for the simplest of economies [e.g. the one-good economy in Solow (1956)], $\Gamma_C^{\,t}(K, S)$ is so complicated a set, that, nothing directly can be gleaned about the nature of policies that preserve options. Second, and more importantly, it is an unsatisfactory approach to the notion of intergenerational justice, because it pays no heed to the *worth* of options [Dasgupta (1993), Chapter 3]. But worth cannot be measured except in terms of well-being. So we are back full circle to notions of aggregate well-being. To be sure, uncertainties about current stocks (e.g. numbers of species), and about future needs, wants, technology, climate, and so forth, need to be introduced; say, in terms of the expected value of aggregate well-being. But this is only to remind us of a central truth: the worth of keeping future generations' options open should be seen as a derived value. In other words, the worth should be assessed in terms of an overarching notion of aggregate well-being. The theory of option values (Section 13) is based on this insight.

11. Project evaluation and the measurement of net national product

There are two ways of assessing changes in social well-being.[40] One would be to measure the value of changes in the constituents of well-being (utility and freedoms), and the other would be to measure the value of the alterations in the commodity determinants of well-being (goods and services that are inputs in the production of well-being). The former procedure measures the value of alterations in various "outputs" (e.g. indices of health, education, and other social indicators), and the latter evaluates the aggregate value of changes in the "inputs" of the production of well-being (viz. net national product). A key theorem in modern resource allocation theory is that, provided certain technical restrictions are met, for any conception of social well-being, and for any set of technological, transaction, information, and ecological constraints, there exists a set of shadow (or accounting) prices of goods and services that can be used in the estimation of real national product. The index in question has the following property: small investment projects that improve the index are at once those that increase social well-being.[41] We may state the matter more generally: provided the set of accounting prices is unaffected, an improvement in the index owing to an alteration in economic activities reflects an increase in social well-being. This is the sense in which real national product measures aggregate well-being. Moreover, the sense persists no matter what is the basis upon which social well-being is founded. In particular, the use of real national product in measuring changes in aggregate well-being is *not* restricted to utilitarian ethics.

The theorem should be well-known, but it often goes unrecognized in development economics, and today the use of national income as an indicator of economic development is held in disrepute. For example, Anand and Ravallion (1993) criticize the use of national income in assessing relative well-beings in poor countries, on grounds that income is a measure of

---

[40] In what follows, we will use the terms "aggregate well-being" and "social well-being" interchangeably.

[41] See Dasgupta (1993, Chapters *7 and *10). The technical restrictions amount to the requirement that the Kuhn–Tucker Theorem is usable; i.e. that both the set of feasible allocations and the ethical ordering reflected by the aggregate well-being function are convex (see Appendix 2). The assumption of convexity is dubious for pollution problems, and we will study the question in Section 15. Nevertheless, in a wide range of circumstances, it is possible to separate out the "non-convex" sector, estimate real national income (or product) for the "convex" sector, and present an estimate of the desired index as a combination of the real product of the convex sector and estimates of stocks and their changes in the non-convex sectors. This is a simple inference from Weitzman (1970) and Portes (1971).

opulence, and not of well-being (nor, as they say, of "capability" [see Sen (1992)]. They assert that using the former for the purposes of measuring the latter constitutes a philosophical error, and imply that development planners would have been better placed to make recommendations in poor countries if they had only read their Aristotle, a thinker who had earlier talked about human development. The authors divide national income into personal income and public services, and show that there are a number of countries with a better-than-average personal income per head that display worse-than-average social indicators, such as health and basic education.

But it has long been a tenet of resource allocation theory that public health and basic education ought not to be a matter of private consumption alone. One reason for this view is that they both display strong externalities, and are at once merit goods [Musgrave (1959)]. Another reason is that the credit and savings markets work especially badly for the poor in poor countries. In short, the theory has always informed us that a community's personal consumption would not tell us much about its health and education statistics. As this is standard fare in public economics, one can but conclude that if the majority of poor countries have a bad record in the provision of public services, it is not due to philosophical error on the part of their leaderships, nor a lack of knowledge of resource allocation theory: it is something else. In any event, reliance on national income as an indicator of aggregate well-being does not reflect any particular brand of ethics. Its justification rests on a technical result in economics, and is independent of the ethical stance that is adopted.

To be sure, if real national product is to reflect social well-being, accounting prices should be used. Recall that the accounting price of a resource is the increase in the maximum value of aggregate well-being if a unit more of the resource were made available costlessly. (It is a Lagrange multiplier.) Accounting prices are, therefore, the differences between market prices and optimum taxes and subsidies. This provides us with the sense in which it is important for poor countries to "get their prices right". Moreover, by real national product for an intertemporal economy, we mean real *net* national product (NNP). The accounting value of the depreciation of fixed capital (and by this we mean both manufactured and natural capital) needs to be deducted if the index of national product is to play the role we are assigning to it here [Dasgupta and Heal (1979), Dasgupta and Mäler (1991), Mäler (1991), Lutz (1993)]. Assume for simplicity that labour is supplied inelastically and that the labour market clears (see Appendix 2 for extensions). In this case, NNP in a closed economy, when correctly measured, reads as follows:

NNP = *Consumption + net investment in physical capital + the value of the net change in human capital + the value of the net change in the stock of natural capital – the value of current environmental damages.*[42]

$$(6)$$

We are regarding consumption as the numeraire in our measure of NNP. So the "values" referred to in equation (6) are consumption values, and they are evaluated with the help of shadow prices. In Appendix 2 we will present an account of how net national product ought ideally to be computed in an intertemporal economy. We will study an optimizing economy there. The optimization exercize enables one to estimate accounting prices. These prices can then in principle be used for the purposes of project and policy evaluation even in an economy that is currently far off the optimum [Little and Mirrlees (1974), Squire and Van der Taak (1975)].

An alternative way is to think of public policy as a sequence of reforms. Accounting prices in this framework would be estimated from the *prevailing* structure of production and consumption (and not from the optimum). Consider now an indefinite sequence of improvements of this kind; that is, at each stage small projects are evaluated at the prevailing marginal valuations, and only socially profitable projects are accepted. Such an adjustment process is called the *gradient process* (also called the *hill-climbing method*). If the economy has a strong convex structure, such a sequence of project selections would eventually lead the economy to the optimal consumption and production point. In short, the gradient process converges to the optimum [see Arrow and Hurwicz (1958), for a formal demonstration, and Dasgupta, Marglin and Sen (1972), and Ahmad and Stern (1990), for applications]. Expression (6) reflects the correct notion of NNP in both frameworks.[43]

It is useful to note here that the convention of regarding expenditures on public health and education as part of final demand implicitly equates the cost of their provision with the contribution they make to aggregate well-being. This in all probability results in an underestimate in poor countries.[44] We should note as well that current defensive expenditure against damages to the flow of environmental amenities ought to be included in the estimation of final demand. Similarly, investment in the stock of environmental defensive capital should be included in NNP.

By "investment", we mean the value of net changes in capital assets, and not changes in the value of these assets. This means that anticipated capital gains

---

[42] In an open economy the value of net exports ought to be deducted from equation (4). [See Sefton and Weale (1994)].

[43] For a simplified exposition of the connection between these two modes of analysis (reforms and optimization), see Dasgupta (1982a, Chapter 5).

[44] If education is regarded as a merit good, and not merely as instrumental in raising productivity, then its accounting price would be that much higher.

(or losses) should not be included in NNP (see Appendix 2). As an example, the value of the *net* decrease in the stock of oil and natural gas (net of new discoveries, that is) ought to be deducted from GNP when NNP is estimated. Answer to the question as to how we should estimate NNP should not be a matter of opinion today: it is a matter of fact.

It is as well to remark that our motivation for developing the idea of NNP (both here and in Appendix 2) has been considerably different from those who have written on the matter in recent years [e.g. Solow (1986), Hartwick (1990, 1994), Asheim (1994)]. Our account has been prompted by the desire to obtain a linear index that could serve as a criterion for judging the worthwhileness of small policy changes. To stress this in this chapter, we are emphasizing the link between project evaluation and NNP. Thus, our account is prompted by policy questions. The motivation in the writings of Solow, Hartwick, and Asheim, lies elsewhere. They ask if there exists a (possibly non-linear) index, resembling the ideal index of NNP (but not necessarily identical to it), that measures the return on the present discounted value of the flow of social well-being (i.e. aggregate well-being) along the optimal path.

In Appendix 2 we will link our account with that of these authors. We will see there that these authors identify NNP with what in optimal control theory is called the *current-value Hamiltonian*. Economists in the past have, however, sought to measure ideal output by means of a *linear* index. This is understandable: if an index is to have operational use, it needs to be linear; otherwise one would have to estimate changes in consumer surpluses for each and every commodity, inclusive of environmental services. We will therefore, seek to develop a linear index. We will see that, unless social well-being is a linear function of its arguments, the current-value Hamiltonian is not the same object as NNP.

Current estimates of NNP are biased because depreciation of environmental resources is not deducted from GNP. Stated another way, NNP estimates are biased because a biased set of prices is in use. Prices imputed to environmental resources on site are usually zero. This amounts to regarding the depreciation of environmental capital as zero. But these resources are scarce goods, so we know that their shadow prices are positive. Profits attributed to projects that degrade the environment are therefore higher than the social profits they generate. This means in turn that wrong sets of projects get chosen – in both the private and public sectors.

The extent of the bias will obviously vary from project to project, and from country to country. But it can be substantial. In their work on the depreciation of natural resources in Costa Rica, Solorzano et al. (1991) have estimated that, in 1989 the depreciation of three resources – forests, soil, and fisheries – amounted to about 10 percent of gross domestic product and over a third of gross capital accumulation. Resource-intensive projects look better than they actually are. Installed technologies are usually unfriendly towards the environment.

12. Biases in technological adaptation

One can go further: the bias extends to the prior stage of research and development. When environmental resources are underpriced, there is little incentive on anyone's part to develop technologies that economise on their use. The extent of the distortion created by this underpricing will vary from country to country. Poor countries inevitably have to rely on the flow of new knowledge produced in advanced industrial economies. Nevertheless, poor countries need to have the capability for basic research. The structure of shadow prices there is likely to be different from those in advanced industrial countries, most especially for non-traded goods and services. Even when it is publicly available, basic knowledge is not necessarily usable by scientists and technologists, unless they themselves have a feel for basic research. Often enough, ideas developed in foreign lands are merely transplanted to the local economy; whereas, they ought instead to be modified to suit local ecological conditions before being adopted. This is where the use of shadow prices is of help. It creates the right set of incentives both among developers and users of technologies. Adaptation is itself a creative exercise. Unhappily, as matters stand, it is often bypassed. There is loss in this.

There is further loss associated with a different kind of bias: that arising from biased demand. For example, wherever household demands for goods and services in the market reflect in the main male (or for that matter, female) concerns, the direction of technological change would be expected to follow suit. Among poor countries, we would expect technological inventions in farm equipment and techniques of production to be forthcoming in regions where cultivation is a male activity (there would be a demand for them); we would not observe much in the way of process innovations in threshing, winnowing, the grinding of grain in the home, and in the preparation of food. Thus, cooking in South Asia is a central route to respiratory illnesses among women: women sit hunched over ovens fuelled by cowdung, or wood, or leaves. It is inconceivable that improvements in design are not possible to realize. But entrepreneurs have little incentive to bring about such technological innovations. Household demand for them would be expected to be low.

The argument extends to collective activity in general, and State activity in particular. In poor communities, men typically have the bulk of the political voice. We should then expect public decisions over rural investment and environmental preservation also to be guided by male preferences, not female needs. Over afforestation in the drylands, for example, we should expect women to favour planting for fuelwood and men for fruit trees, because it is the women and children who collect fuelwood, while men control cash income. And fruit can be sold in the market. Such evidence on this as we are aware of is only anecdotal. But as it is confirmed by theory, it is reasonable to imagine that this must quite generally be true.

Such biases in NNP as we have identified here occur in advanced industrial countries as well. So then why do we stress their importance in the context of poor countries? The reason is that poor people in poor countries cannot cope with the same margin of error as people living in rich countries can: a 10 percent drop in the standard of living imposes greater hardship on a poor household than a rich one. Recall too that the rural poor are especially dependent upon their local environmental resource-base (Sections 1 and 3). Losses in well-being due to an underpricing of this base are absorbed by them disproportionately. The estimation of accounting prices of environmental resources should now be high on the agenda of research in the economics of poor countries.

13. Environmental accounting prices: The valuation problem

How we should estimate accounting prices is a complex question. But it is not uniformly complex. There are now standard techniques of evaluation for commodities like irrigation water, fisheries, timber, and agricultural soil.[45] The same techniques can be used for estimating losses associated with water-logging and overgrazing. They rely on the fact that the environmental resources in question are inputs in the production of tradeable goods. As long as the flow of all other inputs in production are held constant, the accounting value of changes in their supply can be estimated directly from the value of the resulting changes in outputs.

For commodities such as firewood and drinking and cooking water, the matter is more complex: they are inputs in household production.[46] This means that we need estimates of household production functions. As an example, transportation costs (in particular energy costs as measured in calories) for women and children would be less were the sources of fuelwood and water not far away and receding. As a first approximation, the value of water or fuelwood resources for household production can be estimated from these energy needs. In some situations (as on occasion with fuelwood), the resource

---

[45] See, for example, Brown and McGuire (1967) for irrigation water; Clark (1976), Cooper (1975) and Dasgupta (1982a) for fisheries; Magrath and Arens (1989) and Repetto et al (1989) for soil fertility; Newcombe (1984) and Anderson (1987) for forestry; and Solorzano et al. (1991) for the latter three.

[46] The classic on household production is Becker (1981).

is a substitute for a tradeable input (for example, paraffin or kerosine); in others (as with cooking water) it is a complement to tradeable inputs (for example, food grain). Such facts allow us to estimate accounting prices of non-marketed goods in terms of the accounting prices of marketed goods [Mäler (1974)]. In Appendix 1 we will develop the household production function approach to the estimation of accounting prices in greater detail.[47]

The approach outlined above allows us to capture only the known use-value of a resource. As it happens, its shadow price may well exceed this. Why? The reason is that there may be additional values embodied in a resource stock. One additional value, applicable to living resources, is their intrinsic worth *as* living resources. (It is absurd to suppose that the value of a blue whale is embodied entirely in its flesh and oil, or that the value of the "game" in Kenyan safari parks is simply the present-discounted value of tourists' willing-ness-to-pay). The idea of "intrinsic worth" of living things is inherent not only within traditional religious systems of ethics, but also in the modern "utilitarian" tradition. Therefore, the question is not so much whether living things possess intrinsic worth, but rather, about ways of assessing this worth. It is almost impossible to get a quantitative handle on intrinsic worth. So the right thing to do is to take note of it, keep an eye on it, and call attention to it in public debate if the resource is threatened with extinction.

What is the point of basing shadow prices solely on use-value when we know that resources often possess intrinsic value as well? It is that such estimates provide us with *biased* shadow prices, and this can be useful information. For example, in his classic paper on the optimal rate of harvest of blue whales, Spence (1974) took the shadow price of these creatures to be the market value of their flesh, a seemingly absurd and repugnant move. But he showed that under a wide range of plausible parametric conditions, it would be most profitable commercially for the international whaling industry to agree on a moratorium until the desired long run population size were reached, and for the industry to subsequently harvest the creatures at a rate equal to the population's (optimal) sustainable yield.[48] In other words, preservation is recommended solely on commercial ground. But if preservation is justified

---

[47] A second approach to the estimation of accounting prices of environmental resources is based on contingent valuation methods (or CVMs). They involve asking concerned individuals to reveal their equivalent (or compensating) valuation of hypothetical changes in the flow of environmental services. CVMs are useful in the case of amenities, and their applications have so far been confined to advanced industrial countries. As we are not focusing on amenities in this chapter, we will not develop the ideas underlying CVMs any further. The most complete acccount to date on CVMs is Mitchell and Carson (1989). See also the report on the NOAA Panel on Contingent Valuation (co-chaired by K.J. Arrow and R.M. Solow) in the *Federal Register*, 58(10), 15 January 1993.

[48] During the moratorium the whale population grows at the fastest possible rate. In his numerical computations, the commerically most-profitable duration of the moratorium was found to be some 10–15 years.

when the shadow values of blue whales are estimated from their market prices, the recommendation would, obviously, be reinforced if their intrinsic worth were to be added. This was the point of Spence's exercize.

There is another source of value of environmental resources, which is more amenable to quantification. It arises from a combination of two things common to them: uncertainty in their future use-values, and irreversibility in their use. (Genetic material in tropical forests provides a prime example). The twin presence of uncertainty and irreversibility implies that, even if the social well-being function were neutral to risk, it would not do to estimate the accounting price of an environmental resource solely on the basis of the expected benefit from its future use. Irreversibility in its use implies that preservation of its stock has an additional value – the value of extending society's set of future options. (We discussed this in a wider context in Section 9). Future options have an additional worth because, with the passage of time, more information is expected to be forthcoming about the resource's use-value. This additional worth is often called an *option value*. The accounting price of a resource is the sum of its use-value and its option value.[49]

Part III: Poverty, institutions, and the environment

14. Markets and their failure: Unidirectional and reciprocal externalities

All this has been from what one may call the "programming" or "operations research" side of things. It is an essential viewpoint, but it is limited. By way of its complement, there is the institutional side, with all its attendant difficulties. We earlier observed that the market price of environmental resources in situ is often nil, even though they are clearly of value. Why? The blanket answer is "market failure", but the sharper answer is provided by environmental externalities, arising from incomplete property rights and information and transaction costs. We turn to this.

By a market we will mean an institution that makes available to interested parties the opportunity to negotiate courses of action. Now interested parties would be unable to negotiate courses of actions if property rights were to be either incompletely specified, or insubstantially enforced (see below). Furthermore, market outcomes (i.e. the outcome of private, decentralized negotiations) are typically inefficient if much information of relevance to the negotiation process is privately held. Environmental resources, by virtue of their physical characteristics, present especial difficulties in each of these regards.

---

[49] The pioneering works are Arrow and Fisher (1974) and Henry (1974). See also Dasgupta (1982a), Fisher and Hanemann (1986) and Mäler (1989).

Consequently, markets for environmental resources often do not exist, and they are prone to malfunction when they do exist. In this section we will focus on the implications of incomplete markets. In Sections 15–17 and 19 we will touch upon the implications on the design of institutions of the fact that much information is privately held. We will note there that certain patterns of "centralized" coordination are required as supplements to markets. But for reasons of space, our treatment will be sketchy. (On the design of resource allocation mechanisms see e.g. Groves and Ledyard (1977), d'Aspremont and Gerard-Varet (1979), Dasgupta, Hammond and Maskin (1979, 1980), Dasgupta (1980), Laffont and Maskin (1982), Farrell (1987).

Market failure is prominent in those hidden interactions that are *unidirectional*; for example deforestation in the uplands, which can inflict damages on the lowlands in watersheds.[50] It pays first to concentrate on the assignment of property rights before seeking remedies. The common law in many poor countries, if we are permitted to use this expression in a universal context, *de facto* recognizes polluters' rights, and not those of the pollutees. Translated into our present example, this means that the timber merchant who has obtained a concession in the upland forest is under no obligation to compensate farmers in the lowlands. If the farmers wish to reduce the risk of heightened floods, they will have to compensate the timber merchant for reducing the rate of deforestation. Stated this way, the matter does look morally bizarre, but that is how things would be with polluters' rights. Had property rights been the other way round, i.e. one of pollutees' rights, the boots would have been on the other set of feet, and it would have been the timber merchant who would have had to pay compensation to the farmers for the right to inflict the damages that go with deforestation. However, even if the law were to see the matter in this light, there would be enforcement problems. When the cause of damages is hundreds of miles away, when the timber concession has been awarded to public land by government, and when the victims are thousands of impoverished farmers, the issue of a negotiated outcome does not usually arise. Judged even from the viewpoint of Pareto efficiency, a system of polluters' rights in such an example would be disastrous. The private cost of logging being lower than its social (or accounting) cost, we would expect excessive deforestation.

When the shadow prices of environmental resources are higher than their

---

[50] Watersheds are fairly self-contained ecological systems. The most critical sector of a watershed is forest cover. The forest not only offers direct yield to its population, it maintains ecological balance and water regime, dampens floods and droughts, retards wind and water erosion and sedimentation. Watershed lowlands are typically used for the production of staple food, and are usually flat plains of alluvial and heavy soil. See Easter, Dixon and Hufschmidt (1986) and Rogers (1992) for an account of the economics of watersheds. The classification of externalities into two categories, "unidirectional" and "reciprocal" (see below in the text), follows Dasgupta (1982a).

market prices, resource-based goods can be presumed to be underpriced in the market. Naturally, the less roundabout, or less "distant", is the production of the final good from its resource base, the greater is this underpricing, in percentage terms. Put another way, the lower is the value-added to the resource, the larger is the extent of this underpricing of the final product. We may then conclude that, when unidirectional externalities are present in countries that export primary products, there is an implicit subsidy on such products, possibly on a massive scale. Moreover, the subsidy is paid not by the general public via taxation, but by some of the most disadvantaged members of society: the sharecropper, the small landholder or tenant farmer, the forest dweller, the fisherman, and so on. The subsidy is hidden from public scrutiny; that is why nobody talks of it. But it is there. It is real. We should be in a position to estimate such subsidies. As of now, we have no estimate.[51]

In some parts of the world, community leaders, non-government organizations, and a free press (where they exist) have been known to galvanize activity on behalf of the relatively powerless pollutees. In recent years this has happened on a number of occasions in different contexts. One of the most publicized has been the Chipko Movement in India, which involved the threatened disfranchisement of historical users of forest products. This was occasioned by the State's claiming its rights over what was stated to be "public property" and then embarking on a logging operation. The connection between environmental protection and civil and political rights is a close one. As a general rule, political and civil liberties are instrumentally powerful in protecting the environmental resource-base, at least when compared with the absence of such liberties in countries run by authoritarian regimes [Dasgupta (1993)].

We will see in Section 17 that matters can be quite different for economic and ecological interactions that are *reciprocal*. Here, each party's actions affect all. Reciprocal externalities are the hallmark of *common property resources*, such as grazing lands, forests, fisheries, the atmosphere, aquifers, village tanks, ponds, and lakes. They are often common property because private property rights are for a number of reasons difficult to define (e.g. in the case of mobile resources, such as air). Even when definable, they are on occasion difficult to enforce (e.g. in the case of forest products in mountainous terrains). However, unlike public goods, consumption of common property resources is rivalrous: it is possible for at least one party to increase its consumption at the expense of others' consumption of them. Resources such as local forests, grazing lands,

---

[51] But see Dixon (1992) and Hodgson and Dixon (1992) for an attempt at such an estimation for the Bacuit Bay and the El Nido watershed on Palawan, in the Philippines. The cause of damages (to tourism and fisheries) was due to logging in the uplands. Dixon's computations were incomplete, but such as they were, the analysis did point to the desirability of a reduction on logging.

village ponds, and rivulets, are often common property because that is how they have been since time immemorial. Moreover, in poor countries they have remained common property for long because they are basic needs and are at the same time geographically contained. Rivers may be long, but they are narrow, and do not run through everyone's land. Upstream farmers would have untold advantages over downstream farmers were they in a position to turn off the "tap". Exclusive private territoriality over them would leave non-owners at the mercy of the owners at the "bargaining table", most especially in societies where markets are thin. No society could risk the institution of private-property rights over such resources.[52] However, unless there is collective action at some level, a common property is over-exploited: the private cost of using the resource falls short of its shadow price. This was the point of Scott Gordon's article [see Gordon (1954), see also Scott (1955), Milliman (1956)]. It was popularized subsequently by Hardin (1968), who coined the phrase, "the tragedy of the commons".[53]

Economic analysis is thought by some to have implied that common-property resources can be managed only through centralized coordination and control, where by a "centralized agency" is meant the government, or some agency external to the community of users. Referring to solutions to the problem of the commons in the theoretical literature, Wade (1987, p. 220) writes: "The prevailing answer runs as follows: when people are in a situation where they could mutually benefit if all of them restrained their use of a common-pool resource, they will not do so unless an external agency enforces a suitable rule". And he proceeds to describe enforcement mechanisms in his sample of villages which do not rely on external agencies.

Wade's is a bad reading of modern economic analysis. The theory of games has unravelled a number of institutional mechanisms (ranging from taxes to quantity controls) that can in principle support effective allocations of common property resources. The theory makes clear, and has made clear for some time, that enforcement of the controlled allocation can in a variety of circumstances be undertaken by the users themselves [Dasgupta and Heal (1979), Chapter 3]. In many cases, such participatory arrangements of control may well be the most desirable option (see below).[54]

---

[52] Rulers had control over such resources in many early societies. But that was not the same as private property rights. Rulers were obliged to make them available to the ruled. Indeed, one of the assumed duties of rulers was to expand such resource bases.

[53] It should be noted that a resource being common-property does not mean that people have free access to it. Often, only those households with a historical right of access are permitted by the community to avail themselves of local common-property resources (see below).

[54] Not everyone writing on the subject has misread the literature. For illuminating accounts of the way communities have jointly controlled common-property resources, see Feeny et al. (1990), Ostrüm (1990), and Stevenson (1991). Seabright (1993) contains a good theoretical discussion of the problems.

Common-property problems can rear their head through all sorts of un-suspected sources. The introduction of cotton as an export crop in Tanzania was successful in increasing farmers' incomes. But other than for the purchase of cattle, there were few alternative forms of saving. The quantity of livestock increased significantly, placing communal grazing lands under stress – to the extent that herds declined through an increase in their mortality rate.

As always, monitoring, enforcement, information, and transaction costs play a critical role in the relative efficacy of the mechanisms that can be used for controlling common-property resources. It matters whether the common property is geographically contained (contrast a village pond with the open seas); it matters whether the users know one another and whether they are large in number (contrast a village grazing ground with a tuna fishery); and it matters whether individual use can easily be monitored, so as to prevent "free-riding" (contrast the use of a village tube-well with littering the streets of a metropolis; or the grazing of cattle in the village commons with firewood collection from forests in mountainous terrain). We will have something more to say on methods of control in Sections 15 and 17. The confirmation of theory by current evidence on the fate of different categories of common property resources has been one of the pleasing features of modern economic analysis.

Public concerns about environmental degradation are often prompted by disasters, such as nuclear leakage or floods.[55] The environmental impact of large undertakings (e.g. dams and irrigation systems, such as the Narmada Project in India) also catch the public eye. This is not surprising. Large-scale effects caused by single happenings are easy to detect. They thereby invite debate. In contrast, the examples of environmental externalities offered for study here are not so easy to detect. They often involve large numbers of resource users, each inflicting only a tiny damage on each of the others, which, however, sum to a substantial amount; usually, over an extended period of time. It would seem that much of the environmental degradation in poor countries is due to this kind of subtle interaction that creeps up over time, and not due to large projects [Repetto (1988)].

15. Property rights, Coase's theorem, and non-convexities

Modern resource allocation theory is in great part grounded on the assumption that technological transformation possibilities, ecological interactions, and individual preferences are all convex.[56] Two of the fundamental theorems of

---

[55] Kreimer and Munasinghe (1991) is an excellent collection of studies on the management of natural disasters.
[56] The classic exposition of this is Koopmans (1957).

economics concern the existence of competitive equilibrium allocations and the implementation of Pareto-efficient allocations by means of competitive markets. Both require the convexity assumption.[57] They also require that *all* commodities and services have competitive markets. In this section we will first study the link between property rights and market exchanges, and then discuss the limitations of the convexity assumption in environmental economics.

In the previous section we studied the implications of an absence of certain types of markets. We noted there that interested parties would be unable to negotiate efficient courses of actions if property rights were either incompletely specified or insubstantially enforced. The link between property rights, transaction costs, and the nature of resource allocations was studied in a famous article by Coase (1960), who attempted to demonstrate the neutrality of the assignment of initial property rights on allocative efficiency, provided transaction costs are nil. As the Coase theorem is often alluded to in the environmental literature, it will pay to study it.

Consider agent A, who is engaged in an activity that, as a byproduct, is damaging to agent B. In Figure 39.3 the marginal private cost to B has been drawn as an upward sloping function of the level of A's activity, and the marginal private benefit to A has been drawn as a downward sloping function. Coase's observation was that the intersection of the two curves is independent of whether A has the right to pollute or whether B has the right not to be polluted.[58] If transaction costs are nil, then bargaining between the two parties could be expected to lead to the point of intersection, and, therefore to an efficient level of pollution ($\hat{X}$ in Figure 39.3). The assignment of initial property rights affects the distribution of income, but is irrelevant from an efficiency perspective.

The above example is prototypical of the argument underlying Coase's theorem. As we have just seen, it invokes several assumptions. They are that (i) the negotiation game is common knowledge among participants; (ii) "transaction" costs are nil; (iii) the game is convex; and (iv) there are only two parties to the negotiation. For this reason the theorem has been much studied for its validity. Here we will ignore the fact that in negotiations over environmental resources, much information is likely to be privately held; a fact that makes certain patterns of centralized coordination and "control" desirable [on which see, Dasgupta, Hammond and Maskin (1980), Dasgupta (1982a),

---

[57] Aumann (1966) showed that the requirement that preferences be convex is not necessary in large economies. We should also note that a third theorem of modern welfare economics, which says that competitive equilibrium allocations are Pareto efficient, does not require the convexity assumption.

[58] In wording the matter this way, we are taking liberties with the legal language. It was one of the points of Coase's article that the question of which party should be thought of as inflicting harm on which other party is itself dependent upon the structure of property rights.

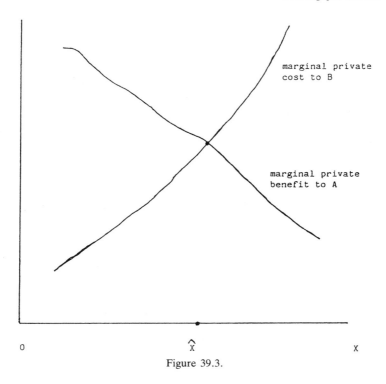

marginal private
cost to B

marginal private
benefit to A

O $\hat{x}$ X

Figure 39.3.

Farrell (1987)]. In the previous section we observed that transaction costs are often in the nature of fixed costs. This too affords a reason for "government" involvement in environmental matters.[59] In this section we will, therefore, concentrate on the desirability of "centralized" involvement when assumptions (iii) and (iv) are violated.

Suppose then that there are more than two parties engaged in a negotiation. Matters can now be very different from the prediction of the Coase theorem, and the very existence of a bargained outcome (let alone whether it leads to an efficient allocation) can depend upon the assignment of property rights. Consider, as an example, the "garbage game", studied by Shapley and Shubik (1969) and Starrett (1973).

Each of 3 parties possesses a bag of garbage which must be deposited in someone's yard. The utility of having n garbage bags in one's yard is $-n$ ($n = 0, 1, 2, 3$).[60] We will suppose that the underlying bargaining game is one

---

[59] This means that assumptions (ii) and (iii) are not unrelated.

[60] Fractional amounts can be incorporated without affecting the analysis.

whose solution is the set of core allocations. We will study two alternative property-rights regimes.

Assume to begin with that parties have the right to dump their garbage on their neighbours (even without permission, that is). It is a simple matter to confirm that the resulting game has an empty core: any allocation that is proposed would be blocked by some two-member coalition. (This is formally the same as the famous voting paradox of Condorcet.) Suppose instead, that each party has a right to as pure an environment as he is able to attain, subject to his having to absorb his own garbage. With these property rights the resulting game has a unique core allocation: it consists of each party retaining his own bag of garbage. It may be noted that this is also a competitive equilibrium allocation, in that it would be sustained by a price system in which a party would have to pay a unit of "utility" to a neighbour for the right to deposit his garbage in the neighbour's yard.

As noted earlier, the convexity assumption has been central to resource allocation theory. But the assumption is especially inappropriate when the environment is included in the domain of discourse. In this connection, it is useful to distinguish in a rough and ready manner two types of non-convexities: exogenous and endogenous. The former are non-convexities at the technological and ecological levels, and they cannot be made to disappear through institutional reform. Key examples are economies-of-scale in production, non-convexities associated with the fact that one cannot be at more than one location at any given time, synergistic effects between different pollutants, non-linear dose-response relationships in the environmental impacts of pollutants, and threshold effects in growth functions of populations.[61] The latter type of non-convexities is dependent upon economic and legal institutions. They are non-convexities that arise under one system of institutions and are suppressed under another. The garbage game we have just studied provides an illustration in the context of negotiation games embodied in the notion of the core. It will now pay to look at the matter from the perspective of competitive markets.

In a seminal pair of articles, Baumol and Bradford (1972) and Starrett (1972) showed that there are underlying non-convexities associated with external diseconomies that can be neutralized by institutional reform. Consider a firm located upstream, whose production activity generates a pollutant as a byproduct. The effluent is deposited in the river, whose water is an input in the production activities of a community downstream. The downstream community is concerned with its own well-being, and can make an appropriate decision concerning its economic activities for every level of effluent, X, in the river. In Figures 39.4 and 39.5 we denote the community's (maximal) well-being as a

---

[61] For further discussion, see Dasgupta (1982a).

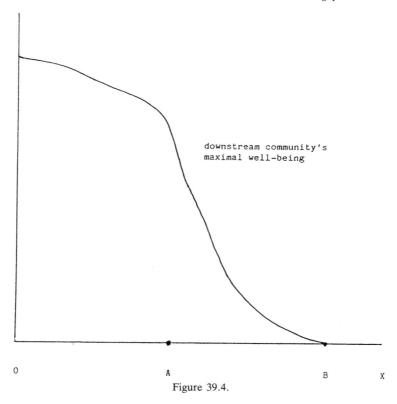

downstream community's
maximal well-being

0   A   B   X

Figure 39.4.

function of X. By definition, the effluent is bad. So the community's well-being is a declining function of X. It must also be bounded below, since the community has the option of migrating to another location (albeit at a cost), or altering its lifestyle and ceasing to be dependent upon river water (again at a cost). It follows that well-being cannot be concave over the entire X-axis. Figure 39.4 depicts the case where the non-concavity is sharp, with the community's well-being falling dramatically in the neighbourhood of $X = A$, and becoming zero soon thereafter, at B (the point at which the community migrates). In Figure 39.5 the non-concavity is "smooth", with the community's well-being tailing off as X increases. (This is the case where it does not pay the community to migrate or alter its lifestyle). The community's well-being in either case is non-concave, and it means that the set of feasible combinations of pollution level and the community's well-being is non-convex.

   Arrow (1971) showed why it is difficult to believe that competitive prices for externalities (or Lindahl prices, as they are sometimes called) can form even when private property rights are well-defined and enforceable. The reason is

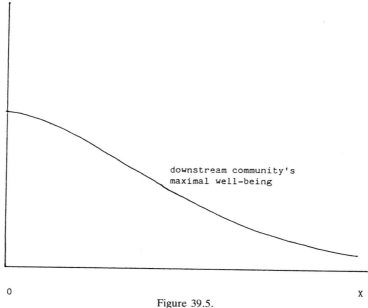

Figure 39.5.

that markets for externalities are typically "thin" (e.g. bilateral, as in the Coasian Figure 39.3). The Baumol-Bradford-Starrett non-convexities imply something more powerful: in the presence of external diseconomies, Lindahl equilibria typically do not exist even if property rights are well-defined and enforceable. This is simple to prove in our example. If the price of a unit of pollution were to be positive (i.e. the upstream firm has to pay the community for each unit of effluent), the community would demand an infinite quantity and migrate. If it were to be either negative or zero, the community's demand would be nil, but the firm's supply would be positive. In no case would market demand for X match its market supply.

But now consider an alternative institutional structure. Markets for externalities are prohibited, and the State imposes a tax on each unit of pollution. The upstream firm is entitled to pollute as much as it cares to, but it has to pay the tax. It takes the tax rate as given and chooses its profit-maximizing level of X. In this scheme the downstream community has no say on the level of X. The optimal pollution tax is one that maximizes aggregate well-being (which includes the community's well-being and the polluting firm's profit, among other things). If the only non-convexities of the system are the Baumol–Bradford–Starrett non-convexities, then a tax equilibrium exists (see below). The reason it exists is that, under the tax scheme the question of equating demand and supply of pollution does not arise: the downstream community does not get to make a demand, and the Baumol–Bradford–Starrett non-convexity is unable to play its detrimental role as regards the existence of a tax equilibrium. This then is the Pigovian solution to the problem of externalities. The example is one among many that make irresistible the Pigovian moral, that patterns of taxation and prohibitions will often be required if environmental problems are to be reduced. (We offered other examples in the previous section). It provides the reason for the attitude we are adopting in this chapter concerning public policy.

But there are problems even with this. Vestiges of the Baumol-Bradford-Starrett non-convexities remain in the Pigovian solution.[62] There can be multiple tax equilibria, and the government in these circumstances would be required to conduct global cost-benefit analysis if it were to try to locate the optimal rate of tax on pollution. This is seen most easily in the case where the downstream community's well-being as a function of X has the shape given in Figure 39.4. It will be noticed that the community's marginal loss in well-being due to pollution (i.e. negative of the slope of the curve LB in Figure 39.4) increases with X until $X \simeq A$, after which it falls rapidly to zero at $X = B$, and it remains zero thereafter. In Figure 39.6 the marginal loss in the community's well-being, as a function of X, has been drawn as the curve CDEBX. Assume now that the marginal gain in profit enjoyed by the upstream firm is a declining function of X. In Figure 39.6 this curve has been drawn as FDX_3, and it depicts a case where it is zero at $X = X_3$, a point at which the community downstream would not operate.

Imagine for expositional ease that market prices of all commodities, excepting for the pollutant, equal their accounting prices. Assume next that the socially optimal level of pollution is the amount at which the sum of the upstream firm's profits and the downstream community's well-being is maximized.[63] Then it is an easy matter to check that there are three tax equilibria in Figure 39.6: X_1, X_2 and X_3 (the points at which the marginal gain in the firm's profit equals the marginal loss in the community's well-being). Of these, X_1 and X_3 are local maxima of aggregate well-being, and X_2 is a local minimum. Suppose that the global optimum is X_1 (as in Figure 39.7), with an implied tax rate t^*. Suppose also that by the time the government notices the problem, the flow of pollutants is at a rate a bit in excess of X_2. In this case marginal social cost-benefit analysis of pollution changes would not deliver: it would lead eventually to the conclusion that X_3 is the optimum. To be sure, X_3 is a local optimum; but the global optimum (X_1) will have been missed.

So the Pigovian solution to the problem of environmental pollution raises its

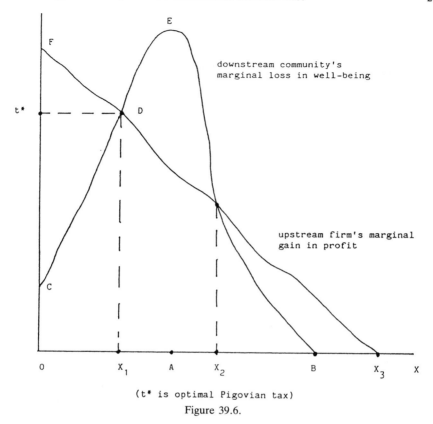

(t* is optimal Pigovian tax)

Figure 39.6.

own problems. Global cost-benefit analysis requires information of a kind that is hard to obtain. It involves the government having to know about possible states of affair that are far removed from where the economy currently finds itself. The tension between weaknesses of market solutions, on the one hand, and government interventions, on the other, is a recurrent theme in environmental economics.

16. Land rights[64]

Property rights on land have assumed a bewildering variety across regions. For example, land rights in sub-Saharan Africa have traditionally been quite

---

[64] This section has been taken from Dasgupta (1993, Chapter 10).

P. Dasgupta and K.-G. Mäler

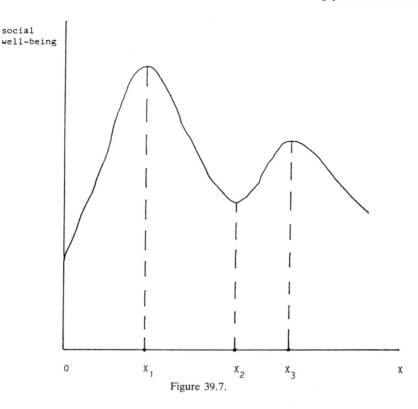

Figure 39.7.

different from those in, say, South Asia. Chance events have undoubtedly played a role in the way patterns of land tenure developed in various parts of the world, but so have economic, demographic, and ecological circumstances. We observed earlier that rights to assets that offer multiple services are often complex. Thus, someone may have the right to cultivate a piece of land (in many contexts if he has inherited it from his father, in others if he is the one to have cleared it), while others may share the right to the products of the trees growing on this land, while still others may have a concurrent right to graze their animals on the stubble following each harvest, and so forth. On occasion, the person who has the right to cultivate a piece of land does not have the right to rent it, or to sell it, and on most occasions he does not have the right to divert water-flows through it. These last are often group rights [Breslin and Chapin (1984), Feder and Noronha (1987)]. However, for clarity it pays to think of polar cases, which are *territorial* (or private property) systems, and *communal* property systems. Even these on occasion can be hard to distinguish in practice. For example, social groups could assert territorial rights over land

and at the same time practise reciprocity over access. This would have much the same effect as controlled communal ownership of all the lands. Or it could be the other way round: ownership could be communal across groups, but residence could be confined to given territories. Right of access to resources by one group from the territories of another would have to be monitored to avoid free-riding. But this would look pretty much like private ownership with reciprocity over access [Cashdan (1983)].

Two aspects of spatially-spread resource bases are of vital importance: *density* and *predictability* [Dyson-Hudson and Smith (1978), Smith (1987)]. By density we mean the average value of the resource, say per square mile; and by predictability we mean the inverse of the variance in the value of the resource per unit of time per square mile, with the allied assumptions that the probability distributions are not overly correlated across spatial groupings of land, and not overly correlated over time. Two extreme types of spatially-spread resources are then of particular interest. The first is characterized by both high density and high predictability (for example, river valleys), and the second by low density and low predictability (for example, semi-arid scrub-lands and grasslands). Resource allocation theory informs us that communities would tend to institute private property rights over the former category and remain geographically stable. The theory also tells us that communities would be dispersed and mobile were they dependent upon the second category of resources. The prevalence of nomadic herdsmen in the Sahel is an instance of this.[65] In any event, we would expect a greater incidence of common property resources in regions where resources have low density and low predictability.

Field studies in India reported in Agarwal and Narain (1989), Chopra, Kadekodi and Murti (1989), and C.S.E (1990) are consistent with these observatons. Hill (1963), Cohen (1980), Netting (1985), Feder and Noronha (1987), Feder and Feeny (1991), and Migot-Adholla et al. (1991) have provided accounts of the evolution of land tenure systems in sub-Saharan Africa that also are consistent with our reasoning. In Africa land rights were typically held by groups, not by individuals. This has recently been trans-formed, a good deal by State fiat (which often claimed ownership, as in Ethiopia, Mauritania, Zaire, Zambia, Nigeria, and Tanzania), and some by the individuals themselves, who break with traditional norms of ownership when land values rise.

Resource density increases with investment and technological improvements; for example terracing, or the introduction of high-yielding varieties of wheat.

---

[65] The payoff (or utility) to a community is the net return per unit of time spent in harvesting the resource and in defending it. For a review of the evidence, see Smith (1987). Boserup's well-known thesis [see Boserup (1965)], that high population density is usually associated with private property rights and the use of the plough, is somewhat different from the classification we are discussing in the text.

Predictability can be made to increase at the same time; for example by the creation of irrigation facilities. (Poor countries today account for about 75 percent of the world's irrigated land area.) The opening of new markets for cash crops also raises resource density. Changing patterns of land tenure often observed in poor countries can be explained along the lines we have outlined (Ensminger, 1990). We will go more deeply into these issues in the next section.

17. Public failure and the erosion of local commons[66]

There is a vast difference between *global* commons and *local* commons. The open seas are common-property resources, as are usually village ponds. As economic analysis makes clear [Dasgupta and Heal (1979), Chapter 3], what are problems for the former are by no means necessarily problems for the latter. However, it is the global commons, and popular writings on them (for example, the influential article by Hardin, 1968), that have shaped popular images of *all* common-property resources. This has been unfortunate, because, unlike global commons, the source of the problems associated with the management of local commons is often not the users, but other agencies. The images invoked by "the tragedy of the commons" are mostly not the right ones when applied to local commons. As noted in Section 14, local commons (such as village ponds and tanks, pastures and threshing grounds, watershed drainage and riverbeds, and sources of fuelwood, medicinal herbs, bamboo, palm products, resin, gum, and so forth) are not open for use to all in any society. In most cases they are open only to those having historical rights, through kinship ties, community membership, and so forth. Those having historical rights-of-use tend, not surprisingly, to be protective of these resources. Local commons are easy enough to monitor, so their use is often regulated in great detail by the community; either through the practice and enforcement of norms of behaviour, or through deliberate allocation of use.[67]

Wade (1987, 1988) has conducted an empirical investigation of community-based allocation rules. Forty-one South Indian villages were studied, and it was found, for example, that downstream villages had an elaborate set of rules, enforced by fines, for regulating the use of water from irrigation canals. Most villages had similar arrangements for the use of grazing land. In an earlier work on the Kuna tribe in Panama, Howe (1986) described the intricate set of social sanctions that are imposed upon those who violate norms of behaviour designed to protect their source of fresh water. Even the iniquitous caste

---

[66] This section is based on Dasgupta and Mäler (1991).
[67] Further differences between the management problems that the local and global commons present are discussed in Section 23.

system of India has been found to provide an institutional means of checks and balances by which communal environmental resources have been protected [Gadgil and Malhotra (1983)].

It is important to caution against romanticising local common-property resource management. Beteille (1983), for example, contains examples of how access to the local commons is often restricted to the privileged (e.g. caste Hindus). Rampant inequities exist in rural community practices. We are laying stress on the fact the local commons are not unmanaged; we are not claiming that they are invariably managed in an equitable way.

The extent of common-property resources as a proportion of total assets in a community varies greatly across ecological zones. In India they appear to be most prominent in arid regions, mountain regions, and unirrigated areas. They are least prominent in humid regions and river valleys [Agarwal and Narain (1989), Chopra, Kadekodi and Murty (1989)]. In the previous section we provided an explanation for this in terms of relative resource predictability and density. An almost immediate empirical corollary of this is that income inequalities are less where common-property resources are more prominent. However, aggregate income is a different matter, and it is the arid and mountain regions and unirrigated areas that are the poorest. This needs to be borne in mind when policy is devised. As may be expected, even within dry regions, dependence on common-property resources falls with rising wealth across households. The links between undernourishment, destitution, and an erosion of the rural common-property resource base are close and subtle. They have been explored analytically in Dasgupta (1993, Chapter 16).

In an important and interesting article, Jodha (1986) used data from over eighty villages in twenty-one dry districts from seven states in India to estimate that among poor families the proportion of income based directly on common-property resources is for the most part in the range 15–25 percent [see also Jodha (1990)]. This is a non-trivial proportion. Moreover, as sources of income they are often complementary to private-property resources, which are in the main labour, milch and draft animals, cultivation land and crops, common agricultural tools (e.g. ploughs, harrows, levellers, and hoes), fodder-cutting and rope-making machines, and seeds. Common-property resources also provide the rural poor with partial protection in times of unusual economic stress. For landless people they may be the only non-human asset at their disposal. A number of resources (such as fuelwood and water for home use, berries and nuts, medicinal herbs, resin and gum) are the responsibility of women and children.[68]

---

[68] The most complete account we have read of the centrality of local forest products in the lives of the rural poor is Falconer and Arnold (1989) and Falconer (1990) on Central and West Africa. The importance of common-property resources for women's well-being in historical times has been stressed by Humphries (1990) in her work on 18th century rural England. The parallels with modern-day poor societies are remarkable.

A similar picture emerges from Hecht, Anderson and May (1988), who describe in rich detail the importance of the extraction of babassu products among the landless in the Brazilian state of Maranhão. The support that such extraction activity offers the poorest of the poor, most especially the women among them, is striking. These extractive products are an important source of cash income in the period between agricultural-crop harvests [see also Murphy and Murphy (1985), and for a similar picture in the West African forest zone, see Falconer (1990)].

It is not difficult to see why common-property resources matter greatly to the poorest of the rural poor in a society, or therefore, to understand the mechanisms by which such people may well get disfranchised from the economy even while in the aggregate the society enjoys economic growth. If you are steeped in social norms of behaviour and understand community contractual obligations, you do not calculate every five minutes how you should behave. You follow the norms. This saves on costs all round, not only for you as an "actor", but also for you as "policeman" and "judge".[69] It is also the natural thing for you to do if you have internalized the norms. But this is sustainable so long as the background environment remains pretty much constant. It will not be sustainable if the social environment changes suddenly. You may even be destroyed. It is this heightened vulnerability, often more real than perceived, which is the cause of some of the greatest tragedies in contemporary society. They descend upon people who are, in the best of circumstances, acutely vulnerable.

Sources that trigger destitution by this means vary. The erosion of common-property resource bases can come about in the wake of shifting populations (accompanying the growth process itself), rising populations and the consequent pressure on these resources, technological progress, unreflective public policies, predatory governments, and thieving aristocracies. There is now an accumulation of evidence on this range of causes, and in what follows we will present an outline of the findings in three sets of studies.

1. In his work on the drylands of India, Jodha (1986) noted a decline in the geographical area covering common-property resources ranging from 26 to 63 percent over a twenty-year period. This was in part due to the privatization of land, a good deal of which in his sample had been awarded to the rural non-poor. He also noted a decline in the productivity of common-property resources on account of population growth among the user community. In an earlier work, Jodha (1980) identified an increase in subsistence requirements of

---

[69] Provided people are sufficiently far-sighted, norms of behaviour that sustain cooperation can be shown to be self-enforcing (i.e. are subgame-perfect Nash equilibria) in stationary environments. For a demonstration of this in the context of repeated games amongst infinitely-lived agents, see Friedman (1971), Aumann and Shapley (1976), Fudenberg and Maskin (1986), and Abreu (1988); and in the context of overlapping generations, see Dasgupta (1993, Chapter 8).

the farming community and a rise in the profitability of land from cropping and grazing as a central reason for increased desertification in the state of Rajasthan. Jodha argued that, ironically, it was government land reform programmes in this area, unaccompanied by investment in improving the productive base, that had triggered the process.

2. Ensminger's (1990) study of the privatization of common grazing lands among the Orma in northeastern Kenya indicates that the transformation took place with the consent of the elders of the tribe. She attributes this willingness to changing transaction costs brought about by cheaper transportation and widening markets. The elders were, quite naturally, from the stronger families, and it does not go unnoted by Ensminger that privatization has accentuated inequalities. However, she provides no data to tell whether the process has increased the prevalence of destitution among the economically weak.

3. In an earlier, much-neglected work on the Amazon basin, Feder (1977, 1979) described how massive private investment in the expansion of beef-cattle production in fragile ecological conditions has been supported by domestic governments in the form of tax concessions and provision of infrastructure, and loans from international agencies, such as the World Bank. The degradation of vast tracts of valuable environmental resources was accompanied by the disfranchisement of large numbers of small farmers and agricultural labourers from the economy. At best it made destitutes of traditional forest dwellers; at worst it simply eliminated them [see also Barraclough (1977), Hecht (1985)]. The evidence suggest that during the decades of the 1960s and 1970s protein intake by the rural poor declined even while the production of beef increased dramatically. Much of the beef was destined for exports, for use by fast-food chains.[70]

These matters, which are an instance of the intricate link between economic, social, and financial institutions, have been taken up anew by Repetto (1988), Mahar (1988), and Binswanger (1991). The latter in particular has shown how in Brazil the exemption from taxation of virtually all agricultural income (allied to the fact that logging is regarded as proof of land occupancy) has provided strong incentives to the rich to acquire forest lands and then deforest them. The subsidy the government has provided to the private sector to undertake deforestation has been so large, that it is arguable that a reduction in this activity is in *Brazil's* interests, and not merely in the interest of the rest of the world. This has implications for international negotiations. The current consensus appears to be that Brazil in the aggregate has much to lose from reducing its rate of deforestation. If this were true, there would be a case for

---

[70] Durham (1979) provides a compelling analysis of the 1969 "Soccer War" between El Salvador and Honduras. The explanation he provides of the disfranchisement of the poor is based not on reduced land-man ratios, but on the expansion of commercial agriculture by the largest landholders in the region.

the rest of the world to subsidize her if she is to restrain herself. But it is not at all clear if the consensus is correct.

The sources of the transformation of common property resources into private resources described in the three sets of studies mentioned above are different. Consequently, the ways in which they have had an impact on those with historical rights have been different. But each is understandable and believable. (Noronha, 1994, provides an illuminating discussion of a number of other case-studies). Since the impact of such forms of privatization are confirmed by economic theory, the findings of these case studies are almost certainly not unrepresentative. They suggest that privatization of village commons and forest lands, while hallowed at the altar of efficiency, can have disastrous distributional consequences, disfranchising entire classes of people from economic citizenship.[71] They also show that public ownership of such resources as forest lands is by no means necessarily a good basis for a resource allocation mechanism. Decision-makers are in these cases usually far removed from site (living as they do in imperial capitals), they have little knowledge of the ecology of such matters, their time-horizons are often short, and they are in many instances overly influenced by interest-groups far removed from the resource in question.

All this is not at all to suggest that rural development is to be avoided. It is to say that resource allocation mechanisms that do not take advantage of dispersed information, that are insensitive to hidden (and often not-so-hidden) economic and ecological interactions (what economists would call "general equilibrium effects"), that do not take the long-view, and that do not give a sufficiently large weight to the claims of the poorest within rural populations (particularly the women and children in these populations) are going to prove environmentally disastrous. It appears that, during the process of economic development there is a close link between environmental protection and the well-being of the poor, most especially the most vulnerable among the poor. Elaboration of this link has been one of the most compelling achievements at the interface of anthropology, economics, and nutrition science.

18. Environmental degradation and children as producer goods

In poor countries children are not only durable "consumer goods" [e.g. serving the cult of the ancestor; see Caldwell and Caldwell (1987, 1990) they are useful also as security for old age (Cain, 1982, 1983)]. Both have been much studied.

---

[71] For alternative demonstrations of this theorem, see Cohen and Weitzman (1975) and Dasgupta and Heal (1979, Chapter 3). The analysis in these works assumes that the property is perfectly divisible. Often, in poor communities an asset is a common property because it is indivisible [see Noronha (1992)]. Privatization of any such property increases inequality.

In fact, children serve also as income-earning assets; that is, as producer goods. This provides households in these parts with an additional motivation for having children. The motivation has been recognized in the demographic literature [Mueller (1976)], but its possible consequences have not been much explored.[72]

We noted earlier that poor countries for the most part are biomass-based subsistence economies. Production throughput is low. Households there do not have access to the sources of domestic energy that are available to households in advanced industrial countries. Nor do they have water on tap. (In the semi-arid and arid regions, water supply is not even close at hand). This means that the relative prices of alternative sources of energy and water faced by rural households in poor countries are quite different from those faced by households elsewhere. Indirect sources (e.g. tap water nearby) are often prohibitively expensive for the household. As we will see presently, this provides a link between high fertility, degradation of the environmental resource-base of a rural community, and an accentuation of hardship among its members.

From about the age of six, children in poor households in poor countries mind their siblings and domestic animals, fetch water, and collect fuelwood, dung, and fodder. These are complementary to other household activities. They are necessary on a daily basis if the household is to survive. As many as 5 hours a day may be required for obtaining the bare essential amount of firewood, dung, and fodder. (One should contrast this with the direct time spent by households in acquiring water and fuel in advanced industrial economies, which is nil.)

All this may be expected to relate to the high fertility and low literacy rates in rural areas of most poor countries. Poverty, the thinness of markets, and an absence of basic amenities make it essential for households to engage in a number of complementary production activities: cultivation, cattle grazing, fetching water, collecting fodder and fuelwood, cooking food, and producing simple marketable products. Each is time-consuming. Labour productivity is low not only because capital is scarce, but also because environmental resources are scarce.[73] Children are then continually needed as workers by their parents, even when the parents are in their prime. A small household simply is not viable. Each household needs many hands, and under certain circumstances the overall usefulness of each additional hand increases with declining resource availability. In their study of work allocation among rural households in the foothills of the Himalayas, C.S.E (1990) recorded that children in the age range 10–15 work one-and-a-half times the number of hours

---

[72] Exceptions are Dasgupta and Mäler (1991), Nerlove and Meyer (1991), and Dasgupta (1992).
[73] Cooking in a poor household is a vertically-integrated activity: nothing is processed to begin with. It is time-intensive.

adult males do, their tasks consisting of collecting fuelwood, dung, and fodder, grazing domestic animals, performing household chores, and marketing. Now, a high rate of fertility and population growth further damages the environmental resource base (to the extent that this consists of unprotected common property), which in turn in a wide range of circumstances (viz. if households discount the future at a high rate) provides further (private) incentives for large families, which in turn further damages the resource base, and so on, until some countervailing set of factors (whether public policy, or some form of feedback that lowers the productivity of additional children) stops the spiralling process. But by the time this happens, millions of lives have usually suffered.[74] Such an explosive process can in principle be set off by any number of factors. Government or private usurpation of resources to which rural communities have had historical access is a potential source of the problem; as are breakdowns of collective agreements among users of common-property resources. Indeed, even a marginal decline in compliance can trigger the process of cumulative causation. The static efficiency loss associated with minor violations is, to be sure, small, but over time the effect can be large.

As workers, children add to household income. They are often costless to rear by the time they are adolescents. This line of argument has been emphasized by Mueller (1976) and Lindert (1980, 1983). Cain (1977) has studied data from the village Char Gopalpur in Bangladesh. He showed that male children become net producers at as early an age as 12 years, and work as many hours a day as an adult. Using a zero (calorie) rate of interest, he estimated that male children compensate for their own cumulative consumption by the age of 15. This may not be typical in Bangladesh. We cite it, nevertheless, to show the vast difference in the motivation for having children between households in rich countries and poor households in poor countries.

It appears then that the transfer of "material" resources over a life-cycle in poor households in poor countries is from offspring in the aggregate to their parents. The qualification is important. We have seen no study that includes in the calculation of resource transfers the value of time forgone in the rearing of children, nor the risks borne by the mother during the process of reproduction. These amount to resource transfers from parents to their children. There is nevertheless a sense in which children are more valuable to parents as producers of income within poor households in poor countries than they are in rich communities. So we will take it that the flow of resources in such communities is from the offspring to their parents. However, it is not mere poverty that leads to this directional flow; it is poverty in alliance with

---

[74] World Bank (1991) has provided weak confirmation of the thesis in the context of parts of sub-Saharan Africa.

immobility. If people are mobile, poor parents are not able to effect this transfer readily. In these circumstances, much of the motivation for having children is absent, and even a poor society may display a move towards the "demographic transition"; that is, the transition from high to low fertility.[75] But this is not so in the Indian sub-continent and sub-Saharan Africa, and its absence makes for a strong parental motivation for having large families.

In many societies (e.g. in the Indian sub-continent), daughters are a net drain on parental resources (dowries can be bankrupting), and this goes some way towards explaining the preference parents there show for sons (Sopher, 1980). It also helps explain why daughters in their childhood are expected to work relatively harder for their parents. All this is in sharp contrast with advanced industrial nations, where material resources are transferred on average from the adult to the young. In a long sequence of writings, Caldwell [Caldwell (1976, 1977a,b, 1981, 1982)] has argued that whether a society has made the demographic transition is related to the direction of the intergenerational flow of resources [see also Willis (1982)].

The motivation for fertility we have been emphasizing here springs from a general absence of certain basic needs in rural parts of poor countries: public-health services, old-age security, water, and sources of fuel. Children are born in poverty, and they are raised in poverty. A large proportion suffer from undernourishment. They remain illiterate, and are often both stunted and wasted. Undernourishment retards their cognitive (and often motor) development [Dasgupta (1993) Chapter 14]. Labour productivity is dismally low also because of a lack of infrastructure, such as roads. With this background, it is hard to make sense of the oft-expressed suggestion [e.g. Simon (1977, 1981)] that there are increasing-returns-to-scale in population size even in poor countries, that human beings are a valuable resource. They are potentially valuable as doers of things and as originators of ideas, but in order for human beings to be able to achieve them, they require inputs of the means for development. Moreover, historical evidence on the way pressure of population has led to changes in the organization of production, property rights, and ways of doing things, which is what Boserup (1965, 1981) studied in her far-reaching work, also does not seem to address the population problem as it exists in sub-Saharan Africa and the Indian sub-continent today. Admittedly, the central message in these writings is that the spectre of the Malthusian trap is not to be taken seriously. But we should be permitted to ask of these modern writers what policy flows from their visions. The Boserup–Simon thesis (if we may be permitted to amalgamate two sets of writings) implies that households

---

[75] See Sundstrum and David (1988) for an empirical investigation of this in the context of antebellum America.

confer an external benefit to the community when they reproduce. This means that fertility ought to be subsidized. We have not seen this implication advocated by its proponents.

19. Work allocation among women and children, and the desirable locus of environmental decisions

The links between environmental degradation and an accentuation of depriva-tion and hardship can take forms that even today are not always appreciated. The gathering of fuelwood and fodder, and the fetching of water for domestic use in most rural communities fall upon women, and, as we have seen in the previous section, upon children as well. When allied to household chores and their farming obligations, the work-load of women in South Asia in terms of time is often one-and-a-half to two-and-a-half times that of men.[76] This work-load has over the years increased directly as a consequence of receding resources. Now it should be remembered that we are speaking of a category of people of whom over 50 percent suffer from iron deficiency, of whom only a little under 50 percent suffer from wastage, and who in some parts of the world work fifteen to sixteen hours a day during the busy agricultural season (Dasgupta, 1993). Thus communities in the drylands of the Indian sub-continent and in sub-Saharan Africa today often live miles away from fuelwood and fodder sources, and permanent water sources. As noted earlier, women and children spend up to 5 hours a day collecting water during the dry season in these parts. The consequence is that anything between 10 and 25 percent of daily daytime energy expenditure is required for the purposes of collecting water.[77]

A similar problem is associated with fodder and fuelwood collection. In northern India, for example, some 75 percent of firewood for domestic use comes from twigs and fallen branches. A substantial part of the remaining fraction comes from cowdung. From data now available from the drylands of India on time allocation on the part of women in fuelwood collection, the energy costs in this activity would seem to be also in the range 10 to 25 percent. In Appendix 1 we will see that estimates of the energy cost of collection are essential ingredients in the calculation of the shadow prices of fuelwood and water.

Information concerning the ecology of local commons is often dispersed, and

---

[76] See, for example, Cecelski (1987), Fernandez and Menon (1987), Kumar and Hotchkiss (1988), and C.S.E (1990).
[77] See Chen (1983) for a review of the link between improved water supply and health benefits among the rural poor.

is usually in the hands of the historical users, who, as we observed earlier, are often the women of rural populations. There are exceptions, of course, but as a general rule this makes it desirable that local commons be protected as commons, and that decisions regarding local commons be left in the hands of the users themselves. This is because the local commons will almost certainly remain the single source of vital complementary and insurance goods for poor people for a long time to come. To be sure, it is essential not only that governments provide infrastructure and credit and insurance facilities, but also that they make available to users new information concerning technology, ecology, and widening markets. However, there is little case for centralized control. Quite the contrary: there is a case for facilitating the growth of local, community decison-making, in particular decision-making by women, since it is the women who are the actual users of these resources and thus know something about the ecology of the matter. More generally, there is an urgent case for the State to ensure that local decision-making is undertaken in an open way. This would help to prevent the economically powerful among rural communities from usurping control over such decisions.[78] This tension – the simultaneous need for increased decentralization of rural decision-making, and for government involvement in ensuring that the seat of local decisions is not usurped by the powerful – poses the central dilemma in the political economy of rural poverty. The large, often fragmented, literature on local common-property resources is beginning to offer an unequivocal impression that during the process of economic development the protection and promotion of environmental resources would best be served if a constant public eye were kept on the conditions of the poorest of the poor in society. Environmental economics and the economics of destitution are tied to each other in an intricate web. We should not have expected it otherwise.

20. Computable general equilibrium modelling

The environmental impact of alterations in property rights or macroeconomic policies (Sections 14–17) can be large: changes in one sector can have substantial, and often unforeseen, effects on other sectors. Computable general equilibrium models (or CGE models) provide a means of identifying and determining the magnitudes of such impacts. In large part, though, existing CGE models are based on the hypothesis that competitive markets exist for all

[78] The need for reinforcing the capacity of rural communities to make decisions about matters pertinent to them is the subject of a special issue of *The Administrator* (Lal Bahadur Shastri National Academy of Administration, New Delhi), 35 (1990). On the role of local organizations in rural development, see Esman and Uphoff (1984) and Baland and Platteau (1993).

goods and services.[79] It is a matter of some urgency that CGE models be extended, so that the "general equilibrium" effects of large-scale policy changes may be studied in second-best economies; for example, those in which labour and credit markets do not clear, or where certain commodities do not have markets. One interesting study that has moved in this direction is Unemo (1993). She has investigated the environmental link between Botswana's two main export goods: beef and diamond.

Beef-cattle in Botswana are grazed in semi-arid regions. This land, assumed fixed in size, is in the main communally owned, and its use would appear to be unorganized. Letting X be the number of cows in the grazing land and $F(X)$ the quantity of beef produced, Unema has assumed that $F''(X) < 0$ for all X. She has modelled land as an open access resource, and so has equated the market price of beef (relative to a cow) with the average output of beef per cow $(F(X)/X)$, not the marginal output. This is an extreme form of the problem of the commons, and is the source of stress on land in her model. The rest of the economy has been modelled in a Walrasian fashion.

The purpose of the exercize was to conduct numerical experiments, in which the impact of changes in macroeconomic parameters on cattle herds could be assessed quantitatively. Unemo has shown such impacts to be substantial. For example, she found that a 5 percent drop in the world price of diamonds would lead to an increase in the size of herds by 12 percent. The mechanism by which this occurs in her model involves the domestic cost of capital: a fall in the price of diamonds makes cattle a better form of private investment. Even if open-access cattle grazing were sustainable prior to the fall in diamond prices, it could well be that it would be unsustainable subsequent to the fall. In short, a drop in the price of diamond prices could well have a deleterious effect on grazing lands. CGE models are good at detecting this type of intersectoral linkages.

21. International institutional failure and the erosion of global commons

Global commons in general pose a different type of problem from that of local commons. Free access to the atmosphere, to watersheds, and to large bodies of water, such as the oceans, are a cause of inefficiency in the allocation of resources. In the case of the atmosphere (for example, over global warming), even the option of "voting with one's feet" is unavailable. Furthermore, future generations are not directly represented in today's forum. Their interests are

---

[79] Dixon et al. (1991) contains a good review of CGE models and their rationale. There are also several softwares available; both for constructing and for solving such models (e.g. the General Algebraic Modelling System, developed at the World Bank).

included only indirectly, through transactions between co-existing generations. The inefficiencies and inequities that are involved with the use of the global commons are, therefore, not merely static, but are also intergenerational.[80] From this it follows that the international community needs consciously to design systems that improve upon existing resource allocation mechanisms.

The most complicated international environmental problems, like the local commons, are characterized by reciprocal externalities: countries both contribute to environmental damages and suffer from them. Emissions of greenhouse gases are an instance of this, and in Section 10 we studied the implications of this on social cost-benefit analysis at a global level. Now, a central problem with greenhouse emissions is that, even though reciprocal, countries do not inflict damages on others in equal amounts. Thus, for a cooperative outcome to be achievable, some financial transfers are necessary, if only in an implicit manner. Several alternatives suggest themselves; debt relief for the preservation of the Amazon being one that has most frequently been discussed.

This is not to say that agreements cannot be reached without side-payments; it is only to say that they will tend to be less efficient. Barrett (1990) has argued, for example, that one should not expect all countries to sign the Montreal protocol on emissions of chlorofluorocarbons (CFCs): if a bargaining equilibrium exists, it involves only some countries signing the protocol. The reason is that if only a few countries were to sign the protocol, national benefits from further reduction in CFC emission would be high. This would induce more countries to sign. However, if many countries were to sign the protocol, national benefits from further reduction would be small, and it would then not be worth a country's while to sign the agreement.

Direct (side) payments among countries for solving environmental problems have not been common. When made, side payments have tended to be non-pecuniary; for example, trade and military concessions [Krutilla (1966), Kneese (1988)]. Recently, an agreement has been reached on reducing the production and use of CFCs in developing countries. This has involved the creation of an international fund for technological transfers to these countries. It is a promising development.

One broad category of allocation mechanisms well worth exploring in the international context involves making the global commons quasi-private. The basic idea, which originated in Dales (1968), is similar to the principle currently being experimented within the U.S.A. The idea, if extended to the international sphere, would have the community of nations set bounds on the total use of the global commons, such as the atmosphere; have it allocate an initial distribution of transferable national rights which add up to the aggregate

---

[80] See Mäler (1990) for a more detailed discussion of these issues. Dasgupta, Mäler, and Vercelli (1994) is a collection of essays on various aspects of the economics of transnational commons.

bound; and allow the final allocation among different users to be determined by competitive markets.[81]

To give an example, consider the emission of greenhouse gases. Suppose it is desired by the community of nations that emissions should be reduced to a prescribed global level. Units of the various gases would then be so chosen that all gases have the same (expected) effect on global climate. (In other words, at the margin the emission of one unit of any one gas would have the same (expected) climatic effect as the emission of one unit of any other gas). The scheme would allow countries to exchange permits for one gas for permits for any other. Countries would receive an initial assignment of marketable permits. It transpires that under a wide range of circumstances, this scheme has informational advantages over both taxes and quantity controls on individual emissions.[82] Furthermore, if the permits were to refer to *net* emissions (i.e. net of absorption of carbon dioxide by green plants), the scheme would provide an incentive for countries with fast-growing tropical rain forests to earn export revenue by encouraging forest growth and then selling permits to other countries. The scheme also has the advantage that the necessary side-payments required to induce all (or most) countries to participate in the agreement can be made through the initial distribution of emission permits. Countries that do not expect severe damages from global warming would also wish to participate if they were to be provided initially with a sufficient number of permits (or rights).

The sticking point will clearly be over reaching an agreement on the initial distribution of permits among nations.[83] But if the bound that is set on annual aggregate greenhouse emissions were approximately optimal, it would always be possible *in principle* to distribute the initial set of rights in such a way that all countries have an incentive to join the scheme. Having said this, it is important to note that in practice it is difficult to come up with a *rule* that would accomplish the assignment of initial rights [Barrett (1992)]. So progress in this sphere of international cooperation can be expected to be slow. Nevertheless, one cannot overemphasise the fact that there are large potential gains to be enjoyed from international cooperation. A scheme involving the issue of marketable permits in principle offers a way in which all nations can enjoy these gains. The argument that "national sovereignty" would be

---

[81] See Tietenberg (1980, 1990) for reviews of the experience that has been accumulated with such schemes in the United States. See also Dasgupta (1982a) and Mäler (1990) for mathematical formalizations of these schemes under varying environmental circumstances. The motivation behind these formalizations is that they enable us to calculate the efficiency gains realizable by such resource allocation mechanisms.

[82] See Dasgupta, Hammond and Maskin (1980) for a formal analysis of optimal incentive schemes for pollution control.

[83] How a national government allocates the nation's rights among agencies within the country is a different matter.

endangered is in fact no argument, for the point about global commons is precisely that they are beyond the realm of national sovereignty.

22. Trade and the environment

Links between international trade and the environment are often alluded to, and it has not been uncommon to view growth in trade as a harbinger of a deteriorating environment [e.g. Daly (1993)]. The analysis we have offered in this chapter suggests that, stated as baldly as we have, the view is false: it does not recognize the heterogeneity of environmental problems (Sections 3–5); it does not distinguish between the volume and composition effects of a growth in trade on the world's production of goods and services (Sections 5, 17–19); it does not say if the growth is allied to international agreements on transfrontier pollution (Section 21) and a reduction in domestic market failure (Sections 14–16); and it is silent on whether the growth is brought about by a removal of government-induced distortions (Sections 5 and 17). The conclusions in these earlier sections are now relevant. To be sure, increased world trade is often associated with a relocation of production units in accordance with relative international labour, capital, and resource costs. Moreover, countries differ in regard to local environmental standards; but insofar as the resulting pollution is local, this is a matter of national sovereignty. The argument that lobbies would succeed in lowering environmental standards in countries that have high standards, in order to meet competition from countries with low standards, is not dissimilar to the concern people have that trade with low-wage countries would eventually lower wages in high-wage countries. However, it is possible to design tax-subsidy schemes to offset the additional cost of higher standards while retaining some of the gains from trade.[84] Above all, the argument for trade protection arising from the thought that countries with lower environmental standards will become sinks for other countries' pollutants, is to be resisted because of the kinds of considerations that were outlined in Sections 3 and 4.

A variant of these economic considerations formed the intellectual background of an argument in a widely-publicized memorandum issued in 1991 by the Chief Economist of the World Bank to his staff for discussion. It suggested that trade in pollutants should be encouraged between rich and poor nations because of at least two reasons: (i) poor countries (e.g. sub-Saharan Africa) suffer from lower industrial pollution than those in the West; (ii) being poor, they could be expected to value environmental quality less at the margin.

The memorandum was much criticized in the international press, mostly

---

[84] Low (1992) and Srinivasan (1993) contain discussions of these matters.

along the lines that it read altogether too much like saying: let the poor eat pollution. The arguments we offered in Sections 4 and 5 imply that this is misplaced criticism. On the other hand, the discussions in Sections 15 and 17 imply that there are two reasons why we should be wary of the recommendation. First, it is based implicitly on the assumption that there are no significant non-convexities associated with environmental pollution. In the presence of such non-convexities, it would not make sense to spread pollution evenly across geographical locations. Within municipalities, for example, household and industrial waste are typically deposited in "rubbish dumps". This is a social response to the presence of environmental non-convexities. We may now enlarge on this observation. Assuming that it is true that poor countries currently enjoy a better environment as regards industrial waste, it could well be that global well-being would be enhanced if their environment were protected and promoted, and if selected sites in rich countries were used as global centres of deposits for industrial effluents.

The second reason one should be circumspect about the recommendation is that it does not take note of the fact that the poor in poor countries are not the same as poor countries. There are both rich and poor people in poor countries. Typically, the rich in these countries do not absorb anything like the environmental risks that the poor are forced to accept (e.g. health risks at work). In addition, the rich enjoy political advantages. Furthermore, there is nothing resembling a free press, nor open debate, in a majority of poor countries. It is then all too possible to imagine that if trade in industrial pollutants were to be encouraged, the poor in poor countries would be made to absorb the health risks (industrial pollutants are usually spatially localized public bads), and the rich in poor countries would grasp the income accruing from the trade (a private benefit). This should make for a difference in our attitude towards the proposal. As elsewhere in economics, the issue of governance lies somewhere at the heart of the matter.

23. Contract agreements and the structure of authority[85]

A striking difference between local and global environmental problems is this: unlike agreements on the use of, say, local commons, there is no obvious central authority that can enforce agreements among nations over the use of transnational commons. To be sure, there are international authorities that have the mandate to act as overseers. But they do not possess the coercive powers of national governments; so they are unable to enforce agreements with anything like the same force.

---

[85] This section is taken from Dasgupta (1993).

Insights into the range of options open in the international sphere can be obtained by asking a prior question: How are agreements enforced in the case of local environmental problems? Broadly speaking, there would appear to be three mechanisms by which this is achieved. (Of course, none may work in a particular context, in which case people will find themselves in a hole they cannot easily get out of, and what could have been mutually beneficial agreements will not take place.)

In the first mechanism the agreement is translated into a contract, and is enforced by an established structure of power and authority. This may be the national government, but it need not be. In rural communities, for example, the structure of power and authority are in some cases vested in tribal elders (as within nomadic tribes in sub-Saharan Africa), in others in dominant landowners (such as the zamindars of eastern India), feudal lords (as in the state of Rajasthan in India), chieftains, and priests. On occasions there are even attempts at making rural communities mini-republics. Village Panchayats in India try to assume such a form. The idea there is to elect offices, the officials being entrusted with the power to settle disputes, enforce contracts (whether explicit or only tacit), communicate with higher levels of State authority, and so forth. Wade's account (Wade, 1987) of the collective management of common-property resources in South India describes such a mechanism of enforcement in detail.[86]

The question why such a structure of authority as may exist is accepted by people is a higher-order one, akin to the question why people accept the authority of government. The answer is that general acceptance itself is a Nash equilibrium: when all others accept the structure of authority, each has an incentive to accept it. Contrariwise, when a sufficiently large number don't accept it, individual incentives to accept it weaken, and the system unravels rapidly. General acceptance of the structure of authority is held together by its own bootstraps, so to speak.

The second mechanism consists in the development of a disposition to abide by agreements, a disposition that is formed through the process of communal living, role modelling, education, and the experiencing of rewards and punishments. This process begins at the earliest stages of our lives. We internalize social norms, such as that of paying our dues, keeping agreements, returning a favour; and higher-order norms, as for example frowning on people who break social norms, and so forth. By internalizing such norms as keeping agreements, a person makes the springs of his actions contain the norm. The person therefore feels shame or guilt in violating a norm, and this prevents him from doing so, or, at the very least, it puts a break on his violating it unless

---

[86] See also Gadgil and Guha (1992) for a narrative on India's ecological history as seen from this perspective.

other considerations are found by him to be overriding. In short, his upbringing ensures that he has a disposition to obey the norm. When he does violate it,
neither guilt nor shame is typically absent, but the act will have been
rationalized by him. A general disposition to abide by agreements, to be
truthful, to trust one another, and to act with justice is an essential lubricant of
societies. Communities where the disposition is pervasive save enormously on
transaction costs. There lies its instrumental virtue.[87] In the world as we know
it, such a disposition is present in varying degrees. When we refrain from
breaking the law, it is not always because of a fear of being caught. On the
other hand, if relative to the gravity of the misdemeanour the private benefit
from malfeasance were high, some transgressions could be expected to take
place. Punishment assumes its role as a deterrence because of the latter fact.

However, where people repeatedly encounter one another in similar situations, agreements could be reached and kept even if people were not
trustworthy and even if a higher authority were not there to enforce the
agreements. This is a third kind of mechanism. How does this argument work?
A simple set of contexts in which it works is where far-sighted people know
both one another and the environment, where they expect to interact
repeatedly under the same circumstances, and where all this is common
knowledge.[88] For expositional purposes, it helps to simplify further and to
consider circumstances where actions are observable, and where there is
perfect recall on each person's part of how others have behaved in the past.[89]
One idea is to require norms of behaviour to be supplemented by an entire
sequence of meta- (i.e. higher-order) norms, all of which can be succinctly
stated in the form of a basic norm, requiring each party to abide by the
agreement with any other if and only if that other party is *deserving*. We now
assume that the social norm requires all parties to start the process of repeated
interactions by co-operating. By recursion, it is then possible for any party at
any date to determine who is deserving and who is not. If someone is found to
be non-deserving in any period, the norm enjoins each of the other parties to
impose a sanction on him for that period. (This amounts to non-cooperation
with him for that period). In long, the norm requires that sanctions be imposed
upon those in violation of an agreement; upon those who fail to impose
sanctions upon those in violation of the agreement; upon those who fail to
impose sanctions upon those who fail to impose sanctions upon those in

---

[87] See Dasgupta (1988) for further discussion of the value of trust in a community.
[88] See Kreps and Wilson (1982), Milgrom and Roberts (1982), Kreps et al. (1982), and Benoit
and Krishna (1985) for demonstrations that co-operative behaviour is possible even when people
know that the interactions will be for a (large) finite number of periods. For a non-technical
discussion of the force of the assumption of common knowledge, see Binmore and Dasgupta
(1986) and Aumann (1987).
[89] Each of these qualifications can be relaxed. See Radner (1981) for weakening the first
qualification, and Sabourian (1988) for relaxing the second.

violation of the agreement; . . . and so on, indefinitely. (This is the sequence of meta-norms mentioned earlier). Provided agents are sufficiently far-sighted to give sufficient weight to their future gains from cooperation, this basic norm, which tells each agent to cooperate with (and only with) deserving agents, can lift communities out of a number of potentially troublesome social situations, including the repeated Prisoners' Dilemma. The reason each agent conforms to the basic norm when a sufficient number of others conform is pure and simple self-interest. If an agent does not conform, he will suffer from sanctions for the duration of his non-conformism. It will be noticed, however, that since continual co-operation is an equilibrium outcome, there will be no deviance along this equilibrium path, and so no sanctions will be observed. The meta-norms pertain to behaviour off the equilibrium path.

This sort of argument, which has been established in a general setting only recently [e.g. Fudenberg and Maskin (1986), Abreu (1988)], has been put to effective use in explaining the emergence of a number of institutions which facilitated the growth of trade in medieval Europe. Greif (1993), for example, has shown how the Maghribi traders during the eleventh century in Fustat and across the Mediterranean acted as a collective to impose sanctions on agents who violated their commercial codes. Greif, Milgrom and Weingast (1994) have offered an account of the rise of merchant guilds in late medieval Europe. These guilds afforded protection to members against unjustified seizure of their property by city-states. Guilds decided if and when a trade embargo was warranted against the city. In a related work, Milgrom, North and Weingast (1990) have analysed the role of merchant courts in the Champagne fairs. These courts facilitated members in imposing sanctions on transgressors of agreements.

A somewhat reverse set of actions occurred as well in medieval Europe, where transgressions by a party were sometimes met by the rest of society imposing sanctions on the entire kinship of the party, or on the guild to which the transgressor belonged. The norm provided collectives with a natural incentive to monitor their own members' behaviour. (For a different instance of this, the context being the use of local common-property resources, see Howe, 1986.)[90]

As matters stand, international agreements on environmental matters could be expected to be sustained by the latter two mechanisms in the list we have just discussed, not by the first. There is currently no world body with the kind of authority and power that national governments in principle enjoy. Ultimately, though it is the second route that offers the strongest hopes for the

---

[90] Those among readers who are game theorists will recognize that the strategy we have identified is not renegotiation-proof. On an application of this requirement for international agreements on biodiversity, see Barrett (1994).

emergence of collective responsibility over the transnational commons. However, institutional changes are easier to bring about than changes in personal and collective attitudes; or so it would seem. Social scientists typically take "preferences" and "demands" as given and try to devise policies that would be expected to improve matters collectively. This is the spirit in which environmental economics has developed, and there is an enormous amount to be said for it. But in the process of following this research strategy we should not play down the strictures of those social thinkers who have urged the rich to curb their material demands, to alter their preferences in such ways as to better husband the earth's limited resources. If such strictures seem quaint in today's world, it may be because we are psychologically uncomfortable with this kind of vocabulary. But that is not an argument for not taking them seriously.

Appendices

Introduction

In Sections 11–13 we outlined the use of accounting prices in project appraisal and national income accounting. The purpose of these appendices is to develop a few of the more technical arguments that are involved in this.

In Section 13 we argued that in poor countries household production functions offer a useful venue for estimating the accounting prices of environmental goods and services. Appendix 1 contains a discussion of a number of issues that arise if the aim is to assess public policies that affect only a small portion of an economy (e.g. a rural community). The point of view to be adopted in Appendix 1 will be that economic appraisal is an aspect of policy reform. Analysis of policy reforms involves calculating the probable effects on general well-being of marginal changes in some set of control variables (for example, public investments). This enables one to make recommendations on the direction in which the controls ought to be altered. One way of doing this is to make use of accounting prices for goods and services: the art consists in trying to estimate such prices from features of the economy as it currently is, and is expected to be [Dasgupta, Marglin and Sen (1972), Boadway (1978), Blitzer, Dasgupta and Stiglitz (1981), Dinwiddy and Teal (1987), Ahmad and Stern (1990)]. Often it makes sense to assume more strongly that the rest of the economy is, to a first approximation, unaffected by what happens to the segment that is under scrutiny [Dasgupta, Marglin and Sen (1972), Chapter 19; Anderson (1987), Hodgson and Dixon (1992)].

Although related, this approach to the estimation and use of accounting prices is different from the one where the government is involved in an overall optimization exercize [Little and Mirrlees (1974)].[91] In Appendix 2 we will follow this latter route. Our aim will be to derive formulae for accounting prices and to develop the concept of net national product.

Appendix 1

The valuation of environmental resources: Public policy as reform

Let us begin with an example of fuelwood (or water) collection. We take the unit of analysis to be a household.[92] To fix ideas, consider a reduced form of the model. Assume that a representative household's daily energy intake is c, and that x is its harvest of fuelwood (or water) per day. Denote by S the stock of fuelwood (or water) resources in the locality, and by $e(S)$ the energy cost of bringing home a unit of fuelwood (or water). Obviously, $e(S)$ is a decreasing function of S. Equally obviously, the household's production of goods and services (e.g. cooked food, heating) is an increasing function of x. It follows that household well-being is an increasing function of both the net energy intake $(c - e(S)x)$ and x. Write this as $W(c - e(S)x, x)$. Assume for simplicity that the household chooses x so as to maximize W. We write the maximized value as $V(c, S)$. It is the indirect well-being function.

Suppose next that there are M households that rely on the resource. For an additive aggregate well-being function (see Section 9), the shadow price of the resource is simply $-M(dc/dS)_W = MV_S/V_c = -Me'(S)x$. (Here V_S and V_c denote the partial derivatives of V, and $(dc/dS)_W$ denotes the marginal rate of substitution between c and S in the indirect well-being function.)[93] In a more detailed model, c will be endogenous, and the effect of Mx on future values of S will also be taken into account. We turn to a few generalizations.[94]

A household's production function can be written as

$$q = f(y, S),$$

where y is the vector of net demands for goods and services transacted in the market; S is a vector of environmental stocks; and q is the household's production of goods and services. Without undue loss of generality, we will

[91] The connection between the two approaches is discussed in Dasgupta (1972, 1982a).
[92] This has shortcomings (see Dasgupta, 1993, Chapters 11–12), because a household typically consists of more than one individual. But it will not matter here. Our aim is to sketch the technical problems that are involved, nothing more.
[93] Fredriksson and Persson (1989) have used this framework for estimating the social benefits of improved water supply in Manicaland, Zimbabwe.
[94] The discussion that follows is based on Mäler (1985, 1993).

regard q and S as scalars. Interest lies in the case where S does not have a market. The task is to estimate the value of a change in S in terms of changes in the values of q and y. This leads to a taxonomy based on what the analyst can observe and what he (or she) is able to value. We will consider a few cases.

(1) The simplest is one where q is measurable. Assume that household well-being depends solely on q. Suppose now that q and y can be transacted in markets, and so have market prices associated with them. We wish to estimate the social value of an increase in S. If the increase is marginal (i.e. it is not expected to have any effect on prices), its value is the marginal change in well-being that accompanies it. In short, y is held constant in this exercize. If the increase in S is large, but nevertheless it does not affect market prices, the social value of the increase needs to be measured as the difference between maximum household well-being after and before the increase, taking optimal adjustments in y into account. Anderson's (1987) study of the benefits and costs of establishing shelterbelts and farm forestry in the arid zone of Nigeria, is a fine example of this "partial" approach to cost-benefit analysis.[95]

(2) q may not be easily quantifiable. This would be so if q were an amenity (e.g. if S were a recreational area). In many such cases, there are inputs in the production of q that *can* be valued and that are at the same time substitutes or complement of S. Consider, as an example, the "travel cost" method for valuing recreational facilities. Regard y to be a "weak complement" of S if the value imputed to S is zero when the demand for y is zero (see Mäler, 1974). The travel cost method involves counting the number of visitors to the place (preferably the number of visitor days). But travel costs are not the same for all visitors. In our notation, different people face different prices for y. The demand curve for q can be estimated by taking a sample of visitors, and recording their travel costs and durations of visit. Survey techniques also enable one to infer how the demand curve would shift if the recreational area were to change in quality. This information enables one to estimate the change in consumer-surplus, which, under the assumption of weak complementarity, measures the value of the change in quality.

In some cases, y is a perfect substitute for S. The production function can then be written as $q = f(y + B(S))$, where B is an increasing function of S. A marginal increase in S would lead to an increase in q by $f'(.)B'(S)$. If, however, y were simultaneously reduced by the amount $-B'(S)$, output would not be affected. Suppose now that p is the accounting price of y. Then the accounting price of S is $pB'(S)$. Of course, we could so choose units that $B(S) = S$. In this case the accounting price of S is p.

There are a number of examples where this technique is of use. For example, the corrosion of material structures due to air pollution can be offset

---

[95] Anderson also explores the the risks that are involved in farm forestry programmes.

by preventive care (e.g. painting the structures more frequently, replacing the corroded material more often). Expenditures on these preventive measures are a good measure of the social costs of corrosion. Similarly, the value of improved water supplies can be estimated from the reduced cost of obtaining water. And so forth.

Appendix 2

Net national product in a dynamic economy

A2.1. The economics of optimal control

In Section 11 and Appendix 1 we sketched a number of methods that are currently available for estimating shadow prices of environmental resources in situ. We now seek to put shadow prices to use in judging the relative desirability of alternative economic activities. Of particular interest to us is social cost-benefit analysis of investment projects. The measurement of real national income is intimately connected to this. The index we seek is net national product (NNP) as a measure of aggregate well-being.[96] We will show that the question how we should measure it for the purposes of social cost-benefit analysis is not a matter of opinion, it has an unambiguous answer. We need a formal model to establish this. In this appendix we present what we hope is a canonical model of an optimizing economy for doing so.[97]

Our aim here is to display the connection between accounting prices, rules for project evaluation, and national product accounting in a context that is simple, but that has sufficient structure to allow us to obtain a number of prescriptions alluded to in the body of the chapter. In order to keep to what, for our purposes in this chapter, are essential matters, we will ignore the kinds of "second-best" constraints (for example, market disequilibria) that have been the centre of attention in the literature on project evaluation in poor countries; as, for example, in Dasgupta, Marglin and Sen (1972) and Little and Mirrlees (1974). The principles we will develop here carry over to disequilibrium situations. For expositional ease, we will restrict ourselves to a closed economy.

We will take it that the aggregate well-being function*al* is the (possibly discounted) integral of the flow of instantaneous social well-being (as in (1) in Section 9). Let us begin by recalling the main features of intertemporal

---

[96] There are other purposes to which the idea of national product has been put; for example, as a measure of economic activity. They require different treatments. We are not concerned with them here.

[97] This appendix is taken from Dasgupta and Mäler (1991) and Mäler (1991).

optimization exercizes.[98] The theory of intertemporal planning tells us to choose current controls (for example, current consumptions and the mix of current investments) in such a way as to maximize the current-value Hamiltonian of the underlying optimization problem. As is well known, the current-value Hamiltonian is the sum of the flow of current well-being and the shadow value of all net investments currently being undertaken. (The optimization exercize generates the entire set of intertemporal shadow prices.)[99] It will be seen in Section A2.3 that if accounting prices are approximately constant over time, then the current-value Hamiltonian measures the return on the value of all capital assets. In short, it is in such circumstances a measure of the return on wealth. This provides us with a connection between the current-value Hamiltonian and real net national product. In fact, NNP is a linearized version of the current-value Hamiltonian, the linearization amounting to representing the current flow of well-being by the shadow value of all the determinants of current well-being. In the simplest of cases, where current well-being depends solely on current consumption, NNP reduces to the sum of the accounting value of an economy's consumptions and the accounting value of the changes in its stocks of real capital assets.

The Hamiltonian calculus in fact implies something more. It implies that the present discounted sum of today's current value Hamiltonian is equal to the maximum present discounted value of the flow of social well-being (equation A13 below). This was not seen immediately as an implication of the mathematical theory of programming, although it should have been transparent from the work of Arrow and Kurz (1970) and Solow (1974a). Each of these matters will be illustrated in our formal model.

A2.2. NNP in a deterministic environment

We consider an economy that has a multi-purpose, man-made, perfectly durable capital good, whose stock is denoted by K_1. If L_1 is the labour effort combined with this, the flow of output is taken to be $Y = F(K_1, L_1)$, where $F(.)$ is an aggregate production function.[100] The economy enjoys in addition two sorts of environmental-resource stocks: clean air, K_2, and forests, K_3. Clean air

---

[98] The best economics treatment of all this is still Arrow and Kurz (1970).

[99] The current-value Hamiltonian in general also contains terms reflecting the social cost of breaking any additional (second-best) constraint that happens to characterize the optimization problem. As mentioned in the text, we ignore such additional constraints for the sake of expositional ease.

[100] In what follows we assume that all functions satisfy conditions which ensure that the planning problem defined below is a concave programme. We are not going to spell out each and every such assumption, because they will be familiar to the reader. For example, we assume that $F(.)$ is concave.

is valued directly, whereas, forests have two derived values: they help keep the atmosphere (or air) "clean", and they provide fuelwood, which too is valued directly (for warmth or for cooking). Finally, we take it that there is a flow of environmental amenities, Z, which directly affects aggregate well-being.

Forests enjoy a natural regeneration rate, but labour effort can increase it. Thus we denote by $H(L_2)$ the rate of regeneration of forests, where L_2 is labour input for this task, and where $H(.)$ is, for low values of L_2 at least, an increasing function. Let X denote the rate of consumption of fuelwood. Collecting this involves labour effort. Let this be L_3. Presumably, the larger the forest stock the less is the effort required (in calorie requirements, say). We remarked on this earlier. We thus assume that $X = N(K_3, L_3)$, where $N(.)$ is an increasing, concave function of its two arguments.

Output Y is a basic consumption good, and this consumption is also valued directly. However, we take it that the production of Y involves pollution as a byproduct. This reduces the quality of the atmosphere both as a stock and as a flow of amenities. We assume however that it is possible to take defensive measure against both these ill-effects. Firstly, society can invest in technologies (e.g. stack-gas scrubbers) for reducing the emission of pollutants, and we denote the stock of this defensive capital by K_4. If P denotes the emission of pollutants, we have $P = A(K_4, Y)$, where A is a convex function, decreasing in K_4 and increasing in Y. Secondly, society can mitigate damages to the flow of amenities by expending a portion of final output, at a rate R. We assume that the resulting flow of amenities has the functional form, $Z = J(R, P)$, where J is increasing in R and decreasing in P.

There are thus four things that can be done with output Y: it can be consumed (we denote the rate of consumption by C); it can be reinvested to increase the stock of K_1; it can be invested in the accumulation of K_4; and it can be used, at rate R, to counter the damages to the flow of environmental amenities. Let Q denote the expenditure on the accumulation of K_4.

Now, the environment as a stock tries to regenerate itself at a rate which is an increasing function of the stock of forests, $G(K_3)$. The net rate of regeneration is the difference between this and the emission of pollutants from production of Y. We can therefore express the dynamics of the economy in terms of the following equations:

$$dK_1/dt = F(K_1, L_1) - C - Q - R \tag{A1}$$

$$dK_2/dt = G(K_3) - A(K_4, F[K_1, L_1]) \tag{A2}$$

$$dK_3/dt = H(L_2) - X \tag{A3}$$

$$dK_4/dt = Q \tag{A4}$$

$$X = N(K_3, L_3) \tag{A5}$$

and

$$Z = J[R, A(K_4, F[K_1, L_1])] . \tag{A6}$$

The current flow of aggregate well-being, W, is taken to be an increasing function of aggregate consumption, C; the output of fuelwood, X; the flow of environmental amenities, Z; and the quality of the atmospheric stock, K_2. However, it is a decreasing function of total labour effort, $L = L_1 + L_2 + L_3$. (As noted in the text, labour effort could be measured in calories). We thus have

$$W(C, X, Z, K_2, L_1 + L_2 + L_3) .$$

Stocks of the four types of assets are given at the initial date; the instantaneous control variables are C, Q, R, X, Z, L_1, L_2 and L_3. The objective is to maximize the (discounted) sum of the flow of aggregate well-being over the indefinite future; that is

$$\int_0^\infty W(C, X, Z, K_2, L_1 + L_2 + L_3)e^{-\delta t} \, dt , \text{ where } \delta > 0 \text{ (see Section 9)} .$$

We take well-being to be the numeraire. Letting p, q, r and s denote the (spot) shadow prices of the four capital goods, K_1, K_2, K_3 and K_4 respectively, and letting v be the imputed marginal value of the flow of environmental amenities, we can use equations (A1)–(A6) to express the current-value Hamiltonian, V, of the optimization problem as:

$$\begin{aligned}
V = {} & W(C, N(K_3, L_3), Z, K_2, L_1 + L_2 + L_3) + p[F(K_1, L_1) \\
& - C - Q - R] + q[G(K_3) - A(K_4, F[K_1, L_1])] \\
& + r[H(L_2) - N(K_3, \quad L_3)] + sQ + v(J[R, \quad A(K_4, \quad F[K_1, \quad L_1])] - Z) .
\end{aligned} \tag{A7}$$

Recall that the theory of optimum control instructs us to choose the control variables at each date so as to maximize (A7).[101] Writing by W_C the partial derivative of W with respect to C, and so forth, it is then immediate that, along an optimal programme the control variables and the shadow prices must satisfy

---

[101] Notice that we have used equation (A5) to eliminate X, and so we are left with 6 direct control variables.

the conditions:

(i) $W_C = p$;   (ii) $W_X N_2 + W_L = r N_2$;   (iii) $W_Z = v$;

(iv) $W_L = [q A_2 - v J_2 - p] F_2$;   (v) $W_L = r\, dH(L_2)/dL_2$;

(vi) $p = v J_1$; (vii) $p = s$.[102]   (A8)

Moreover, the accounting prices, p, q, r, and s satisfy the auxiliary conditions:

(1) $dp/dt = -\partial V/\partial K_1 + \delta p$;   (2) $dq/dt = -\partial V/\partial K_2 + \delta q$;

(3) $dr/dt = -\partial V/\partial K_3 + \delta r$;   (4) $ds/dt = -\partial V/\partial K_4 + \delta s$.   (A9)

Interpreting these conditions is today a routine matter. Conditions (A8) tell us what kinds of information we need for estimating accounting prices. (A9) are the intertemporal arbitrage conditions that must be satisfied by accounting prices. We may now derive the correct expression for net national product (NNP) from equation (A7): it is the linear support of the Hamiltonian, the normal to the support being given by the vector of accounting prices.

It will pay us now to introduce time into the notation. Let us denote by O_t^*; the vector of all the non-price arguments in the Hamiltonian function along the optimal programme at date t. Thus:

$$O_t^* = (C_t^*,\, Z_t^*,\, Q_t^*,\, R_t^*,\, K_{1t}^*,\, K_{2t}^*,\, K_{3t}^*,\, K_{4t}^*,\, L_{1t}^*,\, L_{2t}^*,\, L_3 t^*) .$$

Write $I_{it} \equiv dK_{it}/dt$, for $i = 1, 2, 3, 4$. Consider now a small perturbation at t round O_t^*. Denote the perturbed programme as an unstarred vector, and dO_t as the perturbation itself. It follows from taking the Taylor expansion around O^*; that the current-value Hamiltonian along the perturbed programme is:

$$V(O_t) = V(O_t^*) + W_C\, dC_t + W_X\, dX_t + W_Z\, dZ_t + W_L(dL_{1t} + dL_{2t} + dL_{3t})$$
$$+ p\, dI_{1t} + q\, dI_{2t} + r\, dI_{3t} + s\, dI_{4t} ,$$

where $Z^* = J[R^*,\, A(K_4^*,\, F[K_1^*,\, L_1^*])]$.   (A10)

Equation (A10) tells us how to measure net national product. Let $\{O_t\}$ denote an arbitrary intertemporal programme. NNP at date t, which we write as NNP_t, in the optimizing economy, measured in well-being numeraire, is the

---

[102] F_2 stands for the partial derivative of F with respect to its second argument, L_1; and as mentioned earlier, $L = L_1 + L_2 + L_3$. We have used this same notation for the derivatives of $N(.)$, $J(.)$ and $A(.)$.

term representing the linear support term in expression (A10). So,

$$NNP_t = W_C C_t + W_X X_t + W_Z J[R_t, \ A(K_{4t}, \ F[K_{1t}, \ L_{1t}])]$$
$$+ W_L (L_{1t} + L_{2t} + L_{3t}) + p \ dK_1/dt + q \ dK_2/dt + r \ dK_3/dt$$
$$+ s \ dK_4/dt .^{103} \tag{A11}$$

Notice that all resources and outputs are valued at the prices that sustain the optimal programme $\{O_t^*\}$.[104] In order to stress the points we want to make here, we have chosen to work with a most aggregate model. Ideally, (income) distributional issues will find reflection in the well-being functional. These considerations can easily be translated into the estimates of shadow prices (see Dasgupta, Marglin and Sen, 1972).

Why should expression (A11) be regarded as the correct measure of net national product? The clue lies in expression (A10). Suppose we are involved in the choice of projects. A marginal project is a perturbation on the current programme. Suppressing the index for time once again, the project is the 10-vector $(dC, dX, dR, dL_1, dL_2, dL_3, dI_1, dI_2, dI_3, dI_4)$, where $I_i = dK_i/dt$, $(i = 1, 2, 3, 4)$; and dC, and so on, are small changes in C, and so forth. If the project records an increase in NNP_t (the increase will be marginal of course), it will record an increase in the current-value Hamiltonian, evaluated at the prices supporting the optimal programme. Recall that optimal control theory asks us to maximize the current-value Hamiltonian. Moreover, we are assuming that the planning problem is concave. So, choosing projects that increase NNP (i.e. they are socially profitable) increase the current-value Hamiltonian as well and, therefore, they should be regarded as desirable. Along an optimal programme the social profitability of the last project is nil. Therefore, its contribution to NNP is nil. This follows from the fact that the controls are chosen so as to maximize expression (A7). This is the justification. All this is well-known, and our purpose here is to obtain some additional insights. Expression (A11) tells us:

(a) If wages were equal to the marginal ill-being of work effort, wages would not be part of NNP. In short, the shadow wage bill ought to be deducted from gross output when we estimate NNP. Although our formal model is based on the assumption that the labour market clears, our result that the shadow wage bill ought to be deducted holds true even if the labour market were not to

---

[103] We may divide the whole expression by W_C to express NNP in aggregate consumption numeraire. It should also be recalled that by assumption W_L is *negative*.

[104] But recall the alternative framework mentioned in Sections 10–12, in which accounting prices are estimated from the prevailing structure of production and consumption. See Dasgupta, Marglin and Sen (1972).

clear. (If labour is supplied inelastically, it is a matter of indifference whether the wage bill in this optimizing economy is deducted from NNP).

By labour here we have so far meant raw labour. If a part of the wage bill is a return on the accumulation of human capital, that part would be included in NNP.

(b) Current defensive expenditure, R, against damages to the flow of environmental amenities should be included in the estimation of final demand [see the third term in expression (A9)].

(c) Investments in the stock of environmental defensive capital should be included in NNP [see the final term of expression (A11)].

(d) Expenditures that enhance the environment find expression in the value imputed to changes in the environmental resource stock. We may conclude that this change should not be included in estimates of NNP [notice the absence of sQ in expression (A11)].

(e) The value of changes in the environmental resource base (K_2 and K_3) should be included in NNP. However, anticipated capital gains (or losses) are not part of NNP.

A2.3. *The Hamiltonian and the return on aggregate well-being*

Differentiate expression (A7) and use conditions (A9) to confirm that along the optimal programme:

$$dV_t^*/dt = \delta(p\ dK_1/dt + q\ dK_2/dt + r\ dK_3/dt + s\ dK_4/dt)$$
$$= \delta(V_t^* - W_t^*)\,, \tag{A12}$$

where W_t^* is the flow of optimal aggregate well-being.

This is a differential equation in V_t^* which integrates to:

$$V_t^* = \delta \int_t^\infty W_\tau^* e^{-\delta(\tau - t)}\ d\tau, \text{ and thus} \tag{A13}$$

$$V_t^* \int_t^\infty e^{-\delta(\tau - t)}\ d\tau = \int_t^\infty W_\tau^* e^{-\delta(\tau - t)}\ d\tau\,. \tag{A14}$$

Equation (A13) says that the current-value Hamiltonian is the return on the present discounted value of the flow of well-being (i.e. aggregate well-being) along the optimal path. Equivalently, equation (A14) says that the present discounted value of a constant flow of today's current-value Hamiltonian measures the present discounted value of the flow of social well-being along the optimal path. Equations (A13) and (A14) have been the object of study in Solow (1986), Hartwick (1990, 1994) and Asheim (1994). Solow assumed that $W(.) = C$ (i.e. that the flow of social well-being is linear in consumption). In this case the Hamiltonian *is* NNP. Asheim and Hartwick , on the other hand, work with strictly concave social well-being functions. They identify NNP with the Hamiltonian so as to make the connection between their notion of NNP with the return on the present discounted value of the flow of well-being along the optimal path. In Section 11 we observed why NNP has always been thought of as a *linear* index.

Under certain special circumstances, the current-value Hamiltonian equals the return on the aggregate value of capital stocks (inclusive of the environmental resource-base, measured at current accounting prices). The special circumstances amount to the case where the optimum is approximately a steady state, so that accounting prices are constant over time.

To see this, define $K \equiv pK_1 + qK_2 + rK_3 + sK_4$ as the aggregate capital stock in the economy. The first part of equation (A12) can then, as an approximation, be written as:

$$V_t^* = \delta K_t .$$

If, as would generally be the case, the optimal path is not a steady state, the current-value Hamiltonian equals the return on the sum of the values of all net investments in the past. This follows directly from equation (A12).

A2.4. Future uncertainty

We will now extend the analysis for the case where there is future uncertainty. As an example, we could imagine the discovery and installation of cleaner production technologies which make existing abatement technologies less valuable. For simplicity of exposition, we will assume that such discoveries are uninfluenced by policy, for example, research and development policy.[105]

It is most informative to consider discrete events. We may imagine that at some random future date, T, an event occurs which is expected to affect the value of the then existing stocks of capital. We consider the problem from the vantage point of the present, which we denote by $t = 0$; where t, as always, denotes time. Let us assume that there is a (subjective) probability density function, π^t, over the date of its occurrence. (We are thus supposing for

---

[105] Research and development policy can be easily incorporated into our analysis (see Dasgupta, Heal and Mujumdar, 1977). The following account builds on Dasgupta and Heal (1974), Dasgupta and Stiglitz (1981), and Dasgupta (1982b). These earlier contributions, however, did not address the measurement of NNP, our present concern.

expositional ease that the event will occur at some future date). From this we may define the cumulative function Φ^t.

We take it that the social good is reflected by the expected value of the sum of the discounted flow of future aggregate well-being. If the event in question were to occur at date T, the economy in question would enter a new production and ecological regime. We shall continue to rely on the notation developed in the previous section. As is proper, we use dynamic programming, and proceed to work backwards. Thus, let K_i^T (with $i = 1, 2, 3, 4$) denote the stocks of the four assets at date T. Following an optimal economic policy subsequent to the occurrence of the event would yield an expected flow of aggregate well-being. This flow we discount back to T. This capitalized value of the flow of well-being will clearly be a function of K_i^T. Let us denote this by $B(K_1^T, K_2^T, K_3^T, K_4^T)$. It is now possible to show that until the event occurs (i.e. for $t < T$), the optimal policy is to pretend that the event will never occur, and to assume that the flow of aggregate well-being is given, not by $W(.)$, as in Section A2.1, but by $(1 - \Phi^t)W(.) + \pi^t B(.)$. [See Dasgupta and Heal (1974)]. Suppressing the subscript for time, we may then conclude from the analysis of the previous section that NNP at any date prior to the occurrence of the event is given by the expression:

$$NNP = (1 - \Phi)[W_C C + W_X X + W_Z J[R, A(K_4, F[K_1, L_1])]$$
$$+ W_L(L_1 + L_2 + L_3) + p \, dK_1/dt + q \, dK_2/dt + r \, dK_3/dt$$
$$+ s \, dK_4/dt] .$$
$$(A15)$$

Notice that if the event is not expected to occur ever, then $\pi^t = 0$ for all t, and consequently, $(1 - \Phi^t) = 1$ for all t. In this case expression (A15) reduces to expression (A11). Notice that the accounting prices that appear in expression (A15) are Arrow–Debreu contingent commodity prices. Notice too that while we have used the same notation for the accounting prices in expressions (A11) and (A15), their values are quite different. This is because future possibilities in the two economies are different.

References

Abreu, D. (1988) 'On the theory of infinitely repeated games with discounting', *Econometrica*, 56:383–396.

Agarwal, A. and Narain, S. (1989) *Towards green villages: A strategy for environmentally sound and participatory rural development* (New Delhi: Centre for Science and Environment).

Ahmad, E. and Stern, N. (1990) *The theory and practice of tax reform for developing countries* (Cambridge: Cambridge University).

Anand, S. and Ravallion, M. (1993) 'Human development in poor countries: On the role of private incomes and public services', *Journal of Economic Perspectives*, 7:133–150.

Anderson, D. (1987) *The economics of afforestation* (Baltimore: Johns Hopkins University Press).

d'Arge, R., Ayres, R. and Kneese, A.V. (1970) *Economics and the environment: A materials balance approach* (Baltimore: Johns Hopkins University Press).

Arrow, K.J. (1971) 'Political and economic evaluation of social effects of externalities', in: M. Intriligator ed., *Frontiers of quantitative economics*, Vol. I (Amsterdam: North Holland).

Arrow, K.J. and Fisher, A. (1974) 'Preservation, uncertainty and irreversibility', *Quarterly Journal of Economics*, 88:312–319.

Arrow, K.J. and Kurz, M. (1970) *Public investment, the rate of return and optimal fiscal policy* (Baltimore: Johns Hopkins University Press).

Asheim, G. (1994) 'Net national product as an indicator of sustainability', *Scandinavian Journal of Economics*, 96:257–265.

d'Aspremont, C. and Gerard-Varet, L. (1979) 'Incentives and incomplete information', *Journal of Public Economics*, 11:25–45.

Aumann, R. (1966) 'Existence of competitive equilibria in markets with a continuum of traders', *Econometrica*, 34:1–17.

Aumann, R. (1987), 'Game theory', in: J. Eatwell, M. Milgate and P. Newman eds., *The new Palgrave* (London: Macmillan).

Aumann, R. and Shapley, L. (1976) 'Long-term competition: A game theoretic analysis', mimeo., Department of Mathematics, Hebrew University.

Ayres, R. and Kneese, A.V. (1969) 'Production, consumption and externalities', *American Economic Review*, 59:282–297.

Baland, J.-M. and Platteau, J.-P. (1993) *A multidisciplinary analysis of local-level management of environmental resources* (Rome: Food and Agricultural Organization).

Barghouti, S. and Lallement, D. (1988) 'Water management: Problems and potentials in the Sahelian and Sudanian zones', in: Falloux and Mukendi (1988).

Barraclough, S. (1977) 'Agricultural production prospects in Latin America', *World Development*, 5:459–476.

Barrett, S. (1990) 'The problem of global environmental protection', *Oxford Review of Economic Policy*, 6:68–79.

Barrett, S. (1992) 'Acceptable' allocations of tradeable carbon emission entitlements in a global warming treaty', in UNCTAD ed., *Combating global warming: Study on a global system of tradeable carbon emission entitlements* (New York: United Nations).

Barrett, S. (1994) 'On biodiversity conservation', in: C. Perrings et al. (1994).

Baumol, W.M. and Bradford, D. (1972) 'Detrimental externalities and non-convexity of the production set', *Economica*, 39:160–176.

Baumol, W.M. and Oates, W. (1975) *The theory of environmental policy* (Englewood Cliffs, NJ: Prentice-Hall).

Bayliss Smith, T. (1981) 'Seasonality and labour in the rural energy balance', in: R. Chambers, R. Longhurst and A. Pacey eds., *Seasonal dimensions to rural poverty* (London: Francis Pinter).

Becker, G. (1981) *A treatise on the family* (Cambridge, MA: Harvard University Press).

Benoit, J.-P. and Krishna, V. (1985), 'Finitely repeated games', *Econometrica*, 53:905–922.

Beteille, A. ed. (1983) *Equality and inequality: Theory and practice* (Delhi: Oxford University Press).

Binmore, K. and Dasgupta, P. (1986), 'Game theory: A survey', in: K. Binmore and P. Dasgupta, eds., *Economic Organizations as Games* (Oxford: Basil Blackwell).

Binswanger, H. (1991) 'Brazilian policies that encourage deforestation in the Amazon', *World Development*, 19, 7:821–829.

Binswanger, H. and Rosenzweig, M. (1986) 'Credit markets, wealth and endowments in rural south India', Report No. 59, Agriculture and rural development department, World Bank.

Blitzer, C., Dasgupta, P. and Stiglitz, J. (1981) 'Project appraisal and foreign exchange constraints', *Economic Journal*, 91:58–74.

Boadway, R. (1978) 'A note on the treatment of foreign exchange in project evaluation', *Economica*, 45:391–399.

Boserup, E. (1965) *The conditions of agricultural growth* (London: Allen & Unwin).

Boserup, E. (1981) *Population growth and technological change: A study of long-term trends* (Chicago: Chicago University Press).

Breslin, P. and Chapin, M. (1984) 'Conservation Kuna-style', *Grassroots Development*, 8:26–35.

Broome, J. (1992) *Counting the cost of global warming* (Cambridge: White Horse).

Brown, G. and McGuire, C.B. (1967) 'A socially optimal pricing policy for a public water agency', *Water Resources Research*, 3:33–43.

Cain, M. (1977) 'The economic activities of children in a village in Bangladesh', *Population and Development Review*, 3:201–227.

Cain, M. (1982) 'Perspectives on family and fertility in developing countries', *Population Studies*, 36:159–175.

Cain, M. (1983) 'Fertility as an adjustment to risk', *Population and Development Review*, 9:688–702.

Caldwell, J. (1976) 'Toward a restatement of demographic theory', *Population and Development Review*, 2:321–366.

Caldwell, J. (1977a) 'The economic rationality of high fertility: An investigation illustrated with Nigerian data', *Population Studies*, 31:5–27.

Caldwell, J. (1977b) *The persistence of high fertility: Population prospects in the Third World* (Canberra: Australian National University).

Caldwell, J. (1981) 'The mechanism of demographic change in historical perspective', *Population Studies*, 35:5–27.

Caldwell, J. (1982) *Theory of fertility decline* (New York: Academic Press).

Caldwell, J. and Caldwell, P. (1987) 'The cultural context of high fertility in sub-Saharan Africa', *Population and Development Review*, 13:409–437.

Caldwell, J. and Caldwell, P. (1990) 'High fertility in sub-Saharan Africa', *Scientifc American*, 262 (May) 118–125.

Cashdan, E. (1983) 'Territoriality among human foragers: Ecological models and an application to four bushmen groups', *Current Anthropology*, 24, 1:47–55.

Cecelski, E. (1987) 'Energy and rural women's work: Crisis, response and policy alternatives', *International Labour Review*, 126, 1:41–64.

Chakravarty, S. (1969) *Capital and development planning* (Cambridge, MA.: MIT Press).

Chen, L.C. (1983) 'Evaluating the health benefits of improved water supply through assessment of nutritional status in developing countries', in: B.R. Underwood ed., *Nutrition intervention strategies in national development* (New York: Academic Press).

Chichilnisky, G. (1994) 'What is sustainable development?', mimeo., Department of Economics, Columbia University.

Chopra, K., Kadekodi, G.K. and Murti, M.N. (1989) *Participatory development: People and common property resources* (New Delhi: Sage).

Clark, C.W. (1976) *Mathematical bioeconomics: The optimal management of renewable resources* (New York: John Wiley).

Clark, W.C. (1989) 'Managing planet earth', *Scientific American*, 261 (September) 46–55.

Coase, R. (1960) 'The problem of social cost', *Journal of Law and Economics*, 3:1–44.

Cohen, J. (1980) 'Land tenure and rural development in Africa', in: R.H. Bates and M.F. Lofchie eds., *Agricultural development in Africa: Issues of public policy* (New York: Praeger).

Cohen, J.S. and Weitzman, M.L. (1975) 'A Marxian view of enclosures', *Journal of Development Economics*, 1:287–336.

Cooper, R. (1975) 'An economist's view of the oceans', *Journal of World Trade Law*, 9:357–377.

Costanza, R. ed. (1991) *Ecological economics: The science and management of sustainability* (New York: Columbia University Press).

Cowen, T. and Parfit, D. (1992) 'Against the social discount rate', in: P. Laslett and J.S. Fishkin eds., *Justice between age groups and generations* (New Haven, CT: Yale University Press).

C.S.E. (1982, 1985) *The state of India's environment: A citizens' report* (New Delhi: Centre for Science and Environment).

C.S.E. (1990) *Human-nature interactions in a central Himalayan village: A case study of village Bemru* (New Delhi: Centre for Science and Environment).

Dales J.H. (1968) *Pollution, property and prices* (Toronto: University of Toronto Press).

Daly, H.E. (1993) 'The perils of free trade', *Scientific American*, 269 (November), 5:50–55.

Daly, H.E. and Cobb, J.B. (1991) *For the common good: Redirecting the economy towards community, the environment, and a sustainable future* (London: Greenprint).

Dasgupta, P. (1969) 'On the concept of optimum population', *Review of Economic Studies*, 36.

Dasgupta, P. (1972) 'A comparative analysis of the UNIDO guidelines and the OECD manual', *Bulletin of the Oxford University Institute of Economics and Statistics*, 34.

Dasgupta, P. (1980) 'Decentralization and rights', *Economica*, 47.

Dasgupta, P. (1982a) *The control of resources* (Oxford: Basil Blackwell).

Dasgupta, P. (1982b) 'Resource depletion, research and development, and the social rate of discount', in: R.C. Lind ed., *Discounting for time and risk in energy policy* (Baltimore: Johns Hopkins University Press).

Dasgupta, P. (1988) 'Trust as a commodity', in: D. Gambetta ed., *Trust: Making and breaking agreements* (Oxford: Basil Blackwell).

Dasgupta, P. (1989) 'Exhaustible resources', in: L. Friday and R. Laskey eds., *The fragile environment* (Cambridge: Cambridge University Press).

Dasgupta, P. (1992) 'Population, resources, and poverty', *Ambio*, 21:95–101.

Dasgupta, P. (1993) *An inquiry into well-being and destitution* (Oxford: Clarendon Press).

Dasgupta, P. (1994) 'Foreword', in: C. Perrings et al. (1994).

Dasgupta, P., Folke, C. and Mäler, K.-G. (1994), 'The environmental resource-base and human welfare', in: H. Landsberg and K. Lindahl-Kiessling eds., *Population, economic progress, and the environment* (Oxford: Oxford University Press).

Dasgupta, P., Hammond, P. and Maskin, E. (1979) 'The implementation of social choice rules: Some basic results in incentive compatibility', *Review of Economic Studies*, 46:185–216.

Dasgupta, P., Hammond, P. and Maskin, E. (1980) 'On imperfect information and optimal pollution control', *Review of Economic Studies*, 47:857–860.

Dasgupta, P. and Heal, G.M. (1974) 'The optimal depletion of exhaustible resources', *Review of Economic Studies* (Symposium on the economics of exhaustible resources), 41.

Dasgupta, P. and Heal, G.M. (1979) *Economic theory and exhaustible resources* (Cambridge: Cambridge University Press).

Dasgupta, P., Heal, G.M. and Mujumdar, M. (1977) 'Resource depletion and research and development', in: M. Intriligator ed., *Frontiers of quantitative economics*, Vol. III (Amsterdam: North Holland).

Dasgupta, P. and Mäler, K.-G. (1991) 'The environment and emerging development issues', *Proceedings of the annual world bank conference on development economics* (Supplement to the *World Bank Economic Review* and the *World Bank Research Observer*).

Dasgupta, P. and Mäler, K.-G. eds. (1994) *The environment and emerging development issues* (Oxford: Oxford University Press), forthcoming (1995).

Dasgupta, P., Mäler, K.-G. and Vercelli, A. eds. (1994) *The economics of transnational commons* (Oxford: Oxford University Press), forthcoming, 1995.

Dasgupta, P., Marglin, S. and Sen, A. (1972) *Guidelines for project evaluation* (New York: United Nations).

Dasgupta, P. and Stiglitz, J.E. (1981) 'Resource depletion under technological uncertainty', *Econometrica*, 49:85–104.

Dinwiddy, C. and Teal, F. (1987) 'Shadow prices for non-traded goods in a tax-distorted economy: Formulae and values', *Journal of Public Economics*, 33:207–221.

Dixon, J.A. (1994) 'Analysis and management of watersheds', in: P. Dasgupta, and K.-G. Mäler eds. (1994).

Dixon, J.A., James, D.E. and Sherman, P.B. (1989): *The economics of dryland management* (London: Earthscan Publications).

Dixon, P.B. et al. (1991) *Notes and problems in applied general equilibrium economics* (Amsterdam: North Holland).

Durham, W.H. (1979) *Scarcity and survival in central America: Ecological origins of the soccer war* (Stanford: Stanford University Press).

Dyson-Hudson, R. and Smith, E.A. (1978) 'Human territoriality: An ecological reassessment', *American Anthropologist*, 80, 1:21–41.

Easter, K.W., Dixon, J.A. and Hufschmidt, M. eds. (1986) *Watershed resources management: An integrated framework with studies from Asia and the Pacific* (Boulder, CO: Westview Press).

Ehrlich, P., Ehrlich, A. and Holdren, J. (1977) *Ecoscience: Population, resources and the environment* (San Francisco: W.H. Freeman).

Ehrlich, P. and Roughgarden, J. (1987) *The science of ecology* (New York: Macmillan)

Ensminger, J. (1990) 'Co-opting the elders: The political economy of state incorporation in Africa', *American Anthropologist*, 92:662–675.

Esman, M.J. and Uphoff, N.T. (1984) *Local organizations: Intermediaries in rural development* (Ithaca, NY: Cornell University Press).

Falconer, J. (1990) *The major significance of 'minor' forest products* (Rome: FAO).

Falconer, J. and Arnold, J.E.M. (1989) *Household food security and forestry: An analysis of socio-economic issues* (Rome: FAO).

Falkenmark, M. (1986) 'Fresh water: Time for a modified approach', *Ambio*, 15:192–200.

Falkenmark, M. (1989) 'The massive water scarcity now facing Africa: Why isn't it being addressed?', *Ambio*, 18:112–118.

Falkenmark, M. and Chapman, T. eds. (1989) *Comparative hydrology: An ecological approach to land and water resources* (Paris: UNESCO).

Falloux, F. and Mukendi, A. eds. (1988) *Desification control and renewable resource management in the Sahelian and Sudanian zones of West Africa*, World Bank Technical Paper No. 70.

Farrell, J. (1987) 'Information and the Coase theorem', *Journal of Economic Prespectives*, 1:113–129.

Feder, E. (1977) 'Agribusiness and the elimination of Latin America's rural proletariat', *World Development*, 5:559–571.

Feder, E. (1979) 'Agricultural resources in underdeveloped countries: Competition between man and animal', *Economic and Political Weekly*, 14, August: 1345–1366.

Feder, G. and Feeny, D. (1991) 'Land tenure and property rights: Theory and implications for development policy', *World Bank Economic Review*, 5:135–153.

Feder, G. and Noronha, R. (1987) 'Land rights and agricultural development in sub-Saharan Africa', *World Bank Research Observer*, 2:143–169.

Feeny, D. et al. (1990) 'The tragedy of the commons: Twenty-two years later', *Human Ecology*, 18, 1:1–19.

Fernandes, R. and Menon, G. (1987) Tribal women and the forest economy (New Delhi: Indian Social Institute).

Fisher, A. and Hanemann, M. (1986) 'Option value and the extinction of species', *Advances in Applied Microeconomics*, 4:169–190.

Fredriksson, P. and Persson, A. (1989) 'Health, water and sanitation programmes in Zimbabwe', mimeo., Stockholm School of Economics.

Friedman, J. (1971) 'A non-cooperative equilibrium for supergames', *Review of Economic Studies*, 38.

Fudenberg, D. and Maskin, E. (1986) 'The folk theorem in repeated games with discounting and with incomplete information', *Econometrica*, 54:533–554.

Gadgil, M. and Guha, R. (1992), *This fissured land: An ecological history of India* (Delhi: Oxford University Press).

Gadgil, M. and Malhotra, K.C. (1983) 'Adaptive significance of the Indian caste system: An ecological perspective', *Annals of Human Biology*, 10:465–478.

Georgescu-Roegen, N. (1971) *The entropy law and the economic process* (Cambridge, MA: Harvard University Press).

Gigengack, A.R. et al. (1990) 'Global modelling of dryland degradation', in: Dixon, James and Sherman, eds. (1990).

Gordon, H. Scott (1954) 'The economic theory of common-property resources', *Journal of Political Economy*, 62:124–142.

Greif, A. (1993), 'Contract enforceability and economic institutions in early trade: The Maghribi traders' coalition', *American Economic Review*, 83:525–548.

Greif, A., Milgrom, P. and Weingast, B. (1994), 'Coordination, commitment, and enforcement: The case of the merchant guild', *Journal of Political Economy*, 102, forthcoming.

Gross, D.R. and Underwood, B.A. (1971) 'Technological change and caloric cost: Sisal agriculture in north-eastern Brazil', *American Anthropologist*, 73:725–740.

Grossman, G. (1993) 'Pollution and growth: What do we know?', in: I. Goldin and A. Winters eds., *Sustainable economic development: Domestic and international policy* (Cambridge: Cambridge University Press), forthcoming, 1994.

Groves, T. and Ledyard, J. (1977) 'Optimal allocation of public goods: A solution to the free-rider problem', *Econometrica*, 45:783–809.

Hahn, F.H. (1970) 'Savings and uncertainty', *Review of Economic Studies*, 37:21–24.

Hamilton, L.S. and King, P.N. (1983) *Tropical forested watersheds: Hydrologic and soils response to major uses or conversions* (Boulder, CO: Westview Press).

Hardin, G. (1968) 'The tragedy of the commons', *Science*, 162:1243–1248.

Hartwick , J. (1990) 'Natural resource, national accounting, and economic depreciation', *Journal of Public Economics*, 43:291–304.

Hartwick , J. (1994) 'National wealth and net national product', *Scandinavian Journal of Economics*, 96:253–256.

Hartwick , J. and Olewiler , N. (1986) *The economics of natural resource use* (New York: Harper & Row).

Hecht, S. (1985) 'Environment, development and politics: Capital accumulation and the livestock sector in eastern Amazonia', *World Development*, 13:663–685.

Hecht, S., Anderson, A.B. and May, P (1988) 'The subsidy from nature: Shifting cultivation, successsional palm forests and rural development', *Human Organization*, 47:25–35.

Henderson, J.V. and Tugwell, M. (1979), 'Exploitation of the lobster fishery: Some empirical results', *Journal of Environmental Economics and Management*, 6:287–296.

Henry, C. (1974) 'Investment decisions under uncertainty: The irreversibility effect', *American Economic Review*, 64:1006–1012.

Higgins, G.M. et al. (1982) *Potential population supporting capacities of lands in developing countries* (Rome: Food and Agriculture Organization).

Hill, P. (1963) *The migrant cocoa-farmers of southern Ghana* (Cambridge: Cambridge University Press).

Hodgson, G. and Dixon, J. (1992) 'Sedimentation damage to marine resources: Environmental and economic analysis', in: J.B. Marsh ed., *Resources and environment in Asia's marine sector* (London: Taylor & Francis).

Hoff, K. and Stiglitz, J.E. (1990) 'Introduction: Imperfect information and rural credit markets: Puzzles and policy perspectives', *World Bank Economic Review*, 4:235–250.

Holling, C.S. (1987) 'Simplifying the complex: The paradigms of ecological function and structure', *European Journal of Operations Research*, 30:139–146.

Holling, C.S. (1992) 'Cross-scale morphology, geometry and dynamics of ecosystems', *Ecological Monographs*, 62:447–502.

Howe, J. (1986) The Kuna gathering (Austin, TX: University of Texas Press).

Humphries, J. (1990) 'Enclosures, common rights, and women: The proletarianization of families in the late eighteenth and early nineteenth centuries', *Journal of Economic History*, 50:17–42.

Jodha, N.S. (1980) 'The process of desertification and the choice of interventions', *Economic and Political Weekly*, 15, August:1351–1356.

Jodha, N.S. (1986) 'Common property resources and the rural poor', *Economic and Political Weekly*, 21, July: 1169–1181.

Jodha, N.S. (1990) 'Rural common property resources: contributions and crises', *Economic and Political Weekly*, 25 (*Quarterly Review of Agriculture*), A65–A78.

Kanninen, B.J. and Kriström, B. (1993) 'Welfare benefit estimation and income distribution', revised version of Beijer discussion paper Series No. 20, Beijer International Institute of Ecological Economics, Stockholm.

Kennedy, E. and Oniang'o, R. (1990) 'Health and nutrition effects of sugarcane production in south-western Kenya', *Food and Nutrition Bulletin*, 12 (4), 261–267.

Kneese, A. (1988) 'Environmental stress and political conflict: Salinity in the Colorado river', mimeo., resources for the future, Washington DC.

Koopmans, T.C. (1957) 'The price system and the allocation of resources', in: *Three essays on the state of economic science* (New York: McGraw Hill).

Koopmans, T.C. (1960) 'Stationary ordinal utility and impatience', *Econometrica*, 28:287–309.

Koopmans, T.C. (1965) 'On the concept of optimal economic growth', *Pontificiae Academiae Scientiarum Scripta Varia*, 28. Reprinted in *The Econometric Approach to Development Planning*, 1966 (Amsterdam: North Holland).

Koopmans, T.C. (1967) 'Objectives, constraints and outcomes in optimal growth models', *Econometrica*, 35:1–15.

Koopmans, T.C. (1972a) 'Representation of preference orderings with independent components of consumption', in: C.B. McGuire and R. Radner, eds., *Decision and Organization* (Amsterdam: North Holland).

Koopmans, T.C. (1972b) 'Representation of preference orderings over time', in: C.B. McGuire and R. Radner, eds., *Decision and Organization* (Amsterdam: North Holland).

Kreimer, A. and Munasinghe, M. eds. (1991) *Managing natural disasters and the environment* (Washington DC: World Bank).

Kreps, D. et al. (1982), 'Rational cooperation in the finitely repeated prisoners' dilemma', *Journal of Economic Theory*, 27:245–252.

Kreps, D. and Wilson, R. (1982), 'Reputation and incomplete information', *Journal of Economic Theory*, 27:253–279.

Krutilla, J. (1966) 'The international Columbia river treaty: An economic evaluation', in: A. Kneese and S. Smith eds., *Water Research* (Baltimore: Johns Hopkins University Press).

Kumar, S.K. and Hotchkiss, D. (1988) 'Consequences of deforestation for women's time allocation, agricultural production, and nutrition in hill areas of Nepal', Research report 69, International Food Policy Research Institute (Washington DC).

Laffont, J.J. and Maskin, E. (1982) 'The theory of incentives: An overview', in: W. Hildenbrand ed., *Advances in Economic Theory* (Cambridge: Cambridge University Press).

Leach, G. (1975) 'Energy and food production', *Food Policy*, 1:62–73.

Levhari, D. and Srinivasan, T.N. (1969) 'Optimal savings under uncertainty', *Review of Economic Studies*, 36:27–38.

Lindahl, E.R. (1958), 'Some controversial questions in the theory of taxation', in: R.A. Musgrave and A.T. Peacock eds., *Classics in the theory of public finance* (London: Macmillan). Originally published in Swedish, in 1928.

Lindert, P. (1980) 'Child cost and economic development', in: R. Easterlin ed., *Population and economic change in developing countries* (Chicago: University of Chicago Press).

Lindert, P. (1983) 'The changing economic costs and benefits of having children', in: R.A. Bulatao and R.D. Lee eds., *Determinants of fertility in developing countries* (New York: Academic Press).

Little, I.M.D. and Mirrlees, J.A. (1974) *Project appraisal and planning for developing countries* (London: Heinemann)

Low, P. ed. (1992) *International trade and the environment*, World Bank discussion papers 159 (Washington, DC: World Bank).

Lutz, E., ed. (1993) *Toward improved accounting for the environment* (Washington, DC: World Bank).

Mabbut, J. (1984) 'A new global assessment of the status and trends of desertification', *Environmental Conservation*, 11:103–113.

Magrath, W. and Arens, P. (1989) 'The costs of soil erosion in Java: A natural resource accounting approach', World Bank Environmental Department Working Paper No. 18.

Mahar, D. (1988) 'Government policies and deforestation in Brazil's Amazon region', World Bank Environment Department Working Paper No. 7.

Mäler, K.G. (1974) *Environmental economics: A theoretical enquiry* (Baltimore: Johns Hopkins University Press).

Mäler, K.G. (1985) 'Welfare economics and the environment', in: A.V. Kneese and J.L. Sweeney eds., *Handbook of Natural Resource and Energy Economics*, Vol. I (Amsterdam: North Holland).

Mäler, K.G. (1989) 'Environmental resources, risk and Bayesian decision rules', mimeo. Stockholm School of Economics.

Mäler, K.G. (1990) 'International environmental problems', *Oxford Review of Economic Policy*, 6, 1:80–108.

Mäler, K.-G. (1991) 'National accounting and environmental resources', *Journal of Environmental Economics and Resources*, 1(1), 1–15.

Mäler, K.-G. (1993) 'Multiple use of environmental resources: A household production function approach to valuing resources', Beijer Discussion Series No. 4, Beijer International Institute of Ecological Economics, Stockholm.

Mäler, K.-G. et al. (1992) 'The Baltic drainage-basin programme', mimeo., Beijer International Institute of Ecological Economics, Stockholm.

May, R.M. (1972) 'Will a large complex system be stable?', Nature, 238:413–414.

May, R.M. and MacArthur, R.H. (1972) 'Niche overlap as a function of environmental variability', Proceedings of the National Academy of Sciences of the U.S., 69:5:1109–1113.

Meade, J.E. (1973) The theory of externalities (Geneva: Institute Universitaire de Hautes Etudes Internationales).

Migot-Adholla, S. et al. (1991) 'Indigenous land rights systems in sub-Saharan Africa: A constraint on productivity', World Bank Economic Review, 5:155–175.

Milgrom, P., North, D. and Weingast, B. (1990), 'The role of institutions in the revival of trade: The law merchant, private judges, and the champagne fairs', Economics and Politics, 2:1–23.

Milgrom, P. and Roberts, J. (1982), 'Predation, reputation and entry deterrance', Journal of Economic Theory, 27:280–312.

Milliman, J.W. (1956) 'Commodities and price systems and use of water supplies', Southern Economic Journal, 22:426–437.

Mirrlees, J.A. (1965) 'Optimum accumulation under uncertainty', mimeo., Faculty of Economics, University of Cambridge.

Mirrlees, J.A. (1967) 'Optimal growth when technology is changing', Review of Economic Studies, 34:95–124.

Mirrlees, J.A. (1974) 'Optimum accumulation under uncertainty: The case of stationary returns on investment', in: J. Dreze ed., Allocation under uncertainty: Equilibrium and optimality (London: Macmillan).

Mitchell, R.C. and Carson, R.T. (1989) Using surveys to value public goods: The contingent valuation method (Washington, DC: Resources for the future).

Mueller, E. (1976) 'The economic value of children in peasant agriculture', in: R.G. Ridker ed., Population and development: The search for selective interventions (Baltimore: Johns Hopkins University Press).

Murphy, Y. and Murphy, R. (1985) Women of the forest (New York: Columbia University Press).

Musgrave, R. (1959) Theory of public finance (New York: McGraw Hill).

Musu, I. (1994) 'On optimal sustainable endogenous growth', mimeo. Department of Economics, University of Venice.

Nelson, R. (1988) 'Dryland management: The 'desertification' problem', World Bank Environmental Department Paper No. 8.

Nerlove, M. and Meyer, A. (1991) 'Endogenous fertility and the environment: A parable of firewood', in: P. Dasgupta and K.-G. Mäler eds., The environment and emerging development issues (Oxford: Clarendon Press), forthcoming 1994.

Netting, R. (1985) Hill farmers of Nigeria: Cultural ecology of the Kofyar of the Jos Plateau (Seattle: University of Washington Press).

Newcombe, K. (1984) 'An economic justification of rural afforestation: The case of Ethiopia', Energy Department Paper No. 16, World Bank, Washington, D.C.

Nordhaus, W.D. (1991) 'To slow or not to slow: The economics of the greenhouse effect', Economic Journal 101:920–937.

Noronha, R. (1994) 'Common property resource management in traditional societies', in: P. Dasgupta and K.-G. Mäler eds. (1994).

Norse, D. (1985) 'Nutritional implications of resource policies and technological change', in M. Biswas and P. Pinstrup-Andersen eds., Nutrition and development (Oxford: Oxford University Press).

Olsen, W.K. (1987) 'Manmade 'drought' in Rayalaseema', Economic and Political Weekly, 22, March: 441–443.

Ostrüm, E. (1990) Governing the commons: The evolution of institutions for collective action (Cambridge: Cambridge University Press).

Panayotou, T. (1992) 'Environmental "Kuznets" curves: Empirical tests and policy implications', mimeo., Harvard Institute for International Development, Harvard University.

Parfit, D. (1984) Reasons and persons (Oxford: Oxford University Press).

Payne, P. (1985) 'The nature of malnutrition', in: M. Biswas and P. Pinstrup-Andersen eds. (1985).

Pearce, D., Barbier, E. and Markandya, A. (1988) 'Sustainable development and cost-benefit analysis', Paper presented at the Canadian assessment workshop on integrating economic and environment assessment.

Perrings, C. et al. (1994) *Biodiversity loss: Economic and ecological perspectives* (Cambridge: Cambridge University).

Phelps, E.S. (1962) 'The accumulation of risky capital: A sequential analysis', *Econometrica*, 30:729–743.

Pigou, A.C. (1920) *The economics of welfare* (London: Macmillan).

Portes, R. (1971) 'Decentralized planning procedures and centrally planned economies', *American Economics Review* (Papers & Proceedings), 61:422–429.

Radner, R. (1967) 'Efficiency prices for infinite horizon production programmes', *Review of Economic Studies*, 34:51–66.

Radner, R. (1981), 'Monitoring cooperative agreements in a repeated principle-agent relationship', *Econometrica*, 49:1127–1148.

Ramsey, F. (1928) 'A mathematical theory of saving', *Economic Journal*, 38:543–559.

Reij, C., Mulder, P. and Begemann, L. (1988) 'Water harvesting for plant production', World Bank Technical Paper No. 91.

Repetto, R. (1988) 'Economic policy reform for natural resource conservation', World Bank Environment Department Working Paper No. 4.

Repetto, R. et al (1989) *Wasting assets: Natural resources and the national income accounts* (Washington, DC: World Resources Institute).

Rogers, P. (1994) 'International river basins: Pervasive unidirectional externalities', in: P. Dasgupta, K.-G. Mäler, and A. Vercelli eds. (1994).

Rosenzweig, M. and Wolpin, K.I. (1985) 'Specific experience, household structure and intergenerational transfers: Farm family land and labour arrangements in developing countries', *Quarterly Journal of Economics*, 100:961–987.

Rowthorn, R. and Brown, G. (1994) 'Biodiversity, economic growth, and the discount rate', Discussion Series #94-02, Institute for Economic Research, University of Washington, Seattle.

Sabourian, H. (1988), 'Repeated games: A survey', in: F.H. Hahn ed., *The economic theory of missing markets, information, and games* (Oxford: Basil Blackwell).

Schultze, E.D. and Mooney, H.A. eds. (1993) *Biodiversity and Ecosystem Function* (Berlin: Springer-Verlag).

Scott, A.D. (1955) 'The fishery: The objectives of sole ownership' *Journal of Political Economy*, 63:116–124.

Seabright, P. (1993) 'Managing local commons: Theoretical issues in incentive design', *Journal of Economic Perspectives*, 7:113–134.

Sefton, J. and Weale, M. (1994) 'Natural resources and the net national product: The case of foreign trade', mimeo., Department of Economics, University of Cambridge.

Sen, A. (1992) *Inequality Reexamined* (Oxford: Clarendon Press).

Shapley, L.S. and Shubik, M. (1969) 'On the core of an economic system with externalities', *American Economic Review*, 59:678–684.

Simon, J. (1977) *The economics of population growth* (Princeton, NJ: Princeton University Press).

Simon, J. (1981) *The ultimate resources* (Princeton, NJ: Princeton University Press).

Smith, E.A. (1987) 'Optimization theory in anthropology: Applications and critiques', in: J. Dupre ed., *The latest and the best: Essays on evolution and optimality* (Cambridge, MA: MIT Press).

Solorzano, R. et al. (1991) *Accounts overdue: Natural resource depreciation in Costa Rica* (Washington, DC: World Resources Institute).

Solow, R.M. (1956) 'A contribution to the theory of economic growth', *Quarterly Journal of Economics*, 70:65–94.

Solow, R.M. (1974a) 'Intergenerational equity and exhaustible resources', *Review of Economic Studies* (Symposium in the Economics of Exhaustible Resources), 41:29–4.

Solow, R.M. (1974b) 'The economics of resources, or the resources of economics', *American Economic Review* (Papers & Proceedings), 64:1–14.

Solow, R.M. (1986) 'On the intergenerational allocation of exhaustible resources', *Scandinavian Journal of Economics*, 88:141–149.

Solow, R.M. (1991) 'Sustainability – An economist's perspective', Department of Economics, Massachusetts Institute of Technology.

Sopher, D. (1980) 'Sex disparity in Indian literacy', in: D. Sopher ed., *An exploration of India: Geographical perspectives on society and culture* (Ithaca, NY: Cornell University Press).

Spence, A.M. (1974) 'Blue whales and optimal control theory', in: H. Göttinger ed., *Systems Approaches and Environmental Problems* (Göttingen: Vandenhoek and Ruprecht).

Squire, L. and Van der Taak, H. (1975) *Economic analysis of projects* (Baltimore: Johns Hopkins University Press).

Srinivasan, T.N. (1993) 'Environment, economic development and international trade', Occasional Paper No. 13, Bureau of Economic Studies, Macalester College, St. Paul, MN; reprinted in *Pacific and Asian Journal of Energy* 3:43–62.

Starrett, D.A. (1972) 'Fundamental non-convexities in the theory of externalities', *Journal of Economics Theory*, 4:180–199.

Starrett, D.A. (1973) 'A note on externalities and the core', *Econometrica*, 41:179–183.

Stein, D.L. ed. (1989) *Lectures in the sciences of complexity* Redwood City, CA.: Addison-Wesley).

Stevenson, G.G. (1991) *Common property resources: A general theory and land use applications* (Cambridge: Cambridge University Press).

Sundstrum, W.A. and David, P.A. (1988) 'Old age security motives, labour markets and farm family fertility in Antebellum America', *Explorations in Economic History*, 25:164–197.

Tietenberg , T. (1980) 'Transferable discharge permits and the control of stationary source air pollution: A survey and synthesis', *Land Economics*, 56:391–416.

Tietenberg , T. (1988) *Environmental and natural resource economics*, 2nd edn. (Glenview, IL: Scott, Forsman).

Tietenberg , T. (1990) 'Economic instruments for environmental regulation', *Oxford Review of Economic Policy*, 6, 1:17–33.

Tilman, D. and Downing, J.A. (1994) 'Biodiversity and stability in grasslands', *Nature*, 367 (6461) 363–365.

Unemo, L. (1993) 'Environmental impact of government policies and of external shocks in Botswana: A CGE-model approach', Beijer Discussion Paper No. 26, Beijer International Institute of Ecological Economics, Stockholm.

UNEP (1984) *General assessment of progress in the implementation of the plan of action to combat desertification 1978–1984*, Report of the Executive Director (Nairobi: United Nations Environment Programme).

United Nations (1990) *Overall socioeconomic perspectives of the world economy to the year 2000* (New York: UN Department of International Economic and Social Affairs).

Vitousek, P., Ehrlich, P., Ehrlich, A. and Mason, P. (1986) 'Human appropriation of the products of Photosynthesis', *BioScience*, 36:368–373.

von Amsberg, J. (1993) 'Project evaluation and the depletion of natural capital: An application of the sustainability principle', World Bank Environment Department Working Paper No. 56.

von Braun, J. and Kennedy, E. (1986) 'Commercialization of subsistence agriculture: Income and nutritional effects in developing countries', Working Paper on Commercialization of Agriculture and Nutrition No. 1, International Food Research Institute, Washington, D.C.

Wade, R. (1987) 'The management of common property resources: Finding a cooperative solution', *World Bank Research Observer*, 2.

Wade, R. (1988) *Village republics: Economic conditions for collective action in South India* (Cambridge: Cambridge University Press).

Walker, B.H. (1993) 'Rangeland ecology: Understanding and managing change', *Ambio*, 22:80–87.

Weitzman, M.L. (1970) 'Optimal growth with scale-economies in the creation of overhead capital', *Review of Economic Studies*, 37:555–570.

Weitzman, M.L. (1992) 'On diversity', *Quarterly Journal of Economics*, 107:363–405.

Weitzman, M.L. (1993) 'What to preserve? An application of diversity theory to crane preservation', *Quarterly Journal of Economics*, 108:157–173.

Willis, R. (1982) 'The direction of intergenerational transfers and the demographic transition: The

Caldwell hypothesis revisited', in: J. Ben-Porath, ed., *Income distribution and the family* (Supplement to Population and Development Review, 8).

Wilson, E.O. (1992) *The diversity of life* (New York: W.W. Norton).

World Bank (1991) *The population, agriculture and environmental Nexus in sub-Saharan Africa* (Washington, DC: World Bank).

World Bank (1992) *World development report* (New York: Oxford University Press).

World Commission (1987) *Our common future* (New York: Oxford University Press).

Zylics, T. (1990) 'Miljopolitik for fore detta centralplanerade Ekonomier', *Ekonomisk Debatt*, 4, 361–368.

INDEX

Note: linked page numbers are often used as a space-saver so entries on these pages may not necessarily be continuous.

2570, 2792; Economic Commission for
Africa 2852; Educational, Scientific and
Cultural Organization 2393; EP 2380;
infrastructure 2778-2779; International
Comparisons Project 2583; National
Household Capability Programme 2565;
technology 2253
United States 2492; agricultural land relations
2672, 2696-2697, 2706, 2708, 2710-2711,
2717, 2723, 2725; AID 2779; American
Chamber of Commerce 2271; Bureau of
Indian Affairs (institutions) 2335;
Computable General Equilibrium model
2093; Constitution of the 2312; consumer
price index 1846; data 1791-1792, 1805,
1811, 1814; econometric tools 1819, 1835,
1850, 1854-1855; foreign aid 2515; human
capital investments 1919-1920, 1929, 1933,
1939; human resources 1953; infrastructure
2780, 2786; institutions 2320, 2323-2325,
2337; links among individuals/households/
families 1983, 1987, 1997, 2001;
Longitudinal Survey of Youth 2127;
macroeconomic data 1847; Patent and
Trade Mark office 2229; policy lessons post
Second World War 2524; poverty 2559,
2584, 2596, 2615; poverty, institutions and
environment 2386, 2391, 2431, 2435-2436;
public investment 2792, 2796-2797, 2808,
2811; savings, credit and insurance 2134,
2135, 2153, 2155, 2160, 2173, 2190-2191,
2193; Savings and Loans Associations 2176;
schooling/wages/farm output 2784;
structural adjustment 2859, 2875, 2894;
technology 2228-2229, 2231, 2234, 2252-
2253, 2267, 2269-2270, 2277, 2282; trade
and industrial policy reform 2939-2940,
2949, 2951, 2957; University of
Pennsylvania 1779, 1808; university systems
2233; wages and labor supply 1965-1966,
1971; Washington consensus 2928
Uphoff, N.T. 2433
urbanization 1788, 1790, 1794, 1797, 2591,
2604-2605, 2628, 2637; bias 2563, 2600,
2634; consumers 2280; formal sector 2601,
2605; informal sector 2600-2601, 2605, 2615,
2617, 2637; and poverty 2599-2602, 2610,
2615, 2637
Uruguay 2348, 2523, 2536, 2799, 2800; Round
2060, 2282, 2989
Usher, D. 2562
usufructuary mortgage 2181
usufructuary rights 2663
Uzawa, H. 2489, 2777, 2984

vagrancy laws 2673-2677, 2691, 2747-2749,
2751, 2755

Vail, L. 2755
Vakil, C.N. 2561
Valdés, A. 2526-2528, 2537-2538, 2594, 2737,
2931
Valdés, S. 2901
valuation methods 2409
van de Walle, D. 1983, 2593, 2602-2603, 2608-
2609, 2612, 2632-2633
van der Gaag, J. 1789, 1831, 1928, 1935,
1937, 1961, 1965, 1967, 2507, 2575, 2613,
2631, 2798, 2819-2821, 2825, 2879
van der Heyden, L. 2069
van der Laan G. 2072
van der Mensbrugghe, D. 2060, 2064
Van der Taak, H. 2405
van Ginneken, J. 1921
van Praag, B.M.S. 2575
van Wijnbergen, S. 2051, 2091, 2610, 2881,
2930, 2961, 2964
Varian, H. 2038, 2041, 2153, 2182, 2186-2187
VARs *see* vector autoregressions
Vartia, Y.O. 2574
Vashishtha, P. 2116
Vaughan, B. 1953
Veblen, T. 2305
vector autoregressions 1849
Vegh, C. 2875
Velez, E. 1967
Venezuela 1814, 2599, 2614, 2687, 2731, 2746,
2938
Vercelli, A. 2435
Vernon, R. 2226, 2261
Vietnam 1835, 2166, 2683, 2688-2690, 2726,
2731, 2734
Vijverberg, W. 1961-1962, 1964, 1966-1967,
2704
villages 1790-1791, 1797, 1800, 1817-1818,
1828, 1830-1831, 1892, 2155; *see also*
agriculture; rural
Villanueva, D. 2878-2879
Viner, J. 2846
Virmani, A. 1851-1852
Visaria, P. 2586, 2589, 2591, 2598, 2626
Vishny, R. 2943, 2952-2953, 2993
Viteri, F. 1915
Vitousek, P. 2399
Vogel, R.C. 2172, 2174
Vogel, R.J. 2827
Vogelsang, I. 2958
Volterra, V. 2375
von Amsberg, J. 2394
von Braun, J. 1978, 1994, 1997, 2024, 2380,
2589, 2609
von Neumann, J. 2401, 2984
von Thuenen 2664
Vosti, S.A. 2571